EARLY CHILDHOOD EDUCATION

3rd Edition

Early Childhood Education

Creative Learning Activities

Barbara Day
University of North Carolina, Chapel Hill

Macmillan Publishing Company
New York

Acknowledgments

Special recognition and many thanks to:

1. The teachers and administrative staffs of the Frank Porter Graham Child Development Center; University of North Carolina, Chapel Hill; the Jeffreys Grove School; Wake County School System, Raleigh, North Carolina; and the Elizabeth Seawell Elementary School, the Glenwood Elementary School, the Estes Hills Elementary School: Chapel Hill-Carrboro City Schools, Chapel Hill, North Carolina, the Montessori Day School, North Carolina; the Overton Pre-School; Carolina Friends School, Chapel Hill, North Carolina; the Duke School for Children, Durham, North Carolina; Kiddlington Infant School, Oxford, England; the Eno Valley Elementary School, Durham County Schools, Durham, North Carolina; Hickory Grove Elementary School, Charlotte-Mecklenburg Schools, Charlotte, North Carolina; Demonstration Classroom, the University of North Carolina at Chapel Hill; Creswell Elementary School, Creswell, North Carolina; and North End Elementary School, Roxboro, North Carolina, for their cooperation and support in allowing most of the photographs in this book to be taken in their classrooms and learning centers.

2. Graduate students in early childhood education and colleagues including Cheryl Anderson, Sara Bell, Ed Bostley, Rachel Hilbert, Charlotte Hundley, Marshall McCorkle, Margie McFarland, Nancy Miles, and Jane Seawell at the University of North Carolina, Chapel Hill, for their enthusiasm, ideas, and interest in this publication.

3. Tempe Thomas at the University of North Carolina, Chapel Hill, for her tireless dedication and invaluable contributions in editing this book.

4. Barbara Smith and Janine Castro, graphic artists, for the excellent illustrations throughout this book.

Macmillan Publishing Company
866 Third Avenue, New York, New York 10022

Collier Macmillan Canada, Inc.

Library of Congress Cataloging-in-Publication Data
Day, Barbara, 1938–
  Early childhood education.
  Bibliography: p.
  Includes index.
  1. Open plan schools. 2. Creative activities and seatwork. 3. Education, Primary. I. Title.
LB1029.06D38 1988   372.13   87-18507
ISBN 0-02-327930-3

Printing: 4 5 6 7   Year: 9 0 1 2 3 4

ISBN 0-02-327930-3

To our Daughter, Susan, who brings
us pride, love, and happiness

and

To our Godchildren: Billy, Beth,
David, Andrew, Vince, John, Rachel,
and Barbara who now share with us the
joys of adolescence and young adulthood.

Contents

Introduction

Early Childhood Education: Creative Learning Activities, 3rd Edition is designed to help early childhood teachers, administrators, and supervisors provide a creative learning environment for young children. Such an environment is developmentally oriented and child centered. It invites individual and group learning through exploration and investigation.

Designing and operating a creative learning environment is a complex task, one that requires careful planning and organization of both the curriculum and the classroom environment. Effective curriculum organization consists of (1) a variety of learning centers containing experiential activities that accommodate children's individual developmental levels and learning styles, (2) skills groups that are used for direct instruction in specific curriculum areas, and (3) integrated approaches (i.e., units of study, thematic approaches, extended interest areas) that incorporate curriculum content across many subject areas to make learning meaningful and useful within the broad context of the child's world.

Systematic organization and management structure the environment to facilitate learning within such a curriculum. Color coding, contracts, and social-behavioral discipline methods are three effective organization and management techniques. Color coding learning centers and the materials, books, and activities within them creates order in a complex environment by enabling children to independently identify, work with, and replace materials. Contracts, written plans for each child's day, enable teachers to individualize learning experiences and plan a balanced program. Contracts also enable children to independently stay on task and to develop initiative and responsibility in carrying out assignments and selecting free-choice activities. Finally, effective social-behavioral classroom management techniques help minimize discipline problems and develop children's self-responsibility and control.

Three characteristics of an open and creative learning environment—active involvement, experience-based learning, and individualization—are essential for effective learning. Children learn by doing, and therefore the curriculum is structured to promote their active participation. Learning centers provide a variety of experiences through which children can actively seek and discover knowledge about themselves and their world. The curriculum then becomes a series of integrated experiences that build on previous learning and stimulate new learning and experiences. Teachers structure and guide the learning process based on their knowledge of the abilities and background of each child. Because children have unique developmental needs, learning styles, and interests, teachers tailor the learning process to fit each child. In an open learning environment, where caring teachers systematically plan and organize individualized learning experiences, each child can be creative and discover the many joys that learning has to offer.

Many historical precedents lend credibility to the open education approach. The European educator Pestalozzi (1746–1827) proposed that the young child learns best through activity and sense perception. Pestalozzi's learning through discovery

1

approach influenced Froebel (1782–1852), the father of the kindergarten, who proposed that the curriculum reflect the interests, impulses, and capacities of the specific group of children involved. Froebel observed that play is the child's main vehicle for learning, and he further proposed that a curriculum for young children be based on the child's natural desire to play and discover. Creative and open education values and utilizes play as a natural process of discovery. Maria Montessori (1870–1952), Italian physician and educator, stressed the use of a prepared environment to meet children's need to order and organize their world. Montessori recommended and used active involvement of children in the learning process, multi-age grouping, and self-correcting materials, all of which are features that have been incorporated in the open classroom.

John Dewey (1859–1952), a major figure in the progressive education movement, advocated many of the same principles associated with creative and open learning. The expression of individual pupil interest, learning through experience, and the acquisition of skills necessary for success in everyday life are but a few of the principles that Dewey found necessary for a sound learning experience. These principles, along with those expressed by Pestalozzi, Froebel, Montessori, and Piaget, validate the concept of creative learning. It is not merely another education fad or a flash-in-the-pan approach; rather, it is an approach based on traditional philosophies relating to the education of young children. And it works!

The classroom environment must reflect these principles, and a great deal of planning must be done by the teacher to accomplish this end. In a learning environment with children ranging in chronological age from 5 to 8, and whose actual developmental span is far greater, a tremendous amount of diversified materials is necessary to meet individual needs, interests, and abilities. The environment must be one that provides for all areas of development, including the specific social, emotional, motor, and cognitive requirements of early childhood. Such an environment is based on the following beliefs:

1. Children grow and develop at different rates and each child's rate is separate and distinct from that of any other child. This rate of development is often unrelated to chronological age.
2. Children are naturally curious and eager to learn, and they learn best when they are able to follow many of their own interests and desires to learn.
3. Learning is something children do rather than something that is done to them.
4. Play is a child's way of working and learning.
5. Children learn from each other; they learn to experience a sense of responsibility and achievement, to respect themselves and others, and to learn how to learn.
6. A rich learning environment, one deliberately designed with much to explore and to discover, is essential in helping young children to learn basic skills. Concrete and sensory materials are a vital part of this environment, since they are basic learning devices for the young child.
7. Basic skill development is considered essential in an open education learning environment; however, a variety of creative approaches to teaching and learning, including an integrated day, is suggested.
8. The development of initiative and self-reliance is encouraged in an atmosphere of trust and structured freedom.
9. Each child is a unique individual and must be appreciated and valued for his or her individuality in all areas.

An early childhood learning environment should be a comfortable, colorful place where children and adults can live together in a happy and relaxed atmosphere. This environment can be designed for large complexes or open-spaced schools where teachers work together in teams, or it may be designed for self-contained open classrooms. Physical structure does not determine openness; however, it may facilitate the process. The inside area should be carpeted, if possible, and large enough to allow for fluidity of movement and also to provide open space for group activities such as creative dramatics. The space can then be divided with movable walls or partitions to provide small spaces for special tutoring or quiet, individual, or small-group activities. There should be many windows, and there should be easy access to the outside, which is a vital part of the total learning environment.

Learning centers or areas provide the core of an early childhood learning environment, and this volume discusses ten such centers. The discussion of each learning center includes: environmental resources, materials (commercial and teacher-made), objectives, and suggested activities. The suggestions for each center are a sample of appropriate activities, and are not intended to be all-inclusive. Basic textbooks and other resource materials will continue to be part of the total program.

The possibilities for centers are limitless. Centers should contain self-correcting activities at various levels of difficulty that require a minimum of teacher direction. An attractive center will invite investigation and provide opportunities for children to learn through exploration. Some centers may be prepared by the teacher to accomplish a specific objective. Others may be an eclectic arrangement of interesting items where children find their own purposes. Still other centers may be assembled spontaneously to meet the particular interest of the moment.

An important element of this environment is its "openness." Activities flow from one area to another and every possibility for optimal use of space is explored. There may, of course, be physical limitations, depending on the design of the structure, but whenever possible, the flow should include the outdoors, halls, a parent room or space where parents are involved with children, and perhaps the kitchens and cafeterias of the school. Learning centers and areas should be well planned to allow ease of movement and accessibility.

The organization of the learning areas changes with changing needs. Often the curriculum is an evolving, rather than a prescriptive one. Choice is provided, depending on the needs and interests of each child. Children demonstrate responsibility as they move from center to center and complete the assignments. Children and adults are open and sensitive to each other, and there is frequent contact between individual students and teachers.

How might an open early childhood learning environment appear to an observer? Imagine yourself visiting an environment such as this for the first time.

You have heard of an open learning environment such as the one you are about to visit, but somehow you feel that it will be different from the verbal descriptions. You finally reach the building, and you are impressed by the outdoor learning environment. You notice the flower and vegetable gardens, the play equipment, the animals, and many children of various ages engaged in a number of activities. As you move closer, you see that the outside is ordered into different sections (cement patios and grassy areas) and that doors lead to the inside from these areas. One child is sitting in a small rocking chair on the grassy area reading *Charlotte's Web*. A small group of children on the patio are "building a city" with blocks. A young boy comes up to you, says "hello," asks your name, and hands you a yellow flower. You walk to another area that houses animals. There are fine homemade cages and pens containing chickens, ducks, rabbits, and guinea pigs. The animals are being fed and cared for by enthusiastic children. A 7-year-old girl is instructing a 5-year-old boy in how to hold a rabbit correctly.

Around the school is a play area with gymnastic equipment, tire swings, slides, climbing poles, and other apparatus. You turn your attention briefly to a small red-haired boy who is measuring the slide ladder with a measuring tape and recording it in a notebook.

Over on another sheltered patio, children are moving freely from the inside to the outside. There is one child with an easel and paints; two children are making birdhouses at the woodworking bench. A 6-year-old girl is sitting on the patio writing about bugs in a notebook. Three older children are sitting at the brightly painted round table (once used for telephone wire) playing a math game.

From this patio you can see inside the classroom area, as you could from the other outside areas. As you walk into the room, you get the same feeling of action and spontaneity that you did observing the children outside. There are few individual desks in the room. Instead, there are tables supporting what look like interest or learning centers. There are also special work-study tables in an area where the teacher meets with small skills-groups in reading and mathematics. On one side of the room is an arts and crafts area. Two children are making animals out of juice cans and construction paper. In the adjacent corner is a math area, with measuring materials, several sets of Cuisenaire rods, and graph paper. Two boys are charting the weights of three baby guinea pigs born the week before. A third child who has tired of painting joins them in their task. There is a daybed near the math area. Two boys are stretched out drawing pictures of each other. In what looks to be a language arts center, a woman, possibly a parent, is typing a story being dictated by two 5-year-olds. In the reading corner an older child is reading to a younger one who is stretched out on an oval rug. You spot another mother near a science area holding a small, squirming infant while talking to a group of three or four children about baby mammals.

As you are looking around the room, you are seeing children ages 5 to 8 engaged in many different activities, some in groups and some alone. They are writing, reading, listening, talking, building, painting. They seem to be getting along extremely well. You suddenly feel that something is missing—the teacher. As you search the room, you see several adults interacting with the children. Which is the teacher? You are told by a polite 5-year-old that "That is the teacher," the woman calmly writing on the blackboard, unattended. She turns at a request for her presence at a "tea party" prepared and served by a group of boys and girls and joins them with a smile.

What is this experience all about? What does it tell you about this classroom? It is a creative learning environment to be sure, but what does that mean? In essence, it is an environment where teachers, parents, and children are finding their own ways of expressing and exploring what they have to offer each other. Everyone learns from each other. Each person is a facilitator of learning. There is a wealth of materials and experiences, all very carefully organized. The children are learning to be independent, to follow directions, to be self-motivated, to explore, to inquire, and to discover. Of utmost importance, these children are experiencing the joy of learning.

This book is intended to aid you in helping young children find joy and challenge through a variety of creative learning activities. This third edition includes a new chapter on creativity, many new suggested activities, and further discussion of the theory and research that provide direction and support for the development of creative learning activities.

1

Creative Learning

What is creativity? Is creativity an important and appropriate goal for early childhood education? If so, how does the creative process work and what can educators do to support and enhance the development of creativity? The answers to these questions provide the conceptual background for the remainder of this book on creative learning activities.

Creativity is a difficult concept to define. People often think of creativity as a unique gift possessed by artists, musicians, writers, architects, scientists, and others who create original ideas, art forms, and structures. From a broader perspective, creativity is a way of thinking, acting, or making something that is original for the individual and is valued by that person and by others (Mayesky, Neuman, & Wlodkowski, 1985). A person does not have to be the first to think, do, or make something in order for it to be a creative act; the creative significance lies in its originality and value for the individual and others. From this perspective, one can see that creativity is a quality that everyone possesses in varying degrees. For young children, who are just beginning to explore the world around them and to acquire language and the countless other ways in which they can express themselves, almost all acts are creative.

The Importance of Creativity

Assuming that everyone has some creative capacity, the question remains as to whether and why it is important for early childhood educators to nurture and enhance creativity. Is creative learning (or learning to be creative) an appropriate goal of early education and the educational system in general? Or is it more appropriate to focus on teaching "the basics," i.e., traditionally accepted knowledge and ideas, practical skills, and standard methods of expression? Over the past two decades, open and creative education in America has been criticized for offering too many "soft" choices and not enough "hard" skills that children need to succeed in school and become productive citizens. Yet over the same period, American government and industry have suffered from lack of creative vision and innovative skill in solving the complex economic, political, and social problems of today's rapidly changing world. The issue

5

of appropriate goals is not an either/or question; the answer is both/and! Creativity involves both the hard realm of practical skills and knowledge and the soft realm of imagination and intuitive impulse. In essence, creativity is the integration of imagination and practical skills.

To enable children to make this integration, to help them be creative, is an appropriate goal of education, and it is a goal that American society has traditionally valued and required. Respect and demand for creativity is inherent in the individual rights and the general process of government established by our constitution. The Bill of Rights guarantees freedoms that allow and encourage innovative thinking, expression, and action within the bounds of the common good. Our participative system of government, which the people themselves maintain, assess, and improve through the electoral process, requires the creative capacity within us all. To quote from a recent editorial on American education, "creativity has powered America's success . . ." and, "if we are to fulfill our next destiny in the world—'to help the indigent majority of mankind to struggle upward toward a better life,' as he [historian Arnold Toynbee] put it—then America must 'treasure and foster all the creative ability she has in her' " (Geyer, 1987).

The Creative Process

Although it is beyond the scope of early education to solve world problems, to encourage creative thinking is an appropriate and attainable goal. Creative thinking is a critical part of everyday tasks such as counting, reading, writing, deciphering someone else's writing, and solving problems (Trostle & Yawkey, 1981). Different writers have suggested that creativity is an inherited ability, that it is a personality trait, or that it develops as a result of environmental influences. Creativity probably stems from all three sources, and educators' concern is with the source over which they have control, the learning environment.

In order to design a learning environment that supports the creative process, we must first understand how that process works. Some researchers suggest that creativity is a purely cognitive process. Guilford (1968) proposed that creative thinking involves "the interaction of the cognitive traits of fluency, flexibility, elaboration, and originality." Other researchers support the view that the creative process involves the whole person, not only the cognitive domain. Torrance (1962) proposed that before creativity reaches the realm of logic, it is first nurtured in the emotional, the irrational, the preconscious.

Mayesky et al. (1985) support the latter view. They designed a two-part model for creative activity. The first part of creative activity leads to the discovery of ideas, answers, or solutions. This part involves the intuitive processes of imagination and speculation. The second part of creative activity leads to proving or disproving the ideas discovered in the first part. This involves the learned skills of evaluation and analysis.

When the creative process is broken down in this way, educators can begin to see how to support it. To support the first part, discovery, young children must have opportunities to use their imagination, play with ideas, and generally reflect on the world around them. To support the second part, proving, children must acquire knowledge (relevant facts) and basic analysis and evaluation skills. Although there is no guaranteed formula for producing creative geniuses (Torrance & Torrance, 1973),

researchers have found that certain factors can enhance the creativity already present in a child. These factors can be categorized as teacher attitudes and behaviors, teaching strategies, and environmental characteristics.

Teacher Attitudes and Behaviors

Teachers play an important role in the development of children's creativity. The first way in which they do this is being aware of what creative behaviors are, and supporting creative behaviors by praising those behaviors and by providing opportunities for those behaviors to occur. George Maxim (1985), in his book, *The Very Young,* describes the characteristics of very creative children. According to Maxim, creative children:

- have amazingly long attention spans when involved in creative endeavors
- have a surprising capacity for organization and demonstrate a need for order
- are able to return to familiar things and see them in different ways and in greater depth
- learn a great deal through fantasy and solve many of their problems of development by using fantasy
- enjoy "playing" with words and seem to be natural storytellers

Such characteristics are present to some degree in all children, not only the creatively gifted. Teachers must remember that every child has the capacity to be creative and should be encouraged to do so. Mayesky et al. (1985) have made several suggestions for identifying creativity in children. Teachers should provide free periods when materials are available and children can do whatever they wish with the materials; they should question children in ways that permit them to freely express opinions and ideas; and they should encourage children to share experiences. Mayesky et al. (1985) further suggest eight ways in which teachers can help children express their natural creative tendencies. These are as follows:

1. help children accept change
2. help children realize that some problems have no easy answers
3. help children realize that many problems have a number of possible answers
4. help children learn to evaluate and accept their own feelings
5. reward children for being creative
6. help children feel joy in their creative productions and in working through a problem
7. help children appreciate themselves for being different
8. help children develop perseverance

Teachers can also promote creativity by modeling creative behavior. Smith (1966) proposed that teachers must see themselves as the "bridging engineers" between the research they have read and the students they must teach. Teachers are the agents who put theory to work, and they must model intelligent, open-minded, and creative behavior for their students. Torrance (1962) found that students with more creative teachers produce more creative work than students with less creative teachers. Whether motivation, imitation, or both create this effect is unknown. The important point is that modeling creative behavior works.

What are the characteristics of creative teachers? Creative teachers are confident in their own abilities, as well as those of their students. They balance freedom and necessary limits, realizing that if students do not have enough room to explore and make mistakes, they will not be able to grow (Smith, 1966). Creative teachers are sensitive listeners, respect their students' ideas, and help students explore and test those ideas (Hilgard, 1959). They know their students' capabilities, and teach children that they should strive for their own goals, not someone else's (Smith, 1966).

In addition, Hilgard (1959) says, "We must allow sensitivity to new ideas, perhaps tolerating a little foolishness. We must not develop critical abilities to the point that anything unproven is stupid or anything weak is altogether wrong." For the creative classroom to flourish, teachers must reward creativity, differences among children, and originality, rather than likeness or conformity. By doing this, they help students recognize the worth of their own creative talent (Smith, 1966). Creative teachers are organized and careful planners, but they do not overplan to the point that they lose the flexibility to seize the moment. They give their students room to invent (Smith, 1966). Above all, creative teachers continually evaluate and refine the methods and strategies that work for themselves and their unique students; they cannot always copy what has been successful with other teachers and students.

Teaching Strategies

In addition to general teacher attitudes and behaviors, researchers have also found that certain teaching strategies can be used to promote creativity. Such strategies include teaching problem-solving and creative thinking skills, the creative-aesthetic approach, questioning strategies, and play. Teachers can combine elements from these strategies to create an approach that works for them and their students.

Problem-Solving and Creative Thinking Skills

Several researchers have evaluated the effects of problem-solving training. Torrance and Torrance (1973) defined problem-solving skills as:

1. Becoming aware of problems and missing information;
2. Defining the problem;
3. Retrieving, assimilating, and accommodating information from one's own life experiences;
4. Coming up with alternative solutions;
5. Using criteria to evaluate solutions;
6. Testing the most promising solutions;
7. Deciding which solution is best; and
8. Working out plans and details for implementing the solution.

Severeide and Sugawara (1985) used these skills to train primary grade students to think creatively. Students were taught the skills through a method called chunking, i.e., breaking down the creative problem-solving process into chunks or strategies. Students who were taught these skills scored higher on tests of creativity than students who were not taught the skills. Shaklee and Amos (1985) used a similar strategy, breaking down problem-solving skills into fact finding, problem finding, idea finding, solution finding, and acceptance finding. In their experiment, they used learning centers that stressed self-expression, language skills, problem-solving, and logical thinking. They found that this environment encouraged "sensitivity and awareness of problems, questioning strategies and discussion, generating a wide variety of ideas, and deferred judgment during idea finding" (Shaklee & Amos, 1985). In spite of these positive findings, they found no significant increase in creative thinking after a six-week treatment.

Another researcher has suggested that preschoolers can be taught creative thinking skills more effectively than elementary school children. Khatena, in a 1971 study involving disadvantaged preschoolers, trained the experimental group in three creative thinking strategies: breaking away from the obvious and commonplace, restructuring, and synthesis. Khatena found that children's scores on tests of creative thinking were significantly higher after this training. The practical implication of all these studies for teachers may be that it is important to begin developing creative thinking skills as early as possible, and that children should be taught specific creative thinking skills as well as generic problem-solving skills.

Creative-Aesthetic Approach

In the creative-aesthetic approach to learning, creative thinking skills are combined with aesthetic activities. The objective of this approach is to develop intellectual skills, abilities, and attitudes that will be useful in later learning (Torrance, 1969). In this approach, activities are designed to bring out creative thinking, problem solving, fluency of ideas, fluency in verbal expression, and auditory and visual awareness and discrimination.

In a study of the creative-aesthetic approach, the activities chosen were art and the active use of materials, music, rhythms, and creative dancing. Also included were food preparation, sharing or dividing food, and measuring objects. Further, beginning reading, phonics, games, number games, and dramatizations of children's own writing were all part of the curriculum. The children in the experiment showed substantial growth in verbal fluency, flexibility, and originality. Severeide and Sugawara (1985) found that the creative-aesthetic approach was effective in increasing creative thinking.

Questioning Strategies

Certain questioning strategies have also been found to be effective in promoting creative thinking. Children learn to ask their peers the same kinds of questions that adults ask them (Cliatt, Shaw, & Sherwood, 1980). If children are only asked questions with predictable answers, they will ask such questions, and may tend to focus on the obvious rather than the possibilities. Ozgener (1970) found that more creative thinking occurred when evaluative divergent questions were asked than when only cognitive-memory questions were asked. One example of the many divergent thinking questions that can be used with young children is "What other things could you do with these materials?"

Play

Play is one of the most popular strategies for teaching creative thinking. Smith and Dutton (1979) found that students performed a specific task better through play than through being trained to perform the task. Half of the children in their experiment were trained to get a marble out of a box by fitting blocks and sticks together in a certain way. They were given eight minutes of instruction time. The other half of the students were given eight minutes to play with the materials and discover how to perform the task. Those who played performed the task faster than those who were trained. This is important for teachers to remember since direct instruction is often thought of as the most efficient way of teaching. Interestingly, the researchers also observed that motivation did not seem to be as high in the students who played. The conclusions that might be drawn from this are (1) that children engaged in play are more motivated than they appear and/or (2) that even when highly motivated children are taught through direct instruction they may learn better and faster through play. As noted in the introduction to this book, early childhood specialists have traditionally agreed that play is the child's main vehicle for learning.

Trostle and Yawkey (1981) developed seven strategies to enhance play. They are:

1. *Physical Cues.* Teachers permit children to use the objects they want to. Teachers provide and help children find materials that are interesting and useful, and are also safe.
2. *Adult Playfulness.* When teachers act out creative roles, children will soon model the process. For example, the teacher could pretend to be a robot while the children give the robot commands.
3. *Exploration.* Teachers provide time for children to explore new objects and materials before using them in creative thinking.
4. *Oral Cues.* Teachers use "idea sparkers" to expand creativity. For example, the teacher asks a child playing with a doll how he or she might show the doll walking to the store to buy some bread.
5. *Descriptions.* Teachers elaborate on what the student have already said and make it more visually descriptive.
6. *Modifying Objects.* Teachers remove objects that have lost their creative appeal, and change them to make them more interesting.
7. *Adding Objects.* During children's role playing, teachers may provide additional relevant objects that the children create a use for in their play.

Environmental Characteristics

Just as important as teacher behavior and special teaching strategies is the general environment in which learning occurs. If a safe and stimulating environment is provided that fosters creativity, then children will naturally seek out the possibilities. Children's expressive attempts are intrinsically motivated. According to Schachtel, "the motivation lies in the need to relate to the external world" (quoted in Busse & Mansfield, 1980).

Naturally inquisitive, children venture out, relate to the environment, and learn that the environment reacts to them. Children's perceptions of the positive or negative reactions to their probings determine the likelihood of future investigations and their understanding of the limits within that environment. Limits direct children's energies elsewhere, and are a natural part of understanding how the world operates. The teacher's task is to construct a learning environment that welcomes exploration and has meaningful and necessary limits, rather than arbitrary limits that inhibit creativity.

Maxim (1985) lists environmental conditions that stimulate creative behavior:

1. Time limits are removed from activities in which children are deeply involved.
2. A free, open atmosphere is established where open expression is encouraged.
3. The children are allowed to share ideas and to stimulate one another's thinking.
4. Conditions producing stress and anxiety are removed from the environment.

Khatena (1971) stressed that the environment must include stimulating concrete materials, since young children's "stage of cognitive development allows them to handle nonverbal materials where it will not permit them to handle verbal material." For the concrete materials to be beneficial, they must be played with and manipulated (Torrance, 1959, as cited by Smith, 1966). A variety of materials are important in building both children's knowledge base and creative ability. As Smith (1966) noted, knowledge, facts, and skills are necessary "to aid in the divergent thinking process." Children can play with and manipulate knowledge, facts, and skills, as well as concrete materials, in the fantasies they create in their dramatic play.

Conclusion

In summary, children tend to be more creative in an environment where adults are warm and encouraging; where many concrete materials and activities are challenging, rewarding, expressive, and open-ended; where there is time and freedom for children to learn and practice skills at their own pace; and where there are many opportunities to explore, inquire, and discover. The remainder of this book describes in detail the structure, organization, and materials and activities that create such an environment.

The structural framework recommended for a creative learning environment consists of a variety of learning centers with materials and activities that stimulate and satisfy children's natural desire to explore and learn about themselves and the world around them. The organizational and management techniques suggested—color coding, contracts, and behavioral-social management techniques—give children the support, security, and confidence to learn effectively and creatively.

The benefits of a creative learning environment are immeasurable for the children and teachers involved. Children want to bring out new ideas, have new experiences, and express themselves openly (Mayesky et al., 1985). In an environment that values and enhances the development of their individuality and their potential for creative thinking and learning new skills, children will feel good about themselves and will fully experience the joy of seeking and finding many solutions to life's challenges. Teachers will experience the joy of developing closer relationships (and having fewer discipline problems) with children, appreciating the uniqueness and individuality of each child, and helping children realize their full creative potential.

References

Busse, T. V., & Mansfield, R. S. (1980). Theories of the Creative Process: A Review and a Perspective. *The Journal of Creative Behavior, 14,* 91–103.

Cliatt, M. J., Shaw, J. M., & Sherwood, J. M. (1980). Effects of Training on the Divergent-Thinking Abilities of Kindergarten Children. *Child Development, 51,* 1061–1064.

Geyer, G. A. (1987, July 30). Creativity Has Powered America's Success. *The News and Observer,* p. 19A.

Guilford, J. P. (1968). *Intelligence, Creativity, and Their Educational Implications.* San Diego: Robert R. Knapp.

Hilgard, E. (1959). Creativity and Problem Solving. In Harold H. Anderson, *Creativity and Its Cultivation.* New York: Harper and Brothers.

Khatena, J. (1971). Teaching Disadvantaged Preschool Children to Think Creatively with Pictures. *Journal of Psychology, 62,* (5), 384–386.

Maxim, G. W. (1985). Creativity: Encouraging the Spirit of Wonder and Magic. In G. W. Maxim, *The Very Young* (pp. 359–402). Belmont, Ca.: Wadsworth Publishing Company.

Mayesky, M., Neuman, D., & Wlodkowski, R. J. (1985). *Creative Activities for Young Children* (3rd ed.). New York: Delmar Publishers.

Ozgener, E. S. (1970). Teachers Need to Ask Creative Type Questions. (ERIC Document Reproduction Service No. ED 160–207.)

Severeide, R., & Sugawara, A. I. (1985, November). The Effectiveness of Creative Experiences in Enhancing Creative Development. (ERIC Document Reproduction Service No. 258–375.)

Shaklee, B. D., & Amos, N. G. (1985, November). The Effectiveness of Teaching Creative Problem Solving Techniques to Enhance the Problem Solving Ability of Kindergarten Students. (ERIC Document Reproduction Service No. 264–292.)

Smith, J. A. (1966). *Setting Conditions for Creative Teaching in the Elementary School.* Boston: Allyn and Bacon.

Smith, P. K., & Dutton, S. (1979). Play and Training in Direct and Innovative Problem-Solving. *Child Development, 50,* 830–836.

Torrance, E. P. (1962). Cultural Discontinuities and the Development of Originality of Thinking. *Exceptional Children, 29,* 2–13.

Torrance, E. P. (1969). A 3-Year Study of the Influence of a Creative-Aesthetic Approach to School Readiness and Beginning Reading and Arithmetic on Creative Development. (ERIC Document Reproduction Service No. 41–419.)

Torrance, E. P., & Torrance, P. (1973). *Is Creativity Teachable?* Phi Delta Kappan, Bloomington, Ind.

Trostle, S. L., & Yawkey, T. D. (1981). Creative Thinking and the Education of Young Children: The Fourth Basic Skill. (ERIC Document Reproduction Service No. 204–015.)

2

Organizing the Learning Environment and Guiding Young Children

A well organized and creative early childhood learning environment reflects children's interests, developmental levels, and learning styles. It is humanistic and personalized, and it facilitates responsibility for discovery and learning in children. Such an environment is organized so that children work directly with the teacher both individually and in small groups, engage in independent activities planned by the teacher, and spend time on their own free-choice activities. Key components in organizing the environment and guiding children within it include: learning centers with a variety of multi-level and self-correcting materials, color coding of learning materials, contracts designed jointly by the student and the teacher, behavioral-social management techniques, parent involvement, and comprehensive evaluation.

Developmental Assumptions and Goals

The first step in organizing a creative, effective, and appropriate early childhood program is to state developmental assumptions and goals for the children involved. These assumptions and goals then form the basis for designing an environment, teaching strategies, and activities that fit with young children's developmental levels and learning styles.

The work of the Swiss psychologist Jean Piaget (1896–1980) has provided comprehensive insight into the development of young children. Piaget's theory has been supported in concept and practice by early leaders such as Pestalozzi, Montessori, Froebel, and Dewey, as well as by modern researchers and practitioners. Current professional standards articulated by the National Association for the Education of Young Children (NAEYC) cite the application of child development knowledge as the first and foremost determinant of the quality of early education programs (*Developmentally Appropriate Practice,* 1986). Following is a brief summary of Piaget's observations about how young children learn and develop.

14

According to Piaget, children from two to seven years of age are in the preoperational stage of development. Children at this stage are eager learners, constantly exploring, manipulating, and experimenting with the environment in order to learn more about it. They are rapidly acquiring language, and are eager to know and use new words. Within the range of preoperational development, there are many levels, and individual children develop at their own unique rates in the different domains of cognitive-intellectual, psychosocial, and physical-motor development.

In the area of cognitive-intellectual development, children this age are just beginning to develop reasoning powers. They generally focus on one aspect of an object or situation and have difficulty discriminating between perception and reality. Preoperational children develop cognitive abilities by performing concrete operations and then reflecting on what happens, rather than by being "taught" abstract rules.

According to Piaget, play is one of the most important learning activities of young children. As young children develop they tend to progress from solitary observational kinds of play to more active cooperative forms of play. Young children's play both reflects and promotes their development in all areas. Through play, young children solve problems, acquire enriched meaning for language and ideas, express and meet emotional needs, try out new roles and activities, develop social relationships and skills, exercise and develop muscles, and generally explore and make sense of the world around them (Leeper, Witherspoon, & Day, 1984). The importance of play as the young child's natural learning vehicle cannot be overemphasized; the learning environment should accommodate and promote many different kinds and levels of play.

In the area of psychosocial development, Piaget observed that children of this age are becoming less egocentric, and are gradually learning to see the viewpoints of other people. They are easily influenced and molded by home and school activities. Attending school, being with other students, and being with the teacher can be strong motivators for the child (Evans, 1975). A nonthreatening, secure, and yet challenging learning atmosphere is important in utilizing these intrinsic sources of motivation. Young children need and respond to praise, smiles, encouragement, or any positive acknowledgment for a job well done. Because of their development away from a self-centered base, encouragement and esteem-building help to strengthen the children's self-images and to promote gains in learning.

In the area of physical-motor development, fine motor skills such as grasping, lacing, and other finger manipulations generally lag behind gross motor development. Preoperational children need experience with large objects that can be easily manipulated. As practice increases their skill, they can move on to work with smaller, finer objects. Exercise to maintain the large muscle skills of running, jumping, climbing, pulling, and pushing is important.

The High/Scope Curriculum Comparison Project (Schweinhart, Weikart, & Larner, 1986; Weikart, Epstein, Schweinhart, & Bond, 1978), a 15-year evaluation of the short- and long-term effects of three preschool programs for disadvantaged children, supports the application of Piaget's child development theory in early childhood curriculum. The programs compared in the study were a traditional child-centered nursery school, the open-framework High/Scope model, and a direct instruction program. The programs differed primarily in the amount of child-initiated activity as opposed to teacher-initiated activity, and in the focus on narrow academic goals as opposed to broader social development goals.

The traditional nursery school program and the High/Scope curriculum involved a high degree of child-initiated activity, included play and experiential learning activities, and had social development goals. The traditional nursery school focused on social development and self-esteem. Children in this program initiated their own free-play activities with the teacher playing a supportive but noninterfering role. The High/Scope program focused on social and physical development as well as general cognitive development. In this program teachers and children planned and initiated activities together, and teachers organized the environment with experiences and interest centers to promote active learning. The direct instruction program focused exclusively on developing clearly-defined academic skills, with the teacher initiating closely prescribed interaction sequences and students playing a responsive role.

The researchers found that although children in all three programs achieved and maintained significant gains in IQ and academic achievement, participants in the two programs featuring child-initiated activities reported more positive social behavior patterns at age 15 than participants from the direct instruction program. Specifically, they reported having committed half as many acts of delinquency, participating more in sports and extracurricular activities, and believing that their families regarded them more favorably. Lawrence Schweinhart suggests that the difference may have occurred because the traditional nursery school and High/Scope program had explicit social goals for the children, promoted greater self-responsibility and initiative by giving children some control over their activities, and addressed the children's total needs and interests instead of focusing only on academic performance (Schweinhart, 1986).

From this background of Piaget's child development theory and findings from the High/Scope Curriculum Comparison Study, the following developmental assumptions and goals can be drawn. These assumptions clearly support a creative approach to early education that allows for active exploration, experimentation, and inquiry within an environment that is both open and carefully structured to meet a broad range of developmental needs and goals.

1. Children grow and develop at unique, individual rates that are often unrelated to chronological age. (Many learning activities at a variety of challenge levels should be provided in an effort to meet the needs of all children. Even within the range of preoperational learning there are many levels.)
2. Children's natural curiosity and eagerness to learn are enhanced if children are free to follow many of their natural interests. (Piaget has said that children learn best through direct, immediate involvement with the environment. They learn through sensory input of observation, manipulation, and testing.)
3. Learning is what children do; it is not something that is done to them. (The child must be directly involved in doing the learning. Telling the child may result in empty verbalizations.)
4. Play is the child's way of working and learning. (Children acquire many skills through play. They try new roles, solve problems, learn how to make sense of the environment, and practice social skills.)
5. Children learn many things from each other, including respect for themselves and others, ways of learning how to learn, and a sense of responsibility and achievement. (Bloom [1981] has described "such basic characteristics of 'learning to learn' as the ability to receive instruction from adults, deferring gratification of reward, and the more generalized motivation to learn. It also includes the basic attitudes toward school and teacher.")

6. A specially constructed, rich learning environment, filled with concrete and sensory learning materials, is essential in helping children to learn. (The environment is the vehicle for learning, and it must provide the materials the child needs for exploration and learning.)

7. The integrated day, involving centers-oriented, simultaneously occurring activities within the learning environment, is one of the creative approaches to the development of basic skills. (Life is a spectrum of all types of overlapping skills and activities. An integrated approach helps the child to see how the newly acquired skills fit into a broader realm of experiences, thus providing a reason for learning. Children can see how learning "school skills" will help them in everyday life.)

8. In a learning atmosphere based on trust and structured freedom, children are encouraged to use their own initiative and to be self-reliant. (Children need reassurance and security but they also need intriguing challenge. They need and respond to praise for a job well done.)

9. The uniqueness of the child, as reflected in his or her individuality and learning style, should be appreciated and valued.

10. Young children are experiencing rapid and important development in many areas: cognitive-intellectual, psychosocial, and physical-motor. An appropriate program supports development in all areas, rather than focusing solely on cognitive development.

In addition, the National Academy of Early Childhood Programs presents ten components of group programs for young children, which are included in the Academy's Criteria for High Quality Early Childhood Programs (Accreditation Criteria & Procedures, 1986). A high-quality childhood program, as defined by the Academy, is one that "meets the needs of and promotes the physical, social, emotional, and cognitive development of the children and adults—parents, staff, and administrators—who are involved in the program." The ten components are as follows:

1. Interactions between children and staff provide opportunities for children to develop an understanding of self and others and are characterized by warmth, personal respect, individuality, positive support, and responsiveness. Staff facilitate interactions among children to provide opportunities for development of social skills and intellectual growth.

2. The curriculum encourages children to be actively involved in the learning process, to experience a variety of developmentally appropriate activities and materials, and to pursue their own interests in the context of life in the community and the world.

3. Parents are well informed about and welcome as observers and contributors to the program.

4. The program is staffed by adults who understand child development and who recognize and provide for children's needs.

5. The program is efficiently and effectively administered, with attention to the needs and desires of children, parents, and staff.

6. The program is sufficiently staffed to meet the needs of and promote the physical, social, emotional, and cognitive development of children.

7. The indoor and outdoor physical environment fosters optimal growth and development through opportunities for exploration and learning.

8. The health and safety of children and adults are protected and enhanced.

9. The nutritional needs of children and adults are met in a manner that promotes physical, social, emotional, and cognitive development.

10. Systematic assessment of the effectiveness of the program in meeting its goals for children, parents, and staff is conducted to ensure that good quality care and education are provided and maintained.

Organizing for Creative Learning

Based on the assumptions justifying a developmental approach to the education of young children, it appears that the learning environment in which such education can occur is one that is creative, individualized, stimulating, and experiential. A program organized around learning centers provides this kind of environment by giving children opportunities to play, experiment, and discover as they engage in activities that help them with problem-solving, learning basic skills, and understanding new concepts.

Learning Centers

Learning centers are carefully designed areas that contain a variety of learning activities and materials drawn from the classroom's basic skills program and from the themes and units being pursued. In learning centers children can manipulate objects, engage in conversation and role-playing, and learn at their own levels. Learning center experiences may be adapted to the individual child's learning style, ability, maturity, experience, and interest. Some activities may be required of all students, others may be assigned only for some students, and others may be optional. Learning centers enable children to develop independent learning skills because of the self-directing and self-correcting nature of many learning center materials.

One of the most significant features of the learning center approach is that each child can work at his or her own pace, with materials designed to meet his or her particular needs and level of learning. This requires careful planning and construction of materials to provide an individually appropriate foundation and structure for learning. Centers incorporate inquiry, discovery, and direct instruction, all of which channel the child's eagerness to learn toward individualized educational goals and result in broad educational achievement.

Before proceeding to a discussion of the core centers that could be utilized within a classroom setting, the rationale for and positive outcomes of a center-based learning environment should be understood:

1. A good early childhood program must focus on clearly defined goals and objectives. A developmental program with learning centers meets this criterion. Learning centers provide a succession of carefully focused and structured experiences that promote the development of academic, communication, and social skills; a positive self-concept, independence, and the ability to make choices; and values such as respecting, helping, and understanding others.

2. Effective early childhood programs accommodate individual developmental levels and needs. The learning center approach is most responsive to the needs and potential of children by offering a variety of experiences through which children can develop at their own unique rates.

3. Learning centers capitalize on children's natural curiosity, desire to learn, and active learning styles by providing for active experimentation, inquiry, and discovery. Centers make learning attractive and meaningful as children learn practical skills and concepts, and have the freedom to chose and initiate some activities based on their own interests.

With this rationale in mind, teachers can design a creative centers-based environment. To begin with, teachers should set up the number and kinds of centers they feel can be managed and kept in order. Later, more centers can be added and the original centers can be expanded with new activities to reflect the changing developmental levels and learning needs of the students. The first centers that teachers implement should be those in which children need the least teacher direction and contact. The purpose of the centers and directions for using materials and doing activities should be simple and clear. The centers should incorporate materials with which children are familiar from their experience at home, so that they will feel confident, secure, and thus, motivated to engage in center activities. By beginning in this way teachers can comfortably orient themselves and their students to the centers approach.

What centers might be included in a creative learning environment and what materials and activities might those centers contain? Following are examples of the core centers and program components that are typically found in early childhood classrooms.

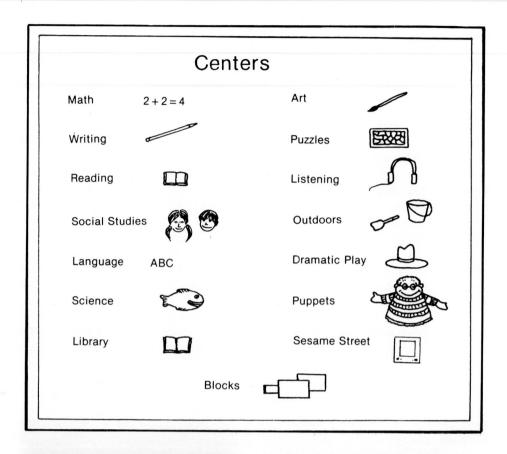

Centers

Math	$2 + 2 = 4$	Art	
Writing		Puzzles	
Reading		Listening	
Social Studies		Outdoors	
Language	ABC	Dramatic Play	
Science		Puppets	
Library		Sesame Street	
	Blocks		

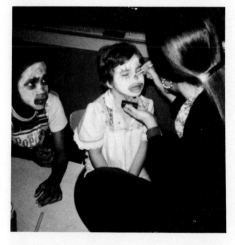

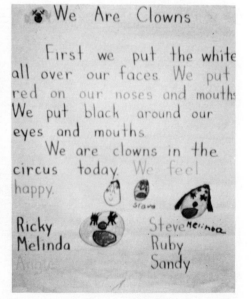

We Are Clowns

First we put the white all over our faces. We put red on our noses and mouths. We put black around our eyes and mouths.

We are clowns in the circus today. We feel happy.

Ricky   Steve
Melinda   Ruby
                 Sandy

Blocks Center

Activities with blocks give children the opportunity to experience the joy and mastery of building and creating; to engage in dramatic play; to develop social interaction and cooperation skills; to develop coordination, visual perception, and large and small motor skills; and to develop concepts in all curriculum content areas. Through activities with blocks, children can learn about measurement, gravity, spatial relationships, and language usage, among other things.

The blocks center might include unit blocks of all sizes and shapes, alphabet blocks, and accessories for building and decorating such as small people and animal figures, puppets, spools, wheeled toys, carpet squares, dominos, and so on. These materials and others like them give children the tools for a wide range of creative play and learning activities.

Communication: The Language Arts Centers

Communications skills cross all content fields and form an important foundation for the child's current and future success in school and life in general. Key communication skills include listening, reading, speaking, and writing.

A variety of learning centers can be designed to promote development in the language arts. A books area could include picture books, read-and-do books, comics, magazines, and catalogues. The books area should be a quiet, comfortable, and cozy place that allows for concentration and thought. Another language arts center could include materials for more active pursuits such as handwriting practice, directed

reading activities, language experience activities, dictation and composition of stories and books, puppets for enactment of stories, and other language expansion materials. Both small group instruction and individual study could occur in this center. A third area to promote communication skills, as well as investigation in all content areas, is a research center. This center would contain picture dictionaries, child encyclopedias, telephone directories, newspapers, slides, reference books, and information cards.

Fine Arts Centers

As with the language arts, several centers may be devoted to the fine arts. A music and listening area might include tapes, read-along stories, records, and rhythm in-

struments for accompanying or creating music. Activities in music centers include listening, singing, marching, playing instruments, and composing. An activity that taps both music and art skills is actually making and playing simple folk instruments. Music centers must be carefully planned and monitored by teachers to avoid distracting conflict between quiet and noisy activities.

Music and art centers help children develop aesthetic appreciation and expressive skills that will be rewarding and enriching throughout life. Music and art activities also enhance children's perceptual, language, gross and fine motor, social, and emotional development.

An art center would include a variety of materials for cutting, pasting, painting, drawing, sculpting, and craft making. The art center should also include "beautiful junk" such as ribbons, wallpaper scraps, cloth samples, shells, jewelry, boxes, wire, and cans for use in creative projects. The teacher might also set up a separate clay center with a special table or surface on which children can manipulate and experiment with several kinds of clay. Modeling clay, play dough, salt and flour clay, and natural clay from areas around the school can all be used along with objects for sculpting, pressing, cutting, and molding the clay.

Home Living and Creative Dramatics Centers

Home living and creative dramatics centers can provide valuable learning experiences for teachers as well as children. By observing children engaged in dramatic play, teachers can gain important insight into the child's world and developmental needs. Children learn and grow through dramatic play. It helps them build cooperative social relationships, practice and improve language and problem-solving skills, express and understand their emotions, and enhance sensorimotor skills, divergent thinking, and creativity. In addition to dramatic play, home living center activities such as cooking and stitchery help children learn to follow directions and think logically, develop small muscle skills and eye-hand coordination, acquire knowledge of good nutrition, and gain a sense of personal competence and achievement.

A home living and creative dramatics center might contain child-sized furniture and appliances; cooking, cleaning, and sewing equipment; dishes and tableware; and baby dolls and accessories. The center also includes props and materials for creating a variety of settings such as a store, a post office, or a hospital. The center may have an adjoining dress-up area with old clothes, costumes, shoes, and various trade and dressy hats.

Science and Mathematics Investigation Centers

Science and mathematics investigation centers provide opportunities to discover basic concepts through games, exploration, and experimentation. In keeping with young children's developmental level, activities in these centers help children understand abstract concepts through guided manipulation and investigation of concrete objects. Science and math center activities incorporate the scientific processes of observation, classification, measurement, computation, experimentation, and prediction in order to develop the basic process skills that are the framework for science and math education.

Materials for science centers include magnifying glasses, microscopes, scales, beakers, eyedroppers, prisms, yardsticks, litmus paper, and clocks. Natural objects for exploration include rocks, wood, leaves, water, soil, seeds, shells, flowers, plants, and household chemicals such as salt and vinegar. Indoor or outdoor gardens may be part of a science center. A living things center might include an antfarm, aquarium, earthworm farm, turtles, frogs, hamsters, guinea pigs, or other small animals that can be observed and cared for by the students.

Math centers would include materials such as math games, an abacus, play money, measuring cups, number blocks, adding machines, Cuisinaire rods, dominos, playing cards, number puzzles, geometric forms, number and fraction boards, and collections of all kinds (buttons, coins, marbles, sticks, etc.).

Movement

Although movement activities occur in open space rather than within the bounds of a learning center, movement is a central part of any early childhood program, and should be introduced along with the core learning centers. Movement activities help children to express themselves and to develop motor skills, confidence in the operation of their own bodies, and a positive self-concept. An appropriate movement program fits the developmental levels, skills, and experiences of the children involved. It begins with general exploration of individual body movements and progresses to more complex combined movements and cooperative movements with partners. Rather than demonstrating concepts and movements for children to imitate, teachers pose problems for children to explore creatively and successfully at their own skill levels. Examples of such challenges are: How wide is your space? If you keep one foot still and move the other, can you make your space wider? Pretend you are a cloud moving on a windy day. Can you move your arms in different directions? In front of you? Sideways? Behind you?

The resources required for a movement program are a large open area, music, floor mats, objects for manipulation such as balls, ropes, and hoops, a balance board, and a drum or tambourine for signalling changes in movement. Movement activities include body rolls, crawling, skipping, swaying, running, balancing, rhythmic activities, and many others.

Outdoor Play

Another core component of early childhood programs that occurs outside of a learning center is outdoor play. The outdoors is a natural learning environment and an extension of the activities from indoor learning centers. Children can practice math skills outdoors by measuring and counting natural objects. They can develop language arts skills by talking, writing, and reading about the many experiences they enjoy outdoors. Children can engage in dramatic play and the creative arts using natural outdoor objects or materials brought from inside the classroom. The outdoor environment is healthy and refreshing, and gives children needed freedom to make noise, move actively, and exercise large muscles.

Possibilities for outdoor activities include spontaneous and directed play, obstacle and movement courses, exercises, jump rope, carpentry, building playhouses such as teepees and tents, and exploration of nature via a nature trail, garden, or animals kept outdoors. Outdoor play equipment includes structures for climbing on or crawling through, swings, sawhorses, benches, low balance beams, sandpiles, slides, wading pools, and telephone wire spools. Activities and play materials in the outdoor world are limited only by the imagination.

People and Places: The Social Studies Centers

Social studies deal with the human experience and provide children with the knowledge, values, and skills to become responsible individuals and cooperative, constructive participants in small groups and the larger community. The social studies curriculum can and should be integrated with activities in all learning centers.

Possibilities for specific social studies centers abound. One center could focus on self-awareness and control. Activities in this center might include recording personal facts and histories, expressing feelings about different kinds of people, things, and activities, writing or role-playing responses to hypothetical situations, and drawing pictures of feelings. Other centers can focus on different people and places. These centers can involve one aspect of many places (such as food or dress around the world) or they can involve many aspects of one culture. For example, a center on Japan might include Japanese arts and crafts, maps, costumes, foods, models of the terrain and typical dwellings, and language activities such as drawing Japanese symbols or writing Haiku, a form of Japanese poetry.

Still other centers can focus on community awareness, specific occupations, and lifestyles, such as life on the farm. In conjunction with center activities, general classroom discussions and activities (small group problem-solving tasks, formulating classrooms rules, setting up and running a pretend store or bank, mock elections, etc.) can promote the development of social interaction skills and understanding of basic social science concepts.

Sand and Water Play Centers

Playing in sand and water is natural and fun for children. It is a sensory experience that provides many opportunities for learning. Through sand and water play activities children develop math concepts by measuring and noting equivalencies and differences. They learn about physical properties and develop classification skills by differentiating floating versus nonfloating and absorbent verus nonabsorbent materials. They develop language and communication skills through dramatic play with sand and water, and by tracing letters in sand or labeling bottles filled with sand or water. Children also develop large muscles by digging, hauling, and building with sand.

Activities in sand and water play centers include floating and sinking experiments;

weighing, measuring, and comparing quantities; building boats and having boat races; drawing letters, shapes, and numbers in the sand; experimenting with food color and water; making maps and building communities in the sand; and painting with water colors. Materials for these centers include plastic containers, corks, sponges, measuring spoons and containers, brushes, funnels, straws, pitchers, food color, tempera paints, spades, buckets, and wheelbarrows.

Woodworking Center

Woodworking provides opportunities for creative expression and emotional release, cooperative work and problem-solving, practical application and development of math skills and concepts (measuring, equality, proportion), and development of large and small muscle skills and eye-hand coordination. Children enjoy woodworking and gain a sense of accomplishment in their own work and appreciation for the property and work of others.

The basic woodworking operations are sanding, gluing, hammering, holding (with a vise or clamp), fastening (with screws), drilling, and sawing. Woodworking projects involving these operations are making napkin holders, birdhouses and feeders, trucks and cars, puzzles, buildings, and people and animal figures. Children may create objects in woodworking centers that relate to their activities in other learning centers. Materials for a woodworking center include a sturdy workbench, woodworking tools, large wood materials such as plywood, small wood materials such as popsicle sticks, building accessories such as wheels, linoleum, bottle tops, and safety and cleanup supplies. Teachers must carefully organize and supervise woodworking activities to ensure the children's safety and success.

Arrangement of Learning Centers

Once centers are selected for classroom use, the next step is to devise a classroom floorplan. In addition to learning centers, two important areas in the floor plan are open space and an individual storage area. The open space accommodates indoor movement activities and large group activities. Individual storage space for each child provides a sense of privacy and a place to keep personal items, clothing, and rain gear.

The placement and arrangement of learning centers should be planned to make the best use of the space available and to avoid interference between noisy and quiet activities. Low bookshelves, portable chalkboards, low cabinets or tables, and arrangements of child sized chairs and furniture can be used to separate center areas and to store and display materials. The overall arrangement should facilitate comfortable movement and efficient transitions among centers and other areas of the classroom.

Several researchers have found relationships between classroom arrangement and spatial features and children's behavior. Much of this research was conducted in classrooms operating learning centers in preschool settings.

Kritchevsky, Prescott, and Walling (1977) identified several principles concerning the relationship between spatial arrangement and behavior in young children. The spaces arranged by teachers in classrooms encourage children to move in one direction or another, enter or leave an area, to pause or to pass by without attending. Space invites children to talk with others, hurry or move calmly, touch others or leave them alone, combine materials or keep them separated. When behavior encouraged by the environment is expected and desired, teachers are more likely to respond in positive ways that support activities and learning. When the resulting behavior is unexpected or unwanted, teachers tend to recite rules, redirect, scold, or restrain children. In either situation, spatial organization is a strong influence on both teacher and child behavior.

Weinstein (1977) found that changes in the physical setting of a classroom can produce changes in student behavior in predictable, desirable directions. Changes in the classroom environment modified children's spatial patterns (children moved into centers they had previously avoided) and broadened the range of behaviors previously exhibited (children exhibited less "large physical activity," for example). However, she too found that environmental factors only influenced the children's behavior if the activities/materials available were of interest to the children. She concluded that environmental changes intended to increase a desirable behavior will have maximum impact when the inclination to engage in the activity is already present. Weinstein (1979), in a review of the research on the physical environment of the school, also suggests that the learning centers of "subsettings" of early child-hood classrooms do indeed exert "coercive power" over the inhabitants, constrain-ing certain behaviors and encouraging others. She states that different educational activities have varying environmental requirements, that different individuals may require different types of environments in order to function effectively, and that "susceptibility" to different environmental factors may vary with developmental age.

Altman and Wohlwill (1978) point out that young children may be particularly sensitive to modification of the environment. Morrow and Weinstein (1982) suggest that if this is true, then the opportunity for achieving a positive impact on develop-ment may be correspondingly greater in the case of the young child. They contend that a well-designed classroom facilitates behaviors that enhance cognitive develop-ment. They agree with Phyfe-Perkins (1979), who suggests that the "skill of arranging the early childhood environment to support the maximum involvement of children with materials and with each other is a skill that can and should be taught." Chapter 13 includes several classroom designs that can help teachers effectively arrange classrooms with learning centers.

Effectiveness of Learning Centers

Researchers have examined whether and when learning centers and the classrooms operating them are effective. Some have compared the impact of different types of learning materials and activities on pupil involvement. Others have studied student behavior and engagement rates in various classroom groupings (small group, large group, independent seatwork, and independent activity in learning centers). Others have focused on the impact of management techniques in complex centers-oriented classrooms as well as the effectiveness of such classrooms compared with class-rooms using whole and small group instruction. On the whole, the research sum-marized here suggests that classrooms operating several learning centers are indeed effective when the classroom is well managed and the centers include a variety of appropriate materials.

Rosenthal (1974) found that the length of stay in an activity setting (i.e., learning center) was attributable to the center's holding power rather than to the child's attention span. Other researchers have found that the complexity, variety, and format of materials and activities are all factors that influence pupil involvement, length of attention, and behavior.

Jones (1973) found that providing learning areas with materials of a high level of complexity usually promoted involvement and a fairly long attention span for pupils, combined with independence from teacher assistance and direction. A low level of complexity brought frequent activity change, physical movement, shorter attention span, and a need for adult direction and assistance.

In two different studies, Kounin and Sherman (1979) looked for a significant relationship between the amount of variety the teacher builds into a classroom activity segment and the amount of pupil involvement. Variety had no relationship to pupil involvement in teacher-led segments of the school day; however, there was a substantial relationship between high variety and pupil involvement when children were working independently. Children in first and second grades were much more involved in high variety segments than were children in low variety segments.

Investigations have also shown that pupil involvement can be related to whether or not the activity format calls for active input of stimuli or passive availability of materials and events. In a study of third graders the average pupil involvement scores in all active input segments was 85 percent. It was 75 percent during passive availability segments (Gump, 1967). Another study involving grades one through five showed pupil involvement in recitation segments (active input) to be 85 percent, yet only 65 percent in seatwork (passive availability) segments. Misconduct beyond simple noninvolved behavior was almost four times as frequent in the seatwork segments (Kounin, Friesen, & Norton, 1966).

Numerous studies have addressed the effect of various grouping structures on student behavior. These studies have reported conflicting findings. Many investigations have concluded that there are no demonstrated differences between student engagement rates during different classroom groupings (Cooley & Leinhardt, 1980; Probst, 1980; Cornbleth & Korth, 1980). However, other studies have reported that large group structures are superior in producing higher engagement rates (Ruff, 1978; Filby, 1978; Easton, Muirhead, Frederick, & Vanderwicken, 1979).

Still others have found that engagement rates of students are higher during small-group work than during independent seatwork or conventional large-group instruction (Peterson, Marx, & Clark, 1978; Slavin, 1980; Sharan, 1980; Hess & Takanishi, 1974). For example, Webb (1982) found that the degree of giving and receiving help in small groups is positively related to student achievement. Peterson (1979) found that only small effects on achievement were attributable to large group, teacher-led, direct instruction, with the difference between this instruction and an individual or open approach only one-tenth of a standard deviation. Further, Peterson found that nondirect rather than direct instruction was more often associated with creativity and problem solving.

Linn (1980) found that a combination of direct instruction, such as lectures and demonstrations with the teacher functioning as group leader, followed by free-choice experiences, such as those found in learning centers, increased children's learning more than either direct instruction or free-choice experiences alone.

Classrooms with several learning centers are very complex settings. Teachers operating these classrooms must manage many simultaneously occurring segments or activities. Teachers in this complex setting face significant organizational and management challenges. Researchers have studied the impact of management techniques in complex classrooms, as well as the comparative effectiveness of complex classrooms with classrooms that rely primarily on teacher-led large and small group instruction.

Gump (1967) notes that overlapping segments are common in elementary class-rooms (for example, a small group of children may be reading with the teacher, while the rest of the children are engaged in seatwork). Doyle (1977) has noted that beginning teachers try to adapt to the complexity of the classroom by localizing attention to one region of the classroom and being engrossed in one activity at a time. He found that this strategy was not generally successful. Kounin (1970) found that where teachers were able to deal with simultaneous segments without becoming immersed in one situation to the exclusion of the others, pupils were more involved in the teacher-led segments and less deviant in the pupil-initiative segments. It was especially important that the pupil-initiative segments have activities that the students could manage.

Wasik and Day (cited in Day & Drake, 1983) studied a multiaged kindergarten and first grade classroom that created a multitask, active input type of learning environment through the use of learning centers and contracts. These students spent over half their time working independently (kindergarten 54.97 percent; first grade 54.50 percent), without direct adult supervision. Wasik and Day reported that the overall rate of appropriate, on-task behavior exhibited by the children while working independently was over 88 percent. The overall rate of on-task behavior exhibited by the children while working under the supervision of an adult was over 94 percent. The children had the least amount of aggressive/resistive behavior when they were in learning centers. Some centers showed no instances of aggressive behavior over a two-year period. The work-study areas (used for completing independent seatwork) were the least productive places in the classroom for the first graders in this study.

However, even the intrinsic interest and strong signal systems of small-group tasks and learning center activities may not keep students attentive unless the activities are well managed. For this reason, classes having a wide range of concurrent activities sometimes show lower achievement gains than classes with only one or two activities occurring simultaneously (McDonald & Elias, 1976; Stallings, 1980). This is because some teachers in multitask settings are unable to supervise the work behavior of all students (Rosenshine, 1979; Berliner, 1979). These findings have led some researchers to recommend less small-group work and more whole-class instruction (Medley, 1979; Brophy, 1979).

Wilson (1983) suggests that in highly differentiated classrooms, complex strategies of management and coordination are necessary. The classroom characterized by high task complexity differs markedly from the more routine classroom since more activities take place and since children change activities more often. He states that engagement in a class with complex task arrangements depends on the fit of the management system with the task arrangement. He also hypothesized that student engagement would be higher in well-managed complex classrooms because teachers would, of necessity, foster interdependency among the children by encouraging them to take over some of the management functions usually performed by the teacher. These children would be sharing information with one another and working together to solve problems. Wilson designed a study that investigated the engagement rates of students who were taught science through the use of learning centers (a "high-complexity" task arrangement) and students in math classes where everyone was working on the same assignment at a given time (a "low-complexity" task arrangement). The area of greatest difference in management between high- and low-complexity task arrangements was in the delegation of authority. Significantly more working together and peer task talk occurred in high- as compared to low-complexity task arrangements. Students set up materials, allocated necessary resources, and answered each other's questions regarding what to do next and how to do it. Engagement was also higher in the high-complexity condition.

In conclusion, the research on classrooms organized with learning centers suggests that good classroom management and selection of engaging appropriate activities are keys to learning center effectiveness. Based on this research and the earlier discussion of child development, the conditions for effective learning center usage can be stated as follows:

1. The development of an effective management system that is clearly understood by teacher and children.
2. The teacher's genuine knowledge of each student's ability and achievement level, prior experiences, maturity, and learning style, and the use of this knowledge in planning goals and objectives for the program.
3. Attractive, well-organized centers that are rich in materials at a variety of developmental levels and that provide feedback for the child of how he or she is progressing.
4. The instruction of children in how to use the centers materials and equipment effectively.
5. Provision of much individual and group planning, guidance, and evaluation of activities.
6. Understanding by the children of the purpose of and expectations for effective use of materials in centers, including responsibility for maintaining simple records of their activities.
7. Integration of skills and concepts into centers to ensure that all centers activities have a valid purpose.

Management Techniques

The goal of a classroom management system is to enable both teachers and students to comfortably and effectively accomplish their purposes. A good management system establishes the structure that permits creative learning. Structure frees teachers to focus on planning, facilitating, evaluating, and supporting individualized learning. Structure frees children to learn with security, independence, and provides the freedom to satisfy their unique needs, learning styles, and interests. Three major components of an effective classroom management system are color coding, contracts, and social-behavioral discipline techniques.

Color Coding

The systematic use of color and symbols helps children function independently and successfully in a complex learning environment. Children can quickly learn a color-coding system even if they do not yet possess reading skills. Colors and symbols can be used to identify learning centers, to manage children's movement in and out of centers, and to enable children to independently find and replace assigned materials.

A special symbol and color code help children identify and locate each center. The symbol identifies what is learned in the center. The color code helps children easily locate the center in the classroom. For example, the art center's symbol might be a paintbrush and its color code blue. A card would be hung at the entrance to each center with its symbol and color code.

To manage traffic in and out of the centers, the card at the center's entrance would also indicate the number of children allowed in the center at one time. That number of color-coded clothespins would be attached to the bottom of the card. For example, the art center might allow ten children and thus have ten blue clothespins. The clothespins are children's "tickets" to the centers. Children must pin on the clothespin upon entering the center, wear it while using the center, and replace it on the card upon leaving. When no clothespins are on the card, the center is full, and children must choose another activity until a clothespin is available.

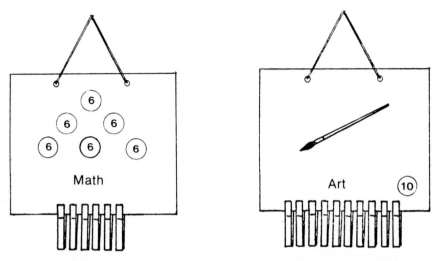

To help children find and replace assigned materials within the centers, all learning center materials and activities can be labeled with stickers of different shapes and colors.

Contact paper in three basic colors may be cut into various shapes ($\bigcirc$, $\square$, $\triangle$, $\square$). These shapes are then attached to each game or activity and to the shelf where it belongs. Each basic color can represent a different level of difficulty. For example, label the easiest activities with yellow shapes, middle-level activities with red, and the most difficult activities with green shapes. This enables the teacher to assign activities on an individualized basis. This also enables children to use and replace materials easily and correctly. This task is extremely important in developing overall responsibility for the environment.

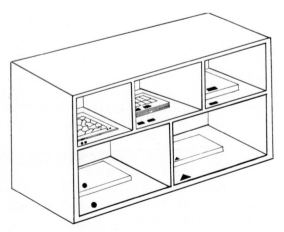

Classroom libraries can also be organized by color coding and symbol systems to categorize books by topic and difficulty. In addition to color coding, word labeling can be used to build word recognition, association, and meaning skills.

Color coding is a simple and efficient way to manage traffic, keep materials in order, and help children function responsibly and independently in a complex environment. A second management technique that supports responsibility and independence is a contract system.

Contracts

A contract is an agreed-upon individualized activity outline that incorporates teacher direction and guidance with student interests. Contracts create shared purpose between teacher and child. They provide structure that enables children to operate successfully in a complex environment at the same time they enable teachers to structure that environment by planning and coordinating the children's activities within it.

Contracts have benefits for teachers, parents, and children. For teachers, contracts are an efficient and effective mechanism to promote on-task behavior, to organize traffic flow, to monitor and control the variety and frequency of learning center visits, and to evaluate children daily. Contracts give parents a daily record of their children's activities so that they can track progress and follow up with the teacher when needed. Teachers can send contracts home daily along with children's work products and special notes. Contracts enable students to independently handle their learning center activities and transitions, to work at their own pace and skill level since contracts are individualized, to choose some activities that fit their own interests, and to be personally responsible and accountable for each day's work.

Daily check-in and evaluation meetings between children and the teacher (or a teacher aide if one is available) are key to the success of the contract system. Although the teacher monitors each student's activity throughout the day, making sure

that the contract is understood and the student is able to do the assigned activities, an evaluation meeting allows for general review, feedback, updating records, and planning future activities. The daily check-in helps the teacher know students better, and to accurately pinpoint developmental progress and needs. As a result of daily evaluation with all students, the teacher can also evaluate and maintain overall program success.

The flexibility of the contract system is as broad as the creative range and needs of the teacher and children using it. A contract may cover one day's activities or several. It can also cover one subject area or several. Contracts can be entirely individual in design or may be developed for small group usage. The contract format can be varied to fit the child's learning level. Some contracts may involve a few steps, pictorial diagrams, and color coding. Others may be simple, but more direct, with written instructions only.

Day and Drake, in *Early Childhood Education: Curriculum Organization and Classroom Management* (1983), describe four levels of contracts. The contract sequence starts with those for very young children and/or nonreaders and progresses through those designed for children working at third- and fourth-grade levels.

Stage 1 Contracts

Stage 1 contracts are simple picture contracts. The teacher or the child color codes the contract by using crayon to underline the name of the center with the same color as the center's clothespin chart. For example, the art clothespins and chart are dark blue; whenever art appears on the contract, it is underlined in dark blue. Children have two clues to help them use the contract: (1) they read the center symbol, a paint brush, as "art"; and (2) they match the dark blue underlining on their contract to the dark blue clothespin chart that hangs beside the art center. After completing the art activity, the children check off art on their contract and refer to their contract to move to another center. At the end of the contract the phrase "pick a clothespin" indicates that the child can select a free choice center.

Stage 1 Contract

Stage 2 Contracts

Some children will use only clothespins, or use only picture contracts, longer than others. When children can effectively follow a picture contract, they are ready to begin Stage 2. This contract level will add some required center activities as well as a minimal amount of reading. The required activities give the children responsibility for specific tasks. This structure helps children develop independent work habits and also reinforces teacher-designated skills. To follow this contract the child needs to recognize the center symbols, match shapes, and read three-color words. These contracts are easily used by children with limited reading and writing skills.

Children using Stage 1 and 2 contracts can begin to work in centers independent of the teacher. Contracts can also begin to cover a longer period of the child's day. The children can copy their assigned task from the board, or the teacher can fill in the contract for them. The standardized coding system used on the contracts—"Do the activity," "Play the red △ game"—provides a format that allows the same series of contracts to be used over and over again.

Rather than spending time each afternoon designing contracts with specific tasks such as "Look up Benjamin Franklin" or "Do the magnet experiment" written on them, the teacher has a standard contract form for each day of the week.

Stage 2 Contract

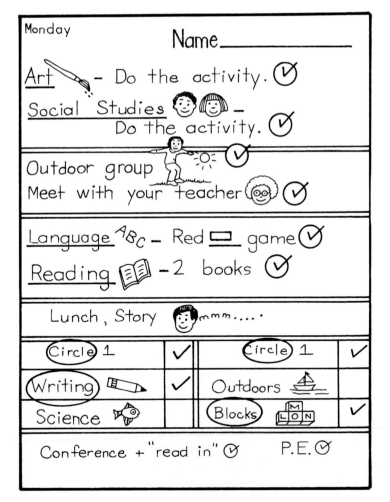

Stage 3 Contracts

Stage 3 contracts require more proficient reading and writing skills. Children fill these contracts out for themselves by copying assigned tasks from the chalkboard. Then they select free choices from a chart that lists the available centers, selecting one free choice center from each side of the centers chart. The chart is designed so that the child must select one center from the more difficult or cognitively oriented centers and one from the psychomotor/creative areas.

Stage 3 Contract

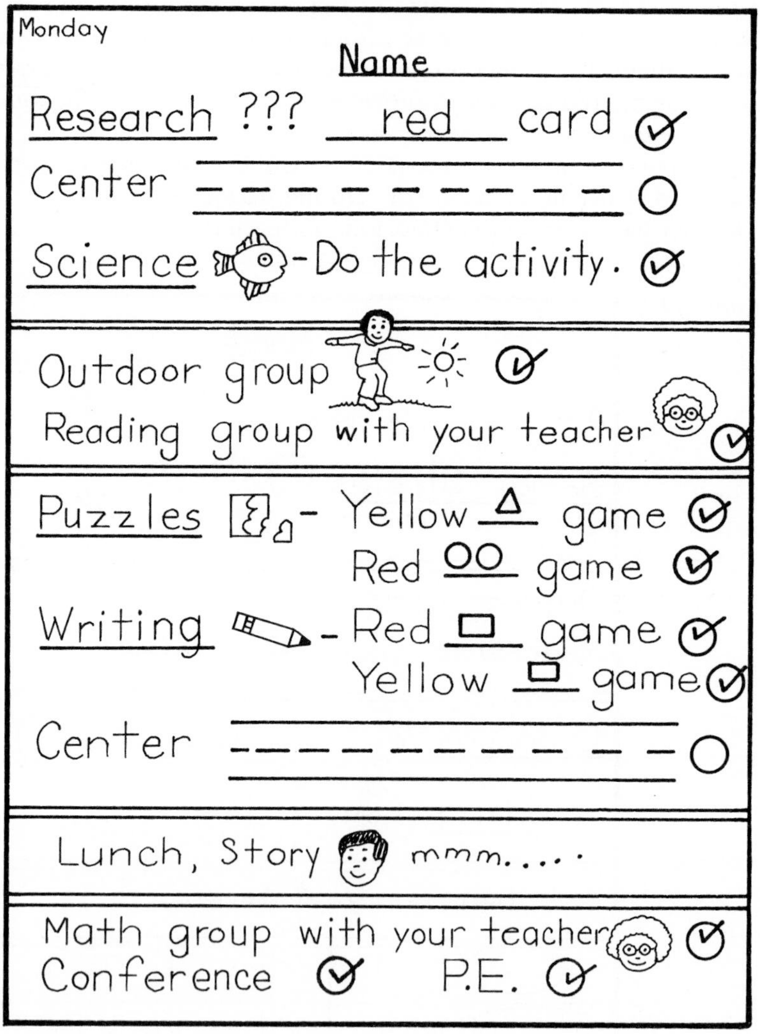
Monday
Name
Research ??? red card
Center
Science - Do the activity.
Outdoor group
Reading group with your teacher
Puzzles - Yellow game
Red game
Writing - Red game
Yellow game
Center
Lunch, Story mmm.....
Math group with your teacher
Conference P.E.

Stage 4 Contracts

Stage 4 contracts require children to keep written diaries of their activities. Children write in specifics about what they completed in the science center, what their creative story was about, and so forth.

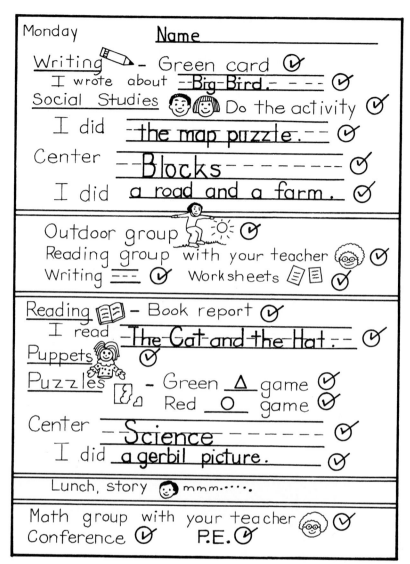

Stage 4 Contract

Whatever contract format is used, it should be clear and manageable to the child using it. Materials for contracts should be easily accessible, and teachers should thoroughly orient children to the symbols and system used so that they can work confidently and effectively with contracts. Individual folders to hold the contract, pencils, and papers will help children keep their work together and record their own progress, and will provide a sense of pride in managing that responsibility.

The children's day includes spending approximately one-third of their time with the teacher, one third on independent activities planned by the teacher, and one-third on their free choice activities. Thus the material on the contracts is usually a combination of follow-up on skills being taught, introduction of new unit concepts, and focus on their own special interests. The contracts must be planned to vary the required centers so that each center is visited two or three times a week. Sample contracts, Monday through Friday, illustrate this program.

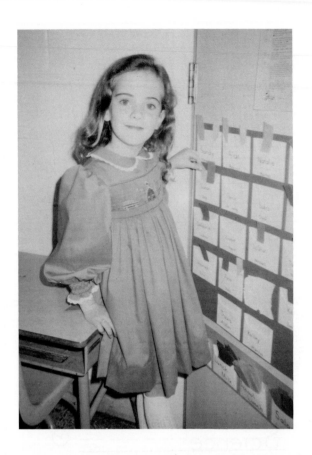

S-Mon.   Name _____

☐ Blocks

☐ Science   Do the activity.

☐ Language   Yellow _____game
                    Red _____game

☐ Outdoor group

☐ Meet with your teacher

☐ Math   123   Green _____game
                 Red _____game

☐ Research   ?   Yellow card

☐ Dramatic Play

Circle 2			Circle 2		
Games			Writing		
Outdoors			Reading		
Blocks			Listening		

Lunch, story

☐ UNC - TV
☐ Meet with your afternoon group

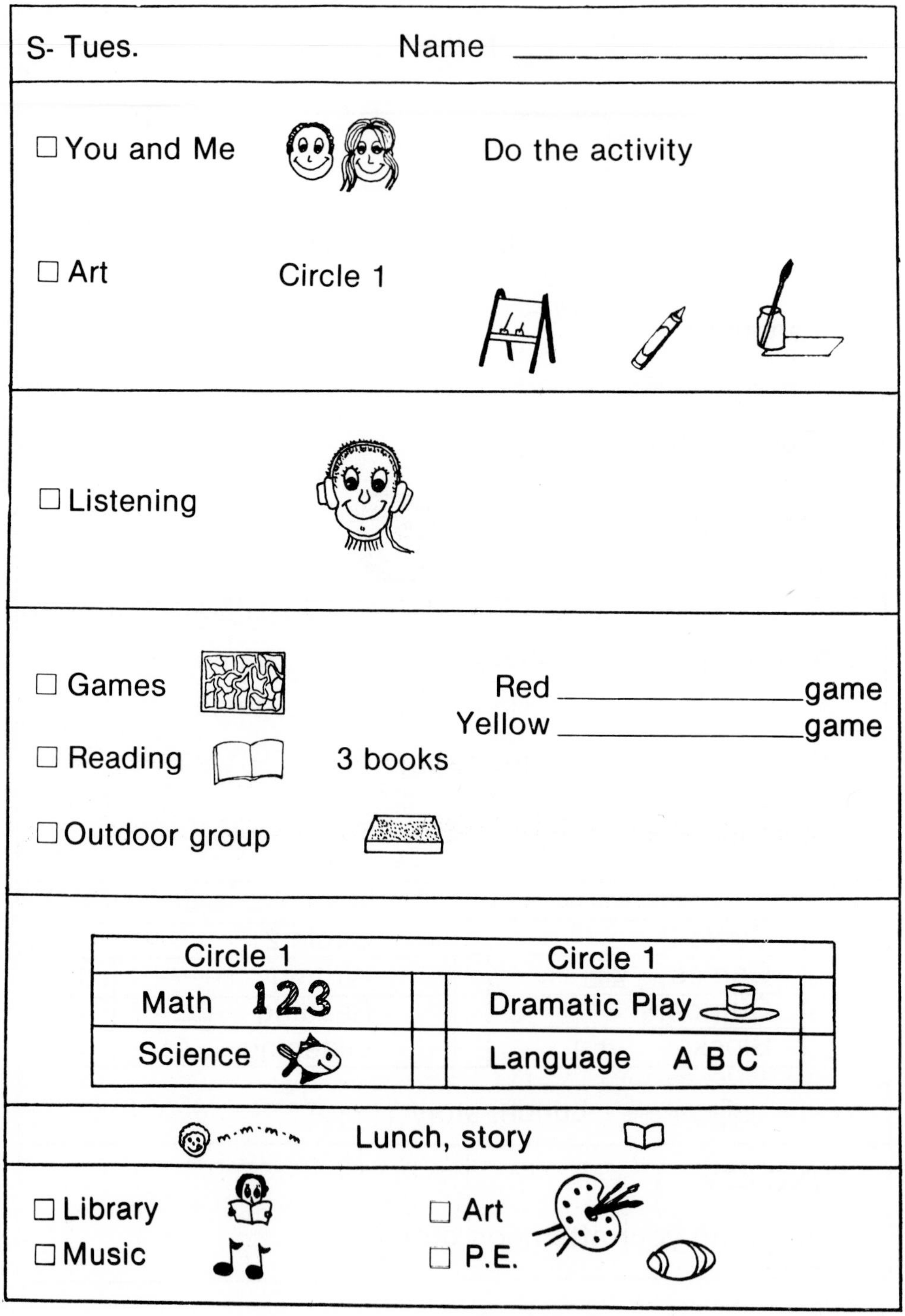

S- Tues.   Name _____

☐ You and Me   😊🧑   Do the activity

☐ Art   Circle 1

☐ Listening

☐ Games   Red _____game
                 Yellow _____game

☐ Reading   📖   3 books

☐ Outdoor group

Circle 1		Circle 1	
Math **123**		Dramatic Play 🎩	
Science 🐟		Language A B C	

Lunch, story   📖

☐ Library 📖   ☐ Art 🎨
☐ Music 🎵   ☐ P.E.

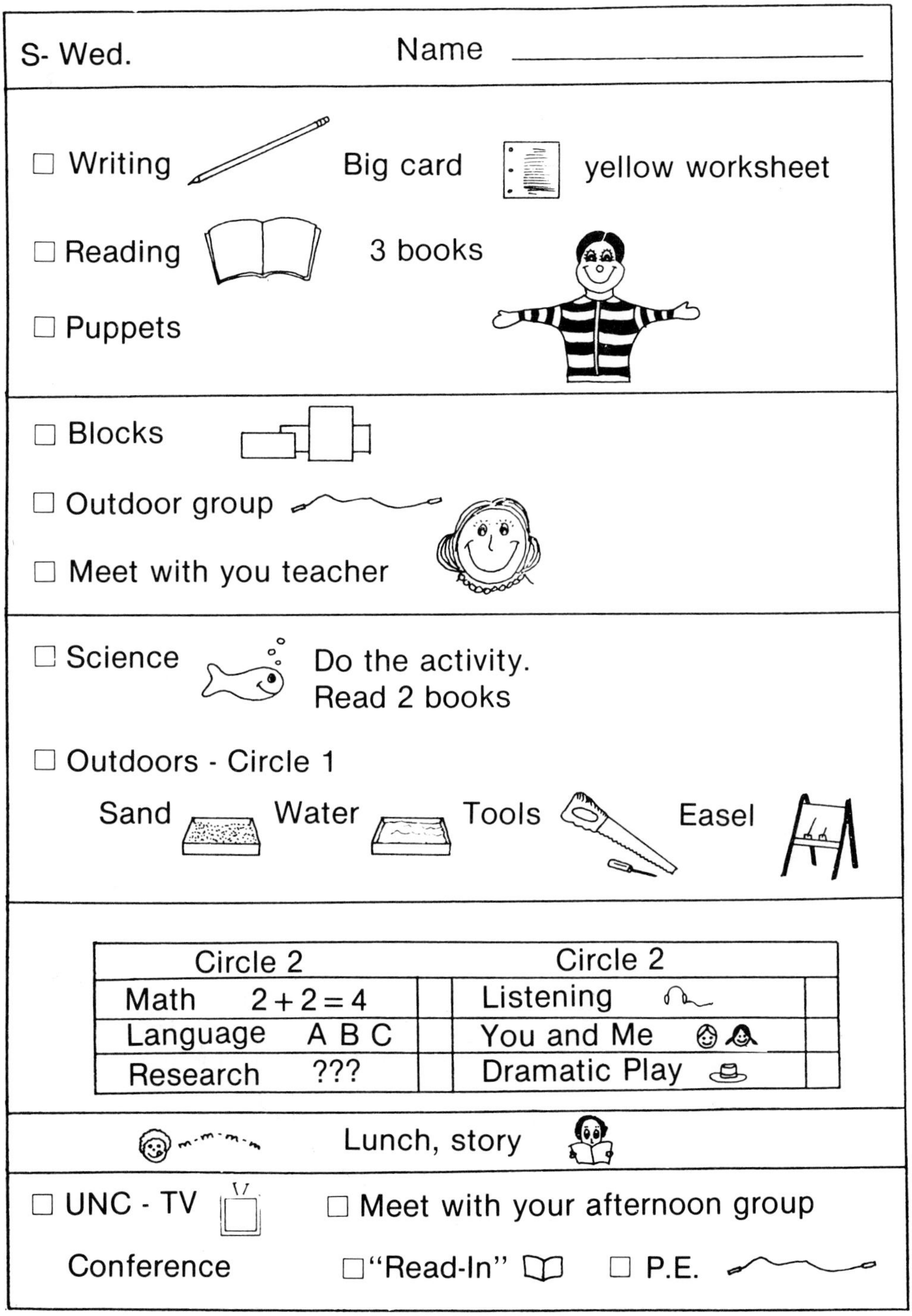

S- Wed.   Name _____

☐ Writing   Big card   yellow worksheet

☐ Reading   3 books

☐ Puppets

☐ Blocks

☐ Outdoor group

☐ Meet with you teacher

☐ Science   Do the activity.
                   Read 2 books

☐ Outdoors - Circle 1

Sand   Water   Tools   Easel

Circle 2		Circle 2	
Math	2 + 2 = 4	Listening	
Language	A B C	You and Me	
Research	???	Dramatic Play	

Lunch, story

☐ UNC - TV   ☐ Meet with your afternoon group

Conference   ☐ "Read-In"   ☐ P.E.

S- Thur.   Name _____

☐ Class Meeting [?]   Special activities in 🐟

☐ Meet with your teacher 😊

☐ You and Me   Do the activity.
                     Read 2 books.

☐ Games   Yellow _____game
                     Red _____game.
☐ Writing   Yellow _____game.
                     Red _____game.

☐ Library   Get a new book

☐ Language   ABC   Yellow _____game.
                     Red _____game.

☐ Outdoor group

Circle 1		Circle 1	
Math 678		Dramatic Play	
Reading		Outdoors	

Lunch, story

☐ UNC - TV   ▣

☐ Meet with your afternoon group

S- Fri.   Name _____

☐ Writing   ✏   Yellow worksheet

☐ Math   **123**   Yellow _____game

☐ Meet with your teacher.

☐ Art   Do the activity or use the

☐ Outdoor group

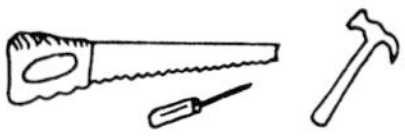

☐ Library    ☐ Dramatic Play

☐ Listening    ☐ Puppets

Circle 2	Circle 2	
You and Me ☺ 🙎	Reading 📖	
Research ? ? ?	Blocks	
Language A B C	Games	

Lunch, story

☐ UNC - TV   ☐

☐ Meet with your afternoon group

Recent research indicates that classrooms operating learning centers and using a contract system promote on-task behavior. Day and Drake (1986) found that children in classrooms that featured eight or more learning centers operating all day, that were multiaged (5- and 6-year-old children grouped together), and that used contracts had on-task behavior rates of 92 percent. As a result of these high rates of on-task behavior, children in these developmental classrooms actually received 120 more hours of schooling (20 more school days) over the entire school year than did children in the study whose classrooms did not include learning centers and contracts.

This study investigated the relationship between various types of early childhood classroom environments and the on-task behavior rates generated by the children in each program. For this purpose the classroom environment was defined in terms of the number of simultaneous activity segments operating at any one time (Wilson, 1983). Eighteen kindergarten and first grade classrooms were observed and then categorized into five different organizational patterns:

Type 1.   Six-year-old children in classrooms that operated for most of the school day with only one or two simultaneous activity segments.

Type 2.   Five-year-old children in classrooms that operated multiple activity segments (including eight or more learning centers) for the first hour of the school day, then operated only one or two simultaneous activities for the rest of the school day.

Type 3.   Six-year-old children in classrooms that operated multiple activity segments during the morning. The afternoon included only one or two simultaneous activity segments.

Type 4.   Five-year-old children in classrooms that had multiple activity segments operating all day.

Type 5.   Five- and six-year-old children in classrooms that operated multiple activity segments all day and used written contracts as a management technique.

Children in Type 5 classrooms were grouped in 5-year-old kindergarten programs (Type 5a), 6-year-old first grade programs (Type 5b), and multiaged 5- and 6-year-old programs (Type 5c). Table 1 shows the on-task behavior rates generated by each type of classroom.

Types 1, 2, and 3, which either had limited or no simultaneous activity, had similar on-task behavior rates of approximately 78 percent. A small positive change in

TABLE 1   Percentage of On-Task Behavior by Classroom Type

Type	Activities	Time	Contract	On-Task Behavior
1	1–2	—	no	79%
2	multiple	1 hr/day	no	79%
3	multiple	½ day	no	78%
4	multiple	all day	no	81%
5A	multiple	all day	yes	85%
5B	multiple	all day	yes	87%
5C	multiple	all day	yes	92%

TABLE 2 Percentage of On-Task Behavior for 5-Year-Olds

Music 100	Water 100	Outside 98
Listening 93	Sensory/Motor 88	Math 84
Housekeeping 81		Science 80
	Study Area 78	
Research 75	Writing 75	Cooking 72
	Reading 29	

TABLE 3 Percentage of On-Task Behavior for 6-Year-Olds

Math 100	Sensory/Motor 100	Outside 100
Reading 93	Art 97	Sand 91
Science 89	Blocks 88	Listening 86
Writing 85		Cooking 82
	Study 78	
	Housekeeping 60	

on-task behavior rates was produced by Type 4 classrooms, which operated multiple activity segments for the entire day (82 percent).

However, pronounced changes in on-task behavior rates were observed in the Type 5 classrooms, which combined the all-day use of multiple activity segments with the use of written contracts. This interaction generated on-task behavior rates as high as 92 percent.

Tables 2 and 3 illustrate that 5- and 6-year-old children in this study had higher on-task behavior rates when working in learning centers than when engaged in seatwork activities. These results suggest that young children need classrooms that feature a variety of learning experiences.

A particularly interesting example of the interaction between the developmental readiness of children for an activity and the on-task behavior rates generated by that activity was seen in the reading centers studied. Five-year-olds in this study had on-task rates of 29 percent when observed in reading centers. Six-year-old children had an on-task rate of 93 percent in reading centers. Clearly, reading centers, as they are typically designed in early childhood classrooms, are not involving 5-year-old children, most of whom are nonreaders. Implications of this research suggest a need for reorganization of reading centers for 5-year-olds so that stimuli other than print are included. For example, books with tape recordings of their content might interest 5-year-olds more than books alone.

These results suggest that a complex early childhood environment featuring learning centers in conjunction with an appropriate management system can achieve rates of on-task behavior higher than those achieved in less complex classrooms that rely largely on large- and small-group instruction and seatwork assignments.

Social-Behavioral Discipline Techniques

Discipline techniques comprise the third major component of an effective classroom management system. Scott Peck (1978) has defined discipline as the set of tools for solving life's problems. Discipline techniques in an early childhood classroom are the tools with which teachers and children prevent and resolve behavioral problems. The ultimate purpose of discipline is to develop children's self-responsibility and control, important goals of any early childhood education program. Day and Drake (1986) suggest that discipline has external and internal components. External discipline refers to how the classroom environment influences the child's behavior. Internal discipline refers to the child's own ability to behave in appropriate ways. Effective external discipline helps a young child develop internal discipline.

The organization and management techniques described thus far in this chapter create conditions that enhance discipline. Stimulating and developmentally appropriate learning center activities provide natural conditions for children to stay on task and behave appropriately. Color coding and contracts help children understand what they are expected to do and how to do it independently and responsibly. In general, appropriate tasks, clear expectations, regular monitoring and feedback, consistent routines and rules, and an accepting, supportive atmosphere, are characteristic of well organized creative learning environments, and are proactive means of developing internal discipline and avoiding discipline problems.

Even in the most effective classroom environment, where every effort has been made to eliminate frustration and anxiety, problems will sometimes occur. Many factors, such as home problems, poor nutrition, ill health, or just lack of sleep, will influence and interfere with children's ability to behave appropriately. Therefore teachers need an effective social-behavioral management system for directing student behavior. Three effective systems are described in the following paragraphs. From these systems and others, early childhood teachers can draw techniques and ideas to create a behavior management system that fits their own personalities and management styles.

Reality Therapy Approach

William Glasser (1978) has developed a positive, reality-based approach to behavior management. Glasser's approach includes seven steps to successful behavior reorientation. The steps are based on positive, nonthreatening, and helpful communication and reorientation techniques. Reality therapy deals with the present reality, not the subconscious, ill-defined, and unknown causes of behavior. Reality therapy involves children in confronting behavior, identifying consequences, and planning and committing to appropriate future behavior. Through this method children learn to assume responsibility for their actions and to become aware of how they influence events and create their own outcomes. Easily learned and readily incorporated into classroom activities, the seven steps are as follows:

1. Establish communication.
   Communication is established within the classroom by building self-esteem and trust. Communication has already developed prior to a confrontation.
2. Ask the child to assume responsibility.
   When inappropriate behavior occurs, ask the child to describe what happened and to assume responsibility for his or her part in it.
3. Discuss the effect of the action.
   Ask the child how his or her actions affected the situation. Direct the child to look at what the consequences were or could have been. The teacher does not tell the child, but rather encourages the child to think through consequences from a logical point of view.

4. Make a plan.

   The teacher asks the child to think through how to handle the situation better next time. This may be done in the time-out area. When the child has had time to devise a plan, the teacher and child discuss it. The plan should be simple, easy to remember, realistic, and attainable.

5. Get a commitment.

   The child agrees to stick to the plan, and the teacher agrees to help. A handshake helps to seal the deal.

6. Help the child stick to the plan.

   Praise efforts that show the child is sticking to the plan. The teacher should also praise other related appropriate behaviors. This encourages the child to maintain good behavior.

7. Accept no excuses.

   Hold the child accountable for sticking to the plan. If the child needs help remembering the plan, the teacher might use the time-out area to provide an opportunity to "think about it." The time-out area can also be used for removing the child from the area in which the behavior problem generally occurs. This might prevent problems before they occur. The point is to help children direct their own behavior and develop internal control mechanisms based not on fear, but on knowledge of logical consequences and outcomes.

The key to success of this or any social-behavioral management system is clear communication to the child that he or she is lovable, capable, important, respected, and cherished. The child is not "inappropriate," only the behavior is. Positive reinforcement for good work, task orientation, good social interaction, and problem solving should be frequent and continual and can be in the form of praise, a hug, a touch accompanied by praise, a simple reward, or a special privilege. Such communication of self-worth is important in altering behavior in a more appropriate direction. Children need to know what they are doing right more than they need to know what they are doing wrong.

One positive way of reinforcing and enhancing self-esteem is through the use of a compliment box or some other system that gives children the opportunity to praise each other verbally. If a compliment box is used, the contents should be read daily. Children who observe others making an effort to behave appropriately could seek help from the teacher or an aide in writing out a short compliment and then placing it in the box. Children feel good about giving a compliment, and peer recognition while receiving a compliment is very reinforcing. Compliments can be anonymous or signed, and can be shared at a special group meeting each day. The teacher and aide could monitor the compliment box to be certain that all children receive compliments (the teacher or aide could insert compliments also). The compliment box idea is a pleasant way in which to use peer influence to boost appropriate behavior.

Managing Surface Behavior

Redl's methods for managing surface behavior and maintaining a successful learning atmosphere incorporate helpful, nonthreatening teacher guidance methods for developing children's internal behavioral controls. Redl's suggested techniques are summarized in the following paragraphs (cited in Long & Newman, 1980).

The four major alternatives for managing surface behavior are permitting behavior, tolerating behavior, interfering with behavior, and preventive planning. Each alternative is described below.

Permitting Behavior

Rather than focusing on what children cannot do, focus on what children are allowed to do. Emphasizing appropriate accepted behavior avoids unnecessary testing and resistance to limits. Teachers should define what behavior is expected, appropriate times, places, and conditions for the behavior, and limitations or boundaries. For example:

> Tell children where and when they may run or shout (e.g., outdoors or in the gym).
> Tell children when they may move freely about the room (e.g., lavatory visits or going from center to center).
> Tell children when and where they may be messy (e.g., outdoors).

Tolerating Behavior

Under certain circumstances teachers may tolerate what would ordinarily be considered inappropriate behavior. There are three basic conditions for tolerating behavior.

1. Learner's leeway.
   Mistakes often occur when a child is learning new concepts, experimenting, or trying to gain status in the group. At such a time, the teacher can discuss "good" and "poor" mistakes with the child. A good mistake results from logical efforts to act appropriately. A poor mistake results from impulsive illogical action.
2. Behavior that reflects a child's developmental stage.
   Age-typical behavior will naturally change as the child matures. Efforts to inhibit such behavior are generally ineffective, and may produce results worse than the original behavior.
3. Behavior that is symptomatic of a disease.
   Behaviors that result from physical discomfort or emotional disorders are beyond the child's internal controls and require understanding and constructive support from the teacher.

Interfering with Behavior

Some classroom behaviors must be dealt with immediately and directly. Intervention should occur before the teacher becomes frustrated by the behavior and responds too severely. Effective intervention helps the child get back on task without disrupting the classroom. There are several criteria for intervention:

1. *Reality dangers.* The teacher recognizes that consequences of a certain act are physically dangerous.
2. *Psychological protection.* The teacher recognizes that psychological harm is a consequence of a particular behavior.
3. *Protection against too much excitement.* The teacher intervenes before the child becomes too excited, anxious, or frustrated.

4. *Protection of property.* The teacher intervenes before damage occurs.
5. *Protection of an ongoing program.* The teacher keeps the group on task without letting one child disrupt activities.
6. *Protection against negative contagion.* The teacher asks one child to stop a behavior that could spread to other students and disrupt the lesson.
7. *Highlighting a value area or school policy.* The teacher interferes because the behavior relates to an important school policy or rule. The teacher uses the situation to illustrate the policy or rule.
8. *Avoidance of a conflict with the outside world.* The teacher interferes to prevent problems with other classes or the public.
9. *Protection of a teacher's inner comfort.* The teacher interferes to protect himself or herself from abuse.

Redl also includes "instant" techniques for stopping inappropriate behavior. These techniques should not be used in the place of a sound, underlying behavior management program. The advantage of these techniques is that they are easily implemented, and they save the self-respect of the child by not focusing on him or her in the group.

1. *Planned ignoring.* The teacher ignores minor problem behaviors in order to cause extinction and to avoid reinforcing the child's need for inappropriate attention.
2. *Signal interference.* The teacher uses nonverbal signals, such as eye contact, coughing, frowning, or body posture, to communicate disapproval of the behavior.
3. *Proximity control.* The teacher stations herself or himself near the child having difficulty and operates as a source of protection, strength, and identification.
4. *Interest boosting.* The teacher uses the child's natural interest areas to help boost success in a lesser-liked subject. The teacher lets the child know he or she is interested in the child.
5. *Tension decontamination through humor.* The teacher uses humor to dispel anxiety or tension.
6. *Hurdle lessons.* The teacher should be aware that the child may sometimes become frustrated and need help with the classroom assignment. The key is to give the child the help needed before it is sought from other sources.
7. *Restructuring the classroom program.* Teachers should constantly evaluate their methods to be sure that children are learning as effectively as possible.
8. *Support from routine.* The teacher provides daily routine and structure to give the child security.
9. *Direct appeal to values area.* The teacher can appeal to the child's own sense of fairness, logical consequences, group identification, or teacher's own power of authority.
10. *Removing seductive objects.* The teacher removes items that compete for the child's attention during the lesson.
11. *Antiseptic bouncing.* The teacher sees that the child is reaching a point where the verbal controls are ineffective. The teacher may "bounce" or remove the child from the immediate environment by asking the child to run an errand, get water, or be excused. This is not a punishment but, rather, a way of protecting the child and helping all students involved to calm down.

12. *Physical restraint.* If a child completely loses control the teacher should calmly, but securely, physically restrain the child and thus avoid injury to that child and others.

Preventive Planning. Redl suggests that the preferable avenue for avoiding disruptive behavior is continual planning and evaluation to maintain the best classroom procedures and the healthiest learning environment for children.

Although not specified as such by Redl, it is helpful, in preventive planning, to discuss with the children early in the year (perhaps during the first week of school) a simple, concise set of class rules. These should be easily remembered and should reflect both teacher and student input. An example of a set of five rules for young children might include:

1. Use words to solve problems.
2. Speak and walk softly in the classroom.
3. Always put away materials and games after using them.
4. Respect the property and rights of others.
5. Have a task to do.

Rules need to be positive and reflect what the child *can* rather than *cannot* do. A colorful, easily understood poster of rules should be displayed where children can see it readily. A cartoon or appropriate symbol may be added to each rule to help the child remember what it means. Also, children should be able to offer suggestions, as a class, for the development of new rules as situations call for them (addition of a new center, pet added to the classroom, etc.). Children will be more apt to follow rules that they have helped to create. Such rules help to establish a preventive foundation for behavior control.

Implementing the Time-Out Technique. The use of time-out may also be helpful in developing internal behavioral control mechanisms. Time-out refers to the removal of any offending stimulus from the child, and is usually accomplished by placing the child in a special area, chair, or enclosure that prohibits the child from receiving any attention from the teacher or peers. The time-out area is also free from any distractions or rewarding activities. The purpose of time-out is to provide a time and place for calming down, and for reflecting and redirecting behavior. A child can choose to use the time-out area independently or can be placed there. The teacher should convey to the child that time-out is not a punishment per se, but an opportunity to collect oneself and to calm down. Sometimes the teacher may request the formulation of a plan before leaving the time-out area, as suggested in the Glasser approach. Time-out is useful because it gives both the teacher and the child time to think and plan before rushing into an inappropriate response.

Teacher Effectiveness Training

Gordon places communication as being of primary importance (Curwin & Mendler, 1980; Rinne, 1984). He lists the following as being roadblocks to communication: 1) ordering, commanding, directing; 2) warning, threatening; 3) moralizing, preaching, giving "shoulds" and "oughts"; 4) advising, offering solutions or suggestions; 5) teaching, lecturing, giving logical arguments; 6) judging, criticizing, disagreeing, blaming; 7) name-calling, stereotyping, labeling; 8) interpreting, analyzing, diagnosing; 9) praising, agreeing, giving positive evaluations; 10) reassuring, sympathizing, consoling, supporting; 11) withdrawing, distracting, being sarcastic, humoring, diverting, and; 12) questioning, probing, interrogating, and cross-examining (Curwin & Mendler, 1980).

This method provides teachers with a model for communication that includes "active listening," "I messages," "problem ownership," and "negotiation" (Curwin & Mendler, 1980; Rinne, 1984). Active listening is a process that involves one person listening carefully to what another has expressed and then feeding back the message to convey understanding. This approach is utilized by the teacher when a student "owns" the problem. Convey empathy and understanding to a student who's experiencing a problem, and through this process, help the student find his own solutions. "I messages" are used when the student's behavior has a real concrete or tangible effect upon the teacher's ability to function. Teacher-owned problems are dealt with through the use of "I messages" (Curwin & Mendler, 1980). These messages include a description of the student's behavior that is causing the teacher to have a problem; what the tangible or concrete effect is upon the teacher; and how this makes the teacher feel (Curwin & Mendler, 1980; Rinne, 1984). "Problem ownership" involves negotiation and problem solving rather than having a power struggle. Give all students a voice in the classroom rules. "Negotiation" is the setting up of a social contract in the classroom (Curwin & Mendler, 1980).

Gordon's method helps the student to solve his own problem. The problem-solving process includes: 1) define the problem according to the perceptions of both sides, then agree on exactly what it is that both parties want solved (Rinne, 1984); 2) generate possible solutions through a brainstorming process; 3) evaluate the solutions by crossing out any solution that is objectionable to either party (Rinne, 1984; Faber & Mazlish, 1980; Crary, 1979); 4) make the decision by choosing the best solution through consensus; 5) decide who will implement the decision by assigning clear responsibilities; and 6) assess the success of the solution (Rinne, 1984; Crary, 1979). Search for the kinds of solutions that meet both the students' and the teachers' needs as individuals (Faber & Mazlish, 1980). Class meetings are used to establish rules that all of the students will follow (Rinne, 1984).

Parent Involvement

In organizing the learning environment effectively, the role of parents should be considered. The Parent Education Follow-Through Program at the University of North Carolina at Chapel Hill, outlines six suggestions for roles that a parent might play in the learning process:

1. *Audience*—listening to the child read, give reports, recite, and so on.
2. *Classroom volunteer*—working with individuals or small groups within the classroom.
3. *Teacher of own child*—instructing the child at home, following through with classroom assignments.
4. *Paraprofessional*—working with child in the areas of nutrition, physical growth, development, and so on.
5. *Decision maker*—acting as a member of a policy review board.
6. *Learner*—extending own education to better educate the child (Olmstead, 1979).

Parent involvement through these channels provides the primary avenue for the child's acquisition of the best education possible. Parents are their children's first and most important teachers, having already had the greatest influence on their children's development prior to their entrance into public school. Parents want to and should be involved closely in the education of their children.

One way of bridging the home-school gap is through frequent communication between home and school. The individual learning contract and accompanying papers should go home daily to give parents the opportunity to review that day's activities. Parents should be invited to visit the classroom frequently to observe, discuss the child's progress, or participate in other ways in which the parent might feel comfortable (e.g., leading a song session, reading a story, leading an art lesson, tutoring an individual child). Parents should be allowed to feel their importance in the union of home and school in building the child's education.

Another way of keeping communication open is by sending notes and letters home frequently. These can be in the form of informative communiqués telling about an upcoming event, offering suggestions for follow-up or at-home activities for parent and child to do together, or a progress letter that indicates the successes as well as any difficulties that the child may be having. Invitations to class plays or special presentations, thank-you letters for special parental help, and recipes for repeating at home are all good examples of communication with the home. The teacher should be willing to begin and to maintain an open communication between home and school.

To promote the home-school relationship, a special night could be arranged for parents to meet in their child's classroom, take a tour with the teacher or child, and see the centers and contracts used by the child during the day. This special night could also include a time for parents to view examples of games and activities they could make for use at home with their child. Materials and instructions for making the games and activities could also be provided so that parents could actually take home an instructional item they had made during the meeting.

Parents are a key factor in their child's education, and they should feel welcomed by the school and, especially, by their child's teacher. Conferences, letters, phone calls, and frequent periodic checks facilitate good home-school communications and aid in the education of the child.

Conclusion

A carefully organized learning environment can meet the needs of children and make learning a more meaningful and joyful experience. The factor that determines success or failure is the teacher's conviction in the creative and open learning philosophy. Teachers must adapt the system to their teaching styles and beliefs about children and learning so that they feel comfortable and capable. Teachers' attitudes are crucial, for they affect and shape the psychological environment for the group of children. Teachers must view each child as a human being, unique from all others. They must realize that each child is motivated in different ways, reacts differently to stimuli, and in turn learns in different ways and at differing rates. Thus a child-centered learning environment is essential. If the child is the raison d'être of schools, then he or she must be the central focus for the teacher and the learning environment.

The physical arrangement of the learning environment should consist of a variety of learning centers containing a wide assortment of materials that are both self-corrective and open-ended. An ideal situation would be a unit of teachers employing team teaching and multiaging, as it would serve to supply a larger area and provide more centers and more equipment for the children. It would also provide more supervision in the various centers and would capitalize on the strengths of each teacher. As stated previously, however, the physical facility does not determine openness; it facilitates it. Obviously, learning can occur in a self-contained or open-spaced learning environment. There is no one arrangement that is best or prescribed for all teachers. Teachers and children must work to find out the best organizational plan for their learning and working together, depending upon the physical space available. Whatever the arrangement of learning centers may be, effective learning necessitates a well-organized environment where children respect materials and use them in a meaningful way, and where the care of this environment and the appropriate storage of materials are dependent upon all who work and learn there. For very young children the materials may need to be color coded according to the various learning centers. These centers must be changed, expanded, and contracted to provide for continuous growth of the children. All available space should be utilized for learning, both inside and outdoors.

Creative and open learning occurs in a healthy and trusting social environment, where children retain their individuality while participating as members of a large social group. Both individual and group interests are held in high esteem by all. Children learn from everything around them, including other people; therefore, it is most important that the school be a place where children learn good social attitudes. It must be a place where children learn internal self-discipline through positive social values—a place where teachers, through time spent with individuals, are able to develop feelings of personal worth in each child.

A good learning environment further emphasizes an integrated approach to curriculum and instruction, where children are given an opportunity to explore, select from, and react to a rich and varying environment that is well planned, inviting, encouraging, and challenging. A balance of intellectual, social, emotional, physical, and aesthetic growth is provided for each child. The interests of children stem from the kinds of learning materials available to them. The curriculum is reflected in the learning environment through the careful planning of teachers and is based on the needs and interests of children whom the teachers know so well. The teacher's instructional goals must be clear, yet provide flexibility for children to engage in activities that are genuinely rewarding for them. Learning skills in various subject areas go on simultaneously while the children work in a variety of learning centers.

Such an open learning approach provides many advantages and answers to questions asked for years by educators and children alike. In the words of John Dewey, "The difference between the esthetic and the intellectual is thus one of the places where emphasis falls in the constant rhythm that marks the interaction of the live creature with his surroundings" (cited in Eisner, 1982, p. ix).

References

Accreditation Criteria & Procedures. (1986). Washington, D.C.: National Association for the Education of Young Children.

Altman, I., & Wohlwill, J. F. (1978). *Children and the Environment.* New York: Plenum.

Berliner, D. C. (1979). Tempus educare. In P. L. Peterson & H. J. Wahlberg (Eds.), *Research on Teaching* (pp. 120–135). Berkeley, Ca.: McCrutchen.

Bloom, B. S. (1981). *All the Children Learning.* New York: McGraw-Hill.

Brophy, J. E. (1979). Teacher Behavior and Its Effects. *Journal of Educational Psychology, 71,* 733–750.

Cooley, W., & Leinhardt, G. (1980). The Instructional Dimensions Study. *Educational Evaluation and Policy Analysis, 2,* 7–24.

Cornbleth, C., & Korth, W. (1980). Context Factors and Individual Differences in Pupil Involvement in Learning Activities. *Journal of Educational Research, 73,* 318–323.

Crary, E. (1979). *Without Spanking or Spoiling: A Practical Approach to Toddler and Preschool Guidance.* Seattle, Washington: Parenting Press.

Curwin, R. L. & Mendler, A. N. (1980). *The Discipline Book: A Complete Guide to School and Classroom Management.* Reston, Va.: Reston Publishing Company.

Day, B. D., & Drake, K. N. (1986). Developmental and Experimental Programs: The Key to Quality Education and Care of Young Children. *Educational Leadership, 44* (3), 24–27.

Day, B. D., & Drake, K. N. (1983). *Early Childhood Education: Curriculm Organization and Classroom Management.* Alexandria, Va.: Association for Supervision and Curriculum Development.

Developmentally Appropriate Practice. (1986). Washington, D.C.: National Association for the Education of Young Children.

Doyle, W. (1977). Learning the Classroom Environment: An Ecological Analysis. *Journal of Teacher Education, 28,* 51–55.

Easton, J. Q., Muirhead, R. S., Frederick, W. C., & Vanderwicken, S. (1979). *Relationships Among Student Time on Task Orientation of Teachers, and Instructional Grouping in Elementary Reading Classes.* Paper presented at the meeting of the American Educational Research Association, San Francisco, 1979. (ERIC Document Reproduction Service No. ED 169–503.)

Eisner, E. W. (1982). *Cognition and Curriculum.* New York: Longman.

Evans, E. D. (1975). *Contemporary Influence in Early Childhood Education* (2nd ed.). New York: Holt, Rinehart, & Winston.

Faber, A. & Mazlish, E. (1980). *How to Talk So Kids Will Listen and Listen So Kids Will Talk.* New York: Avon Books.

Filby, N. (1978). How Teachers Produce "Academic Learning Time": Instructional Variables Related to Student Engagement. In C. W. Fisher (Ed.), *Selected Findings from Phase III-B of the Beginning Teacher Evaluation Study.* San Francisco: Far West Laboratory for Educational Research. (ERIC Document Reproduction Service No. ED 160–639.)

Glasser, W. (1978). Notes from his lecture at the University of North Carolina at Greensboro, February.

Gump, P. V. (1967). *The Classroom Behavior Setting: Its Nature and Relation to Student Behavior.* (U.S. Office of Education Final Report, Project No. 2453; Bureau Report No. 5–0334). Lawrence, Kans.: University of Kansas Press.

Hess, R. D., & Takanishi, R. (1974). *The Relationship of Teacher Behavior and School Characteristics to Students' Engagement* (Technical Report No. 42.). Stanford, Ca.: Stanford Center for Research and Development in Teaching.

Jones, E. (1973). *Dimensions of Teaching-Learning Environments: Handbook for Teachers.* Pasadena, Ca.: Pacific Oaks College Bookstore.

Kounin, J. S. (1970). *Discipline and Group Management in Classrooms.* New York: Holt, Rinehart, & Winston.

Kounin, J. S., Freisen, W., & Norton, A. E. (1966). Managing Emotionally Disturbed Children in Regular Classrooms. *Journal of Educational Psychology, 57,* 1–13.

Kounin, J. S., & Sherman, L. W. (1979). School Environments as Behavior Settings. *Theory into Practice, 13,* 145–151.

Kritchevsky, S., Prescott, E., & Walling, L. (1977). *Planning Environments for Young Children:*

Physical Space (2nd ed.). Washington, D.C.: National Association for the Education of Young Children.

Leeper, S. H., Witherspoon, R. L., & Day, B. D. (1984). *Good Schools for Young Children* (5th ed.). New York: Macmillan.

Linn, M. C. (1980). Free-Choice Experiences: How Do They Help Children Learn? *Science Education, 64,* 237–48.

Long, N., & Newman, R. (1980). Managing Surface Behavior of Children in School. In N. J. Long, W. C. Morse, & R. G. Newman (Eds.), *Conflict in the Classroom.* Belmont, Ca.: Wadsworth.

McDonald, F. J., & Elias, P. J. (1976). The Effects of Teaching Performance on Pupil Learning. *Beginning Teacher Evaluation Study, Phase II, Vol. 1.* Princeton, N.J.: Educational Testing Service.

Medley, D. M. (1979). The Effectiveness of Teachers. In P. L. Peterson & H. J. Walberg (Eds.), *Research on Teaching* (pp. 11–27). Berkeley, Ca.: McCutchan.

Morrow, L. M., & Weinstein, C. S. (1982). Increasing Children's Use of Literature Through Program and Physical Design Changes. *The Elementary School Journal, 83,* 131–137.

Olmstead, P. (1979). Lecture-Handout: Parent Roles in Parental Involvement. *Parent Education Follow-Through Program.* Chapel Hill, N.C.: University of North Carolina.

Peck, S. (1978). *The Road Less Traveled.* New York: Simon & Schuster.

Peterson, P. L. (1979). Direct Instruction Reconsidered. In P. L. Peterson & H. J. Walberg (Eds.), *Research on Teaching* (pp. 57–69). Berkeley, Ca.: McCutchan.

Peterson, P. L., Marx, R., & Clark, C. (1978). Teacher Planning, Teacher Behavior, and Student Achievement. *American Educational Research Journal, 15,* 417–432.

Phyfe-Perkins, E. (1979). *Children's Behavior in Preschool Settings: A Review of Research Concerning the Influence of the Physical Environment.* (ERIC Document Reproduction Service No. ED 168–722.)

Probst, D. (1980). *A Study of Time on Task in Three Teachers' Classrooms Using Different Instructional Modes* (Technical Report No. 562). Madison, Wis.: University of Wisconsin, Research and Development Center for Individualized Schooling.

Rinne, C. H. (1984). *Attention: The Fundamentals of Classroom Control.* Columbus, OH: Charles E. Merrill.

Rosenshine, B. V. (1979). Content Time and Direct Instruction. In P. L. Petersen & H. J. Walberg (Eds.), *Research on Teaching* (pp. 28–56). Berkeley, Ca.: McCutchan.

Rosenthal, B. A. (1974). An Ecological Study of Free Play in the Nursery School (Doctoral dissertation, Wayne State University, 1973). *Dissertation Abstracts International, 34,* 4004A–4005A.

Ruff, F. (1978). *Instructional Variables and Student Achievement in Reading and Mathematics: A Synthesis of Recent Process-Product Research.* Unpublished manuscript, Research for Better Schools, Philadelphia.

Schweinhart, L. J. (1986). Research Findings Support Child Development Programs. *Educational Leadership, 44* (3), p. 16.

Schweinhart, L. J., Weikart, D. P., & Larner, M. B. (1986). Consequences of Three Curriculum Models Through Age 15. *Early Childhood Research Quarterly, 1,* 15–35.

Sharan, S. (1980). Cooperative Learning in Small Groups: Recent Methods and Effects on Achievement, Attitudes, and Ethnic Relations. *Review of Educational Research, 50,* 241–271.

Slavin, R. W. (1980). Effects of Student Teams and Peer Tutoring on Academic Achievement and Time on Task. *Journal of Experimental Education, 48,* 253–257.

Stallings, J. A. (1980). Allocated Academic Learning Time Revisited, or Beyond Time on Task. *Educational Researcher, 19* (11), 11–16.

Webb, N. M. (1982). Student Interaction on Learning in Small Groups. *Review of Educational Research, 50,* 421–455.

Weikart, D. P., Epstein, A. S., Schweinhart, L. J., & Bond, J. T. (1978). The Ypsilanti Preschool

Curriculum Demonstration Project: Preschool Years and Longitudinal Results. *Monographs of the High/Scope Educational Research Foundation, 4,* Ypsilanti, MI: High/Scope Press.

Weinstein, C. S. (1977). Modifying Student Behavior in an Open Classroom Through Changes in the Physical Design. *American Educational Research Journal, 14,* 259–260.

Weinstein, C. S. (1979). The Physical Environment of the School: A Review of the Research. *Review of Educational Research, 49,* 594–600.

Wilson, B. L. (1983, April). *Effect of Task and Authority Structures on Student Task Engagement.* Paper presented at the meeting of the American Educational Research Association, Montreal, Quebec, Canada. (ERIC Document Reproduction Service No. ED 230–416.)

3

Blocks

"Play is the way children learn what none can teach them." Children explore the world around them and grow through this environmental interaction. As an integral part of the early childhood program, block play provides children with both basic skills and creative outlets.

Blocks are a dramatic material in an early childhood program. The children can create something in three-dimensional boldness to see, to touch, to reach through, and even to crash. To build, use, change, destroy, and build again at will is mastery.

Growing mastery gives children joy in their work. Even 3-year-old children work a long time, striving to build what satisfies them. The child's very persistence and involvement with blocks help to make this material a valuable learning experience.

The highly manipulative nature of blocks ensures the development of eye-hand coordination, visual perception, and large and small muscle growth. In addition, blocks assist in the development of self-concept, promote social interaction and co-operation, and provide opportunities for dramatic play and emotional release. Rogers (1985) found that kindergarten children playing with both large hollow and unit blocks exhibited higher incidences of positive social behavior than negative social behavior.

Blocks play provides many opportunities for concept development in all major curriculum content areas. For example, mathematical concepts include measurement, area and spatial relationships, fractions, and broader areas such as seriation and size relationships. Also, children may discover scientific principles such as balance, gravity, and stability, as they begin to work with ramps and inclined planes. Blocks also encourage extensive oral communication and support and provide support language experiences such as dictating and writing labels, sentences, and stories. Building houses, stores, hospitals, airports, streets, bridges, and harbors not only represents beginning model making and mapping skills, but also serves in understanding such social science concepts as neighborhood and community.

Success or failure of the blocks center is usually correlated with the role of the teacher. As a facilitator of learning, the teacher must set the stage by providing the necessary raw materials in an environment organized for exploration and inquiry, a watchful eye and a listening ear, and, perhaps most important, skillful questions and comments that pave the way for new understandings. Teachers may use some of the examples following to help to focus and stimulate learning:

> *"You used a lot of blocks." "He has only a few blocks." "He needs five more blocks."* (number concepts, language development, comparison of quantity)
>
> *"Can you find another block just like this one?"* (matching, classifying according to size and shape)
>
> *"How can you make this road as long as that one?" "How can you make this side as high as that one?"* (language development, measurement, defining spatial relationships, problem solving)
>
> *"I wonder what would happen if we put this block here?"* (experimentation, testing)
>
> *"How can we connect these two blocks?"* (problem solving, language development)
>
> *"Look, two square blocks are as long as, or equal to, one rectangle." "This rectangle is half as long as this rectangle."* (fractions, measurement, spatial relationships, language development, labeling)
>
> *"Can you make the same pattern with your blocks that I have made with my blocks?"* (comparison, patterns)
>
> *"Try to make the other side the same as this side."* (symmetry)
>
> *"Can you think of a sentence/story to tell about your block creation?"* (written language)

Comments and questions such as these offer information subtly, confirm conclusions, pose problems that open new doors for exploration and discovery, and may be as important as the act of building itself. Sometimes the mere presence of the

teacher in the center, perhaps just sitting or quietly observing, will reinforce the message that what the children do there is of great value and importance. Occasionally children need help with technical problems such as bridging, making a roof for an enclosure, building a ramp or steps, or connecting roads. If children are really "stuck," help them solve their problems. There is nothing wrong with teaching a skill that will enable them to move ahead in their general building activity.

Of equal importance to the success of the block-building center are the teacher's efforts in preparing the physical environment and in providing a sense of "structured freedom" necessary for creative and organized play. Basic resources needed for the block center include the blocks themselves, a storage area, and an appropriately sized physical space for building.

Stages of Block Building

Just as children undergo stages of development, they also progress with their building techniques. The stages of block building as described by Harriet Johnson (1962) are as follows:

Stage 1: (under the age of 2)   Blocks are not used for building. The child carries one or two blocks around, making vast discoveries about the blocks themselves, turning them over and over, throwing them, pushing them, standing them on end. The child at this stage learns all facets of one block before moving to two, three, or more blocks.

Stage 2: (age 2 or 3) Actual building begins. Rows become the fascination, either horizontally or vertically; repeated patterns are typical to this stage— one block is often pushed along to become a car or a train.

Stage 3: (age 3) Bridging begins to occur. Two blocks with a space between them are spanned by a third one; there is still some horizontal or vertical building at this stage, and bridging illustrates a problem-solving technique discovered by the child builder.

Stage 4: (ages 2, 3, or 4) Four blocks are placed so they form an enclosed space. Children learn about insideness and outsideness of space; combined with bridging, sophisticated building occurs.

Stage 5: (age 4) Patterns begin to appear. Symmetry can be seen at this level of ability in building; buildings do not have names but become more elaborate.

Stage 6: (ages 4 to 6) Prior to this stage, a structure was named as an exercise in itself; now the child begins the dramatic play and the name of the building is related directly to the function of the building.

Stage 7: (ages 5 and up) Block play begins to reproduce or symbolize true-to-life structures. Building becomes an integral element of dramatic play ideas.

Environmental Resources

Unit blocks of various sizes and shapes and in appropriate quantities are obviously the primary material for construction. These solid wooden blocks are based on a single unit (approximately $1\frac{1}{2}'' \times 3'' \times 5''$); are designed in various shapes (double and quadruple units, ramps, curves, triangles, cylinders, switches, buttresses, Gothic arches); and, despite their seemingly high initial cost, are possibly the most durable, functional, and creative material in the early childhood classroom. Most important, children must have enough blocks to work with; nothing will diminish the value and interest of construction activities more quickly than will an insufficient quantity of unit blocks.

The diagram below shows the shapes and names of the recommended unit blocks.

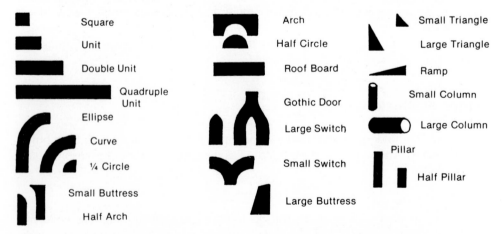

Square	Arch	Small Triangle
Unit	Half Circle	Large Triangle
Double Unit	Roof Board	Ramp
Quadruple Unit	Gothic Door	Small Column
Ellipse	Large Switch	Large Column
Curve	Small Switch	Pillar
¼ Circle	Large Buttress	Half Pillar
Small Buttress		
Half Arch		

*Reprinted by permission of Monroe D. Cohen and the Association for Childhood Education International, 3615 Wisconsin Avenue, N.W., Washington, D.C. Copyright © 1976 by the Association.

The number of unit blocks required for a block center varies depending on the age of the children. Below are some general recommendations.

Classroom Situation	Number of Blocks Recommended for Purchase		
	Year 1	Year 2	Year 3
Nursery school group (16 to 20 children, ages 3 to 5)	150	150	150
Kindergarten group (20 to 24 children, ages 4 to 6)	350	200	200
Early elementary school group (ages 6 to 10)	Two complete sets, large floor building blocks		

*Reprinted by permission of Monroe D. Cohen and the Association for Childhood Education International, 3615 Wisconsin Avenue, N.W., Washington, D.C. Copyright © 1976 by the Association.

Block Shape	At 3 Years	At 4 Years	At 5 Years
Half units	48	48	60
Units	108	192	220
Double units	96	140	190
Quadruple units	48	48	72
Pillars	24	48	72
Small cylinders	20	32	40
Large cylinders	20	24	32
Circular curves	12	16	20
Elliptical curves	8	16	20
Pairs of triangles— small	8	16	18
Pairs of triangles— large	4	8	12
Floor boards—11"	12	30	60
Roof boards—22"	0	12	20
Ramps	12	32	40
Half pillars	0	12	16
Y switches	2	2	4
Right angle switches and/or switches	0	4	8

Source: Jessie Stanton, Alma Weisberg, and the faculty of the Bank Street School for Children, *Play Equipment for the Nursery School* (New York: Bank Street College of Education).

    The storage area, whether permanent shelving or a freestanding cabinet, should be of an appropriate height for young children and large enough to group blocks of the same size and shape in an orderly manner. If a freestanding cabinet is used, the shelving should have a back to prevent blocks from falling out the other side. Contact paper labels cut in the shape and size of blocks show where each type of block is stored. Labels are applied to the front left-hand corner of each shelf (which helps children with the idea of reading left to right); they are placed lengthwise so that blocks can be discriminated one from another. (Remember, the ends of the unit, double unit, quadruple unit, etc., all look the same.) Labels for blocks that are stored standing up might be placed on the back of the shelf. In order to make the

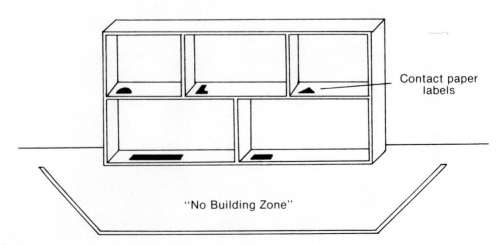

Contact paper labels

"No Building Zone"

storage area accessible, a "No Building Zone" can be marked off with masking tape. This area allows children to remove blocks and accessories freely without accidentally knocking over someone else's structure.

The building space in the center must be large enough to accommodate several children working on different structures simultaneously. Noise will be reduced if the space is carpeted; industrial-type carpeting is best, because its smooth surface permits better balance for block structures. The actual space for building should be clearly defined and visible. The use of a rug or carpet may itself provide sufficient demarcation, but if the room is fully carpeted or the center has no rug covering, lines made from masking tape will easily define building limits.

Management techniques are frequently incorporated into the physical setting and structure of the block-building center. These include: appropriate space, defining work space, and proper storage. Additional rules may be necessary. The best rules are frequently those that the children establish themselves with the help and guidance of the teacher. Many block areas have "reminders" such as:

> Blocks are for building, not for throwing, hitting, or knocking together to make noise.
> Always ask someone if he or she wishes help with his or her building.
> If you build too close to someone else, accidents may happen.
> Remember: only four (three, two, or whatever) builders are to be in the center at a time.
> Build only as high as you can reach standing with your feet on the floor.
> Work quietly and quickly when cleaning up.

Frequently the rules of the block center are the same as those for the entire classroom; in either case, always emphasize the constructive nature of block building.

If at all possible, allow some buildings to remain up at the end of the day. (Although this may be difficult to accomplish in programs that serve two groups of children a day, this could be done occasionally when a child feels especially proud of his or her building.) The teacher might have available laminated stop signs as reminders to other builders and those who clean up *not* to take down a certain building.

Accessories often make the difference between a "good" blocks center and a "great" one. Possibilities are limitless, provided that both teacher and children use their imaginations!

Small plastic or wooden people figures (often available in family or community worker sets)

Tiles, carpet squares, wallpaper (can be used as floors)

Large- and small-wheel toys such as trucks, trains, tractors, and airplanes

Miniature traffic signs

Small wooden or rubber animals (containers labeled "Zoo" and "Farm" provide a good sorting activity at cleanup time)

Miniature furniture

Magic markers, pencils, small cards, sentence strips (for labeling; store in small boxes or cans covered with contact paper)

Puppets

Tool kits (for dramatic play)

Thin pieces of rubber tubing (for gasoline pumps)

Pulleys

Dry cell batteries with lights (to illuminate building interiors)

Planks

Packing crates, boxes, ropes

Old steering wheel

Books related to building and construction

Objects used to "decorate" buildings:
  Dominos
  Shells (scallop, clam)
  Variety of small plastic containers, lids
  Popsicle sticks
  Large dried beans
  Small colored cubes (1" or 2 cm)
  Spools (thread and textile mill)
  Parquetry blocks
  Assorted colored wooden table blocks
  Lumber scraps (sanded)
  Pebbles, stones

Other building materials:
  Lego blocks (large and small)
  Tinker Toys
  Lincoln logs
  Large hollow blocks (plastic or wooden)

Easter grass (excellent for animal food)

Scraps of fabric

Styrofoam pebbles

Small flags

Art box (paper, crayons, string, clay, scissors, Scotch tape, masking tape, etc.)

Block cart (use a wooden crate and add wheels and a handle; this will make an excellent cart for the children to move the blocks outside)

Milk carton blocks (cut off the pouring end of two milk cartons; put one inside of the other; these will make good hollow blocks; use half-pint, pint, quart, and half-gallon cartons)

Blocks from wood scraps (sand and varnish or paint scrap 2" × 4" bits of wood from a construction site)

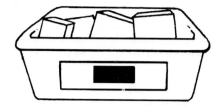

Large plastic tubs or wash basins make excellent containers for accessories. There might be a different container for each different accessory; containers could be labeled with a photograph or a drawing of the particular accessory, with the label covered with clear contact paper for extra durability.

Cleanup

Cleaning up the block-building center can be a frustrating and seemingly never-ending chore, or it can be a fun and enjoyable learning experience. Always warn the children and set a time limit before cleanup: "We will need to start cleaning up in ten minutes." This provides the child with a sense of security and a chance to complete his or her structure. Another reminder might be given a little later: "Five more minutes until cleanup." When cleanup does begin, decisions should be made as to who is responsible for various tasks. The teacher might help with cleanup, particularly during the first few weeks of school, with the adult involvement and interaction providing both model and structure for what can be a very confusing and possibly chaotic activity. Once the children fully understand the process, the teacher can still provide suggestions or directions to make the daily chore as varied and interesting as possible:

Each person carries ten blocks to the shelves (or eight, or as many blocks as the child's age, etc.)

Assign a different kind of block to each child: "Tamika, you're in charge of the squares." "Joanna, the small triangles." "Edmond, can you clean up the curved blocks?"

Put away all accessories before cleaning up blocks.

Organize an "assembly line" of cleanup; this is a fine way to initiate a cooperative task.

Compose a "cleanup song" to add a little merriment to the occasion.

Ask children to put away blocks that are longer or shorter than their feet.

Begin with blocks that are closest to the shelf and work outward.

The "director" of cleanup holds up a certain block and children must put up that particular one before going to another.

"Jack, put away five cylinders and seven ramps, and then tell me how many you cleaned up all together."

"Clean up all the blocks that are longer than the one I'm holding, Connie."

The following objectives can help focus learning in the block center:

1. To enjoy the block area by working with the blocks for fun.
2. To orient the builder to his or her body in space.
3. To improve small and large muscle coordination by working with and building with blocks.

4. To role-play with the animals, people, and/or puppets.
5. To learn to share ideas and work together in a group while taking turns with the blocks.
6. To develop genuine respect for other's work.
7. To make the inquiry approach to learning valuable and real to the child.
8. To develop concepts of big, little, more than, less than, equal to, shapes and sizes.
9. To develop a sense of pattern and symmetry.
10. To use materials to create the child's world as he or she sees it.
11. To be able to express oneself nonverbally and to release emotions in an acceptable form.
12. To explore the dynamics of balance through construction.

Suggested Activities

1. *Map Study.* Use blocks for defining map study. Children might take a walk around the block or the school community, return to school, and use blocks to make a model of what they saw. (Examples are streets, paths, buildings, shopping center or stores, trees, church, etc.). The children can also draw their structure on paper.
2. *Bridge.* After a visit to a river (or a film on rivers), some children might be interested in constructing a bridge, boats, and so on.
3. *Defining Special Areas.* Colored (or plain) masking tape can be used to define special areas such as coastlines, rivers, and streams (blue) and roads, highways, streets, and airport runways (gray or red). A whole community might be planned this way that could later be "mapped out" with crayons and paper, allowing the children to make a two-dimensional representation of their three-dimensional model.
4. *Signs.* Have children bring in shopping bags displaying store logos or labels.

These designs and words can be cut out, pasted on small pieces of posterboard and laminated, resulting in small miniature "signs" that children can use to label their buildings. Best of all, even very young children and other "nonreaders" can usually read and recognize familiar signs!

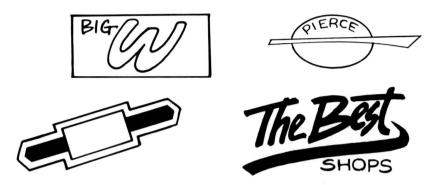

5. *Sentence Strips.* In addition to allowing children to make their own labels, the teacher can prepare a set of labels on sentence strips in advance. Once laminated, these strips may be stored in a small can near the center; children can come and select the label they need. A small picture or illustration added next to the word may help young prereaders.

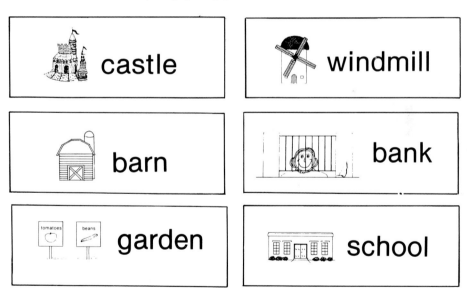

6. *Language Experience Stories.* Encourage children to dictate, write, or type labels, sentences, or stories about their constructions. (Providing pencils, markers, sentence strips, and writing paper nearby or in the center will facilitate this.) Language experience stories could be written on chart paper and later illustrated by the children or written on smaller sheets of paper and later collected and "bound" in a book for the reading center. These books could also be illustrated with drawings or the teacher could take photographs of the structures ("instant" cameras are best for young children because they provide "instant gratification") and tape or glue them onto the pages.

We built a barn.

There are places for the cows

and horses to sleep.

There are four salt blocks for

the cows.

We built a loft for hay.

There are places for the

animals to eat and drink.

Miles   Joan   Kyle

We built Kenan Stadium.

It has Kenan Field House

and the Bell Tower.

We put in the upper decks.

The end zone seats are

slanted.

The goal posts are made

two different ways.

Pam   Carol

We built a train station.
We built a place for people
to buy something to eat while
they wait for the train. Our
train has a big engine and a
caboose, too! The train
track goes forever and
ever! On top of the engine
is a big smokestack.

Jon   Susan   Keith

We made a castle. It
had a nice gate at the front.
It had a watch tower and
a place to keep the prisoners.
There is a wall around our
castle. It has an archway
in the center. There is a
see-saw for the kids.

Linda Richie Denise

7. *Task Cards.* Task cards may provide specific directions for a step-by-step assignment, or they may simply serve as a visual reminder (particularly for prereaders) of a suggested task. Teacher-made drawings or pictures cut from magazines might be used to illustrate the cards.

Can you build a map of your body?

Build a
three-ring

CIRCUS.

How would you build a
tightrope for the trapeze
artist?

Send in
the clowns!

Where would the
audience sit?

Can you make these
letters with blocks?

A R k
m   b

YOU JUST CAUGHT A LION!
BUILD A CAGE.

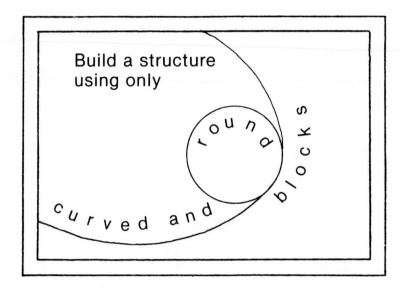

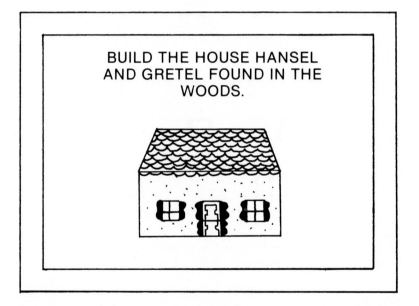

Encourage the children to tell about their structures. This encourages verbal expression.

8. *Task Card Variation.* A variation on task cards for the older or more mature blockbuilder may be a "record-keeping worksheet." These worksheets should be used only occasionally, yet they add a new dimension in allowing the child to record his or her own experiences as well as reinforcing numerous skills such as counting, graphing, and writing.

Write the number of how many blocks of each kind used inside the block shape.

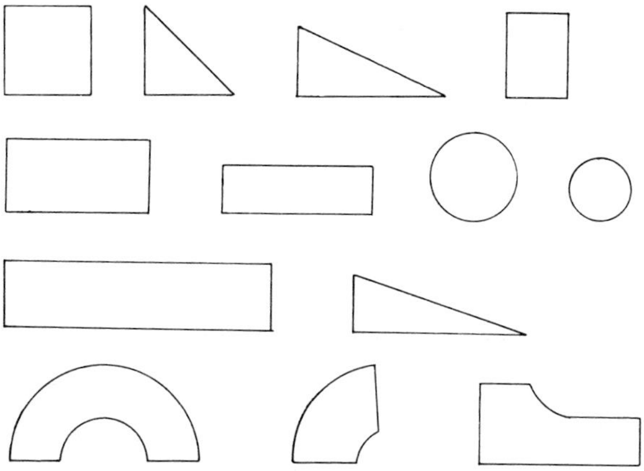

I built

_____

....

_____

Name_____Date_____

Write 2 sentences about your building.

_____

_____

Use ☐ to measure:

How tall is your building? _____

How long?_____

How wide? _____

Estimate how many blocks you
    used. _____

Name _____

If ☐ equals 1 unit, then:

☐ is the same as how many ☐

◪ is the same as how many ☐

▭ is equal to how many ☐

BONUS*BONUS*BONUS*BONUS*BONUS*BONUS

◺ is the same as how many ☐

◺ ◺ is the same as how many ☐

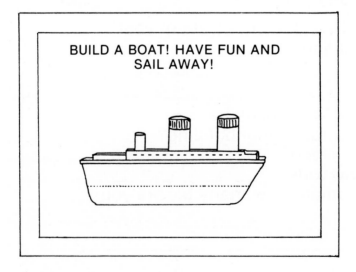

BUILD A BOAT! HAVE FUN AND
SAIL AWAY!

1. Build a tower as tall as your friend.

2. Then draw a picture of it and give it to him.

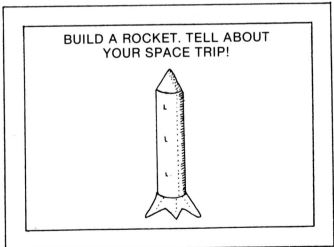

BUILD A ROCKET. TELL ABOUT
YOUR SPACE TRIP!

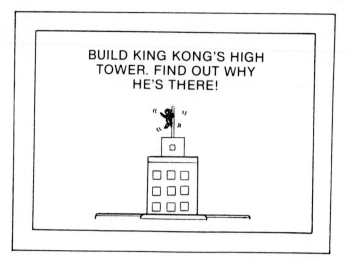

9. **"Sample" Building Cards.** The teacher can prepare "sample" building cards by mounting pictures or photographs of different kinds of structures (for example, apartment highrises, the Eiffel Tower, a barn, coliseum, igloo) on posterboard. The child could select one from a box or file of the cards, try to "reproduce" the structure, and then prop the card against the building to share his or her work with others.

10. **Define Individual Building Areas.** For a change of pace (and new possibilities in using space), use masking tape to define individual building areas. Unusual building spaces such as triangles, long narrow rectangles, and hexagons provide new challenges in problem solving.

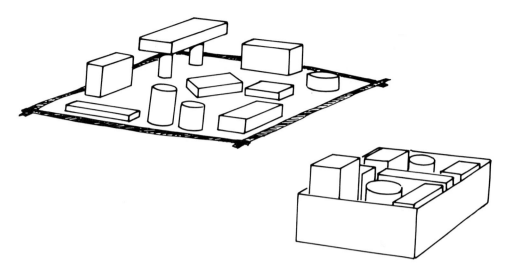

11. ***Trace and Match.*** Trace around the shape of several blocks and have the child match. This activity is good to use with young children learning shape recognition.

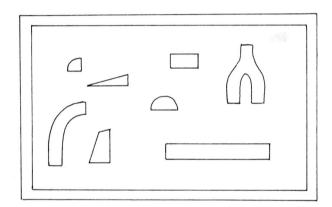

12. ***Sequencing.*** Sequencing activities can also be structured in a similar manner with prepared mats of traced shapes. Provide a limited number of blocks to be used. Move the other blocks out of the center.

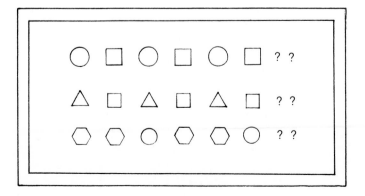

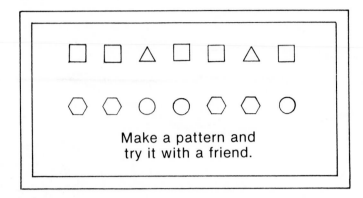

Make a pattern and
try it with a friend.

13. *Blueprints.* Full-sized sheets of posterboard may be prepared as "blueprints" by tracing block shapes in various designs or sequences. When taped vertically to the side of a storage cabinet or "cubbie," the child can match and reproduce the design exactly—a fine exercise in visual discrimination and sequencing.

14. *Horizontal Blueprints.* Posterboard sheets can also be placed directly on the floor for the child to build on top; these "horizontal blueprints" prove to be valuable exercises in open-ended problem solving.

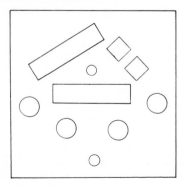

15. *Area and Volume.* Tape off an area or give a child a square to fill up or cover with blocks; in doing so, the child will be working with the concept of *area.* If given a cardboard box to fill to the brim, the child will be exploring the concept of *volume.* Can you do it more than one way? If you use bigger blocks, what happens to the number you use?

16. *Visual Discrimination.* The teacher (or another child) could build a structure in advance and have the other children duplicate it—an excellent activity in visual discrimination and spacing. Talk to the child about the similarities and differences.

17. *Ratio.* How many different ways can you reproduce a structure identically? Using different-sized blocks will develop the concept of *ratio.*

18. *Build a Maze.* Show children a maze. Explain how it is made. Encourage the builders to construct one, and use the class pet, cars, or, if large enough, even classmates to explore the maze.

Today we built a train station.

Our train has a big engine and a caboose too.
The train track has a

19. *Partnership Activity.* Assign a partner to the child and have them work together. This is effective when children have had vast experience with blocks and it encourages a new friendship.

20. *Add a Block.* With a small or medium-sized group of children, allow each child to add one block at a time, to create a group structure. This cooperative activity provides maximum opportunity for teacher-pupil interaction and discussion as well as an exercise in group creativity.

21. *Role Play.* Children might make puppets in the art area to use for role play in the block center. These might be added to cars, boats, or airplanes made in the woodworking center.

22. *Limit Block Use.* Limiting the number of blocks or the shape of blocks used for a day will create new problem-solving situations for the child. If, for example, each child may use only 17 blocks, questions arise not only of *"what* can you build?" but also "how many *different* buildings can be made?" Both the teacher and the children will be pleasantly surprised at the wide range of structures that can develop.

23. *Low Enclosures.* Encourage children to construct low enclosures for imaginative eating, sleeping, and so on.

24. *Simple Machines.* Working with blocks naturally may lead to discussion of simple machines, particularly considering frequent work with inclined planes and ramps. If the school or classroom has models of other simple machines, these items might be placed in the blocks center as accessories.

25. *Lighting.* A high-powered Tensor or gooseneck lamp added to the center will allow opportunities to discover principles with light and shadows.

26. *Creative Construction.* Children's books may instigate creative construction, particularly if one is occasionally placed in the center as a visual reminder. For instance, Virginia Lee Burton's *Little House* may result in a large replica of the city, with the "little house" right in the middle. Likewise, David Macaulay's *Cathedral* (Houghton Mifflin, 1973) can produce miniature Notre Dames, complete with flying buttresses!

27. *Creative Construction.* An object or leaflet gathered during a field trip may also result in fine, creative buildings if placed on display in the block-building center. A firefighter's helmet might produce the fire station that was visited; a pamphlet from Cape Canaveral might result in the Columbia space shuttle or rockets to visit galaxies unknown!

28. *A New Center.* A new center might be developed using the blocks, and the ingenuity of the children. (For example, store, post office.)

29. *Small-Scale Constructions.* Lincoln logs, Tinker Toys, and other sets and kits can be used to do small-scale construction on a table or a designated floor area. (These can be easily stored.)

30. *Outside Block Play.* Move the blocks outside. Some of the large pieces from the center might remain out at all times. Outdoor space is more conducive to larger building of objects (forts, submarine, etc.).

31. *Temporary Constructions.* Have a pile of scrap lumber outside the classroom for building temporary constructions in the outdoors. Children can build something much larger outside than they can inside.

32. *Weekly Theme.* Use the block center to reinforce the weekly theme in the classroom. For example, for winter/snow, build a snow fort, make a snowmobile, and drive away in it.

33. *Relate to Other Studies.* Encourage the children to use the blocks throughout the curriculum: in math for counting, in science for building a weather station.

References

Johnson, H. (1982). *The Act of Block Building.* New York: Bank Street College Publications.
Rogers, D. L. (1985). Relationships Between Block Play and Social Development of Young Children. *Early Child Development and Care, 20,* 245–261.

4

Communication: The Language Arts

Language Arts in the Elementary School

Much of the young child's life depends on his or her ability to communicate in some way. Communication spans all content fields. For this reason, language arts becomes the foundation of school programs and life in general. The language arts skills are a series of interrelated thinking processes. They are listening, speaking, reading, and writing. Language activities can be divided into two groups: the *receptive* and the *expressive*. Receptive activities involve *reading* and *listening;* expressive activities involve *speaking* and *writing*. All four of these aspects of the language arts are equally important in the development of good language use and understanding in the young child.

Teachers can encourage and develop language skills in an atmosphere of warmth and creativity. Language models in the child's environment are a powerful influence on language development. However, a language environment that encourages comfortable social patterns and interactions *with* a variety of models will help the child to develop communication skills. The effective teacher will continually promote language interactions encouraging children to question and engage in dialogue. The language arts field is a world of code-breaking processes that open the doors to well-developed oral and written communication.

Mayesky, Neuman, and Wlodkowski (1985) state that ability in one language skill is not always directly related to competence in another. For example, many young children are far better speakers than listeners. In addition, because development is highly individualized, in early elementary grades it is very common for children to perform at different levels of skill in reading, writing, and comprehension. Mayesky et al. stress the idea that in early childhood programs, language arts experiences must take into consideration the developmental levels of children in each distinct part of language development.

DiStefano, Dole, and Marzano (1984) provide goals for language arts instruction that include reading, listening, writing, and speaking activities. The goals are as follows:

82

1. To create in young minds a desire to learn and a love of learning through language. Educators must see to it that they instruct in such a way that they encourage learning through many forms and medias. Children should be taught so they will value and love language in all its forms and see a need and purpose in the various roles and functions of language.
2. To enable each child to communicate effectively with others. Effective communication involves listening to what someone is saying to others, speaking, reading, and writing.
3. To develop each child's fullest potential in listening, speaking, reading, and writing abilities. In order to learn how to communicate effectively with others, children need to learn specifics as to how to spell, how to write clearly and legibly, how to pronounce multisyllabic words, and how to write a letter.

In summary, according to DiStefano et al. language arts instruction must include teaching positive attitudes, thought and language processes, and specific content.

Furthermore, DiStefano et al. state that in order to implement the goals previously mentioned, one needs a framework from which to examine the components of the language arts to see how they relate to each other and to thinking and language. In their model of language arts (Figure 1), thinking is central and permeates the model. The dashed lines in the model enclosing the forms of language reflect the fact that thinking and language are interrelated.

Norton (1985) maintains that the development of thinking skills is essential for all subjects. "A well-balanced curriculum must develop children's thinking capacities as well as increase their knowledge." The National Council of Teachers of English (1983) identifies the following creative, logical, and critical thinking objectives:

In the area of creative thinking, students should learn
- that originality derives from the uniqueness of the individual's perception, not necessarily from an innate talent.
- that inventiveness involves seeing new relationships.
- that creative thinking derives from their ability not only to look, but to see; not only to hear, but to listen; not only to imitate, but to innovate; not only to observe, but to experience the excitement of fresh perception.

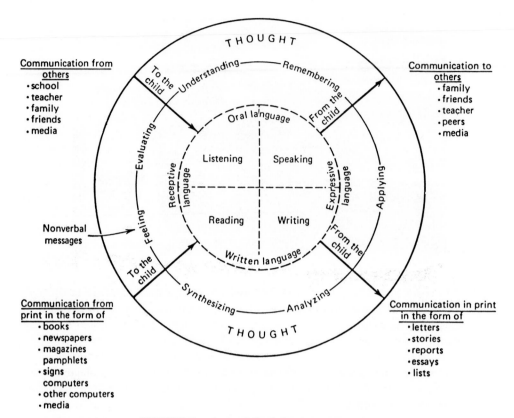

FIGURE 1 *A model of the language arts.*

In the area of logical thinking, students should learn
- to create hypotheses and predict outcomes.
- to test the validity of an assertion by examining the evidence.
- to understand logical relationships.
- to construct logical sequences and understand the conclusions to which they lead.
- to detect fallacies in reasoning.
- to recognize that "how to think" is different from "what to think."

In the area of critical thinking, students should learn
- to ask questions in order to discover meaning.
- to differentiate between subjective and objective viewpoints; to discriminate between opinion and fact.
- to evaluate the intentions and messages of speakers and writers, especially at attempts to manipulate the language in order to deceive.
- to make judgments based on criteria that can be supported and explained.

To fully understand how language operates, one must look at thinking in general (DiStefano et al., 1984). Thought interrelated with language forms the basis of language arts instruction. As defined by cognitive psychologists, thought is the symbolic, mental representation of the environment. Thought is the coding of what one perceives with his or her senses, and these representations or codifications of perceptual information are stored in memory. There are three different stages of the memory process that have been identified: sensory information storage, short-term memory, and long-term memory. Sensory information storage feeds short-term memory, which in turn feeds long-term memory. Long-term memory enables a person to interpret information being processed through sensory information storage and short-term memory. DiStefano et al. state that thinking is also related to a person's interpretation system. Human beings "try to make sense out of what they perceive—they interpret all information as meaningful and consistent with the knowledge they already possess." Finally, thinking is limited by a child's level of cognitive development. According to Piaget, thinking develops from the concrete to the abstract. Specifically, from birth to age two, thought is very little more than sensation, the coding of information sent to the brain via the senses (the sensorimotor stage). From ages two to seven, the preoperational stage, the child begins to produce mental images of static things and situations.

In addition to thinking, speaking is an important language activity. Mayesky et al. (1985) maintain that speech is a form of language in which words or sounds are used to convey meanings. The ability to speak is not necessarily related to the ability to understand. They also note that in the development of speech, there are great differences among children in the age at which they begin to learn to speak and the rate with which they achieve competence. Burns and Broman (1983) state that by the time children come to school they have usually already developed a large speaking vocabulary. The purpose of an oral language program, then, is not necessarily to get children to talk, but to develop skills they already possess. The National Council of Teachers of English (1983) also provides objectives for speaking, which include:

Students should learn
- to speak clearly and expressively about their ideas and concerns.
- to adapt words and strategies according to varying situations and audiences, from one-to-one conversations to formal, large-group settings.
- to participate productively and harmoniously in both small and large groups.
- to present arguments in orderly and convincing ways.
- to interpret and assess various kinds of communication, including intonation, pause, gesture, and body language that accompany speaking.

According to Burns and Broman (1983), oral language involves both informational and fictitional use. The informational or factual uses include conversation, discussion, description, oral reporting, and conducting meetings and interviews. The fictitional uses of language include dramatization and storytelling. They also state that in order to teach spoken language effectively, teachers must use a variety of methods and materials and relate speaking to the other language arts and other areas of the curriculum.

Another expressive activity other than speaking involves writing. Mayesky et al. (1985) claim that in early childhood programs, it is not the goal to have young children "practice" letters and words. Instead, the goal is to provide young children with opportunities to practice the eye-hand coordination and small-muscle skills needed to be able to write. Writing can be divided into two subcategories: hand-writing, spelling, grammar, usage, and the mechanics of writing; and composition and creative writing.

Burns and Broman (1983) state that the primary purpose of handwriting is to express meaning. The pupil should have a purpose for writing, even in the earliest stages of writing instruction. Also, the objectives of handwriting instruction include the following: helping pupils recognize and accept the importance of good hand-writing, developing pride in and a critical attitude toward their own handwriting, acquiring suitable speed in handwriting, and developing habits of neatness and or-derly arrangement in written work. Norton (1985) also stresses that handwriting should be taught within the broader context of composition and communication, rather than as the subject of isolated drills. "Many language arts authorities fear that if handwriting practice is a predominately isolated drill, or if handwriting is given more importance than the developmental process of composing, children may think handwriting is an end in itself, instead of a means to self-expression and commu-nication."

Like handwriting, spelling is not an end it itself (Norton, 1985). The major objec-tive is effective written communication. Gentry (1982) identifies and describes de-velopmental stages in learning to spell that appear to be consistent in young chil-dren:

1. *Precommunicative stage.* The child first uses symbols from the alphabet to represent words; there is, however, no knowledge of letter-sound correspon-dence.
2. *Semiphonetic stage.* The child, approximately five years old, begins to use sounds heard in words. Spelling is abbreviated; one, two, or three letters may represent a whole word (BRZ = birds).
3. *Phonetic stage.* The child, approximately five to six years old, spells words according to the entire sound structure of the word being spelled (STRET = street, KOM = come).
4. *Transitional stage.* The child, approximately six years plus, begins to assimi-late conventional alternatives for representing sounds; includes vowels in every

syllable; uses familiar spelling patterns; and intersperses standard spelling with phonetic spelling.

5. *Correct stage.* The child's knowledge of the English orthographic system and its rules are established; formal spelling instruction facilitates growth. The child recognizes when words do not look right.

Norton (1985) states that if the educator's goal is to develop effective spellers, the spelling program must be formulated on objectives enhancing the students' independent spelling skills. Also the spelling program must include many opportunities for writing for an audience.

Furthermore, according to Burns and Broman (1983), grammar describes the human communication system. There are three approaches to grammar: the traditional approach, the structural approach, and the transformational approach. The traditional approach is prescriptive, defining socially preferred ways of communicating. "There is 'good' grammar and 'bad' grammar; there is a 'correct' way to speak and an 'incorrect' way to speak." The structural approach is descriptive, describing the ways we communicate and our arrangement of the elements of communication—words, sounds, and units of meaning. Structural grammar has little to do with rules for proper grammar. The transformational approach defines grammar as the set of rules we intuitively know and use in order to communicate. It focuses on language as an "underlying form that can be expressed through speech and through writing."

Finally, composition and creative writing are also important parts of writing. The National Council of Teachers of English (1983) provides guidelines for the enhancement of written composition. According to the NCTE "Essentials of English," students should:

1. Learn to write clearly and honestly.
2. Recognize that writing is a way to learn and develop personally as well as a way to communicate with others.
3. Learn ways to generate ideas for writing, to select and arrange them, to find appropriate modes for expressing them, and to evaluate and revise what they have written.
4. Learn to adapt expression to various audiences.
5. Learn the techniques of writing for appealing to others and persuading them.
6. Develop their talents for creative and imaginative expression.
7. Recognize that precision in punctuation, capitalization, spelling, and other elements of manuscript form is part of the total effectiveness of writing.

Creative writing, according to Norton (1985), has a function that goes beyond the communication of information. It includes writing that is original in nature and that uses both imaginative and experimental thinking. Norton stresses that creative writing cannot be taught in the same way many other skills are taught. Instruction in creative development must stimulate and encourage the student in self-awareness, as well as in written skills.

Following the expressive activity of writing, reading is a receptive activity critical to the language arts experience. The National Council of Teachers of English (1983) present the following objectives for reading, emphasizing the desired outcomes of a reading program and suggesting the relationships among reading and other areas of language arts:

1. Recognize that reading functions in their lives as a pleasurable activity as well as a means of acquiring knowledge.
2. Learn from the very beginning to approach reading as a search for meaning.
3. Develop the necessary reading skills to comprehend material appearing in a variety of forms.
4. Learn to read accurately and make valid inferences.
5. Learn to judge literature critically on the basis of personal response and literary quality.

Reading

Reading is the process of constructing meaning from the text. It is the identification of written symbols, combined with previous experiences, to gain meaning. An overall goal of reading is to give children a foundation for lifelong literacy.

The background knowledge the children bring to the material allows them to grasp the meaning. In schema theory, the role of past experiences is important in learning to read and for continued understanding of concepts in learning. We can comprehend better because we have the necessary schemata, or structure of knowledge, in our minds. A major implication from schema theory is that strong emphasis should be given to building background knowledge, prereading preparation, and comprehension follow-through activities. Some appropriate experiences that develop concepts and vocabulary are opportunities for using manipulatives, role playing in other subject areas, planned field trips, and hands-on activities in math and science. The teacher can also provide an environment that is rich in varied, suitable, and interesting reading material. Allow time for children to read independently. Reading to children can also stimulate the language of individual children.

Many approaches are possible in teaching reading and reading skills. Probably the most widely used is the basal reader approach. This system, which involves the use of a graded set of reading books, is based on the idea that the skills needed for word attack, comprehension, and the use of reading as a source for learning must be systematically organized. Skills and vocabulary are presented in a developmental and sequential manner. Basal programs usually provide an introduction to new vocabulary, a purpose for reading, an opportunity to read silently and orally if desired, questions for comprehension development, and practice with specific skills. Disadvantages of this program include a vocabulary not based on the vocabulary and experiences of the child, little or no child input, little student-student interaction, and little room for individualization.

The directed reading-thinking approach (DR-TA) is similar to, yet different from, the basal or directed reading activity method. The purposes for reading using DR-TA are set by the group through predictions about the reading rather than by the author of the text. The interaction is truly a group discussion during which students are encouraged to think and contribute, supporting and refuting the predictions made. Comprehension skills are taught by the pupils themselves as they reread to define their individual purposes further. Word-attack skills are usually taught after the reading according to pupil needs. In this method, the teacher serves as a moderator of group discussion, with the text as the source of authority.

The language experience approach, a popular method of reading instruction, gives each child a chance to use his or her own speech patterns, experiences, thoughts, and ideas during all parts of the school day. As the child speaks, the teacher writes down *exactly* what is said. The child begins to get the idea that print is talk written down and that he or she can read it. This is a very individualized approach, presented in a creative and purposeful way. The student's interest and individual personal involvement are great assets of this program, and culturally disadvantaged students can benefit greatly from this approach.

The individualized reading program is also gaining in popularity. Educators have found that children learn at different rates and in different ways and that learning may be more effective if each student's individual needs and interests are met at the student's own learning rate. In this program, because the student selects his or her own reading material, the child has a greater interest in the reading. Skills are taught through these selections. Individual conferences with the teacher, during which the teacher can become aware of each child's individual skill needs, are a vital component of this program. These skills can be developed through individual programs or small-group sessions. Record keeping is another vital part of the program. This can be quite time consuming, but it must be done accurately to ensure uninterrupted progress. Students share books and projects with other students and thus become exposed to others' interests as well as their own. Three requirements of this program on the part of the teacher are (1) tremendous amounts of reading materials, (2) an awareness of the pupils' interests, and (3) a clear knowledge of skills needed in each individual program.

Any of these approaches to teaching reading can be quite effective if used in the proper setting and matched to the particular child's needs and interests. Mayesky et al. (1985) state that the readiness to read involves a complex combination of mental, physical, and emotional skills. A child must have enough skill in visual discrimination in order to recognize and distinguish between shapes and to "read" pictures.

Finally, listening is the last activity essential to language arts. Norton (1985) notes that recent research indicates that elementary children spend over 50 percent of their classroom time listening rather than speaking or reading. DiStefano et al. (1984) present three components of listening: physiological, attention, and comprehension. The physiological component has two subcategories. The first is auditory acuity, the ability to hear, and the second is auditory perception, which consists of the ability to discriminate among sounds, to blend sounds together, and to hold sequences of sounds in memory. Attention deals with focusing, becoming aware, and selecting cues from the environment to attend. Comprehension is concerned with getting meaning from what is heard or associating the sounds to something already known. Burns and Broman (1983) suggest that there are four levels of listening: literal, interpretive, critical, and creative. Literal listening is easier for children to learn and includes being able to identify main ideas, describe details, and recognize cause-and-effect relationships and sequence. Interpretive listening involves more complex skills such as drawing conclusions, making generalizations, recognizing the objective of speech content, and identifying implied main ideas. Another complex skill is critical listening. Children begin to recognize speakers' bias and propaganda techniques, to differentiate fact from opinion, and to determine whether data being presented are appropriate or accurate. The last listening level, creative listening, requires the imagination to produce new ideas based on what is being said.

In conclusion, thinking, speaking, writing, reading, and listening are all important aspects of the language arts. Burns and Broman (1983) state that the language arts program has a major objective: to help children use language more effectively. To meet this objective, teachers must provide activities that integrate and develop thinking, speaking, writing, reading, and listening skills.

Reading Materials

Books: child-made, high interest level (varying ability levels), paperbacks and comics
Books with coordinating records or tapes
Books with coordinating filmstrips
Resource books such as children's encyclopedias, science library, Childcraft
Newspapers: class, local, and city (current)
Magazines (popular as well as children's)
Catalogs
Stories: child-written and commercial

Talk-starter picture cards
Puppets
Flannel board with flannel objects, labels, letters, story characters
Magnetic board, letters
Lotto games
Matching picture and letter games
Parquetry blocks, designs
Puzzles (variety of topics and number of pieces)
Spelling and reading games
Crossword puzzles
Tapes: blank, teacher-made, and commercially prepared

Reading Objectives

1. To develop an understanding of the relationship between oral language and written symbols.
2. To foster success and satisfaction in beginning reading.
3. To develop a basic sight vocabulary.
4. To develop word-attack skills, picture and context clues, structural analysis.
5. To further develop comprehension and interpretive skills and to read for meaning.
6. To develop the ability to read silently.
7. To develop the ability to read orally with proper expression.
8. To develop a desire to read for achievement, pleasure, information, and understanding.
9. To encourage independent reading and thinking, for information and recreation.
10. To apply skills in other content areas through reading.

Environmental Resources

1 to 2 tables and 2 to 4 chairs
Small table with typewriter

Low shelves used also as a divider
Rocking chair, easy chairs, couch
Carpet, rug, or carpet squares
Pillows or floor cushions
Book rack
Open storage for records and tapes
Carrels for individual usage
Electrical outlets

Materials for K–2 Children in Language Arts

Tape recorder, earphones
Paper: lined and unlined, white and colored
Sentence strips
Blackboard
Pencils
Markers
Crayons
Paints
Brushes
Various scrap materials that can be used for book covers
Manipulative letters: wood, sandpaper, pipe cleaners, plastic, cardboard
Cans labeled with a letter each: small cans with small letters, large cans with
    capital letters in another color
Pictures of animals (farm)
Pictures of animals (wild)
Pictures of vegetables
Pictures of fruits
Pictures of birds
Pictures of flowers

Various other pictures of different groups of things and places
Wide variety of books of interest to children including
    Mother Goose and nursery rhymes
    ABC books
    Counting books

Stories
Stories of the country, seasons, and nature
Stories of other countries
Realistic animal stories
Fanciful animal stories
Modern fanciful stories
Folk and fairy tales
Poetry
Informational books
Series of pictures (for putting in correct sequence)
Dramatic play equipment
Dress-up clothes
Props
Furniture
Films
Cards with words on them
Many cards for children to write their own words on
Groups of cards with rhyming words (self-correcting with other word on back)
Groups of cards with rhyming pictures (self-correcting)
ABC Bingo game
Groups of pictures with one different for visual discrimination
Tiles with letters on each
Play and real telephones
Mirror (full child body length)

Suggested Reading Readiness Activities

Auditory Discrimination

For the following activities, the objective is auditory discrimination. The child will work with environmental sounds and speech sounds.

1. *Sound Boxes.* A child shakes the contact-covered milk cartons on little place-mats. Matching letters are on the bottom of each pair. The more advanced student may then add the labels that are included. Labels have picture clues on the backs. Sounds included are pennies, paper clips, rice, flour, bells, beans, and macaroni.

2. *Sound Cards.* Make cards with three pictures on them. The child says the words and puts a paper clip over the one that does not have the same beginning sound. The answer is coded on the back.

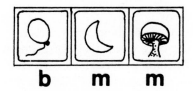

3. *Sound Tracks.* Give the children track boards that are alike. The teacher claps his or her hands and the children move that number of spaces. All should finish together.

4. *Art Fun.* Have children draw objects that begin with the same sound.

5. *Tape Recorder.* The child will recognize familiar sounds. Make a tape recording (in advance) of indoor and outdoor sounds. Some examples are children singing, bell ringing, teacher talking, lawn mowers, and dogs barking. Ask the children to draw or name the sounds they hear.

6. *Musical Sounds.* The child will distinguish between types of sounds a particular instrument makes. Hide several musical instruments or put them in a box. Have the children close their eyes. Play one instrument and have the children guess the instrument.

Sequencing

For the following activities, the objective is sequencing.

1. *Fire Pictures.* A child will look at four laminated pictures of events that happen during a fire: someone at a phone calling the fire department, fire fighters hearing alarm and sliding down poles, fire fighters on truck rushing to the fire, fire fighters putting out the fire. The child tries to put the cards in proper sequence. These are self-correcting with each picture numbered as to its place in the event.

2. *Sequence Cards.* The child examines the story cards and places them in order from left to right. A star on each holder indicates left, the starting point. Cards are self-correcting and numbered on the back.

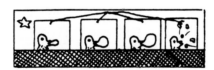

3. *Comic Strips.* Sequencing cards are made from comic strips. A child arranges them in the correct order and can tape record his or her own interpretation of the sequences.

4. *Musical Sequence.* The child will be able to repeat sound sequences. Gather several types of instruments with different sounds—triangle, drum, tambourine, sandpaper blocks, rhythm sticks. Make a sound with three instruments, one at a time. Ask the children to tell you which comes first, second, and third. Add new instruments and increase the number. This can also be done with body sounds—clapping, stamping, snapping fingers.

Visual Discrimination

For the following activities, the objective is visual discrimination.

1. *Look-alikes.* Two columns of pictures are presented on posterboard. The pictures have a look-alike mate, shown on the board in a different way. The child matches the look-alikes by connecting each piece of yarn to the correct picture.

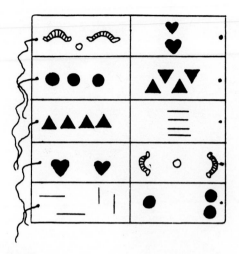

2. *Little Rugs.* Make little wallpaper squares. A child spreads out the squares and attempts to place matching "rugs" on top of each other. The rugs differ in color, pattern, and texture. Identical shapes on the back indicate correct matches.

3. *Outline Game.* Put objects into a bag. A child selects one object from the bag to match the picture. If correct, the object is kept. If incorrect, it goes back in the bag. The one with the most matches is the winner.

4. *Fish Game.* Children are provided with construction paper fish of various length from 2″ to 7″ and are directed to arrange the fish by length.

5. *Lotto.* Make a card for each child, and divide it into nine to twelve squares with a different letter in each square. Then make a set of small cards to fit over the squares. Make three for each letter. Players take turns drawing cards and matching them to letters on their big card. The player who fills his or her card first wins.

Circle the two teddy bears that look alike.

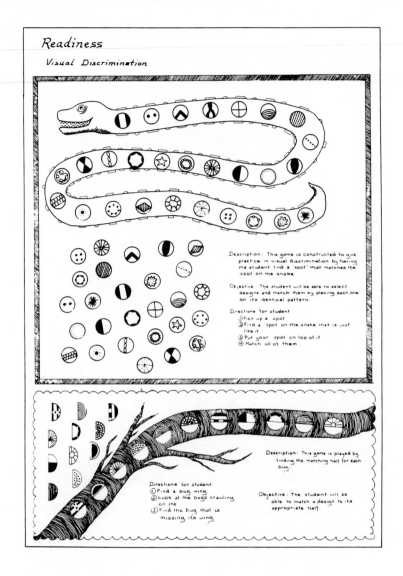

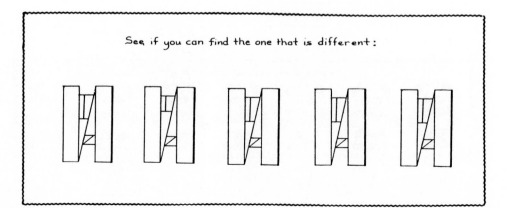

Stare at the items in the toy chest. Look away. See how many you can name without looking back.

6. *Missing Objects.* The children will be able to name the object that he or she does not see. Make a collection of several objects. Display these objects. Then put them in a bag, shake it, and take the objects out again. Leave one object in the bag. The child guesses what object is left in the bag.

7. *Match-a-Word.* The child will recognize and match words. Prepare a chart that looks like water. Write some selected words on the chart. Make some cards shaped like fish that have these words on them. The child places the "fish" in the water on the word that matches.

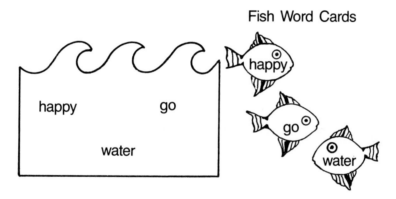

Fish Word Cards

8. *Silhouettes.* The children will distinguish facial shapes. Make silhouettes of each child and have the children guess who it is. To make the silhouettes, tape white paper on the wall and use a film projector light. Have the child stand about one foot from the wall, facing sideways. Trace the child's head. Cut out carefully and mount on black paper. These make nice gifts.

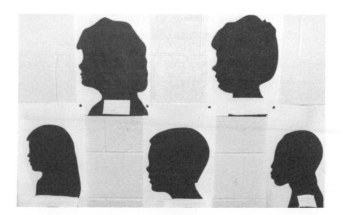

Alphabet Recognition

For the following activities, the objective is alphabet recognition.

1. *Umbrella Game.* Using posterboard or tagboard, draw a large umbrella containing capital letters. Out of another sheet of tagboard, cut out raindrops containing lowercase letters. Have the children match these raindrops to the letters on the umbrella.

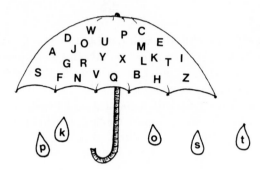

2. *"Go Fish" Card Game.* Make four cards for each letter. (Up to ten letters can be used at once.) Players take turns asking for cards: "Give me all your A's." The winner has the most "books" at the end of the game.
3. *Point the Arrow Game.* Make a large card and divide into six sections. Each section will have an arrow attached next to the capital letter. The child points the arrow and matches it to the lowercase letter.

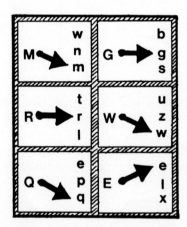

4. *Alphabet Puzzles.* Using posterboard or tagboard, cut large rectangular cards. Put a capital letter on one side and a lowercase letter on the other. Cut down the middle.

5. *Sewing Cards.* Trace 6″ letters on tagboard, cut out and punch holes. Let children color and decorate letters. Children "sew" cards with shoelaces or yarn to become familiar with letter shapes. (You may want to use wax on the ends of the yarn to prevent fraying.)

6. *Footprints.* Make a colorful set of footprints. Left feet have uppercase alphabet letters; right feet, lowercase. The children arrange them in order across the room or in circles.

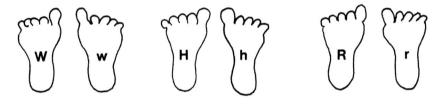

7. *Alphabet Worm.* On heavy paper, draw a worm with a body of 27 connecting circles, all containing capital letters. On a separate sheet, draw and cut out matching circles, all containing lowercase letters. The children match the letters.

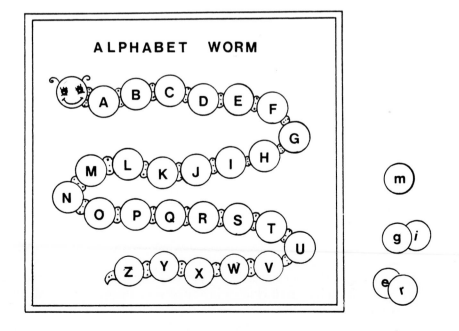

ALPHABET WORM

Variation. Use a larger circle for the worm's head and let the children build the worm by putting the letters in alphabetical order.

8. *Alphabet Train.* Train cars are made from milk cartons covered in contact paper, each with a letter on the side. After arranging in alphabetical order, the children remove objects from the locomotive and place them in the correct car.

9. *Alphabet Fish.* Using orange construction paper, cut out many small fish, each containing letters (both upper- and lowercase). Glue a paper clip on each one. A child uses a magnetic fishing pole and tries to identify the letters on each fish caught. Each child is provided with a paper "fishbowl" (which he or she may draw) and may glue on the fish that he or she recognized.

10. *Alphabet Land.* Make a game board and set of alphabet playing cards. A player moves along by picking a card, saying the letter, and placing his or her marker on that letter. He or she then returns the card to the bottom of the deck. The first one to Alphabet Land is the winner.

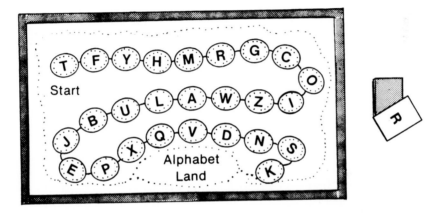

11. *Sandpaper or Cloth Letters.* Make a set of 26 sandpaper letters. The children can feel the shape of the letters and play with them in various ways.

12. *ABC Concentration.* Make two sets of letter cards (52). Players place cards face down and alternate turning over two cards. If they match, the player may keep them. The one with the most matching pairs is the winner.

13. *ABC Bingo.* Make individual cards with six letters of the alphabet on each card. Then make a large card on which to place the letters that have been called.

14. *Find Me a Home.* Children find a home for a set of 26 cloth letters. To do this, the child must match the cloth letter with a letter written on the flap of the envelope.

15. *Shape Bingo.* Make cards as illustrated. Play (like Bingo) by holding up cards with shapes while players mark their cards. The first to fill his or her card wins. (Include 10 to 15 shapes.)

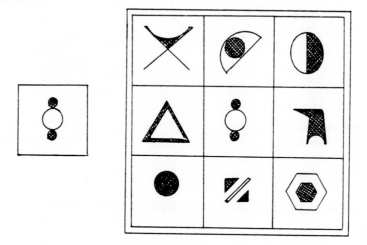

Suggested Activities: Phonetic Analysis

Consonant Sounds: Beginning Sounds and Ending Sounds

For the following activities, the objective is beginning sounds.

1. *Collages.* Find large sheets of paper and write consonants at the top of each. Children will find words or pictures in magazines or newspapers that begin with these letters. After they cut them out, they glue them on to make collages. The children can write their names on or beside their pictures.

2. *Ring Around the Pictures.* Glue or draw pictures on tagboard and write one consonant at the top of each. The children tell what the picture is and decide which ones begin with the letter at the top. They either place a jar ring around the correct ones or circle them with a grease pencil, if laminated. This can also be a worksheet activity.

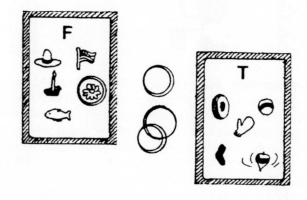

3. *Sound Pictures.* This is a worksheet activity. Make a ditto like the one illustrated. Have the children draw anything in the squares that begins with that particular letter.

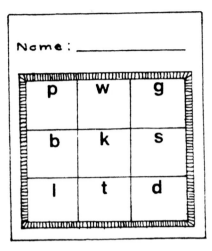

4. *Turtle Toss.* Draw a turtle on a piece of tagboard. Write (or tape so they can be changed) one consonant in each section of its back. The child tosses a bean bag onto the turtle (on the floor) and names a word that begins with the letter on which the bean bag landed. (Points can be kept.)

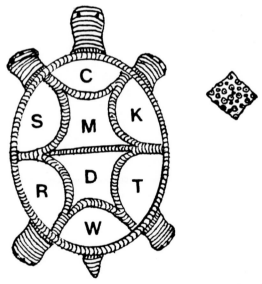

5. *Flannel Board Activity.* The student puts a letter card at the top of the flannel board and puts all the picture cards on the board, along with the "Yes" and "No" cards. He or she puts a "Yes" card under the picture if it begins with the letter at the top and a "No" card under the picture if it does not begin with that letter.

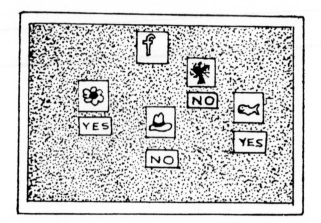

6. *Snake.* Make a playing board out of posterboard. Players "snake" their way to the finish line, giving a word beginning with whatever letter landed upon. A few spaces are red and a few are black. If the player lands on red, he or she must go back two spaces. If the player lands on black, an extra spin is awarded. If the player cannot supply a word, he or she returns to the last space.

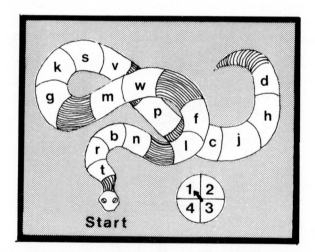

7. *Go Fishing.* Make a pole with a yardstick, string, and magnet. Make fish with pictures and paper clips on them. Each child fishes for a fish, says a word, and identifies the beginning letter. If correct, the child keeps the fish.
   Variation. Put a letter on the fish and have the student say a word beginning with that letter.

8. *Sort the Pictures.* Make a chart with consonant letters and hooks under the letters. The child sorts given pictures by hanging the picture under the appropriate letter.
   Variation. Have the child cut out his or her own pictures from magazines or draw pictures, attach them to a card, and then sort the pictures according to beginning or ending sounds.

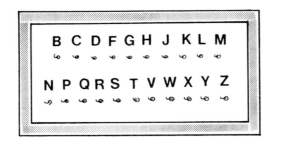

9. *Picture Houses.* Make houses for different initial consonants. Make picture cards for each house. Have the children place pictures in slots of the correct house.

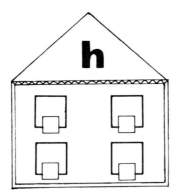

10. *Word Animal.* Make an animal out of tagboard. Leave slots to slide a strip of consonant letters, blends, or digraphs through to make sensible words (or nonsense words).

11. *Consonant Lotto.* Divide tagboard into nine sections. Write a consonant in each section. Make a picture card for each initial consonant. The children look at the pictures, decide on their initial consonant, and match the pictures to the nine sections.

    Variation. This can also be made into a flower by outlining the flower and writing in the letters. This can be on a cork board or flannel board or used with "Post-It" tape. The child can pin, stick, or place each petal inside the correct outlined petal.

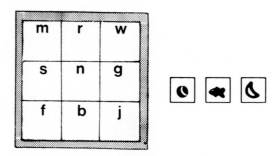

12. *Letter Wheel.* Make a wheel from tagboard, divide into sections, and put pictures in each section. Put the initial consonant and another consonant at the edge of the wheel. Punch holes above each letter. The child will look at the picture, choose one of the letters, and put his or her pencil in the hole over the letter. When the child turns the card over, the correct letter will have an arrow pointing to it.

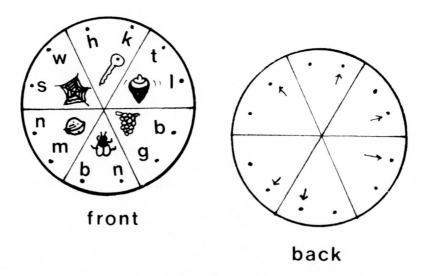

front

back

13. *String It.* Draw pictures on one side of a piece of tagboard and write their initial consonants on the other side. Make small holes beside each letter and picture. Knot string underneath pictures and pull through hole. Children should match pictures and consonants by connecting the string. To be self-correcting, glue a 1″ piece of different colored yarn on the back of the card beside each consonant hole. (Shoelaces may also be used.)

14. *Feely Bag.* This can be a small-group or an individual activity. Fill a bag with objects and have the students reach into the bag, pull out an object, name it, and name the consonant heard at the beginning of the word. (Points can be scored for each correct answer. The child with the most points is the winner.) This can lead into a language experience story.

15. *Sound Puppets.* Make puppets representing initial consonant sounds. The teacher may use them to introduce new sounds; children may use them as a follow-up activity on their own.

16. *Cassette Activity.* Make a cassette tape by recording words familiar to the students. Make a task card or worksheet with the picture of each word, followed by three consonants. The student listens to the word, looks at the picture, and circles the correct letter.

17. *Name the Beginning Sound.* When given a stack of cards with a picture on each card, the child pronounces the word for that picture and fills in the correct beginning consonant using a waxed pencil (or crayon). The card is then turned over to check for the correct response.

18. *Initial Sound Match.* Make cards with four pictures. The children must arrange them so that any sides "touching" must have matching initial sounds. They must name the initial sound they match.

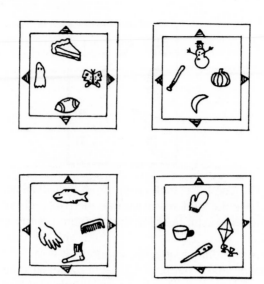

19. *Puzzle Circles.* Cut circles into puzzles. Put a picture of an object on one half and the letter on the other. Children are to match pictures with initial consonant sounds.

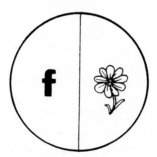

20. *Freddy Fish.* Make a large orange fish on which to display children's pictures of things with initial "f" sounds. This may be adapted to any initial consonant (Danny Duck, Katy Kangaroo, etc.).

21. *Rhymes.* The child will be able to identify beginning sounds. Have them guess these rhymes.

I'm thinking of a word that begins with m and rhymes with cat.

I'm thinking of a word that begins with s and rhymes with ring.

22. *It's All in a Name.* The child will be able to identify beginning sounds of words. Copy each child's names across a piece of paper and have them find pictures (or draw pictures) that begin with the same sounds as the letters in the name.

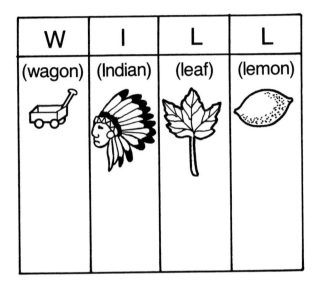

23. *Animal Cages.* Make animal cards and "cages." Have the child identify each animal and then place it in the plastic berry cage with the correct beginning letter. Letters are written under each animal for self-checking.

24. *"Drag Race" Track Game.* Draw a race track on tagboard. Make a spinner and four "cars" for markers. Divide the track into sections, each containing a consonant letter. The child spins and moves that number of spaces, naming the letter and one word that begins with the letter. If a mistake is made, the player returns to "Start." The first one to get to the finish line is the winner.

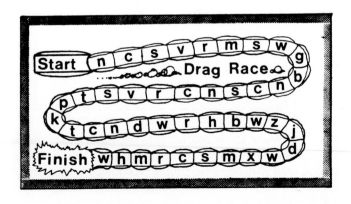

25. *Consonant Containers.* Glue styrofoam hamburger containers to tagboard. Write a different consonant on the lid of each. Place picture cards in one container. The child chooses a card, says the word, and puts it in the container with that beginning consonant written on the lid.

26. *Flannel Board Activity.* Have student match and name pairs of cards that begin alike and place them side by side on the flannel board.

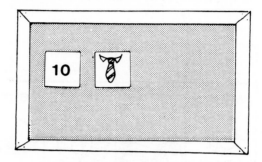

27. *Alphabet Coloring.* This is a worksheet activity. The student is to color the flower by the first letter sound of the colors. For example, color *Y* spaces yellow. Do not use colors that begin with the same letter (black, brown, or blue). This can also be used for patches on a scarecrow.

28. *Flannel Board Activity.* Have the students place picture cards in the correct initial consonant row, according to their beginning sound.

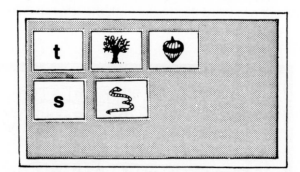

29. *Drive-U-Nuts.* Make cards according to the illustration. The student matches beginning consonant sounds by arranging cards on the board so that each side of one card matches a beginning word of a picture or letter on the side of the adjacent card. This is a challenge, because there is only one possible solution for all the cards to fit on the board.

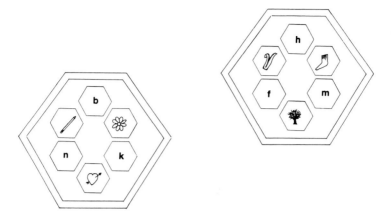

30. *Find the Consonant.* Make charts where children can paste words with the correct initial consonant.

31. *Consonant Sound Books.* The teacher provides "books" representing 21 consonants. The children cut pictures from magazines that begin with the same sound as the consonant on that book. The children may want to make their own consonant sound book and either draw or glue in pictures.

32. *Twister.* Make a "Twister" game from an old sheet of heavy paper taped to the floor. The circles have pictures on them. The spinner has initial consonants on it. The children spin and place a hand or foot on a picture with that beginning sound. (This is noisy, but fun!)

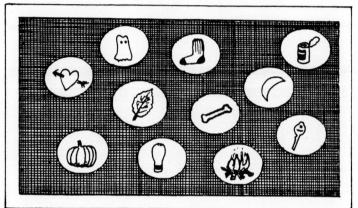
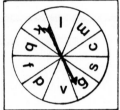

33. *Matching Beginning Sounds.* Make this game using tagboard with letters and pictures. The child will draw a line from the letter to the picture of the object with that beginning sound. (This game can also be played using ending sounds.)

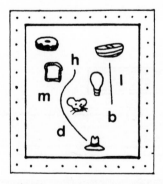

34. *Pizza Party Pictures.* Glue pictures of words that begin with consonants to a cardboard pizza tray. Write consonants on clothespins. Have the child clip the clothespins beside the picture of the word beginning with that letter.

35. *Sort-a-Sound.* You will need a 3″×5″ file box, unruled index cards, and a set of alphabet dividers. Glue or draw on the cards pictures of objects that start with the initial consonants. Write the word on the back of the card. Have the child file each card behind the correct letter. (This also reinforces alphabetical order.) The children can make the cards themselves. (The same box can be used when initial vowels are studied.)

36. *Checkers.* Place letters on a checkerboard. The players must say a word beginning with the letter on which they land.

37. *Create a Picture.* Have the children draw a picture and label the objects with their beginning letter.

Group Activities—Beginning Sounds

1. *Treasure Hunt.* Hide 10 to 20 small picture cards for each initial consonant being practiced. Give each team a letter and tell the players that they must look for cards picturing objects that begin with that letter. The first team to find all of its cards wins.

2. *Class Walk.* Have a class walk, looking for things that begin with a certain letter. Follow with a language experience story.

3. *The Guessing Game.* Blindfolded students try to identify and name the beginning sounds by touching the objects.

4. *Going on a Trip.* "Today we are going on an imaginary trip. I'm going to take

an apple." The first child must "take" something that begins with b, the next c, and so on. (This also reinforces alphabetical order.)

5. *Name It.* Say a child's name and have children name other objects in the room that begin with the same sound.
6. *I Spy.* "I spy something that begins like ball." The children guess what the object is. Children as well as teachers can make up "I spy" sentences.
7. *Ball Toss.* Say a word and toss the ball to someone. That person must say a word beginning with the same sound and then toss the ball to someone else.

For the following activities, the objective is ending sounds.

1. *Wall Mural.* The child will be able to identify ending sounds. Divide a large piece of paper mounted on the wall (or a bulletin board) into squares. Write a letter in each square. Have the children draw or paste pictures that have the same ending sound as the letter.

Ending Sounds					
g	⬤	l	m	★	r
s	🎩	t	n	✋	d

2. *Leaves on a Tree.* The child will be able to identify ending sounds. Draw several trees with an ending sound on the trunk. Make several leaves with various pictures. The child places the leaf picture on the tree that has that ending sound.

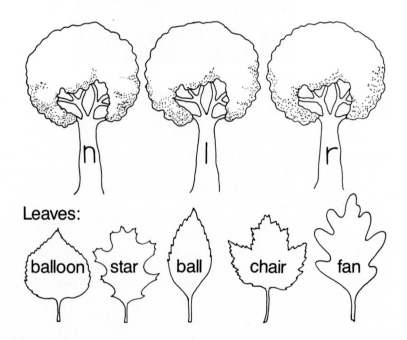

Leaves: balloon, star, ball, chair, fan

For the following activities, the objective is beginning and ending sounds.

1. *Initial and/or Final Consonant Sound Bingo.* Make a variety of Bingo-style cards. Cut clear, simple pictures from magazines or old workbooks. As these are held up, each player places a marker on the matching letter. The usual Bingo rules apply.

2. *Sort the Objects.* Using 21 cans representing the 21 consonant sounds, have the child sort objects according to the beginning or ending sound.

3. *Auto-Matic.* Make cars, wheels, and cards as illustrated. The child places a picture card on the "door" of the car and looks for wheels with beginning and ending sounds.

4. *Bean Bag Throw.* Make a board as shown. Using a bean bag, the players take turns tossing it onto the playing board. If the bean bag lands on a letter, the child identifies the letter and says a word that begins (or ends) with that letter. If a child misses a letter, he or she will "go to jail" and remain there until someone misses. If the bean bag lands in jail, the turn is lost.

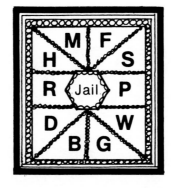

Card Games

1. *"All Show."* Each child spreads out cards with consonant letters. After a word is called out, the children select a card with its beginning sound. When they hear "All Show," they hold up their card for the teacher to check.

2. *Consonant Rummy.* Using 3″ × 5″ index cards, design a set of playing cards

with a picture card and a pair of word cards beginning with each consonant. Print the rules on one of the cards:

a. Deal seven cards to each player.

b. Any three cards with the same beginning sound makes a book.

c. Take turns drawing a card from the deck.

d. Lay one card face up each turn.

e. The first player left with no cards is the winner.

3. *Changeover.* Make cards with letters and pictures as shown. The dealer gives five cards to each player and puts the rest of the deck in the center of the players. The player to the left of the dealer plays any card, pronouncing the sound as it is played. The next child plays a card having a word beginning with the same letter. If the child cannot play from his or her hand, up to three more cards are drawn. If a "changeover" card is drawn, that card may be played and a new sound can be named. The first player out of cards is the winner. (This game resembles Crazy Eights.)

Consonant Blends and Digraphs

For the following activities, the objective is to identify blends and digraphs.

1. *Blends Race.* Make a track game out of tagboard. Fill in with blends and write the directions on the game board:

a. Spin the spinner.

b. Move that number of spaces.

c. If you can say a word with that blend, you may stay. If you cannot, go back to the space where you were.

d. The first player to arrive in the middle is the winner.

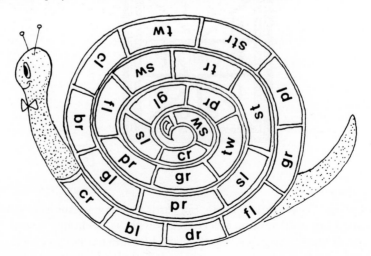

2. **Blend Wheel.** Make one large circle and one small circle. Print blend on small circle and word endings on large circle. After laminating, pin together in the center with a brad. By turning the circle, new words are made.

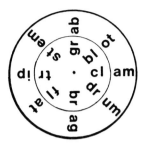

3. **Digraph Concentration.** Make a set of cards with pictures and digraphs written on them. The player or players place cards face down and try to match each card.

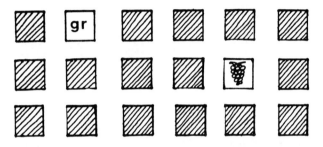

4. **Digraph Fish Game.** Make self-correcting fish cards. The child picks a fish, looks at the picture, and tries to decide which letters are missing. The player can open up the fish to see if the response is correct.

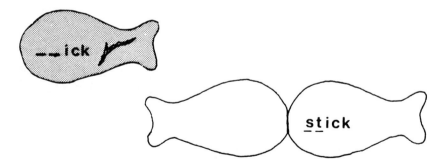

5. **Stories and Pictures.** Have children write stories that have words with blends and digraphs in them.

   Write a story about five things you would like to have that begin with *tr*.

   Write a story about a *cl*umsy *cl*own. Use as many *cl* words as you can.

6. **Pocket Chart.** The child will identify consonant blends and digraphs. Make a pocket chart and label each one with a blend or digraph. Make some cards with pictures and/or words on them. Have the child place them in the pocket to show the sound heard in the word.

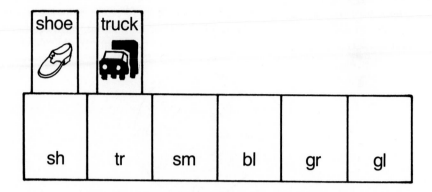

7. *Mobiles.* Make a mobile of pictures that have the same consonant blends and digraphs.

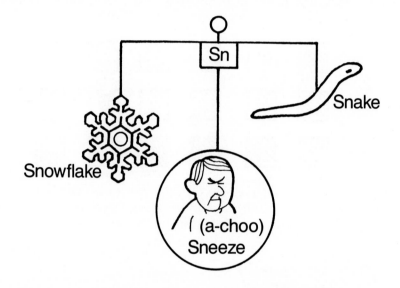

Distinguishing Short and Long Vowels

For the following activities, the objective is to identify long and short vowel sounds.

1. *Vowel Lotto.* Make vowel boards and picture cards as shown. Give the child a vowel board with one of the ten long and short vowel sounds along with sound picture cards. After saying the picture, have the child sort the pictures according to vowel sounds. Responses can be self-correcting.

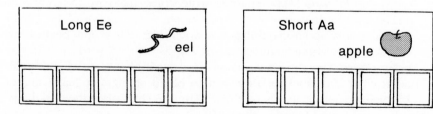

2. *Mr. Short and Ms. Long.* Use one piece of cardboard covered with contact paper. Make one short, fat owl and one long-nosed bird. Make two pockets, one for each character, and supply a small box for holding word strips. Make any number of word strips with long and short vowel words for the children to put in the appropriate pocket.

3. *Vowel Cutout.* Give the child a vowel letter made from construction paper and several magazines. Have the child cut out pictures with that vowel sound and glue them into the letter.

4. *Mountain Climb Game.* Use a piece of cardboard (covered with contact paper) with a scene of houses and mountains. Make a snake-shaped path with short vowel words printed on the spaces, a spinner with numbers 1 to 3, and markers for players. Print the rules on the game board:

   a. Two or four people may play.

   b. Turn spinner to determine first player. The player with the highest number goes first.

   c. Turn spinner and move that number of spaces.

   d. Say the word on which you stop.

   e. If you miss the word, go back to start.

   f. The winner is the player who lands on "Home" first.

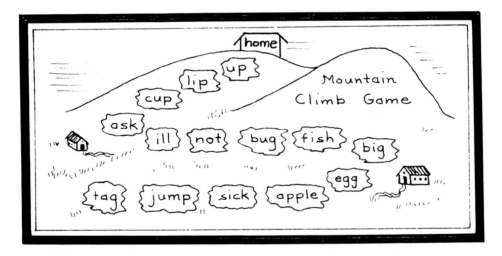

5. *Magic "e" Game.* You will need one piece of tagboard, two plastic caps from aerosol cans (one black, one white), one picture of a magician, and strips of paper with magic "e" words and short vowel words written on them. Make a red felt brim for black hat and a red felt brim for white cap. Words are color coded—blue strips for long vowel words and red strips for short vowel words.

   Two to four children play. Each player takes one strip from the black hat. If the word has a long vowel sound, the child may hold it. If the word has a short vowel sound, the child puts it in the cap. The strips of words can be mixed and sorted into two piles.

6. *Vowel Word Flower.* Make a flower and staple it to a straw. The center has a short vowel and the petals have consonants. Challenge the players to see who can make the most words from his or her flower.

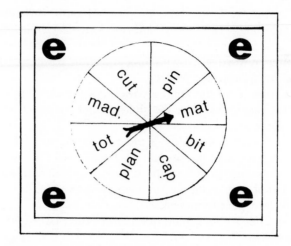

7. *Silent "e" Wheel.* Make a board as shown. The rules are as follows:
   a. Spin the arrow.
   b. Make a sentence with the word on the board.
   c. Make another sentence after the silent "e" has been added.
8. *Fishing for Vowels.* A box containing fish (made from tagboard) with short vowel words is placed on the floor. Fish have paper clip noses so they can be caught by a magnet on a fishing pole. If the child can say the word, he or she may keep the fish.
9. *Vowel Clowns.* Make five clowns with the different vowels for their noses. The child chooses from a stack of short vowel "hats" the hat that each clown will wear.

10. *Vowel Match.* Make picture cards and a picture board with various long and short vowel words. The children match picture cards with corresponding pictures having the same vowel sounds.
11. ***Think and Choose Vowel Game.*** Words with long and short vowel sounds are printed on flower petal shapes of colored paper. They are sorted into pots, one marked long and one marked short.

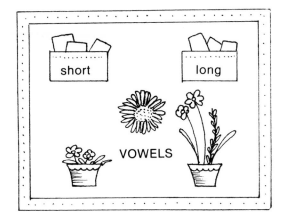

12. ***Oscar Octopus.*** Draw a large octopus. Have the children draw and cut out things beginning with the *o* sound. Have them glue their cutouts onto Oscar's arms. Variations can be made using other short vowel characters: Adam Ant, Eddie Egghead, and so on.

13. ***Mr. Short and Ms. Long.*** Make cards with long and short vowel sounds. Place the words in a box. The children are to read the words and place them in the pockets of Mr. Short and Ms. Long.

14. *Vowel Cards.* Make a deck of 40 cards with words and pictures of long and short vowel sounds (four for each). This can be used for various games such as Go Fishing, or the deck can be divided and used for Concentration.

15. *Sort-a-Long-Vowel and Sort-a-Short-Vowel.* Use an egg carton with a vowel in each holder. Student may sort picture or word cards into appropriate holders according to vowel sounds.

16. *Categories.* Ask the children to name some animals with short vowel sounds—cat, duck, pig. Ask them to name some kinds of weather with long vowel sounds—snow, rain.

My Vowel Contract

Name _____

1. I will use the records and the sheets of Listen and Do, lessons 12, 14, 16, 18, 20. ◯

2. I will divide a big sheet of paper into 10 parts and draw 2 pictures of each vowel sound. ◯

3. I will use the Language Master cards on vowels. ◯

4. I will play "Vowel Bingo" with a friend. ◯

5. I will do the red cards from the Reading Box that are numbered 14, 15 + 20. ◯

6. I will make a vowel book. On each page I will put pictures of a different vowel sound. ◯

Evaluation:
   I will show what I learned orally and on a written sheet during my conference on Thursday.

A Sample Contract on Vowels

This contract has been mutually negotiated. Therefore, activities and evaluation procedures have already been chosen. The student has been introduced to vowel sounds but is having a lot of trouble with their mastery. If the child feels that he or she has mastered them before completing all the activities, he or she has the option of renegotiating the contract and having an evaluation earlier. If the child feels that he or she does not have enough time, he or she may wish to expand the activities and lengthen the time before evaluation. This contract is set up to last a week and a half.

Recognizing Rhyming Words

For the following activities, the objective is to identify rhyming words.

1. *Rhyme Time.* Make a track as shown. Players roll a number cube and move around the track saying a word that rhymes with the one on which they land.

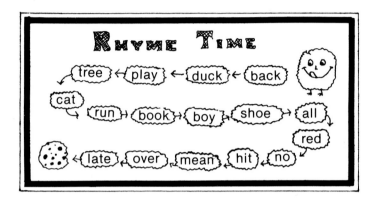

2. *Mrs. No-Rhyme Card Game.* Make 36 cards containing rhyming words and one Mrs. No-Rhyme card. Players shuffle and deal all the cards. Players pick from each other, trying to match all their rhyming cards. Three matches make a complete set. The player who ends up with Mrs. No-Rhyme loses.

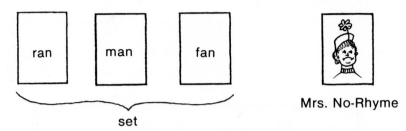

3. *Rhyme-O.* Make playing cards (3″ × 5″) with words that rhyme. Deal four cards to each player. The dealer becomes "it." He or she may ask opponent for a card to match the one held. Player may say, "Do you have a card that rhymes with *cat?*" If opponent has it, he or she must give it to the player. If not, opponent says, "No-Rhyme-O," and "it" loses a turn to the player on the right, after drawing a card from the stack. If the player draws a card that rhymes with the one asked, he or she gets another turn. If the card drawn is not a rhyming word, it is returned to the bottom of the stack. The player with the most books wins the game.

4. *Rhyme Time Concentration.* Make a set of 20 rhyming word picture cards. Player or players place cards face down and pick two at a time for each turn, trying to pick two cards that rhyme. The player with the most matches is the winner. Cards are made self-correcting by writing the numbers on the back.

5. *Family Word Endings Game.* Use a piece of rectangular-shaped tagboard, 38 numbered squares of various colored construction paper with word endings printed on them, two playing card plastic boxes, 50 squares with consonants, and 38 strips numbered 1 to 38.

   One to five players take ten consonants from the box. The first player draws a number strip and finds the square with that number on it. Five points are earned if the player can use one of the consonants with the word ending.

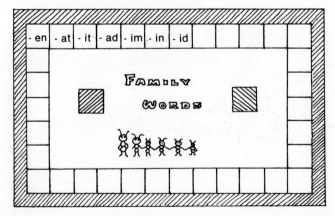

6. *Be a Star.* Make a star with centers and points. The child puts five points on each star center so that the points make a star and rhyme with the word in the center. Check by looking at the backs of the pieces for matching designs.

7. *Monster's Word Wheel.* In the Monster's open mouth appear simple words in the same word family. (Examples are the "at," "an" and "en" families.) The child turns the wheel and uses picture clues to read the words. The wheels are interchangeable.

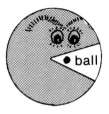

8. *Rhyming Time.* Make a track as shown, using between 10 and 25 footsteps. Write the directions in the game board.

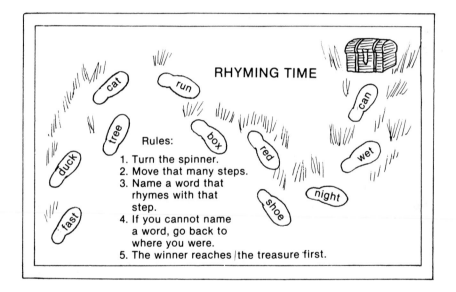

9. *Matching Rhyming Words.* Rule two pieces of tagboard into nine squares each. Draw a picture in each square of the first sheet. For each picture on the first sheet, draw a rhyming picture on the second sheet. Cut the pictures on the second sheet into separate cards. Put the cards in an envelope and clip the envelopes to the first, uncut sheet.

10. *Cups and Saucers.* Made with tagboard and pictures (either drawn or from magazines), this game can be played by matching the cup and saucer with rhyming words. Answer can be placed on the backs for self-correction.

11. *Rhyming Puzzles.* Use colored tagboard and laminate. Include rhyming words and pictures. The activity is self-correcting.

12. **Rhyming Words Hat.** Children can pull strip through the hat as they make and say the rhyming words.

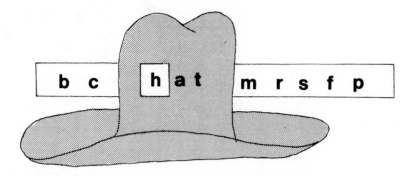

13. **House of Rhyme.** The child will be able to identify rhyming words. Make several large houses. Have the children place the rhyming words (printed on doors and windows) on the appropriate house.

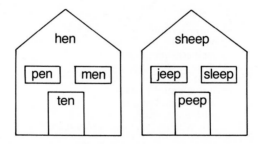

14. **Rhyming Clowns.** The child will be able to identify rhyming words. Make a bulletin board display of several clowns holding balloons. Have the children place words on the balloons that rhyme.

Suggested Activities: Structural Analysis

For the following activities, the objective is to identify contractions and be able to identify the words making up the contraction.

1. *Contraction Line.* Make thirty cards; divide each by a diagonal line. On the left side of the diagonal, write two words that can be made into a contraction (in black). On the right side, write a contraction in red. The students deal all the cards but one. This one is placed on the table, and the students take turns trying to match contractions and contraction words (like dominos). The first one to use all cards is the winner.

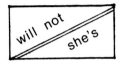  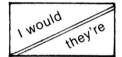 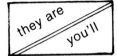

2. *Contraction Flowers.* On a big board, outline a flower with lots of petals. Write contractions inside the outlined petals. Now make petals with the two words from which the contractions are made. The student should place each petal inside the correct outlined petal. (A self-correcting answer card can be made.)

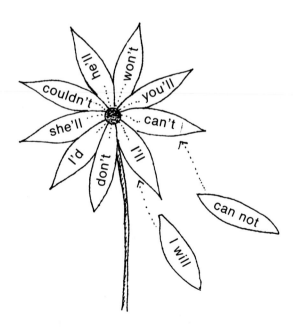

3. *Contraction Car.* Draw a large car on a piece of posterboard and cut it out. Select contractions and print them on cards. Print the two words making up the contraction on the two wheels. The student completes the activity by placing various contractions on the car and matching them with the correct wheel.

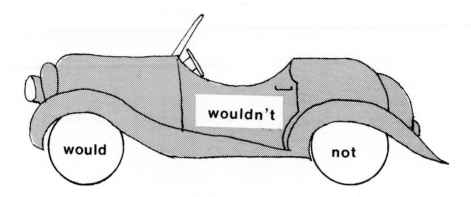

4. *Tachistoscope.* A tachistoscope is made by folding a piece of construction paper on the middle line and sealing the end flap with rubber cement. Cut out the windows and the triangle at the bottom. For the insert, fold a sheet of paper in half. Write contractions on one side and two words making up that contraction on the other side. The child inserts the card, reads the contraction, uses it in a sentence, and turns it over to check the answer.

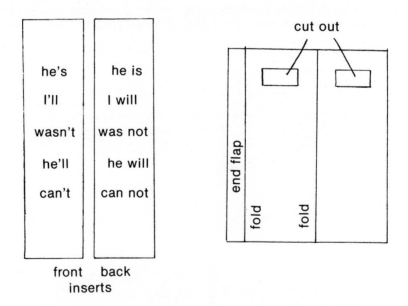

5. *Contraction Wheel.* Use colored tagboard and laminate. Match contraction clothespins with word pairs on the wheel. Make it self-correcting by placing answers on the back of the wheel and clothespins.

6. *Corresponding Clothespins.* Make a long board listing contractions. Take twice as many clothespins as you have words and make $1'' \times \frac{1}{2}''$ covers for them. Write the words that make up the contractions on the covers and glue these to the clothespins. The student clips the proper clothespins to the board. The board can be self-correcting on the back through color, letter, or number coding.

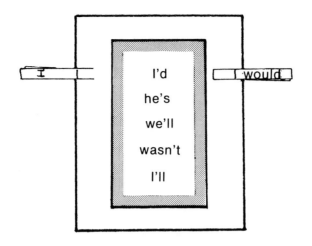

7. *Snoopy Game.* The child will identify contractions. Draw a Snoopy dog and label with contractions. Label the doghouse with the words that make up the contractions. The child places Snoopy on the appropriate doghouse.

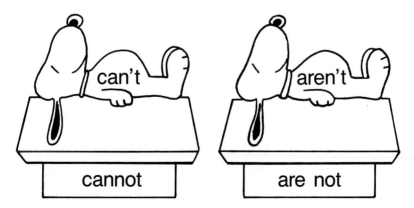

8. *Go Sailing.* The child will identify contractions. Draw a sailboat and write the words making up the contraction on the boat. Write the contraction on the sail. The child matches the sail to the appropriate boat.

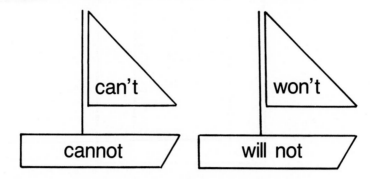

Recognizing Root Words, Suffixes, and Prefixes

The objective for the following activities is to recognize root words, suffixes, and prefixes.

1. *Prefix or Suffix Wheels.* These laminated tagboard wheels have removable centers on which are printed common root words. The child inserts a center (attached to a brad), turns the wheel, and reads the words made. The wheel has either prefixes or suffixes. All combinations make a word. The child can then write the word, determine its meaning, and write it in a sentence. (Inflected endings may also be used.)

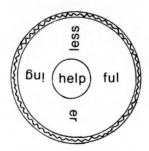

2. *Slides.* Make a tachistoscope by using a standard prefix and different root

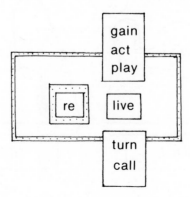

words or one root word and different suffixes. The student may write the new words and use them in a sentence.

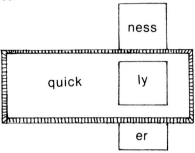

3. ***Root Word Match.*** Make nine cards with words printed around all four sides. The middle card has a dot. The words should have prefixes, suffixes, or inflected endings. The board should be made as illustrated. Blank cards hold the places and the card in the center has a dot. The student places the cards on the board so that any two sides of cards that are beside each other have the same root word. The student then matches all the cards on the board. (Two players may divide the cards and compete.)

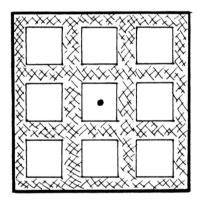

4. ***Root Word Sort.*** Make a 28″ × 14″ pocket folder. Write root words on these pockets. Make cards to fit in the pockets with words on them that have prefixes and suffixes added. Have the students "file" the cards in the correct pocket. They must pronounce the root word each time. (Prefix and suffix folders can be made and the same cards used.) An answer-key card can be attached to the back of the folder.

5. *Affix Affinity.* Print words with prefixes and suffixes on 3″×5″ index cards. Print the word in black and underline the prefix or suffix in red. Have the students who are playing (two or three) shuffle the cards and place them face down in ten to twelve stacks. Turn the top card up on each stack. The players find words with a prefix or suffix in common. They may race each other or go in turns. When a match is made, the player pronounces the words and identifies the common prefix or suffix. If correct, he or she may keep the cards and turn up the top card in the two stacks. The player at the end with the most cards wins.

6. *Roll and Score.* Make a board with a blank playing card in each number position. Print words with prefixes and/or suffixes on 60 playing cards. Students shuffle the cards and place ten face down on top of the blank place-holders. Two to four students can play. Each player rolls a die and draws a card from the corresponding number. He or she must identify the prefix or suffix and the root word and say the word. If correct, the number on the die is the number of points scored. The player with the highest score wins.

Roll and Score

1

2

3

4

5

6

7. *Word Pyramid.* This can be a team competition or an individual activity. Given a root word, the team or person must build a "word pyramid" on the board or on paper, adding prefixes, suffixes, and so on. If a team activity, the team with the largest pyramid wins. A flannel board can be used with blue felt root words, pink felt prefixes, and yellow felt suffixes.

law
lawful
unlawful
unlawfully

8. *Petals and Flowers.* This is made with a cloth-covered material bolt on which a cloth flower is glued. Players choose a root word. They score for every prefix or suffix petal they can add to the root word flower center. A score of 20 wins.

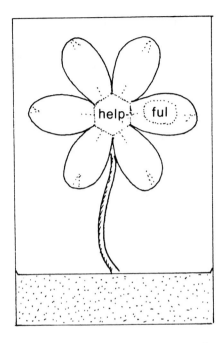

9. *Batters Up.* This game is made on a piece of cardboard. Draw a baseball diamond. On first base, make a pocket with prefixes; on second base, make a pocket of root words; on third, make a pocket of suffixes. Players choose a root word. If they can add a prefix, they get a double and go to second base. If they can add a suffix, they get a triple and go to third base. If they can add both a prefix and suffix, they score a home run! Player with the most home runs is the winner.

10. *Form and Reform.* This game can be made on a manila folder. Balloons make up the game board. On each balloon is a root word. If the player lands on that balloon, he or she must supply either a prefix or a suffix for that word. First player to go through the balloons twice is the winner.

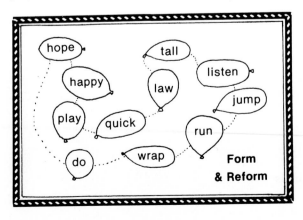

11. *"Rooty" the Bug.* Rooty has three parts. His head is a prefix, his body is a suffix, and his thorax is the root word. The folder has three pockets containing prefixes, suffixes, and root words. Students see (and draw) all the Rooty bugs that they can make.

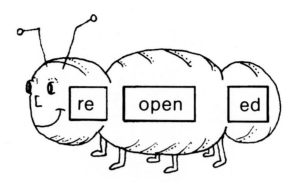

12. *Root Word Tour.* Make a track as shown. Two or more players can play. The first player rolls the die and draws the top card. He or she must say the whole word, say the root word, and spell the prefix or suffix. If correct, the player moves the number shown on the die. If the player lands on a red space, he or she must go back two spaces.

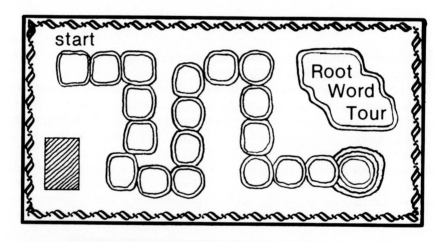

13. *Prefix-Suffix Bean Bag Toss.* Use oil cloth, a window shade, or a large piece of tagboard. The student should say a word containing the prefix or suffix in the block on which the bean bag lands when thrown.

14. *Change and Turn.* The child will use prefixes and suffixes to form new words. See how many new words can be made by adding prefixes and suffixes.

happy	happily
unhappy	happiest

Forming Plurals

For the following activities, the objective is the formation of plurals.

1. ***The Plural Clown.*** Cut out or draw a clown with three pockets. On each pocket, write a singular or plural word (depending on degree of difficulty) that forms its plural in a different way *(s, es, ies).* Print the singular of these words on tagboard squares. Have students read a word and make it plural by placing it in the correct pocket. (Answers may be color coded.)

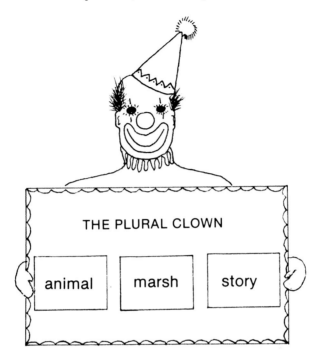

2. ***Foldover Endings.*** Write root words on the front of flashcards, and write the appropriate plural ending (or other inflected ending) on the back of the card. When the card is folded, the ending should be properly positioned at the end of the root word. By manipulating these cards, the students can *see* how plurals (or other endings) are added. The student should guess at the ending, fold over the flap, read the word, and write it in a sentence.

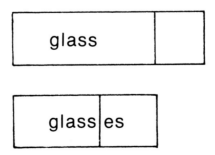

Recognizing Compound Words

For the following activities, the objective is to recognize compound words.

1. ***Spin the Answer.*** Make two circles, one larger with the end of compound words around the outside and one smaller with the beginning of compound

words around the outside. Connect the two in the center with a brad. The student must rotate the wheels to form compound words that answer questions on the worksheet. They can then write a story using these words.

2. *Compound Combo.* Make 10 to 20 cards with the beginning of compound words. From two to six children may play. The dealer shuffles and deals the cards. The first player finding two words that make a compound word places the two cards on the table, pronounces it, and uses it in a sentence. After all have done this, the dealer chooses a card from his or her hand and places it on the table. The players look for a word card that can be joined with it. After one of the players places the appropriate card on the table, he or she says the new word, uses it in a sentence, and places a new card on the table. The first player to run out of cards wins. (The game can be made into Old Maid by placing a contraction card in the pack.)

3. *Word Factory.* Make a game board with 20 green cards (beginnings of compound words) and 20 yellow cards (endings of compound words). The board itself will have blank green and yellow cards. Place the cards face up on the correct color spots. The players (two to four) take turns making words by combining a green and a yellow card. If the word is correct, the player gets the points assigned to each of the two stacks. After all the cards have been used, the player with the most points wins. (A mastery list may be used.)

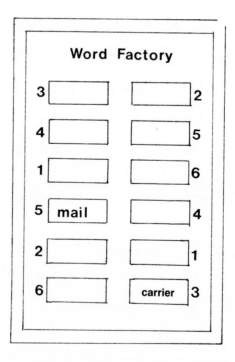

4. *Help the Rabbit Find Its Tail.* The rabbit, word cards, and word tails can be made with tagboard and laminated. Several possible answers may be placed on the backs of the word cards and word tails. A student or small group of children can put together the rabbit and tails that make compound words.

5. *Compound Word Wheel.* This can be made with laminated tagboard. Clothes-pins are made to match with a word on the tagboard, thus making it a compound word. (The same sort of wheels can be made for antonyms, synonyms, and homonyms.)

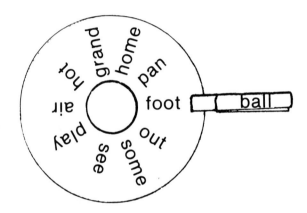

6. *Compound Word Puzzle.* Write compound words on cards and cut down the middle of each card. The children then fit the pieces together.
7. *Spinning Wheels.* The child will be able to identify compound words. Draw a car and write several words on the wheels. Attach a circle (with a wedge cut out) to the wheels. The child turns the wheels to make a compound word.

Comprehension

The development of reading comprehension is a complex task. According to recent research, reading comprehension is influenced by the total reading program, the child's personality, motivation, and habits, the out-of-school environment, and prior knowledge. Areas in comprehension include:

1. Following directions
2. Multiple meanings

3. Context and picture clues
4. Classification
5. Sentence structure
6. Pronoun antecedents
7. Sequence, recall
8. Details, recall
9. Main idea
10. Summarization
11. Characterization
12. Comparisons, associations, relationships
13. Inferences
14. Predictions
15. Generalizations, conclusions
16. Judgments, analysis

Skills such as these are interrelated and should not be broken down into subskills for practice. These skills should be developed as a whole within the context of a reading selection. Comprehension can be practiced through questioning, cloze procedures, retelling, and other activities involved in the reading process of gaining meaning through print.

Speaking

Oral language is an important facet of the school curriculum. Educators realize the importance of personal expression and communication in furthering the educational process. The more that children are allowed to talk and are encouraged to express themselves, the better their concept and vocabulary development, articulation, and consequently, their reading and thinking skills.

Children need many experiences and activities to involve them in hands-on exploration of their environment. A dominant goal is to enrich and expand their knowledge and understanding of their world and to enable them to express themselves effectively.

Children bring to school a basic competency in oral language. By age six, a child has acquired most of the adult patterns of speech. The role of the teacher is to provide an array of experiences that will move the children beyond basic competency to a more masterful fluency. Demonstrating interest in what children say will increase oral fluency. Young children enjoy talking with the teacher, with other children, and in small group situations. Oral language can be developed through puppetry, creative play, drama, formal and informal conversation, choral speaking, and oral reading. Literature is also an important stimulus for oral language. Critical and creative thinking can be well developed and expressed by children through oral language activities.

Speaking Objectives

1. To communicate with others.
2. To develop powers of expression.
3. To acquire better speech patterns.
4. To expand vocabularies.

5. To share experiences with others.
6. To use speech as a tool to adjust to social situations.
7. To contribute information to the class.
8. To begin to participate in group planning.
9. To discuss problems together and arrive at solutions that represent the best thinking of the group.
10. To develop new and clarifying concepts and relate to past experiences.
11. To help plan, carry out, and evaluate activities within the level of maturity.
12. To take advantage of opportunities for developing language through a variety of experiences.
13. To express thoughts and feelings.
14. To become more expressive through dramatic play.
15. To make friends with others.
16. To communicate in an organized way.
17. To participate in group discussions.

Suggested Speaking Activities

1. *Creative Expression Center.* The child will become more expressive during dramatic play. Have many centers for creative play—with a dollhouse, sand and water, materials for housekeeping and dressing up, and trains and trucks.
2. *Explanation Activity.* The child will share knowledge with others. Have older children help explain things to younger children—as art activities, words, and activity cards.
3. *Teacher Reading.* The teacher will model speech patterns for the child. Read good literature to the children—to expose them to varied language models. Always encourage discussion of the stories.
4. *Teacher Listening.* The children will develop powers of expression and expand vocabularies. Listen to children explain their errors in vocabulary, or give them correct vocabulary words. Help them to clarify and make their speech more accurate.
5. *Displays.* The child will communicate with others. Have interesting objects, displays, or animals for children to talk about and discuss.
6. *Free Conversation.* The child will communicate with others. Allow students to talk freely among themselves. Always have time to talk with children individually.
7. *Student Reading.* The child will use speech as a tool of communication. Have children read to one another and take turns reading in small groups.
8. *Student Recordings.* The child will express thoughts and feelings. Have them record their thoughts, what they have learned, or stories they have heard on the tape recorder.
9. *Student Storytelling.* The child will express thoughts. Encourage them to make up and tell stories that they feel will go along with different pieces of music.
10. *Teacher-Student Storytelling.* The child will contribute to a group activity. Begin telling a story. Go around a small group having each child add something to the story and one child end it.
11. *Sequencing Cards.* The child will be able to communicate in an organized way. Use sequencing cards (with pictures on them) that, when put together in the proper order, will form a story. Have children play with these cards,

put them in the proper order, and tell the teacher or a friend what story they form.

12. *Wordless Books.* The child will expand vocabulary and share experiences with others. Use wordless books—books with good illustrations, but no writing. Have one child tell another his or her version of the story.

13. *Games.* The child will share experiences with others. Having children bring in their favorite games and teach their friends how to play them.

14. *New Vocabulary.* The child will expand vocabulary. Introduce new vocabulary words that convey action by having children act the words out.

15. *Flashcards.* The child will communicate with others. Have children play with flashcards of many opposite words and match the words that are opposite. They can play this as a game with a friend, to see who can come up with the most pairs.

16. *Events and Objects.* The child will contribute information to the class. Have at a time when children can bring interesting objects to school to discuss or can relate recent events that are very significant to them.

17. *"How Many" Games.* The child will participate in group discussions. Play such games as "How many red things can you find in this room?" "How many big things?" "How many round things?"

18. *Dramatizations.* The child will become expressive in dramatic play. Have children dramatize stories, events, or their responses to certain situations. This may also be done with puppets and a puppet stage.

19. *Pictures.* The child will express thoughts and feelings. Bring in pictures—copies of good works of art—that children can describe, tell stories about, and discuss their reactions to. They can do this among themselves or with the teacher.

20. *Telephones.* The child will use speech as a tool of communication. Have children play with telephones and toy microphones.

21. *Audiovisual Aids.* The child will expand vocabulary. Use records, tapes, films, and slides to extend vocabulary and provide opportunities for discussion.

22. *Finger Plays.* The child will gain practice in speaking orally. Use finger plays to help children to develop language concepts—such as order, number, left, right, up, down—and gain practice in speaking.

23. *Poetry.* The child will express thoughts and feelings. Encourage the children to dramatize poetry. One child may dramatize a poem while another child reads it. All forms of creative dramatics, freely improvised and carried out by the children themselves, are excellent for spontaneity and freedom of expression.

24. *"Feely Box."* The child will expand vocabulary. Use a "feely box" to develop a vocabulary of descriptive words. A child reaches into a box containing different objects, selects one, and feels it without looking. The child describes the object to other children without telling them what it is.

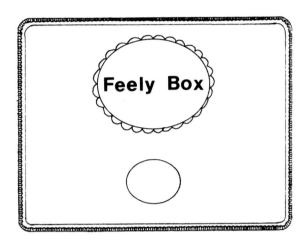

25. *Mystery Box.* The child will be able to express thoughts. Prepare a mystery box with the help of a few children who give clues for others to guess.
26. *Tell a Story.* The child will share experiences with others. Create a story about the day's work, activities, excursion, or other interesting happening.

27. *Story Starters.* The child will become expressive in thoughts and feelings. Prepare a box of story starters. Have the child select one of the story starters and tell the story to the group.
28. *Categories.* The children will be able to sort ideas and expand vocabularies.

Name a category and have the children name all of the things that fit into that category.

29. *Filmstrip stories.* The child will develop powers of expression. Select a filmstrip that does not have words written in. Have the children make up a story about the filmstrip.

30. *Field Trips and Class Activities.* The children will participate in group planning and develop language through experiences. After field trips and class activities, have the children tell about the experience. Write the account in story form on a chart. Have the children read the story back.

31. *Stories.* The children will be able to discuss solutions together and arrive at the best solution. Read a story to the children. Before reading the conclusion, ask the children to tell what they think the outcome will be.

32. *Riddles.* The child will develop oral skills and contribute information to the class. Set aside a time for each child to bring a riddle to read to the group.

33. *Interviews.* The child will develop communication with others and develop skills using speech as a tool in social situations. Have one child interview another child. They should ask for information about each other; for example, "Tell me about your favorite pet," or "What is your favorite thing to do?" These interviews could be tape-recorded.

Listening

Developing listening skills is an important part of language arts. It is through listening, naturally, that a child is first aware of language and begins to imitate sounds. Listening is the identification of oral symbols that, combined with background experiences, produce meaning. Listening implies attention and responsive thought, be it casual or critical. It requires effort on the part of the listener. As a result, children need to be taught *how* to listen and how to think about what they have heard. A child's listening vocabulary far surpasses his or her speaking, reading, or writing vocabularies; through listening, children can learn concepts and ideas otherwise unavailable to them.

Structure the classroom to promote listening. The teacher can model good listening habits to the children by *being* a good listener. Some purpose for listening should be stated.

Children with short listening spans need to lengthen them gradually through opportunities to listen to a variety of things that are based on their own experiences at first and later on the experiences of others. This involves a broadening of a child's own experiences through participation in many concrete situations, which he or she can see as well as hear. Children should learn to listen, understand, and respond to many different situations.

Viewing and Listening Equipment

Language Master 101 and other language experience machines
Record player and records
Tape recorder and tapes (regular and/or cassette)
Super-8 projector and film loops
Slide, filmstrip, and picture viewers, filmstrips
Slide projector and slides
Earphones (eight to twelve separate or two sets of six), jacks
Film projector and film
Screen
Overhead projector, transparencies (blank and prepared)
TV, radio, walkie-talkie
Programmed materials
Filmstrips with coordinating records
Camera and film
Two-way telephone

Listening Objectives

1. To learn how to follow directions.
2. To gain information.
3. To be able to carry out activities.
4. To enjoy stories and poems.
5. To share pleasing experiences with others.
6. To increase vocabulary.
7. To improve sentence patterns.
8. To acquire imitative ways of enunciating and inflecting.
9. To respond to physical stimuli.
10. To listen critically.
11. To listen appreciatively.
12. To recall information.

Suggested Listening Activities

1. *Concealed Sounds.* The child will identify sounds. Have the children play games in which objects that make sounds are hidden by one child and the other children try to identify the objects.
2. *Musical Notes.* The child will be able to distinguish pitch and melodic

movement. Play notes on the piano to see if the children can tell half steps from whole steps. Also, see if they can tell high notes from low notes on the piano or other musical instruments.

3. *Reading.* The child will enjoy poetry, stories, and rhymes. Read the best stories, rhymes, and poems to the children often.

4. *Listening Games.* The child will acquire imitative ways of enunciating and reflecting and learn how to follow directions. Teach the children finger plays, songs, and poems, to which they must naturally listen carefully to learn.

5. *Music Composition.* The child will listen appreciatively. Have the children compare various pieces of music or songs, noting tempo, rhythm, pitch, tone, and so on.

6. *Poetry Reading.* The child will listen appreciatively. Read poems to the children. Have them give their reactions, tell what mood the poem put them in, and what it meant to them.

7. *Poetry Discussion: Comparisons.* The child will listen to gain information. Have the children compare poems on the same subject, such as winter or spring, trying to see how each poem makes its point and describes its subject.

8. *Poetry Discussion: Contrasts.* The child will listen critically. Have the children contrast poems that are different, such as one that is happy and another that is sad.

9. *Music Recordings.* The child will listen appreciatively. Use recordings of music and songs of various moods and types. Use the radio for special broadcasts or to find out about the weather or news.

10. *Listening to Sounds.* The child will identify sounds of the environment. Encourage children who are nearby to pay attention to particular sounds, some of which are very soft and others of which are a little louder, such as the rain, wind, a goldfish or tadpole, a church bell, a bird, a sunny day, a wasp.

11. *Tape Recordings.* The child will identify sounds of the environment. Tape some common sounds and have the children identify them—the sound of an electric mixer, a car door slamming, running water, brushing teeth.

12. *Listening-Memory Game.* The child will follow sequence and recall information. Play a game that taps both listening and memory, for example, "I took a trip to Zanzibar." The first child might say, "I took a trip to Zanzibar and I took along my toothbrush." The next child might say, "I took a trip to Zanzibar and I took along my toothbrush and comb." And so it would go, as many objects would be added to the list, and each child would have to remember them all and add one more. This game can be played well with small groups of children.

13. *Traveling Game.* The child will follow the sequence of action in a story. Do "a traveling tale," in which one child begins a story and every other child adds something in turn. Each child must listen to figure out what he or she will add.

14. *Listening to Silence.* The child will listen for environmental sounds. Have children listen next to a wall, a floor, or a window to see if they can hear anything or tell what is going on.

15. *Listening to Quiet.* The child will listen for environmental sounds. Have children listen when they are all quiet to see if they can still distinguish noises and sounds.

16. *Listening to Tapes.* The child will listen to develop language skills. Have children listen to tapes of stories, teacher made or commercial. Let them

make tapes of their own voices and the voices of other children so that they can play them back and listen.

17. *Identifying Voices.* The child will identify familiar voices. Tape the voices of many different children. Play back the tapes and have the children identify the voices.

18. *Play "Tick-Tock Where Is the Clock?"* The child will respond to physical stimuli. Hide a loudly ticking clock while children cover their eyes. Then ask children, "Tick-tock where is the clock?" Choose two or three children to hunt. The child who finds the clock hides it next.

19. *Play "What Did I Do?"* The child will recognize sounds. Have the children sit in a semicircle. One child goes behind the semicircle and performs some action such as skipping, running, hopping, jumping, clapping; he or she then goes before the group and asks, "What did I do?" The child who answers correctly becomes "it" next.

20. *Play "Listen and Tell."* The child will respond to sounds in the environment. Have the children close their eyes and listen. They must tell what they hear.

21. *Play "What Is This?"* The child will identify familiar sounds. Have the children take turns imitating some noise (an animal, a machine, etc.). Others guess what it is.

22. *Play "Do This."* The child will be able to imitate sound sequences. Tap on a drum or table, then ask the children to imitate you. For example, you may tap one long and two short taps, or you can make the sound patterns by clapping.

23. *Play "Find the Bell."* The child will respond to physical stimuli. Have one child leave the room. Another child is given a small bell to hold loosely. When the first child comes back into the room, all children wave their hands (imitating a bell-ringing motion) until "it" finds the bell.

24. *A Pocketful of Poems.* The child will develop an appreciation of poetry. Make a bulletin board or a center display with pockets. Each child has his or her name on a pocket. The children are to collect poems and put them in their pockets for the teacher to read aloud. Students can also illustrate their poems.

25. *Poetry and Singing.* The child will respond to the rhythm of poetry. Introduce young children to poetry through singing. Through songs, children can respond to the rhythm of poetry.

26. *Oral Directions.* The child will learn how to follow directions. Give children a set of directions and ask them to follow them exactly. For example: "Stand up and raise your right hand"; "Shake your left foot"; "Clap three times"; "Turn around and sit back down."

27. *Play "Who Is Talking?"* The child will be able to discriminate vocal sounds. Select five or six children to stand somewhere in the classroom. Have the other children turn their backs to them. Touch one student and have him or her say something. The others try to guess who is talking. The one who guesses correctly trades places with the one who was talking.

28. *A Sound Walk.* The child will be able to listen critically and recall information. Have the children walk outside or perhaps inside the building. When they return, see how many different sounds they remember hearing.

29. *Listening with Art.* The child follows written directions to carry out an art activity. Give each student a 9″ × 12″ piece of construction paper and a 2″ × 12″ strip. Demonstrate as you ask children to fold their paper in half lengthwise, and in half lengthwise again. Line up the edges of the paper. Keep the papers folded and ask the children to fold the paper in half widthwise, and in half widthwise again. When the children unfold their papers, there should be 16 boxes. Have them turn the paper so that the long side is at the top, and draw lines with a crayon as shown:

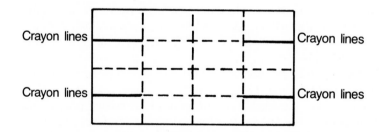

Tell the children to cut slits along the crayon lines. Then the children bend the paper along the lines between the slits and overlap the corners. Glue the corners in place. When all four corners are glued, glue the basket handle. This basket can be used for many special occasions. The students will enjoy decorating the basket.

30. *Poetry.* The child will be able to replace missing words in a poem as an attempt to improve language skills. Read a poem to the children. Then read the poem again, omitting some of the rhyming words. Ask the children to supply the missing words.

Writing

Writing is a skill of expressive language. It includes the formation of letters and the skill of composing. The child's emotional, physical, and intellectual development is reflected by the ability to write. Small motor development and hand-eye coordination are involved in the ability to write. The functional skills of writing include handwriting, spelling, punctuation, and capitalization. These skills are learned best in practical, usable situations. A good foundation in oral language contributes to readiness for creative writing. Creative writing emphasizes thought rather than form. The three stages of writing are precomposing, composing, and rewriting. In the precomposing stage, the child is brainstorming. The composing stage is where the actual writing takes place. In the rewriting stage, the child, with the help of the teacher, proofreads and revises the writing. Care should be taken to maintain the enthusiasm of the child for writing.

The teacher can create an environment that encourages writing. A writing center would be beneficial. Lots of small motor activities and opportunities for creative writing are essential in the language arts curriculum. The beginning writer needs pleasant, relaxing activities and encouragement from the teacher. Children should begin to appreciate the beauty of language and how they can use it to express their feelings. Various experiences with oral language, good literature, and concrete observations, along with the chance to express themselves freely in an independent, open atmosphere, help children to develop thoughtful, original writing.

Writing Materials

Paper: lined, plain white paper, construction paper of various colors, shapes, and
> sizes; chart paper, index cards, canary second sheets

Pencils, crayons, water colors, magic markers, scissors, and other equipment necessary for making individual books and stories

Pictionaries, dictionaries, and a high-frequency word list

Picture file, story starter file (mounted pictures for writing about titles, stories, and words)

Photographs (current snapshots of children and activities)

Books with blank pages and open-ended titles

Chalkboard; white and various colors of chalk

Mailbox

Book jackets

Word boxes

Writing Objectives

1. To write with a purpose.
2. To write in complete sentences when appropriate.
3. To use correct punctuation and capitalization.
4. To spell words well enough to be understood, according to known skills.
5. To write legibly and neatly.
6. To sequence ideas clearly.
7. To choose appropriate words.
8. To write in a variety of forms.
9. To write for others to read.
10. To form letters correctly.
11. To evaluate one's own handwriting.

Writing Areas

Writing can be divided into four areas:
1. Handwriting
2. Spelling

3. Creative writing
4. Punctuation and capitalization

Suggested Writing Activities

Handwriting

1. *Letters.* The child can feel, trace, and compare manuscript and cursive letters. Letters can be made by the teacher and/or children out of felt, sandpaper, wood, masonite, or clay with letter cookie cutters. Children use these
   letters to feel, trace with their fingers, trace around with a pencil or crayon,
   stack for visual discrimination, compare upper- and lowercase, and compare
   cursive and manuscript writing. Rubber letter stamps with stamp pads in different colors are also fun.
2. *Frame It.* The child will be motivated to write his or her best. Buy several
   inexpensive frames for the writing center. They can be with or without glass.
   Children who do their very best writing may have their writing put in the
   frame for a week.

3. *Autograph Book.* The child will practice writing neatly and legibly. Put an
   autograph book in the writing center. The class collects autographs of the
   class members who write in their very best handwriting.
4. *Sand Box.* The child will practice formation of letters. Have children who
   are just learning to write practice in sand. Salt may also be used. Line the

bottom of a shoe box lid with black paper, and fill with three tablespoons of salt or sand.

5. *Alphabet Fish.* The child will practice letter formation. Write letters on cut-out fish. Attach a paper clip to each one. Make a fishing pole out of a yard-stick, string, and a magnet. Players fish, pull out a fish, and reproduce the letter on the fish on their paper or on the board before they can keep their fish.

6. *Bingo.* The child will learn to recognize letters. To learn to recognize cursive letters, have children play Bingo with Bingo cards of cursive upper- and lowercase letters. The first to get a row of letters up, down, or across is the next caller.

7. *Secret Code for Letters.* Students can create their own alphabets by creating their own code for letters. Have them write messages to leave in the center. The next students can try to figure out the messages.

8. *Secret Code for Numbers.* Give the children a secret code where certain numbers stand for letters. Give them a message and let them try to figure it out. Then have them write the message in their best handwriting.

9. *Poem Booklets.* The child will be able to write neatly and legibly. Have the children copy poems in their poem booklets. Have them illustrate the poem according to what they think the poem is about. A decorated cover completes the booklet.

10. *Mystery Sheet.* The child will practice letter formation. Give the children a ditto sheet where the letters have been written in order, with some left out. The children are to fill in the missing letters in their best writing. Let the children practice making alphabet sheets for others in the class. Reinforce the fact that the "guide letters" must be perfectly done.

11. *Introduce Cursive.* The child will be introduced to cursive writing. To introduce cursives show a large sheet of transparency with a cursive story or letter. Discuss what cursive means. Note differences between cursive and manuscript. Read them the story. Point out letters they may recognize. Then take dictation from them in cursive.

12. *Error Sentences.* The child will evaluate handwriting and adjust for error. Write sentences on the board with errors in letter size, spacing, heights, and form. Discuss and have the students write the sentences correctly—to "correct" *your* sentences.

13. *Word Lists.* The child will be able to practice writing neatly and legibly. Have charts on display throughout the room where children can "list" words in their best handwriting. Topics may include vocabulary words learned from science or social studies units.

14. *Charts.* The child will be able to practice writing neatly and legibly. Special charts can be reserved for children to write stories in their best handwriting.

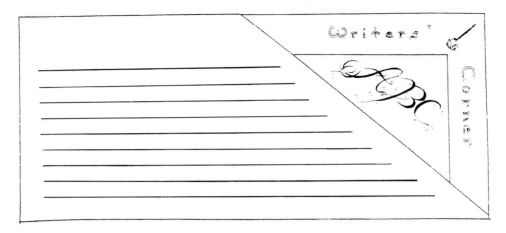

15. *Skill Sheets.* The child will practice handwriting skills and A, B, C order. Make charts or skill sheets where children can arrange words in A, B, C order. Encourage students to use their best handwriting.

Put the ice cream flavors in A-B-C order :

Vanilla	Chocolate	Peach	Mint	Banana
Lime	Pineapple	Lemon	Jelly-Bean	Strawberry
Cherry	Raspberry	Peppermint	Fudge Ripple	Butterscotch

1. _____   4. _____   7. _____   10. _____   13. _____

2. _____   5. _____   8. _____   11. _____   14. _____

3. _____   6. _____   9. _____   12. _____   15. _____

16. *Word Builders.* The child will practice handwriting skills. Have the students build words using their best handwriting.

How many words can you make from the word **Earthquake?**

17. *Riddle Box.* The children will be able to practice writing neatly and legibly. Have the children write riddles in their best handwriting. Place these riddles in a box to be shared with the group later.

18. *Telephone Book.* The child will be able to practice writing neatly and legibly. Make a collection of the names and phone numbers of the children. Have each child make a telephone book and write his or her name and number in his or her best handwriting. This is also good practice for alphabetical order.

19. *Self-Evaluation.* The child will be able to appraise his or her own handwriting and find areas for improvement. Have children examine their own handwriting practice. Ask them to tell what things should be corrected.

20. *Color-coded Manuscript Cards.* The child will be able to practice the formation of letters. Make a set of cards that show the formation of letters by steps. Use a different color for each stroke. Make the cards for all letters. Start each letter formation with a green stroke ("Go") and end with a red stroke ("Stop"). These cards may be placed in a center or used for individual practice.

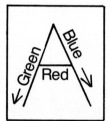 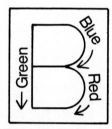 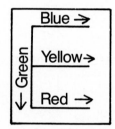

21. *Practice Writing Cards.* The child will practice letter formation. Cut tagboard to fit duplicating machine and make a stencil of handwriting lines. Run paper through machine one sheet at a time. Place square containing upper- and lowercase letter and picture of objects with the initial sound of the letter on each card. Use magic marker to show formation of letters using arrows and numbers. Laminate. Children use erasable pens to practice letters. You can also put basic vocabulary words on back of the card for children to practice writing.

Spelling

In the following activities, the child will be able to spell words and develop an awareness of correct and incorrect spelling.

1. *Stand to Spell.* Construct large letters of the alphabet and distribute to the class or group. The leader calls out a word, and the people with those letters that make up the word come to the front of the group and arrange themselves in the right order. The group checks the spelling. For variety, a clothesline can be strung up and the cards hung with clothespins in correct order.

2. *"Tap and Say."* Letters may be placed randomly on the floor, a piece of paper, or a chalkboard. Players point to or tap letters to spell words. "Phonics Hopscotch" may be played by hopping to letters in the correct order.

3. *Computer Spelling.* Decorate a cardboard box to look like a computer on

one side. Cut a slot in the side. Put spelling words on the "computer cards." Write half the cards in one color, half in another color. Each team has its own color of words. Team members take turns spelling correctly the plural of the words drawn and feeding it into the computer if correct. The team with the most cards in the computer wins.

4. *Anagrams.* Have the children help make four sets of 1″ alphabet cards. Put them in a box. Players put all the cards face down and draw five. They then try to form words with their letters in crossword puzzle style, scoring one point for each letter used. A new card is drawn for each one used. Player with the most points after all cards are used or time is up wins.

5. *Word Turning.* Change one letter at a time in words to form new words. Definitions may be given as clues. Children can make up their own (tear, dear, deaf, leaf, loaf, loan, loon, noon).

6. *Spelling Booklet.* Young children can make a spelling booklet with a page for each letter. On these pages, the children write the words that they can spell on the correct initial letter page. They can really see their progress this way, and so can parents!

7. *Dictionaries.* Older children can make dictionaries on subjects of interest. Pronunciation, syllabification, and spelling of the word with different endings may be included.

8. *Letters.* Letters to be manipulated into words and sentences can be made out of felt, sandpaper, or construction paper. Rubber letter stamps can also be used.

9. *Crossword Puzzles.* Crossword puzzles are great to reinforce spelling and help stop tendencies to juggle letters. They are self-correcting, and children can work alone or as partners to pool knowledge.

10. *Hangman.* This popular children's game reinforces spelling. Players try to guess a word letter by letter before the "man is hung."

11. *Ghost.* Ghost is a game in which players continue to add letters to a word without being the one who brings the word to an end. Affixes of all kinds can be used as long as it is a real word.

12. *Scrabble.* Games such as scrabble are great for spelling practice. Games can be made with tagboard letters and a game board. Many new words are learned, and the dictionary is used often.

13. *Track Games.* Track games can be made in which the child must spell the called-out word correctly before he or she can move on. Children enjoy the competition, and spelling is encouraged.

14. *Independent Reading.* Encourage independent reading.

15. *Word Groups.* Give children groups of words that follow a spelling pattern and allow them to discover the rule for themselves.

16. *Rhyming Words.* The child will write a word that rhymes with selected spelling words.

17. *Word Search.* The child will visually discriminate and circle the spelling words. From the selected words to spell, make a word search. This can be done as a group activity or an individual activity.

18. *Spelling Contract.* The child will practice spelling words orally. Have the child write the words on a piece of paper. The child is to find a friend or an adult to call out the words for him or her to spell. The person who calls out the words signs the contract. Each child should have five people to sign the contract before test time.

19. *Spelling Squares.* The child will practice spelling new words and perhaps use a dictionary. Ask the child to write as many words as possible using the letters in the squares.

		Two-letter words	Three-letter words	Four-letter words	Longer words
c t u o					
m a g r					
p s e i					

Creative Writing

In the following activities, the child will develop prewriting and composition skills. In general, provide as many experiences, visitors, and class visits to museums, factories, and parks. Always encourage lively discussion among the children concerning what they have learned. From oral language and the discussion of many ideas will come the fluency and thought content necessary for writing.

1. *Picture Books.* For preschool children you need to have a number of well-illustrated picture books from which the children can tell stories. This gives them the feel of an imaginative creation and of the sequence of a story. Later these can be written down.

2. *Reading.* Choose subjects (such as animals, family, friends, trips) and read selections from children's books. Have children write on that particular subject, integrating their own experiences with what they have heard.

3. *Writing.* Have the children write about how they perceive an object in the

environment (an ant hill, a kitchen stove, or the school cafeteria). Have them observe color, shape, and texture and describe the object through the way it is observed in the five different senses.

4. *Description.* Bring interesting objects to class that the children can examine for color, shape, and texture (fabrics).

5. *Perception.* Encourage children to write not only about their own perceptions of objects (how objects make them feel) but also how they feel about events, situations, persons, seasons.

6. *Collections.* Have children bring to school collections of objects that represent the qualities of a particular season. Encourage them to make a display of all the objects brought. Their own feelings and thoughts, and perhaps poems, will result.

7. *Dictation.* Children can dictate individually or participate as the group dictates and the teacher writes such things as captions for pictures, experience charts, invitations, thank-you notes, charts about pets, experiments, or some other item of group interest.

8. *Flower Story Wheel.* Cut flowers from posterboard and fasten with a brad to a large posterboard. The student spins all four flowers. The petal closest to the marker indicates setting, description, character, and action to be included in the original story.

9. *TV.* Cut a rectangle in the back of a cardboard box. Cut holes for dowel rods to fit into both sides of the TV. Draw a continuous action story on a roll of paper. Staple paper to dowels in a scroll-like fashion, after the rolls have been placed in the TV. Caption for the TV might read, "Become a TV script writer. Write your own dialogue for this story." Instead of drawing your own story, you might cut out stories from comic books or from magazines.

10. *Pick a Bundle from the Basket.* Place a basket of bundles (made by using colorful laminated tagboard) in the writing center or perhaps on the floor in a reading nook. The bundles contain a variety of words taken from reading books or from appropriate areas of interest or projects ongoing in the learning area. Students may write a story using words on the bundles.

11. *Poems.* Select poems for illustration and copying or give the child an idea for a poem of his or her own.

12. *Writing at the Chalkboard.* Encourage children to write or sketch on the board. You might put some kind of starting idea on the board such as "What I Did Last Night," "A Funny Thing Happened to Me," "Draw Here. . .".

13. *Mailbox.* Place a mailbox in or out of the classroom to encourage children to communicate in writing. Notes, invitations, thank-you's, get-well notes, and so on can go through this channel. Mail can be sent through a classroom mail carrier.

14. *Idea Exchange Box.* Students write suggestions for interesting activities such as cooking experiences, science experiments, good books to read.

15. *Typewriter* (**standard size**). This equipment allows the child to manipulate while learning letter symbols and word forms. It can be used when the child dictates a story. (Here, the child is able to see his talk appear.) The child may type his own story, science experiment, and so on.

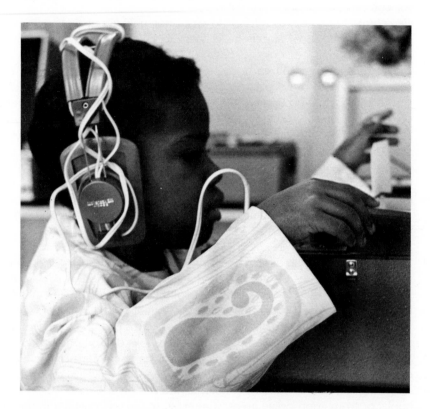

16. *Making Booklets.* Use *comic strips* and either erase wording for creative writing or leave for reading pleasure. Or make books in *particular shapes:* "What Is Round?" "If I Were a Monster." Or *compose books* in which all children have an opportunity to write "My Favorite TV Show," "Our Families on Vacation," and so on.
17. *Case Stories.* Make a briefcase out of poster paper and fill with small "cases," each with a title for a mystery story.

18. *It's Magic.* Make a large poster with a picture of a magic potion or a geni. Children "break the spell" by writing a story. Examples are "Help! I've been turned into a toad!" and "Save me! I'm inside a teapot."

19. ***Crazy Giraffe.*** Make a giraffe and put pockets labeled "people," "places," and "events" on its neck. Have the children choose a card from each pocket and write a "tall tale."

20. ***The Big Lick.*** Make ten large ice cream cones with a story idea on each cone.

I had to make up a new ice cream flavor.

21. ***Chicken Chatter.*** Make an egg carton containing plastic eggs with a story starter on each egg.

22. ***Ideas to Boot.*** Make a large boot containing words to be drawn out and used for writing a story. Draw ten words and write a story.

23. *"Things to Do."* Make a "things to do" file that involves writing. Children may add their own ideas.
    a. Look out the window and find three things that are moving. Describe them.
    b. Draw a picture of three animals. Write about the one you like best.
    c. Look at the aquarium. Write about what it would be like to be a fish.
24. *What Kind of Sentence?* Use cardboard covered in colorful contact paper. Staple four library card holders or envelopes on the cardboard, three holders representative of a different kind of sentence and the fourth holder containing a variety of sentences. A child or small group of children may sort the sentences into the correct holder.
25. *Clever Clovers.* The clover can be made by using different-colored laminated tagboard. Place them in a colorful box (covered with contact paper) in the writing center.
26. *Make a Story.* Write a story on sentence strips. Mix up and clip together. The students arrange the strips in order.
27. *Picture Files.* Contact a box. Fill it with mounted pictures on tagboard. Select pictures that are appealing to children. On some cards, include story starters and vocabulary words relevant to the pictures. Leave others with only pictures.

28. *Story Tapes.* Tapes of stories already started can encourage students to then write an ending to the story.
29. *Puppet Shows.* Puppet shows for which children create the dialogue provide excellent opportunities to practice writing skills.
30. *Poetry Files.* Poetry files can stimulate the writing of rhymes, free verse, or haiku.
31. *Story Starter File.* A file with index cards—color coded by subject area—is used as a story starter. Each child has a title or a beginning paragraph of a story.
32. *Newspaper.* Small groups take turns reporting the day's events. The "Editor of the Day" might use the typewriter to make the final copy.
33. *Photos.* Polaroid photos of children's current experiences stimulate children to verbalize and discuss sequence of events and perhaps to write about the event.
34. *Music.* Play a musical selection, preferably without words, for the students. Ask them to write down what the music makes them think of.
35. *Picture Books.* The children will be able to express and write creative ideas. At the same time, they will develop skills of writing with a purpose, sequenc-

ing ideas clearly, and writing a variety of forms. Select some books that do not have words. Have the children write a story to go along with the pictures.

36. *Pockets.* The child will be able to write creatively. Prepare a duplicating master in the shape of a pocket with lines for writing. Have the students write a story about a pocket or the ways a pocket can be used.

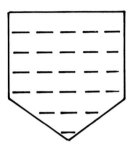

37. *Sequence Cards.* The child will be able to organize thoughts and write them in a logical way. Mount sequence cards on tagboard. Laminate. Have the children arrange the sequence cards in the correct order and write a story about the events.

38. *Shape Booklets.* The child will write with a purpose. Cut writing paper into shapes—animals, flowers, clothing, and others. Have the students write sentences or stories about the shape. Children can add a cover that they illustrate.

39. *Kinds of Sentences.* The child will write with a purpose. Show children a picture and ask them to write questions about the picture. With other pictures or the same picture, ask them to write statements and exclamatory sentences.

Punctuation and Capitalization

1. *Punctuation Paradise.* This is a game for teaching punctuation. Make a game board and use these rules:
   a. Each player places a marker on the board.
   b. Roll die and move correct number of spaces. Give a sentence that contains the punctuation.
   c. Continue until a player reaches "Paradise."

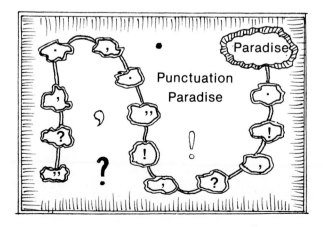

2. *Tic-Tac-Toe.* The child will recognize punctuation marks. Have students play as you would normally do so, but give a sentence and use the mark of punctuation, rather than the usual *X* or *O.*

?	,	"
.	!	?
,	"	.

3. *Sentence Scramble.* The child will be able to unscramble the words and supply the correct punctuation mark at the end. Prepare several sentences without punctuation marks at the end on sentence strips. Cut the sentences apart. Prepare cards with appropriate punctuation marks. Scramble the words in each sentence. Display the mixed-up sentence on a flannel board, pocket chart, or some other means of display. Ask the children to unscramble the sentence and select one of the punctuation marks on the cards to be used at the end of the sentence.

4. *Confusing Paragraph.* The students will be able to supply the correct punctuation and capitalization. Prepare a paragraph on a chart that has no marks of punctuation or capital letters. Ask the children to read the paragraph and supply the missing capital letters and punctuation.

5. *Seashell Punctuation.* The child will be able to select the correct punctuation to be used with a sentence. Prepare a seashell with punctuation marks on each section. Prepare cards with several different kinds of sentences. Label each card with the correct answer on the back. The child will match the sentence to the correct punctuation mark and attach it to the paper clip on the shell. The child can flip the card to check the answers.

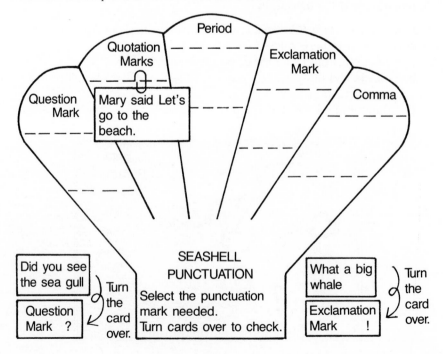

The Computer in Language Arts

The computer is a valuable resource in the language arts program. When introducing the computer to young children, you may need to develop some computer literacy skills. Young children will need to know how to operate the computer and how to use the programs. It is helpful for the teacher to be able to run the program before introducing it to the children. Look for programs that provide feedback to children or establish some interaction and dialogue. Some types of programs are skill-and-drill programs and programs for word processing and writing. The computer offers a way to reinforce reading and writing skills that is highly motivating to children.

Other Approaches to Language Arts

Fairy Tales

Language arts may also be taught by integrating the language arts unit into all the centers. An example of this sort of approach is a "Fairy Tales" unit, which follows.

I Love Fairy Tales

General Objective: To create enjoyment of fairy tales through center activities.

Fairy Tale Center: To recall familiar fairy tale stories.

Using an overhead projector, a transparency of fairly tale characters can be shown on a wall for the children to observe. There will also be a stencil (same as transparency) for the children to color. For the transparency, use *Creative Expression: Lower Primary,* by Billy Leon Shumate, Miliken Publishing Company, St. Louis, Missouri.

Books and Records to Be Used
Cinderella
Little Red Riding Hood
The Gingerbread Boy
The Three Bears
Hansel and Gretel
The Three Billy Goats Gruff
The Three Little Pigs
Peter Rabbit and Other Tales

Games: Commercial
A flannel board can be used with flannel characters. Sequence cards may be obtained from Scholastic Magazines, Inc. Sequence pictures for *The Three Bears* and *The Three Billy Goats Gruff* may be obtained from ABC and the Rand Series.

Games: Teacher-Made
1. Match pictures. *Materials:* A piece of tagboard with a line drawn in the center. Write the words "Real" on one side and "Make-Believe" on the other side. Put a picture on each side so the child will see the difference. Make cards with pictures on them. *Activity:* Place cards in correct category.

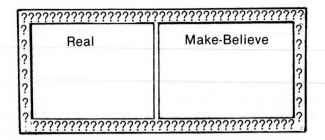

2. Match the jigsaw puzzle. *Materials:* On a piece of tagboard place a picture and the title of the story. Then cite it. *Activity:* Match the title to the picture.
3. Make task cards. Use title of fairy tale and put a picture under it.

The Gingerbread Man

Evaluation: Through observation and talking with the children.

Listening and Viewing Center: To enjoy stories by listening and viewing.

Filmstrips with Cassettes

Little Red Hen
Little Red Riding Hood
Peter Rabbit
The Three Little Pigs
The Ugly Duckling

Filmstrips with Records

Cinderella, Parts 1 and 2
Snow White and the Seven Dwarfs, Parts 1 and 2
The Three Little Pigs
The Tortoise and the Hare
The Ugly Duckling
Aladdin and the Wonderful Lamp
Goldilocks and the Three Bears
The Gingerbread Man

Equipment for the Listening and Viewing Center

1. Filmstrip with a matching record
2. Filmstrip with cassette

3. Filmstrip previewer
4. Filmstrip projector
5. Head sets
6. Record player
7. Cassette deck

Teacher-Made Activity: A task card will be used in this center telling the children which filmstrips they may use. Another task card will instruct children to draw a picture about the filmstrip.

Evaluation: Through observing the children while they watch the filmstrip.

Puzzle and Game Center: To develop eye-hand coordination and enjoyment.

Puzzles

Aladdin and His Lamp (14 pieces)
Cinderella (10 pieces)
Snow White (10 pieces)
Three Pigs (12 pieces)
Red Riding Hood (9 pieces)
Three Bears (14 pieces)
Jack and the Beanstalk (14 pieces)
Gingerbread Boy (6 pieces)
Billy Goats Gruff (12 pieces)

Teacher-Made Games

1. Eye-hand coordination. *Materials:* Draw a fairy tale character on tagboard. Then cut it out. Take a hole puncher and punch around the picture. *Activity:* Thread the yarn through the holes and complete the picture.
2. Match pictures. *Materials:* Tagboard (sectioned into nine squares). Put a fairy tale picture in each square. Make cards to match. *Activity:* Match the card to the picture on the tagboard.
3. Recall fairy tale stories. *Materials:* Tagboard (cut into cards). Place a character or an event from a fairy tale story on the card. *Activity:* Step on the cards and say the name of the fairy tale story.

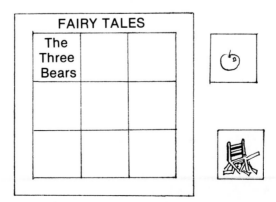

Evaluation: Through observing children playing the games.

The Cooking Center: To read and follow directions on recipe; to enjoy cooking.

Teacher-Made Activities: Write the recipe on a piece of tagboard. Make tasks cards (with directions) for the children to follow.

Recipes

1. *Gingerbread Man.* Ingredients: ½ cup butter or margarine, 1 cup sugar, 1 egg, 1½ cups flour, 1 teaspoon baking powder, 1 teaspoon ginger. Cream butter and sugar together. Add egg. Mix in flour, baking powder, and ginger. Roll out this dough. Cut out shape of man. Bake at 375°F until brown.

2. *Peanut Butter Candy Bears.* Ingredients: 1 cup peanut butter, 1 cup instant nonfat dry milk, 1 tablespoon honey, food coloring. Mix peanut butter and instant nonfat dry milk in a large mixing bowl. Stir in honey. The mixture should look like light-brown clay; add a little more powdered milk if it is too sticky. To make "bears," take 1 teaspoon of the mixture for the body and ½ teaspoon for the head; knead each piece well and roll gently between palms to form balls. Place head on body. Pinch ears in the head or use tiny amounts of dough for the ears. Using a toothpick, paint on eyes and mouth with food coloring. Makes about 24 candies. Candies keep fresh in an airtight container for a few days.

3. *Applesauce.* Ingredients: 4 medium cooking apples, quartered and cored, 1 cup water, ½ cup brown sugar (packed), ¼ teaspoon cinnamon, ⅛ teaspoon nutmeg. Heat apples and water over medium heat to boiling. Reduce heat, simmer, stirring occasionally 5 to 10 minutes or until tender. Strain. Stir in brown sugar, cinnamon, and nutmeg; heat to boiling.

4. *Banana Gingerbread Delight.* Ingredients: 4 to 5 ripe medium bananas peeled (2 cups mashed), 3 tablespoons lemon juice, 1 package (4 oz) gingerbread mix, 1 cup golden raisins. Sprinkle bananas with juice and mash with potato masher. Add to gingerbread mix and beat until well mixed. Fold in raisins and pour batter into well-greased gingerbread mold. Bake at 350° for 35 to 40 minutes. Allow to stand in mold for 10 minutes; then unmold onto serving plate. Decorate with vanilla butter cream icing and raisins.

5. *Bits of Gold.* Ingredients: ¼ cup vegetable oil, ½ cup apple juice concentrate, ½ can pineapple tidbits, 1 egg, 2 tsp. vanilla, 1 cup grated carrots, 2¼ cups rolled oats, ½ cup wheat germ, ½ cup chopped nuts. Mix ingredients in a large bowl. Drop bite-size amounts on a cookie sheet. Bake at 350° for 20 minutes. Cool.

Evaluation: Through observing children.

Block Center: To build a construction and to enjoy working with blocks.

Teacher-Made Activity: Make task cards telling the children what to build. Put a picture on each task card. Have a tape recorder under the task card to tell the children more about what they are going to build. For example, "Hello children! Today your task card says to build a bridge. I want you to try and build the bridge that the Three Billy Goats Gruff crossed. Have a good time!"

Evaluation: Through observation of the finished construction.

Dramatic or Pretend Center: To act out a fairly tale with other children or with puppets they have made.

Commercial Materials: Props, clothing, puppet stage.

Teacher-Made Materials: Make tasks cards with title of fairy tale and put a picture with it. The children can use them to decide which fairy tale they want to do.

Evaluation: Through observation and talking with the children.

Creative Writing Center: To create their own fairy tale through writing or dictation.

Teacher-Made Games

1. *A fairy tale book* with construction paper and writing paper in it. The children are to color a picture or their fairy tale and then write a story about it. If a child cannot write his or her story, he or she may dictate it to an adult.
2. *Story starters.* Place a picture on a card with a sentence starter under it.
3. *Capture the magic wand.* The children use their imaginations and vocabularies to make up sentences. *Materials:* a piece of tagboard and some words or pictures. *Activity:* Who can get it to the magic wand first? It takes _____ points. (You may choose the amount of points you want the children to play to.)

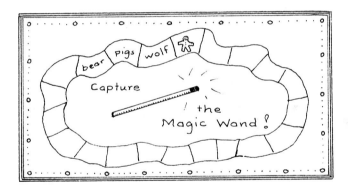

   a. Roll the die and move.
   b. Use the word you land on in the longest fairy tale sentence you can. You get 1 point for each word in your sentence.
   c. The player who gets the most points first gets the magic wand.

Evaluation: Through reading the stories and observing the children playing games.

Language Art Center: To recall a fairy tale by drawing a picture or writing about it.

Teacher-Made Games

1. *Writing a Story:* Recall and write about an event in a fairy tale story. *Materials:* In a folder place a picture of the fairy tale with sight words under the picture. On the other side place writing paper. *Activity:* Write about an event in the story using the sight vocabulary words.

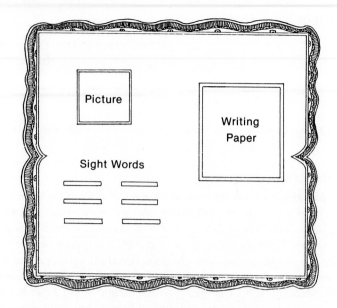

2. *Fairy Tale Picture Book.* Recall a fairy tale story. *Materials:* Construction paper and yarn. *Activity:* Draw a picture of your favorite fairy tale.

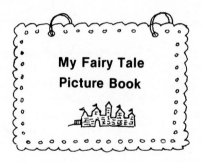

3. *Make a Story.* Recall the events in this story. *Materials:* Write a fairy tale story on a piece of tagboard. Make sentence strips with words on them. *Activity:* Place the word card in the correct slot to make a story.

4. *Word Games.* Sound out words. *Materials:* Tagboard with pocket strips. Make cards with picture and cards with letters. *Activity:* Place picture card in pocket. Then put letter cards in the pocket to spell the word of the picture. The spelling of the word is on the back of the picture.

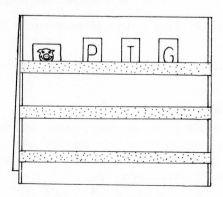

Evaluation: Through observing the children playing games.

Math Center: To learn about numbers and sets by playing games.

Teacher-Made Games

1. *Matching Wheel.* Match number with correct set. *Materials:* Cut a wheel out of tagboard. Then divide it into parts. Place a picture in each part. Take clothespins and write numbers on them. *Activity:* Match clothespin with the correct picture.

2. *Number Line Games:* Recognize sets and match them with the correct number. *Materials:* A sentence strip with numbers on it. Put pictures on another sentence strip and cut them so they will fix or match on the number line. *Activity:* Count objects and put the card on that number. The number will be on the back of the picture.

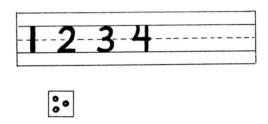

3. *Fill-in-the-Blank Game.* Count objects and place the correct number in the blank. *Materials:* Cut tagboard into twelve cards and place a picture on each card. Then draw a line for the blank and write the word of the picture next to the blank. *Activity:* Count the objects on the card and place the correct number in the blank.

Evaluation: Through observing the children playing games.

Art Center: To enjoy making a fairy tale character.

Provide various quantities of materials in this center, so the children can make what they want. Some of the things should be paint, paintbrushes, crayons, material, tongue depressors, paper bags, construction paper, paste, glue, scissors, yarn, felt, and magazines. There should also be a mural with a fairy tale title for the children to re-create the story.

Teacher-Made Games

To recall the events in the fairy tale. *Materials:* A large piece of paper with a title on it. *Activity:* The children will draw an event or a character on the mural.

Evaluation: Through looking at the children's finished product and having the child tell about what he or she made.

Science Center: To plant a bean seed and watch it grow, much like the story *Jack and the Beanstalk. Materials:* Milk cartons in which to put the seed and dirt. *Activity:* The child will plant the bean seed in the dirt.

Teacher-Made Materials: Task cards with directions for the children to follow.

Evaluation: Through interest that the children show in watching their seed grow into a plant.

Other Activities

1. Invite the school librarian to talk with the children about fairy tales.
2. Use a video tape recorder to film the children in action. Then as a group see the film and talk about it.
3. Show movies to the class:

   Hansel and Gretel
   The Little Red Hen
   Little Red Riding Hood
   The Shoemaker and the Elves
   The Ugly Duckling

Contract: There will be two contracts—one for letting the children write about what they have done and one for having the children color in the art center.

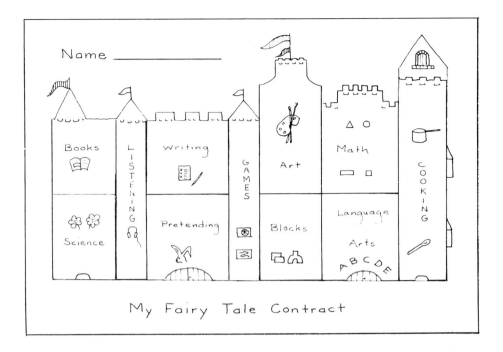

Alphabet Center

An alternative way in which to teach a language arts skill is by setting up a center in the classroom for that particular skill. The following drawing is a sample Alphabet Center.

Suggested Alphabet-Related Activities

1. ***Rain on My Umbrella.*** This is a letter recognition game that can be used to match letters that are the same. It may also be used to match upper- and lowercase letters.

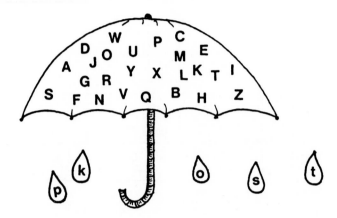

2. ***Mystery Containers.*** Fill different boxes with items that begin with the letter sound being studied. Children are shown an object and try to guess the sound.

3. ***Feed-Me Poster.*** Draw a hungry lion on tagboard or heavy posterboard. At the corner, fasten a milk carton using brads. On the milk carton place a card for a letter sound that is being studied (clip it on so that letters may be changed). In an envelope attached to the back, place several picture cards; some of these cards begin with the letter sound on the milk carton and some do not. The child must "feed" the lion the letter cards that begin with the specified sound.

4. ***Match the Letter Cards.*** Make a set of cards containing all the upper- and lowercase letters that are to be matched with yarn. Have children match the letters.

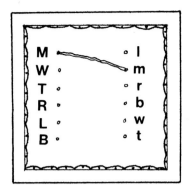

5. *Letter-Shaped Books.* Construct book covers and cut paper to fit them so that the outline of the book represents the shape of a letter of the alphabet. Have children cut from magazines and newspapers all kinds of examples of that letter in printed form. Paste the examples in the books.

6. *First-Sound Sorting Boxes.* Make three boxes, each designated with one letter. Objects are to be sorted according to their initial sounds (for example, "n": notebook, needle, nine, necklace, nuts, nail). Letters in boxes can be changed according to what is being studied. Have the children sort the objects into the boxes matching the initial sound of each object with the appropriate letter.

7. *Sets of Alphabet Cards.* Make two sets of capital letters and two sets of lowercase letters. Have children match capital to capital, lowercase to lowercase, and capital to lowercase. The sets may be made from any type of paper.

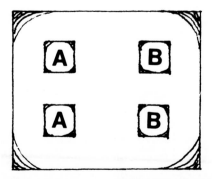

8. *Shoestring Chart* (for use with alphabet cards and beginning sound pictures). Construct a chart with small pockets that can hold the letter and pic-

ture cards, which are, therefore, interchangeable. Use shoestrings to match the cards across the board. Post an envelope on the back to hold all cards until needed.

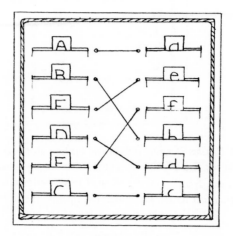

9. *Letter Boxes.* Cover half-pint milk cartons (tops removed). Use tagboard alphabet strips for sorting into these boxes. Have the child sort the letter cards into the boxes with the matching letters. The box can be used for upper- and lowercase letters. Paper clip letters onto boxes so that they may be changed.

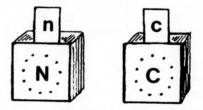

10. *Beginning Letter Sound Picture Cards.* On colorful tagboard, paste several pictures beginning with letter sounds that the children have studied. A set of alphabet squares goes along with this game. Have children place these letter squares on the board covering the pictures that begin with their sounds.

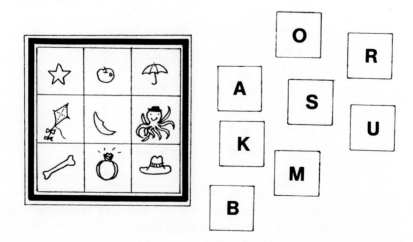

11. ***Octopus Match.*** Construct a game board on which the arms of the octopus serve as holders for cards that are to be matched. What is matched depends upon the learning skills that are being taught at that particular time. As a first step, the child may match letters that are the same. He or she may then match upper- and lowercase letters and finally match letters and pictures that begin with that letter. Cards are matched with yarn.

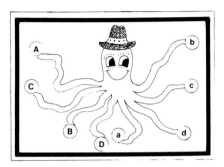

12. ***Phonics Arrow Game.*** Cut squares of tagboard. On each square, print a letter, affix a tagboard arrow, and paste up three pictures at the bottom of the square, only one of which begins with the letter sound being studied. Have the child take the phonics card and look at the letter whose sound he or she is to listen for. Then have the child name the pictures at the bottom of the card and find the picture desired. Have the child turn the arrow to the picture whose beginning sound matches the letter at the top of the card. When the child is finished, have him or her turn the arrow back to the top of the card.

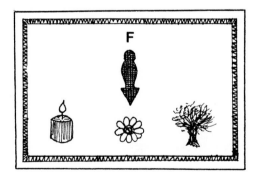

13. ***Phonics Boards.*** Construct nine 18″ × 24″ tagboards. Each board should present three beginning letter sounds accompanied by approximately ten pictures for each sound. Ring the pictures that begin with the same sound with plastic rings or plastic bracelets. The child says the name of each object and rings the ones that begin with a particular sound.

  Variation. Construct a board containing three letters with ten pictures pasted on it for each letter. Have the child decide which letter to work with and circle it with a ring. Then have the child circle the ten pictures that begin with that sound using a ring for each picture.

14. *Alphabet Train.* Make a train of 26 cars from half-pint milk cartons. Each car stands for a letter of the alphabet. Put two or more objects beginning with each sound of the alphabet inside the train cars (for example, Aa = apple, alligator, Dd = doll, duck). Have the child take each object and sort into the proper alphabet car according to its beginning sound.

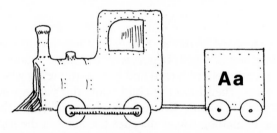

15. *Mystery Fill Box.* Cut in the side of a large ice cream container. Attach the upper part of a child's sock to this so that the child may reach through the sock into the opening. The child will try to feel and guess the object beginning with a certain letter sound. The top of the carton may be removed to see if he or she is correct.

16. *The "B" Barn.* Using different letters on the barn, have the children cut out pictures beginning with those letters.

Other Alphabet-Related Activities

1. *Block-Building Task Cards.* Have the child choose various letter task cards that instruct him or her to build something that begins with the letter sound shown. The child then draws the construction.

2. *Spatter Painting.* Have available letter stencils, wire screen, newspapers, an old toothbrush, construction paper, and tempera paint. Have children place letter or letters on light-colored construction paper. Using thin tempera paint, spray with toothbrush through the screen.

3. *Placemats.* Make letter designs on placemats using construction paper or other suitable materials. Placemats may be used in housekeeping corner or taken home to parents.

4. *Paintings.* At the painting easel, have each child paint a picture onto a letter-shaped piece of paper, perhaps something that begins with the letter shown on the paper.

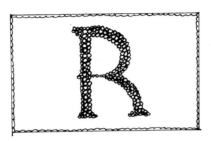

5. *Potato Printing.* You will need a large potato paring knife, construction paper, and tempera paint. Cut potato in half. On the flat side, mark a letter shape. Cut around the shape. Pour a small amount of liquid into a jar lid. Dip the design into the paint and print on construction paper.

6. *Tube Prints.* You will need a piece of old inner tube, a block of wood, white glue, scissors, tempera paint, a shallow pan, and newsprint. Make a letter on paper. Repeat the shape on a piece of inner tube. Cut it out. Imprint the shape on a piece of wood about the same size as the shape. Allow to dry. Place the stamp in a shallow pan containing tempera. Gently press the printer on the paper you are printing.

7. *Letter Stamps.* Supply a set of letter stamps and printing ink for the child to print with (commercial materials).

8. *Clay or Play-Dough.* Let children use these materials to fashion letters. Have a set of alphabet letters nearby for reference.

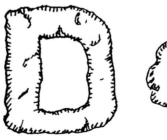

9. *Fingerpaint Alphabet Letters.* Show children how they can make letter designs when finger painting. Encourage large strokes with fingers and fists. Repetition of some letters will make an interesting design.

10. *Sponge Print Letters.* Use a small sponge held by clothespin to dip into various colors of tempera paint placed in a muffin tin or half-pint milk cartons. Transfer sponge print to paper.

11. *Hole-Punch Letters.* Use small sheets of light cardboard, oaktag, and so on.

Have child make a letter (for example, by tracing wooden letters). The child can then punch holes around the shape of the letter with a hole puncher.

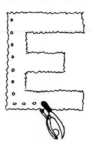

12. *Letter Cards.* Make a set of cards, each listing several letters. Have the children choose a card, find some junk that begins with the letters selected, and arrange the junk onto a collage.

13. *Letter Mosaics.* On light cardboard, draw a letter from which the children make decorative letters by gluing on seeds, torn paper, cereal, beans, etc.

14. *Sew on Burlap.* Trace letters on burlap and have the children follow the pattern with a needle and yarn.

15. *Yarn Letters.* Have child use yarn or string to make letters that can be pasted onto construction paper.

16. *Letter Collage.* Using letter stencils, have the child trace the letters that he or she chooses onto construction paper (or fabrics). Then have the child cut out the letters and put them onto a background material to make a collage.

Contract for a Center on "Nyms"

Name: _____ *Date:* _____

Contract Skill: "Nyms"—antonyms, synonyms, homonyms.

Objective: To learn about "nyms" and to be able to

1. Distinguish between antonyms and synonyms.
2. Give examples of antonyms and synonyms.
3. Choose the appropriate form of a homonym according to context.

Activities: I will check the activities I have completed.

Monday

1. By myself, I will do one of these:

_____ antonym picture match.

_____ antonym directions game.

_____ antonym picture-word match.

2. With a friend I will do one of these:

_____ antonym circle.

_____ Fish-for-a-Nym (using only the antonym fish).

Tuesday

1. By myself I will do

_____ synonym picture-word match.

2. With a friend or friends I will do one of these:

_____ play Spin-a-Nym.

_____ Fish-for-a-Nym (using only the synonym fish).

Wednesday

1. By myself I will do both of these:

_____ Nym crossword puzzle.

_____ Fill-in-a-Nym.

2. With a friend or friends I will do one of these:

_____ Spin-a-Nym.

_____ Fish-for-a-Nym (using both antonyms and synonym fish).

Thursday

1. By myself I will do

_____ homonym-picture word match.

_____ "How Many Homonyms?" activity sheet.

2. With a friend or friends I will:

_____ Fish-for-a-Nym (using all three sets of fish).

_____ play Nym-a-Roo.

Evaluation: I will show what I learned orally in conference and by taking the skills test on Friday.

(These concepts have been introduced and developed during group time. The purpose of these center activities is reinforcement of the concepts of nyms and further skill development.)

Contract for Prefixes, Suffixes, and Contractions

Name: _____ *Date:* _____

Objectives:

1. To recognize base words.
2. To write base words.
3. To add prefixes to base words.
4. To add suffixes to base words.
5. To use prefix words in sentences.
6. To use suffix words in sentences.
7. To recognize contractions.
8. To write contractions.
9. To use contractions in sentences.

I will work in the learning center on the following:

Date Completed

1. I will write five base words on a sheet of paper. _____
2. I will work with the "Mr. T. Prefix" by placing his feathers to make new words. _____
3. I will say five base words to a friend. _____
4. I will use a prefix worksheet and follow the directions. I will ask my teacher to help me with the directions. _____
5. I will use the "Kite Suffix Word Eater" by placing all the words that have a suffix into the kite's mouth and keep the other word cards in my hand. _____
6. I will use a suffix worksheet and follow the directions. I will ask the teacher to help me with the directions. _____
7. I will use the "Mailbox Contractions" activity by taking out all contractions and word cards. Then I will match the contraction card with the word card. _____

8. I will use a contraction worksheet and follow the directions. I will ask my teacher to help me with the directions if I need help. _____

Evaluation

1. I will use answer sheets that are provided with the activities.
2. I will meet with my teacher for a conference every day.
3. I will do the final worksheet that my teacher gives me when I have completed my activities.

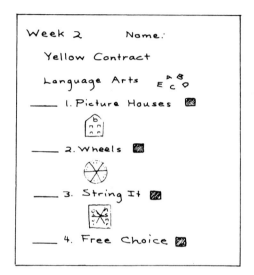

Considerations of Teacher-Made Learning Materials

1. *Self-directed.* It is hoped that the materials you design will provide many opportunities for independent work. Make sure that the directions are clear and

are written on the child's skill level. Have the needed materials already assembled.

2. *Self-correcting.* Children can monitor their own progress if they are able to check behind themselves. Providing answers allows instant feedback.

3. *Attractiveness.* Make the materials fun and colorful. Choose topics that are appealing to the children and let that be your format. Skills can be incorporated to almost anything.

4. *Focus.* Try not to complicate the activity by addressing too many skills at a time. This can lead to unnecessary frustration.

5. *Interchangeability.* When making materials, keep in mind that, while using the same format (once the children have learned directions), you can plug in many different skills, simply by making a few changes.

    For a board game, instead of limiting it to one variation, use materials that will allow for change. For example, laminate game boards with blank spaces. Then you can make cards to use with it. By spraying artists' adhesive (found in artists' supply stores), these parts will adhere yet can be remounted without difficulty. Other formats, for example, Bingo, Lotto, and Twister, can be changed easily.

6. *Adaptability.* Each activity should have at least two different versions, depending on the skill level of the child. For example, a game calling for initial consonant sounds could be a more advanced version of a simple letter recognition game.

7. *Versatility.* When designing materials, use a great variety of formats: file folder games, Lotto games, board games, and so on.

8. *Durability.* Laminate or cover with clear contact paper whenever possible. Some game boards can even be made of masonite or plywood, especially if the skills can be interchanged.

Evaluation and Assessment

There are many ways in which to evaluate progress in the language arts. Evaluation is positive and continuous, and pupils are evaluated in terms of each individual's abilities and progress. It helps the teacher to determine what the student *can* and *does* do with regard to skills and concepts, attitudes, and habits. Evaluation can be of a survey, formative, diagnostic, and summative nature. Errors are not used *against* the children but are used *for* them in future planning, in cooperation between teacher and student.

Some uses of assessment are

1. To diagnose needs and plan further instruction and experiences.
2. To see progress during certain time periods.
3. To build confidence in students by helping them to determine their strengths and progress made.
4. To communicate with parents, special teachers, and so on.
5. To evaluate one's *own* teaching goals, objectives, environment, techniques, and materials.

Ways in which to evaluate and assess in the language arts include

1. Teacher observation, individual conferences, and anecdotal records.
2. Evaluation of nonverbal, individual classwork.
3. Self-evaluation by the student.
4. Teacher-made tests, oral tests, performance tests, skill records, checklists, and standardized tests.
5. Evaluation through verbal activities.
6. Parent conferences.

Teachers should use several or all of these methods to evaluate their students and plan for their further learning.

References

Alexander, J. E., (1983). *Teaching Reading* (2nd Ed.). Boston: Little, Brown and Company.

Beckman, C., Simmons, R., and Thomas, N. (1982). *Channels to Children: Early Childhood Activity Guide for Holidays and Seasons.* Colorado Springs, Colo.: Channels to Children.

Burke, E. M. (1986). *Early Childhood Literature: For Love of Child and Book.* Boston: Allyn and Bacon, Inc.

Burns, P. C., and Broman, B. L. (1983). *The Language Arts in Childhood Education.* (5th Ed.). Boston: Houghton Mifflin Co.

Dickson, W., and Raymond, M. W. (1984). *Language Arts Computer Book.* Reston, Va.: Reston Publishing Company, Inc.

DiStefano, P., Dole, J., and Marzano, R. (1984). *Elementary Language Arts.* New York: John Wiley & Sons.

Forte, I., and MacKenzie, J. (1975). *Kids' Stuff: Reading and Language Experiences.* Nashville, Tenn.: Incentive Publications.

Foust, S. J., Vurnakes, C. D., Simpson, R. J., Bemer, L., and Wolf, K. (1984). *Centers Galore* (Book 5). Greensboro, N.C.: The Education Center.

Fox, S. E., and Allen, V. G., (1983). *The Language Arts: An Integrated Approach.* New York: Holt, Rinehart and Winston.

Jewell, M. G., and Zintz, M. V. (1986). *Learning to Read Naturally.* Dubuque, Iowa: Kendall/Hunt Publishing Company.

La Penta, M. (1983). *Macmillan Early Skills Program: Listening Skills.* New York: Macmillan Educational Company.

Mason, J. M., and Au, K. H. (1986). *Reading Instruction for Today.* Glenview, Ill.: Scott, Foresman and Company.

Mayesky, M. (1986). *Creative Activities for Children in the Early Primary Grades.* Albany, N.Y.: Delmar Publishers, Inc.

Mayesky, M., Neuman, D., and Wlodkowski, R. J. (1985). *Creative Activities for Young Children.* (3rd Ed.). Albany, N. Y.: Delmar Publishers, Inc.

Murdock, C. V. (1984). *Macmillan Early Skills Program: Writing Skills.* New York: Macmillan Educational Company.

Norton, D. E. (1985). *The Effective Teaching of Language Arts.* (2nd Ed.). Columbus: Charles E. Merrill Publishing Co.

Rose, K. (1982). *Teaching Language Arts to Children.* New York: Harcourt Brace Jovanovich, Inc.

Spache, G. D., and Spache, E. B. (1986). *Reading in the Elementary School.* (5th Ed.). Boston: Allyn and Bacon, Inc.

Stewig, J. W. (1983). *Exploring Language Arts in the Elementary Classroom.* New York: Holt, Rinehart and Winston.

Stewig, J. W. (1982). *Teaching Language Arts in Early Childhood.* New York: Holt, Rinehart and Winston.

Warren, J. (1983). *Super Snacks.* Alderwood Manor, Wash.: Warren Publishing House.

Yawkey, T. D., Askov, E. N., Cartwright, C. A., Dupuis, M. M., Fairchild, S. H., and Yawkey, M. L. (1981). *Language Arts and the Young Child.* Itasca, Ill.: F. E. Peacock Publishers, Inc.

5
The Fine Arts

Music

Music is a natural and pleasurable part of children's lives and the world around them. Children hear the music of nature in the concert of cicadas on a summer evening, in the purring of a kitten, in the rush of wind before a storm, and in the crash of waves against the shore. Children make music from birth onward. There is music in the cooing and babbling of infants, in the spontaneous singing and dancing of young children, and in the rhythm and chant of school children jumping rope. Music offers many vehicles for expression and a diverse range of responses.

A unique feature of music is that it is available to anyone at any time. We intellectually capture and retain our music experiences. When we conceptualize music, we hear it. Because we can intellectually hear sounds, we can create music in our minds. A dramatic example of this was Beethoven's ability to compose even after he became totally deaf. Holshan called this process "audiation" from the verb "to audiate" or hear in the mind. Audiation and aural perception differ because the source of aural perception is sound from the external world, whereas the source of audiation is the internal world of the mind (cited in Mark, 1986).

Music is one of the earliest abilities to emerge in children's development (Gardner, 1983). Researchers report that children as young as two months have demonstrated the ability to match pitches (Papousek, 1982), and that by three years of age children can easily recognize and faithfully sing familiar songs (Davidson et al., 1981). By age three or four, children create tunes spontaneously as they engage in a variety of play activities (Winner, 1982). These childish musical play activities constitute the necessary early steps in the child's natural artistic development. This phenomenon is closely parallel to the naturally inquisitive language explorations essential to the development of language proficiency (Gardner, 1983; Chosky et al., 1986).

The early ability to re-create songs and engage in experimental creative music making is only the beginning of children's music potential. A variety of daily musical activities are essential to enhance the development of each child's musical artistry. Children's relationships with music include singing, dancing, creating, composing, and listening. It is not difficult to develop these relationships because music is so readily available and easy to produce. Children's voices and bodies are natural musical instruments—singing, chanting, humming, whistling, clapping hands, snapping fingers, and tapping feet are all ways in which children produce music with only their physical resources.

Music education has many developmental benefits. Rhythmic activities such as marching, clapping, or singing to a beat, promote the development of concentration and gross and fine motor skills. Playing instruments also promotes the development of concentration and fine motor skills. Listening to music expands perceptive and attentive skills. Singing and creating songs enhance linguistic and emotional expression. Translating the symbolic language of music into sounds helps develop children's capacity to deal with abstract concepts. Successful creative experience with

music builds children's self-confidence and self-esteem. Perhaps most important, music education fosters children's aesthetic growth, giving them the experiences and skills to appreciate and create the beauty of music throughout their lives.

Further, music can be naturally incorporated in all curriculum areas. Music is science, made of sound waves, each with different frequencies, lengths, and intensities. Music is history, articulating the tenor, values, and events of every age. Music is social studies, expressing the nature and spirit of different peoples and cultures. Music is math, involving measure, counting, and dividing. Music is language, giving rich meaning and expression to words and ideas.

Young children bring to school an inherent love of music, natural musical abilities, and a wealth of musical experiences. Children are naturally receptive to music, and through music they develop, learn, and create. Music is an integral part of the creative learning environment, one that requires only the teacher's willingness to appreciate, support, and enjoy students' musical development.

Supplies

Paper:
  Chart paper
  Manuscript paper
  Drawing paper
  Writing paper
Books:
  Song books
  Children's books about music
  Musical story books
Pictures:
  Instruments
  Composers
Records
Tapes
Equipment:
  Record player
  Tape recorder
  Radio
  Television
  Listening center with headphones

Rhythm Instruments

Clicking instruments (tone blocks, wood blocks, coconut shells)
Ringing instruments (wrist bells, jingle sticks, sleigh bells, gong)
Rattling or swishing instruments (sand blocks, rattles, gourds, handcastas)
Booming or thudding instruments (all kinds of drums)
Scratching or scraping instruments (notched rhythm sticks, notched tone blocks,
  rhythm board, gourd rasp)

Melody Instruments

Hand bells
Resonator bells
Step bells
Tuned glass (bottles from cord)
Xylophone
Marimba
Flutophone

Harmony Instruments

Accordian
Guitar
Mandolin
Ukulele
Banjo
Autoharp
Keyboard

Objectives of the Music Program

The purpose of the music program is to provide children with opportunities to:

1. express themselves freely through music.
2. derive pleasure from musical experiences.
3. develop an understanding of the elements of music.
4. experiment with creating and performing music.
5. broaden their knowledge of music.
6. experience and respond to a wide variety of music.

The Music Program

All music is made up of certain elements or ingredients that may be mixed or scrambled to give it vitality and spice. Perception of these elements is essential to musical growth. As children become familiar with the components of music, they become more aware of how those components may be manipulated to produce different sounds and effects. Knowledge of the whole is augmented by an understanding of the parts.

To clarify the concept of these parts, children must have musical experiences that clearly illustrate their existence. Once awakened to an element, children can explore and experiment with its qualities. Through these exposures they will begin to understand the unique contribution of each and the effect it has on the whole. The basic elements of music include rhythm, tempo, dynamics, timbre, melody, harmony, form, and style.

Rhythm.   According to Newman (1984), rhythm is the measured movement of music through time. Schafer (1976) says rhythm is direction, and he equates it to an arrow in a Klee painting. Definitions, however, are never adequate to describe rhythm. Rhythm is more easily felt than discussed.

Although rhythm is naturally employed and experienced by all children, they may not equate these common occurrences with the occurrence of rhythm in music. By helping them relate natural rhythm to musical rhythm, the teacher builds on familiar experiences to promote growth.

Tempo.   Tempo is concerned with how quickly or slowly notes are produced. According to Newman (1984), tempo is the pace of music.

Dynamics.   Dynamics is concerned with amplitude or how loud or soft the music is.

Timbre.   Timbre or tone color is the element that gives an instrument a particular sound that distinguishes it from all other instruments.

Melody.   The melody is often called the tune. It is the element that emerges to the surface and is most easily remembered (White, 1968). Melody is composed of a line of single tones that has contour, that moves up, down, or repeats. Each tone has a definite *pitch* ranging from high to low.

Harmony.   Harmony is created by playing two or more tones at the same time.

Form.   The form of a piece of music is its construction plan. It is the design pattern by which the elements of harmony, melody, and rhythm are interrelated. Although form may be difficult to perceive in some music, it is quite easily detected in poetry and in the simple melodies of childhood.

By dissecting a song into basic phrases, these patterns are made quite obvious. The ABA structure (verse, chorus, verse) is dominant in children's music, although other similar and equally simple arrangements exist.

Style

When all of the other elements of music are combined, they create style. Style is distinctly individual, and yet also a characteristic of the music of a people, region, or era.

Objectives for the Basic Elements of Music

To develop concepts regarding the basic elements of music children will:

1. explore and experiment with the characteristics of each element
2. evidence the use of each element in a musical setting
3. express each element through song, movement, or instrumentation
4. reproduce symbolically the qualities of an element
5. observe and listen to how other musicians have manipulated these elements in their compositions

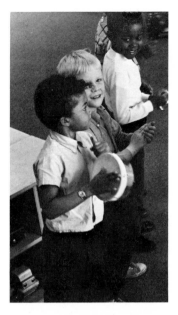 

Activities Involving the Basic Elements of Music

Sound Collage

1. Select one characteristic of sound (high/low, soft/loud).
2. Find or make pictures that illustrate that characteristic.
3. Create a sound collage.

Rhythmic Light Show

1. Use a flashlight in a darkened room.
2. Use the flashlight to follow a rhythm.
   Variation: Cover the flashlight with colored cellophane to create color moods.

Sound Search

1. Close your eyes.
2. Listen to the sounds as someone plays a rhythm instrument.
3. Try to identify it.

Tone Color

1. Listen to recordings in which a specific instrument is played alone.
2. Look at a picture of the instrument as the music plays.
3. Listen to another recording in which the instrument appears but has a lesser part.
4. Try to identify the instrument when it appears.
   Variation: Records may be symbolically coded to represent the different instruments.

Form

1. Listen to melodies constructed in basic ABA form.
2. Use puppets to represent A and B.
3. Use the puppets to indicate the change from chorus to verse to chorus.
4. Repeat with more complicated forms.
   Variation: Select a partner to be A or B.

Draw an Instrument

1. Make an outline of your favorite instrument.
2. Cut and paste clothing for the instrument.
3. Use colors, textures, etc. that you feel reflect the instrument's personality.
4. Put the dressed instruments on a bulletin board.

Sound Sculptures

1. Listen to a selected recording.
2. As you listen play with clay.
3. Compare final sculptures.

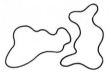

Musical Paintings

1. Listen to a musical selection.
2. As you listen paint.
3. Compare paintings.

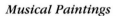

  sponge paint

finger paint

 print

Mechanical Rhythm

1. Select a partner.
2. Pick a machine.
3. One of you is the machine; the other is the noise it makes.
4. Let others guess what you are.

Style Discrimination

1. Listen to several recordings.
2. Each should depict a distinct style.
3. Select the style you like best.
4. Tell why.

Style Characteristics

1. Listen to several records that demonstrate one particular style (rock and roll, jazz, folk music etc.).
2. Tell what you thought made the different records alike.
3. What elements were the same or similar?

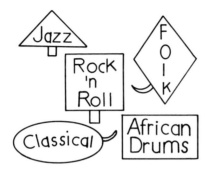

Picture Production

1. Draw a picture.
2. Write a story about it.
3. Use rhythm instruments and harmony instruments to accompany your story.

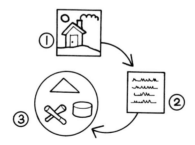

Animal Rhythms

1. Select an animal.
2. Move like that animal.
3. Have classmates try to guess what you are.
4. Try to clap to the rhythm of each animal as it is imitated.

Name Clapping

1. Clap to the rhythm of your own name.
2. Try your first name.
3. Note how many times you clapped.
4. Clap your first and last name.
5. Note how many times you clapped.
6. Compare with classmates.
7. Try to clap their names.

3 claps   2 claps

1 clap

How many claps in all?

Film Fantasy

1. Listen to a musical selection.
2. Use magic markers to draw on 16 mm film or sheets of transparency paper as you listen.
3. "Play" what you drew on a film projector or overhead projector.
4. Compare your film to those of your classmates.
   Variation: Make one long motion picture by taping everyone's together.

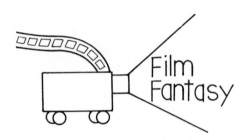

Sounds Around You

1. Cut out pictures of sound producers you hear daily.
2. Draw sound makers too.
3. Make a collage of the sounds in your environment.
4. Compare.

Sounds Are Different

1. Use your collage.
2. Look for sounds that are soft, loud, bumpy, etc.
3. Try to find many types.

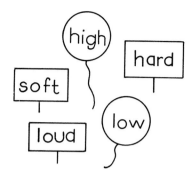

Stylistic Drawings

1. Listen to several recordings of one particular style.
2. As you listen, draw.
3. Discuss and compare drawings.

Shoebox Sound Production

1. Cut a circle or rectangle close to one end of a shoebox cover.
2. Put the cover back on the box.
3. Stretch different width rubber bands over the hole.
4. Pluck the strings.
5. Make as many different sounds as you can.

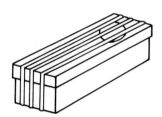

Kazoo

1. Use a cardboard lining of a toilet paper roll.
2. Use a pencil to make a small hole about 1 inch from one end.
3. Cover that end with waxed paper.
4. Stretch waxed paper tightly and secure with a rubber band.
5. Hold the open end over your mouth.
6. Pucker your lips and blow.
7. Experiment.
8. Try to hum a melody.

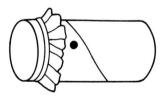

Make a Melody

1. Use a glockenspiel that has been color coded.
2. Compose or reproduce a simple melody.

3. Keep track by using squares of colored paper.
4. Glue the squares to a piece of paper.
5. Each square should represent a note played on the instrument.
6. Play your melody again.

Responsive Rhythm

1. Listen to a musical selection.
2. The selection suggests an animal or animals.
3. Try to guess the animals as they are portrayed.
4. Move with the music.

Rhythmical Endings

1. Use your body.
2. Imitate a frog and hop from lily pad to lily pad.
3. Fall off the pad and into the water.
4. Be a yo-yo that suddenly breaks.
5. Think of an ending yourself.
6. Change tempo.

Resource Materials: Basic Elements of Music

Teacher References:
   Children's songs in ABA form:

   "Did You Ever See a Lassie?"
   "Who Built the Ark?"
   "The Little White Duck"
   "Oh, Susannah"
   "Oh, Dear! What Can the Matter Be?"
   "Bobby Shaftoe"

Song books that contain one or more of the above songs:

Sally Go Round the Sun (Fowke, 1969)
Jim Along, Josie (Langstaff, 1970)
This Is Music (McCall, 1965)

Music that creates pictures:

Hansel and Gretel, Humperdinck
Carnival of the Animals, Saint-Säens
Through the Kaleidoscope, Perry
Peter and the Wolf, Prokofiev
Thunder and Lightning, Strauss
The Flight of the Bumble Bee, Rimsky-Korsakov
The Viennese Musical Clock, Kodály

Chants:

Larrick, Nancy. *The Wheels of the Bus Go Round and Round.* San Carlos, Calif.:
   Golden Gate Junior Books, 1972.

Other references:

Dietz, Betty Warner, and Michael Babatunda Olantunji. *Musical Instruments of Africa.* New York: John Day Co., 1965.

McLeish, Kenneth, and Valerie McLeish. *The Oxford First Companion to Music.* London: Oxford University Press, 1982.

Musical Experiences

All musical experiences involve the basic elements of music, but the experiences themselves take a variety of forms. In early childhood education these forms include singing, listening, rhythmic movement, playing instruments, and composing music. Children need many opportunities to explore these forms because each provides a different way of achieving the development of musical concepts.

Listening

Since music is basically an aural art, all musical experiences are contingent upon the children's ability to listen. Musical development relies on the ability to perceive, identify, and discriminate between sounds. Through guided listening experiences, children may expand their understanding of the elements of music. As they develop these musical concepts and their aural acuity, they also extend their range of responses. The more they can "hear" in music the more occasions they have to react.

Objectives for Listening

To further develop musical concepts and their powers of selective listening, children will:

1. listen and respond to a variety of music.
2. distinguish between natural and man-made sounds.
3. interpret music by talking about it, moving to it, and drawing it.
4. discuss what they hear in music.
5. identify elements of music as they exist in a composition.
6. reproduce a particular melody, rhythm, or tempo by singing, playing an instrument, or moving.

Listening Activities

Sound Search

1. Bring a happy sound to school.
2. Share and compare happy sounds with others.
   Variation: Bring other kinds of sounds (scary, sad, etc.).

Sounds Surround Us

1. Close your eyes.
2. Listen carefully to the sounds around you and inside you.
3. Categorize these sounds according to dynamics, rhythm, pitch, tempo, etc.

Word Sounds

1. Discover words that have a particular sound, such as bumpy, watery, syrupy, etc.
2. Discover words that suggest movement.

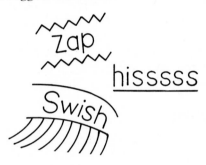

Story Music

1. Listen to or read the story.
2. Listen to the instruments of the orchestra retell the story.
3. Discuss how musical patterns and instruments were used to recreate the mood of the story.
   Variation: After hearing the story, but prior to listening to the music, discuss how you think the music and story will be correlated.

Mood Match

1. Listen to the musical selection.
2. Choose from a series of art prints the one you feel best expresses the feeling of the music.
3. Discuss and defend your choice.

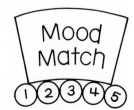

The Orchestra

1. Look at a picture of a symphony orchestra.
2. Listen as the orchestra plays.
3. Follow the music from section to section as different groups of instruments are featured or predominate.

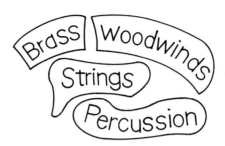

Musical Story Starters

1. Listen to a musical selection.
2. Write a story about what you heard.

Instrument Scrapbook

1. Look for pictures of musical instruments in magazines and catalogs.
2. Identify them.
3. Classify them according to type.
4. Make a scrapbook.
5. Include pictures of musicians and composers.
6. Make comments beside your pictures.

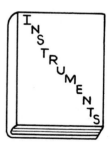

Instrument Categories

1. Look at pictures of musical instruments and observe how they are arranged into different categories (strings, etc.).
2. Pick one category.
3. Make a list of the instruments that fit that category.
4. Make a list of their common characteristics.

Melody

1. Listen to a melody.
2. Get a set of bells that has been numbered or color coded.

3. Use a chart that uses numbers or colors to show the melody.
4. Follow the order on the chart to play.
5. Change the tempo, the dynamics.
6. Practice and experiment.

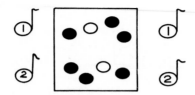

Reference Materials for Listening

Musical picture books

Fantasia Pictorial Series
A series of beautifully illustrated books from Japan, distributed in America by
   Silver Burdett, Morristown, N.J. Included in the series:
      "Carnival of the Animals"
      "William Tell"
      "The Nutcracker"
Bunche, Jane. *An Introduction to the Instruments of the Orchestra.* New York:
   Golden Press, 1962.
Commins, Dorothy Berliner. *All About the Symphony Orchestra and What it Plays.*
   New York: Random House, 1961.
Dietz, Betty Warner, and Michael Babatunde Olantunji. *Musical Instruments of
   Africa.* New York: John Day, 1965.
Greene, Carla. *Let's Learn About the Orchestra.* Irving-on-Hudson, N.Y.: Harvey
   House Inc., 1967.
Headington, Christopher. *The Orchestra and Its Instruments.* New York: World
   Publishing Company, 1963.
Kettlekamp, Larry. *Singing Strings.* New York: William Morrow and Co., 1958.
Lacey, Marion. *Picture Book of Musical Instruments.* Boston: Lothrop, Lee and
   Shepard Co., 1942.
Shippen, Katherine B., and Anco Seidlova. *The Heritage of Music.* New York: Vi-
   king Press, 1963.
Skolsky, Syd. *The Music Box.* New York: Dutton, 1946.
Weissman, Dick. *Music Making in America.* New York: Frederick Ungar Pub. Co.,
   1982.

Singing

Many music educators, among them Myers (1950), Matthews (1953), and Raebeck
and Wheeler (1964), consider singing the most important musical experience for
the young child. Singing is important not only because it is fun and personally satisfying, but also because in the process of singing the child is exposed to the basic
elements of music.

Children naturally love to sing. Early on they attempt to control their babbles and
coos to create tone patterns. As they develop control of their singing voices, they
pass through stages that closely parallel language development (Greenberg, 1979).

Initially, they just make sounds. Then they experiment with sounds. By the end of the third stage they are able to approximate singing. By the age of three, most children have reached the fourth stage and are singing accurately within a limited range. By the age of four, most children have reached the fifth and final stage and are able to sing accurately within an expanded range. However, these stages are only approximate. Many children entering school have not reached stage four or five; and they may never reach them without encouragement, assistance, and musical experiences (Greenberg, 1979)

The musical education that young children receive should reflect an understanding of this developmental process. The ability to sing accurately is a question of readiness. Thus, the teacher's expectations should be consistent with the child's abilities. The teacher's role is to provide the meaningful experiences that will help children progress.

Song Selection

Good songs for young children have certain characteristics:

1. vocal range: limited
2. words: simple, meaningful, and easy to remember
3. rhythm: definite, prompts response
4. length: short
5. effect: pleasure
6. subject matter: appropriate for grade level; the lower the grade the more important it is that it reflect the child's environment
7. quality: aesthetically beautiful

Songs in a limited vocal range:

"A-Tisket, A-Tasket"
"Go Tell Aunt Rhodie"
"Hokey Pokey"
"Hot Cross Buns"
"It's Raining, It's Pouring"
"Jingle Bells"
"Mary Had a Little Lamb"
"Rain, Rain Go Away"
"Baa, Baa, Black Sheep"
"Hickory, Dickory Dock"
"Erie Canal"

Introducing and Teaching Songs

Rote Method.   The rote method may be used to teach short songs as a whole or longer songs as phrases. In either case the child is required to listen carefully. The rote method is preferred in early childhood education because it does not rely on reading skills.

To present the song the teacher may use his or her own voice, an instrument, or a recording. Any teacher who feels unsure of his or her own voice can still easily provide the experience by using records and tapes.

Objectives for Singing

To further develop musical concepts and the ability to sing, children will:

1. explore the variety of sounds they can create with their own voices.
2. express themselves through spontaneous singing.
3. experience and describe dynamics as the ability of sounds to be soft or loud.
4. experience and describe rhythm as the steady pulse of a composition.
5. experience and describe the tempo as how quickly or slowly the music moves.
6. experience and describe the melody as the ability of a single tone to move up, down, or repeat.
7. use their singing voices alone and in a group.

Suggested Activities for Singing

Explore: Use your voice but not words to attempt the following:

1. charm a snake
2. tickle a whale
3. direct traffic
4. pet a porcupine
5. put yourself to sleep
6. crack an egg

Create: Make up a sound for others to identify or describe.
Experiment: Use your voice to become:

1. a marshmallow
2. a red balloon
3. barbed wire

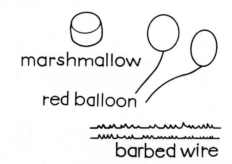

marshmallow

red balloon

barbed wire

Sound Classification

1. Make a list of sounds.
2. Select one or more categories for the list.
3. Use your voice to try to imitate the sounds.

soft   loud

low   high

Rhythmical Recital

1. Recite a poem, nursery rhyme, or chant.
2. Move to the beat as you recite.

Chants

1. Learn a new chant from a friend, your teacher, or a book.
2. Clap as you say the chant.
3. Teach your chant to another friend.

Songs

1. Listen to a new song.
2. Learn the melody and the words.
3. Practice singing the song alone and with the group.

Song Patterns

1. Use an ABA form.
2. Make up a short song using this pattern.
3. Sing your song.

Form Match

1. Listen to a selection of songs.
2. Try to match songs with patterns (ABA, ABBA, etc.).

Being Me

(Self-concept)   Words and music by Dottie Rambo

1. If   I   were a bird   I could   fly   High as the
2. If   I   were a bell   I could   chime,   Ring ding-a-

stars   in the   sky.   But a   bird I'll never be so I'm-happy you
ling   all the time.   But a   bell I'll never be so I'm-happy you

see just being   me,   being   me.   Being   me, being
see just being   me,   being   me.   Being   me, being

free,   being   all I can   be.   I can pass every test cause I'll
free,   being   all I can   be.   I can always be myself (better than

give it my best just being me,   being   me.
an-y-bod-y else) just being me,   being   me.

Sing.

Happy Song

(Rhythm Instruments Reading Music)   Early American Folk Song

When I'm happy,   hear me sing;   When I'm happy,   hear me sing;

When I'm happy,   hear me   sing; Tra, la, la, la,   Tra, la, la, la,

2. When I'm happy, hear me play;
   When I'm happy, hear me play;
   I will play my Indian drum;
   Rum, tum, tum, tum, Rum, tum, tum
3. Triangle; Ting, ting, ting, ting, Ting, ting, ting, ting,
4. Tambourine; Shake, shake, shake
5. Castanets; Clack, clack, clack
Let the song continue with other instruments.

I'm a Little Popcorn

(Tune: I'm a Little Teapot)   (Creative movement.)

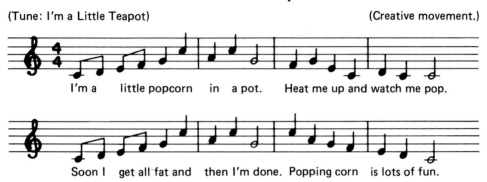

I'm a   little popcorn   in   a pot.   Heat me up and watch me pop.

Soon I   get all fat and   then I'm done.   Popping corn   is lots of fun.

Children can make motions to go with the song.

Simon Says for Everybody

(Body Movement)

(Tune: If You're Happy And You Know It)   Words by Juanita Shippey

Simon says for everybody swing your arms Simon says for everybody, swing your

arms.   Simon says for everybody swing your arms, swing your arms. Simon

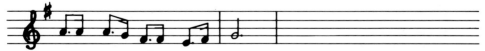

says for everybody   swing your arms.

b. swing legs, feet, elbows
c. shake head, feet
d. wiggle nose, mouth, fingers, toes
e. stomp feet
f. cross feet, legs, arms, hands
g. open mouth, close mouth

This Is the Way the Worm Crawls

(Tune: Here We Go Round the Mulberry Bush)   Words by Juanita Shippey

This is the way the worm crawls the worm crawls the worm crawls

This is the way the worm crawls, so early in the day.

2. the birdie flaps
3. the bunny hops
4. the frog jumps
5. the fishy swims
6. the elephant stomps
7. the lion roars

Johnny Works with One Hammer

(Tempo and Meter)

John-ny works with one hammer, one hammer, one hammer. John-ny works with

one hammer. Then he works with two.

Last verse Now he goes to sleep.

2. two hammers
3. three hammers
4. four hammers

Children begin hammering with one hand slowly to the beat. as the song progresses, it gets faster and children use both hands and feet as hammers.

Dance of Greeting

Movement
Listening
Responding

Bow to your part-ner. Bow to your neighbor Stamp! Stamp! And

turn yourself around   1. Join hands and circle left-   Circle left together,
                         2. Join hands and circle right-   Circle right together,

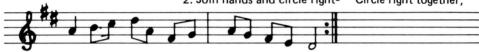

Join hands and circle left, to-gether here we go.
Join hands and circle right, to-gether here we go.

3) Join hands we're walking in,
   We're walking in together,
   Join hands and back again,
   Together here we go!

4) Now take your partner's arm
   And swing around together,
   Now take your partner's arm,
   Together, here we go!

Instruments

Instruments allow children to reproduce and create music. They offer yet another outlet for expression. As children play, they also manipulate the elements of music and experience for themselves the effects of those elements.

Orff instruments are the ones most commonly used in early childhood education. The melodic instruments include glockenspiels, metallophones, and xylophones. Rhythm instruments include hand drums, tambourines, triangles, woodblocks, cymbals, rattles, and jingle bells. However, neither the availability nor the lack of these instruments should prevent the creative production of sounds. Many instruments are cheaply and easily made, and natural substitutes exist for others.

Objectives for Playing Instruments

To develop musical concepts through playing instruments children will:

1. explore the sounds made by different instruments.
2. use instruments to illustrate musical elements.
3. dance, sing, move, and listen to the sounds of their own instruments.
4. experiment with playing many instruments.

5. create and reproduce simple melodies using an instrument.
6. listen to the ways others have used instruments to produce sounds.

The Rhythm Band

Although the quality of manufactured instruments is superior to that of homemade instruments, the cost is sometimes prohibitive. The following activities allow children to create their own set of rhythm instruments and noisemakers.

Rhythm Sticks

1. Use 2 pencils or 2 ½-inch round dowels.
2. Play by striking sticks together.
3. Describe the sound.
4. Experiment with creating sounds and producing beats.

Wood Blocks

1. Use a piece of wood that is easy to hold.
2. Sand the wood until it is smooth.
3. Play by hitting the block with a mallet.
4. Describe the sound.
5. Experiment with creating sound patterns.

Sandpaper Blocks

1. Nail or glue emery cloth or sandpaper to one side of a wooden block.
2. Prepare 2 wooden blocks.

3. Play by rubbing sandpapered surfaces together.
4. Describe the sound.
5. Experiment with the blocks.

Clinkers

1. Use 2 coconut shells.
2. Play by hitting shells together.

Gong

1. Use an old license plate (the older the better).
2. Strike with a mallet to play.
3. Describe the sound.

Shaker

1. Use 2 small paper plates.
2. Between them put a few beans or some rice.
3. Lace or staple the plates together.
4. Shake to play.
5. Describe the sound.
6. Experiment with sound patterns.

Chocallo (Latin American Shaker)

1. Use the cardboard tube from a roll of paper towels.
2. Put beans, rice, or popcorn into the tube.
3. Cover both ends and seal.
4. Decorate.
5. Play by shaking.
6. Describe the sound.
7. Experiment with the shaker.

Maracas

1. Use a frozen juice can that has a plastic lid.
2. Use a hammer and nail to make a hole through the center of the metal end.
3. Insert a dowel, pencil, or stick. Make it fit snuggly.
4. Push the stick in until the top of it reaches the top of the can.
5. Put in beans or rice.
6. Cover with plastic top.
7. Nail plastic to the stick.
8. Play by shaking.
9. Experiment with playing the maracas.

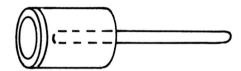

Tambourine

1. Use bottle caps and a ping-pong paddle.
2. Attach caps around the edge with cup hooks.

3. Screw hook through the center of the cap.
4. Bend hooks completely over.
5. Play by shaking.
6. Experiment with playing the tambourine.

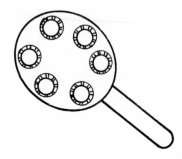

Rattles

1. Use a plastic bottle, spice can, pill box, etc.
2. Put pebbles, beans, rice, or popcorn inside.
3. Decorate the container with paint.
4. Shake to play.
5. Describe the sound.

Jingle Instrument

1. Use a set of metal measuring spoons.
2. Play by slapping them into your hand.
3. Describe the sound.

Wrist or Ankle Bells

1. Lace 2 or 3 bells through a shoe string.
2. Tie to wrist or ankle.
3. Move to shake your bells.

Kazoo

1. Use a piece of waxed paper over a clean comb.
2. Play by pressing your lips against the paper and humming.
3. Try to hum a little tune.

Musical Characterization

1. Use a story you already know, or write a new one.
2. Use instruments to represent the story characters.
3. Read your story, and accompany yourself with selected instruments.

Explore

1. Use your box of rhythm instruments.
2. Find one instrument to make an animal sound, a mechanical sound, etc.
3. Compare your selection to the selections of classmates.

Song Writing

1. Use a glockenspiel or xylophone that has been color coded.
2. Make up a short song.

3. Use colored squares to keep track of each note.
4. Glue colored squares in proper sequence to another sheet of paper.
5. Try to replay your song.

Song Accompaniment

1. Select a familiar song.
2. Select a rhythm instrument to play.
3. Sing and play at the same time.

Play and March

1. Listen as the march is played.
2. Select a rhythm instrument to play as you march.
3. Play and march.

Garden Hose Sounds

1. Cut garden hose into different lengths.
2. Blow through the end of a length.
3. Describe the sounds made by the different lengths of hose.

Get the Beat

1. Use a rhythm instrument.
2. Use the instrument to make different beats.
3. Select and use instruments to imitate the following:
   a. the ticking of a clock
   b. a fast or slow walk
   c. a dripping faucet
   d. the beat of your heart

Sound Effects

1. Create a monster story.
2. Select instruments to make horrible noises.

Play Partner

1. Select a partner.
2. Play an instrument to direct the way your partner moves.
3. Reverse roles.

Comical Sounds

1. Use a comic strip.
2. Select an instrument or instruments to make the sound effects for each frame.
3. Read and play the comic strip for a classmate.

Chant

1. Select a familiar chant.
2. Play it rather than saying it.
3. Change tempo.
4. Could you use different instruments for different voices?
5. Try to characterize.
6. Select an instrument to be a relative's voice.

Found Sound

1. Look at a selected art print.
2. Select an instrument to match the mood of the picture.
3. Discuss and defend your selection.

Outline Sound

1. Look at an outline.
2. Select an instrument to describe the outline musically.

Spelling Fun

1. Use a current list of spelling words.
2. Select an instrument to depict the character of each word.
3. Compare and contrast your selection with those of classmates.

Folk Instruments for Children to Make

Bull-roarer. This instrument is also known as the "thunder stick." The Indians used it to provide a roaring sound behind their drums. Take a soft, light piece of wood 2″ wide and ½″ thick. Shape it so that one end measures 1¼″ across and the other end is rounded off. Sand off the edges and drill a hole into the untapered end of the wood. Run a piece of strong lightweight string through the hole and knot it securely. Make a loop for your finger in the opposite end and whirl the roarer in a circle in front of your body. It can be decorated with painted Indian symbols.

Bottle chimes. Construct a frame to hold a dowel rod from which bottles will be hung. Tie bottles with corks to dowel rod after filling them with varying amounts of water. Tap them to produce different sounds.

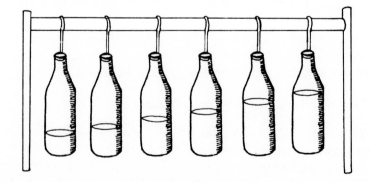

Double flowerpot drum. This drum is designed from a Nigerian double drum. The lacings can be loosened or tightened to create different sounds. Glue or tape two plastic flowerpots together at the small end. Cut out inner tubing about 1″ larger than the flowerpot openings. Puncture holes all around the edge of the tubing circle, 2″ apart and ½″ from the edge. Soak the inner tube and some heavy string or rawhide lacing in lukewarm water for 30 minutes before they are used. Thread laces through holes in tubing evenly from the lower drumhead to the upper drumhead so that the heads are tight enough to elicit clear sounds. Dry it for 12 hours, and do not handle it until it is dry.

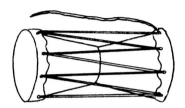

Movement Activities

Color Movement

1. Select a color.
2. Move like that color.

March Creatively

1. Listen to a Sousa march.
2. March around the room.
3. Be an instrument in a marching band.
4. Be a person watching the parade.
5. Be an animal trying to keep in step.

Dance

1. Listen to a musical selection.
2. Dance freely as you listen.
3. Use scarves and other props as you dance.

Move to the Melody

1. Listen to a song.
2. Move your body to demonstrate the pitch, rhythm, tempo, and dynamics.

Action Song

1. Listen to a song that suggests movements.
2. Act out the movements that are suggested.

Music Instruction Approaches

It is gratifying to realize that more than 90% of the school districts in this country employ music specialists to teach general classroom music to all children in the elementary grades (Peters & Miller, 1982). Unfortunately, even in many schools that employ highly trained music specialists well versed in the contemporary methodologies (e.g., Orff, Kodaly, Dalcroze), musical activities rarely occur on a daily basis and sometimes only once a week. Consequently, musical instruction is often limited to only musical games rather than substantive music teaching/learning. A variety of daily musical activities are essential in maximizing music learning. Music specialists need the assistance of the classroom teacher in maintaining a daily musical environment in the classroom (Bostley, 1985). Such a partnership does not require unusual *musical talent* or *skills* on the part of the classroom teacher. The music specialist should establish the musical goals and objectives as well as the teaching/learning strategies, and initiate each step of the instruction. The classroom teacher should lead the children in carrying out and practicing the specific musical objectives demonstrated by the specialist. The initial requirement of the classroom teacher is to recognize the importance of musical artistic development in children and to be willing to learn with the children and to assist in their musical development.

Through aculturation children acquire varying degrees of musical competencies between infancy and the middle school years. These competencies (musical intelligence), tend to be of an intuitive nature and, lacking a planned, structured spiral curricular musical program, remain as such without much appreciable maturation even into adulthood (MMCP, 1970). To accomplish the goals and objectives of music education, a multifaceted instruction program should be structured that will help each child:

1. develop performance skills at the appropriate age level through singing, movement, and use of instruments (psychomotor activities);
2. develop listening skills such as tonal memory, melodic and rhythmic recognition and conservation (Zimmerman, 1971), decision-making on the expressive qualities of music, and ultimately making intelligent critical musical judgments (affective domain);
3. acquire specific musical knowledge including the reading and writing of simple music notation, as well as learning appropriate historical facts about composers and their musical eras (cognitive and music literacy development);
4. appreciate music as an art through the gradual comprehension of the various components of music (melody, rhythm, harmony, timbre, dynamics, etc.) through performance, listening, and creative activities (the cultivation of music consumers and audiences at all ages);
5. incorporate acquired musical skills to confidently make music individually or in groups;
6. ultimately inculcate, in a maturing manner, a deep appreciation of and for music and to instill confidence about personal musical abilities and perceptions.

Within the past quarter-century American music educators have incorporated the musical instruction approaches of Orff, Kodaly, and Dalcroze into the music education program of the general classroom (Chosky, 1986). The basic goals of these three approaches are consistent with the goals listed above. In addition to the Orff, Kodaly, and Dalcroze approaches which were specifically developed for the general classroom, it may prove valuable to gain an understanding of another musical instruction approach; the Suzuki "Talent Education" method.

Suzuki Talent Education

Suzuki's intent was to initiate effective violin instruction for children as early as possible, even three years of age, when they were most curious and sensitive to learning and following directions. His philosophy is compactly described in the title of his book, *Nurtured By Love* (1969). Suzuki insists on a totally sympathetic musical atmosphere both with parents in the home setting as well as with teachers and peers in a school setting. One parent is required to actually take violin lessons and practice regularly with the child. In addition, recordings of quality music professionally performed are used in the lesson and at home to provide ideal musical role models in which to emulate. Such a situation provides more than merely an awareness by parents and teachers of the child's musical activity but provides a sharing empathy and greater understanding among all concerned with the nature of the child's musical learning task. Patterning general music instruction after Suzuki's philosophy may be as appropriate for general classroom music education as it has been in teaching the violin.

Although it is not practical to totally superimpose Suzuki's instruction expectations upon the general music education of children, the music activities that follow, and the desired competencies described, will be illustrated within this framework. These goals and musical activities will provide the classroom teacher with some practical guidelines in leading the musical development of their young students. Indeed, in keeping with the philosophy of Suzuki, musically untrained classroom teachers should find the music activities conducive to learning.

Zoltan Kodaly and Early Singing Experiences

In designing musical learning strategies for children at any age, it is important to utilize the natural musical abilities which children already possess. The most common skill that children exhibit at an early age is singing (Gardner, 1983; Winner, 1982) which is central in the Orff, Kodaly, and Dalcroze methodologies. Of the three, Zoltan Kodaly used singing (solfege with hand signals to indicate pitches) almost exclusively, whereas Emile Jacques-Dalcroze emphasized the significance of rhythm through movement and the development of physical coordination. Carl Orff introduced the use of quality instruments as well as vocal chanting in his approach to musical instruction.

American music educators have included the highlights from each approach in devising an appropriate music instruction program for early childhood instruction (Chosky et al., 1986).

In the Kodaly Musical Training sequence for very young children (ages 3–9), their first songs consist of the three-, four-, and five-note melodies typical of familiar nursery rhymes and folk songs from different cultures. Based on the tonic solfa, hand signs, and rhythmic syllables, children gain a gradual sensitivity and understanding of melody and rhythm. The music specialist may very well wish to use the Kodaly method and the following activities will help to acquaint teachers to the approach as well as provide simple musical activities for their children.

Solfege is merely labelling musical pitches with syllables. The major scale is illustrated with standard notation and "solfa" syllables as follows:

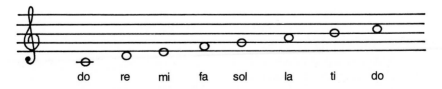

The use of *solfa* helps tonal memory for the child by incorporating easily learned words or syllables into the music vocabulary. The musical segment:

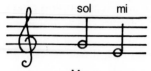

Ma - ry   is a familiar playground vocalization of one child calling to another. These pitches of *sol* and *mi* seem to be a naturally learned interval. The answering sequence of pitches include the pitch *la* which is a natural extension of the young child's vocal repertoire.

Where are you hiding?

Utilizing what appears to be a natural ability of the young child, a variety of musical activities can be devised around these pitches. The following is a good example of a simple musical call and answer sequence. One group sings in imitation of the teacher, "guess what?" and in like manner the second group responds "guess what?" The first group then sings "Mary has a birthday!" and the second group imitates the same tune.

Guess what?

Ma - ry   has   a   birth - day!

To modify the repetitiveness of the melody yet retain use of the same pitches and syllables, the activity could continue as follows: "How old is Mary?" (a question has a natural vocal rise at the end). The response is: "Mary is five years old" adding the tonic *do*. Such a declamation has a natural vocal fall for a resolution.

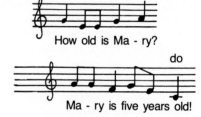

How old is Ma - ry?

Ma - ry is five years old!

In this method Kodaly adapted the Curwin hand signals to provide visual and physical cues in helping children acquire a sense of melodic direction and pitch-interval relationships of "skips" and "steps." The first musical scale example above is made up of pitch intervals called "steps" because of the closeness of each pitch. This is in contrast to wider intervals, called "skips," which are illustrated in the "Call" and "Answer" activity. To help children control their voices in accurately singing melodic steps and skips, the hand signals are strategically formed in front of the body to indicate melodic direction and a relative physical interval between the pitches. The music specialist may wish to use

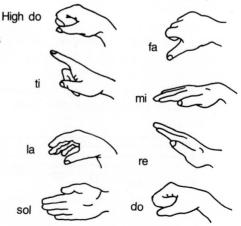

hand signals. If so, the children should learn to imitate the teacher in using the hand signals as well.

Many music teachers attempt to isolate the elements of music with the desire to more effectively emphasize the learning probability for the young children. Typically, rhythmic games are very popular as musical activities. Should the music specialist wish to use the Kodaly system, specific rhythmic syllables used are as follows:

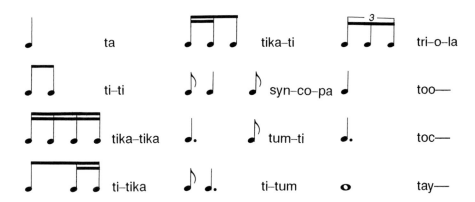

In rhythmic activities, the introduction of musical symbolism is most effective if used first with songs containing a familiar text. For simplicity's sake, music in duple time of two beats to the measure of quadruple time (also referred to as "common time") with four beats to the measure should be the choice for initial instruction in counting and learning notation.

Teachers should select a simple song like "Rain, rain go away" and have the children imitate them. This song fits nicely to the series of pitches utilized in the "call and answer" song.

Rain , rain go a - way, come a - gain an - oth - er day .

First the melody should be practiced, and then hand symbols can be added if desired. If teachers use hand signals, the children should imitate them. The songs with only two or three pitches will be ideal for learning the signals. Then the children can be asked to clap as they sing. With some practice they will quickly adapt both the hand signals and clapping to singing. Some will clap the pulsation or beat, others will clap each syllable (also referred to as melodic or surface rhythm). It will become important that the children eventually be able to have the patience to only clap the beat while singing the melodic rhythm (which will become more evident in the movement activities of Dalcroze and the instrumental accompaniment of Orff).

At this point a simple pulsation notation should be placed on the chalk board or other convenient display board (felt and magnetic boards are ideal for these activities). ♩♩♩♩ The teacher can ask the children to identify the number of symbols on the board and then count them in imitation of the demonstration. Selecting a pitch such as *sol,* the teacher should demonstrate counting the symbols in a chant (a recitation type singing on one pitch, e.g., *sol*):

and ask the children to imitate. The response will be easy. Now using *sol* as the first pitch of the illustrated song, the children can be asked to chant the count and clap by themselves as the teacher superimposes the song on their chant. This is building complexity into the rhythmic activity by reintroducing the melody to their rhythmic accompaniment. Now the teacher should divide the class in half and challenge one group to sing the melody while the other group chants the count with clapping.

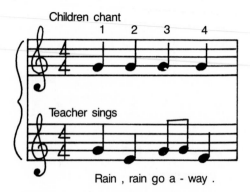

The actual counting activity should begin without the visual reference to a notational system. When the children are comfortable with a repetitive-rote accomplishment of counting the song, then the teacher should introduce the notation indicating that "this is just what you were singing!" After sufficient repetitions of the counting-chanting activity while looking at the notation (as they count, the teacher points to each symbol in turn), the teacher should then redirect their attention away from the notation for a final trial. At this point the children have sufficient experience to be divided into two groups to combine singing the song with chanting the count. The group that chants the count may easily be pulled into the melody rather than remaining in the chant. This is satisfactory and should even be praised with the very young children because it will become an activity goal in the near future.

This two-group activity can remain the basis of learning melody and rhythm throughout the school year with the addition of different songs borrowed from song series or invented by the teacher for special occasions. Seasonal events provide excellent material for such activities. The children may be assisted in composing short poems about Halloween, Thanksgiving, Christmas, Valentine's Day, etc., and then the teacher can compose a simple song for their poems based on *so, mi, la,* and *do.*

With older children (ages 6–9), as they gain sufficient familiarity with solfege, they can be asked to compose their own melody for their songs (although at first the teacher should provide only two pitches such as *sol* and *mi,* then with proficiency add other pitches one at a time). This activity may seem more reasonable after the description of the Orff approach using various rhythm and melodic instruments.

Emile Jacques-Dalcroze Eurhythmics

It has been generally assumed that rhythm (the "beat") is the most powerful musical influence on children. Research supports the theory that melodic and rhythmic perception tend to develop concurrently in children (Petzold, 1966; Bostley, 1986). Nonetheless, many music teachers place initial instructional emphasis on rhythmic activities. " 'Dalcroze Eurhythmics' is an approach to music education based on the premise that rhythm is the primary element of music, and that the source for all musical rhythm may be found in the natural rhythms of the human body" (Chosky et al., 1986). Although the Curwin hand signals are not an aspect of the Dalcroze method, *solfege* is as important as it is in the Kodaly method.

As already mentioned, within any of these musical methodologies, the point of departure in the learning process is the realm of competencies the child already possesses and easily demonstrates. Dalcroze observed that while the child, who *could not* rhythmically perform well (maintain tempo or pulse while trying to learn a new musical competency such as singing a new song) in a musical setting, was very capable of naturally walking in tempo. He also observed that as children began to concentrate while listening to music, they also naturally tapped their feet and moved their bodies in a responsive manner to the expression of the music (dynamics, tempo, harmonic complexity, etc.). "The students themselves were the instruments, he realized; not the piano, violin, flute or drum [producing the musical sounds], but the students themselves" (Chosky et al., 1986).

The most natural physical activity to accompany the musical program for very young children is clapping hands to the pulse of the music. The children will find this an easy, pleasurable activity. Using a song or nursery rhyme which is familiar, the teacher should ask them to clap while they listen to the song, and next ask them to clap while they sing the song. The teacher should observe and compare the nature of their clapping under both circumstances. While listening the children should naturally tend to clap "only" the beat. While singing they will probably clap the melodic rhythmic patterns as well as the beat. Generally a competency goal of clapping is simply to find and maintain the pulse or "beat" of the song. In both instances, children as young as three are capable of accurately accomplishing this simple task.

Two musical goals encompassing kinesthetic-psychomotor and listening skills are involved with clapping the music: (1) establish a sense of beat and (2) become aware of the physical control involved in clapping.

The music specialist should explain simply to the children the goal of maintaining the beat while singing. The teacher will be able to observe and help the children practice this objective in daily singing by demonstrating that several syllables may occur on each beat "but we only clap on certain words (syllables) that fall on the beat." An example is the following familiar song, "Here we go round the mulberry bush." Any musical note may receive the beat. In this example, the dotted quarter-note ♩. receives one count and is subdivided into three eighth-notes ♪♪♪ , therefore, there are four beats in the measure and the time signature could have been illustrated as: 𝄴. instead of 12/8 .

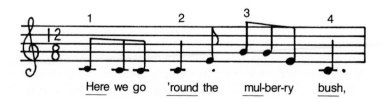

Here we go 'round the mul-ber-ry bush,

The beat occurs on "Here" - "round" - "Mul" - "bush." The rest of the words are important because the song does not make sense without the words, but the children should be asked to imitate the teacher in only singing in rhythm those words that fall on the beat while everyone claps in a steady beat. After a couple of trials in which they are reminded to have "patience" and wait for the beat, the teacher should supply the other words (syllables) while clapping.

As part of this activity the teacher will quickly notice that the clap sound only lasts a split-second, yet the actual beat has a much greater

Here (we go) round (-the) mul-(ber-ry) bush

ILLUSTRATE: Chant: Here   round   mul   bush

Clap: ∧——→ ∧——→∧——→ ∧

duration, extending until the next clapping sound. It is important for the teacher to understand the nature of rhythmic duration in which a single clap or sound of the beat does not necessarily represent, in actual sound, the length of the beat.

This can be demonstrated to the children by pointing out the manner in which they clap. Teachers should ask the children to listen and watch carefully as they perform the following: slowly chant on any pitch, One - Two - Three - Four and clap hands to each count. While chanting and clapping, teachers should slowly separate their hands after each beat in preparation for the next beat to the extent that they are actually choreographing the motion of the arms and hands. This is a physical action which will encompass the full duration of the beat, and when the children imitate this on a regular daily basis, they will begin to capture the true feeling of the beat. As they demonstrate, teachers should direct children to feel the arm muscles pull the hands and arms away from each other, then reverse the motion to force the hands to meet again to clap the next beat.

The next step is to repeat the clapping exercise but this time chant "One-and-a-Two-and-a-Three-and-a-Four-and-a." Teachers should instruct the children to notice the flow of their arms as they chant each syllable ("and-a" are now verbal subdivisions of the beat; teachers should still clap only on the actual count while the arm muscles pull the hands apart and then reverse the motion on "and-a"). The actual clap occurs on the numbered count, but the teacher's arms and hands should be moving away gracefully during the subdivision and, like a clock pendulum, gracefully returning in preparation for the next clap on the next numbered beat. The children should be able to imitate likewise and also chant the new count with the subdivisions.

Now "Here we go round the mulberry bush" should be reintroduced, demonstrating the same process as with numbers and syllables. The word "Here" is beat "One," and "we-go" are the subdivision equivalents to "and-a." This process may be used on any song and will quickly lead to careful, more discriminant listening as well as developing a sense for pulsation and the subdivisions of the beat as found in the melody (surface rhythm) of the songs.

"Movement comes very naturally to children. . . . Children love to run, hop, bounce, skip, and slide rather than walk" (Leeper, Witherspoon, & Day, 1984). Such movement activities become an important aspect of the Dalcroze method and follow the clapping objectives described above. "Movement patterns of children appear at different times in their lives. Some appear in infancy; some, later at two, three, even four years" (Leeper et al., 1984). Consequently, teachers may find many children in preschool unable to walk or march "in-time" to songs, especially if they are both singing and walking or trying to march while playing a rhythm instrument at the same time. Yet Dalcroze observed that most youngsters tend to naturally walk "in tempo." The difference in the two activities is that natural walking is just that, an unthinking, natural occurrence, but in reality it is a learned accomplishment before it becomes a natural phenomenon. Adding singing and enforcing a specific tempo complicates the walking activity and at first may be too complex for very young children to accomplish. Sitting in a circle and clapping as described above is a first good step. Then merely walking to a comfortable tempo would be a next step (perhaps to the count of "hup-two-three-four in a military manner), and finally teachers can add a recording to the count.

Before adding too much complexity to a movement activity, the teacher should have the children walk behind each other to a regular rhythm, either to a comfortable song or count (a "follow-the-leader" activity). If teachers are able to play an instrument or sing a song, they should gradually alter the tempo, first getting slower, then speeding up a little. They should make the change very gradual and observe the children's reactions. If they slow their speed in accordance with the tempo change, the teacher should ask them what they are observing and what they are doing in response. Some youngsters will respond that you "are getting slower," (or faster as the case may be) and so are they. This is the response the teacher should look for.

As in the clapping in which teachers trained the children to control the entire motion of their arms, they should now ask children to carefully pick up one foot and place it in front of the other, then pick up the other foot and place it in front of the first as they "slowly" walk to the song.

As teachers sing or play a song faster, they should ask the children to carefully place their foot quickly in front of the other, etc. At quicker tempos, rather than quickly moving around the room, teachers should demonstrate quick, short steps with slow forward movement to control the walking-marching activity. The feet will move quickly but the actual forward motion will be slow.

The two simple objectives, establishing a sense of beat and physical control in clapping, can occupy several weeks of daily musical activities and can be easily adapted to any song for variety. The same activities can be transferred to the use of instruments, and indeed, these movement activities are preparation for more abstract control of music. The use of instruments will be a very good demonstration of musical understanding and individual artistic development and control.

The Orff "Schulwerk"

Children like to sing, and they like musical activities that involve movement, but there is nothing more exciting than playing a musical instrument, even if it only involves hitting two rhythm sticks together. As is true in both the Kodaly and Dalcroze methods, the use of chant and singing is also the central aspect in the Orff approach to music education for children in the general classroom. Unique to the Orff approach is the inclusion of a wide variety of instruments. The instruments designed by Orff are high quality, sturdy, professional-type instruments including xylophones, metallophones, glockenspiels, and non-pitched rhythmic instruments that produce high quality musical tones. Quality instruments are required to insure accurate development of children's tonal acuity for timbre, melody, and harmony.

Most preschools and elementary classrooms will not be able to invest in a com-

plete set of "Orff" instruments. It is recommended that at least one soprano xylophone (illustrated above) be purchased for each classroom and be available in the music learning center for easy access by the children. This instrument has a pleasing, mellow tone that does not interfere with other classroom activities once the children become acclimated to it.

A variety of instruments is included in the Orff approach to enable the children to become more creative in their musical activities and to gain a deeper appreciation of music through a variety of encounters with music making. The use of instruments is important, but the approach is not an instrumental program. Gaining artistic proficiency on mallet or other percussion instruments is not the goal, rather, the goal is the inclusion of a variety of timbres and the acquisition of music reading to more fully understand the art of music. The instruments are actually used to accompany and help refine the children's singing technique. Nonetheless, proper handling of the instruments (as illustrated below) should be expected of the children. The clapping demonstration in the previous section of "Dalcroze" will be an important pre-

requisite to learning to control the instruments. The child should learn to transfer the arm muscle demonstrations to the forward motion of making a mallet strike a tone bar and then pulling the mallet away, trying to "pull" the sound out of the instrument rather than "beat" the sound from the instrument.

Before the children are introduced to musical instruments in the Orff approach, they are encouraged to use different parts of their bodies as musical rhythmic instruments. If teachers borrow the activity from the previous section describing the Dalcroze method, they should have the children clap on the beat to "One-Two-Three-Four" as before, but now for the subdivisions, have them snap their fingers. A variation is to have children clap their hands and tap their feet to the "beat," then quickly touch their knees then shoulders "in tempo" to each subdivision of "and-a." This adds a greater dimension to body control and coordination and, although children of preschool age are capable of accomplishing these activities, such activities may best follow refinement of walking, clapping, and singing.

The use of rhythm instruments is merely an extension of clapping and body rhythms, and once the class understands what is meant by the beat and the subdivisions of the beat, a variety of instruments may be substituted. A felt, magnetic, or chalk board should be available in the classroom. Any symbol may be used to indicate music notation, although even very young children will quickly adapt to standard musical symbols (Bostley, 1986). Therefore, it is recommended to begin with standard musical notation.

First the teacher should place one musical note on the board, ♩ , and ask a volunteer to clap the "picture." The teacher should select a child at least four years old, so that the initial attempt will be easily accomplished. Next the teacher should ask the class to imitate. The teacher should follow this simple exercise by adding

three horizontal musical notes on the board, ♩ ♩ ♩ ♩ , and ask for another volunteer to clap the musical picture. If there is difficulty, the teacher should demonstrate and then ask if anyone knows how many musical notes are on the board. Once the children understand the total number, the teacher should ask everyone to count while a volunteer claps and the teacher points, from left to right, to each note.

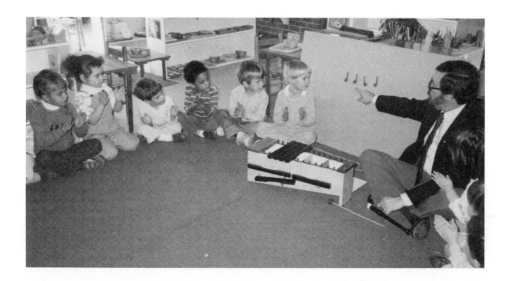

The teacher should repeat the exercise by having the children tap their feet and pat their knees and shoulders, etc., in imitation of the earlier body-rhythm exercise. Now the teacher can test their sense of physical direction of the musical notated pitches as well as their temporal sense of rhythm. The teacher should place four horizontal notes at the bottom of the board, followed by four more notes midway up the board, and finally four more notes at the top of the board as illustrated below.

The teacher should inform the children that each group of notes either represents the toes, the waist, or the shoulders of their body and they are to figure which part of the body to tap when the teacher points to a given group. With minimal practice, they will be able to count and tap their feet when the teacher points to the bottom four notes, and then shift to the waist or shoulders as the teacher points to the other groups. In due time they will not need the identifying words illustrated above, merely the spatially related notes will denote the behavioral expectancy.

The teacher should rearrange the notes and test their speed in responding to the following:

The teacher should now substitute words for the count such as "Tap Your Feet-Feet, Tap Your Waist-Waist, Tap Your Shoul-ders." The teacher should chant pitches corresponding to the relative interval, such as a low voice for "feet," and a high voice for "shoul-ders." Then ask the children to sing or chant in imitation of the demonstration. This involves coordinating body control, rhythmic and pitch sensitivity, and the relationship of rhythm-pitch to a notation.

The teacher should shift the above procedure to rhythm instruments. For the lowest group of four notes, have one child sit and play a hand drum instead of tapping his feet. Have a second child squat and play the middle group of four notes on the claves, and finally have a third child stand and play the highest four notes with a triangle. The teacher should note that each instrument, while not having a fixed, designated pitch, tends to provide a relative lower or higher sound. In this instance, a hand drum usually sounds lower than the other two instruments and the triangle has the highest pitch. The teacher could ask the children if the triangle should be played while pointing to the lowest pitch. In this manner the teacher will begin to test their musical, aural perceptions and gradually help them develop pitch and melodic discrimination.

The teacher should return to the song "Mulberry bush." Substitute a hand drum or wood block for indicating ("playing") the beat. Draw a picture of the instrument on the chalk board, this symbol ✕ indicating claves (two crossed wooden sticks), and place the beats next to the symbol (this symbol now becomes a "clef" sign);

✕ ♩ ♩ ♩ ♩ Two or more instrumental notations would develop a simple score by adding a "triangle clef" to the "clave clef" as illustrated below:

Adding the text to the score would help to indicate the beat for the words and the instruments, and would also illustrate the space necessary for including the subdivisions of the beat. Even a third clef sign indicating the hand drum becomes a logical addition easily accepted by six year-olds.

Here	we	go	round - the	mul-berry	bush;
	1		2	3	4
△	♩		♩	♩	♩
✕	♩		♩	♩	♩
○	♩		♩	♩	♩

Now returning to the previous series of examples, the teacher should repeat that sequence with a soprano or alto xylophone substituted for the "body instrument." First, place only one tone bar on the instrument (the lowest "C" will be satisfactory). Then place only one note on the chalk board and ask a volunteer to play that note on the xylophone, and follow by adding three more notes and have volunteers play the four notes. In the illustration, a simple drawing of a xylophone, to relative scale, will serve as a meaningful clef sign.

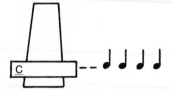

The teacher should add a second tone bar "G" to the instrument and draw the clef sign as illustrated. Also add a second group of four notes.

Finally, add a third tone bar to the instrument and draw the notation as illustrated to the right.

Of course this is indentical to the previous "body instrument" and rhythm exercises, and now the teacher may try to combine these previous exercises by having a

child play the xylophone while other children play the hand drum, claves, and the triangle and the rest of the class use their feet, waist, and shoulders as the teacher points to each group of notes. When this seems fairly well coordinated, then have the children sing the count on the pitches of the xylophone. The xylophone player can play each pitch as the teacher asks the class to sing that pitch.

The above series of exercises may take several weeks for preschool children and perhaps only a few days for youngsters in third grade. The teacher will have to evaluate their progress and not move quicker than their demonstrated abilities. The music specialist should help the teacher in assessing the students' capabilities. All of the above exercises have been successful with four-year-old children.

Art

Art is visual language. It is the silent but dynamic voice of cultures past and present. In one sense it serves as a pictorial history of society; in another sense it serves as a reflector of society today.

We live in a visual world. "Art is one of those things which like air and soil is everywhere about us, but which we rarely stop to consider" (Read, 1945). We tend to confine our concept of art to those objects that drape the walls and decorate the halls of museums and art galleries, rather than to acknowledge that art is part of our daily lives.

Many things are communicated to us through art. The bright wrapping of a candy bar suggests the tasty delights to be found within; the street sign's symbolic representation of children crossing reminds us to slow down and drive more cautiously. As observers we respond, however unconsciously, to these stimuli.

But we are not only observers; we are also creators. We create when we decorate a cake, fashion a doll's house, arrange flowers in a vase, or stack blocks for a playhouse. We experience and participate in art every day even though the quality of our responses and artistic abilities may differ. The greater our repertoire of responses and the more satisfying our efforts at expression, the more comfortably we function.

One of the main goals of education is to help us achieve a sense of harmony and balance with the world around us. "Art education, as an essential part of the educative process, may well mean the difference between a flexible, creative human being and one who will have difficulty relating to his environment" (Lowenfeld & Brittain, 1982).

No early childhood program would be complete without an art component. It is generally agreed that art is an essential part of the curriculum. However, accepting art education in principle does not necessarily insure its effectiveness in practice. Efforts by local, state, and federal agencies to develop, promote, and support an art curriculum are ineffectual unless teachers find significance in art. They must believe that art is as vital to the child's educational development as reading or math. To reach that understanding and then to respond effectively, teachers must appreciate the unique relationship between children and their art and the process that children go through in creating art.

Creative art begins with a mark, a splash, a dab of color carelessly placed and incidentally constructed. At whatever age these dabs and splashes occur, they constitute the beginning of children's creative expression. The further development of artistic expression will depend on the quality of children's experience with art. A large part of that experience will occur in an educational setting. "Teachers and parents need to understand that the creative impulse is like a tender plant to be nourished and valued. Early on the subject of Art is not so much taught as encouraged and not so much learned as experienced" (Bryant, 1983).

For children art is a means of expression, a tool they can use to make visual representations of their world. These representations should not be compared with adult art; their meaning and significance may only be apparent to the children who create them. In developing their artistic abilities, children pass through four stages. According to Lowenfeld and Brittain (1982) these stages are sequential even though different children may reach various stages at different times. A description of each stage helps teachers understand the general characteristics of children and their art at any particular time.

Scribbling.   "Although the child expresses himself vocally very early in life, his first permanent record usually takes the form of a scribble at the age of eighteen months or so" (Lowenfeld & Brittain, 1982). Initially these marks appear randomly and spontaneously, but eventually children will grasp the idea that their motions have some relationship to their marks. For a while they will be preoccupied with perfecting their motor control. Once they have attained that control, the marks themselves will gain meaning and they will start to name their scribbles.

During the scribbling stage children need encouragement and many opportunities to practice. Scribbling should be viewed not as a mindless activity but as the necessary precursor to more elaborate forms of expression.

Preschematic.   At about age four children enter the preschematic stage. During this phase they try to make what they draw stand for something in the real world; they are developing their forms of schema. According to Paine (1949), these symbols will be children's own representations of how they feel about what they see.

Color becomes important during this stage, not because colors bear any relationship to the symbols, but because the use of colors has emotional implications. Blue trees, purple houses, and pink oceans reflect a child's personal taste and should not be treated as improper selections. "Since color is an emotional outlet how could anyone direct what another should see?" (Paine, 1949).

The preschematic stage is characterized by flexibility. In their attempts at representation, children are constantly changing their forms and colors. They draw things according to their understanding and feelings about them; they do not draw things as they look, even to themselves (Bryant, 1983).

Schematic.   The schematic stage lasts from about age seven to age nine. During this stage the children develop their concepts more fully. Their drawings indicate an integration with the environment with regard to space, and their colors are more naturalistic. Their symbols become standardized. According to Lindstrom (1957), all elements of the picture now relate to each other, although the design and composition may not follow conventional rules.

During the schematic stage, through the development of a set of symbols or schema, children are bringing order and structure to their drawings.   "Creative thinking is not disorganized thinking, rather it is the ability to redefine and reorganize in a flexible manner those forms and elements with which we are familiar" (Lowenfeld & Brittain, 1982). As children develop patterns and logical arrangements, they also take their first step towards abstract thinking, which is based entirely on symbols.

Dawning Realism.   This stage lasts from about age nine to age eleven. It represents the beginning of a more adult approach to art. Much of the creative element is lost from children's art when they reach this stage because, according to Paine (1949), they will now attempt to reproduce nature as they see it, not as they feel it.

It is most likely that early childhood teachers will encounter children in either the preschematic or schematic stages, since these stages occur from about age four to nine. Recognizing and understanding the elements of each stage will help the teacher plan a more effective art program. In planning a program teachers must remember that their role is to stimulate and encourage rather than to instruct and define. The lessons should not get in the way of the expression.

"The role of the teacher in helping children increase the range of their perceptual awareness should be that of a catalyst, one who encourages exploration of ways to see, rather than one who directs learning to see" (Paine, 1949). By providing children with the opportunities and materials for expression, the teacher helps them find new ways to deal with their environment, and offers them alternative ways to respond. The more flexible and creative children become, the easier it will be for them to function within their society.

Art Appreciation

When art is approached as a way of life rather than as a subject, the teacher's role is to enlighten rather than to instruct. Helping children see their own world and the natural elements of their environment sponsors growth in their visual reservoir. Exposing children to fine art allows them to experience the effect of these works, gives them opportunities to see how others have approached and solved a "creative" problem, and increases their range of responses when faced with a similar situation.

Perhaps teachers' first step in helping children develop aesthetic tastes is to design their classroom so that it reflects their own appreciation of art. Children's art should be prominently and attractively displayed, art prints and other examples of fine art should appear throughout the classroom, and in general the physical appearance of the room should show a regard for beauty.

Secondly, teachers should strive to promote a creative atmosphere. Children should be given many opportunities to discuss works of art, including their own and that of their peers. They should be allowed to discover how elements of art relate to their environment and how themes of current art projects exist in their surroundings. For example, when collages are introduced children should discuss their own products as well as those of other artists. The illustrations in children's books may be used to demonstrate one way this form of art is currently relevant to them. The celebrated illustrator Marcia Brown believes that the books children see help them form an approach to their visual world of order, rhythm, and interesting arrangement of color (cited in Viguers, 1958).

Finally, teachers should relate art to all aspects of the curriculum. An art element exists in everything that children study, learn about, and produce. Although the most obvious application of art is in the study of cultures and history, the only limitations for melding art and any subject are the self-imposed restrictions that result from a closed mind.

It is only through constant exposure and an expanded awareness that children fully develop their array of artistic devices and establish a set of criteria for judging artistic accomplishments.

Objectives of the Art Program

The purpose of the art program is to allow children opportunities to:

1. identify and discuss art forms.
2. use art to demonstrate concepts, communicate ideas, and express feelings.
3. increase their repertoire of responses to a creative art problem.
4. find pleasure in art as creators and observers.
5. gain experience in using many types of art media.
6. develop and utilize an art vocabulary.
7. recognize the cultural significance and historical value of art.
8. utilize and improve motor skills.
9. develop an awareness of the natural and man-made forms of art that surround them.

Environmental Resources

Storage space: cabinets, shelves, containers, baskets, and boxes should allow the children easy access to a variety of media (it should be well organized to encourage independence).

Containers

    Crates. Nail or screw together coke, pear, or peach crates and paint them.

Files. Obtain a large box and shoe boxes to fit it. Cut off the ends of the shoe boxes but leave the lids on.

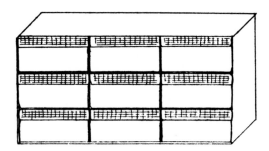

Containers. Obtain 3-gallon ice cream containers. Paint or cover them. Arrange them to allow for easy access by the child.

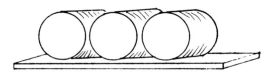 

Cleanup equipment: buckets, sponges, and mops (should be accessible to the children).
Working space: tables, easels, countertops, floor, or outdoor space.
Aprons or substitutes: old shirts, newspaper held with clothespins, or plastic.

Art Supplies

Paper: a wide variety in many sizes and colors

Construction paper
Manila
Fingerpaint paper
Posterboard
Tissue paper
White drawing paper
Butcher block
Newsprint
Architect's drawing paper

General Office Supplies

Scissors: right- and left-handed
Rulers
Paper punch
Brads
Common pins
Stapler and staples
Compasses
Paper clips
Tape
Sticky tack

Marking, Stamping, and Painting Media

Pencils
Paints: tempera, fingerpaint, and water colors
Indian ink and stamp pad
Chalk
Crayons
Food coloring
Magic markers (washable and permanent)
Charcoal

Brushes: a wide variety of sizes and bristle textures

Plaster of Paris

Clay: Natural, modeling, and playdough

Adhesives

White paste
White glue
Rubber cement
Glue sticks

Household Items

Iron, sponges, liquid starch, talcum powder, hair spray, aluminum foil, waxed paper, toothpicks, straws, and needles

Beautiful Junk: Almost anything can be used for an art project, and a wide variety of recyclable materials will extend and enrich an art program:

Cans: coffee, juice, and spice
Boxes of many shapes and sizes
Coat hangers
Telephone wire
Styrofoam trays
Inner tubes
Cloth scraps
Lace and ribbon

Felt
Cord, yard, string, and thread
Blankets and sheets
Magazines, greeting cards, and newspapers
Cardboard
Wallpaper samples
Paper bags
Shells, seeds, dried flowers
Jewelry

Teacher-Made Supplies and Tips

1. *Scissors holders.* Holders can be made from gallon milk or bleach containers. Simply punch holes in the container and place scissors in holes with the points to the inside. Egg cartons turned upside down with slits in each mound also make excellent holders.

2. *Paint containers.* Containers can range from muffin tins and plastic egg cartons to plastic soft drink cartons with baby food jars in them. These work especially well outdoors as well as indoors because they are large and not easily tipped over. Place one brush in each container; this prevents colors from getting mixed and makes cleanup easier.

3. *Crayon containers.* Juice and vegetable cans painted or covered with contact paper work very well.

4. *Cardboard carpentry*
   Clay or crayon tables. Make a table of tri-wall cardboard. Cut a hole in the center of the table for a dishpan so that the dishpan will fit down in the table. Use this dishpan as a common crayon holder or for clay. The dishpan can be easily removed and washed.
   Easels. Easels to use on the floor, a table top, or outside can easily be made from tri-wall by joining two pieces together and using string on the sides to keep it upright and in an inverted "V" shape.

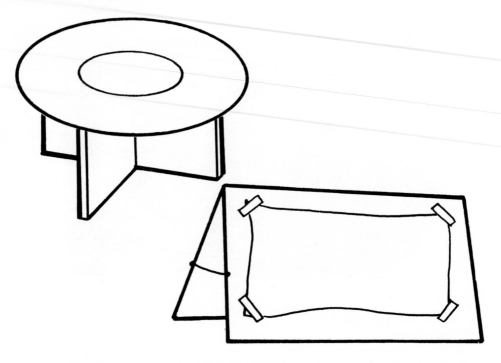

5. *White glue containers.* Glue can be watered down slightly to go farther. Good containers are those with a small tip-up pour spout, such as antibacterial soap containers.
6. Chalk dust problems may be reduced by dampening the paper with liquid starch, thinned white tempera, thinned white glue, thinned wheat paste, or a mixture of 1 part sugar and 2 parts water.
7. Crayon pieces may be melted down in muffin trays in a warm oven. These chubbies or cookies are nice for rubbings.
8. Printing with tempera is easier if the tray is lined with a sponge or paper towel.
9. Splatter paint frames may be constructed by nailing wire screening to a cigar box or wooden frame. Vegetable brushes and toothbrushes make good tools for splatter painting.
10. A card file for art activities helps organize the program.
11. Smocks for painting may be easily made by
    a. cutting an opening for head and arms from the bottom of a trash bag; and
    b. stapling together 3 thicknesses of newspaper front and back and wrapping the newspaper to make a collar and attaching it.

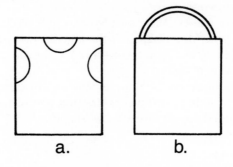

a.   b.

12. *Pottery clay* (if a kiln is not available)
    Pottery clay
    Yellow dextrin
    Mix 1 teaspoon of yellow dextrin to 1 pound of moist clay. Knead the dextrin thoroughly into the clay. It dries quickly, so use it immediately.
13. *Clay containers.* Airtight coffee cans and plastic food containers are excellent ways to keep clay moist and always ready for use.
14. *Sewing storage.* A large box in which smaller boxes containing needles, toothpicks, pins, buttons, lace, ribbons, tape, and elastic can be placed is an easy way to keep sewing materials together.
15. *Paper scrap boxes.* By keeping two or more scrap boxes of paper, children will be able to choose the size paper they want more easily.

Recipes

Salt Paint

⅓ cup salt
¼ tsp. food coloring
Spread in pan to dry.

Sand Paint

½ cup sand (washed, dried, and sifted)
1 tbsp. powdered tempera

Playdough

1 cup flour
1 cup water
1 tbsp. oil
1 tbsp. alum
½ cup salt
2 tbsp. vanilla
food coloring
Mix dry ingredients. Add oil and water. Cook over medium heat until like mashed potatoes. Remove from heat. Add vanilla and color. Divide into balls. Work in color. Store in tightly covered container.

Playdough (uncooked)

4 cups flour mixed with
1 cup salt
Add powdered tempera paint coloring to this mixture.
Add water until the mixture is soft and workable, but not sticky.
Store in an airtight container.

Finger Paint

Liquid starch may be used in combination with powdered paint for color. Add 1 tablespoon glycerin as a preservative and store in an airtight container. (Glycerin can be bought readily at the drugstore and makes an excellent preservative for all types of paints, such an finger and tempera.)

Great Stuff

½ cup corn starch
¼ cup cold water
1 cup salt
½ cup water

Mix ½ cup corn starch and ¼ cup water. Stir 1 cup salt into ½ cup water and heat. Pour heated mixture into corn starch mixture. Mix thoroughly. (Small objects take 2–3 days to dry.)

Soap Bubbles

wire coat hanger
1 tablespoon liquid detergent
2 tablespoons water
4 drops corn syrup
dish

Pour 4 drops of corn syrup into the dish and carefully add the water and detergent. Mix gently. Bend the coat hanger hook to make a loop.

The Basic Elements of Art

Color

Although children manipulate color according to their stage of development, experimenting with color is a pleasurable experience for most children regardless of their expertise. An understanding of the contribution color makes to any composition helps children improve their own use of color.   Pleasing results in design and composition depend on color harmony (Paine, 1949).

To develop their awareness of color children will:

1. identify the primary colors.
2. mix the secondary colors.

3. use color in a variety of ways.
4. describe colors in terms of the emotions they evoke.
5. observe ways others have used color.
6. observe color in nature.

Suggested Activities

Explore

1. Use blue and yellow tempera.
2. Fold a piece of newsprint in half.
3. On one half put a spoonful of blue.
4. On the other half put a spoonful of yellow.
5. Refold.
6. Rub hard across the newsprint.
7. Use circular motions.
8. Open and unfold.
9. You should have created a new color.
   Variation: Use any combination of primary colors.

Color Mix

1. Obtain a mixing tray with three primary colors.
2. Experiment with mixing these colors to form secondary colors.

Color Collage

1. Decide on a color theme.
2. Cut out pictures that color from magazines.
3. Find natural objects that are that color.
4. Glue pictures and objects to construction paper.

Color Walk

1. Get a paper bag.
2. Go outside and collect objects of many colors.
3. Discuss your collection with classmates.

Color Wheel

1. Cut three discs from tissue paper.   (Teacher may precut.)
2. Cut one yellow, one blue, and one red.
3. Arrange on construction paper so they overlap to form the secondary colors.
4. Glue.

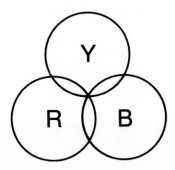

Color Feelings

1. Select a color.
2. Write a sentence to describe your color.
3. Use a sheet of construction paper.
4. Illustrate your sentence, and include pictures of other feelings that you experience when you think of that color.

Children's Literature

Adoff, Arnold. *Black Is Brown Is Tan*. New York: Harper, 1973.
Becker, Edna. *900 Buckets of Paint*. Nashville, Tenn.: Abingdon Press, 1949.
Brown, Margaret. *The Color Kittens*. New York: Golden Press, 1967.
Crews, Donald. *Freight Train*. New York: Greenwillow, 1978.
Emberly, Ed. *Green Says Go*. Boston, Mass.: Little, Brown, 1968.
Grossman, Barney, and Broom, Gladys. *Black Means . . .* New York: Hill and Wang, 1970.
Johnson, Crockett. *Harold and the Purple Crayon*. New York: Harper and Row, 1955.
McGovern, Ann. *Black is Beautiful*. New York: Four Winds Press, 1969.
Miles, Miska. *Apricot ABC*. Boston, Mass.: Little, Brown, 1969.
O'Neil, Mary. *Hailstones and Halibut Bones*. Garden City, N.Y.: Doubleday, 1961.
Tester, Sylvia Root. *A World of Color*. Elgin, Ill.: The Child's World, 1939.

Artists

Cassatt, Mary
Cezanne, Paul
Chagall, Marc
Degas, Edgar
Matisse, Henri
Monet, Claude
O'Keefe, Georgia
Renoir, Pierre Auguste
Wyeth, Andrew

Texture

The three-dimensional quality of a surface is called texture. It may be an intrinsic factor or one that is artificially created. Texture is used and created in many ways in art.

To develop their awareness of texture as a basic element of art, children will:

1. experience, recognize, and describe textures.
2. create textures by using a wide variety of materials.
3. use a variety of textures.
4. observe the textures of natural and man-made objects.
5. observe how others have created and simulated texture in their compositions.

Suggested Activities

Texture Walk

1. Get a piece of newsprint and some crayons. (Chubbies are recommended.)
2. Collect texture rubbings of objects inside and outside the classroom.
3. Cover the object with newsprint.
4. Rub hard over the surface with side of crayon.
5. Discuss your rubbings with classmates.

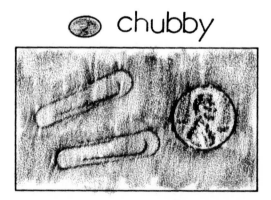

chubby

Texture Rubbings Picture

1. Arrange pieces of precut sandpaper and tagboard on a piece of construction paper.

2. Glue these to paper.
3. Cover with newsprint.
4. Rub over newsprint with side of crayon.

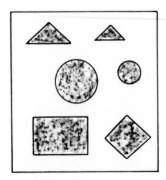

Sand Painting

1. Paint a picture with white glue.
2. Use brush or Q-tip to apply.
3. Sprinkle with colored sand.

Tray Art

1. Draw designs in a tray filled with flour, salt, cornmeal, or sand.
2. Use your fingers and other objects.

Flour Pictures

1. Spread 1 cup of flour on tray

2. Draw a picture with your finger.

3. Use the objects to decorate.

Fluffy Pictures

1. Decide on an animal or shape to make.
2. Suggestions are lambs, clouds, ducks, or chicks.
3. Use cotton balls.
4. Color the balls if desired by shaking them in a bag with a little dry tempera.
5. Glue balls to construction paper.
6. Add detail with crayons and magic markers.

Cutting Texture

1. Fold 3″ × 4″ piece of fadeless paper into a triangle.
2. Make 2–3 diagonal slits along the fold.
3. Unfold paper and lay it flat.
4. Each cut will have formed a triangle.
5. Gently pull the point of one triangle down.
6. Pull down as far as it will go.
7. Crease it on the fold.
8. Repeat until all slits are folded.
9. Mount on construction paper.

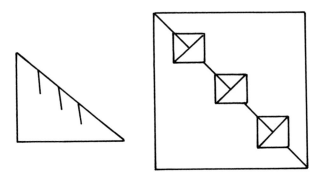

Texture Collection

1. Select a texture theme (soft, hard, smooth, rough, etc.).
2. Find objects at home and in the classroom that have that texture.
3. Display your collection in the classroom.
4. Discuss your collection with classmates.

Children's Literature

Gibson, M. T. *What Is Your Favorite Thing to Touch?* New York: Grosset & Dunlap, 1965.
Levitin, Sonia. *A Single Speckled Egg.* New York: Paranassus, 1976.
Showers, Paul. *Find Out by Touching.* New York: Thomas Y. Crowell, 1961.

Artists

Gaugin, Paul
Picasso, Pablo
Seurat, Georges

Line

Children can be encouraged to see lines as they exist in nature and as they occur in deliberate patterns and forms. "Take a walk with a line" is the encouragement that artist Paul Klee offered his students (cited in Moore, 1968).

Lines have direction and destination; they create rhythm and movement. They are one of the basic elements of art.

To develop their ability to see and use line within a composition, children will:

1. describe lines as wide, thin, zigzag, crooked, etc.
2. use lines to create a sense of movement.
3. use lines to create overall patterns.
4. observe how others have used the line element within their compositions.
5. observe lines as they occur in nature.

Suggested Activities

String Print Line Design

1. Wrap string randomly around a block of wood.
2. Paint the string with tempera.
3. Press the painted side against a sheet of newsprint.
4. Repeat until design is completed.

(wrapped wood)

Design Lines

1. Make brushes by notching the ends of strips of cardboard.
2. Dip the tips of these brushes into tempera.
3. Touch or drag the brush across a sheet of construction paper.
4. Repeat until the design is completed.

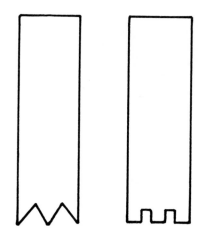

Abstract Line Design

1. Scribble with black crayon on construction paper.
2. Make big scribbles and thick, dark lines.
3. Do not let scribbles touch the edges.
4. Color each space with crayon.
5. Cut around the scribble.
6. Glue onto construction paper.

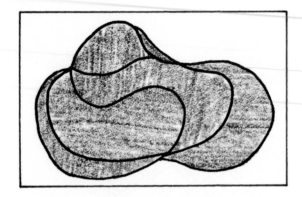

Spiderweb Catch

1. Locate a spiderweb.
2. Sprinkle it with talcum powder.
3. Carefully lift it onto a piece of black construction paper.
4. Ask the teacher to spray web with a fixative.

Children's Literature

Downer, Marion. *Discovering Design.* New York: Lothrop, Lee and Shepard Co., 1947.
Zemach, Margot, ed. *It Could Always Be Worse.* New York: Farrar, 1976.

Artists

Klee, Paul
Matisse, Henri
Miro, Joan
Van Gogh, Vincent

Shape

Shape is important to the composition of design and a necessary tool for visual expression of ideas. An understanding of shapes and their function in design is important in children's artistic development.

To develop their awareness of shapes, children will:

1. identify geometric shapes.
2. use shapes to create designs.
3. observe the shape of natural and man-made objects.
4. observe how others have used shapes and form in their compositions.

Suggested Activities

Shape Pictures

1. Cut out a collection of geometric shapes. (Teacher may precut.)
2. Arrange these on construction paper to form a design.
3. Glue.

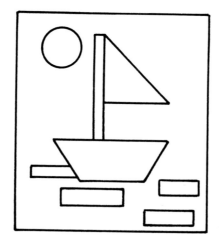

Sponge Pictures

1. Use sponges that are precut into geometric shapes.
2. Dip sponges in tempera.
3. Print by pressing sponge onto construction paper.
4. Fill the paper with your design.

Stamp Pictures

1. Use alphabet or number stamps.
2. Select one stamp.

3. Press stamp onto stamp pad.
4. Press onto construction paper.
5. Repeat.
6. Fill the paper with a design.

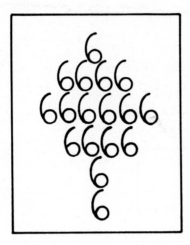

Magazine Hunt

1. Select a shape as a theme.
2. Look in magazines.
3. Cut out pictures of that shape.
4. Arrange pictures on construction paper.
5. Glue.
   Variation: Outline the shapes with black crayon.

Children's Literature

Emberly, Ed. *The Wing on a Flea.* Boston: Little, Brown, 1961.
Lerner, Sharon. *Square Is a Shape.* Minneapolis, Minn.: Lerner Press, 1974.
Lewis, Stephen. *Zoo City.* New York: Greenwillow Books, 1976.
Reiss, John J. *Shapes.* Scarsdale, N.Y.: Bradbury Press Inc., 1974.

Schlein, Miriam. *Shapes.* Reading, Mass.: Addison-Wesley, 1952.
Seuss, Dr. *The Shape of Me and Other Stuff.* New York: Beginner Books, 1973.

Artists

Albers, Malevich
Braque, Georges
Klee, Paul
Matisse, Henri
Mondrian, Piet
Picasso, Pablo

Space Relationships

In a well-constructed composition the proportions are balanced and varied. Equal importance is placed on used and unused space (Paine, 1949). All elements relate to one another to create a harmonious design.

An understanding of these concepts is basic to children's artistic development. The better their grasp of these ideas, the more flexible their responses.

To develop their awareness of space relationships, children will:

1. explore the concept of negative space.
2. experiment with ways to create large and small spaces.
3. develop concepts of over/under, inside/outside, near/far, etc.
4. use these concepts in solving "creative" problems.
5. observe how others have manipulated space relationships in their compositions.

Suggested Activities

Space Walk

1. Participate in a class space walk.
2. Walk around inside and outside.
3. Observe the spaces you pass through.
4. Discuss the walk with your classmates.

Negative/Positive Pictures

1. Get a piece of 9 × 12 construction paper and a 6 × 9 piece of fadeless paper. (Fadeless is preferred because it has a white back.)
2. Select contrasting colors.
3. Cut into the smaller piece on the long edge.
4. Go in and out on the same edge.
5. Do not cut through other edges.
6. Match negative to positive in the center of the construction paper.
7. Glue.
   Variation: Cut smaller piece of paper in half. Place two halves together and cut. Arrange accordingly.

Expanded Geometric Shapes

1. Select a geometric shape from precut shapes.
2. Cut the shape apart in parallel sections.
3. Select a piece of construction paper in contrasting color.

4. Arrange sections in order on construction paper.
5. Leave space between each section.
6. Glue.

Pizza

1. Get a cardboard circle.
2. Cut out pizza toppings from scrap paper.
3. Mix dry red tempera with liquid starch.
4. Brush tempera onto cardboard.
5. Put on toppings.
6. Sprinkle top with cornmeal "cheese."

Overlapping Paper Picture

1. Decide on a theme: suggestions are city buildings, cars on a street, crowds of people, etc.
2. Cut objects out of scrap paper.
3. Arrange objects so that they overlap to create a realistic design.
4. Glue to construction paper.

Children's Literature

Macauley, David. *Castle.* Boston, Mass.: Houghton Mifflin, 1977.
————. *Cathedral.* Boston, Mass.: Houghton Mifflin, 1973.
————. *Underground.* Boston, Mass.: Houghton Mifflin, 1976.

Artists

Léger, Fernand
Mû Ch'i
Rembrandt, Van Rijn

Art Media

Crayons

Crayons are an excellent and commonly used tool for elementary children. Each child should have many opportunities to explore the use of crayons.
To develop their skill in using crayons, children will:

1. experiment with ways to manipulate crayons to achieve different effects.
2. create textural effects by varying the degree of thickness with which color is applied.
3. use this medium with other media.
4. observe ways others have used crayon in their compositions.

Suggested Activities

Rainbows

1. Get a piece of newsprint.
2. Experiment with using the flat side of a crayon to make broad strokes.

3. Practice.
4. Get a sheet of white drawing paper.
5. Use flat side of crayons to make a rainbow.

Crayon Texture

1. Draw with crayon on a piece of precut sandpaper.
2. Cover sandpaper with white paper.
3. Ask the teacher to press this with a warm iron.
4. Two pictures will result.
5. Mount both on construction paper.
6. Glue.

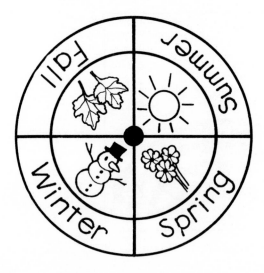

Family Portrait

1. Get a piece of paper.
2. Use crayon to draw a family portrait.
3. Explore various ways to use crayons to make thin and thick lines, dots, etc.

Season Wheel

1. Cut two unequal size circles from construction paper.
2. One circle should be about an inch larger than the other.
3. Join two circles in center with a brad.
4. Divide each circle into four sections.
5. On each outside segment print the name of one of the four seasons.
6. Decorate each inner segment with symbols of that season.

Indian Tepees

1. Cut paper bags into triangles.
2. Use crayons to decorate each triangle with Indian symbols.
3. Arrange various size tepees on construction paper.
4. Glue.
5. Create background of Indian village with crayon.

Frosty Picture

Caution: Epsom salts are poisonous.

1. Get a piece of blue construction paper.
2. Use crayon to draw a snowy day picture.
3. Paint over this with an Epsom salt mixture. (4 oz. Epsom salts dissolved in 1 pint hot water.)
4. Crystals will appear on surface.

Snakes

1. Get a white paper plate.
2. Color both sides with crayon.
3. Cut each plate around and around in a spiral.
4. Draw an eye on one end.

Children's Literature

Goble, Paul. *The Girl Who Loved Wild Horses.* Scarsdale, N.Y.: Bradbury, 1978.
Keats, Ezra Jack. *A Snowy Day.* New York: Greenwillow Books, 1963.

Artists

Hoffman, Hans
Picasso, Pablo

Tempera

Tempera is another commonly used art medium for young children. Children can use tempera to paint, print, wash, etc.

To develop their ability to use tempera in a variety of ways, children will:

1. manipulate a brush using tempera.
2. explore the many ways to use tempera.
3. use tempera with a wide variety of other media.
4. observe how others have used tempera.

Suggested Activities

Explore

1. Get a piece of newsprint.
2. Use tempera and a variety of brushes.
3. For brushes include pine branches, Q-tips, scouring pads, bones, feathers, etc.
4. Experiment with making different kinds of lines.

Accidental Design

1. Fold a piece of construction paper in half.
2. Spoon a blob of tempera on one half.
3. Refold.
4. Rub hand over paper.
5. Open.
6. Name the shape you have made.

Blown Painting

1. Get a piece of construction paper.
2. At one end put a spoonful of runny tempera.
3. Blow through a straw to make tempera flow in many directions.

Rain Paintings

1. Sprinkle 2–3 different colors of dry tempera on construction paper.
2. Set paper outside in rain.
3. Watch the rain do the painting.

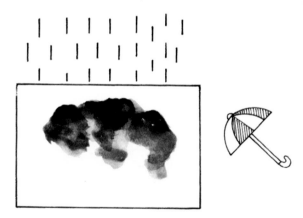

Tempera Wash

1. Use crayons to create a jungle picture.
2. Apply a heavy coating of crayon by pressing hard.
3. "Wash" over drawing with sponge or brush dipped in diluted green tempera.

Tempera Prints

1. Line a tray with a paper towel or a sponge.
2. Pour in thick tempera paint.
3. Arrange an assortment of beautiful junk (bolts,, nuts, spools, etc.).
4. Dip an object in tempera.
5. Print on newsprint.
6. Experiment.
7. Get a piece of construction paper.
8. Create an overall design by printing with beautiful junk.

Tempera Stencil

1. Fold a piece of waxed paper or construction paper into a rectangle.
2. Cut out pieces along the fold.
3. Open and flatten paper.
4. Tape cut paper to another piece of construction paper.
5. Make a pounce by wrapping several cotton balls in a small piece of cotton cloth and closing with a rubber band. (See discussion of pouncing below.)
6. Pour tempera into tray lined with sponge or paper towel.
7. Dip pouncer into tempera.
8. Remove excess paint by printing first on newsprint.
9. Lightly pounce color over stencil.
10. Remove stencil.

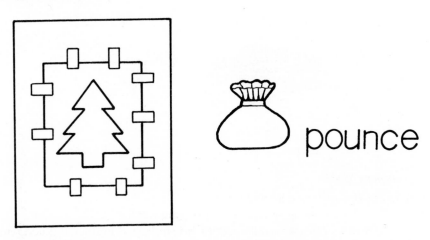

Pouncing

This process would fit nicely into kindergarten or first grade if used in its simplest form. In advanced techniques it can be used by older children.

Touch the pouncer in the paint first, then on folded newspaper to unload excess paint and spread it evenly over the surface of the tool. Then lightly pounce the color over pattern in the stencil. More than one color may be used if each is used lightly.

Pulverized chalk or dry tempera may be used in place of the paint, except that a rubbing motion may be necessary with the pouncer.

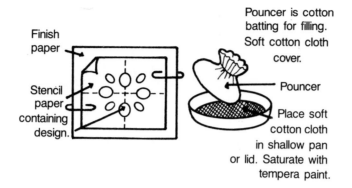

Finish paper

Stencil paper containing design.

Pouncer is cotton batting for filling. Soft cotton cloth cover.

Pouncer

Place soft cotton cloth in shallow pan or lid. Saturate with tempera paint.

Tempra Painting

1. Get a piece of newsprint.
2. Explore using brushes of different textures and widths.
3. Hold the brushes at different angles to see what effect this has on your mark.
4. Get a piece of construction paper.
5. Use different brushes and colors to create a picture of yourself.

Tempera Rubber Cement Resist

1. Paint a picture using rubber cement.
2. Allow to dry.
3. Paint over the cement with tempera.
4. Allow to dry.
5. Use eraser to remove rubber cement.

Children's Literature

Lewis, Stephen. *Zoo City.* New York: Greenwillow Books, 1976.

Artists

Cassatt, Mary   Degas, Edgar
Cezanne, Paul   Renoir, Pierre Auguste
Chagall, Marc

Chalk

Chalk is a popular drawing material that offers many possibilities for expression. To develop their ability to effectively use chalk, children will:

1. explore the different ways to use chalk to create lines, texture, and shades.
2. experiment with blending colors of chalk.
3. use chalk with other media.
4. observe how others have used chalk as a tool for expression.

Suggested Activities

Explore

1. Get a piece of newsprint.
2. Explore ways to grasp and position chalk.
3. Experiment with making different marks.
4. Note the effect your grasp and chalk position has on your mark.

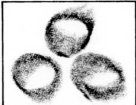

Use side to make circles.

Use tip to make dots.

Chalk Picture

1. Experiment with using chalk to create a picture.
2. Try blending some of the colors.
3. Try to use different ways of grasping the chalk.
4. Make circles, dots, thick lines, and thin lines.

Use side to make wide lines.

Use tip to make thin lines.

Cave Drawing

1. Wrinkle a piece of brown paper.
2. Use chalk to create a cave drawing.
3. Ask teacher to spray with hair spray or other fixative.

Children's Literature

Bate, Norman. *When Cave Men Painted.* New York: Charles Scribner's Sons, 1963.

Artists

Cassatt, Mary
Degas, Edgar
Renoir, Pierre Auguste
Reubens, Peter Paul

Clay

Clay is a versatile, inexpensive material that has high appeal. Children enjoy manipulating clay and experimenting with its plastic properties. It is a texturally pleasing and responsive medium that has many uses in the art curriculum.

To develop their ability to use clay, children will:

1. explore the properties of clay.
2. experiment with manipulating clay.
3. shape and form objects from clay.
4. use clay in a variety of ways.
5. observe how others have manipulated and used clay as a means of expression.

Suggested Activities

Explore

1. Obtain a ball of clay, playdough, or great stuff.
2. Experiment with the clay by twisting, pulling, pressing, etc.
3. Make a 3-dimensional object.

Fossil Print

1. Roll out a ball of clay until it is about ¼ inch thick. (Use a rolling pin or round can.)
2. Press the ribbed side of a shell into the clay.
3. Let the print dry.
   Variation: Put dried weeds on waxed paper. Press clay into weeds.

High-Relief Sculpture

1. Roll out a ball of clay until it is about ½ inch thick.
2. Make a circle as large around as a dinner plate.
3. Crumple a piece of newspaper into a ball.
4. Center clay slab on top of ball.
5. The center represents your face.
6. Create facial detail by imprinting and adding on pieces of clay.
7. Let dry.

Clay Slab Shapes

1. Roll out a piece of clay until is is about ¼ inch thick.
2. Use cookie cutters or dull knife to cut out shapes.
3. Create texture by imprinting and adding clay.
4. Allow to dry.
5. Paint with tempera if desired.

Clay Beads

1. Roll bits of clay into ¼ inch balls.
2. Pierce each ball through the center using a needle or opened paper clip.
3. Allow to dry.
4. Decorate with magic marker or tempera.
5. Use with paper beads (see Thanksgiving project), colored pasta, or dyed seeds to make an Indian necklace.

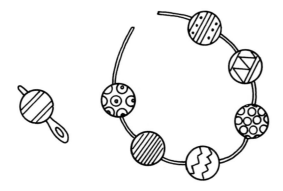

Children's Literature

Hawkinson, John. *A Ball of Clay.* Chicago: Albert Whitman & Co., 1974.
Price, Christine. *Arts of Clay.* New York: Charles Scribner's Sons, 1977.
Val Baker, Denys. *The Young Potter.* New York: Frederick Warne Co., 1963.

Artists

Artigas, Jose
Miro, Joan

Art Methods

Collage

Collages are a fun way for children to express ideas. The word *collage* comes from the French verb *coller,* meaning to stick. Collages are created by sticking pieces of paper, cloth, etc. to a background. They are useful for improving the child's sense of pattern, color, and texture.

To develop their ability to use collages children will:

1. explore ways to create design using a variety of materials.
2. observe how others have used the collage format.

Suggested Activities

Nature Collage

1. Collect assorted natural materials (seeds, pods, twigs, leaves, etc.).
2. Arrange on heavy cardboard or tagboard.
3. Glue with white glue.

Face Collage

1. Get a small paper plate.
2. Use beautiful junk to create a face on the plate.
3. Glue with white glue.

Seed Collage

1. Press a ball of great stuff or playdough into a plastic lid.
2. Arrange seeds and beans on top of playdough.
3. Press seeds into playdough.
4. Allow to dry.

"I" Collage

1. Cut a big capital "I" from butcher block paper. (Teacher may precut.)
2. Fill it with pictures, drawings, and words that represent things you can do.

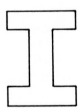

Patchwork Collage

1. Divide a piece of cardboard into several rectangular spaces using a pencil and ruler.

2. Fill each rectangle with one type of beautiful junk.
3. Glue with white glue.

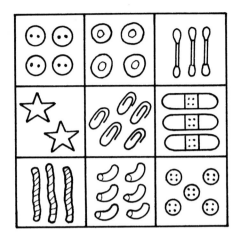

Tissue Paper Collage

1. Lay a piece of plastic wrap on a 9×12 piece of newsprint.
2. Paint the plastic with a mixture of ½ glue to ½ water.
3. Tear tissue paper into irregular shapes.
4. Lay tissue on glue covered wrap.
5. Overlap tissue paper until entire piece of wrap is covered.
6. Allow to dry overnight.
7. Peel wrap from tissue paper.
8. Hang finished products in the window.

Children's Literature

Brown, Marcia. *Shadow.* New York: Charles Scribner's Sons, 1982.
Fisher, Aileen Lucia. *Do Bears Have Mothers, Too?* New York: Crowell, 1973.
Keats, Ezra Jack. *Louis.* New York: Greenwillow, 1975.
———. *The Snowy Day.* New York: Scholastic Book Service, 1971.
McDermott, Gerald. *The Stonecutter.* New York: Viking Press, 1975.

Artists

Braque, Georges
Matisse, Henri
Picasso, Pablo

Weaving

Weaving allows children to work with many textures and colors and to develop the over/under concept of the process. With teacher assistance, children can make simple looms from paper, cardboard, onion sacks, etc.

To develop their ability to use weaving children will:

1. practice weaving.
2. use weaving to create designs and products.
3. make simple looms.
4. observe how others have used weaving for creative expression.

Suggested Activities

Paper Looms

1. Fold a piece of 12 × 18 construction paper in half.
2. Beginning on the fold make cuts.
3. Stop 2 inches from the top.

fold

Cardboard Looms

1. Measure and draw a line across top and bottom of a piece of cardboard about ½ inch from the edge.
2. Cut an uneven number of slits from the edge to the line at about ½ inch intervals.
3. Cut top and bottom.
4. Begin warping by pulling string through the first slit at top of loom.
5. Tape string to back of loom.
6. Carry string across front of loom to first slit at bottom of loom.
7. Go behind tab created by first and second slits.
8. Carry string across front of loom to second slit at top.
9. Repeat until all slits are used. Tape string to back of loom.

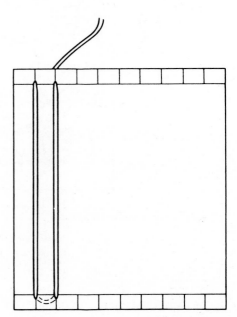

Yarn Weaving

1. Make a cardboard loom.
2. Use yarn for warp and weft.
3. Weave.
4. Tie yarn ends together in back.
5. Slip woven piece off loom.
6. Insert a dowel and use as a wall hanging.
   Variation: Weave in dried grasses and other natural materials.

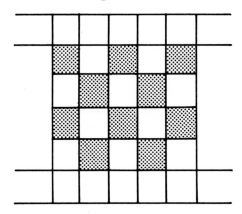

Placemat

1. Make a paper loom.
2. Cut strips of construction paper slightly longer than loom.
3. Use strips to weave.
4. Trim ends and glue.

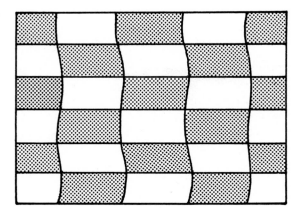

Magazine Photo

1. Make a paper loom.
2. Cut a large photograph from a magazine.
3. Cut a strip from the photo.
4. Use strip to weave. (Strip is the weft.)
5. To avoid confusion weave each strip before cutting the next.
6. Cut strips in succession.
   Note: Use magazines with high quality paper (*National Geographic,* for example).

Artists

Albers, Anni

Printing

Printing is another way of creating art that can extend children's array of artistic devices.

To develop their ability to use printing, children will:

1. experiment with different ways to print.
2. create designs and patterns using printing.
3. observe how others have used printing as a method of expression.

Suggested Activities

Fingerprints

1. Get a sheet of newsprint.
2. Press one of your fingers onto a stamp pad or onto a tray filled with thickened tempera.
3. Press your finger onto the newsprint.
4. Experiment. Use different fingers, etc.
5. Add details with magic markers and crayons.

Monoprints

1. Apply fingerpaint to a washable surface.
2. Use fingers, Q-tips, and brush tips to draw a picture.
3. Cover the picture with fingerpaint paper (shiny side down).
4. Rub over the paper.
5. Remove.
6. Your picture has been printed on the paper.
   Note: A plastic cutting board makes a good washable surface.

Styrofoam Prints

1. Get a styrofoam tray.
2. Draw a picture using permanent magic markers.

3. These markers will dissolve the foam.
4. Use a brush or sponge to apply a thin layer of tempera to the surface of the tray.
5. Place a piece of construction paper over tempera.
6. Rub.

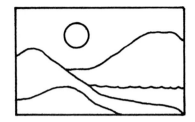

Vegetable/Fruit Prints

1. Use any variety of halved and quartered fruits or vegetables.
2. Select one and press cut surface into a tray of tempera.
3. Press on newsprint.
4. Experiment.
5. Create different shapes and designs.
6. Get a piece of construction paper.
7. Print an overall pattern or design.

Children's Literature

Baker, Betty. *And Me, Coyote.* New York: Macmillan Publishing Co., 1982.
Brown, Marcia. *All Butterflies.* New York: Charles Scribner's Sons, 1974.
Gag, Wanda. *Millions of Cats.* New York: Coward-McCann, Inc., 1928.
Katz, Marjorie. *Fingerprint Owls and Other Fantasies.* New York: M. Evans and Company, 1972.
MacStravic, Suellen. *Print Making.* Minneapolis, Minn.: Lerner Publishing Co., 1973.
Rockwell, Harlow. *Printmaking.* Garden City, N.Y.: Doubleday & Co., 1973.

Sculpture

Sculpture is the creation of three-dimensional objects by taking from, adding to, or assembling materials (Lansing & Richards, 1981). It is yet another vehicle for the expression and communication of ideas.

To develop their ability to use sculpture, children will:

1. create three-dimensional objects using a variety of materials.
2. observe how others have used sculpture as a means of expression.

Suggested Activities

Animals

1. Gather a collection of beautiful junk (scraps of wood, paper, towel rolls, nuts, bolts, etc.).
2. Arrange pieces to create a 3-dimensional animal.
3. Glue pieces together with white glue.

Cities/Neighborhoods

1. Arrange various size boxes to create a setting.
2. The boxes may be houses or office buildings.
3. Glue boxes together with white glue.
4. Paint with tempera.
5. Decorate with beautiful junk and crayons.

Paper Sculpture

1. Experiment with cutting, rolling, curling, and folding paper scraps so they are not flat.
2. Arrange on construction paper.
3. Glue.

Eskimo Mask

1. Get a white paper plate for the center.
2. Use crayon and scraps to make your face on the plate.
3. Glue 5 popsicle sticks to the back of the plate.
4. Allow sticks to project around the edge of the plate.
5. Decide on 5 things you would like to be better at doing. (This is a lucky mask.)
6. Use paper scraps to make a symbol for each of these 5 things.
7. Glue each symbol to the end of one of the popsicle sticks.

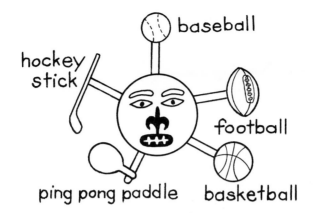

Totem Pole

1. Experiment with stacking various boxes to form a totem pole.
2. Glue boxes together with white glue.
3. Paint with tempera.
4. Decorate with paper.

Edible Sculpture

1. Use vegetables and fruits.
2. Use toothpicks to hold pieces together.
3. Make an animal, person, or object.

Children's Literature

Comins, Jeremy. *Eskimo Crafts and Their Cultural Backgrounds.* New York: Lothrop, Lee and Shepard, 1975.

Glubock, Shirley. *The Art of the Southwest Indians.* New York: Macmillan Publishing Co., 1971.

Hammond, Penny, and Thomas, Katrina. *My Skyscraper City.* Garden City, N.Y.: Doubleday, 1963.

Oppenheim, Joanne. *Have You Seen Roads?* New York: Young Scott Books, 1969.

Artists

Arp, Jean
da Vinci, Leonardo
Marisol, Escobar
Nevelson, Louise
Rodin, Auguste

Stitchery

Even though children may not be able to perform intricate stitches, they enjoy and are able to do simple sewing projects.

To develop beginning skills in sewing, children will:

1. use sewing as a way of creating.
2. sew on a variety of materials.
3. observe how others have used sewing as a method of expression.

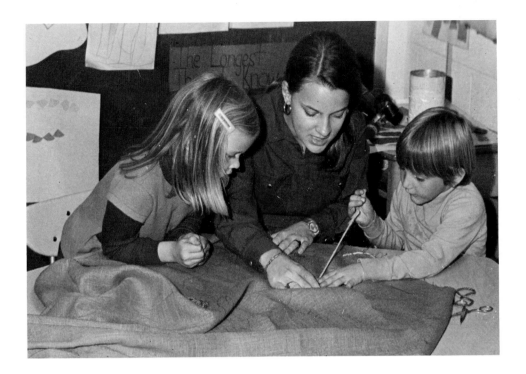

Suggested Activities

Burlap Names

1. Print your name on a piece of burlap with a magic marker.
2. Thread a large, blunt needle with yarn.
3. Sew around outline of your name with yarn.

Wire Screen Picture

1. Get a piece of wire screen that has been precut and taped around the edges.
2. Thread a large blunt needle with yarn.
3. Go in and out of the holes in the screen with the needle.
4. Use different colors of yarn.

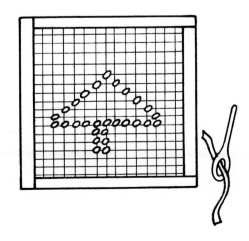

Sewing Cards

1. Get a piece of stiff paper or cardboard.
2. Use a hole punch to make holes around edges.
3. Thread large, blunt needle with yarn.
4. Sew by going in and out of the holes.

Miscellaneous Activities

Murals. Murals are large pictures. The average classroom mural is from four to eight feet long. Younger children do not view a mural activity as a cooperative adventure. However, by the third grade, children can plan and work together on a mural. It should be emphasized to the students that, whatever the chosen topic, it should allow for several students to work on it.

Suggested mural topics include
    People walking in a city
    Children playing games on the playground
    Children getting on a bus
    Books I have liked
    A trip under water
    A parade
    Circus acts

Bookbinding. Children like to make books to display their pictures or stories. Sharing their books can increase their self-esteem and pride in "writing" their own book.

Open-fold books. Use cardboard of various sizes, staples, thread, and colored tape. Cloth is taped to the cardboard to make the back. (Contact paper may also be used.) The pages can be stapled or sewn to the spine.

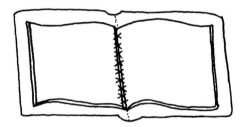

Accordian books. The child glues or staples his or her work to pieces of covered cardboard. The pieces can be sewn together.

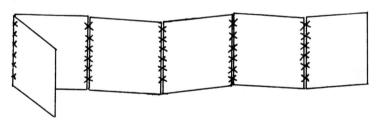

Puppets. Children enjoy not only making puppets but also performing, watching, and listening to puppets. They like to create their own puppet characters. "Beautiful junk" can be used to decorate, dress, and enhance the "personality" of the puppet. A simple puppet rack is handy for the storing and safekeeping

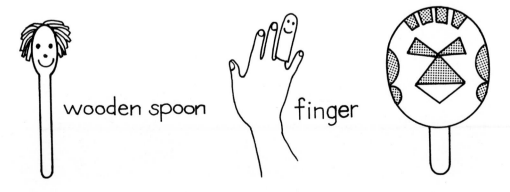

wooden spoon   finger

of puppets. To make one, use small/large detergent bottles bolted to scrap lumber.

Types of puppets for children to make include

Wooden spoon puppets
Cardboard tube puppets
Mask puppets
Vegetable puppets
Plastic bottle puppets
Finger puppets
Paper bag puppets
Tree/limb/root puppets (let the children go out and find the limb/root form that they would like to use to create their character)

paper bag

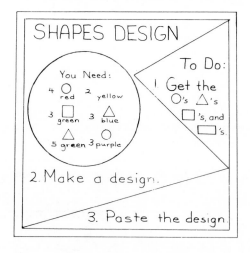

Activity Cards

Teacher-made art activity cards can contain directions for a specific project or a general suggestion to stimualte creative activity.

SHAPES DESIGN

You Need:
4 ◯ red   2 △ yellow
3 ☐ green   3 △ blue
5 △ green   3 ◯ purple

To Do:
1. Get the ◯'s △'s ☐'s, and ▭'s.
2. Make a design.
3. Paste the design.

GREEN MONTAGE

You Need: ✂ scissors   🖊 paste   ☐ paper
📄📄 magazines

To Do:
1. Cut out green pictures ✂
2. Paste them on your paper. 🖊 ☐
3. Put your trash 🗑 in the ▽ trash can.

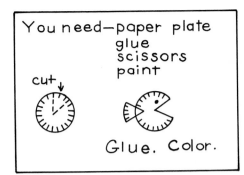

Holiday and Seasonal Activities

Fall

Leaf People

1. Use construction paper for background.
2. Trace around collected leaves.
3. Arrange tracings to create a design.
4. Use crayon and magic markers to make leaf shapes into people.

Leaf Print

1. Arrange collected leaves on construction paper.
2. Place arrangement under splatter paint screen.
3. Dip vegetable brush or toothbrush in tempera.
4. Draw brush across screen to make paint splatter.
5. Remove from screen.
6. Lift off leaves.

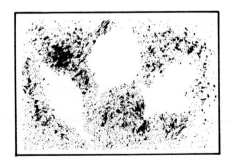

Pumpkin Patch

1. Use white glue to draw a pumpkin patch on construction paper.
2. Shake cotton balls in paper bag with a little dry, orange tempera.
3. Press balls onto glued surface.
4. Twist around pumpkins with a piece of green yarn to create a vine.

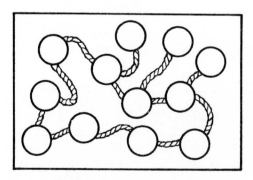

Fall Trees

1. Get a piece of blue construction paper.
2. Use brown crayon to draw a tree trunk and branches.
3. Dip sponges in trays of orange, red, and yellow tempera.
4. Print by pressing sponge on paper.
5. Repeat to form leaves on tree.
   Variation: Use brown shoe polish to draw tree trunk and branches.

Columbus Day: Ship in a bottle

1. Cut a bottle shape from blue construction paper.
2. Use scraps of brown, black, and white construction paper to design a sailing ship.
3. Add detail with crayon and magic marker.
4. Glue ship onto bottle shape.
5. Cover the entire front with a piece of plastic wrap and tape to back.

Columbus Day: Sailing ships

1. Use ½ walnut shell.
2. Place a small dab of clay in shell.
3. Glue a white triangular sail to a toothpick.
4. Insert toothpick into clay.
5. Try sailing your ship in a basin of water.

Halloween: Scary night

1. Use crayons to draw a Halloween picture.
2. Press down hard with crayon and use bright colors.
3. Use a sponge or brush to "wash" over picture with diluted tempera.
   Note: Craypas work well.

Halloween: Spiderweb

1. Line a round cake tin with a piece of black construction paper.
2. Place a tablespoon of white glue in the center of the paper.
3. Put a marble in the pan.
4. Roll the marble around to create a spiderweb effect.

Halloween: Ghost print

1. Spread a tablespoon of white tempera on a washable surface.
2. Smooth out the paint with your hand.
3. Use fingers to create 2 eyes and a mouth.
4. Cover with a sheet of black paper.
5. Rub across the back of the paper with your hand.
6. Lift off paper.

Halloween: Bouncing spiders

1. Tie 4 six-inch pieces of black yarn in the middle with a 12-inch piece of black yarn.
2. Wrap a ball of clay around the center.
3. Cover the knot with clay.
4. Let the short ends of the yarn stick out of the clay to form the spider's legs.
5. Allow to dry.
6. Bounce spider from 12-inch piece of yarn.

Thanksgiving: Handful of thanks

1. Use bright colored construction paper.
2. Trace around your hand with a crayon.
3. On each finger print something for which you are thankful.

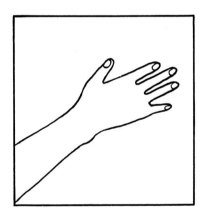

Thanksgiving: Indian Necklace

1. Cut small triangles and rectangles from magazine pictures.
2. Roll these shapes over a knitting needle and secure ends with glue.
3. Allow to dry.
4. Slip off needle.
5. Shellac if desired.
6. String with clay beads and colored pasta to make a necklace.

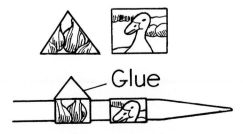

Thanksgiving: Mural

1. Work with classmates.
2. Create a mural of the first Thanksgiving.
3. Use a long sheet of butcher block paper.
4. Use tempera to paint figures.
5. Glue on paper figures.

Thanksgiving: Pinecone Turkey

1. Lay a pinecone on its side.
2. Cut feathers from construction paper.
3. Glue feathers on to pinecone.
4. Cut head and neck from scraps.
5. Glue onto body.

Thanksgiving: Melon-seed necklace

1. Wash the seeds from a honeydew melon or a canteloupe.
2. Put seeds into a bowl.
3. Add food coloring.
4. Let sit for a little while.
5. Remove seeds and allow to dry overnight on a paper towel.
6. Thread a needle with thin dental floss.
7. String seeds.

Winter

Ice Cube Pictures

1. Fill ice cube trays with water.
2. Insert a popsicle stick into each cube.
3. Freeze (outside if possible).
4. Cover table with newspaper.

5. Sprinkle dry tempera onto fingerpaint paper.
6. Rub ice cube over paint.
7. Watch the ice melt into color.

Torn Paper Snowman

1. Tear pieces of white construction paper into 3 large snowball shapes.
2. Arrange pieces on blue construction paper to make a snowman.
3. Glue.
4. Add detail with paper and cloth scraps and chalk.

Snow Scapes

1. Press playdough into margarine lid.
2. Stick 2–3 pinecones into play dough.
3. Spray cones with snow spray.
4. Cut out paper figures and add to snow scene.

Hanukkah: Star of David

1. Cut out 2 blue triangles from construction paper.
2. Paste one over the other to form a Star of David.
3. Glue to construction paper or hang from string.

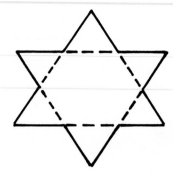

Hanukkah: Menorah

1. Roll out an 8-inch snake from playdough.
2. Press snake down on a 1″ × 8″ strip of cardboard.
3. Put one tall candle in center.
4. Put 4 smaller candles on each side.

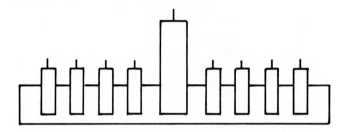

Holiday Cards

1. Fold a 6 × 9 piece of green construction paper in half.
2. Cut out a large triangle to fit on the front of the card.
3. Put the card in the splatter paint frame.
4. Splatter with white tempera by drawing brush across screen.
5. Remove card.
   Variation: For Hanukkah use the Star of David (see above) on blue paper.

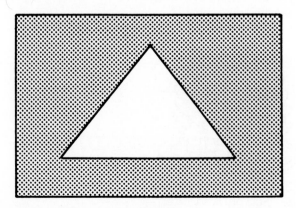

Holiday Wrapping Paper: Printed paper

1. Use halved or quartered fruits or vegetables.
2. Dip selected item in tray of thick tempera.

3. Press onto white tissue paper.
4. Repeat until overall design is created.

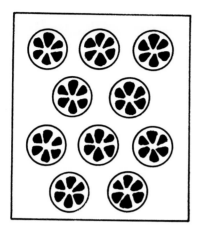

Holiday Wrapping Paper: Dyed paper

1. Fold a piece of white tissue paper into a small rectangle.
2. Dip corners into food coloring or watercolor.
3. Allow colors to bleed and mix.
4. Open paper carefully and allow to dry.

Holiday Gifts: Wall Plaque

1. Stain a piece of scrap lumber with liquid brown shoe polish.
2. Arrange dried flowers, leaves, and other natural materials on wood.
3. Glue with white glue.

Holiday Gifts: Leather vase or pencil holder

1. Tear small pieces of masking tape and stick them onto a small can or jar.
2. Completely cover jar or can with tape.
3. Cover with liquid brown shoe polish to create a leathery effect.

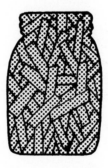

Christmas: Wreath

1. Crumble one large shredded wheat biscuit in a bowl.
2. Mix 5 drops green food coloring with ¼ cup glue.
3. Mix glue and shredded wheat.
4. Pile mix on a margarine lid.
5. Shape into wreath.
6. Decorate with red hots or paper punch circles.
7. Make hole in top with pencil and thread yarn through.
8. Let dry overnight.
9. Pop off lid and add bow.

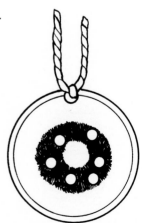

Christmas: Decoration

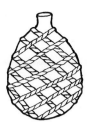

1. Put pieces of yarn in a tray filled with liquid starch.
2. Blow up a balloon and tie.
3. Wrap wet yarn around the expanded balloon.
4. Allow to dry.
5. Pop balloon and remove.
6. Hang ornament with paper clip.

Winter: Bird Food

1. String cranberries and Cheerios on yarn.
2. Drape on trees for birds.

New Year's: Resolution Picture

1. Use crayons and construction paper.
2. Draw a picture to illustrate your resolution.

Valentine's Day: Collage

1. Use scraps, magazine pictures, and beautiful junk to design a card that has a message.

Valentine's Day: Flashy Valentine

1. Mix white glue with dry red tempera.
2. Cut a 3-inch square of oaktag.
3. Cover square with foil.
4. Paint a Valentine picture on foil with glue.
5. Frame or glue on a large red heart.

Valentine's Day: Animals and Flowers

1. Use heart shapes to draw a picture.
2. Add detail with crayons.

Valentine's Day: Lace

1. Fold a square of white paper in half.
2. Fold in half again.
3. Cut out heart shapes and lacy patterns from edges.
4. Open and lay flat.
5. Glue to construction paper.

Valentine's Day: Bleeding Heart

1. Use black magic marker to draw a heart outline on paper towel.
2. Brush water onto the outline.
3. Watch the colors bleed.

Spring

Chicks and Ducks

1. Tear yellow construction paper into rounded shapes.
2. Arrange shapes on construction paper.
3. Glue.
4. Add detail with crayons or magic markers.

Pussy Willows

1. Fold a piece of construction paper in half.
2. Cut a vase from paper.
3. Glue vase to another piece of construction paper.
4. Use crayons to draw branches.
5. Dip finger in black tempera and press onto paper to form buds.
6. Dip little finger in white tempera and press on paper to form pussy willow.

Wash Day

1. Use construction paper.
2. Draw 2 posts with brown crayon.
3. Glue a piece of yarn between posts to make a clothesline.
4. Cut clothes shapes from scrap paper and material.
5. Glue.

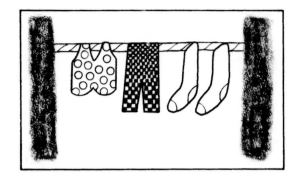

April Fool's Day

1. Use crayons, scraps, and construction paper.
2. Create the facial expression of the victim of an April Fool's joke.

Easter: Cracked Eggs

1. Draw a large egg on white construction paper.
2. Decorate it with crayons and magic markers.
3. Cut out the egg.
4. Cut across the egg with a jagged line to make it appear cracked.
5. Secure halves at one corner with a brad.
6. Use scrap paper to make a chick.
7. Glue chick to bottom half of egg.

Easter: Mosaic Egg

1. Cut white drawing paper into egg shape.
2. Brush surface with water.
3. Cut out small pieces of tissue paper.
4. Cover egg with tissue paper scraps.
5. Brush entire surface with water.
6. Let dry.
7. Remove tissue paper.
8. Colors in tissue will "bleed" onto egg.

Mother's Day Card

1. Collect flowers (whole or petals), leaves, and grasses.
2. Do not use thick flowers or grasses.
3. Arrange flowers on newsprint.
4. Lay flowers between eight thicknesses (4 above/4 below) of newspaper.
5. Place between pages of a heavy book.
6. Let dry for about a week.
7. Remove carefully.
8. Glue to front of card with white glue.

Father's Day Card

1. Draw a small animal outline on newsprint.
2. Place outline on a piece of black construction paper.
3. Cut around outline.
4. Cut through newsprint and black paper.
5. Fold a piece of white construction paper in half.
6. Glue black silhouette to front of card.

Summer

Beach Vacation

1. Get a piece of blue construction paper.
2. Use white glue to draw a sandy beach.
3. Sprinkle on sand.
4. Use white shoe polish to make tips of waves.
5. Cut paper figures from scraps.
6. Glue.

Fourth of July

1. Get Queen Anne's Lace stalks.
2. Dip blossom into red, yellow, or orange tempera.

3. Print by lightly dabbing on paper.
4. Use other colors.

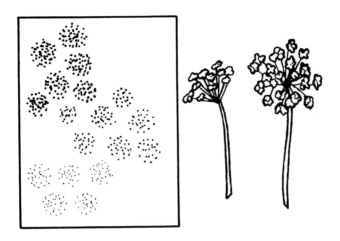

References

Bostley, E. J. (1985). "How to Teach Music as a Daily Discipline," *The School Administrator.* Arlington, Va.: American Association of School Administrators.

Bostley, E. J. (1986). "Children's Musical Cognition as Revealed in Their Created Music Notations," *The Proceedings of the 1986 Southeastern Music Education Symposium.* Athens, Ga.: The University of Georgia Center for Continuing Education.

Bryant, J. C. (1983). *Why Art How Art.* Seattle, Wash.: Special Child Publications.

Chosky, L., et al. (1986). *Teaching Music in the Twentieth Century.* Englewood Cliffs, N.J.: Prentice-Hall, Inc.

Davidson, L., McKernon, P., Gardner, H. (1981). "The Acquisition of Song," *Documentary Report of the Application of Psychology to the Teaching of Music.* Reston, Va.: MENC.

Day, B. (1983). *Early Childhood Education: Creative Learning Activities.* (2nd ed.). New York: Macmillan Publishing Company.

Gardner, H. (1983). *Frames of Mind: The Theory of Multiple Intelligences.* New York: Basic Books, Inc.

Greenberg, M. (1979). *Your Child Needs Music.* Englewood Cliffs, N.J.: Prentice-Hall.

Lansing, K., and Richards, A. E. (1981). *The Elementary Teachers Art Handbook.* New York: Holt, Rinehart and Winston.

Leeper, S. H., Witherspoon, R. L., & Day, B. (1984). *Good Schools For Young Children.* New York: Macmillan.

Lindstrom, M. (1957). *A Study of Normal Development in Children's Modes of Visualization.* Berkley, Calf.: University of California Press.

Lowenfeld, V., and Brittain, W. (1982). *Creative and Mental Growth* (7th Ed.) New York: Macmillan.

MMCP Final Report (1970). Washington, DC: U.S. Office of Education, ED 045 865.

Mark, M. L. (1986). *Contemporary Music Education.* New York: Schirmer Books.

Matthews, P. W. (1953). *You Can Teach Music.* New York: E. P. Dutton & Co., Inc.

Moore, J. G. (1968). *The Many Ways of Seeing.* Cleveland, Ohio: The World Publishing Co.

Myers, L. K. (1950). *Teaching Music in the Elementary School.* Englewood Cliffs, N.J.: Prentice-Hall.

Newman, G. (1984). *Teaching Children Music* (2nd ed.) Dubuque, Iowa: William C. Brown.

Paine, I. L. (1949). *Art Aids* (5th Ed.). Minneapolis, Minn.: Burgess.

Papousek, M. (1982). "Musical Elements in Mother-Infant Dialogues." Austin, Tex.: Paper presented at the International Conference on Infant Studies.

Peters, G. D., and Miller, R. F. (1982). *Music Teaching and Learning.* New York: Longman.

Petzold, R. G. (1966). *Auditory Perception of Musical Sounds by Children in the First Six Grades* (Cooperative Research Project No. 1051). Washington, D.C.: Office of Education.

Raebeck, L. and Wheeler, L. (1964). *New Approaches to Music in the Elementary School.* Dubuque, Iowa: William C. Brown.

Read, H. (1945). *Education Through Art.* New York: Pantheon Books.

Schafer, R. M. (1976). *Creative Music Education.* New York: Schirmer Books.

Suzuki, S. (1969). *Nurtured by Love.* New York: Exposition Press.

Viguers, R. H., et al. (1958). *Illustrators of Children's Books 1946–1956.* Boston: The Horn Book.

White, J. D. (1968). *Understanding and Enjoying Music.* New York: Dodd, Mead and Co.

Winner, E. (1982). *Invented Worlds: The Psychology of the Arts.* Cambridge, Mass.: Harvard University Press.

Suggested Readings

Music

Collier, J. L. (1973). *Jug Bands and Handmade Music.* New York: Grosset & Dunlap, Inc.

Cline, D. "Making Simple Folk Instruments for Children." *Music Educators Journal* 66:6 (February 1980), pp. 58–61.

Frost, B. (1957). *Music Makers.* New York: Maxton Pub.

Gilmore, L. (1962). *Folk Instruments.* Minneapolis, Minnesota: Lerner Publishing Co.

Hawkinson, J., and Faulhaber, M. (1970). *Music Involvement Series Book 1. Music and Instruments for Children to Make.* Chicago: Albert Whitman and Co.

Kettlekamp, L. (1960). *Drums, Rattles and Bells.* New York: William Morrow Co.

Langer, S. K. (1942). *Philosophy in a New Key.* Cambridge, MA: Harvard University Press.

Palisca, C. V. (1964). *Music in Our Schools: A Search for Improvement.* Report of the Yale Seminar on Music Education. Washington, DC: U.S. Department of Health, Education, and Welfare, Office of Education, OE-33033, bulletin 1964, number 28.

Price, C. (1973). *Talking Drums of Africa.* New York: Charles Scribner's Sons.

Art

Athey, I. J., and Rubadeau, D. O., eds. (1970). *Implications of Piaget's Theory.* Waltham, Mass.: Ginn-Blaisdell.

Baer, G. (1979). *Paste, Pencils, Scissors and Crayons.* West Nyack, N.Y.: Parker Publishing Co.

Baer, G. (1982). *Imaginative Art Lessons for Kids and Their Teachers.* West Nyack, N.Y.: Parker Publishing Co.

Baker, L. (1979). *The Art Teacher's Resource Book.* Reston, Va.: Reston Publishing Co.

Barnett, R. R. (1981). *Let Out the Sunshine: A Montessori Approach to Creative Activities.* Dubuque, Iowa: William C. Brown.

Beaney, J. (1970). *Adventures with Collage.* New York: Frederick Warne & Co.

Beswick, B. A. (1983). *Every Child an Artist.* West Nyack, N.Y.: Parker.

Bilus, P., and Sachs, K. (1981). *Integrating Art with the Curriculum Areas.* Washington, D.C.: Department of Education.

Blake, J., and Ernst, B. (1976). *The Great Perpetual Learning Machine.* Boston, Mass.: Little, Brown.

Blau, R., et al. (1977). *Activities for School-age Child Care.* Washington, D.C.: National Association for the Education of Young Children.

Brittain, W. L. (1979). *Creativity, Art and the Young Child.* New York: Macmillan Publishing Co.

Broshnahan, J. P., and Milne, B. W. (1978). *A Calendar of Home/School Activities.* Santa Monica, Calif.: Goodyear.

Brown, S. (Ed.). (1981). *Bubbles, Rainbows and Worms.* Mount Ranier, N.Y.: Gryphon House.

Cole, N. R. (1940). *The Arts in the Classroom.* New York: John Day Co.

Collier, M., et al. (1969). *Kid's Stuff.* Nashville, Tenn.: Incentive Publications.

Comins, J. (1975). *Eskimo Craft and Their Cultural Backgrounds.* New York: Lothrop, Lee and Shepard.

Crane, D. (Ed.). (1982). "Arts and Crafts for Everyone," *Instructor, 92,* 70–79.

D'Amato, J., and D'Amato, A. (1969). *African Crafts for You to Make.* New York: Messner.

Davidson, T., et al. (1976). *The Learning Center Book: An Integrated Approach.* Santa Monico, Calif.: Goodyear.

Dotts, M. F., and Dotts, M. J. (1974). *Clues to Creativity. Vol. I* New York: Friendship Press.

Dotts, M. F., and Dotts, M. J. (1975). *Clues to Creativity. Vol. II.* New York: Friendship Press.

Fleming, B. M., and Hamilton, D. (1977). *Resources for Creative Teaching in Early Childhood Education.* New York: Harcourt Brace Javonovich.

Forte, I., and Pangle, M. (1976). *More Center Stuff for Nooks, Crannies and Corners.* Nashville, Tenn.: Incentive Publications.

Forte, I., et al. (1974). *Pumpkins, Pinwheels and Peppermint Patties.* Nashville, Tenn.: Incentive Publications.

Gaitskell, C. D. (1970). *Children and Their Art.* New York: Harcourt Brace and World, Inc.

Hawkinson, J. (1970). *Paint a Rainbow.* Chicago, Ill.: Albert Whitman.

Hill, B. (1980). "Art Workshop of Classroom Teachers, Part 2," *Instructor, 89,* 77–80.

Horwitz, E. L. (1975). *Contemporary American Folk Artists.* Philadelphia: J. B. Lippincott.

Kaplan, S. N., et al. (1975). *A Young Child Experiences.* Santa Monica, Calif.: Goodyear.

Kohl, M. F. (1985). *Scribble Cookies.* Bellingham, Wash.: Bright Ring Publishing Co.

Kranz, S., and Deley, J. (1970). *The Fourth "R" Art for the Urban School.* New York: Van Nostrand Reinhold.

Kuslan, D. M. (1980). "The Art of Reading," *Instructor, 89,* 102–104.

Lasky, L., and Mukerji, R. (1980). *Art Basic for Young Children.* Washington, D.C.: National Association for the Education of Young People.

Lindstrom, M. (1957). *A Study of Normal Development in Children's Modes of Visualization.* Berkley, Calif.: University of California Press.

Lowenfeld, V. (1957). *Your Child and His Art.* New York: Macmillan.

McFee, J. K. (1961). *Preparation for Art.* San Francisco, Calif.: Wadsworth.

Mason, B. (1946). *The Book of Indian Crafts and Costumes.* New York: A. S. Barnes.

Melzi, K. (1967). *Art in the Primary Schools.* Oxford, England: Alden and Mowbray.

Ott, R. W., and Hurtwitz, A. (Eds.). (1984). *Art in Education: An International Perspective.* University Park, Pa.: Pennsylvania State University Press.

Pattemore, A. W. (1974). *Art and Environment.* New York: Van Nostrand Reinhold.

Pflug, B. (1971). *Boxed-In Doll Houses.* Philadelphia: J. B. Lippincott.

Price, C. (1977). *Arts of Clay.* New York: Charles Scribner's Sons.

Renfro, N. (1983). "It's in the Bag," *Instructor, 93,* 18–20.

Roucher, N. "Step up to a Stage," *Instructor, 96,* 88.

———. "Enter a Personal Moment," *Instructor, 96,* 42.

———. "Walk a Surreal Dog" *Instructor, 96,* 58.

Salomon, J. H. (1928). *The Book of Indian Crafts and Indian Lore.* New York: Harper and Bros.

Schwebel, M. and Ralph, J. (1973). *Piaget in the Classroom.* New York: Basic Books.

Seefeldt, C., and Barbour, N. (1986). *Early Childhood Education: An Introduction.* Columbus, Ohio: Charles E. Merrill.

Sefkow, P. D., and Berger, H. L. (1981). *All Children Create Homes.* Beach, Fla.: Learning Publications.

Sime, M. (1973). *A Child's Eye View.* New York: Harper and Row.

Stephens, L. S. (1983). *Developing Thinking Skills Through Real-Life Activities.* Boston: Allyn and Bacon.

Steven, H. (1963). *Ways with Art.* New York: Reinhold.

Sutherland, Z. (1980). *The Best in Children's Books.* Chicago: University of Chicago Press.

Val Baker, D. (1963). *The Young Potter.* New York: Frederick Warne & Co.

Wachowiak, F. (1985). *Emphasis Art* (4th Ed.). New York: Harper & Row.

Warren, J. (1983). *Crafts.* Palo Alto, Calif.: Monday Morning Books.

Warren, J. (1985). *1.2.3. Art.* Everett, Wash.: Warren Publishing House.

Wolf, A. D. (1984). *Mommy It's a Renoir.* Altoona, Pa.: Parent Child Press.

6

Home Living and Creative Dramatics

The home living and creative dramatics center is a natural setting for rich, stimulating, and enjoyable play and learning experiences. Because play is children's primary mode of learning, dramatic play has tremendous developmental benefits. Such play enables children to grow to their full potential socially, emotionally, intellectually, and physically (Wolfgang, Mackender, & Wolfgang, 1981).

Through dramatic play in this center, children build social relationships with peers while they practice and improve language skills, problem-solving skills, and cooperation. Imaginative play also contributes significantly to children's intellectual development (Mayesky, Neuman, & Wlodkowski, 1985). According to Piaget, imaginative play is one of the purest forms of symbolic thought available to the young child. Divergent thinking and creativity are enhanced when young children pretend with one another (Kostelnik, Whiren, & Stein, 1986). In acting out their fantasies, children can create whatever their imagination will hold (Fein, 1982). In addition, creative play helps children develop a positive self-concept. Through dramatic play, children can begin to manage their problems in an environment in which they have some control. They can try out new roles and tasks, and can safely experiment with solutions to real and imaginary problems. They can also express and come to understand their own emotions as well as the emotions of others.

By observing children engaged in dramatic play, teachers gain invaluable insights into the child's world. Children naturally dramatize and imitate people, animals, objects, and experiences that are familiar to them. As children imitate what they have observed and experienced at home, teachers can learn about their home life. Teachers can learn about children's true feelings as they speak through "pretend" characters. Fears or concerns that are otherwise hidden are easily articulated through puppets and other dramatized characters. When children reveal concerns related to school, such as fear of leaving the classroom or fear of the fire bell, teachers can actively and effectively address those concerns. Teachers may also observe qualities, such as leadership or organizational skill, that they can utilize in other areas of the classroom.

Teachers can also assess children's developmental levels and needs through ob-

293

servation of dramatic play (Eheart & Leavitt, 1985). This information can be used in planning an appropriate individualized program for each child (Hutt & Bhavnani, 1976). In order to do this, teachers should be familiar with how dramatic play generally evolves as children develop. Mayesky et al. (1985) have categorized play into four types:

1. *Solitary Play.* A child plays alone.
2. *Parallel Play.* Children play side by side with other children, but without direct involvement.
3. *Associative Play.* The child is present in a group, for example, participating in a finger play.
4. *Cooperative Play.* Children are mutually involved in a play activity.

The development of dramatic play begins around age two. Toddlers are beginning to engage in dramatic play when they hold the telephone and pretend to talk to someone. At this age, children use realistic props to play. Teachers of toddlers can encourage dramatic play by planning for simple experiences and providing realistic objects. For example, two-year-old children would enjoy feeding and petting a toy puppy after a real puppy had visited the classroom. Very young children may also need to imitate the teacher. Imitation is a stepping-stone to original role-playing, and should not be discouraged.

Around the age of three, children begin to substitute other items for the real object. A three-year-old may still talk on the telephone, but now may use a banana or a block for the receiver. Pictures, stories, and field trips enhance dramatic play in three-year-olds. They may interact verbally, but their play will most often be parallel.

As children further develop, their play becomes more complex. They talk to each other and make plans about their play. A wider range of roles are involved as they become more knowledgeable of real life situations. Teachers may be invited to join in the play, but their presence is not vital to sustaining the play. One of the best ways for teachers of older preschoolers to encourage dramatic play is to provide materials for the children to make props and to add props to complement the children's imaginations.

The dramatic play of most children progresses through three themes. The first theme is domestic scenes. Children in the home living center who cook, clean, and care for the doll are exploring domestic situations. They are role-playing from experience. The second theme is rescue. The "family" is busy in the home living center when suddenly the doll becomes sick or the daddy has a flat tire and cannot get to work. The children have to solve the problem. Often the most socially mature children will introduce the conflict and solve it as the rescue theme begins to emerge in role-play. The third theme is sudden threat. Monsters come out from under beds as the mother is sweeping, or a mean animal chases the children as they play outside (Kostelnik, Whiren, & Stein, 1986).

Once children have played through these themes, they go back and forth through them to satisfy their play needs. One theme may interest them more, and they may spend a great amount of time engaging in that role-play situation. Children's age does not influence the themes they play out as much as opportunities they have had to engage in any dramatic play.

The home living and creative dramatics center can provide endless opportunities for the teacher, as a facilitator of learning, to broaden a child's horizon. The center can be decorated and rearranged to represent an area that pertains to a specific

content of classroom study. Possibilities include creating a home, hospital, post office, grocery store, and more. The change of seasons as well as certain holidays can be easily incorporated in this center. For example, during fall, a child's rake, batons, sweaters, and pom poms might be included in the center. During the winter months, mufflers, mittens, a child's shovel, a holiday apron, candles, candlesticks, and bells may be additions to the center. For spring, the teacher may add baskets, plastic colored eggs, plastic or silk flowers, and a variety of bonnets and hats. The supplies in the home center should reflect the activities in the classroom and extend the skills being taught elsewhere in the classroom, as well as introduce new skills.

Cooking, stitchery, and puppetry are other components of home living and dramatic play. Activities involving food and cooking can be used to help children learn new information; gain new skills; develop positive attitudes about themselves and about learning; and promote good nutrition through nutritious recipes. Children build information in six ways through cooking experiences. They: (1) learn to describe things; (2) learn about tastes; (3) observe changes; (4) learn to express themselves; (5) think more logically; and (6) begin to establish positive nutritional habits. Through cooking experiences children build at least three skills: (1) small-muscle coordination; (2) simple measuring abilities; and (3) social abilities. In addition to gaining information and skills through cooking experiences, children also acquire attitudes including a feeling of being successful, a feeling of having fun, and a determined attitude (Mayesky, Neuman, & Wlodkowski, 1985).

Stitchery projects can also be used in a variety of ways in the classroom. Stitchery provides an excellent opportunity to develop and reinforce eye-hand coordination. Children also learn to follow directions. Stitchery gives the teacher a method to expand and reinforce the other learning activities in the classroom. For example, a child could follow the numbers 1 through 10 sequentially on a sewing card, thereby reinforcing math skills. These activities encourage a feeling of accomplishment while the child is having fun and developing skills.

Puppets are invaluable in the classroom. The home living center should have some ready-made puppets available, which can vary with the seasons, holidays, and units of study. In addition, the home living center should provide children the opportunity of making their own puppets.

In summary, the home living and creative dramatics center provides endless possibilities for learning activities that help all children in the classroom grow intellectually, socially, and/or physically. It also provides teachers, parents, and counselors with valuable opportunities to observe and plan for the enhancement of children's development.

Dramatic Play

Dramatic play activities help to acquaint children with roles, models, and situations in their environment. Drama involves six factors: (1) the use of the five major senses; (2) imagination; (3) the use, mastery, and control of the physical self; (4) speech; (5) the discovery and control of emotion; and (6) intellect (Way, 1967). Through dramatics a child can pretend to be the people or things he finds interesting and can experiment with societal roles. A child can experience conflicts and solve problems and learn to identify and empathize with others. Dramatics offers a variety of communication experiences. Children benefit from creative dramatics in four areas: (1) by developing language arts skills; (2) by improving socialization skills; (3) by

stimulating their creative imagination; and (4) through enjoyment (Heinig & Still-well, 1974). Positive, comfortable feelings can be enhanced within each individual through meaningful experiences in expressive play. Materials may be very simple and should vary according to classroom themes.

Dramatic play is a valuable learning experience. By playing together and creating new roles, children build social relationships. They learn to cooperate as they try to create a dramatic situation. They learn more about the world as they play with children of various backgrounds and knowledge.

Dramatic play is essential to the development of young children. It is one of the ways that children naturally learn. Teachers of young children have a responsibility to allow dramatic play to flourish in their classrooms. Some suggestions for encouraging dramatic play are:

Engage in fun activities for the children to role-play later on their own.
Take part when appropriate.
At other times, let the children control the play.
Guide children who seem to be having trouble by modeling.
Allow the children to work out their conflicts as much as possible. Guide them but do not solve all of their problems for them.
Enjoy the children as they role-play.

Supplies

Sufficient space to allow free movement
Child-sized furniture and appliances (table, chairs, sink, stove, bed, cabinet, ironing board and iron, baby carriage, baby high chair, etc.)
Clothes for dress-up (including various occupational hats such as firefighter, police officer, hardhat, nurse, helmet, cap, etc.)

Props for cooking (pots, pans, tea set, dishes, pot holders, aprons, spoons)
Props for cleaning (broom, mop, dustpan, pail, sponge, empty spray can, rags, feather duster)
Full-length mirror
Added objects as needed for special emphasis

Objectives

1. To act out the children's world as they see it.
2. To act out feelings and emotions in a comfortable setting with an accepting adult.
3. To interact in a variety of roles.
4. To interact with other children and adults in a permissive and informal situation.
5. To develop oral language through creative expression.
6. To imitate characters from stories and films.
7. To provide opportunities for children to create their own stories and actions for their stories.
8. To practice standard American English through social amenities such as using the telephone.
9. To encourage creative expression through mask making and other activities.
10. To develop problem-solving techniques.
11. To enhance divergent thinking.
12. To build social relationships with peers.
13. To enhance sensorimotor skills.

Suggested Activities

1. Role Playing
   Activity Objectives
   a. The children will be able to pretend to be very many different kinds of people and experience many social roles.
   b. The children will be able to better understand the feelings of others and themselves.

2. Mask Making

Activity Objectives

a. The children will make masks to represent themselves.
b. The children will make masks to describe their feelings about a certain subject.
c. The children will make masks for use during a particular holiday or event.
d. The children will make masks for enjoyment and for the feeling of accomplishment.

Types of Masks

Paper plate mask. Use a round paper plate. Make two eyes in the paper circle. Decorate the mask with facial features using crayons or markers. Attach an elastic strip or rubber band to each side.

Paper bag mask. Draw a face on the flat side of a medium- or large-sized paper bag. Decorate facial features using paint, crayons, markers, or fabric scraps. Roll up a cuff at the bottom of the bag. Place bag on child's head and mark spaces for eyes. Remove and cut eye holes.

Box mask. Use a small box for a head mask and a large box for a body mask. Decorate the boxes using various materials to resemble such things as a robot, spaceman, or monster.

Papier-mâché mask. Blow up a round balloon and draw spaces for eyes, nose, and mouth. Dip strips of newspaper into papier-mâché mixture (you may add water to commercially made powder or make your own mixture of wheat paste diluted with warm water).

Molded mask. Construct a basic form for masks by assembling and joining together such items as paper plates, egg cartons, plastic foam balls, paper cups and cones, boxes, and so on. Cover the headlike assembly with aluminum foil and place on a square of waxed paper or foil. Cut a piece of cloth 10 inches larger than the form's base. Dip the cloth into white glue or very heavy starch, drape over the foil and pat and press into shape. Let dry for several days. Then remove form, trim material, and spray paint outside and inside of mask. Add painted features and textured hair. Trim eyeholes and mouth and staple on elastic for wearing (Colvin, 1979).

Produce tray mask. Produce trays are the starting forms for purely decorative 3-D masks. Scrap objects, such as bottle caps, plastic foam packing pieces, yarn, ribbon, buttons, sections of cardboard tubes, and parts cut from plastic bottles can be used singly or in combination to make unique noses, mouths, eyes, brows, and ears. When gluing heavy objects, let white glue set in a small puddle so that it will be a bit thick when you place the object on a tray (Colvin, 1979).

Construction paper mask. Fold a piece of 9″ × 12″ construction paper vertically. Open the paper and hold it against the child's face, marking the place for eyes, nose, and mouth. Add cut paper for ears, eyebrows, hairs, and whiskers. Roll paper strips over a pencil to create curly hair. Features that pop out can be made of paper strips, accordian-pleated, or cut paper can be folded and attached at only one point so that it protrudes (Mayesky, Neuman, & Wlodkowski, 1985).

Eye mask. The child will cover the rims of discarded sun glasses with construction paper, sequins, or stickers to create eye masks. These work well with children who are uncomfortable covering their heads with bags or boxes.

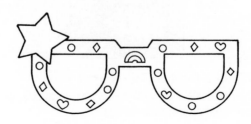

3. Hat Making

> *Helmets.* Cut the bottom and a face size section from a large plastic jug. The child will then decorate the helmet with stickers and bright paper to make a sports or astronaut's helmet.
>
> *Paper hats.* Laminate a large sheet of red paper. Cut a semi-circle, following the diagram. Staple the strip across the back to secure the hat. The child will paste a large number on the front to make a fire fighter's hat.

> Laminate a large sheet of white paper. Enlarge the following diagram onto it to make a nurse's hat.

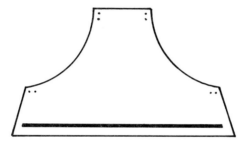

> *Animal ears.* The child will make animal ears by cutting two ears from heavy paper and stapling them onto a band. The teacher may need to assist the child in measuring the band to fit his or her head. Provide pictures of the real animal whose ears the child is making.

4. Expand Play Center. Add materials to create a variety of situations in which the child will be able to role-play numerous occupations.

a. *Post office.* A countertop or top of a bookcase or a window (or a puppet stage), stamps, play money, letters, old Christmas cards, telephone, postcards, mailbag or large shoulder bag, empty envelopes, stamp and ink pad, old magazines, advertisement flyers, badges, index cards, and file and post cards. Mailboxes, such as upside-down shoe boxes with the end cut out, can be placed in several other areas in the room for pick-up and delivery.

b. *Store.* A counter, cash register, play or real money, labeled boxes and cans, a price marker, newspaper ads, advertising bargains, a telephone for receiving orders, calculator, and shopping carts.

c. *Beauty parlor and/or barbershop.* Full-length mirror (turned on its side) on a long table, combs, brushes, wigs, hair clasps, decorative combs, play razor, shaving cream, makeup, rollers, clips, pins, play shampoo, dryer, uniforms, capes, hair nets, and towels.

d. *Election booth.* Refrigerator box, paper ballots, pencils, names of candidates, curtain, official, clipboard with paper, voters.

e. *Public library.* Shelves, books, divider for quiet area, stamp and ink pad for dates, cards, record player, books with records, cassette player, books with cassettes, and posters about authors and/or books. This is a good place to share books the children themselves have written and illustrated.

f. *Playhouse.* A large refrigerator box with doors and windows cut out makes an exciting place to play. Let the children paint or decorate it as they wish. (This can make a good office, library, barbershop, doghouse, etc.)

g. *Laundry area.* A washtub and clothesline on an adjoining outside area add zest to this center. Allow the children to use the tub, with possibly a scrub board to wash the clothes they play with in the center.

h. *Grocery store.* Empty food containers, cash register, play money, plastic or papier-mâché fruits and vegetables, shopping carts, and paper bags.

i. *Hospital.* Stethoscope, masks, rubber hammer, tongue depressors, tissues, hospital gowns, doctor bag, scales, yardstick, measuring tape, clipboard with paper, cotton balls, adhesive bandages, empty pill bottles, play thermometer, hypodermic needle minus needle.

j. *Fishing Pond.* An old wooden crate and a tackle box can turn any cor-

ner into a pond. Provide a fishing pole with a magnet in place of the hook and fish with paper clip noses.

Home Living

Many types of home living activities can be very beneficial in preparing children for many areas of learning. Most children enjoy role-playing a home-life situation. The home center provides an outlet for children to act out feelings that often can't be expressed directly. Generally speaking, people, including children, feel more comfortable sharing their feelings and ideas with others their own age (Jalongo, 1985).

Children can learn to deal with their anxieties as well as act out their fantasies through creative dramatic play. To pretend to do something, the child must have already experienced first-hand (or on television or through stories and pictures) the concepts and roles used in dramatic play. A child's everyday life is the best source of such ideas (Mayesky, Neuman, & Wlodkowski, 1985). The home living center furnishes the appropriate background for this dramatic play. In the home center dramatic play often begins with one child, and others later join in. The home living center presents a familiar and comfortable setting for learning, developing skills, and having fun.

Supplies

Child-sized furniture
Dress-up clothes, costumes, and accessories (jewelry,
     pocketbooks, dress shoes, slippers, scarves)
Blankets, pillows
Tableclothes, placemats
Flower vase with flowers
Tea sets, dishes, pots and pans, silverware, large spoons,
     aprons
Calendar
Clock
Telephone, a classroom telephone book, datebook
Books, magazines, newspapers
Mirrors
Cardboard chest, suitcase, or trunk
Baby equipment and accessories (dolls, bottles, cradles,
     blanket, toys, feeding dish, bibs, baby brush and comb,
     baby high chair, stroller, music box, rocker, toys)

Objectives

1. To find success with the various ways in which one can "set up" a house and practice the manners used in living there.
2. To role-play people in familiar and community settings.
3. To develop and facilitate behavior modification within the child in a comfortable situation.
4. To provide an outlet for children to act out feelings that often can't be expressed directly.

Activities

1. *Role Playing*
   Activity Objectives
   a. The children will be given the opportunity to better understand their own feelings, and in some cases the feelings of others.

b. The children will become more aware of the duties of various family members.

c. The children will develop problem-solving skills when dealing with social situations.

d. The children will develop appropriate manners for the home.

2. *Placemats*

Activity Objective

a. The children will be able to correctly set the table.

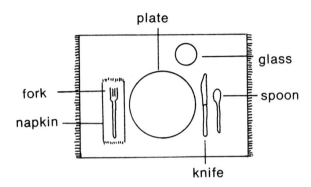

3. *Dollmaking.* Dolls should be of varied ethnic groups, sexes, and ages. Sew together one long piece of material for the body and head. Divide these parts by tying a tight band around the neck. The head should be of equal width and length. The body should be one-and-a-half times the width of the head. The arms should be half as wide as the head and one-and-a-half-times as long. The doll should be stuffed and decorated. Doll equipment should include carriages, cradles, beds, cots, baby bottles, and togs.

Activity Objectives

a. The children will become aware of the relational proportions of body parts.

b. The children will become more aware of the functions of body parts.

4. *Flowermaking.* Simple flowers can be made from scraps of crepe paper, construction paper, and/or tissue paper. The children can draw and cut out basic flower shapes. Using a pencil or the edge of scissors, the children will curl the edges of the flower. For the stems and leaves, use straws, pipe cleaners, wire, or popsicle sticks covered with crepe paper. These may be put into an empty juice can that has been covered in yarn, wallpaper, fabric, or construction paper. This arrangement may be used as a centerpiece on the table.
Activity Objectives
   a. The children will enjoy making an attractive addition to the center.
   b. The children will become more aware of the basic parts of a flower (Cole, Haas, Heller, & Weinberger, 1976).

Stitchery

Stitchery is a favorite activity for many children. Stitchery develops eye-hand coordination, direction-following skills, and feelings of accomplishment. The satisfaction and reinforcement a child feels upon completion of a sewing project make stitchery a worthwhile activity.

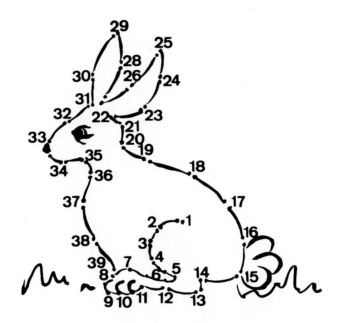

Supplies

Scraps of material	Grocery store meat trays
Yarn, thread, shoelaces	Bobby pins
Burlap	Cellophane tape
Tagboard	Paper punch
Plastic needles	Ribbons
Scissors	

Objectives

(These objectives apply to all of the following activities.)
1. To provide practice in the development of eye-hand coordination.
2. To encourage self-expression and creativity.
3. To gain confidence in starting a project, following directions, and completing it successfully.
4. To develop manual dexterity.

Activities

1. *Sewing Cards.* Make sewing cards by drawing a pattern on tagboard. Punch holes, laminate, and tie a knotted shoelace at one end. The child threads the shoelace through holes to complete the picture.
2. *Pillows.* Make pillows by sewing together two pieces of material and stuffing. Two washcloths sewn together and stuffed also make a nice pillow.
3. *Meat Tray Stitchery.* Draw a design on a styrofoam meat tray; then punch holes using an ice pick. The child uses yarn and a plastic sewing needle to complete the project with a backstitch or a simple cross stitch.

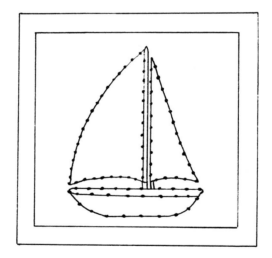

4. *Weaving Cards.* Make weaving cards by making vertical cuts 1″ apart across a piece of tagboard (approximately 8″ × 10″). Using paper or ribbons cut in 12″ lengths, weave over and under alternate strips with a single ribbon or strip of paper. Then, do likewise with a second ribbon, this time weaving under the strips woven over by the first ribbon (Collier, Forte, & MacKenzie, 1981).

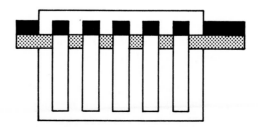

5. *Cross Stitch on Burlap.* Draw design or pattern on a burlap square with a magic marker. The child uses yarn to complete.

6. *Pompon People.* The child will wrap yarn around a 4″ × 5″ piece of cardboard about 100 times. The yarn is then gathered at the middle and tied tightly with another piece of yarn. The cardboard is removed and the yarn loops are snipped. The child can glue eyes, bow ties, and other items to the pompon to create a creature.

7. *Necklaces.* The child will string dough beads, which have been made by the teacher, on heavy thread or shoelaces to make necklaces. Other items can be provided to string, such as thread spools.

8. *Braided Rags.* Cut material scraps into long strips two inches wide. Safety pin three strips together at one end. The child will braid the strips and shape the braid into an oval. The child will sew a few threads through the back to hold the shape.

9. *Sew on Vest.* Make a vest for each child by sewing shoulder seams in two pieces of fabric. The child will sew up the side seams and personalize the vest with fabric scraps, trinkets, ribbon, etc.

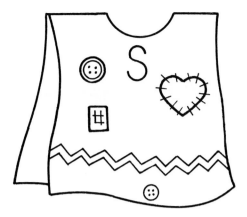

10. *Gifts.* Make gifts for holidays, birthdays, and other special occasions.
11. *Reinforcement.* Use stitchery as a reinforcement activity. Practice alphabet, numerals, shapes, names, and more.

Cooking

Cooking in the classroom can provide a child with many valuable experiences. Reading, direction-following, and math and science concepts are emphasized in each cooking activity. Cooking activities also provide a natural vehicle for nutrition education.

Nutrition is essential to the well-being of students. Nutrition education and health are key factors affecting learning and all areas of development. Nutrition education activities foster child development in the following areas: (1) promotion of language development; (2) promotion of cognitive development; (3) promotion of sensori-motor development; and (4) promotion of social/emotional development (Marotz, Rush, & Cross, 1985). Hungry and malnourished children have many problems relating to school, including problems concentrating, resisting fatigue, and staying alert. Malnutrition also increases susceptibility to infection and may cause children to have gaps in learning due to poor attendance (Oliver & Musgrave, 1984). This center provides an excellent opportunity, through cooking activities, to alleviate hunger in the classroom, promote good nutrition, teach valuable cooking skills, and provide recipes that may be used at home. All of a child's senses are used in food or cooking experiences. Children see, smell, touch, and taste the food, as well as hear the food frying, boiling, popping, etc.

Food activities must meet certain standards. They must be open-ended, challenging, varied, emphasize the doing, involve inexpensive materials, and not be dangerous (Mayesky, Neuman, & Wlodkowski, 1985). The cooking procedure itself is one of cooperation and a selected sequence of tasks.

Supplies

Measuring spoons and cups	Muffin tin
Minute timer	Cookie sheets
Mixing bowls	Paper towels, plates, napkins
Hot plate	Recipe task cards or chart
Toaster oven	Spatula
Saucepans	Grater
Wooden spoons	Sifter
Eggbeater	Whisk
Paring knife	Blender
Cookie cutter	Aluminum foil
Pot holder	Cutting board
Aprons or smocks	Electric fry pan
Dishpans	Colander
Rolling pin	Vegetable brush

Objectives

1. To provide opportunities to work together as a group to achieve a common goal.
2. To provide concrete experiences that promote understanding of concepts related to reading, science, mathematics, social studies, and health.
3. To practice formal skills such as problem solving, following directions, predicting outcomes, quantitative measurement, and so on.
4. To expose children to foods and customs of other cultures or times.
5. To practice manipulative tasks, such as jar opening, pouring, sifting and cutting, which help to develop fine motor skills.
6. To develop nutritious eating patterns.
7. To develop children's positive attitudes about themselves and learning.

Suggested Activities and Recipes

1. *Manipulation and Exploration.* Use containers and cooking materials to encourage these activities.
2. *Language Experience Stories.* Using the cooking experience as a topic for a class or individual story.
3. *Tasting Experiences.* The child will identify familiar foods by tasting them (while unable to see them), will compare and match foods with different textures, and will taste foods that are opposites, such as sweet and sour.
4. *Smelling Experiences.* The child will identify familiar aromas (while unable to see the food) and will match foods that have been placed in small containers by aroma only.
5. *Recipes.* The child will actively participate in a variety of cooking experiences by pouring, mixing, grating, measuring, and following written and spoken instructions.

The first set of recipes is designed to be used with a small group of children and an adult helper. The second set is designed for individual use, perhaps located or set up in a learning center.

Recipes for Small Groups with Adult Helper

Porcupines (no-cook)

You will need: measuring cups
measuring spoons
mixing spoon
mixing bowl
shallow dish
cookie sheets

Ingredients: 3 T honey
                  4 T peanut butter
                  ½ C nonfat dry milk
                  ½ C coconut

Directions:
1. Mix honey and peanut butter
2. Add nonfat dry milk. Mix well.
3. Roll into balls, about ½" in diameter.
4. Roll in coconut
5. Chill until firm.

Stone Soup

You will need: large soup pot
                  hot plate
                  mixing spoon
                  cutting board
                  knife
                  scrub brush

Ingredients: 1 stone   turnips
                  5 beef bouillon cubes   onions
                  1 qt water   tomatoes
                  1 can tomato or V-8 juice celery
                  carrots   beans
                  potatoes   corn
                  cauliflower   peas
                  small bag of noodles

Directions:
1. Scrub the stone well.
2. Dissolve five beef bouillon cubes in 1 quart of water.
3. Add tomato or V-8 juice. Simmer.
4. Add more water when necessary.
5. Wash and chop all vegetables.
6. Add to soup pot all vegetables and cook for 30 minutes.
7. Add a small bag of noodles during last 10 minutes.

Peanut Balls

You will need:
sauce pan
hot plate
blender
mixing bowl
mixing spoon

Ingredients:
½ C raisins or chopped dates
¼ C apple juice concentrate
¼ C peanut butter
¼ C low-fat dry milk
1 tsp. vanilla
1 tsp. cinnamon
1 C Grape Nuts

Directions:
1. Heat raisins or chopped dates and apple juice concentrate in a sauce pan.
2. Boil about 2 minutes.
3. Pour raisins in a blender and puree.
4. Mix raisin puree and remainder of ingredients in a bowl.
5. Shape into balls about ½″ in diameter.
6. Refrigerate.

Stuffed Potatoes

You will need: oven
mixing bowl
potato masher
tablespoon
mixing spoon
cookie sheet

Ingredients: baking potatoes
milk
margarine
cheese
crumbled bacon
(optional)
   diced ham
   choice of cooked vegetables

Directions:
1. Bake potatoes.
2. Cut them in half lengthwise.
3. Scoop the potato from the skin and put it in a mixing bowl.
4. Add milk and butter to creamy consistency.
5. Mash potatoes.
6. Add any optional ingredients.
7. Mix everything well.
8. Put back into potato skins.
9. Place on cookie sheets.
10. Reheat.

Variety Muffins

You will need: sifter
mixing bowl and spoon
measuring cup
measuring spoons
blender
muffin tins
paper liners
cutting board
knife
rubber spatula

Ingredients: 1 C white flour
1 T baking powder
½ tsp. salt
¾ C whole-wheat flour
1 egg
½ C apple juice concentrate

> ¼ C vegetable oil
> ½ C milk
> 1 banana, sliced
> fresh or canned fruit
> (optional)
> > 2 C bran flakes
> > chopped nuts

Directions:

1. Sift the white flour, baking powder, and salt together.
2. Add the whole-wheat flour.
3. In a blender, blend egg, apple juice, vegetable oil, milk, banana.
4. Pour liquid ingredients into dry ingredients.
5. Stir
6. Spoon into muffin tins.
7. Bake at 400°F for 20–25 min.

It is optional to add fresh or canned fruits and/or chopped nuts before filling muffin cups. For bran muffins add 2 cups bran flakes in place of the whole-wheat flour.

Great Granola

You will need: mixing bowls
measuring cup and spoons
cookie sheet
paper towels
wooden spoon

Ingredients: 2 C oatmeal
⅔ C wheat germ
½ C coconut
½ C sunflower seeds
½ C powdered nonfat milk
1 tsp. cinnamon
½ tsp. nutmeg

Directions:

1. Mix the oatmeal, wheat germ, coconut, sunflower seeds, powdered milk, nutmeg, and cinnamon in large mixing bowl.
2. Add honey, oil, and vanilla.
3. Mix well.
4. Spread on cookie sheet.
5. Bake at 375°F for 8–10 minutes.
6. Cool on paper towels (Jenkins, 1982).

Apple Salad

You will need: paring knife
mixing bowel
measuring cups
measuring spoons
wooden spoon

Ingredients: 2 apples
3 celery sticks
½ tsp. lemon juice
½ C mayonnaise
½ C chopped nuts

Directions:
1. Wash apples and cut into quarters.
2. Cut celery and apples into small pieces.
3. Put apples and celery into mixing bowl.
4. Sprinkle with lemon juice.
5. Add nuts and mayonnaise.
6. Mix

Peanut Butter

You will need: a blender

Ingredients: 1 lb. roasted peanuts
few drops of peanut oil
salt to taste

Directions:
1. Shell roasted peanuts.
2. Place peanuts in blender and grind.
3. Add a few drops of peanut oil.
4. Add salt to taste.
5. Refrigerate.

Bagel Bonanza

You will need: blender
spatula
table knife
toaster (optional)

Ingredients: softened cream cheese
chopped walnuts
chopped carrots
raisins
chopped dates
bagels of all kinds—plain, egg, raisin, pumpernickle, whole wheat

Directions:
1. Put cream cheese and other desired ingredients in blender.
2. Blend well.
3. Toast bagels if desired.

Tacos

Ingredients:
2 lbs. ground beef, 2 tomatoes, 2 onions, ½ lb. cheese, ketchup, can of prepared hot dog chili, taco shells.

Tacos

Recipe:
Brown ground beef; add chili.
Shred and grate the vegetables and cheese.
Place all of these in the taco shell.
Top with ketchup.
(This activity is a little more advanced, but it is a very good one to follow a unit of study on Mexico.

Energy Cookies

Ingredients:

4 cups uncooked rolled oats, 3 cups unbleached white flour, 2 cups dates (pitted and chopped), 6 tablespoons milk, 1 cup brown sugar, 1½ cup corn or peanut oil, ½ cup maple syrup.

Recipe:

In large bowl beat together sugar and oil. Add oats, syrup, flour and milk. Mix in dates.

Preheat oven to 350⁰. Oil cookie sheets, roll dough into small balls, and flatten them on cookie sheets.

Bake for 15 to 20 minutes. Let cool.

Makes 60 cookies.

Gingerbread Man

Ingredients:

½ cup butter or margarine, 1 cup sugar, 1 egg, 1½ cups flour, 1 teaspoon baking powder, 1 teaspoon ginger.

Recipe:

Cream butter and sugar together. Add egg. Mix in flour, baking powder, and ginger.

Roll out this dough. Cut out shape of man. Bake at 375⁰ until brown. Try making other shapes too.

Applesauce

You need: apples, plastic serrated knives, a pot, water, sugar, hot plate

Now:

Peel and cut up the apples. Put the apples in a pot of water. Cook until tender. Mash. Add sugar (1½ cup per 6 apples); Cook for 10 more minutes. Add cinnamon if desired. Cool and serve.

Gazpacho

Ingredients:

1 cup chopped tomato, ½ cup green pepper, ½ cup celery ½ cup cucumber, ¼ cup green onion, 2 teaspoons parsley, 1 small clove garlic, ½ tablespoon olive oil, 1 teaspoon salt, ¼ teaspoon black pepper, ½ teaspoon Worchestershire sauce, 2 cups tomato juice

Recipe:

Chop all vegetables, crush garlic clove, combine all ingredients, chill overnight.

Enjoy. (This is a good follow-up recipe after a trip to the market or a unit on foods.)

Girl Salad

Face:	Canned peach half, round side up
Eyes:	Raisins
Nose:	Clove
Mouth:	Cut from maraschino cherry
Collar:	Stand half ring of pineapple on edge
Dress:	Hide a canned pear half under a lettuce leaf skirt and let pear show for petticoat
Slippers:	Tuck cherry halves under the petticoat

Boy Salad

Face:	Canned pear half, using same material for features as girl
Hair:	Shredded carrots or grated cheese
Trousers:	Half a canned peach cut straight at the sides with a notch at the bottom in center
Legs and arms:	Pineapple wedges
Buttons and pocket trim:	Cut from maraschino cherries

Cheddar Cheese Log

You will need:	mixing bowl and spoon shallow dish measuring spoons
Ingredients:	½ lb. Cheddar cheese 3 oz. cream cheese 4 oz. cottage cheese ½ pack onion soup mix 1 T. Worcestershire sauce 2 T chopped parsley ½ C chopped black walnuts variety of breads, bread sticks, crackers (optional)

Directions:
1. Have cheese at room temperature.
2. Place all ingredients except the walnuts in a mixing bowl and mix until well blended.
3. Refrigerate and shape into a log when the mix is cold.
4. Roll in the nuts and keep refrigerated until 2 hours before using.
5. Serve with a variety of crackers, breads, etc. (Selph & Street, 1975).

Cheese Wafers

You will need: table knife
                 cutting board
                 mixing bowl
                 cookie sheet

Ingredients: 7 slices whole wheat bread
                 10 oz. cheddar cheese
                 2 tsp. Worcestershire sauce
                 shortening

Directions:
1. Tear bread into small pieces.
2. Cut cheese into chunks.
3. Mix in bowl with Worcestershire sauce.
4. Press crumbs together firmly into small balls.
5. Place balls on lightly greased baking sheet.
6. Flatten slightly.
7. Bake at 350°F for 5 minutes.
8. Turn wafers and bake 5 minutes more, or until crispy.

Dilled Yogurt Dressing (make ahead)

You will need: blender
                 measuring spoons

Ingredients: 1 C lowfat yogurt
       2 T vinegar
       ½ small onion
       ¼ tsp. salt
       ½ tsp. dill seeds
       ¼ tsp. dry mustard

Directions:
Blend all ingredients in blender.
Serve with fresh vegetable tray including such vegetables as turnips, cauliflower, broccoli, sweet potatoes, zucchini, radishes, etc.

Roasted Pumpkin Seeds

You will need: toaster oven
       paper towels

Ingredients: ¼ C oil
       pumpkin seeds
       salt

Directions:
1. Wash and dry seeds.
2. Pour ¼ cup oil on a cookie sheet.
3. Spread seeds on cookie sheet, coating them well.
4. Bake in 350°F oven until lightly brown.
5. Drain on a paper towel.
6. Sprinkle with salt.

Pumpkin Pudding

You will need: blender
large bowl
baking dish
measuring cups
measuring spoons

Ingredients: 4 pieces whole-wheat bread
½ C milk
½ C orange juice
2 eggs
1 ripe banana, sliced
¼ C apple juice concentrate
2 tsp. cinnamon
1 C canned pumpkin

Directions:
1. Break bread into small pieces and put into blender.
2. Blend well.
3. Place crumbs in a large bowl.
4. Add remaining ingredients to the blender.
5. Add mixture to bread crumbs. Stir together and pour into baking dish.
6. Bake for 50 minutes at 350°F.

Potato Latkes

You will need: frying pan
grater
large bowl and spoon
chopping board
sharp knife
measuring spoons

Ingredients: 6 large potatoes
2 eggs
1 tsp. minced parsley
½ onion
salt
pepper

Directions:
1. Wash potatoes and dry.
2. Grate potatoes into large bowl.
3. Add 2 beaten eggs.
4. Add 1 teaspoon minced parsley.
5. Add ½ chopped onion.
6. Add salt and pepper.
7. Mix well.
8. Flatten to form thin pancakes.
9. Fry until crispy brown.

Mini-Pizzas

You will need: toaster oven
grater
tablespoon

Ingredients: English muffins
                 all natural pizza sauce
                 (optional)
                     pepperoni
                     sausage
                     green pepper

Directions:
1. Place a spoonful of pizza sauce on muffin and spread.
2. Top with grated cheese (other toppings are optional).
3. Place in toaster oven on top brown setting until cheese melts.

Roll-Up Sandwiches

You will need: rolling pin
                 table knife

Ingredients: whole-wheat bread
                 sandwich spread

Directions:
1. Flatten a piece of whole-wheat bread with a rolling pin.
2. Spread sandwich spread on bread (e.g., egg salad, cream cheese, peanut butter).
3. Roll up bread.

Vegetable Patties

You will need: oiled griddle   grater
                 chopping board   sharp knife
                 large bowl and spoon   measuring spoons

Ingredients: 2 T tofu   2 tsp. rolled oats
                 ½ T beaten egg   ½ T chopped onion
                 ½ T grated carrot   1 tsp. chopped green pepper

Directions:
1. Mix all ingredients well in a large bowl.
2. Shape into one patty.
3. Cook 2 minutes on each side.

Fruit Tapioca

Ingredients: 2 cups fruit
                 2 cups water
                 4 tablespoons minute tapioca
                 ½ cup sugar

Place ingredients in a saucepan over low flame.
Boil until clear, stirring frequently.
Fruit suggestions: apricots, cherries, rapsberries, rhubarb

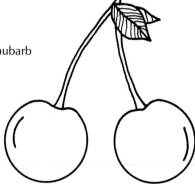

Popcorn

Equipment and ingredients:
A large pot, hot plate or
  popcorn popper.
Popcorn, salt, oil and butter

Put enough popcorn & oil
  to cover bottom of pan.
Add salt and butter to taste

HAYSTACKS

you will need: a large pot
can opener
teaspoon
wax paper

ingredients: 2 packages of butterscotch bits
1 can of chow mein noodles
1 can of peanuts

directions:
1. Melt butterscotch bits in a pot on the stove.
2. Stir in peanuts and chow mein noodles.
3. Drop a teaspoon at a time of the mixture on wax paper.
4. Cool.
5. Eat.

★ Remember : the careful cooks leave the center clean for the next cooks.

Spanish Fruit Salad

2 T. pineapple chunks.
3 T. apple chunks.
2　banana slices.
8　orange slices.
1 t. lemon juice.

In a cup, add
2 T. of pineapple
chunks.

Add 3 chunks
of apple.

Add 2 banana
slices.

Add 8 orange
slices.

Add 1 t. of lemon
juice.

Stir together.

Eat and Enjoy

Recipes for Individuals

Celery Canoes

You will need: table knife
                 vegetable brush

Ingredients: celery stalks
                 cream cheese
                 cheese whiz
                 peanut butter
                 (optional)
                     nuts
                     raisins

Directions:
1. Clean celery.
2. Cut into 3″ lengths.
3. Using knife, fill with cream cheese, cheese whiz, or peanut butter.
4. Optional: Add nuts and raisins.

Egg Salad

You will need: small bowl
                 fork
                 table knives
                 tablespoon

Ingredients: 1 hard boiled egg
                 salt
                 mayonnaise
                 bread

Directions:
1. Peel and wash egg.
2. Mash egg in a small bowl.
3. Add 1 tablespoon mayonnaise and a pinch of salt.
4. Spread on bread.

Jack-O-Lantern Surprise

You will need: table knife

Ingredients: English muffins
                 spreadable orange cheese
                 olives, raisins, peanuts

Directions:
1. Spread cheese over muffins.
2. Use olives, raisins, peanuts to make surprise faces.

Banana-ana Pudding

You will need: measuring spoons
                 bowl and spoon

Ingredients: ½ small banana
                 3 T applesauce
                 1 tsp. plain yogurt

Directions:
1. Mash the banana in a small bowl.
2. Add the applesauce.
3. Stir in the yogurt.

Walking Banana Salad

Substitute honey mixed with granola to create another nutritious banana snack.

Let's Make
A Walking
Banana Salad.

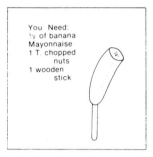

You Need:
½ of banana
Mayonnaise
1 T. chopped
    nuts
1 wooden
    stick

Peel
banana.

Put wooden
stick in end
of banana half.

Spread
banana with
mayonnaise.

Roll in
chopped nuts
Eat! Enjoy!

People Salad

Peach halves, raisins, shredded carrots, cherry slices, pineapple wedges, pear halves, and marshmallows. Encourage the children to create people by putting together a variety of ingredients.

Honey Butter

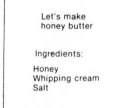

Let's make
honey butter

Ingredients:

Honey
Whipping cream
Salt

1

Pour the whipping
cream into the jar.

2

Add one sprinkle
of salt.

3

Put the lid on the jar and screw on tight.

Take turns shaking the mixture until the cream separates.

4

Pour the cream from the top into a bowl. Leave the butter in the jar.

5

Pour the honey into the jar and stir the mixture.

6

Spread on a piece of bread with a knife.

Eat and enjoy your honey butter treat.

Proportions:
For group of 4 or 5, use 1C whipping cream
shake for 15-20 minutes
Add 2 + honey

Sandwich Spreads

Raisin and Nut

Ingredients: 1 lb. box raisins
2 cups pecans
mayonnaise

Grind the raisins and nuts in a meat grinder. Add the mayonnaise until spreadable.

Egg and Olive

Ingredients: ½ cup chopped olives
6 hard boiled eggs
mayonnaise

Mix the olives and egg together. Add enough mayonnaise to make spreadable.

Pimento Cheese

Ingredients: ½ lb. grated sharp cheese
1 small can pimento
dash of Tabasco
1 tsp. Worcestershire sauce
salt to taste
mayonnaise or salad dressing

Mash pimento with fork and mix with grated cheese. Add Tabasco, Worcestershire, and enough mayonnaise to make spreadable. Add salt to taste.

Drinks

Peanut Butter Milkshake

You will need: measuring cups and spoons
blender

Ingredients: 1 C milk
1 ripe banana
1 T creamy peanut butter

Directions:
1. Put all ingredients in blender.
2. Blend well.

Orange Cooler

You will need: blender
measuring cups

Ingredients: ½ C orange juice concentrate
1 C plain yogurt
1 C milk

Directions:
1. Put all ingredients in blender.
2. Blend well.

Hot Spiced Cider

You will need: sauce pan
hot plate

Ingredients: apple juice
orange juice or cranberry juice
cinnamon stick

Directions:
1. Pour apple juice in sauce pan.
2. Add a small amount of orange juice or cranberry juice.
3. Put cinnamon stick in pan.
4. Simmer for 5 minutes.

Foamy Banana Drink

You will need: blender
tablespoon
measuring cup

Ingredients: 2 C milk
2 bananas, sliced
4 T canned pumpkin
dash cinnamon

Directions:
1. Put all ingredients in blender.
2. Blend well.

Strawberry-Orange Drink

You will need: measuring cup
blender

Ingredients: 1 C orange juice
2 crushed ice cubes
2 strawberries

Directions:
1. Wash and cap strawberries.
2. Put all ingredients in blender.
3. Blend well.

Cantaloupe Sip-Up

You will need: blender
                  measuring cups

Ingredients: 2 C cantaloupe chunks
                  ½ C apple juice concentrate
                  2 C milk

Directions:
1. Put ingredients in blender.
2. Blend well.

Hawaiian Drink

You will need: blender
                  measuring cup

Ingredients: 2 C unsweetened pineapple juice
                  2 eggs
                  2 tsp. vanilla
                  ½ C instant nonfat dry milk
                  2 small bananas, sliced

Directions:
1. Put all ingredients in blender.
2. Blend well.

Egg Nog

You will need: blender
tablespoon
measuring cup

Ingredients: 2 eggs
2 C milk
2 T softened cream cheese
1 banana
4 drops vanilla
dash of cinnamon

Directions:
1. Put all ingredients in blender.
2. Blend well.

Snack Bar

Place toaster, bread, butter, peanut butter, jelly, and butter knives on a table in the center. Allow a few children at a time to have breakfast or a snack as needed for an energy boost. Fresh fruit and cheese snacks may be added as well as classroom recipes. Ask parents to help with the upkeep.

Puppetry

Puppetry experiences are a fascinating form of entertainment for children. Real or make-believe characters can come alive through puppetry and can serve many uses in the classroom. Puppets made by the children can be used to lead singing, teach finger plays, act out nursery rhymes, relieve classroom tension, help develop a feeling for rhythm, help clarify abstract concepts, help demonstrate concrete concepts, and aid in reading. In older children, puppets stimulate creative writing and story telling. Also, puppets provide an avenue for children's self-expression and fantasy. Easy to make and simple to use, puppets enhance any classroom (Mayesky, Neuman, & Wlodkowski, 1985).

Supplies

Scissors, glue, pens, markers
Cloth scraps
Paper bags
Boxes
Costumes
A stage
Materials to decorate puppets (yarn, buttons, trinkets)
Styrofoam balls
Styrofoam cups
Handkerchiefs
Tongue depressors
String
Socks
Paper plates
Spools
Cardboard rolls
Pint-sized milk cartons
Clay or playdough

Objectives

1. To provide a means of self-expression and role playing.
2. To promote verbal and dramatic expression in a variety of situations.
3. To develop an appreciation of various types of literature.
4. To learn how to become a puppet maker.
5. To foster social skills through cooperation in making puppets and performing as a group.
6. To provide a stimulator for creative writing and/or story telling.
7. To reveal the inner world of the child.

Activities

1. Performing with puppets.
2. Role-playing with puppets.
3. Making puppets.
4. Teaching with puppets.
5. Using puppets in introductions.
6. Using puppets as icebreakers.

Finger Puppets

You will need: an old glove
needle and thread
fabric scraps
yarn
markers

Procedure 1:
1. Cut off the finger of a glove.
2. Sew facial features on the finger.

Procedure 2:
1. Draw a figure approximately 5″ tall.
2. Cut it out.
3. Cut holes in the bottom for the child to stick his or her fingers through.
4. The child's fingers will be used for legs.

Procedure 3:
1. Crack raw peanuts.
2. Use shells for puppet.
3. Sew or glue on facial features.

Sock Puppets

You will need:　an old sock
　　　　　　　buttons
　　　　　　　felt scraps
　　　　　　　glue

Procedure:
1. Sew facial features on socks and use for a hand puppet.

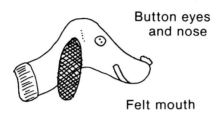

**Button eyes
and nose**

Felt mouth

Felt ears

Wooden Spoon Puppets

You will need:　wooden spoon
　　　　　　　yarn
　　　　　　　string
　　　　　　　material scraps
　　　　　　　glue
　　　　　　　construction paper

Procedure:
1. Draw and cut out character.
2. Glue onto spoon.
3. Glue on yarn, string for hair, and square or half-moon
　 shaped cloth or paper for clothes.

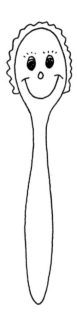

Two-faced Puppet

You will need:　two paper plates
　　　　　　　glue
　　　　　　　sticks
　　　　　　　yarn
　　　　　　　markers
　　　　　　　stapler
　　　　　　　scissors

Procedure:
1. Draw a face on the back of each plate.
2. Add features with varied types of materials.
3. Insert a stick between the plates and glue it into place.
4. Staple edges together.

Milk Carton Puppets

You will need: ½-pint milk carton
construction paper
yarn or string
glue
scissors

Procedure:

1. Cut through the center of a ½-pint milk carton. Cut three sides only. Do not cut the fourth side.
2. Fold the carton in half (the uncut side becomes the hinge).
3. Cut facial features from colored paper and paste them to the carton.
4. Add string or yarn for special emphasis.

To operate the puppet, place four fingers in the top section, and the thumb in the lower section. Spreading and closing the hand makes the puppet's mouth open and shut (Platts, 1972).

Paper Bag Puppets

You will need: brown lunch bag
construction paper
yarn or string
markers
glue
stick

Procedure 1:

1. Stuff the lunch bag with newspaper.
2. Insert a stick.
3. Tie the bottom of bag with string.
4. Add facial features of yarn, construction paper, etc.

Procedure 2:

1. Using crayons or markers draw a character on the bag.
2. Add yarn for special emphasis.
3. The fold of the bottom of the bag makes a good mouth when hand is inserted (Collier, Forte, & MacKenzie, 1981).

Playdough Puppets

You will need: playdough
raisins
cereal
toothpicks
fabric scraps
gravel

Procedure:

1. Place a small amount of playdough onto finger.
2. Mold playdough into face shape covering finger.
3. Add raisins, cereal, gravel, toothpicks, etc. for facial features and added emphasis (Wolfgang, Mackender, & Wolfgang, 1981).

Styrofoam Ball Puppets

You will need: styrofoam ball
sticks
fabric scraps
buttons
felt scraps

Procedure:
1. Insert a stick into styrofoam ball.
2. Cover the styrofoam ball with fabric.
3. Tie the fabric around the stick.
4. Glue on buttons and felt scraps for facial features.

Finger-face puppets. The child will roll a rectangular scrap of paper into a tube and secure it with tape. The puppet is completed by gluing a face or sticker onto the tube. The puppet is then worn on the finger.

Finger-leg puppets. The child will make a finger-leg puppet by cutting two small holes at the bottom of a poster board character. The child inserts two fingers into the holes to make the puppet walk or dance.

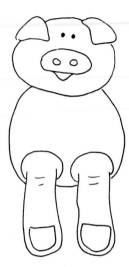

Stick puppets. Either draw your own character on posterboard or cut large faces from a magazine and glue them onto posterboard. Attach this to a dowel stick with staples.

Large people puppets. Draw a character on a piece of cardboard as tall as the height of a child. If need be, this can be easily done by using an opaque projector. Cut the figure out. Cut out a hole for the face as well as holes for the hands.

Body puppets. Large puppets can be made by cutting people or story characters from poster board. A small hole is made for the child's face, and two small slits are cut for the hands. These puppets are more durable if laminated. The child will wear the puppet in dramatic play. Animal puppets are especially appealing to very young children because they can make animal sounds as they wear the puppet.

Some suggestions for stories from which large character puppets can be made are:

The Three Little Pigs
The Billy Goats Gruff
Goldilocks and the Three Bears
The Wizard of Oz
The Gingerbread Man
The Elves and the Shoemaker

Additional Information for Teachers

Basic Four Food Plan

Food Group	Daily Recommended Servings			Foods and Portion Sizes for One Serving	Nutrient Contribution
	Child	Adoles.	Adult		
Milk	3	4	2	milk (skim, whole, low fat, buttermilk)—1 cup cheddar cheese—1½ inch cube or 1–1½ oz. cottage cheese—1 cup, sour cream—1 cup ice cream—1½ cups yogurt—1 cup, cream cheese—16 tbsp. pudding or custard—1 cup	calcium riboflavin protein phosphorus vitamin D

Meat	2	2	2	meat, fish, poultry—lean: 2 oz; with fat: 3–4 oz
				hot dogs—2; bacon—2 slices; sausage—6 oz
				luncheon meats—3 slices or 3 oz
				protein equivalents:
				   eggs—2; peanut butter—5 tbs.
				   dry beans, peas (cooked)—1 cup
				   nuts—2 oz or 8 tbsp.
					protein
					niacin
					iron
					thiamine
					vitamin A

Fruits & Vegetables	4	4	4	cooked fruit or vegetable—½ cup raw or fresh fruit or vegetable—1 cup fresh fruit—1 medium size juice—½ cup grapefruit—½ medium cantaloupe—¼ medium raisins—¼ cup	vitamin A vitamin C fiber iron (dried fruits)
Vitamin A (μg RE)	400–700	800–1000	800–1000	Good sources: spinach, carrots, kale, peas, broccoli, asparagus, brussel sprouts, apricots, peaches, watermelon.	
Vitamin C	45	50–60	60	Good sources: asparagus, broccoli, brussel sprouts, cabbage, citrus juices and fruits, cantaloupe, green pepper, strawberries, sweet potatoes	
Bread & Cereals	4	4	4	bread—1 slice corn bread—2 inch square hamburger/frankfurter roll—½ of the roll cooked cereal—½ cup; dry cereal—1 cup (¾ oz) crackers—4 to 6 biscuits—1 (2 inch diameter) rice, pastas—½ cup; pancake—1 (4 inch diameter)	economical source of energy: thiamine niacin riboflavin fiber iron

Vegetarian Basic Four Food Plan

Food Group	Daily Recommended Servings			Foods and Portion Sizes for One Serving	Nutrient Contribution
	Child	Adoles.	Adult		
Milk & Eggs	3+	4	2+	milk—1 cup cottage cheese—1 cup tofu—1 cup eggs—2 cheese (cheddar, swiss, etc.)—1 ounce slice	vitamin B_{12} calcium vitamin D phosphorus protein
Vegetables		3 or more		Good sources: spinach, carrots, kale, peas, broccoli, asparagus, brussel sprouts, apricots, peaches, watermelon.	vitamin A vitamin C B-complex iron, fiber
Vitamin A (μg RE)	400–700	800–1000	800–1000	Good sources: asparagus, broccoli, brussel sprouts, cabbage, citrus juices and fruits, cantaloupe, green pepper, strawberries, sweet potatoes	
Vitamin C (mg)	45	50–60	60		
Fruits		1 to 4		juice—½ cup raw or fresh fruit—1 cup cooked fruit—½ cup fresh fruit—1 medium size	vitamin A vitamin C iron (dried fruits) fiber
Legumes Breads Grains Nuts Seeds		6 or more (include at least 1 serving of beans)		peanut butter—4 tbs. bread—1 slice cooked cereal—½ cup; dry cereal—1 cup crackers—4–6 pancake—1 (4" diameter) dry beans, peas (cooked)—1 cup nuts & seeds—2 oz or 8 tbsp. rice—½ cup pastas—½ cup	protein thiamin niacin vitamin B_6 folacin vitamin E zinc iron fiber

Books with Background Material for the Teacher

Science Experiences for the Early Childhood Years, Jean Durgin Harlan, Charles E. Merrill Co., Columbus, Ohio, 1976

Beginnings, Teacher's Guide, Science Curriculum Improvement Study, Rand McNally and Company, Chicago, Illinois, 1974

The Organic Living Book, Bernice Kohn, Viking Press, New York, 1972

Good Earth Almanac, 2210 West 75 Street, Suite 305, Prairie Village, Kansas, 66208

Farming in the Classroom—Teachers' Guide, Science Study Aid No. 8, Agricultural Research Service, U.S. Department of Agriculture, Supt. of Documents, Government Printing Office, Washington, D.C.

Gardening in Containers—a Handbook, Brooklyn Botanical Gardens, Brooklyn, N.Y.

Food in History, Reay Tannahill, Stein and Day Publishers, New York, 1973

How Do Your Children Grow? Association for Childhood Education International, 3615 Wisconsin Avenue, N.W., Washington, D.C. 20016

Nutrition and Intellectual Growth in Children, Association for Childhood Education International, 3615 Wisconsin Avenue, N.W., Washington, D.C. 20016

Food Selection for Good Nutrition in Group Feeding, Agricultural Research Service, Dept. of Agriculture, Supt. of Documents, U.S. Government Printing Office, Washington, D.C.

Selection and Care of Fresh Fruits and Vegetables, 1977, United Fresh Fruit & Vegetable Association, 1019 19th Street, N.W., Washington, D.C. 20036

Let's Go Metric (Chapter 7), Frank Donovan, Weybright and Talley, New York, 1974

Books That Can Be Used by the Teacher with Younger Children or Read by Older Children

Milk For You, G. Warren Schloat, Charles Scribner's Sons, New York, 1951

Animals That Give People Milk, Terrance W. McCabe & Harley W. Mitchell, National Dairy Council, Chicago, Illinois, 1970

The Wonderful Egg, G. Warren Schloat, Charles Scribner's Sons, New York, 1952

Plants That Feed Us, Carroll Lane Fenton & Hermine B. Kitchen, John Day & Co., New York 1971 (the story of grains and vegetables)

Foxfire Books, Eliot Wigginton, Doubleday & Co., Garden City, New York

Growing Up, How We Become Alive, Are Born, and Grow, Karl de Schweinitz, Macmillan Co., New York, 1965

The Secret World of the Baby, Beth Day and Margaret Liley, M.D., Random House, New York, 1968

The Little House in the Big Woods, Laura Ingalls Wilder, Harper & Row, New York, 1953

The Little House on the Prairie, Laura Ingalls Wilder, Harper and Row, New York, 1953

Grains, Elizabeth B. Brown, Prentice-Hall, New Jersey, 1977 (history of grain)

Popcorn, Millicent E. Selsam, Morrow, 1976 (history of maize)

Hunters Stew and Hangtown Fry, Lila Perl, (what colonial America ate), Seabury Press, 1977

The Bakery Factory, Aylette Jenness, T. Crowell, 1978

Wild Foods, Lawrence Pringle, Scribner, 1978

Good for Me: All About Food in 32 Bites, Marilyn Burns, Little Brown & Company, Boston, MA, 1978

Fruits We Eat, Carroll Lane Fenton and Hermine B. Kitchen, John Day Co., New York, 1961

Plants in the City, Herman and Nina Schneider, (a good handbook to help introduce plants to children) John Day Co., New York, 1951

The First Book of Food, Ida Scheib, Franklin Watts Publishers, New York, 1956

The Carrot and Other Root Vegetables, Millicent E. Selsam, William Morrow & Co., New York, 1970

We Read About Seeds And How They Grow, Harold E. Tannenbaum and Nathan Sillman, Webster Publishing Co., St. Louis, Missouri, 1960

The Tomato and Other Fruit Vegetables, Millicent E. Selsam, William Morrow & Co., New York, 1970

Eating And Cooking Around the World, Erick Barry, John Day Co., New York, 1963

Plants That Feed the World, Rose E. Frisch, D. Van Nostrand Co., Princeton, New Jersey, 1966

The Wonderful World of Food, John Boyd Orr, Garden City Books, New York, 1958

Plants Are Like That, A. Harris Stone and Peter Plascencia, (a chemistry book about plants for young children) Prentice-Hall, Englewood Cliffs, New Jersey, 1968

The Chemistry of a Lemon, A. Harris Stone and Peter Plascencia, (exciting experiments with lemons) Prentice-Hall, Inc., Englewood Cliffs, New Jersey, 1966

Salt, Augusta Golden, (good experiments for preschool and early primary) Thomas Crowell Co., New York, 1965

The First American Peanut Growing Book, Kathy Mandry, Random House, 1976

Apple Orchard, Irmengarde Eberle, Henry Z. Walck Inc., New York, 1962

And Everything Nice, Eliza K. Cooper (the story of sugar, spice and flavorings) Harcourt Brace and World Inc., New York, 1966

Rice, Food for a Hungry World, Winnefred Hammond, Coward McCann, Inc., New York, 1961

Nothing to Eat but Food, Frank Jupo, (a history of food for young children) E. P. Dutton and Co., Inc., New York, 1954

The First Book of Gardening, Virginia Kirkus, Franklin Watts Inc., New York, 1956

The Indoor Outdoor Grow It Book, S. Sinclair Baker, Random House, New York, 1966

Indoor Outdoor Gardening Book, Cynthia and Alvin Koehler, Grosset & Dunlap, Inc. (Wonder Books), New York, 1969

A Gardening Book: Indoors and Outdoors, Anne B. Walsh, Atheneum, New York, 1976

Kids Gardening: First Indoor Outdoor Gardening Book for Children, Aileen Paul, Doubleday, New York, 1972

References

Cole, A., Haas, C., Heller, E., and Weinberger, B. (1976). *A Pumpkin in a Pear Tree.* Boston: Little, Brown and Company.

Collier, M. J., Forte, I., and MacKenzie, J. (1981). *Kids Stuff.* Nashville, Tenn.: Incentive Publications.

Colvin, M. P. (1979). *Big Holiday Book.* Dansville, N.Y.: Instructor Publications.

Eheart, B. K., and Leavitt, R. L. (1985). "Supporting Toddler Play." *Young Children, 3,* 18–22.

Fein, G. G. (1982). "Pretend Play: New Perspectives." In Janet F. Brown, ed., *Curriculum Planning for Young Children.* Washington, D.C.: National Association for the Education of Young Children, p. 23.

Flemming, B. M., and Hamilton, D. S. (1977). *Resources for Creative Teaching in Early Childhood Education.* New York: Harcourt Brace Jovanovich.

Heinig, R. B., and Stillwell, L. (1974). *Creative Dramatics for the Classroom Teacher.* Englewood Cliffs, N.J.: Prentice-Hall.

Hutt, C. and Bhavnani, R. (1976) "Predictions from Play." In J. S. Bruner et al., ed., *Play: Its Role in Development and Evolution.* New York: Basic, pp. 216–219.

Jalongo, M. R. (1985). "When Young Children Move." *Young Children, 6,* 51–57.

Jenkins, K. S. (1982) *Kinder-Krunchies.* Pleasant Hill, Calif.: Discovery Toys.

Kostelnik, M. J., Whiren, A. P., and Stein, L. C. (1986). "Living with He-Man." *Young Children, 4,* 3–9.

Marotz, L., Rush, J., and Cross, M. (1985). *Health, Safety, and Nutrition for the Young Child.* Albany, N.Y.: Delmar Publications.

Mayesky, M., Neuman, D., and Wlodkowski, R. J. (1985). *Creative Activities for Young Children* (3rd ed.). New York: Delmar Publishers.

Oliver, S. D., and Musgrave, K. O. (1984). *Nutrition: A Teacher Sourcebook of Integrated Activities.* Newton, Mass.: Allyn and Bacon.

Platts, M. E. (1972). *Launch.* Stevensville, Mich.: Educational Service Incorporated.

Selph, A., and Street, B. G. (1975). *Alphabet Soup* (1st ed.). Durham, N.C.: American Printers Limited.

Way, B. (1967). *Development Through Drama.* Atlantic Highlands, N.J.: Humanities Press.

Wolfgang, C. H., Mackender, B., and Wolfgang, M. E. (1981). *Growing and Learning Through Play.* New York: McGraw-Hill.

Investigation in Science and Mathematics

Mathematics and science education have received considerable attention over the past two decades. New curriculum models for science instruction were developed in abundance and used in classrooms across the country. Though they shared some common elements, the models differed in their emphasis on content, process, discovery learning, or problem solving (Bruner, 1960). Today there is still considerable pressure to "improve" our science and mathematics programs. In order to make appropriate decisions regarding approaches to mathematics and science education for young children, teachers must understand the different types of knowledge and how children acquire each type.

Based on Piaget's work, Kamii and DeVries (1977) have identified three different types of knowledge—social, physical, and logical-mathematical. Social knowledge has its source in other people and varies with the culture. Such knowledge is told to the learner by others and is therefore external. Words that name objects, holidays, and rules are examples of social knowledge. Though children appear to learn a great deal by being told, Piaget's research and teachers' observations confirm that young children learn most concepts through direct experience.

Physical knowledge also comes from the external world, but this type of knowledge is the result of actions on objects: touching, smelling, seeing, tasting, listening, etc. Wadsworth (1978) points out that such knowledge comes from the objects themselves and is a form of discovery. Physical knowledge does not have to be reinforced by another person. The child's own observations of the objects' physical nature correct or reinforce the child's learning. The child learns about physical properties by manipulating objects. Gagne (1977, p. 124) writes:

> The great value of concepts as a means of thinking and communicating is the fact that they have *concrete references*. The importance of this characteristic cannot be overemphasized. But since concepts are learned by the human being via language, there is often the danger of losing sight of this concreteness. Learning can become ooververbalized, which means the concepts learned are highly inadequate in their reference to actual situations. The learner, one may note, "does not really know the meaning of the word," even though he can use it correctly in a sentence.

345

In contrast to social and physical knowledge, logical-mathematical or operational knowledge is internal. This kind of knowledge enables the child to classify objects on the basis of their similarities. As Almy and Genishi (1979) point out, the ability to organize one's thoughts in a logical, systematic way is necessary to deal with mathematics and science. Most of Piaget's experiments were directly related to the building of logico-mathematical or operational knowledge. He distinguishes physical knowledge, which is discovered by the child, from logical-mathematical knowledge, which is invented by the child. However, these two kinds of knowledge are closely tied together. Kamii (1973, pp. 214–215) writes:

> Neither physical knowledge nor logico-mathematical knowledge can exist without the other. Pure logic almost exists, but physical knowledge is involved even in the classical example of the child who always found 10 pebbles, whether he counted them left to right, or from right to left. The fact that the pebbles let themselves be ordered is an example of physical knowledge. Physical and logico-mathematical knowledge are thus almost indistinguishable.

Kamii and DeVries (1977) contend that traditional early childhood science programs have treated scientific knowledge as if it were social knowledge. The traditional approach to science, they feel, relies too heavily on verbal instruction and does not provide enough opportunities for children to be discoverers of physical knowledge and builders of logical knowledge.

The "sciencing" approach to learning (McNairy, 1985) may be applied to all educational programs for all ages. This approach has been defined as "the process of active inquiry into and subsequent construction of relationships in both the physical and social world." Specifically this refers to the development and utilization of scientific processes through physical experiences with the environment for the purpose of creative problem solving and developing intelligence. McNairy further defines active inquiry as investigation into or exploration of both objects and ideas. Scientific processes are those processes of inquiry that are basic to all scientific disciplines. There are 11 scientific processes identified by the American Association for the Advancement of Science, several of which can be experienced, in simplified form, by young children and can give opportunities for basic process skills development (Kamii & DeVries, 1977). These processes, which include observation, classification, measurement, computation, experimentation, and prediction, provide a framework for science and mathematics education in the early years.

Children, innately curious, are natural scientists. Eagerly they discover as much as they can about the world around them. Children think, form concepts, and solve problems. They unconsciously use scientific methods as they observe, infer, classify, and reach conclusions. Encouraging the development of scientific and mathematical skills and methods of thinking requires an environment that is rich in interesting objects to explore and manipulate, one that fosters exploration of ideas. It is the teacher's responsibility to capitalize on children's natural curiosity as learning opportunities arise, by helping children focus on relevant details, by asking questions that require judgments and inferences, and by providing opportunities to classify, experiment, and communicate their findings.

The experiences and activities in this chapter are designed to provide opportunities to develop basic process skills and an understanding of the patterns of science and mathematics through the use of hands-on materials. These activities are designed to help young children see relationships and interconnections between science and mathematics as they learn to deal flexibly with scientific and mathematical ideas and concepts. Children do best what they like to do. Although it may be hard work, the challenge of inquiry and discovery is stimulating and fun for children.

Objectives

1. To discover basic math and science concepts by exploration and experimentation (in incidental and contrived situations).
2. To enjoy science and math activities by engaging in various methods of discovery.
3. To use resource materials in problem solving.
4. To use a variety of materials for weighing and measuring.
5. To chart progress and results of experiences.
6. To use the scientific method of problem solving—to observe, identify problem, predict, research, test prediction, and generalize.
7. To manipulate various objects to move from concrete experiences to the abstract.
8. To develop habits of thinking and investigation.
9. To share discovery with others.
10. To find success in these areas.

Environmental Resources

Rugs
Tables
Low shelving for puzzles, games, displays
Windows (preferably low enough for the children to see out)
Clear plastic containers with labels for "raw materials"
Plastic tubs for storing materials and supplies
A sink, preferably with hot and cold water

Science Supplies

Prisms, tuning forks, wood, wire, glass, soil, bottles, candles, batteries
Bolts, switches, pulleys, levers, screws, wheels and axles, planes, and pendulums

Pendulum frame, pendulum bobs, scales (balance, kitchen, spring), weights

Assorted materials for balancing, blocks of various weights, mirrors, lenses

Kaleidoscopes, electric bell, calendars, clocks, hourglass, egg timer, sundial

Bulbs, tape measures, yardstick, meter stick, rulers, dry and liquid measure containers

Rope, drinking straws, food coloring, stopwatch, stethoscope, sponges, keys

Kite, locks, iron filings, magnets, mechanical junk, slinky

An assortment of chemicals from home: vinegar, baking soda, table salt, baking powder, sugar, cream of tartar, rubbing alcohol, epsom salts, iodine, ammonia, and hydrogen peroxide

Fibers: nylon, silk, rayon, linen

Magnifying glasses (hand and large on stand), compass, barometer, flashlight

Objects to smell, taste, touch; gears; strings; color paddles; telescope

Microscopes

Heat, water

Magazines (especially farm and science magazines)

Potting soil, variety of seeds

Hot plate

Thermometers (Celsius and Fahrenheit)

Aquarium and terrarium (empty)

Flowers and plants; animals (alive and preserved)

Rocks and shells

Cages and animal food

Paper and pen for labeling

Chart and graph paper

Resource material, pleasurable nature reading (e.g., *Ranger Rick*)

Watering can, trowel, seeds, flowerpots, incubators, bug house (to keep live insects)

Science Activities

Life Science: Plants

Objectives

1. To be able to distinguish living from nonliving things.
2. To become aware that seeds house dormant baby plants.
3. To understand that each plant has its own unique seed that can only grow into the kind of plant that produced it.
4. To understand that if seeds are planted in soil and are kept moist and receive sunlight, they have the potential to become mature plants.
5. To become aware that gravity, moisture, and sunlight affect plant growth.
6. To become aware that roots, stems, and leaves have tubes or veins running through them that carry liquids to and from the leaves and to and from the roots.
7. To develop an awareness that the fruit of a plant is where the seeds for the plant are produced and found.
8. To become aware that dead flowers left on plants grow into fruits that will eventually contain seeds.

Suggested Experiences

1. *Nature Walk.* Go on a walk. Encourage children to look closely at things outside. Encourage them to handle leaves, grass, soil, rocks, flowers, and to observe carefully. Return to the classroom and ask children to name the things they saw that were living and those that were not. Make a chart listing the children's contributions in two columns.

2. *Beans and Pebbles Experiment.* Provide lima beans, small pebbles the size of lima beans, water, and two equal-size plastic containers. Show the children the lima beans and the small pebbles. Ask them which of the two things is alive and which is not. Ask the children to sort out the lima beans from the pebbles. Ask the children to count out equal numbers of lima beans and pebbles, and place them in separate containers. Tell the children to fill the containers with water and leave overnight. Ask the children what changes if any will occur in the beans and the pebbles overnight. The next day let the children observe the changes in the beans. Encourage them to tell what they observed.

3. *Seeds Observation.* Provide assorted fresh fruits and vegetables, such as apples, oranges, cantaloupe, tomatoes, peas, cucumbers, etc., a knife, paper towels, and a magnifying glass. Ask the children where seeds come from. Allow each child to respond. Show the assorted fruits and vegetables and ask if they know what is inside. Cut the fruits and vegetables and remove the seeds. Ask the children to place the seeds from each kind of fruit or vegetable on a separate paper towel. Allow the seeds to dry. Tell the children to examine the seeds with the magnifying glass. After the seeds have dried for a week, place them on a wet paper towel inside a jar or in a plastic bag to observe possible germination.

4. *Sorting Seeds.* Provide various seeds in a plastic container and an empty egg carton. Show the children the seeds and the egg carton. Ask them to sort the seeds into the sections of the egg carton. Let them guess what plants the different seeds will grow into.

5. *Growing Seeds.* Have available some germinated seeds growing on a moist paper towel and an empty clear plastic glass. Encourage the children to observe the germinated seeds. Ask them to tell which part of the seed grows first, what develops after the roots, and in which direction the roots grow. Place the seeds and the paper towel inside the plastic glass. Then ask one or more children to situate the seeds in the glass so that the roots turn up. Ask the children to observe the seeds the next day to see if the roots are still growing up. (Roots usually curve downward regardless of their position. This is caused by gravity and is called *geotropism.*)

6. *Classifying Leaves.* Ask the children to bring in leaves from home or go on a walk to collect leaves. In the classroom have the children classify the leaves by shape by placing those of the same shape together on poster board. They may be glued on. Ask the children to look up the leaf shapes in a reference book such as *Trees: A Golden Guide,* by Herbert Zim and A. C. Martin, or *Spotter's Guide to Trees of North America,* by Alan Mitchell, to discover their identities. Label the posters with the correct name. Point out that even though leaves of the same variety came from different trees, they have the same shape.

7. *Classifying Evergreens.* Tell children to bring in assorted twigs with leaves from evergreen trees and deciduous trees. Talk about the observable differences in the leaves and the needles. Explain that an evergreen tree does not lose its leaves in the fall, but stays green all year. Have the children make a poster of evergreen twigs and label the varieties. They may refer to reference books for this purpose.

8. *Displays of Live Weeds and Wild Flowers* (these are excellent for helping children understand the concept of diversity). Comparative studies include

   Comparison of weeds found at the school with those found near a pond or creek.

   Comparison of wild flowers found on a slope facing the sun with those found on a slope not facing the sun.

   Comparison of weeds found at a school in the country with those found by a friend in the city, to give children an idea of the diversity of plants found around them and their relationship to the climate.

   Example. Display a beautiful weed (e.g., dandelion or horseweed). Direction card or discussion might evolve around "Why Is This Plant Called a Weed?"

   Collections and classification should be done by children with the assistance of resource materials and the teacher.

9. *Observation-Measurement Charting.* Observe the growth of seeds or plants in the room (height, new leaf, or bloom). Record observations. Measure leaf spread and/or stem growth. Record growth.

10. *Small Garden (for the nature center).* This is a substitute where outdoor gardening is unfeasible. Gardens aid the child's understanding of the concept

of change. (*Note:* With a little direction, the children can make such a garden for themselves.) Materials needed are

A plastic or metal dishpan, although the ideal is a zinc-lined box with a hole for drainage.
A soil mixture (the children will help mix the soils and probably question why).

When the layout is ready, discuss it with interested children. They will offer suggestions. Research (and the teacher) will let them know what is possible in such small gardens. The children should decide on some workable plan, which should be accepted.

Suggestions
  a. A *sunken pond* (made with a dish), with the garden planned around it. Even a small pond will hold a few tadpoles, a snail, and some pond weeds.
  b. A *rockery* (made from snail rocks collected by the children) can be made by placing soil between the rocks in which plants take root. Tiny rock plants can be bought cheaply at dime stores and nurseries or may be donated by the parents.
  c. A *lawn.* Here children can plant different varieties of grass seed.
11. *Outdoor Gardening.* Materials needed are

Tools, child-sized: hoes, rakes, shovels, watering cans, hose, spade, trowels
Land with good soil and sunlight or flower boxes
Thermometers
Wheelbarrows
Seeds, bulbs, and plants

12. *Plant Identical Seeds or Plants.* Use different types of soil, amounts of sunlight, or water. Compare each group.

Suggested Teacher-Made Activities

1. *Seed Identification.* The chart can be made by using tri-wall, cardboard, or tagboard. A sample of each kind of seed with the word under it may be put in the chart. Several additional seeds of the same varieties are placed in a box labeled seeds. Children can find seeds that match and paste them on the chart. Others may want to do research on the various kinds of seeds.

lima beans	corn	pumpkin
rice	grape	orange
peas	cabbage	green beans

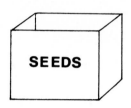

SEEDS

2. *Seed and Plant.* Develop a collection of various seeds familiar to the children. (Get the youngsters to bring in the seeds!) Using tagboard, paste the seeds and a picture of the plant from which the seed came. Make into puzzles that are self-correcting; laminate.
   Variation. Collect leaves and make a leaf identification picture.

Suggested Books for Children

Dewey Decimal Classification Numbers: leaves—581; seeds—581.46; flowers—582.13; trees—582.16.

Aliki, *The Story of Johnny Appleseed.* Englewood Cliffs, N.J.: Prentice-Hall, 1963.

Allen, Gertrude. *Everyday Trees.* Boston: Houghton Mifflin, 1968.

Bulla, Clyde. *A Tree Is a Plant.* New York: Thomas Y. Crowell, 1973.

Cole, Joanna. *Plants in Winter.* New York: Thomas Y. Crowell, 1973.

Cooper, Elizabeth. *Sweet and Delicious Fruits of Tree, Bush and Vine.* Chicago: Children's Press, 1973.

Cooper, Elizabeth. *A Tree Is Something Wonderful.* Chicago: Children's Press, 1972.

Earle, Olive L., and Kantor, Michael. *Nuts.* New York: Morrow, 1976.

Garelick, Mary. *The Tremendous Tree Book.* New York: Scholastic Book Services, 1979.

Gutnik, Martin J. *How Plants Make Food.* Chicago: Children's Press, 1976.

Hammond, Winifred G. *The Riddle of Seeds.* New York: Coward-McCann, 1965.

Jordan, H. J. *How a Seed Grows.* New York: Thomas Y. Crowell, 1960.

Kirkpatrick, Rena K. *Look at Leaves.* Milwaukee: Raintree Children's Books, 1978.

Rodgers, Matilda. *First Book of Tree Identification.* New York: Random House, 1951.

Selsam, Millicent E., and Hunt, Joyce. *A First Look at Leaves*. New York: Scholastic Book Services, 1976.

Selsam, Millicent E., and Hunt, Joyce. *A First Look at the World of Plants*. New York: Walker, 1978.

Resource Books for Teachers

Blough, Glenn O. *Discovering Plants*. New York: McGraw-Hill, 1966.

Hutchins, Ross E. *The Amazing Seeds*. New York: Dodd, Mead, 1965.

Kieran, John. *An Introduction to Trees*. New York: Doubleday, 1966.

Levenson, Elaine. *Teaching Children About Science: Ideas and Activities Every Teacher and Parent Can Use*. Englewood Cliffs, N.J.: Prentice-Hall, 1985.

North Carolina Competence-Based Curriculum. Raleigh, N.C., 1985.

Poling, James. *Leaves*. New York: Holt, 1971.

Shuttlesworth, Dorothy E. *The Hidden Magic of Seeds*. Emmaus, Penn.: Rodale Press, 1976.

Zim, Herbert S., and Martin, A. C. *Trees: A Golden Guide*. Racine, Wis.: Western, 1956.

Animals: Land Animals

Objectives

1. To understand that the world is made up of living and nonliving things.
2. To become aware that most living things are either plants or animals.
3. To develop an awareness that animals live in many places.
4. To understand that all animals need food and water.
5. To understand that each animal needs its own kind of food.
6. To develop an awareness that animals are mobile and move in different ways.
7. To develop an awareness that most animals move, eat, and grow.
8. To develop an awareness that animals adapt to their environment in different ways to aid their survival.
9. To become aware that animals kept in captivity need to be cared for.
10. To begin to develop an appreciation and respect for life and living things.
11. To begin to develop an awareness of how to group animals with similar characteristics or attributes.

Suggested Experiences

1. *Introduction to Animals.* Provide a selection of assorted living and nonliving things, such as various plants, goldfish, parakeets, hamsters, turtles, insects, snails, rocks, seashells, etc. Show the children the assorted living and nonliving things. They should observe at least two or three live animals. Ask them to compare the animals to one another. Discuss how the animals are different, how they are alike, how animals are different from plants, what makes plants and animals alike, whether we are living things, whether we are plants or animals, etc.

   Ask the children to name the largest, then the smallest animal they can think of. Allow them to share their thoughts. Have the children find or make pictures of living and nonliving things. Tell them to sort the pictures into piles of living and nonliving things, and then further sort the pictures of living things into plants and animals. The children can mount the pictures on appropriately labeled posters for display in the classroom.

2. *Caterpillars.* Provide an empty one-quart jar or clear plastic shoebox; a small container for water; a small twig from the tree or plant where the caterpillar was found; some moist soil; a piece of bark; nylon mesh; and a rubber band to secure the mesh as a lid. Place the soil on the bottom of the jar and a piece of bark at a slant against the jar. Place the twig in the water on top of the soil so that the leaves will stay alive longer. Place the caterpillar on the twig. Be sure a twig the caterpillar was crawling on when it was caught is included. For observation provide a magnifying glass; a piece of paper; a ruler; an eye dropper; and water.

Provide opportunities for the children to observe the caterpillars in the jar. Encourage the children to report what they have seen by asking such questions as: What were the caterpillars doing? How much have they eaten? What do the leaves look like after the caterpillars have been on them? Has the caterpillar begun to make a cocoon? Have the children remove the caterpillar from the jar. Place it on a piece of paper. Place a ruler beside the caterpillar. Try to measure its length. Look at it through the magnifying glass. How many segments does it have? Does every segment have legs? How many legs does it have? Hold the paper at a slant. Is the caterpillar able to crawl up a steep slope? What happens when the caterpillar comes to water? What happens when two caterpillars meet? Encourage the children to do as much hands-on activity as possible. Older children will be able to work independently, while younger ones will require more help.

3. *Tadpoles and Frogs.* This is a good springtime experience. Provide a suitable container for pond water, some frog eggs and/or tadpoles, pond water, and pond plants. Place eggs, tadpoles, plants, and pond water in a tank or aquarium. Fill the tank only partially. Children will observe the eggs hatching and the changes in the tadpoles. As the tadpoles grow legs, place rocks in the tank so that the top of some of the rocks come up out of the water. This will provide the maturing tadpoles a way to breathe as their lungs begin to function.

Provide a magnifying glass, leafy vegetables (for a food supplement), extra pond water, fresh water snails if possible (for clean-up), paper and pencil supplies for recording the observable changes.

4. *Grouping Vertebrates.* Provide pictures and small models of assorted vertebrates. Let the children carefully observe the pictures and models. Ask them to think about what makes each animal different from the others. Ask questions such as: Which animals have hair or fur? Do any of the animals have feathers? Do all of the animals have feet? Do any of the animals have rough, scaly skin? Do any of the animals appear to have a smooth, moist skin? Explain to the children that the pictures and models can be divided by the kind of skin the animals have. Tell them that zoologists have divided the animals that have backbones into five large groups or classes of animals. Encourage the children to guess what the five groups or classes of animals with backbones might be. Listen to their ideas and then tell them that the five classes are: mammals, birds, reptiles, amphibians, and fish. Ask the children to sort the models and/or pictures into groups of mammals, birds, reptiles, amphibians, and fish.

5. *Subdividing Mammals into Groups.* Provide mammals to observe (such as children's or classroom pets), a trip to a pet store, or a trip to a farm or a zoo. Ask the children to observe the live mammals. Encourage the children to touch the mammals gently and to use their five senses to observe the mammals. Ask the kind of questions that inspire the children's use of basic process skills. Include questions that require thinking: What kind of animal is this? Can you feel its backbone? Does the animal feel warm or cold when you hold it? How does your body feel when you touch it (warm or cold)? What kind of covering does the animal have? Does it have toenails? What body parts does the animal have that you have? How does the animal move? Does the animal have teeth? Do the animal's teeth look like your teeth?

Suggested Activities

1. *Earthworm Farm.* Use a fairly wide and deep jar or an old aquarium. Fill up to 4″ or 5″ from the top with a layer of small stones; layers of soil of various colors (sand, gravel, dark soil, etc.), well pressed down; and a layer of living turf. Stick a narrow strip of paper down the outside, marked to show where the layers are. Completely cover from bright light (with cloth or black construction paper) or place in a dark place to accelerate burrowing. Keep covered when you are not watching the worms.

    The children can

    Put the earthworms into the farm.
    Observe the disturbances in the earth made by the worms.
    Give them fresh food daily (lettuce, cereal, cornmeal).
    Add moisture to the soil frequently.
    Go in the schoolyard and look for animals living in the soil.

2. *Vivarium* (a home for such creatures as frogs, toads, and salamanders, that live on both land and water). Materials needed are

    A screened wooden box
    Soil to partially fill box
    Shallow dish to serve as a pond

3. *Ant Farm.* Provide this for scientific observation and for watching division of labor.

4. *Animals and Appropriate Cages* (gerbils, mice, rabbits, chicken, snakes). Learning to love and care for pets helps a child to develop a positive attitude toward living creatures.

5. *Walks* (around and about the school, with or without the teacher). Children should be encouraged to look slowly and carefully. They might observe changes of the leaves, nests made by birds and squirrels, sounds made by animals, creatures hiding under stumps, logs, or rocks, a running brook, a mud puddle, a clump of weeds, spider's eggs, the first flower to bloom, a ripening strawberry, erosion of soil, a budding tree, depending upon the location of the school and the season.

6. *Pond or Stream Collections.* (When exploring these areas, children might use a plankton net to collect microscopic animals to observe with their field microscope or to return to the classroom to observe with the microscope.)

7. *Visiting and Exploring River Banks, Quarries, Salt Marshes, a Mountain Stream* (dependent upon location).

8. *Utilization of State Parks.* Their resource people can be utilized as guides for wildlife study and their museums can be used for reference.

9. *Simple Bird Feeders.* Students can make a simple bird feeder either for classroom use or to take home to hang in the yard. Materials needed are a large empty milk carton and a plastic drinking straw. Cut out one of the carton's front panels, leaving about a half-inch border all around. Now make a perch by making a small hole in the bottom edge of the border and inserting the drinking straw well into the hole. Make another hole at the back of the carton exactly opposite the first one. Insert the end of the straw into the second hole

to anchor it. Fill the feeder with suet, orange pieces, birdseed, crackers, and so on. Then attach a hook or string loop to the top for hanging.

Suggested Teacher-Made Activities

1. *Match-by-Land, Water, and Air.* Tape together three pieces of colored tagboard, with pictures on each one depicting land, water, and air. Several pictures of animals representative of each can be mounted on cards. Children can match each picture with the appropriate land, water, and air. Answers can be placed on the back of each card for self-correction.

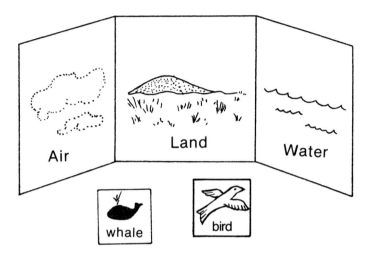

2. *Concentration Habitat Game.* Have children make 20 cards using tagboard and draw pictures of animals and their habitats. Play like Concentration. The person with the most matches wins.

3. *Animals and Their Homes.* These puzzle parts may be made with wood, cardboard, or laminated tagboard. One piece of each puzzle has a picture of an animal; the matching part has a picture of the animal's home. Words may be added if desired and answers placed on the back for self-correction.

4. *Food Chain Train.* Using posterboard, make a train. Find pictures of animals and plants in a food chain and paste on cars. Color code different food chains. The dots make the activity self-correcting.

Variation. Game can also be used to show the water cycle; sequence of seed to plant to flower to fruit; metamorphosis of various insects and frogs.

5. *Ecocycle Circle.* Make a dish or circle containing the names of the elements necessary for animals and plants to live with laminated tagboard. Make sets of picture cards to match the words using the same materials. Make one odd card; the player who plays the odd card on the cycle wins the game. The following words may be used:

Sun
Air
Land
Water
Plants
Meat eater
Plant eater
Decomposer

6. *Name the Animal, Name the Plant.* Find pictures of animals and plants from various environments such as sea animals and sea plants, desert animals and desert plants, pond life, woodland animals and plants, and so on. Paste on tagboard with space for the name of the animal or plant; laminate. The student will match the name of the plant or animal to that picture. The game is self-correcting.

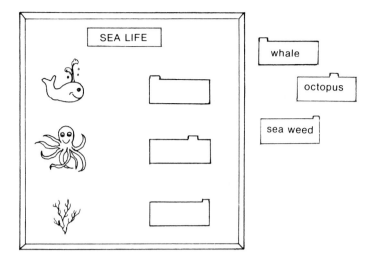

7. *Bird, Mammal, or Fish.* Mount three envelopes or library card holders (each one labeled bird, mammal, or fish) on a board (cardboard, laminated tagboard, or material board). An individual or small group of children can pick picture and word cards from a deck and sort them in the representative pockets. Names are on the back for self-correction.

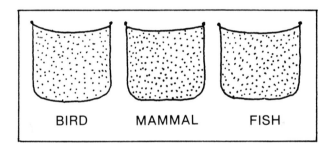

Suggested Books for Children

Dewey Decimal Classification Number for animals is 590 to 595.

Brenner, B. *If You Were an Ant.* New York: Harper, 1973.

Clarkson, J. N. *Tricks Animals Play.* Washington, D.C.: National Geographic Society, 1975.

Cooper, Gale. *Inside of Animals.* Boston: Little, Brown, 1978.

Daly, Kathleen. *Hide and Defend.* New York: Golden Press, 1976.

Freedman, Russel. *When Winter Comes.* New York: Dutton, 1981.

Gallant, R. A. *Me and My Bones.* New York: Doubleday, 1971.

Goldin, Augusta. *Spider Silk.* New York: Thomas Y. Crowell, 1964.

Heller, Ruth. *Chickens Aren't the Only Ones.* New York: Grosset and Dunlap, 1981.

Henrie, F. *Cats.* New York: Watts, 1980.

O'Hagan, Allan, O'Hagan, Judith, and O'Hagan, Caroline. *It's Easy to Have a Caterpillar Visit You.* New York: Lothrop, Lee and Shepard, 1980.

O'Hagan, Allan, O'Hagan, Judith, and O'Hagan, Caroline. *It's Easy to Have a Worm Visit You.* New York: Lothrop, Lee and Shepard, 1980.

O'Hagan, Allan, O'Hagan, Judith, and O'Hagan, Caroline. *It's Easy to Have a Snail Visit You.* New York: Lothrop, Lee and Shepard, 1980.

Piecewicz, Ann Thomas. *See What I Caught!* Englewood Cliffs, N.J.: Prentice-Hall, 1974.

Pringle, Lawrence P. *Twist, Wriggle and Squirm: A Book About Earth Worms.* New York: Thomas Y. Crowell, 1973.

Selsam, Millicent. *A First Look at Animals Without Backbones.* New York: Qalker, 1976.

Selsam, Millicent. *A First Look at Birds.* New York: Scholastic Books, 1981.

Selsam, Millicent. *How to Be a Nature Detective.* New York: Harper and Row, 1963.

Simon, Seymour. *Discovering What Earthworms Do.* New York: McGraw-Hill, 1969.

Stevens, Carla. *The Birth of Sunset's Kittens.* New York: Wm. H. Scott, 1969.

Tarrant, Graham. *Frogs.* Los Angeles: Intervisual Communications, Inc., 1983.

Van Gelder, Richard George. *Whose Nose Is This?* New York: Walker, 1974.

Resource Books for Teachers

Brown, S. E. *Bubbles, Rainbows, and Worms.* Mt. Rainer, Md.: Gryphon House, 1981.

Buck, Margaret. *Where They Go in Winter.* New York: Abingdon Press, 1968.

Farb, P. *The Insects.* New York: Time/Life, 1977.

Hussey, L. J., and Pessino, C. *Collecting Cocoons.* New York: Thomas Y. Crowell, 1953.

Kots, A., and Kots, E., *Insects of North America.* New York: Doubleday, 1971.

Levenson, Elaine. *Teaching Children About Science: Ideas and Activities Every Teacher and Parent Can Use.* Englewood Cliffs, N.J.: Prentice-Hall, 1985.

North Carolina Competence-Based Curriculum. N.C. Department of Public Instruction, Raleigh, N.C., 1985.

Rhine, Richard. *Life in a Bucket of Soil.* New York: Lothrop, 1972.

Shuttlesworth, Dorothy. *The Story of Ants.* New York: Doubleday, 1964.

Simon, H. *Insect Masquerades.* New York: Viking, 1968.

Simon, Seymour. *Pets in a Jar: Collecting and Caring for Small Wild Animals.* New York: Penguin Books, 1979.

Sisson, Edith. *Nature with Children of All Ages.* Englewood Cliffs, N.J.: Prentice-Hall, 1982.

Zim, Herbert. *Insects, a Golden Guide.* New York: Golden Press, 1976.

Zim, Herbert. *Mammals, a Golden Guide.* New York: Golden Press, 1955.

Fish and Ocean Life

Objectives

1. To be able to identify ocean plants and animals.
2. To identify at least five different types of shells.

3. To be able to discuss and show where different sea animals live and what they eat.
4. To be able to discuss what one might see, hear, taste, touch, or smell at the beach.
5. To be able to discuss the duties, responsibilities, and equipment that different sea occupations entail.

Suggested Experiences

1. ***Stock an Aquarium*** (because movement and changes are so easily viewed in the water, an aquarium is perhaps more attractive to children than growing plants). This is excellent for understanding concepts of interrelationships between plants and animals. Materials needed are

   A glass aquarium
   A layer of soil for water plants to root
   A layer of sand to keep the soil down
   Stones and shells for creatures to rest on and hide behind
   Pond water, if available (tap water often needs to be filtered)
   Inhabitants: select creatures that live together harmoniously. Children might like to research to find which ones do.
   Plenty of space
   Snails (important, for they act as scavengers)
   Food for the inhabitants (be careful not to overfeed)
   Pond weed (necessary both for food and to keep the tank clean)
   Filter pump, charcoal, filter fiber, if desired

2. ***Outdoor Exploration and Field Trips.*** These are necessary to encourage and stimulate the young child's natural curiosity about nature.

Suggested Teacher-Made Activities

1. ***Shells from the Seashore.*** Prepare a display table with different shells. Provide reference books and task cards for student research.
2. ***Octopus Science Game.*** Using tagboard, make the octopus and eight multicolored cards on which a question about the sea is written; laminate. At the tip of each leg is an answer to the question. Children read a question and answer the question by poking their pencils into the hole below the answer. To find the correct answer, students flip the octopus's leg up to see if the question card is the same color as the colored circle beneath the octopus's leg. If correct, the colors will be the same.

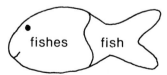 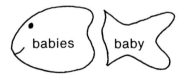

3. ***Fish Root Words.*** Make fish puzzles from tagboard. Children will match the correct fish plural to the fish root word. Game is self-correcting.
4. ***Fish for a Story.*** Make a colorful fish with a pocket from which children will "fish" for story starters. Stories will be posted in the writing center bulletin board.

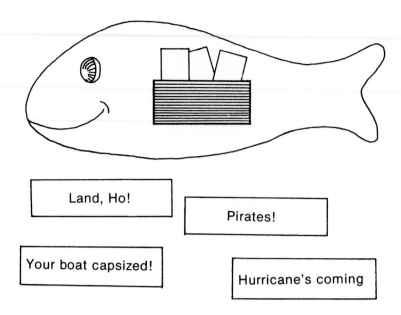

Land, Ho!

Pirates!

Your boat capsized!

Hurricane's coming

5. *Undersea Crayon Resist.* Provide construction paper, crayons, and diluted blue tempera paint. The students draw (with crayon) an underwater sea scene. Then students paint blue tempera over the crayon.
6. *Tools and Trade Match.* Find pictures depicting three different types of occupations related to the sea (fisherman, lifeguard, marine scientist). Put on tagboard. Make cards showing various pieces of equipment that relate to marine occupations; laminate. Put answers on the back of the cards so that game is self-correcting. Have students match the equipment to the occupation.
7. *Sea Life Movement.* Have students perform various movements to music.

   Crab walk
   Hermit crab getting into a shell
   Rocking waves
   Sinking ship
   Jellyfish flop
   Dolphin flip

8. *Go Fishing.* Prepare pictures of animals from both land and sea. Attach a paper clip to each animal. Have the child use a fishing rod to fish for the animals. There will be a magnet attached to the string. As the children fish out the animals, they will sort them according to land and sea. Students can either list and label all the sea animals or draw, color, and label three sea animals, depending on the particular child's ability.

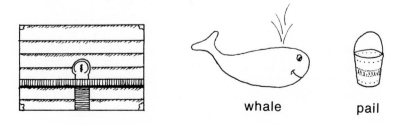

whale   pail

9. *Surf-City Seafood.* Provide construction paper for the students to develop their seafood menus. In the housekeeping center, the children can cook and serve and eat in the Seafood Restaurant.

   Variation. In the art center, the children can draw, color, and cut out paper food for their seafood restaurant.

10. *Seaside Measurement Classification Activity.* Use a large plastic mat and draw in objects found at the beach. Make task cards and x's from construction paper; laminate. The children will place x's on the object, following the directions from the task cards.

Place a blue X over all the things you can play with in the sand.	Place an orange X over all the things you can wear at the beach.	Place a green X over all the things you can play with in the water.

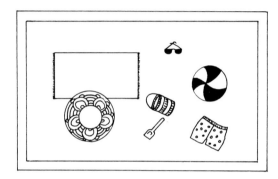

11. *Research Task Cards.* Provide reference books about the sea and sea life. The task cards can be color coded so that children of varying abilities can choose a card on their individual levels.

Find the word sand in My Golden Book Dictionary. Answer these questions: 1. What makes sand? 2. Where do you find sand?	Everyone needs clothes. Turn to page 32-33 in My Golden Book Dictionary. Draw and color two things you can wear at the beach.

Commercial Materials

Books: Nonfiction, used as reference for teacher and students

Houses from the Sea, by Alice E. Goudy
Let's Go to the Seashore, by Harriet Huntington
The Life of Fishes, by Dr. Maunce Burton

All About Whales, by Roy Chapman Andrews
Life Along the Seashore, by Alan Solem
Fish, by Christine Sharr
Watch the Tides, by David Greenhood
Animals of the Sea, a Golden Stamp Book
Seashells, a Golden Stamp Book

Books: Fiction used for enjoyment and motivation

Down to the Beach, by May Garelick
You Will Live Under the Sea, by Fred B. Phleger
One Morning in Maine, by Robert McClosky
Fishes, by Brian Wildsmith
Sam's First Fish, by Leonard Shartall
Good Morning Whale, by Achim Broger and Gisela Kalow
Sand, by Sally Cartwright
Titus Tidewater, by Suzanne Verrier

16mm Films

Exploring the Ocean
We Explore the Beach
We Explore the Ocean Life
I'm No Fool in the Water
The Lighthouse
Fish—A First Inquiry

Filmstrips

"Houses from the Sea"
"Animals of the Sea and Shore"

Children will view the filmstrips in the science center and answer questions about the filmstrips.

Filmstrip and Record

"The Beach"

The filmstrip and record will be placed in the listening center for enjoyment and reinforcement.

The Human Body

Objectives

1. To learn the basic parts of the human body.
2. To name the major parts of the body when shown a picture of the human body (head, neck, arms, hands, fingers, legs, feet, toes, elbows, knees, and wrists).

Suggested Experiences

1. *Look in the Mirror.* Provide a full-length mirror for children to observe themselves.

2. *Identifying Body Parts.* Play games, such as Simon Says (touch your neck, chin, earlobe, eyebrow, etc.).
3. *Life Size Portraits.* Children trace each other on brown wrapping paper. (One child lies down on the paper while the other traces around his/her outline.) Each child paints or colors in his/her own facial features, hair, clothing. The life-size portraits may be cut out and hung in the classroom.
4. *Photo Display.* Take photos of children and display in the room.

Suggested Teacher-Made Activities

1. *Labeling Body Parts.* Make a human figure for the flannel board and labels for major body parts. Make a chart correctly labeling body parts. Let children place labels on the flannel board figure and check themselves for accuracy.
2. *Making Faces.* Make a head shape for the flannel board with no hair, ears, or features. From flannel make several colors and types of hair, eyes, and eyebrows. Make several shapes of noses, ears, and mouths. Let the children experiment with putting the features on the head.

The Five Senses

Objectives

1. To develop a heightened awareness of the five senses and to improve observation skills.
2. To learn the basic functions of the body's senses.
3. To name the sense organs and identify their function.
4. To use the five senses in making observations of objects.

Suggested Experiences

Sound

1. *Sound Direction Experiment.* Children will sit one at a time in a chair with their eyes closed. Ring a bell or tap sicks together. Ask children to guess from which direction the sound came (up, down, behind, to the left, the right, etc.).
2. *Identifying Sounds.* Provide various objects which make sounds (coins, comb, rubber band, sheet of paper, etc.). Show children the objects and ask them to close their eyes. Make noise with one of the objects. Then ask children to guess which object they hear.
3. *Identifying Voices.* Provide a tape recorder and tape for recording children's voices and teacher's voice. Let children identify each other's voices and their own.

Sight and Touch

1. *Describing Attributes.* Provide a set of attribute blocks. Let the children handle the blocks and describe what they are holding. ("I have a large yellow circle"; "I have a small blue triangle.")
2. *Touching Objects.* Make a touching box that the children can reach into without seeing what is inside. This may be done by cutting a hole in the side of the box and hanging a piece of cloth over the hole. Place an object in the box. Ask the children to try to guess what is in the box by feeling the object.

Smell and Taste

1. *Identifying Smells.* Provide baby food jars, paper towels, spices, extracts of vanilla, lemon, and such other food items as fried bacon, onions, etc. Place a wadded-up paper towel in the bottom of each jar. Put a different subject for smelling in each jar. Allow the children with their eyes closed or blindfolded to smell and guess what the odors are.
   Variation: Have two jars of each odor. Let the children match the like odors.
2. *Sorting Flowers.* Provide an assortment of fresh flowers and a flower identification guidebook. Ask children to smell all the flowers and sort the ones with a scent from those with very little odor. Match the real flowers to their pictures in in the guidebook.
3. *Nature Walk.* Discover odors outside by taking a nature walk and gathering soil, leaves, tree twigs, etc. Bring them into the classroom for the children to smell and discuss.
   Variation: Let the children take an odor walk in the classroom to discover how many odors they can find among classroom objects.
4. *Sweet and Salty Experiment.* Provide salt and sugar in two cups. Discuss the difficulty in telling the difference between the two. Ask how they might tell the sugar from the salt. (By tasting them.)
5. *Sweet and Sour Experiment.* Provide lemon juice, vinegar, water, and sugar. Let the children taste each liquid. Discuss how each tastes. Add sugar and water to the lemon juice. Does the lemon juice still taste sour? Do sugar and water change the taste of the vinegar?
6. *Tasting Party.* Provide foods that are salty, sweet, sour, bitter, spicy, and bland. Include foods such as carrots, pickles, cheese, radishes, raisins, grapefruit juice, chocolate milk, whole milk, etc. Talk about the different tastes. Make a list of the foods in each category.

Suggested Teacher-Made Activities

1. *Poster of Senses.* Make a poster with symbols for each of the five senses (an ear, an eye, a nose, a mouth, and a hand) and pictures of things to be identi-

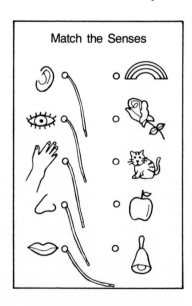

Match the Senses

fied by each sense (a bell, a rainbow, a rose, an apple, and a furry kitten). Laminate. Attach a long shoelace to each symbol. Punch a hole beside each picture. Children can match symbols to the correct pictures by sticking the lace into the correct holes.

2. *Color Paddles.* Using the primary colors, cut out cellophane circles. Glue these into separate circular frames of tagboard. These can be used to learn about the formation of secondary colors from the primary.

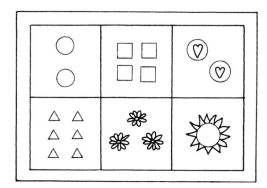

3. *Feel-It Sorting Game.* Laminate tagboard cards of different shapes and with a variety of different textured materials glued on top of each. Students may put on blindfolds and then sort according to shape and texture.

Suggested Books for Children

Dewey Decimal Classification Numbers for the five senses: 372.3, 516.22, 591.4, and 612.

Brenner, Barbara. *Bodies.* New York: Dutton, 1973.

Froman, Robert. *Hot and Cold and in Between.* New York: Young Readers Press, 1971.

Hoban, Tana. *Circles, Triangles and Squares.* New York: Macmillan, 1974.

Ogle, Lucille. *I Spy: A Picture Book of Objects in a Child's Home Environment.* New York: American Heritage Press, 1970.

Van Gelden, Richard. *Whose Nose Is This?* New York: Walker, 1974.

Resource Books for Teachers

Brown, Sam Ed. *Bubbles, Rainbows and Worms: Science Experiments for Pre-School Children.* Mt. Rainier, Md.: Gryphon House, 1981.

Cobb, Vicki. *Science Experiences You Can Eat.* New York: Lippincott, 1972.

Frank, Marjorie. *I Can Make a Rainbow.* Nashville, Tenn.: Incentive Publications, 1976.

Furth, Hans G., and Wach, Harry. *Thinking Goes to School: Piaget's Theory in Practice.* New York: Oxford University Press, 1975.

Hibner, Dixie, and Cromwell, Liz. *Explore and Create.* Livonia, Mich.: Partner Press, 1980.

Knapp, Clifford. "Exploring the Outdoors with Young People." *Science and Children,* October, 1979.

McIntyre, Margaret. *Early Childhood and Science: A Collection of Articles.* Washington, D.C.: National Science Teachers Association, 1984.

North Carolina Competence-Based Curriculum. N.C. Department of Instruction, Raleigh, N.C., 1985.

Wilt, Joy, and Watson, Terre. *Taste and Smell.* Waco, Tex.: Creative Resources, 1978.

Physical Science

Objectives

1. To learn that matter has basic properties such as color, size, shape, texture, sound, and odor.
2. To state properties of various common objects.
3. To distinguish between objects using a single property.
4. To classify objects using a single property.
5. To describe the position of objects using words such as up, over, under, beside, in front of, behind, left, and right.
6. To describe the quantity of objects such as more than, less than, the same as.
7. To describe changes in the environment, such as seasonal changes, the differences in day and night, and how people change as they grow.

Suggested Experiences

1. *Classification.* Provide numerous opportunities for children to classify objects (beads, attribute blocks, pattern blocks, pieces of cloth of different textures, pegs, Cuisenaire rods, etc.).
2. *Location.* Similar objects may be used to play position games in small groups. (Place the blue bead under the chair, on the chair, behind you, on your right, etc.)
3. *Nature Walk.* Walks outside are valuable experiences as seasons change. Ask children to observe changes.
4. *Day and Night.* Talk about appropriate activities for day and night. Let each child contribute to the discussion. Children will then make wall charts titled "Night" and "Day." Provide magazines for finding appropriate pictures to cut out and paste on the proper chart.
5. *Baby Pictures.* Ask children to bring in baby pictures of themselves. Mount them on a poster and let the children guess the identity of the babies. When everyone has had an opportunity to guess, let children write their names under their pictures. If current photographs of the children are available, mount them beside the baby pictures to compare and to observe changes.

Suggested Teacher-Made Activities

1. *Classification Tasks.* Task cards may be prepared for classifying activities and practice. (Place the red beads in the bowl; or, for a greater degree of difficulty, Place the round red beads in the bowl.)
2. *Comparison Tasks.* Task cards may be made for blocks and other manipulatives to reinforce concepts of more than, less than, the same as.
3. *Outdoor Scenes.* Mount pictures of outdoor scenes in all four seasons and pictures of people engaged in outdoor sports appropriate for each season on 4″ × 7″ index cards. Laminate. Have children match appropriate activity and season.

Suggested Books for Children

Branley, F. M. *Light and Darkness.* New York: Thomas Y. Crowell, 1975.
Branley, F. M. *What Makes Day and Night?* New York: Thomas Y. Crowell, 1961.
Bulla, Clyde R. *What Makes a Shadow?* New York: Scholastic Book Services, 1962.
Burningham, John. *Seasons.* New York: Bobbs-Merrill, 1970.
The Colors Book. Encyclopedia Britannica, Inc., 1974.
Hoban, Russell. *Bedtime for Frances.* New York: Harper and Row, 1960.
Simon, Hilda. *The Magic of Color.* New York: Lothrop and Lee, 1981.

Basic Earth Science

Air

Objective

To learn that air is all around us, that it moves, occupies space, and has weight.

Suggested Experiences

1. *Catch Some Air.* Pull an opened plastic bag through the air. Twist the end of bag so the air stays inside. Discuss with the children what is inside the bag. Tell the children to move their arms rapidly around. They will be able to feel their arms pushing air around. Give each child a plastic bag, and tell them all to catch some air. Collect bags afterwards.
2. *Squeeze Some Air.* Provide empty squeeze bottles for the children to squeeze and feel the air coming out of the hole. Let children squeeze the bottle under water and observe the bubbles. Discuss. Put the squeeze bottles in a center for experimentation.
3. *Air and Space Experiment.* Demonstrate that air occupies space by pushing an upside-down glass (or clear plastic cup) down into a bowl of water vertically. This may be observed more readily if a cork is placed on the water first and is seen to float. If the glass or cup is pressed down over the cork it will sink because the water is no longer there to lift it. Place this activity in a center for experimentation.
4. *Balancing Balloons.* Show that air has weight by carefully blowing up two similar balloons to the same size. Using thumb tacks or string, attach each to opposite ends of a yardstick. Hang the yardstick with a piece of string at the center or balance point. Carefully burst one of the balloons with a sharp object. Notice that the end of the yardstick with the inflated balloon tends to be lower. Carefully break this balloon and notice the yardstick tends to balance again.

Suggested Teacher-Made Activities

1. *Bubble Blower.* Prepare a bubble solution as follows:
     2 cups water
     1 to 2 tablespoons liquid soap
     ¼ cup glycerine

Stir to mix well. Pour into 2 or 3 tubs or dishpans. Each child will need several straws and a paper or a styrofoam cup. Make a hole in the side of the cup about one inch from the bottom for the straw to be inserted. Tell children to place the open end of the cup in the bubble solution and then remove the cup. Call attention to the film that has formed across the opening of the cup. Tell the children to hold their cups upside-down and blow slowly through the straws. Large bubbles will form as they blow through the straws. Make task cards asking such questions as: What is inside your bubble? Can you think of a way to make your bubble smaller? Can you think of two ways to remove air from your bubble?

2. *Booklets.* Make booklets with a title such as "Air Works for Us." Provide magazines for the children to find pictures of air at work. Sports magazines are good for pictures of sail boats, sky diving, parachutes, gliders, etc. Children can also find pictures of inflatables, auto and bicycle tires, kites, hair dryers, airplanes, windmills, etc. Children can cut and paste as many pictures as they can find.

   Variation: Pictures can be separated into categories, such as work and play activities.

3. *Paper Airplanes.* Provide materials for making paper airplanes. Demonstrate different methods of folding paper to produce the best glider. Provide a time outdoors for experimenting with these.

4. *Parachutes.* Supply materials for making parachutes using handkerchiefs, pieces of plastic, or paper tied to wooden spools or small balls. Experiment with different materials, making some with a hole in the parachute center. Observe which are more efficient in holding the parachute up the longest. Older children can record the results.

Soil

Objectives

To learn about soil, how sand is formed, how organic matter is formed, that soil is a mixture of organic and inorganic matter, and that soil is important for good plant growth.

Suggested Experiences

1. *Soil Samples.* Have children collect soil samples from the school yard and/or bring samples from home. Yogurt containers or small plastic bags are handy for this purpose. Display samples in the classroom with labels showing where the samples were taken. Try to get as many different samples as possible: clay soil, loam, sand, humus, etc. Provide magnifying glass for observation. Notice that not all soil is the same.

2. *Plant Seeds.* Using the soil samples in milk cartons labeled with the source of the sample, plant seeds in all samples (use the same kind of seed), and give each sample the same amount of water during the next few weeks. Notice in which soil samples the seeds begin to grow first and best. Ask children to record the results.

3. *Making Sand.* Have the students make sand by rubbing together or hammering rocks or shells; have them draw or write their results.

Suggested Teacher-Made Activities

1. *Booklets.* Make booklets for children to record observations and results of experimentation with soil. Younger children can draw their findings and dictate to the teacher for labeling.
2. *Mural.* Children can draw a mural of the steps involving their experimentations. Display in the room or the hallway.
3. *Research Tasks.* Provide resource books about soils, gardens, etc., with colorful pictures if possible. Make research task cards about soils. The task cards can be color coded so that children of varying abilities can choose a card on their individual levels.

Water

Objective

To learn the importance of water to living things.

Suggested Experiences

1. *Free Inquiry.* Provide area (preferably outdoors), materials, and ample time for experimentation. Children will need containers of different sizes, sponges, funnels, strainers, etc. Discuss and record the children's observations.
2. *Sink/Float Experiment.* Provide water and a variety of small items. Let the children discover which ones sink and which ones float. Ask them to record their results individually or as a group on a chart.
3. *Water Use Experiment.* Have the children think of all the ways water helps us. List these on a chart. Discuss the fact that water is essential to life. Plant some seeds. Water some but do not water others. Discuss the results.
4. *Evaporation Experiment.* This is a warm day activity. Provide paint brushes. Allow children to "paint" on the outside of the building with water. When the children notice the water dries, ask them to think about what happened to their pictures. Introduce the word *evaporate.*

Suggested Teacher-Made Activities

1. *Float Away.* Collect a variety of objects, some that float and some that sink. Make the "Float Away" game board and cards as shown; laminate. Provide a

bowl with water and die. Child rolls die and moves that many spaces. If the player lands on a water card, he or she picks a card. "Look at the picture. Will that object float? Answer 'yes' or 'no.'" "Try the object in the water." If correct, the child moves ahead one space. If wrong, the child moves back one space. The winner is the first to reach "Finish."

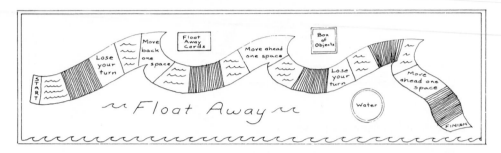

2. *Make a Boat (woodworking).* Provide scrap wood, glue, a hand drill, sandpaper, dowels, and construction paper. Following directions provided by task cards, students sand the bottom of the boat until smooth. Have them drill a hole in the center to place a dowel. They then cut a mast from construction paper and glue to the dowel. Students then glue the dowel into the hole.

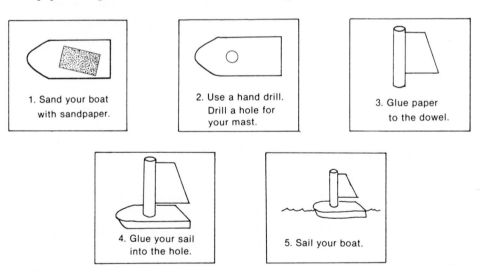

Weather

Objective

To learn that our weather is constantly changing.

Suggested Experiences

1. *Wind Experiment.* Provide paper fans folded accordian-style and a deflated balloon. Tell the children to wave the fans in front of their faces. Ask the children to tell what they feel as they fan themselves quickly (wind). Inflate the balloon and hold by the neck. Ask children what will happen when the balloon is let go. Let go of the balloon. Observe. Discuss what came out of the

balloon and what caused the balloon to move. Explain that wind can make things move; when large masses of air move, weather changes.

2. *Temperature Experiment.* Take children outside. Have them stand in the sun and then in the shade. Let them tell about the difference in temperature. Fill two basins, each with one inch of water. Place one in the shade and one in the sun. Wait about an hour, then observe the temperature in both basins by feeling the water in each basin. Discuss the differences. Use a thermometer to see how many degrees difference there is in the two basins of water. Ask the children to think why it is warmer on a sunny day.

Suggested Teacher-Made Activities

1. *Weather Observation.* On a large chart, keep a weekly record of the weather. Record the temperature in degrees Fahrenheit and Celsius.

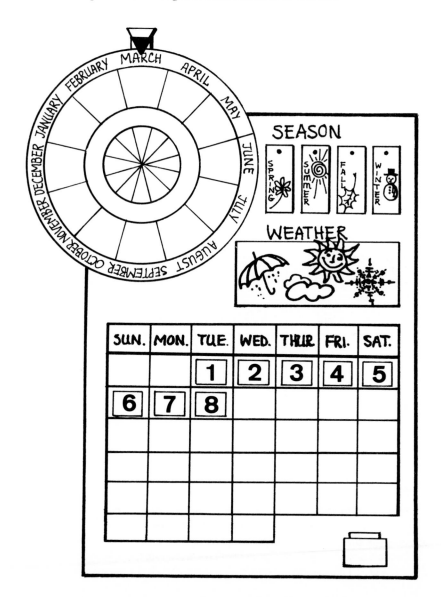

2. *Charting Temperature.* Chart temperature on a graph. Some of the older children can do this with the observation of some younger children. Place thermometers near the chart. The wind could be charted the same way using a weather vane.

NOVEMBER

DEGREES	1	2	3	4	5	6	7	8	9	10	11	*cont.*
80°												
75°												
70°												
65°												
60°												
55°												
50°												

DAY OF THE MONTH

3. *The Date Game.* Using tri-wall, cardboard, laminated tagboard, or material board, mount three pockets made with envelopes or library cold holders. Label the four pockets: Day, Month, Holiday, Season. Make several picture and/or word cards; an individual or small group of children can sort them into the pockets accordingly. Label the back of the cards for self-correction.
4. *The Seasons Game.* Make a seasons matching game with tag board and pictures from magazines of scenes showing different seasons. Select three pictures of each of the four seasons. Glue them on tag board and cut to fit convenient card size. Laminate. Children can match picture cards to poster naming the seasons.

Fall	Winter	Spring	Summer

5. *Seasonal Clothes.* A flannel board figure and clothing suitable for different seasons may be made from felt or felt-backed drawings. Let children dress the figure appropriately for the current weather.
6. *Season Booklets.* Booklets may be made for current season. Pages may include subjects such as "Special Days in Winter," "Clothes I Wear in Winter," "Things I Like to Do in Winter," "The Best Thing About Winter is . . ."

Suggested Books for Children About Air and Water

Dewey Decimal Classification Number for air and water is 551.

Branley, Franklin. *Air Is All Around You*. New York: Thomas Y. Crowell, 1962.

Brewer, Mary. *The Wind Is Air*. New York: Children's Press, 1975.

Milgrom, Harry. *ABC Science Experiments*. New York: Children's Press, 1975.

Mizumura, Lazue. *I See the Winds*. New York: Thomas Y. Crowell, 1966.

Pine, Tillie, and Levine, Joseph. *Water All Around*. New York: Whittlesey House, 1959.

Podendorf, Illa. *The True Book of Science Experiments*. Chicago: Children's Press, 1972.

Scarry, Richard. *Great Big Air Book*. New York: Random House, 1971.

Smith, Henry. *Amazing Air, Science Club*. New York: Lothrop, Lee and Shepard Books, 1982.

Tresselt, Alvin. *Follow the Wind*. New York: Lothrop, Lee and Shepard Books, 1950.

Watson, Philip. *Liquid Magic, Science Club*. New York: Lothrop, Lee and Shepard Books, 1982.

Zolotow, Charlotte. *When the Wind Stops*. New York: Harper and Row, 1962.

Zubrowski, Bernie. *Messing Around with Water Pumps and Siphons*. Boston: Little, Brown, 1981.

Resource Books for Teachers

Arnow, Boris, *Water*. New York: Lothrop, Lee and Shepard, 1980.

Benish, Jean. *Water, Water Everywhere: Science Through Water Waterplay*. Winston-Salem, N.C.: Kaplan Press, 1977.

Bird, John. *Science from Water Play: Teaching Primary Science*. Milwaukee, Wis.: MacDonald-Raintree, 1979.

Levenson, Elaine. *Teaching Children About Science: Ideas and Activities Every Teacher and Parent Can Use*. Englewood Cliffs, N.J.: Prentice-Hall, 1985.

North Carolina Competence-Based Curriculum. N.C. Department of Public Instruction, Raleigh, N.C., 1985.

Suggested Children's Books About Rocks and Soil

Dewey Decimal Classification Number for rocks is 550.

Coldin, Augusta. *Salt*. New York: Thomas Y. Crowell. 1965.

Heavilin, Jay. *Rocks and Gems*. New York: Macmillan, 1964.

Podendorf, Illa. *The True Book of Pebbles and Shells*. Chicago: Children's Press, 1972.

Podendorf, Illa. *The True Book of Rocks and Minerals*. Chicago: Children's Press, 1972.

Severy, O. Irene. *The First Book of the Earth*. New York: Franklin Watts, 1958.

Simon, S. *The Rock Hound Book*. New York: Viking Press, 1973.

Resource Books for Teachers

Raymo, Chet. *The Crust of the Earth: An Armchair Traveler's Guide to the New Geology*. Englewood Cliffs, N.J.: Prentice-Hall, 1983.

Wyler, Rose. *Exploring Earth Science*. Racine, Wis.: Western Publishing, 1973.

Suggested Books for Children About Weather

The Dewey Decimal Classification Number for weather is 551.5.

Blackwood, Paul E. *The How and Why Wonder Book of Weather*. New York: Grosset and Dunlap, 1978.

Branley, Franklyn M. *Flash, Crash, Rumble and Roll: Let's Read and Find Out*. New York: Thomas Y. Crowell, 1964.

Branley, Franklyn M. *Rain and Hail: Let's Read and Find Out*. New York: Thomas Y. Crowell, 1963.

DePaola, Tomie. *The Cloud Book*. New York: Holiday House, 1975.

Gans, Roma. *Water for Dinosaurs and You: Let's Read and Find Out*. New York: Thomas Y. Crowell, 1972.

Updegraff, Imelda and Robert, *Weather*. New York: Penguin Books, 1982.

Webster, David. *Snow Stumpers*. Garden City, N.Y.: The National History Press, 1968.

Resource Books for Teachers

Burnett, Will R., Lehr, Paul E., and Zim, Herbert. *Weather, A Golden Guide*. New York: Golden Press, 1975.

Hitte, Kathryn. *Hurricanes, Tornadoes and Blizzards*. New York: Random House, 1960.

Levenson, Elaine. *Teaching Children About Science: Ideas and Activities Every Teacher and Parent Can Use*. Englewood, Cliffs, N.J.: Prentice-Hall, 1985.

North Carolina Competence-Based Curriculum. N.C. Department of Public Instruction, Raleigh, N.C., 1985.

Stone, A. Harrison, and Spiegel, Herbert. *The Winds of Weather*. Englewood Cliffs, N.J.: Prentice-Hall, 1969.

Mathematics Activities

Objectives

1. To show skill in numeration by

   identifying numerals
   comparing sets
   rote counting
   using one-to-one correspondence
   using ordinal numbers
   classifying objects using specific attributes

2. To show knowledge of whole numbers by

   combining two sets of objects
   determining the larger of two sets of objects
   dividing a set into two equal sets
   determining the value of a set when objects are taken away

3. To show understanding of fractions by

   identifying objects that have been divided into two parts
   identifying objects that have been divided into halves

4. To show use of measurement skills by

using direct comparison to classify and determine the size of objects
identifying before and after
identifying coins and use value
using hour and minute references in daily vocabulary

5. To show skill in geometry by

recognizing simple plane and solid figures
identifying and repeating simple geometric patterns
classifying objects by size, position, and shape building similar figures

6. To show skill with probability and statistics by

reading simple informational charts
reading simple horizontal and vertical bar graphs

Math Supplies

Dominos (large and/or small), flannel sets, and flannel board
Magnetic letters and numbers, magnetic board, fractional parts, and fractional board
Playing cards, checkers and board, chess set and board
Rope (for encompassing areas), puzzles, logs, counting pegs and boards
Blocks of all shapes and sizes, number blocks, parquetry, attribute blocks
Sum stick, adding machine, play money, colored beads, math games, flashcards
Trundle wheel, compass, measuring rods and containers, Cuisenaire rods

Number line, abacus, collections of all types (buttons, coins, stones, sticks, stirrers, macaroni, beans, yarn, marbles, bottle caps)
Egg cartons for making sets
Books (interest and reference)
Catalogs, newspaper ads
Geometric wire forms and patterns
Metric step-on scale, metric platform scale, metric plastic measure set (spoons and cups, 1 ml to 250 ml), balance scale with metric weights 1 g to 50 g

Coin stamps
Calculator
Unifix cubes
Rice and sand (for measuring)
Measuring cups
Geoboards and rubber bands

Suggested Teacher-Made Supplies and Tips

1. *Trundle Wheel.* Cut a circle from any sort of sturdy material (tri-wall, thin plywood, or paneling) 36″ in circumference. Mark the inch measures around the circumference. Attach this to a dowel rod at the center so that the wheel spins like a pinwheel. Glue or nail a small piece of plastic to the dowel so that as the wheel rolls it will make a clicking sound as it passes the 36″ mark. Start the roll at the 1″ mark; when it clicks, it has measured 1 yard. Measures less than a yard can be taken by reading the mark at the dowel. Mark inch measures on the wheel from right to left.

2. *Sorting Material.* Cover coffee cans (with plastic tops) with contact paper. Fill each container with a different kind of bean or macaroni. Acorns or large seeds make good materials. Children can use these for sorting sets or for weaving and measuring.
   Variation. Collect *styrofoam trays* (meat or vegetable) and use for sorting colors, shapes, objects, and so on.

3. *Task Cards.* Develop "things to do and investigate" math and science task cards to pique the child's curiosity. Some cards will be simply questions and pictures, while others might be sample games for the children to play.

4. *Balance Scale.* Balance scales are easily built, but the sturdier the materials you begin with, the longer they last. By making the baskets different colors, children will have an easier time expressing which basket needs more or less to balance.

5. *Tangram.* A tangram (Chinese puzzle) can be made from a square (of any size) of colored tagboard or cardboard, which is then cut into seven pieces.

Bisect the square diagonally. Bisect one of the large triangles. Take the other triangle and use one fourth of the longest side as the side dimension of the square and short side of parallelogram. Cut out carefully. (These can also be cut from tile or linoleum, using a knife as a cutting tool.)

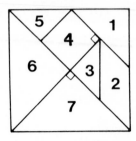

6. *Tangram Cards.* Combine some or all of the tangram pieces to make unique designs. Trace the outside line of these on tagboard to make tangram cards. Geometrical shapes on tagboard make simple cards.
7. *Geoboards.* Geoboards can be made for or by the children. Use a plywood square and 100 nails (10 rows with 10 nails each). Children can use these with colored rubber bands to make designs while discovering shapes and angles.

Manipulating concrete materials is very important for all young children, not just those who require manipulatives as aids for solving problems in addition and subtraction. Because the materials are real, they engage several senses and are enjoyable in their own right. The materials provide motivation for learning and the tools for exploration, discovery, and problem solving. Primary emphasis should be placed on concept development; abstract symbolization will naturally follow when the concept is grasped.

Suggested Experiences

1. *Orientation.* Children should have ample time and opportunity to explore materials on their own. No tasks, other than those the children themselves devise for themselves, should be introduced. After a suitable time (days or weeks, depending on the age and developmental level of the children), simple tasks may be assigned.

2. *Matching Exercise.* Children, paired with identical manipulatives, are asked to work in a matching exercise. One child makes a design, the other copies it.

3. *Imitating Patterns.* Pattern is the underlying theme of mathematics. The skills involving recognizing and using patterns is a valuable problem-solving tool and can have a very real effect on the development of mathematical understanding. Children can be introduced to this concept in activities such as reproducing clapping patterns. The teacher claps a pattern and the children join in. The teacher then claps a pattern, the children listen, and then they duplicate it. As the children become more familiar with this activity, individual children can initiate the clapping pattern as the teacher did, and then the class repeats afterwards. This activity can be expanded to clap and snap patterns.

4. *Making Patterns.* Patterns can be made with children themselves. Seating can be arranged in a line of boy, girl, or standing and sitting.

5. *Identifying Patterns.* Have the children identify patterns visible in the room or on their clothing.

6. *Classifying Activities.* Analytical thinking and clear expression of thoughts develop through classifying activities. Children learn to recognize particular properties of objects, focus on a certain attribute objects have in common, and label with words the property that certain groups have in common. The teacher shows several objects, such as pieces of plastic fruit, and one object that does not belong, such as a cap. The children are asked which object does not belong and why. This activity can be done with shapes, colors, sizes, etc. This can also be done with people. The teacher selects 4 or 5 children, all but one of whom have a common attribute, such as wearing tennis shoes or wearing jeans. Let the other children tell which one doesn't belong.

7. *Collections.* Take the class on a walk outdoors. Before leaving the classroom, decide what the children are going to look for, listen for, or collect

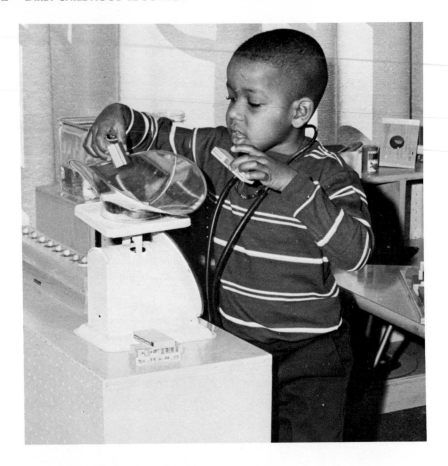

(anything green, things made of metal, signs with numbers, different vehicles, things that are bigger than they are, etc.). Upon returning, a list can be made on a chart, the children can draw what they saw and a booklet can be put together from these drawings, or a display made of the collected items.

9. *Calendar Activities.* Valuable learning occurs when children update the calendar on a daily basis. Children can learn recognition of numbers, ordinal numbers (this is the second day of the month, etc.), before and after (Today is Tuesday. What day comes after Tuesday?), as well as the days of the week and the names of the months.

10. *Using Ordinal Numbers.* Teach ordinal numbers through such everyday experiences as lining up for lunch. (John is the first in line today.)

11. *Using Fractions.* Opportunities for learning about fractions can be found in classroom experiences almost daily. Experiences with food are often meaningful to children. (I am going to cut this apple in half.) How many pieces are there now? If you break your cookie in half, how many pieces will you have?)

12. *Graphing.* Simple graphs can be made with the children's help. Such things as children's favorite ice creams can be charted on a simple graph. Children can readily see that more of them like chocolate, for example, if some visual evidence is placed before them. They could draw their favorite flavor, cut out the picture of the ice cream cone, and place their favorite in the appropriate column (all the vanillas together, the chocolates, etc.).

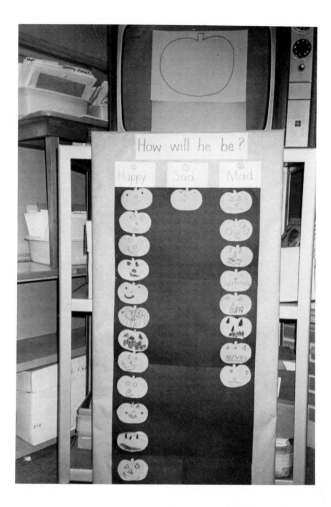

13. *Using Coins.* Names of coins can be learned through play in a school store using play money. Children can also learn the names of coins through the experience of buying their lunch at school. ("Lunch costs 75¢. How many quarters is that?" "You had a dollar today. What coin did you receive as change?")

Suggested Teacher-Made Activities

1. *Pattern Completion.* Make task cards showing the beginning of a pattern for unifix cubes, pattern blocks, beads, etc. Children can duplicate these patterns and extend them as far as space or materials allow.
2. *Pattern Creation.* Cut shapes of different colors (yellow squares, red circles). Have children paste the shapes on a large piece of paper in a pattern of their own design. As the children's skills increase, this activity can be expanded to several shapes and colors.
3. *Sorting Task Cards.* Make cards designating attributes of particular objects to be sorted, such as blue triangles and orange squares, white beans and brown ones.
4. *Same Shape and Different Shape.* Use a manila file folder and paste pockets on the inside. One pocket is labeled Same Shape and the other pocket is

labeled Different Shape, with pictures illustrating same and different. Make ten cards with two objects on each card: five the same and five different. The student is to sort the cards into the correct pockets. The answers are on the back of the folder to make the activity self-checking. For reinforcement, a ditto sheet can be made so that students can record their results.

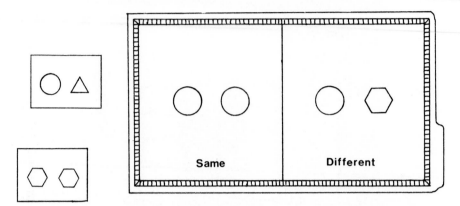

5. *Matching Game.* Making cards for children to sort. Draw or cut out pictures of people in different professions (doctor, police officer, baseball player, grocery store cashier, etc.). Make other cards with pictures of single items used in each profession (bandage, medicine bottle, stethoscope, hospital bed, etc.). Laminate. Have the children sort the cards according to the professional and the appropriate professional tool.

6. *Booklets.* Make booklets at science centers where children classify objects by attributes as they discover them, such as "Things That Float," "Things That Do Not Float," "Things Magnets Will Pick Up," etc.

7. *Shape Bingo.* Laminate tagboard with pictures of familiar objects that are circles, squares, rectangles, and triangles. Play as you would Bingo. The child must recognize the shape to mark his or her block.

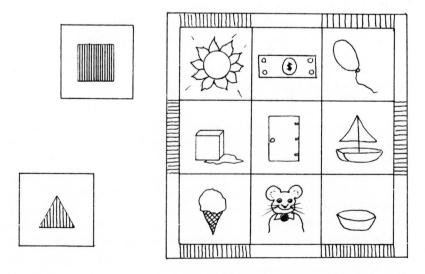

Variation: Make color or number Bingo.

8. *Match-the-Sets Bingo.* This game can be played like regular Bingo or independently. Children must match each set on their cards with the set that is shown on the cards that are drawn. The sets are matched by contents and the number in the set.

9. *Number Mix-up.* Draw the numbers 1 to 10 on a manila folder. These numbers should vary in size. Child matches cutout number to number that is drawn.

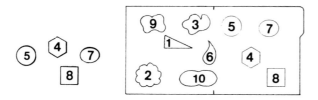

10. *Match the Number.* Use 11″ × 8″ pieces of tagboard, and draw numbers and sets to match each number; laminate. Knot a piece of yarn beside each number. Each number will have a different color yarn. Use a baggie twister on the end of the yarn for a needle. The child will match each number with its set by sewing the yarn through the hole. This activity is color coded on the back for self-checking.

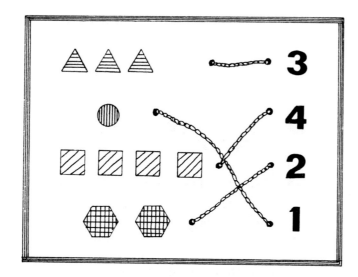

Variation. Game can be used to teach shapes and names for shapes, numbers, and number names, and addition and subtraction facts.

11. *Number Puzzles.* Draw numbers, number names, and sets for the number on tagboard. Draw puzzle lines, laminate and cut into pieces. Children put the puzzle together. For reinforcement provide a ditto sheet for the child to complete once the puzzle is finished.

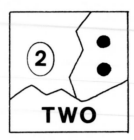

12. *Number Dog.* Cut dog and numbers from tagboard and laminate. Children can put dog together for number sequence. This activity is self-correcting by matching the dog's spots.

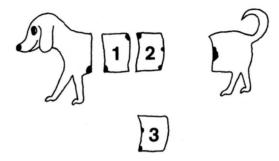

For reinforcement, a ditto sheet can be made on which the child can record the number sequence after completing the puzzle.

13. *Jumping on the Number.* Use 1½ yards of plastic. Draw the numbers 1 to 10 in squares 12″ × 12″. You will need one felt bean bag and two to four players. The first player throws a bag on a number. The child names the number and then jumps to that number. If the child can jump without falling, he or she gets one point. First child who can jump to all the numbers wins.

1	2	3	4	5
6	7	8	9	10

14. **Counting Cards.** Using a rectangular tagboard card, write the numeral 5 (for example). Make five small squares near the bottom of the card. Use clothespins to cover each of the little squares. On the back of the card, place the number word, five.

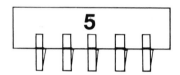

FIVE

15. **Clothes Hanger Counters.** Staple a number card on the neck of a clothes hanger. Clip on clothespins to represent the number shown on the card. This may be used to teach number stories or for drill on missing addends by using two colors for clothespins.

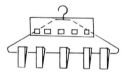

16. **Spool Game.** Using six Tinker Toys and sticks, a student may roll dice and try to get all rolls 1 to 6 and therefore spools 1 to 6. Skills involve counting dots on dice and recognition of numbers 1 to 6.

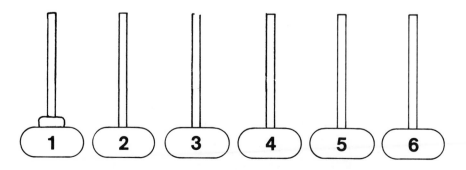

17. *Magic Numbers.* Using posterboard or tagboard, cut large rectangle cards; put a number on each card; laminate; and cut into four pieces. When pieces are put together a number appears. These may be stored in sturdy brown envelopes.

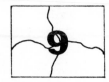

18. *Number Relay.* Make two sets of numerals 1 to 25 on different-colored tagboard and laminate. Designate two teams. Place the numbers, scrambled up, on the floor in front of each team. Team members run to pick up the numbers to place them in sequential order. First team to place the numbers in correct order wins.

19. *Find the Place Value.* Using tagboard, fasteners, and beans, children can use this game to find the place value and record it.

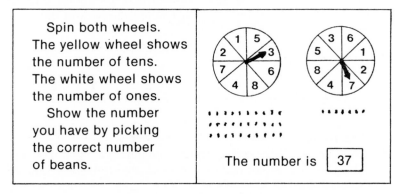

Spin both wheels.
The yellow wheel shows the number of tens.
The white wheel shows the number of ones.
Show the number you have by picking the correct number of beans.

The number is 37

20. *Wheel Turn.* Make three laminated tagboard wheels, each one larger than the other, and place on top of each other. The wheels contain numbers, numerals, and number sets. The student must line up each wheel to match.

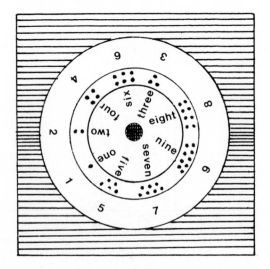

21. *Tic-Tac-Toe.* Use laminated tagboards for all parts of the game (plain board, problem cards, X's and O's). Turn cards face down. Students may take turns taking top card and answering the problem (answers are placed on back of cards for self-correcting). One student takes X's, another takes O's. A student answering the card correctly may put an X or O in any square to try to get three in a row, just as in pencil tic-tac-toe.

22. *Pitch-a-Penny.* A penny is thrown and lands on a square or section. That number is the score. Add points together or subtract whenever the penny lands on that square. The first person to reach a score of 100 wins. This may be made with laminated tagboard, tri-wall, or regular cardboard.

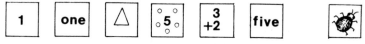

Subtract 10 points			
16	8	4	9
12	15	3	1
2	5	14	6
11	7	10	13

(Left side: Subtract 5 points. Right side: Subtract 5 points. Bottom left: Lose your turn. Bottom right: Take another turn.)

23. *Bad Bug.* Make thirty cards for three sets of ten and laminate. Make one "Bad Bug" card. Three to five players may play. Players take turns drawing one card at a time from each player's hand. As each player gets a match, he or she puts the cards down. The winner is the one with the most matched sets. The loser is the one holding Bad Bug.

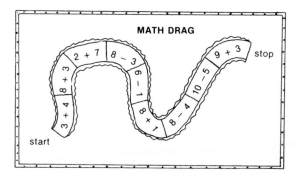

24. *Math Drag.* Use colored tagboard and laminate. One to four children may play the game. Each child throws the dice, moves that number of spaces with his or her car, and adds or subtracts the number within the space he or she lands on to remain there. The first student's car to reach the end of the drag strip wins.

MATH DRAG

25. ***Rubber Dice Cubes.*** Using an electric carving knife, cut foam rubber squares. Use a permanent magic marker to number the cubes 1 to 6 or 4 to 9. Children may use them as dice; they may roll these dice and add the numbers or subtract from the larger number. The dice may be color coded for learning place value; they may be used to learn "less than" and "greater than."

26. ***Number Trains.*** An engine and a caboose are drawn with intermediate cards 1 to 100. Students may use these task cards asking to "Make a train with cars 1 to 10"; "Make a train with cars numbered 68 to 75"; "Make a train with two cars whose numbers add up to 12"; "Make a train with three cards whose numbers add up to 20."

27. ***Math Card Box.*** Various math skill cards may be color coded according to difficulty. Most skill cards have a corresponding answer card that can be found by a number and the color coding. If an answer sheet is not appropriate, this is indicated on the card by a symbol.

Draw objects to match sets	
⬡ ⬡ ⬡	◯
✿ ✿ ✿ ✿	⬭
✎ ✎	△

Make a new set.		
How many?	How many?	How many?
▢ ▢	▢ ▢ ▢	
△	△ △ △ △	
◯◯◯◯	◯	

How many in each set?
Number your paper and
write the number sentences

▢ ▢ ▢
▢ ▢ ▢   ▢ ▢

_____ is greater than _____

◯ ◯ ◯
◯ ◯ ◯   ◯ ◯
◯   ◯

_____ is greater than _____

28. *Bottle Cap Game.* A board, three bottles caps for each player, and a score pad will be needed. The board may be made from contact-covered cardboard and a six-pack plastic divider. Students stand behind a line and toss caps into numbered sections; after three turns the scores are added up.

29. *Number Feet.* Using tagboard, twenty or more feet can be made, each containing a number, numeral, and like set. Laminate for durability. Students may put feet in numerical order and then walk in them or they may rearrange them for adding and subtracting.

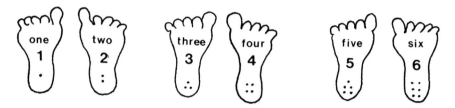

30. *Number Concentration.* Make sixteen cards. On each pair of cards write a number and a set for that number. Use a piece of tagboard to make a game board for Concentration. Place the cards face down on the game board. Play as you would Concentration. Player with the most matches is the winner.

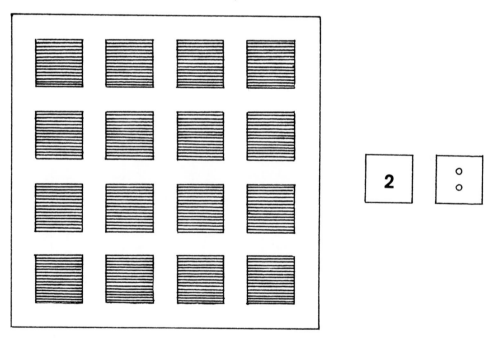

Variation. Concentration can be used to teach numbers and names for numbers, time, fractions, place value [13] [10/111] , names of shapes, and shapes of familiar objects.

31. *Math War.* This may be played with cards made with laminated tagboard and each card containing a subtraction or addition fact. All cards are dealt; each student turns over his or her top card and then subtracts or adds the

numbers on the cards. The student with the highest answer takes both cards. Answers are placed on back of each card for self-correction.

32. *Addition and Subtraction Game.* Ten envelopes or library card holders with numbers from 1 to 10 on each are mounted on a board such as a materials bolt board. A child may choose a card from a pile containing a variety of addition and subtraction facts and place it in the correct pocket. Answers are placed on the back of the cards for self-correction.

33. *Beat the Calculator.* Use flashcards and an easy-to-punch calculator. Up to five children may play. One child has the calculator and all the flashcards are in the deck. Children turn over a flashcard from the deck when it is their turn. If the player can give the correct answer to the problem faster than the person can find the answer on the calculator, then the player gets to keep the flashcard. If not, or if the student gives an incorrect answer, then the card goes on the bottom of the deck. Play for twenty or thirty minutes. Player with the most cards is the winner.
    Variation. This activity can be used to teach multiplication facts, subtraction, and division.

34. *Take a Chance—Add or Subtract.* Two or more children may play this game using an egg carton with a number in the bottom of each section and two dice. Each student shakes the egg carton with the dice inside; dice will land on two numbers. The student can either add or subtract the numbers; each correct answer is worth 1 point. The first to reach a score of 20 wins.

35. *Addition and Subtraction Football.* The game board or "football field" can be made with cardboard, laminated tagboard, or a window shade. Two or more children spin the spinner and advance that number of spaces. Yardage can be gained if the problem is answered correctly. If not, the player must go back to the spot from which he or she advanced. The first person to get to the goal line wins.

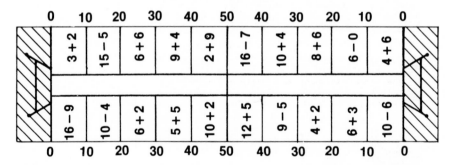

36. *Math Old Flip.* Make forty problem cards. On every tenth card, cut out a picture of Snoopy and place it on the card with the problem; laminate. Up to eight may play. One person turns over the card and finds the answer to the problem. If the answer is correct, the student keeps the card. If incorrect, the card goes back into the pile. If a player gets "Old Flip," all his or her cards must go back into the pile. Play for thirty minutes. Player with the most cards wins.
    Variation. This activity can be used to teach place value, multiplication, and division.

37. *How Many Houses Can You Build?* The object of the game is to find the

roof that matches the house. Use colored tagboard and laminate; a variety of addition, subtraction, multiplication, or division facts can be used.

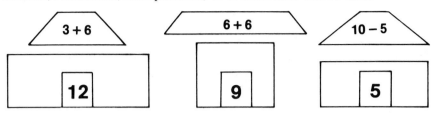

38. *Turn a Card.* Turn a pile of laminated cards containing addition and subtraction facts face down. Students may take turns drawing cards and solving problems; the cards may be placed on the correct answer. Keep score by adding the answers to the cards.

1	2	3	4	5
6	7	8	9	10
11	12	13	14	15

$9-7$

39. *Addo.* Using a variety of addo and problem cards made with tagboard and laminated, a small group of students may play this game just as Bingo is played.

A	D	D	O
9	5	1	6
Free	23	5	8
20	3	4	7

$8-6$

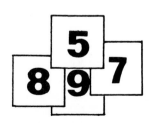

Variations. Change the numbers from 25 to 50, 50 to 75, 75 to 100, and so on. Use numbers in counting by 2's, 3's, 5's, and so on.

40. *Number Houses.* Using colored tagboard, make several houses with windows, each window containing a number fact. Windows open to show correct answers. Laminate before cutting windows. Children slip papers inside house and open windows to write answers. Slide papers out and check. The answers are inside the windows.

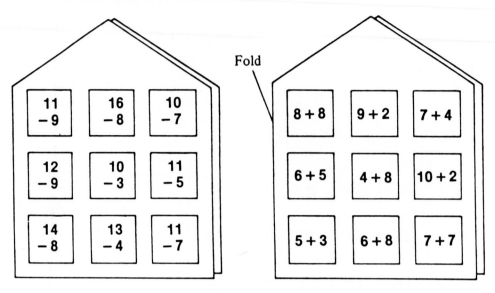

41. *Calendar Game.* Blank calendar and parts may be made by using tagboard; laminate. Children may use the calendar individually or in small groups by filling in the missing parts.
42. *Balance Scale.* Use a balance scale to compare weights and sizes of various objects. Children record results.
   Variation. Select one object. Let the child sort the remaining things according to which are heavier, lighter, or weigh the same.
43. *Money Match.* Make puzzles using coin ink stamps and an amount to match the coin. Use heads and tails of coins.
   Variation. Make puzzles with different coin combinations.
44. *Supermarket Ads, Catalogs.* Use ads or catalogs for on-the-spot shopping. A folder might read "You have $25.00 to spend. What would you buy? List items and prices and place the list in the folder. You might use the adding machine to check your totals."

Suggested Reference Books for Teachers

Baratta-Lorton, Mary. *Mathematics Their Way.* Menlo Park, Calif.: Addison-Wesley, 1976.
Jensen, Rosalie, and Spector, Debora. *Teaching Mathematics to Young Children.* Englewood, Cliffs, N.J.: Prentice-Hall, 1984.
Kamii, Constance. *Number in Preschool and Kindergarten: Educational Implications of Piaget's Theory.* Washington, D.C.: National Association for the Education of Young Children, 1982.
Kamii, Kazuko, and DeClark, Georgia. *Young Children Reinvent Arithmetic: Implications of Piaget's Theory.* New York: Teachers College Press, 1985.

Kay, Evelyn. *Games That Teach for Children Three Through Six.* Minneapolis, Minn.: T. S. Denison and Company, 1981.

North Carolina Competence-Based Curriculum. N.C. Department of Instruction, Raleigh, North Carolina, 1985.

References

Almy, M., and Genishi, C. (1979). *Ways of Studying Children.* New York: Teachers' College Press.

Baratta-Lorton, M. (1976). *Mathematics Their Way.* Menlo Park, Calif.: Addison-Wesley.

Bruner, J. S. (1960). *The Process of Education.* Cambridge: Harvard University Press.

Gagne, R. (1977). *Conditions of Learning, 3rd edition.* New York: Holt, Rinehart and Winston.

Kamii, C. (1973). "Pedagogical Principles Derived from Piaget's Theory: Relevance for Educational Practice." Schwebel, M. and Ralph, J., Eds. *Piaget in the Classroom.* New York: Basic.

Kamii, C., and Devries, R. (1977). "Piaget for Early Education." Day, M. C. and Parker, R., Eds. *The Preschool in Action.* Boston: Allyn and Bacon.

McNairy, M. (1985). "Sciencing: Science Education for Early Childhood." *School Science and Math 85,* (5), 383–393.

Wadsworth, B. (1978) *Piaget for the Classroom Teacher.* New York: Longman.

8

Movement

The need to move and the need to express feelings are present in all human beings at birth. Both needs can be satisfied through a movement education program for young children. Movement education provides opportunities to use movements for creative expression and to develop confidence in the ability to move. An educational movement program can encourage the child to apply problem-solving techniques to explore fantasies and relationships with others. With movement exploration activities children can develop motor skills and knowledge of the operation of their own bodies. In addition, a child's self-concept can grow through the teacher's use of nonjudgmental techniques to show respect for each child's ability (Sullivan, 1982).

Children's skill levels vary according to their experience and development. The amount of encouragement, freedom, and space available will determine the child's overall competence in movement. An atmosphere that contains these essentials must be provided for all children to develop their potential.

For many years, movement has been a part of the curriculum for young children, often disguised by terms such as "rhythm." It continues to be an integral part of the total curriculum, reinforcing and extending the concepts of mathematics, language arts, science, social studies, and other basic areas. Movement can serve as a unifying factor and can enhance the interrelated nature of the curriculum. The elements of a standard movement and dance approach have been defined by Rudolf Laban. These elements are described by Sullivan (1982, p. 3).

Body Awareness. The shape of the body in space, where the different body parts are, how the body moves and rests, the body's behavior when combined with other bodies, how the voice is a part of the body.

Force and Time. Being limp, being energetic, being light, being fluid, being staccato, being slow, being quick.

Space. Where the body is in a room: the level (high—erect posture or in the air, crawling or stooped; low—on the floor), direction (forward, backward, sideways), size (bigness, smallness), path through space, and extensions of the body parts into space.

Locomotion. Movement through space at various levels (lowest—wriggling, rolling, scooting; middle—crawling, crouching, using four limbs (ape walk); highest—walking, running, skipping, galloping, sliding, leaping, hopping, jumping).

Weight. Relationship of body to ground, ways to manage body weight in motion and in relation to others, understanding momentum.

Working with Others. Combining with others to solve problems, to develop trust, to explore strength and sensitivity, to feel a sense of union with others.

Isolations. How various individual body parts (head, shoulders, arms, hands, elbows, wrists, neck, back, upper torso, ribs, hips, legs, knees, ankles, feet) can move (swinging, jerking, twisting, shaking, lifting, tensing, relaxing, becoming fluid, pressing, gliding, floating, flickering, slashing, punching, dabbing).

Repetitions. Getting to know a movement and how it feels when repeated often; being able to repeat a shape or action.

Activities for development of each of these elements are available in the Suggested Activities section.

Two main types of movement are personal movement and functional activity. Personal movement shows the mood or inner state of an individual, while functional activity serves a practical purpose (Lynch-Fraser, 1982). It is appropriate to focus on personal expressive movement with developing young children. Finding appropriate motifs "depends not only on age and development of the child, but on their interests and absorptions at a given time."

The teacher's role in movement is to provide a series of problems that challenges the child and leads to the development of greater skill and expression. Activities must be presented in a developmental sequence, teaching easier movements before more difficult movements. The order of presentation is determined by the needs of the children. For example, preschoolers are not mentally or physically ready for sports. These children need freedom to express themselves in a different way through movement and dance (Coleman, 1985). Their large muscles have not been fully strengthened. Teachers should provide creative activities to develop large muscles.

The teacher begins with a simple problem involving one element of movement and progresses to other elements and combinations according to the maturity and skill demonstrated by the children. Each problem is structured carefully and has

specific objectives to be accomplished. The teacher must anticipate possible responses to the problem and plan additional questions and activities that will help the children to refine their solutions.

When a problem is presented, the children explore it in various ways. There is no one correct response, and all individual efforts must be encouraged. Imitation of other children is to be expected and, for some children, it provides needed security. Most children progress quickly to more original solutions. The teacher does not demonstrate in most instances. Imitation of adult movement is difficult and frustrating for most children and can hinder the development of self-confidence. In movement, the learning process is as important as the product.

During the period of exploration, the teacher circulates, noting problems and progress, asking questions, and occasionally suggesting ideas. Some children may be asked to share their solutions with the group. In general, demonstrations for anyone other than classmates should be avoided. The success of the movement program depends largely upon the attitude and skill of the teacher. If the teacher is enthusiastic, observant, and skillful in phrasing questions, the program will be rewarding for all. The children are naturally motivated, and they learn quickly and easily when they are actively involved and are experiencing success.

The activities that follow begin with general exploration of the individual's body movements and progress to combined movements. Teachers are encouraged to start their movement program with activity 1 and continue in sequence. Skills that are too difficult for particular children or age-groups should be omitted.

Notes to the Teacher

1. Discuss with the children and agree on a signal to be used when it is time to stop and listen.
2. State the problem or challenge briefly, in direct terms.
3. When a piece of equipment is involved, indicate what the children are to do as soon as they get their equipment. Immediate involvement is preferable to

waiting until each child has his or her rope, ball, or bean bag before beginning the activity.

4. Remind the children to avoid collisions with one another when they are working in the general or shared space. This requires constant attention and good body control. It is, therefore, a better learning condition than having the children always move in the same direction.

5. Encourage children to wear comfortable clothing that does not bind or impede free movement of any body part. Barefoot participation is highly recommended if the floor surface is splinter-free. The muscles of the feet work more efficiently and tactile sensation is enhanced when walking barefoot.

6. Avoid demonstrating the movement to prevent preconceived notions about the solutions. Once the children are involved, the children themselves will provide good examples of the solution to the problem. The teacher can point out these solutions to the class with the suggestion that others might want to try that particular solution. Make it clear that such examples represent another way of responding, not the right way to respond.

7. Allow time for practice and creativity. Free choice of any activity for a given time will allow the teacher to observe and suggest individual problems to be solved. Encourage children to make up games to be played with the equipment or apparatus. Children thus become responsible for stating the problem or challenge.

8. Assign and/or allow the children to choose a partner they will work with throughout the movement activities. Change partners often (each week) so that children learn to work with different people.

9. Praise and reinforce children's efforts to explore the limits of their motor ability. Challenge children to create new ways to solve the problems you give.
10. End each movement activity with a closing statement based on the children's experience.

Environmental Resources

Large open area
Audio equipment (record player and record, cassette player and tapes)
Tambourine or drum (for signaling)
Partners

Suggested Activities

1. **Where the Body Moves**

Objective:

To understand and explore personal and shared space. Also to learn movements of direction, level, and pathways.

Materials

Large room
Tambourine or drum for signaling
Partners

Directions:

(a) Discuss with the class the definition of personal space and shared space. Personal space is that space occupied by the individual which does not infringe on the space of another. Shared space or general space is the space the group as a whole uses.

(b) Direct the students to the signaling device, explaining that they are to stop moving at the signal of the tambourine or drum.

(c) Encourage the students to explore their own space.
  (1) How tall is your space? How wide is it?
  (2) If you keep one foot still and move the other, can you make your space wider?
  (3) Touch as much of your space as you can at one time. Can you do this standing up? How about sitting down?
  (4) See how little of your space you can fill at one time.
  (5) In your personal space be a telephone pole—standing tall and straight.
  (6) Now be a jelly fish—you can't stand at all.

(d) Encourage the students to explore their shared space.
  (1) Can you travel about the room, moving quickly, without touching anyone? Try it again and change directions each time you hear the signal. (Use the drum or tambourine every 2–5 seconds.)
  (2) How would you move if all our space were filled with cotton balls? Show me how you would move the cotton balls with different parts of your body.
  (3) Can you travel about the room staying very close to one another without ever touching? How would this look in slow motion? How would you move if you were late to school?
  (4) Pretend like you are a cloud. How would you move on a very windy day? Now move on a very calm day.

(e) Encourage students to work on directions (forward, backward, sideward, diagonally, up, down) in their personal space.
  (1) Can you move your arms in different directions? in front of you? sideward? behind you? How about your feet, can they be moved in different directions? in front of you? sideward? behind you?
  (2) Who can stretch one arm in one direction and the opposite leg in another direction? (This assumes that the concept of "opposite" has been learned.)
  (3) Lay on your back and lift your legs. Can you lift one at a time? Can you lift an arm and a leg at the same time?

(f) Work on directions in the shared space.
  (1) Can you change directions each time you hear the signal?
  (2) Who can hop in more than one direction?
  (3) Can you walk, change directions, and still face the same direction? Can you walk backward without touching anyone?
  (4) In shared space be a glider plane with your arms spread making straight wings. Change directions each time you hear the signal.
  (5) Stand in one place and pretend you are a teapot. Pour out some tea. Be careful not to lose your balance.
  (6) With your partner, see if you can both move in the same direction when the tambourine rattles and in different directions on the tap of the tambourine. (Indicate the different sounds from the tambourine so that the class recognizes the two signals; establish a firm, rhythmic beat.) Try this with music and small groups of three or four. Allow

brief time for practice and then share each group's "directional pattern" with the class.

(g) Work on some different levels (high, middle, low) in students' personal space.

(1) Put yourself at the lowest level possible in your space. Can you move your whole body at this level?

(2) Is it possible to have your head lower than your feet? Is there another way?

(3) Show me how you can keep two different body parts low and one body part high. Can you do it another way?

(h) In the shared space, work on different levels.

(1) Begin your run at one level and end your run at a different level. Can you think of another way to do this?

(2) What level is best for stopping at the end of a run? What level is best for a quick change of direction? (Encourage experimentation with the idea of lowering the body level with a wide stance to stop or turn.)

(3) Can you travel, changing your level and direction on the signal?

(i) Explore pathways as another way to move around (straight, curved, twisted, zigzag).

(1) Can you move forward with a pathway that is not straight? Can you show me a different way?

(2) Who can move like a cockscrew? Can you do it the opposite way?

(3) How would you move if you were an arrow shot from a bow?

(4) Can you make a zigzag pathway? Can you make the same zigzag pathway when you are hopping?

(5) Can you move in one pathway? At the beat of the tambourine, move in a different pathway. Repeat.

Note:

(1) Below is a list of movements that can be used by the teacher to extend any of the given activities. Each of the levels (low, middle, and high) has activities arranged according to difficulty.

Low Level

long body roll	seal walk (using arms, legs
belly crawl	dragging)
moving forward; sitting	sitting up roll (palms; hips; and
moving backward; sitting	legs on the floor)
back on ground; scooting	curled-up roll
hip walking	

Middle Level

crawling	walk on knees and elbows
knee walk	walk holding onto ankles
squatting walk	semicartwheels
frog jumps	four-legged walk—belly up
four-legged walk—belly down	

High Level

walk	tip-toe walk
run	giant steps

pogo jumps

run through held-up large
   scarf

run and hit drum or tambourine with two hands

march/high-knee walk

stomp

straight-leg walk

walk on heels

shuffle (without lifting feet
   from ground)

slide walk (without lifting feet
   from ground)

kicking walk

crossed-over steps—one
   swings out and around in
   front of other

hop

gallop

turn

punch air with fists as you walk

run and jump to hit drum

lunge

run and jump

run and leap

run and freeze in a shape

run and fall down and roll

swinging arm broad jump

skip

run and slide

(Sullivan, 1982, p. 62)

(2) The activities should be spread over a number of days. *Repetition* of these activities will help the children understand each concept.

2. *How the Body Moves*

Objective:

To understand and explore time, force, flow, tensed-relaxed, and relationships associated with different movements.

Materials:

Large open space
Musical equipment
Tambourine or drum for signaling
Bean bags (one per child)
Partners

Directions:

(a) When moving your body in both personal and shared space you can use different time (fast, medium, sudden, sustained).

   (1) Can you be a machine that begins very slowly and then moves faster and faster? Repeat with a change of levels. (Remind the students of low, middle, high levels.)

   (2) When you are ready, travel very quickly until you hear the signal, then stop. Repeat, but on the signal stop and slowly change your level on four drum beats (or tambourine taps). Can you show me a different level this time?

   (3) Move like a train that is having trouble starting. Now move like a race car or a racing horse just out of the gate.

(b) Your body can also move using forces (strong, light).

   (1) How would you travel if you were pushing a heavy box? pulling a loaded wagon?

   (2) Can you walk like a giant? run like a deer?

(3) While the music plays, change from heavy, strong movements to light ones each time you hear the signal.

(4) Again, listen to the music and try to change your movements by force each time the music changes.

(c) In the next activities, see if you can show tensed-relaxed movements.

(1) Can you show me what happens to a popsicle in the sunshine? Move as if you are a cup of water that changes to an ice cube.

(2) Can you slowly tighten all your muscles as the tambourine beats four counts? Now relax them with the next four counts. This time show me a change of body shape (curled, twisted, stretched) as you tighten. Are you able to change your level as you relax?

(3) Can you tighten all at once on one tambourine beat and relax on three counts? Can you slowly tense on three beats and relax completely on one tambourine beat?

(4) Move like an iron man and then like a rag doll when you hear the signal. (Try this to music letting the children alternate their movements at will. Praise any sense of rhythmic pattern exhibited.)

(d) Relationships (near-far, alongside, in front-behind, over-under, leading, following, unison-contrast) can also be expressed in movements. For this activity, pass out bean bags to each child.

(1) Can you place yourself over the bean bag? alongside it? under it? behind it?

(2) On the signal, can you move as far as possible from your spot and then return to your spot on the second signal? Change the level or the force of your movement this time.

(3) Be very still and listen to the music. Then let some part of your body move to the music; let the movement grow bigger until it takes you all over the room. Repeat with a different body part leading.

(4) Mirror your partner's movements when the tambourine rattles and try to contrast your movements with his or hers on taps of the tambourine. (Precede this challenge with a discussion of what it means to mirror and contrast movements. Examples of contrast: fast-slow, up-down, strong-weak, and so on. This may be done to music.)

Note:

These activities should be conducted over a number of days. Provide much repetition in order to promote thorough understanding.

3. ***What the Body Does***

Objectives:

To explore and understand changes in body shape, positions, locomotion movements, nonlocomotion movements.

Materials:

Large open space
Tambourine or drum for signaling
Musical equipment (record player, cassette player with a variety of fast/slow music)

Floor mats (one for every two children)
Partners

Directions:

(a) One way we can see how the body moves and changes is by shape (stretched, curled, twisted, wide, narrow, tall, short).

 (1) Try to make your body as small as possible, now as large as possible.

 (2) Show me a tall, twisted shape; a curled shape at a low level, a wide, stretched shape.

 (3) Is it possible to curl one body part and stretch another?

 (4) Let me see you stretch, then twist, then curl your body. Show me a different way as you change your level. Can you make three different body shapes as you travel about the room?

 (5) As I tap the tambourine four beats, change your body shape.

 (6) With your partner, combine body movements to make a statue.

(b) Now let's move our body parts in different positions (leading, supporting, transferring, receiving, initiating).

 (1) Show me how many ways you can move your head, your arms, your feet and legs, your trunk. This can be done to music as the children combine different body parts in movement in personal space or as they travel the shared space.

 (2) Find a way to make a bridge, supporting your weight on three body parts. Who can show me another way?

 (3) Can you support your weight on one body part and shift your support to two body parts with a smooth movement? Now move from standing on two body parts to three body parts smoothly.

 (4) What is a good way to land after you jump or leap? Why? (Stress the best way to absorb force: by giving with the force, i.e., bending in the hips, knees, and ankle joints when landing.) What is a good way to catch a ball that is moving very fast? Why? ("Give," as if pulling the ball into your midsection.)

 (5) Pretend like you are catching a ball that is moving very fast. Then catch a ball that is moving slowly.

 (6) How would you toss a ball, catch it, and go into a roll on the floor? Can you think of another way to do this? Try another.

(c) Locomotor movements include movements of running, walking, crawling, rolling, hopping, skipping, jumping, leaping, climbing, sliding, galloping, pushing, and pulling. Try some of these locomotor movements.

 (1) When you are ready, move about the room as quickly and quietly as possible, changing directions on the signal. Remember not to touch anyone.

 (2) Can you jump from one foot and land on two? Can you jump backward?

 (3) Who can skip at a high level? Can you skip backward? (Progression for nonskippers: hop two times on the right foot, lifting the left knee high; hop two times on the left foot, lifting the right knee high. As children become proficient, alternate one hop right, one hop left, emphasizing lifting opposite knee high each time. This is the basis for skipping.)

(4) Let me see you travel about the room at a low level, changing your way of moving on the signal (crawling to rolling, to running, to giant steps, and so on).

(5) Begin doing one of the locomotor movements. At the signal change to another. Repeat.

(6) Find a partner. How many ways can you and your partner pull, push, roll each other? (Point out examples of good body mechanics, i.e., getting down low and close to one's partner in order to apply force for pushing or rolling; lining up one's body in the direction of applied force in pulling.)

(7) Do three movements in a row. See if your partner can follow your sequence. Switch roles with your partners.

(d) Nonlocomotor movements include swinging, swaying, twisting, turning, curling, and stretching. The activities we are going to do now will work on these nonlocomotor movements. In addition, we will combine some of the other movements we have previously learned.

(1) Can you swing one body part and then another? Can you swing your whole body? Can you swing with a partner? (Try this with music and/or rhythmic accompaniment.)

(2) With a partner, can you make a very twisted shape? a combined high and low, stretched shape?

(3) As you sway back and forth or from side to side, can you show me different body shapes (curled, stretched, twisted, and so on)? Do this to music.

(4) Can you combine two of these movements? Try to do it another way.

4. *Using Movements of Manipulation*

Objective:

To explore and use effectively manipulatives (ropes, balls, hoops, wands, and balance boards). Also to understand how the body is able to manipulate these materials.

Materials:

Bean Bags	If possible, all children should
Balls	have their own pieces of equip-
Hoops	ment
Wands	
Balance Board	
Partners	

Directions:

(a) Using balls, let's explore some movements.
   (1) How many ways can you move your ball?
   (2) Can you move your ball at a different level?
   (3) Can you travel and move your ball at the same time (walk, toss, and catch; run, tap ball with your feet, and so on).

(4) Each time you hear the signal, change the way you move the ball or
your body. Remember you don't always have to be bouncing the ball.
Repeat a few times in order to allow the children to experiment with
different movements.

(5) Can you and a partner move the ball from one to the other with
good control? What helps you to control the movement of the ball?

(6) Bounce or pass the ball to any person who does not have a ball;
keep balls moving all over the room. (Use as many balls as the group
can control.)

(b) Bean bags can be used like balls to explore movements.

(1) What body part can you use to move your bean bag? Is there another
part? yet another?

(2) Toss and then catch your bean bag with a different body part—other than your hands.

(3) Can you toss your bean bag so it lands in front, behind, beside you?

(4) Can you toss your bean bag and clap once (twice, three times) before you catch it?

(5) Balance your bean bag on a part of your body. Can you move (walk, skip, hop, sway, etc.) while you balance the bean bag?

(6) Can you balance it at a different level? Now try to move at this level.

(c) Let's see if we can use ropes in movement.

(1) How many ways can you move over your rope? What ways can you travel from one end of your rope to the other? Can you move backward along your rope?

(2) Can you jump over your rope while turning it? Can you jump while turning your rope backward?

(3) Can you travel about the room while you turn and jump your rope?

(4) Use your rope at a different level. Can you think of something else to do with your rope at this level?

(5) Can you combine a body movement and a movement with your rope? Is there another way?

(d) Another tool we can use in movement is a hoop. Let's manipulate the hoop while moving.

(1) Lay the hoop on the floor, show me different ways to move around the outside of your hoop. Around the inside of the hoop.

(2) Now pick up your hoop and show me ways to move inside and outside of your hoop.

(3) Can you stretch as you move into your hoop and curl and roll as you move out of your hoop?

(4) Show me a way to stretch as you move into your hoop at a different level.

(5) Who can twirl the hoop around some body part? Show me a different way. Is there another way?

(6) Can you balance the hoop on a body part? Show me a different place to balance the hoop.

(7) How many ways can you move through the hoop as your partner holds it? Can you move through a rolling hoop?

(8) Hold the hoop at a different level. Now see how many ways your partner can go through it.

(e) Wands can help us explore movements, too.

(1) Move around the room slowly using your wand. Can you do it at another level?

(2) Can you stand in your personal space and balance your wand? Is there another way? Now can you move forward or backward balancing the wand?

(3) Now balance the wand on a body part. Then stand up or sit down. Is there another way you can move while balancing the wand?

(4) As you hold the wand with both hands, can you step forward and then backward over the wand?

(5) Can you stand the wand in front of you, turn quickly, and catch the wand before it hits the floor?

(6) Can you and a partner have a tug-of-war holding the wand? Can you do it at a different level?

(7) Can you draw a pathway with your wand, then hop along it?

(8) Show me another way to use the wand that we have not done.

(f) Balance boards are another piece of equipment that we can use to expand our movements.

(1) How can you move from one end of the board to the other with good balance.

(2) Can you walk and dip a foot at the same time?

(3) Try to walk to the middle of the balance board then extend one leg forward—now backward. Can you do it with the other leg?

(4) Can you walk halfway across, then balance, leaning forward with arms held out to the side and the other foot held high in back? (*Hint:* Look straight ahead, not down.)

(5) Who can walk halfway across, stop and then change direction to finish?

(6) As you move across the board, show me two balanced positions before you finish. (Balance is aided by a wide base of support and/or a position which is lower to the floor.)

(7) Can you get into a kneeling position without falling off the board? How about a sitting/squatting position?

(8) Sit on the balance beam and make your body into a V position (legs and arms extended).

(9) As you move across the board, toss and catch a beanbag.

(10) Who can jump off the end of the balance beam, land softly, curl,

and roll? (Mats are needed. *Hint:* Roll on the rounded parts of your body.)

5. *Rhythmic Activities*

Objectives:

To encourage exploration of large and small motor movements with music. In addition, to use combinations of all previously learned movements.

Materials:

Large space
Partners
Music: It is helpful to prepare a cassette with a variety of music pieces so that you will not have to stop the lesson to change the music.

Directions:

(a) We will begin our rhythmic activities working individually.

   (1) Sit comfortably on the floor, close your eyes, and listen to the music. Can you move just your head in time to the music? Now move your head in one direction, pause, and then in another direction, pause, and so on. (Stress the "pause" as being a positive element rather than merely an absence of movement. Such rhythmic pauses are either the logical ending for a movement or the preparation for a new movement. The concept of pause and stillness as a positive element is basic to confident rhythmic responses; it indicates purpose and control.)

(2) Move a joint in you body. Can you move two joints at a time?

(3) Show me how you would use your muscles. Is there another way to move your muscles?

(4) There are some muscles we often forget about—facial muscles. Make your face sad, happy, scared, excited, frustrated.

(5) Show me how many ways your hands and arms can move in response to the music. Now your feet. Can your movements lead you as you dance around the room? How about your feet?

(6) Stand like a floppy rag doll and listen to the drum. Can you start a movement in your trunk that takes you all about the room? (Vary the rhythm of the drum beat, and stress pauses that end a movement or begin a new one.)

(7) Pretend you are an instrument. Can you make your instrument play to the rhythm of the music you hear? Change the way you move when the rhythm of the music changes.

(8) As you move, can you make different body shapes each time you hear a different sound? (Shapes—curled, stretched, twisted, tall, short, narrow, wide. Vary sounds—drum, bell maracas, tambourine, vocal sounds.)

(9) Listen carefully to the music—make up a dance that follows the music. (Use a variety of music types in order to encourage changes in movement.)

(10) Ask the children to suggest various words that describe or depict movement—creeping, dashing, springing, balancing, rising, sinking, growing, flowing, and so on. Make a list of these words and ask each child to choose one or two of them as a theme for a dance. Rhythm instruments or body percussion can provide accompaniment. If the children feel secure, have them share their dances and let the class guess which works served as the themes for each dance. This can also be done as a group effort when working with partners and groups.

(b) Creative movements with music can also be done with a partner. With your partner, we can do the following activities.

(1) Face your partner and do a "mirror dance" with your hands and arms. Can you do a mirror dance with your feet and legs? How about with different facial expressions?

(2) Hold hands with your partner and skip (slide, leap, gallop) until you hear the signal; then find a new partner and continue to move to the music.

(3) Move the same way your partner moves until you hear the tambourine; then move in a different way. (Encourage contrasting movements as well as strong unison movements. This challenge can be either locomotor or nonlocomotor.)

(4) What interesting body shapes can you and your partner make? Can the two of you create an interesting design in the space you share? Practice until you two can make three different designs with various body shapes and levels; then let's do these designs to music. (The concept of purposeful pause is basic in this problem; the children finish one design and prepare for the next, holding the final design longer to give a strong ending to their dance.)

(c) The final way we will explore movement with music is in a group situation.

 (1) Can you move toward the center of the room on the signal and away from the center when you hear the signal again? *Hint:* Remember not to bump anyone. (Recorded music may be used for this. Allow time for controlled movement in the center, occasionally, before sounding the signal to move away from the center.)

 (2) With all the children seated in a circle on the floor, take turns leading a rhythmic pattern with body percussion. Can you work out a rhythmic pattern to your name and share it with the group?

 (3) Assign each small group (three to four children) a movement theme and let them make up a short dance. Suggested themes: "Grow and stretch as flowers do, opening their petals"; "Move as if you were leprechauns creeping out for a frolic in the moonlight"; "Move as if you were calm ocean waves that become rough and tossed by a storm." The theme from a favorite story or poem may be chosen. Remind the children of elements that make movements interesting—change and contrast in direction, level, strength, tempo, pathways, body shapes, and relationships in movements.

Warm-Up and Relaxation

Warm-up activities are important before starting movement activities with children. The warm-up will not only physically prepare them for the upcoming activities, but will also give them a chance to regroup and slowly work their way up to larger, more active movements.

Relaxation activities are very important after a session of physical activity. Relaxing will help children calm down and get settled before they move on to another phase of the day. Relaxation at the end of an active period helps the child release tension and become more fluid (Zion et al., 1986).

Warm-up activities:

1. Tell the children to stand up and stretch as high as they can. Have them sit on the floor with their legs out in front of them and try to touch their toes. Also have them stand up with their feet together and bend down to touch their toes.
2. a. jumping jacks
 b. running in place
 c. rocking horse (lie on stomach, grasp feet with hands and rock)
 d. upper body twists
 e. alternate touching right toe with left hand, left toe with right hand

Relaxation activities:

Tell the children to lie down on the floor with their hands out to their sides. Have them "feel" their bodies against the floor. Ask them to imagine they are floating and all the muscles in their body are very relaxed. Show them how to breath deeply and slowly.

References

Coleman, M. et al. (1984–1985). "Play, Games and Sport: Their Use and Misuse." *Childhood Education, 61,* 192–197.

Lynch-Fraser, D. (1982). *Dance Play—Creative Movement for Very Young Children.* New York: Walker and Co.

Sullivan, M. (1982). *Feeling Strong, Feeling Free: Movement Exploration for Young Children.* Washington, D.C.: Association for the Education of Young Children.

Zion, L. et al. (1986). *The Physical Side of Thinking.* Illinois: Charles C. Thomas.

Suggested Readings on Movement for Teachers

Baker, K. R. (1966). *Let's Play Outdoors* (Rev. ed.). Washington, D.C.: National Association for the Education of Young Children.

Bicanich, D. D., & Manke, C. W. (1978). *Sensori-motor Activity Guide for Preschoolers from Birth to Age Five.* West St. Paul, Minn.: Bicanich & Manke.

Engstrom, G. (Ed.). (1971). *The Significance of the Young Child's Motor Development.* Washington, D.C.: National Association for the Education of Young Children.

Joyce, M. (1973). *First Steps in Teaching Creative Dance: A Handbook for Teachers of Children, Kindergarten Through Sixth Grade.* Palo Alto, Calif.: Mayfield Publishing Co.

Kamii, C., and DeVries, R. (1980). *Group Games in Early Education; Implications of Piaget's Theory.* Washington, D.C.: National Association for the Education of Young Children.

Kogan, S. (1982). *Step by Step: A Complete Movement Education Curriculum from Preschool to 6th Grade.* Byron, Calif.: Front Row Experience.

Stecher, M. B., McElheny, H., and Greenwood, M. (1972). *Joy and Learning Through Music and Movement Improvisations.* New York: Macmillan.

9

Outdoor Play

Young children learn and grow from play. According to Frost and Klein (1983, p. 1), play is universal and essential to humanity. "Since the dawn of civilization, people have left artifacts and records depicting the importance of play to physical, intellectual, emotional, social, and spiritual well-being of the individual." Play is the child's means of communication, discovery, and expression (*Criteria for Selecting Play Equipment for Early Childhood Education: A Reference Book,* 1981). Loving guidance and adequate equipment can open a world where children can unfold and learn to understand themselves and those with whom they live. Pitcher, Lasher, Feinburg, and Braun (1974) emphasize that optimal learning in young children occurs when they play. Therefore, educators of young children must acquaint themselves with the crucial role of play in the development of the individual child.

Play has many functions, all of which are important to the child. Play provides the means for a search for knowledge in human beings and is a vehicle for probing curiosities and minimizing uncertainties in the universe (Pitcher et al., 1974). The different forms of play represent mastery of various skills, capabilities, or experiences, determined by the child's current developmental status and personal life experiences. According to Rogers (1985), the primary function of play is active mastery. Children's play is psychically active if and when they are free to enjoy and to impose something on the environment. Play involving motor skills, such as climbing, jumping, etc., demonstrates the child's exercise and mastery of developing motor skills. Play involving creative or constructive activities—making paintings, working with clay or blocks—demonstrates the joy of self-expression. Play centered on acting out unhappy incidents from the past demonstrates the child's active attempts to master traumatic experiences. Play contributes to mental health by helping the child to regain or maintain emotional equilibrium. Social play involving role-taking with peers demonstrates the child's attempts to understand and master complex social life roles and situations. Finally, play also helps the child develop positive personality traits or attitudinal styles involving perseverance, self-confidence, and social competence.

In addition to the functions mentioned above, Frost and Klein (1983) reiterate the Roberts and Sutton-Smith study which hypothesized that children compensate for stress by playing games to relieve it. Also, playing games aids in the enculturation of the child. In addition, Frost and Klein present the instinct-practice theory of Karl Gross, in which play is viewed as a vehicle for perfecting instincts and skills needed

417

in later life. For example, playing house is a rehearsal for adult roles played by the children around the world.

Play occurs optimally in a pressure-free, safe environment (Pitcher et al., 1974). Children do not play in an environment laden with fear or stress. Jerome Bruner, an American cognitive theorist, maintains that play minimizes the consequences of actions and maximizes learning because in play, one can test limits without risk. Play provides opportunities to try combinations of behavior that under pressure would never be tried. Dr. Joe L. Frost (1986) developed a Playground Maintenance Checklist to keep a child's outdoor area safe (Figure 1).

FIGURE 1 *Playground Maintenance Checklist*

Instructions: *Check the entire playground at least once each month. Train all personnel to be alert to playground hazards, and report them promptly. Avoid the use of hazardous equipment until repaired.*	*Date Checked*	*Repair Needed*	*Date Repaired*
1. Is there an 8- to 10-inch-deep resilient ground cover (sand, pea gravel, shredded wood) under all swings, merry-go-rounds, slides, and climbing equipment? Is the resilient surface compacted or out of place? If concrete or asphalt is under equipment, is the manufactured impact attenuation product in place?			
2. Are there foreign objects or obstructions in the fall zones under and around fixed equipment?			
3. Are there obstructions to interfere with normal play activity?			
4. Are there climbing areas that would allow children to fall more than their reaching height when standing erect?			
5. Are concrete supports sticking above the ground? Are they secure?			
6. Are there sharp edges, broken parts, pinching actions, or loose bolts?			
7. Are there openings that could trap a child's head?			
8. Are there frayed cables, worn ropes, open hooks, or chains that could pinch?			
9. Are timbers rotting, splitting, termite infested, or excessively worn?			
10. Are portable toys such as tricycles and wagons in good repair?			

In providing a pressure-free, safe environment for children to play, the selection of appropriate playthings is important. *Criteria for Selecting Play Equipment for Early Childhood Education: A Reference Book* (1981) states that good play equipment should have the following characteristics: be as free of detail as possible; be versatile in use; be easily comprehended; have large, easily manipulated parts; involve the child in play, including large muscles; encourage cooperative play; have material that is warm and pleasant to touch; be durable; work as intended; be safe; be generous in proportions and quantity; have a price based on durability and design. A good plaything should involve the whole child—body, mind, and spirit—because

FIGURE 1 (Continued)

Instructions: Check the entire playground at least once each month. Train all personnel to be alert to playground hazards, and report them promptly. Avoid the use of hazardous equipment until repaired.	*Date Checked*	*Repair Needed*	*Date Repaired*
11. Are there protrusions that can catch clothing?			
12. Are there crush points or shearing actions such as hinges of seesaws and undercarriages of revolving equipment?			
13. Are swing seats excessively heavy? Do they have protruding parts such as animal noses or legs?			
14. Is the fence at least 4 feet high and in good repair? Can gates be secured?			
15. Are there electrical hazards on the playground such as accessible air conditioners, switch boxes, or power lines?			
16. Are there collections of contaminated water on the playground?			
17. Are there toxic materials on the playground?			
18. Do the grass, trees, and shrubs need care?			
19. Do children wear inappropriate clothing such as capes on climbing and moving equipment?			
20. Does the adult-to-child supervision ratio equal ratios required for indoor activity?			

Source: Frost, J. L. (1986) Playground Maintenance Checklist. Austin, TX: Texas Department of Human Services. Reprinted with permission.

such a toy will stimulate children to do things for themselves. Frost and Klein (1983) suggest that the novelty of a toy is a primary reason for children to explore it. The introduction of a novel object stimulates the child to explore its properties.

Playgrounds are divided into various categories: traditional, contemporary, adventurous, creative, and commercial (Frost & Klein, 1983). Traditional playgrounds are usually part of schools, housing projects, or neighborhood parks and typically contain swings, slides, seesaws, and climbing bars. Contemporary playgrounds are frequently designed by architects and emphasize textures, novel designs, and different heights in aesthetically pleasing arrangements. Most often these playgrounds are somewhat sculptured, frequently based on sand or concrete. Adventure playgrounds provide children raw building materials and tools with which they can build their own play structures. Creative playgrounds include an inexpensive mix of handmade equipment and loose parts. Finally, commercial playgrounds may consist of a massive unit structure containing interior and exterior space for climbing and dramatic play, horizontal tire swings, slides, and a fire fighter's pole and ladder. Some commercial playgrounds comprise an array of specially treated wood structures, including balance beams, chinning bars, obstacle climbers, suspension bridges, etc.

In each of the types of playgrounds mentioned, Frost and Klein (1983) report that certain activities are prevalent. They also present general conclusions from the Frost and Strickland study of creative and commercial playgrounds. The most widely used piece of equipment on the traditional playground tends to be the swing, where on the contemporary playground the sand areas are the most widely used. At adventure playgrounds, the clubhouse is used most. Surprisingly, slides on the traditional playground are rarely used, while they are heavily used on the contemporary playground due to the variety of ways of climbing to the top. In addition, of traditional, contemporary, and adventure playgrounds, children stay the shortest lengths of time at the traditional playground and the longest at the adventure playground. General conclusions from the Frost and Strickland study on creative and commercial playgrounds are: Action-oriented equipment is preferred by children; equipment designed primarily for exercise play is not sufficient to provide for the wide range of children's developmental play needs; children prefer equipment that can be adapted to their play schemes; among equipment tested, only loose parts have equal appeal to children across all grade/age levels; and inexpensive play environments can be superior to expensive ones.

Playgrounds should be developmentally relevant to the play needs of children. Frost and Klein (1983) state that the complexity and variety of playground equipment influences play types, equipment choices, social behavior, and verbal interaction. High complexity in the play environment sustains greater interaction with play objects and less interaction with peers. As the amount of equipment increases, the amount of play increases, and the amount of undesirable behavior and social behavior decreases. On the traditional playground the children engage in exercise play over 77 percent of the time and in dramatic play less than 3 percent of the time. On the creative playground, children engage in dramatic play 40 percent and exercise play 43 percent of the time. In addition, on the traditional playground over 35 percent of the time is spent in solitary and parallel activity, but on the creative playground this activity occupies less than 25 percent of the time.

In the child's world of outdoor play, life is an adventure of sunshine, imagination, and freedom. The outdoors is a natural learning environment for children, and its endless possibilities should be explored at every opportunity. It can be a place for noisy, active pursuits such as kickball or carpentry, or a place for quiet reflection while studying a flower or reading under a shady tree. The outdoor world is limited only by the imagination.

The advantages of using the outdoor classroom are many, and the limitations are few. The health benefits of fresh air, sunshine, and exercise for children are obvious. Rarely is the weather too cold or damp for children to go outside. The addition of a roofed patio area greatly expands the possibilities for using the outdoor classroom during inclement weather. Children have a very real need for freedom—freedom to move, to make noise, and to sometimes make a mess. The outdoors gives them this freedom, far beyond the possibilities of the indoor learning environment.

Opportunities for learning in the basic curriculum areas are present both indoors and out. The outdoor environment simply adds another dimension to the learning process. In mathematics, the skills of counting, sorting, classifying, and measuring can be practiced using natural outdoor objects. Creative material for language arts abounds in the outdoor classroom. There is much to see, to hear, to talk about, to write about, and to read about. Science concepts are learned more easily through hands-on experience with actual objects. The plants, animals, rocks, and sky in the outdoor environment provide this opportunity.

Certain activities such as art, water play, sand play, or carpentry may be offered intermittently in the outdoor classroom because of a lack of space or housekeeping restrictions indoors. The freedom of the outdoors allows these activities to continue on a daily basis with plenty of space and no clean-up difficulties. In fact, virtually all classroom activities may be conducted outside, allowing great flexibility in scheduling, using equipment, and balancing quiet and active tasks. Thus the indoor and the outdoor environments become one world—a world in which children can explore, create, learn, and grow.

Environmental Area

150 square feet of play area per child
Variety of topographical features: mounds, flat, sod and turf, pine needles, and
    sand
Balance of space in the sun and shade
Hard-surfaced area for wheel toys and bouncing balls
Grassy plot for running and romping
Spot for pets, garden, and digging
Sandpit and cover (with brick or concrete surroundings for a place to sit)
Space for water play
Storage space for equipment
Safety precautions
Natural areas with a variety of plant life: trees, shrubs, grass, weeds, flowers
Outdoor weatherproof electrical outlets

Stationary Equipment

Interesting structures or sculptures for climbing
Swings (tire or leather seats)

Platforms for climbing and/or swinging
Large sewer pipes set in concrete
Equipment for crawling and tunneling
Tree trunks
Low horizontal ladders
Low climbing ropes
Wading pool

Portable Equipment

Walking boards of various lengths
Sawhorses of various heights
Wooden steps, wooden ladder
Heavy wooden benches
Low balance beams
Bales of straw
Tires (tractor, automobile, bicycle)
Balls
Bean bags

Jump ropes: long and individual
Transportation equipment: wagons, tricycles, wheelbarrow, go-carts, broomstick
    with sock head
Sand toys
Tools for gardening: shovels, rakes, hoes
Building blocks
Tools for woodwork
Scrap lumber for large construction
Wooden boxes, packing crates, rope handles, cardboard cartons
Planks
Steering wheel and column attached to a heavy box

Parent-Made Equipment and Materials

1. Storage unit to build

2. Wooden climbing structure

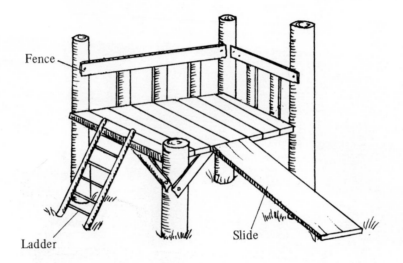

Fence

Ladder

Slide

3. Telephone spools

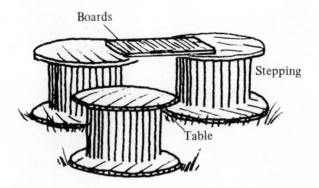

Boards

Stepping

Table

4. Wooden bridges and structures

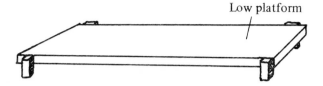

Low platform

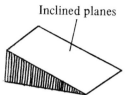

Inclined planes

5. Cans and barrels

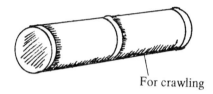

For crawling

6. Tires

Swing (punch holes in bottom
to let out water)

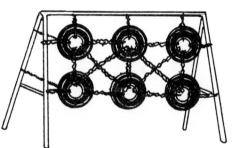

Old swing-set frame held together with rope

Tire bed swing-bolt tires together

7. Rolling slide

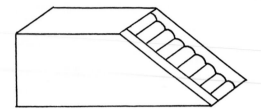

Walk up area (slide is made of
pipes app. 20 inches long)

8. Trees encircled with brick (may be used as a quiet area for small-group teaching, storytelling, or dramatic play)

9. Nets for climbing

Rope should be knotted
at intersections

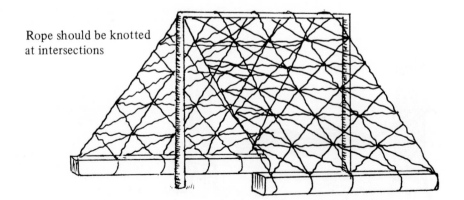

Suggested Activities

1. *Spontaneous and Directed Play.* Structure the outdoor environment so that the child will have many opportunities for spontaneous, creative play as well as directed play. Children should be free to engage in either or both.
2. *Hopscotch.* Paint a hopscotch square on an asphalt area.
3. *Obstacle Course.* Plan an obstacle course requiring crawling through pipes, stepping through tires, climbing, crawling under bars, etc.
4. *Movement Courses.* Instigate active movement courses such as "Station one, gallop like a horse; station two, leap like a frog; station three, bend like a tree in the breeze." Include walking, running, jumping, hopping, galloping, leaping, skipping, climbing, dodging.
5. *Extension of Indoors.* Take out as many indoor activities as possible, for example, painting, blocks, dolls.
6. *Task Cards.* Make task cards of games that the children might enjoy. Remember to make the wordings as simple as possible.
7. *Change Equipment.* Create interesting situations for climbing, crawling, and so on by changing the equipment frequently.
8. *Jump Rope.* Use the jump rope on the ground to create geometric designs and shapes; have the children "walk" the shape.
9. *Large Bag of Rags.* For emotional release, hang a large bag of rags from a tree and use it as a punching bag.
10. *Tussles.* When tussles occur on the playground, allow the children to fight it out—in slow motion.
11. *Rope Net.* Hang a rope net between two trees (good for swinging or climbing).
12. *Exercising.* When they are exercising, ask children to suggest an exercise and let them lead it.
13. *Playhouse Change.* From time to time, place an interesting playhouse on the playground, such as a camping tent or teepee.
14. *Nature Trail.* Create a nature trail for the children to walk through, to explore, and to enjoy (creek, trees, animals, plants, natural habitats of animals).
15. *Carpentry.* Keep tools, wood scraps, nails, and paint in an outdoor storage area for children to build and paint small, temporary objects and structures. Adult assistance is advised here.
16. *Animal Cages.* Keep animals and cages near both indoor and outdoor play environments for children to observe and enjoy throughout the day.

Playground Suggestions

1. Give support and encouragement to the timid and unsure child.
2. Plan activities for the uncoordinated child so that he or she may succeed.
3. Be patient with all types of children in their endeavors.
4. Make the playground an interesting learning situation by adding art, music, reading, sciences, and other activities.
5. Slides need top platforms. Slides built into hills and mounds are safest.
6. Swings should be situated away from heavy traffic areas.
7. Sawdust or sand should be placed under all climbing apparatus.
8. Place trash cans on the playground.

Additional Playground Equipment

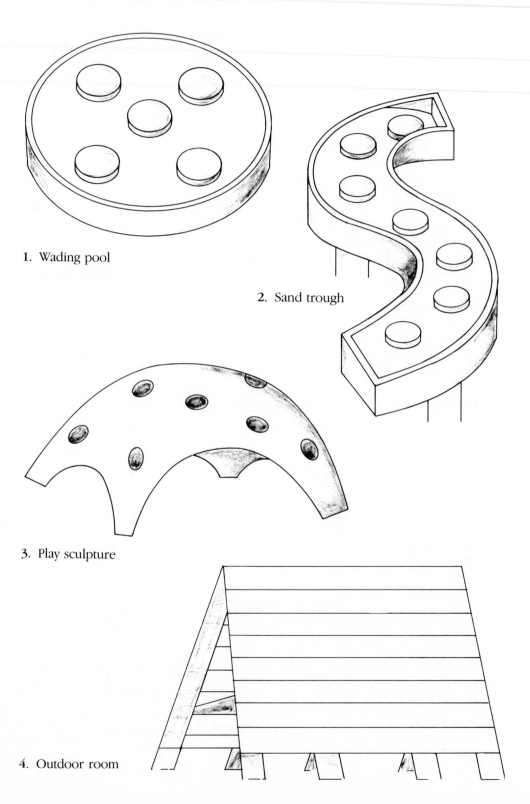

1. Wading pool

2. Sand trough

3. Play sculpture

4. Outdoor room

5. Blocks

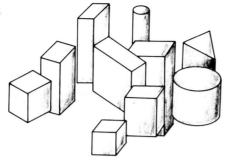

6. Tire walk

7. Slides and tunnel

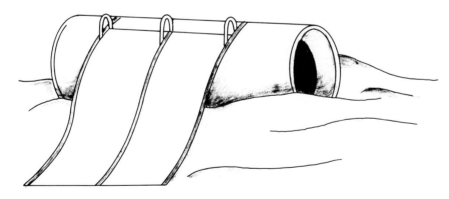

8. Mound

9. Free play area
10. Climbing trees

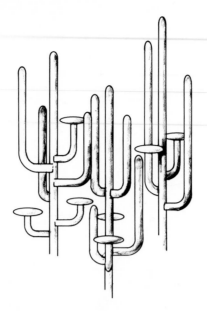

11. Cargo net climber

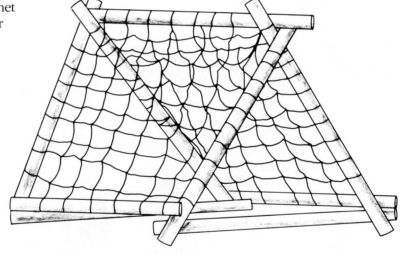

12. Swings

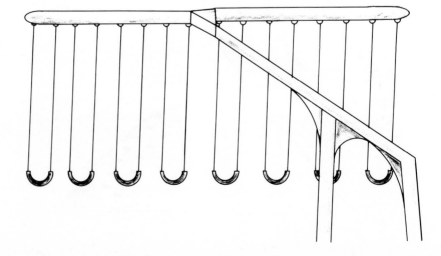

References

Frost, J. L. (1986). Playground Maintenance Checklist. Austin, TX: Texas Department of Human Services.

Frost, J. L. and Klein, B. L. (1983). *Children's Play and Playgrounds.* Austin, Tex.: Playscapes International.

Pitcher, E. G., Lasher, M. G., Feinburg, S. G., and Braun, L. A. (1974). *Helping Young Children Learn* (2nd ed.). Columbus, Ohio: Charles E. Merrill.

Rogers, D. L. (1985). Relationships Between Block Play and Social Development of Young Children. *Early Child Development and Care, 20,* 245–261.

Criteria for Selecting Play Equipment for Early Childhood Education: A Reference Book. (1981). Rifton, N.Y.: Community Playthings.

10

People and Places: The Social Studies

Social studies is the study of people and cultures. It provides a background for group activities that increases students' awareness of their world, nation, state, and community. The social studies program in early childhood education helps children become discerning, capable, and caring citizens committed to a democratic way of life. For children to become effective citizens and decision makers in the family, community, nation, and world, the social studies program develops knowledge of concepts, generalizations, and facts through critical thinking and problem-solving skills. Such a program prepares them to live in a constantly changing world and to be sensitive to social attitudes, values, and beliefs (Martorella, 1985). "Living and functioning in a democracy require informed, knowledgeable people, skillful in every area of social science—able to think, solve problems, and analyze their attitudes, as well as live together effectively" (Seefeldt, 1984, p. 4). Achieving this goal is a life-long process. However, the foundation begins early in the home and is firmly established throughout the elementary school years (Martorella, 1985).

Social studies is the single curriculum area that deals with human experiences entirely. It prepares the student to accept the right and responsibility of citizenship. The social studies program should provide skills, knowledge, attitudes, and values that enable students to become problem solvers and decision makers.

Reflective teachers in early childhood education plan appropriate social studies programs based on the mental, social, and physical growth of young children as described in development research by Jean Piaget, Jerome Bruner, Lawrence Kohlberg, and Erik Erikson. The theories of developmental stages provide meaningful observations on the learning capabilities and limitations of children 4 to 8 years old. Teachers are aware of what to expect from young children and how to nurture their development. These theories imply that children learn through play, exploring, experimenting, and discovering (Martorella, 1985; Seefeldt, 1984).

Day (1983) proposes that a developmental approach in teaching works because it emphasizes "the total child." A developmental program is organized around the needs, interests, and learning styles of children. An active program enables children to participate in experiencing and exploring their social and physical world through observing, predicting, and communicating.

To plan effectively, teachers reflect on the social studies positions and guidelines published by national organizations such as the influential National Council of the Social Studies, as well as the goals and objectives of state and local educational agencies (Jarolimek, 1986). The "near-to-far" approach is the position taken by the North Carolina Department of Public Instruction in teaching social studies at the kindergarten and primary levels. This approach "helps students to better understand their own familiar environment as they examine close at hand environments and people unfamiliar to them."

Competent teachers are interested in what research discovers about young children, data related to teaching, and how to apply them in the classroom. Current research studies on the human brain indicate that the hemispheres have different cognitive styles identified as systematic and intuitive. Studies also suggest that individuals have a learning style preference and a hemispheric preference for perceiving and processing information used in problem solving. Individuals may prefer the left side of the brain to process information systematically in a linear, sequential, logical way. Others may prefer the right side of the brain to process information intuitively, in a holistic, abstract way. Still others prefer a left-right integrated way (Maxin, 1983).

There is an interrelationship between these separate and unique parts working jointly to process information in a complementary manner. "In all kinds of activities, the brain uses both hemispheres, perhaps at times each carrying an equal share of a task" (Edwards, 1979). Yet traditional education programs and teaching strategies stress rational, logical, and analytic thinking with minimal value on innovative, experimental thinking.

However, researchers and educators such as Roger Sperry, Robert Ornstein, Jerome Bruner, and Robert Samples advocate teaching strategies that exercise right-brain thinking. They also stress the use of techniques integrating both halves of the brain. "We must encourage in the social studies classroom not only systematic problem-solving experiences described in Dewey's description of the inquiry process, but also the inventive, intuitive thinking that is associated with *creative discovery*" (Maxim, 1983).

In reviewing early research in social studies education, Jantz and Klawitter (1985) found support for the notion that in processing information children learn through a "combination of verbal and imaginal mediation," or the verbal, analytical left side of the brain and the nonverbal, synthetical right. Children in preschool and the primary grades are still in the formative stages of establishing their learning style and hemispheric preference and need instructional methods that utilize "both brain hemispheres in equal partnership" (Maxim, 1983).

Teaching strategies incorporating both modes of thinking strengthen young children's awareness in learning there "is more than one way of solving problems." Thus, they assemble "a repertoire of problem-solving skills" (Wilkerson, 1986).

The 4MAT is an instructional model designed by Bernice McCarthy (1980) in which teaching strategies speak to learning styles and hemispheric preference. Each of the four learning styles has concepts presented and taught through an eight-step cycle integrating the right mode and left mode of perceiving and processing information. Wilkerson (1986) applied the 4MAT system of instruction to evaluate its effects on academic achievement and retention of learning. The outcome of this study indicates that both academic achievement and long-term retention are facilitated significantly by the 4MAT system of instruction rather than by the textbook approach of instruction.

Students need assistance in understanding themselves and others. They come from many varied backgrounds, bringing with them many different views of life and their world. The way children view themselves and interact with others promotes a positive or negative self-image or awareness.

> John disrupts the class to be noticed because there is no one at home to listen to him and pay attention to his needs.
>
> Susan's parents spend a lot of time with her and she has traveled all over the world. She brings quite a different view of life to the classroom than John.
>
> Mark has a learning problem. He cannot read on his grade level. He is often called "dummy" by his classmates.
>
> Tonya has a constant fear of not being accepted because she is a minority and has had some unfortunate and unhappy experiences.
>
> Rosa comes from another country and speaks very little English. Rosa and Tonya

realize that being different causes them problems in relating to the other students.

Cole is a noisy, outspoken child whose family has passed their prejudices on to
him.

It cannot be assumed that all students will come to the classroom equipped with
the knowledge and readiness required to study the structure of the social science
discipline without assistance (Skeel, 1979). The knowledge and readiness in which
some students need assistance is in the areas of developing a good self-concept,
recognizing and appreciating the global society and its multicultural composition,
providing knowledge of the past and present as a basis for making decisions and
problem solving, developing valuing skills, and learning how to become an active
participant in society.

A social studies program and the teachers in early childhood education nurture a
"sense of self-worth, dignity and a healthy self-concept in each child" (Seefeldt &
Barbour, 1986, p. 394). Being valued and accepted in spite of limitations fosters the
development of concerned citizens. Developing self-esteem, children learn they are
unique individuals sharing similarities with others in their physical and emotional
needs. "The more adequate children feel about themselves, the better able they are
to reach out and relate to others, and to feel a sense of oneness with people and
the things in their world" (Seefeldt & Barbour, 1986, p. 394). As young children
develop a consciousness of who they are, they realize they have choices and decisions to make about themselves, their relationships with others, and their environment.

Research links the development of the young child's sense of self to school performance and social relationships. Self-concept is distinct from, but correlated with,
academic self-concept. There is evidence that final grades and certain higher-level
thinking processes and self-concept are positively correlated (Stanley, 1985).

Banks (1985) suggests that "before individuals can make sound decisions and act
reflectively, they must be helped to clarify their feelings and confused values." Children need to practice clarifying values as they solve problems and make decisions
by recognizing possible alternatives and consequences because "values often determine what knowledge an individual will accept or reject." The age of the children
and their level of moral and cognitive development dictates the appropriate materials and issues to be used in the social studies program on value clarification. Young
children will "understand simple stories and dilemmas that involve values such as
honesty, truth, and loyalty."

Young children have a personal knowledge. "We know something to be true
simply because we believe it to be so" (Jarolimek, 1986). Their personal knowledge
is on a different level than an adult's, because they do not think logically or ab-
stractly. Another way children develop their thinking capabilities is by depending on
reliable and accepted sources, such as parents, teachers, and books. However, the
time comes when the authority sources are challenged (Jarolimek, 1986).

A questioning and curious attitude is a young child's natural way of learning.
Piaget viewed children as being naturally curious about their surroundings and motivated toward exploration. Teachers must, therefore, capitalize on children's pro-
pensity to question and examine and provide activities designed to stimulate students' curiosity about their environment. These activities should nurture a feeling of
continuity with the past and develop a concept of time of the past and present
(Hatcher, 1985). To reinforce this approach, wise teachers provide an environment

in which meaningful learning takes place by presenting concepts within young children's frame of reference. They are guided toward relating the known and familiar with new and unfamiliar information that broadens their knowledge and experience of the concepts (Jantz & Klawitter, 1985). "The conceptual approach to social studies instruction greatly facilitates comprehension, transfer, and mastery of skills" (Banks, 1985).

The content of such a complex subject is condensed into "manageable proportions," which is essential for teachers in planning and teaching and for students in learning. How the concepts are taught is as important as the actual content being taught to young children (Day, 1983).

As part of the SPAN Project, the Research Triangle Institute conducted a survey interviewing social studies teachers in grades K–12. The results of the survey showed that "commercially published textbooks were one of the central tools for teaching social studies" (Superka, Hawke, & Morressett, 1980). In kindergarten through third grade, 65 percent of the classes were taught using textbooks. Lecture, as an instructional strategy, was used by 46 percent of the teachers "just about daily" and by 20 percent "at least once a week." Discussions were used by 60 percent of the teachers "just about daily" and by an additional 37 percent "at least once a week." Periodically teachers used other forms of instruction, such as student reports, library work, role playing, simulation, and "hands on" materials (Superka, et al., 1980).

After interviewing 23 students in the sixth grade and 23 students in the twelfth grade to find out "Why Kids Don't Like Social Studies?" Schug, Todd, and Beery (1984) found that 48 percent of the students, of which 24 percent were elementary students, did not think social studies was important and relevant to them. The students found social studies to be boring and repetitious in content and lacking a variety of activities and teaching methods. These insights suggest improving social studies by giving students more opportunity to be actively involved in their learning, through group projects, field trips, discussions, and independent projects. It appears that students are asking for opportunities to engage in "both left-brain intellect and right-brain intuition" (Crossett, 1983) in the social studies program.

In the Wilkerson study (1986), both the 4MAT group and the textbook group experimented with concrete objects, drew pictures, saw a filmstrip, and completed worksheets. The teachers' appraisal of the textbook strategies and materials appears to confirm the students' reasons for not liking social studies as described by Schug et al. (1984). They were too hard, too rigid, and dull. However, "the 4MAT group was more interested in learning the material, had a more positive attitude toward the lessons, and demonstrated more on task behavior." The children's attitudes toward the two approaches were reflected in the number of activities they liked: the 4MAT group liked 100 percent of their activities, compared to the 48 percent of the textbook group.

The study of *history* places human beings and their activities in a specific time frame, while the study of *geography* represents the stage for the unfolding of history, giving it a place. Developing the skills needed in order to make use of available resources so that a society can obtain what it needs and wants is accomplished through the study of *economics.* The area of *political science* provides an understanding of why and how governments exist, function, and relate to the world. Studying human behavior in group and individual activity is the emphasis in the study of *anthropology, psychology,* and *sociology.*

Traditionally history and geography have been the supportive pillars of the social studies program. Economics, political science, sociology, and anthropology have been

LEFT HEMISPHERE	RIGHT HEMISPHERE
IV. Dynamic Learner: Integrating Application and Experience	I. Innovative Learner: Integrating Experience with "Self"
Step 7: Left mode, analyzing application for relevance, usefulness Instructional strategies: committee reports, murals, graphics, student demonstrations, debates, panel discussions, line graphs, drawings	Step 1: Right mode, creating a personal experience related to concept being taught Instructional strategies: guided imagery, simulations, brainstorming
Step 8: Right mode, doing it and applying to new, more complex experience Instructional strategies: field trips, student presentations to the class	Step 2: Left mode, reflecting/analyzing experience and sharing results with others Instructional strategies: peer discussions, group discussions
III. Common Sense Learner: Practice and Personalization	II. Analytic Learner: Concept Formulation
Step 5: Left mode, practicing defined concepts Instructional strategies: worksheets, workbooks, lab books, quizzes	Step 3: Right mode, integrating reflective analysis into concepts Instructional strategies: informational films with holistic presentation of the concept, concept mapping, art projects
Step 6: Right mode, practicing and adding something of oneself Instructional strategies: set up experiments, design projects of own choice	Step 4: Left mode, developing concepts/skills Instructional strategies: lectures, reading assignments, reference reports

Adapted from McCarthy (1980) & Wilkerson (1986).

blended into the curriculum through these two disciplines (Jarolimek, 1986; Banks, 1985). However, the program in the primary grades, kindergarten through fourth grade, has been predominantly focused on sociological studies. Units have been planned around narrow and limited topics of low-level concepts, like "Our Family" or "Our Town." But these topics can be extended and developed into interdisciplinary units of generalizations and concepts on the young child's cognitive level (Banks, 1985). Jarolimek (1986) suggests some appropriate terms for expressing concepts that make sense to children.

Concept	*For Your Child This Means*
Justice	Being or playing fair
Laws	Rules
Equality of opportunity	Seeing that everyone gets a turn
Cooperation	Working with others
Responsibility	Doing your part or doing your duty

William Bennett, U.S. Secretary of Education, recommends (1986) a social studies curriculum in kindergarten through third grade that extends from the "children's immediate environs and experience to a richer program that will build civic, historical, and geographic literacy" (p. 30). Jarolimek (1986) submits the idea that a "program for building civic competency begins with the introduction of the concepts relating to people living and working together under a system of order that preserves individual freedom."

Freedom is a concept too abstract for young children to grasp. But through teaching strategies providing experiences, play, and discussion, they learn that rules and laws are necessary for orderly living. They also begin to understand their responsibility, as individuals in the group, to be considerate of others' rights.

There are three basic types of social studies skills. They include the academic or intellectual skills, self-management skills, and social participation skills.

The academic, or the scientific, approach increases the ability to identify, define, and state problems; formulate hypotheses; test hypotheses; locate, organize, and interpret information; and draw conclusions (North Carolina Department of Public Instruction, 1985). Many references are available to help formulate behavioral objectives for the academic skills, such as Benjamin Bloom and David Krathwohl's taxonomies of cognitive and affective objectives (Bloom, 1956; Krathwohl, Bloom, & Masia, 1964). The *cognitive* objectives include conceptual, skill, and process objectives. These are arranged by level of complexity. The first three categories are knowledge, comprehension, and application. They are prerequisites for the next three categories, which are analysis, synthesis, and evaluation. Students must have opportunities to move from knowledge and comprehension to higher levels of cognition. The *affective* objectives include values, interest, and attitudes. The awareness of values and attitudes, such as respect for the views of others, freedom of speech, fair play, and equal rights for all, must be developed through a variety of cross-cultural experiences. All of the categories of the affective domain—receiving, responding valuing, organization, and characterization—will enable the student to experience a deeper dimension of meaning and feeling, in and out of school. The categories in the cognitive and affective domain are both very relevant to social studies instruction as well as daily activities (Michaelis, 1976).

The second social studies skill is self-management. Self-management skills should include techniques to develop abilities that will enable students to deal with managing interpersonal and intergroup relations. They need to develop a sensitivity to others, deal with conflict, diversity, and the major societal changes that are currently taking place in the nation and the world (North Carolina Department of Public Instruction, 1985). One of the major societal changes taking place is the widespread movement for freedom and equality of minority groups and women. A second societal change is the increasing involvement in the decision-making and problem-solving processes of both groups and the individual.

The third basic social studies skill, social participation, deals with skills of group discussion, planning, decision making, and accepting responsibility for such decisions. These decisions concern the problems and solutions of interpersonal and intergroup relations (North Carolina Department of Public Instruction, 1985). These skills should be socially acceptable learned behaviors that enable students to listen and interact in ways that elicit positive responses and achieve the desired objectives set for interacting with other students.

In order to help students develop a basis for making decisions and to enable them to become problem solvers, they need a historical perspective. The "concepts of time are slow to develop in a child's mind. It is not until about the age of nine that anything more than a shallow time perspective begins to develop" (Schlereth, 1980). History begins in the "here and now," but experiences of seeing and handling artifacts, visiting a museum, historical markers, or old houses can be a beginning in relating the past to young children. Recognizing holidays helps the children to know about the past and appreciate it (Jarolimek, 1986).

The study of geography provides young children many concrete-direct opportunities to observe, collect, and record data and to use simple charts. They become familiar with the various tools used to study the features of the earth. These are maps, globes, charts, graphs, tables, reference books, and photographs (Maxim, 1983).

Concepts related to anthropology are integrated into most of the other social studies disciplines. Yet children can begin to understand that people in all cultures have the need for love, protection, food, and recreation. Different cultures satisfy their needs through a variety of ways according to their customs and values (Banks, 1985).

Transportation, communication equipment, and technology have made the world a smaller place to live. International problems and concerns face all who live on this planet. Global education is important to address in the social studies program. Opportunities and activities to enable children to recognize and appreciate the global society and its multicultural composition must be provided. Teachers and students must be broadened ethnocentrically. Judging another culture only from one's own point of view affects objectivity. Negative and biased feelings toward different groups must be discussed. Feelings need to be expressed and likes as well as dislikes acknowledged in order to help tomorrow's adults understand and feel the unity that underlies overt human differences (Martin, 1985). Young children learn about other countries through a study on family structure. They learn about countries through music, art, literature, and resource people in the community (Jarolimek, 1986).

Modern technology is making it possible to solve some current problems more satisfactorily. However, along with these technical advances come more complex problems. The concern of quantity and quality of goods and services, energy and resource waste, rising costs of basic needs, population growth in urban areas, pollution and longer life expectancy, require concerted action using self-management skills and techniques (Michaelis, 1976).

Key sociological concepts integrated with economic concepts promote understanding of interdependence and self-worth for young children. Children learn about interdependence from the concepts "scarcity and plenty; the meaning of consumers and producers; and the advantages of division of labors" (Seefeldt & Barbour, 1986).

Social concerns and current affairs are important aspects in the social studies program. The unresolved problems of the present day help children to become aware of being responsible and caring about people (Martorella, 1985). In the past, developing valuing skills and learning how to become an active participant in society have involved a collaboration between the family, church, and school. These basic social institutions are part of the major societal changes that are currently taking place. A mobile population contributes to the change in socialization. Increasing emphasis in individuality encourages less responsiveness to the needs of others. Working mothers, single parents, and reconstituted families have changed the family from a stable and predictable institution to a problematic one.

Although religion still exerts influence, its influence has waned. Recent data indicate that over 50 percent of Americans reject an organized form of religion. Schools must address an educational challenge of enormous magnitude as students enter school with a wide range of individual differences in values and ethics. Social expectations are also changing, placing still another challenge on the school.

The media is a very powerful socializer. Television is the most influential medium. A 1981 Nielsen report found that the average viewing time for children between the ages of six and seven was 26 hours a week and for two- to five-year-olds was 29 hours a week. This is approximately 3½ hours a day. Schools have become less valued as television viewing has increased. Little influence is exerted by the school in determining what children see and what television produces. Much of television's content conflicts with the school's purposes and objectives. Emotion, instant gratification, and entertainment are the focus of television, while rational thinking and delayed satisfaction are among the objectives of the educational system (Cartledge & Milburn, 1986; Stephens, 1985).

Issues that voters must consider in this nuclear age are overwhelming to an intelligent, well-informed adult, yet an 18-year-old encounters this responsibility also. Social concerns and issues to be addressed include global perspective education; energy and environmental education; career education; multiethnic, ethnic, and racial awareness; law-related education; and sex equity. Other issues include teaching about handicapped individuals, the aging, and nuclear issues. Current affairs instruction is important for producing well-informed people. For young children, "making their own news may be the beginning of current events. The experience of contributing to the news story and of sharing news items and events helps children understand the concept of news" (Seefeldt, 1984).

Social studies skills are taught within the content of the disciplines being studied. The teacher carefully plans the development of the skills in a systematic and sequential order. Ample practice of the skills is provided through the regular lessons and units. Social studies skills taught during the program are thinking skills, research skills, chronological and time skills, maps and globe skills, writing skills, social skills, and new technological skills (Martorella, 1985).

Evaluation for achievement in a social studies program is intended to "(1) assess the effectiveness of instruction; (2) determine whether or not instructional goals have been accomplished; and (3) provide feedback to students about their performance" (Banks, 1985). Evaluation techniques are both informal and formal. Informal evaluation techniques are group discussions, observations, checklists, conferences, anecdotal records, work samples, experience summaries, diaries, and logs. Formal evaluation techniques include teacher-made tests, criterion-reference tests, and standardized tests.

In this time of rapid change, increasingly finer judgments must be exercised to address more complex situations. Information alone seldom causes learning to take place and behavior to change. Motivation, incentives, and relevant activities that force choices and responses must be part of the social studies curriculum if the complex social changes are to be addressed.

It is hoped that this chapter will serve as a resource for identifying needs, stating objectives, and implementing activities that will help young children accept the right and responsibility of citizenship as they gain a better understanding of their world.

Objectives

To begin to learn how to solve problems and make decisions at the appropriate level of development.

To become aware of, accept, and value unique qualities of the self and others.

To develop a positive self-concept.

To become more independent and responsible for one's own actions.

To learn to recognize and accept one's own feelings and the feelings of others.

To learn to make value judgments.

To learn to express one's own feelings in acceptable ways.

To develop social interaction skills.

To understand one's role within the family.

To become aware of the needs for rules and laws.

To develop an awareness of the traditions of one's own culture.

To develop an appreciation of America's heritage.

To develop an awareness of varying life-styles within one's own culture.

To develop a general awareness of community and of one's present and future relation to it as a whole.

To become aware of the need for civic responsibility and values.

To develop some concept of the justice system.

To explore some concepts of politics and local government.

To develop an awareness of different people in the community and an understanding of the services they provide.

To explore various people and their cultures around the world.

To learn about the community in the past and present and its relationship to the world at large.

To become aware of a need to change stereotyped attitudes of leaders and minority groups.

To learn about the environment and its relationship to human life and to investigate environmental problems and solutions.

To explore concepts of economics and use of economic resources.

To learn about economic processes, ideas, and problems and to be wise consumers.

To learn and practice skills in reading, following, and interpreting easy maps, globes, graphs, and charts.

To develop an understanding of time and chronology.

To explore the capabilities of the microcomputer and develop an understanding of new technology.

Environmental Resources

Table and four to six chairs
Bulletin board
Storage space
Community resources: people, places, things
Flannel board
Chalkboard

Materials

Social studies textbooks
Activity kits (e.g., community helpers)
Globe and maps
Charts, posters, graphs, and cartoons
SVE study prints, photographs
Reference books
Biographies
Historical fiction books
Periodicals, magazines, and catalogs
Real objects (flags, coins, costumes)
World atlas
Typewriter
Cassette player and cassettes
Record player and headset
Records

Dukane (filmstrips, tapes, or records)
Film loop projector and film loop
Overhead projector and transparencies
Slide projector and color transparency slides
Radio, television
Microcomputer and software
Works of art (paintings, drawings, sculptures, basketing, pottery, architecture)
Art materials (paints, easels, chalk, crayons, clay, paste)
Paper for writing, construction, chart
Cartons and boxes
Blocks and transportation toys
Telephone
Envelopes and stamps
Cooking equipment and utensils
Clothing for dramatic/role play

Suggested Activities: Self-awareness and Interpersonal Relations

1. *Life-Sized Body Outline.* The children will construct and stuff life-sized bodies. They will have their bodies traced by the teacher and another student. They will color or paint in their features and add fabrics, scraps, or other materials for detail. They will cut out the traced body.

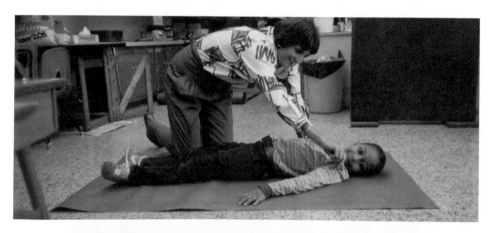

Variation. The children or teacher will staple the trace body to another large piece of paper. They will cut out the second piece of paper to be the back of the body. They will color the back to match the front of the body. They will stuff the body with crushed newspaper and staple edges.

2. *Autobiographies.* The children will write or dictate about themselves.
3. *"Me" Puppet.* The children will make a hand puppet to represent themselves. They will choose from a variety of materials, such as paper plates, socks, paper bags, fabric pieces, buttons, yarn, shredded paper, crayons, paints, and colored markers to make the puppet.
4. *Personal Time Line.* The students will be able to develop time lines of the community after they have had experiences of collecting, observing, and investigating the past in relation to their own experiences. They will first develop a time line showing important personal dates, births of brothers and sisters, dates they started school, lost their first tooth, etc. The students will then create a time line of the important dates and events of the community to help them develop a concept of time as well as identify historical events.
5. *Feeling Chart.* The children will place on a chart a face expressing how they feel during the school day.

Katrina	Susan	Chris
Carol	Jennifer	John

6. *Footprints and/or Hand Collages.* The children will paint or print their feet and hands for a large class mural to show individual differences.
7. *Yum Yum! and Yuck! Books.* The children will express their personal feeling by cutting out magazine pictures or drawing pictures to show the things they like or dislike.
8. *Captions.* The children will write captions about feelings expressed in cartoons.

9. *Friendly Way to Talk Game.* The children will enact the nice and poor way to tell someone something.
10. *People Collages.* The children will cut out pictures from magazines of different kinds of people to arrange on a large piece of construction paper or cardboard. The children or teacher will shellac the completed collages.
11. *What Color Is Happy?* The children will write or dictate a story about the color(s) that make them happy. They will illustrate the stories.
12. *Coat of Arms.* The student will assess strengths and weaknesses by making a coat of arms. A shield is drawn and divided into six equal sections. Each section is devoted to one of the following: (a) people in my family; (b) two things I enjoy doing with my family; (c) two things I do well; (d) two things I would like to do better; (e) one thing I do most in my spare time; (f) my occupation when I grow up. Color and outline the drawings. Print the family name in large letters and mount on black construction paper.

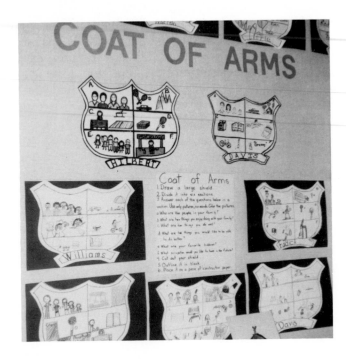

Variation: "About Me." The students will write a personal story using the drawings on the coat of arms as illustrations.

Variation: Show and Tell. The students will make a display of the coat of arms and bring their own family history, family tree, or coat of arms from home to share.

13. *Group Game.* A group of children will invent a group game. The following questions will help the children in planning the game: What is the name of the game? What materials will be needed? How many players will be needed? Will there be teams? What will be the rules? Where can the game be played?

14. *Feelings.* The children will create faces on the flannel board to show expressions of different emotions such as happiness, sadness, anger, surprise. They will use a large flannel face and cutouts of eyes and mouths.

15. *I Like.* The children will make a capital "I" out of paper and print the word LIKE at the top of the letter and their name at the bottom of the letter. They will draw or cut out pictures from magazines showing what foods, sports, subjects, games, people, and hobbies they like.

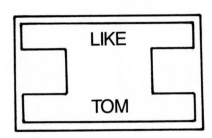

Variation: I Like, I Dislike. The children will draw or cut out pictures showing their likes and dislikes to put on the poster.

16. *My Number Facts.* The children will make a chart writing the appropriate numbers for their birthdate, weight, height, address, phone number, number of people in their family, and their grade level.

My number Facts

Birthday........Feb. 10, 1980
Weight .... 40 lbs.
Height....... 45 ins.
Address...1316 ELm St.
Phone number...368-0219
Family......... 5
Grade.........2

17. *Classroom Mailbox.* The children will make a mailbox, stamps, and envelopes. They will send and receive letters from each other and the teachers. They will take turns delivering the mail.

18. *Yearbook.* The children will make books or use photo albums to develop attractive yearbooks. They will use captions for pages like "Cars in 1989," "Fashions of 1989," "News in 1989," "Songs in 1989," "Me in 1989."

19. *Big Cheese.* The students will be special. Each week a student will be selected to be the *Big Cheese* for the week. He/she fills out a personal data sheet, draws a self-portrait, and furnishes a photograph. This will be displayed on the Big Cheese bulletin board. At the end of the week each class member will fill out a slip telling specific reasons why this person is special. The Big Cheese takes all of the data and slips home in a special folder to keep.

The Big Cheese

_____is
the big cheese!
My address is_____

_____.

_____ is my phone
number. I was born in the town
of_____, in the
state of_____.
My eyes are_____and the
color of my hair is_____.
I wear_____sized shoes.
Some of my favorites:
Colors: _____
Food: _____
Song: _____
TV Program: _____
School Subject: _____
Friends: _____
The people who live at my house are _____

_____.
The things I like to do are _____

_____.

20. **Situation Cards.** The children will use task cards related to particular times
or situations they are studying. The following is a simple card for a study of
manners:

SITUATION. You have made a lovely picture and have given it to someone you
like. The person you have given it to smiles and says, "Thank you."

QUESTION. What would you say to the person?

(In a study of the West, the following card is fairly simple; for older children, the card could delve into more complex social awareness.)

SITUATION. It is the time of the early settlers in the West. You are the parent of a family of five children (three girls, two boys). The other parent is visiting friends. It is nighttime. You hear the hoot of an owl. The cows are making noise out in the pasture. You know that the Indians have been attacking some settlers in the area.

QUESTION. What is upsetting the cows? Was that really an owl hooting? What would you do? What could your community do to guard against Indians? Why did Indians attack settlers?

A teacher or parent will lead the discussions asking questions that will make the children think creatively about the situation.

21. *Hop To It Chart.* Students will accept the role of leader by carrying out specific classroom responsibilities independently as their names appear on the chart.

22. *Assignment Contracts.* The students will carry out assignments independently by writing down the assignments. As they complete them in a specified amount of time, a check is made on the assignment sheet by the student. He/she will place the assignment sheet and the assignment in his/her folder to be checked by the teacher. Daily evaluations will be made.

Daily Assignments			Name:		
Monday			**Thursday**		
Name and number of paper	Check when you finish	Teacher Check	Name and number of paper	Check when you finish	Teacher Check
Tuesday			**Friday**		
Name and number of paper	Check when you finish	Teacher Check	Name and number of paper	Check when you finish	Teacher Check
Wednesday			How many assignments did you complete this week?	what would you like to do better?	
Name and number of paper	Check when you finish	Teacher Check			

Filmstrips

What Is Responsibility?
Personal Success
Who Am I?
Who Do You Think You Are?
Getting Along
Making and Keeping Friends

Films

Beginning Responsibility—Taking Care of Things
Family of the Island: Her Name Is Wasamatha
There's Nobody Else Like You
What Is a Friend?
Why We Need Each Other
What Mary Jo Shared

Suggested Activities: Social Interaction Skills

Intervention to reduce sex-role stereotyping and its effects on sex competencies, attitudes, and behaviors, is needed in the early years. All children need to learn how to interact with people different from themselves, whether the difference is of race, sex, ability levels, etc. (Scott, 1985).

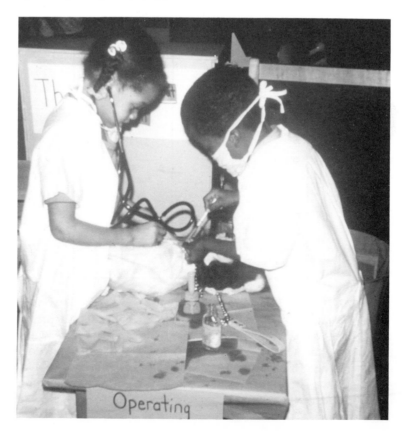

1. *Mixed Sex Small Groupings.* The teacher will create interaction between students by putting both boys and girls in all groupings.
2. *Unisex Labels.* The teacher will label all learning and play activities as appropriate for both boys and girls.
3. *Leadership.* The teacher will provide all pupils with equal roles of leadership in many different situations.
4. *Feelings and Emotions.* The children will engage in role-playing situations that enable boys and girls to vent their feelings by crying.
5. *Assertiveness Training.* The students will use puppets to act out situations in which they might tend to be less apt to speak up for themselves.
6. *Communicating Positive Statements.* The students will improve their social skills and learn to communicate on an equal-status (boy-girl) basis by completing unfinished sentences such as the following (Ellis, 1977):

    I feel best when I _____.

    I am proud that I can _____.

    I have learned that I can _____
    as well as a member of the opposite sex.

    I was surprised that I could _____.

7. *Identifying Prejudices.* The students will engage in an activity to help them recognize some of their feelings by marking the degree of acceptance (Ellis, 1977).

How Do You Feel About These People?			
People	😊	😞	😐
White			
Black			
Boys			
Girls			
Red Haired			
Curly Haired			
Fat			
Tall			
Handicapped			

8. *Female Role Models.* The students will study a selection of women to learn of their important contributions to society in the past and present. Some suggested role models are Abigail Adams, Helen Keller, March Fong Eu, Sarah Winnemucca, and Carmen Delgado Cotaw. The students will do research, read biographies, discuss the historical, social, economic, and political issues present, and the family structures of each model. They will do some creative activity to illustrate their findings, such as shadow boxes, dioramas, time lines, movie-roll boxes, murals, etc. (Women's Educational Equity Act Program, 1985).

ABIGAIL ADAMS
(Nov. 11,1744–Oct. 28, 1818)
by Jean M. Molinari

When Abigail was growing up in the Massachusetts Bay Colony, she seemed to have three families. What do you think that would be like? Because of her health, Abigail was sometimes sent to live at her Grandmother Quincy's house. Other times she lived in the city with her Aunt Smith. Between her long visits to their houses she lived with her parents in the country eight miles away. How would you feel moving around this much? Abigail enjoyed it very much. She felt like a welcome guest in all three houses.

You may find this hard to believe, but girls couldn't go to school when Abigail was growing up. Luckily, her father had a large library of books. She was taught to read by her relatives. Her grandparents were very interested in politics and encouraged her to read, discuss and think about life in the colonies, freedom, people's rights and government. This was how she found out that women did not have any legal rights under British Colonial Laws. Abigail did not think this was fair, but what could she do about it?

When she was 19 years old, she married John Adams. He was a lawyer who wanted to change unjust British laws. It was because of these unjust laws that John became involved in starting a new government for the colonies. His work kept him away from the family home. This was difficult for Abigail. She was glad that John was working on the laws for their new country. She was eager to help him with her ideas about the new government.

Working on the new government in Philadelphia did not pay John any money. It was up to Abigail to take care of all their family business matters. Abigail ran their small farm in Braintree. She provided the food, clothes, and other supplies for the family.

In order to have a new government the Colonies had to become independent from the British. This is what led to the Revolutionary War. Sometimes the war was fought very close to the Adams farm. Abigail was afraid that children might get hurt. She thought that they might have to hide in the woods so the British army would not find them.

Abigail was a very brave woman. One time the British soldiers were very close to her house. Lots of her neighbors had left their farms because they were afraid that the British

soldiers and the American soldiers would fight right on their land. People told Abigail to take her children and leave, too. She and the children stayed. When the American soldiers went by the farm, Abigail gave them food and water. She also gave the soldiers her dishes made of pewter metal. Even though she liked her dishes very much, she and the soldiers melted them and used the soft metal to make bullets. Instead of running away, she stayed to help, and she helped in many ways.

Abigail was responsible for her family's home and money for a long time. One way she earned money was by having John send her things from Europe when he was there working. Abigail made a list of things that were hard to buy in the Colonies, like straight pins. John would send these things to Abigail. She would sell them to her neighbors.

Under Abigail's care the farm grew bigger and bigger as she saved money and bought more land. She taught their five children to read, write, and do arithmetic. When they grew older the boys went to school, but there were still no schools for girls. Luckily, they could learn at home from their mother and the family books, just as Abigail had done.

The education of women was very important to Abigail. She wanted women to be equal with men. She wrote John many letters when he was working on the new government. She asked that the new laws take care of men and women equally. She wanted the new government to listen to what the women had to say.

Abigail taught her children that slavery was wrong. "No one should buy, sell or own another person," she said. When the laws of the new government were written, they allowed people to own slaves. Abigail knew that this was wrong.

To protest the new laws, she wrote many letters. She wrote to friends, family members, and statesmen. In fact, she wrote over 2,000 letters during her life!

Abigail Adams and her family were important people in the beginning years of the United States. Her husband, John, was the second President of the United States. Her son, John Quincy Adams, became the sixth President of the United States. Her husband and her son both learned from Abigail's leadership and often asked for her help.

Abigail did not give up! She was a leader. She was one of the first people in this country to talk and write about equality for women and freedom for slaves.

Abigail Adams (November 11, 1744—October 28, 1818) spoke out for women's rights even before the constitution was written.

Listening Questions

1. How many families did Abigail have when she was growing up?
2. Why didn't Abigail go to school?
3. What did Abigail and the American soldiers do with her pewter dishes?
4. What did Abigail do when she thought something was not fair?

Suggested Activities

Discussion
1. Abigail Adams wanted women to have a voice in the new United States government after the Revolutionary War. She believed that women should have full rights to own property and to vote. Did women have these rights after the Revolutionary War? What are some of the rights women are working for today? Who are some of the leaders of today's women's movement?

Activities
1. Have the whole class imagine that they are growing up during the time of Abigail Adams. Remind them that books are scarce and that there are no public libraries. How will they learn to read and write? Have each student write and then give a short speech in class telling why they think there should be schools

for both girls and boys. In their speeches, they should tell why being able to attend school is important to them.

2. To encourage your students to learn more about American government and how it works, discuss the school's system of authority. Have the class write and send a letter to the student council asking a representative to come to class and answer students' questions. What does the student council do? Who are the members? How does someone become a member? Have the class write a similar letter to the school's Board of Education. Discuss in advance what questions the visitor will be asked. Have each student write down three questions to ask. Have the students write down the answers when they learn them too.

3. After reading the story of Abigail Adams have each student write a letter of advice to someone who decides on new laws: the city mayor, the state governor, or the President of the United States. The letter should offer advice about something the student feels is important.

4. Abigail Adams ran the farm business that supported her family. She conducted business in many different ways to raise money. What types of work do your students' mothers do outside and inside their homes to help support the family? Have each student write a short story about his or her mother and the various kinds of work she does.

Name _____

Key Words

Fill in the blanks with the words that best complete the sentences. Choose from the following words:

business   rights   laws   colony   ideas

1. Abigail found out that women did not have any _____.

2. One _____ Abigail had was selling things to other people.

3. She told John her _____ about equality.

4. The United States was a _____ of the British.

5. Abigail Adams wanted the new _____ to include women's rights.

True or False?

Write T if the statement is true. Write F if the statement is false.

_____ 1. Abigail sold her dishes to the soldiers so they could make bullets.

_____ 2. Abigail Adams was the wife of the second President of the United States.

_____ 3. She wrote over 2,000 important letters.

_____ 4. Abigail believed in freedom for all people.

_____ 5. She supported her farm and her family by her very hard work.

Write On

On another sheet of paper, write a letter to Abigail Adams telling her what it is like to be a child living today. Think about what she would like to know.

Source: Women's Educational Equity Act Program (1985). *Woman as Members of Communities: Third Grade Social Studies.*

9. *Literary Story Paper.* The students will write articles about the female role models for a literary story paper in order to recognize and present these women as independent, worthwhile individuals with an intellectual, political, economic, and social life of their own (Chilcoat, 1985).

10. *Famous Black Americans.* The students will become familiar and appreciate the contributions of some famous black Americans. They will read available books, magazines, and newspapers and study entertainment programs and posters.

Filmstrips

Getting Along
Mixing In
Learning to Live with Others
The Reverend Dr. Martin Luther King
Leading American Negroes

Films

Communication: A First Film
Why We Need Each Other
Home Free
Family of the Island: Her Name Is Wasamatha

Suggested Activities: Community and Career Awareness

1. *Careers or Places Riddles.* The children or the teacher will write riddles about careers or places in the community. For example, "'What would you be if you worked on a farm?"

2. *Then and Now.* The students will learn about their community and become historians by preparing a questionnaire as to the types of schools, businesses, places of entertainment, shopping areas, and other aspects of the community. They will administer the questions to a grandparent or neighbor who has lived in the community at least for 50 years. The students could use a tape recorder; for the very old person, a video should be used for the class to be able to view. The students will compile the responses and make a comparison of the community *then* and *now* (Carroll, 1985).

3. *Picture Album.* The students will bring pictures of old schools, the downtown, homes, fashions, and historical views of the community that families will allow them to borrow from the family album. They will make a wall display of the pictures using black construction paper for the background.

4. *Slide Show.* The Chamber of Commerce may have a prepared slide show of important places in the community that they would share. Parents or other resource people may have slides available to help the students have a better visual image of places in the community.

5. *Community Helpers Task Cards.* The children will match pictures of helpers with the words that identify each picture. Colored shoestrings (or yarn) are used for matching and the back of each card is color coded for self-correction.

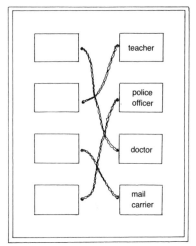

Other community helper charts can include
garbage collector, electrician, plumber,
firefighter, grocer, farmer, butcher, gardener,
librarian, cashier, nurse

Variation: The children will draw in the features of the outlined community helper on laminated cardboard.

6. *Mapping.* After a walk around the neighborhood or community, the children will construct models of streets and landmarks on a table or in the block area.

   Variation. The children will draw a map of the neighborhood or community on brown paper.

7. *Build a Neighborhood.* The children will build a neighborhood or school community using different size milk cartons and boxes.

8. *Public Safety.* The children will draw on the wheel toy area of the playground without rules. They will discuss solutions to the problems that arise.

9. *Puzzle: "People and Their Jobs."* The children will match the picture or name of a person with a picture or name of something the person uses on the job.

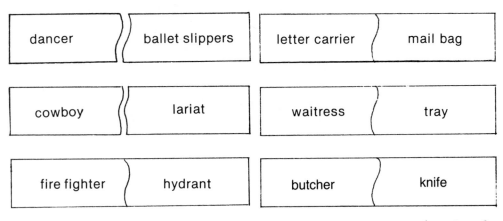

(*continued*)

painter	brushes

diver	fish

jockey	horse

baker	cupcake

police	whistle

farmer	tractor

10. *Places in the City Sorting Game.* The children will sort and classify laminated cutouts of pictures associated with the zoo, library, park, supermarket, post office, department store, hardware store, school, dentist's office, doctor's office, bank, and restaurant.

11. *Working Moms and Dads.* The children will interview their parents about the kind of work they do. They will give oral or written reports about these occupations.

12. *Jobs in the Want Ads.* The children will list jobs advertised in the Want Ads. They will draw a picture of the kind of work a person does on a particular job advertised and do research projects when appropriate.

13. *Slide Down the Community Slide.* The children will play this laminated teacher-made game according to the directions on the card.

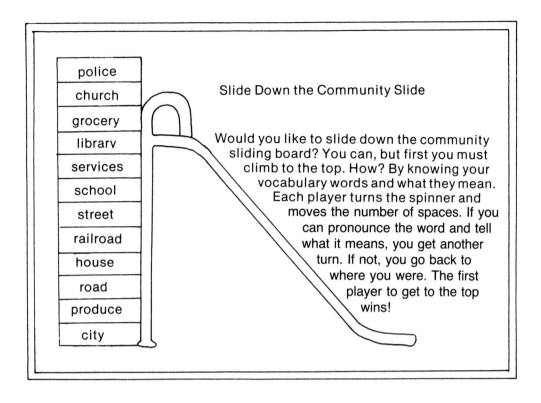

police
church
grocery
library
services
school
street
railroad
house
road
produce
city

Slide Down the Community Slide

Would you like to slide down the community sliding board? You can, but first you must climb to the top. How? By knowing your vocabulary words and what they mean. Each player turns the spinner and moves the number of spaces. If you can pronounce the word and tell what it means, you get another turn. If not, you go back to where you were. The first player to get to the top wins!

14. *Career Awareness Centers and Materials.* The children will go to the career center to use a variety of materials about careers. They will use books, tapes, films, or filmstrips. They will use other materials to role-play. For example:
   a. *Cosmetologist.* Wigs, rollers, clips and pins, comb, brush, mirror (turned horizontal) on table, hairdryer, apron, shampoo container.
   b. *Barber.* Comb, scissors, shaving cream, apron, shampoo containers.
   c. *Secretary.* Dictionary, telephone, typewriter, letters, paper, pen.

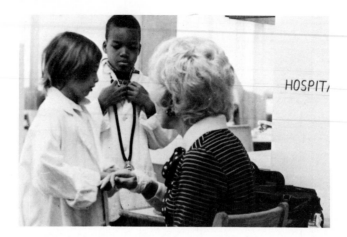

HOSPIT/

  d. *Nurse.* First aid kit, thermometer, nurse's cap.
  e. *Carpenter.* Tools, wood, bib overalls, yardstick, ruler, nails.
  f. *Librarian.* Books, stamp, desk.
  g. *Construction worker.* Wooden toys (bulldozer), hard hats.
  h. *Truck driver.* Truck, traffic signs, cargo.
  i. *Banker.* Puppet stage for window, checkbooks, play money, adding machine.
  j. *Postal worker.* Window, stamps, letter scales, pencil, money.
  k. *Baker.* Stove, cooking utensils, apron, hat.

15. *Resource People.* The children will interview people of different occupations who are invited to the classroom. They will draw pictures about these occupations.
    Variation. The children will give reports about the occupation. These will be oral or written reports.

16. *Community Resources.* The children will take field trips to places in the community to observe people working. They will visit factories, plants, industrial bakeries, farms, radio and TV stations, stables, fish markets, pet shops, florists, grocery stores, lumber yards, zoos, museums, fire stations, and construction sites. They will dictate or write stories and poems, draw or paint pictures, cook or build something they saw on the trip.

17. *Division of Labor.* The children will observe how ants or bees work as a society, using an ant farm, filmstrip, or books.
    Variation. The children will compare and contrast two methods of making baskets. First, the children will make their own baskets. Then they will divide into small groups and assign each child a different job to do in making the baskets like an assembly line.

18. *Mini Field Trips.* A small group of children with a teacher or principal will visit a community resource person or place. They will write a short experience story, report orally, or engage in other activities related to the trip. For example, if the resource is a greenhouse, they will plant seeds and chart growth.
    Photos. The children will have their pictures taken visiting resource people or places on field trips. They will write or dictate stories about the photos.

19. *Role-Playing.* The children will role-play workers that they have learned about, using props such as fire fighter's gear, construction worker's helmets, soldier's uniforms, turn-of-the-century clothes, etc. They will make masks for the roles from large paper bags.

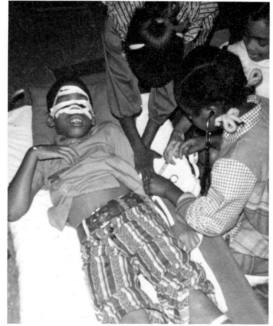

Variation. The children will make puppets from lunch-sized bags to dramatize workers and their jobs.

20. *Working Tools.* The children will be shown trade tools such as plumber's friends, levels, stethoscopes, toy cars, chalkboards. They will discuss who uses the tools and how the tools are used.

21. *Creative Writing.* The students will design a brochure telling why their community is a good place to live. They should include the places of interest, type of climate, location, natural and man-made resources, educational and health-care facilities, and recreation and entertainment opportunities. This should be a culminating activity to the study of the community.

Filmstrips

Community Services: Many People
   Serve Our Community
People Serving Your Community
What Is a Community?
Living in Cities
The Tree That Became a Chair

Films

Home Free
Moving Goods in the Community
Turn Off the Pollution

Suggested Activities: Places

1. *Imaginary.* The children will plan a trip to the beach or the mountains, a hike, a picnic to the park, or a sightseeing trip to Washington, D.C. or the capital city in their state.

2. *Imaginary Place.* The children will make a map of a make-believe place. They will make a map-symbols key and draw the symbols on the map. They will write a story about this place.

3. *Tracing on Maps.* The children will trace routes from their classroom to other places in the school on a laminated map, or from their home to a neighborhood destination.
   Variation. The children will trace routes from their city to other cities or places on maps.

4. *Find Our State Map Game.* The children will play this game using a large laminated map of the United States mounted on cardboard or styrofoam. Taking turns blindfolded, the children will try to pin a picture of the state flower or state bird to their state on the map. The child placing the pin on the state or nearest the state will win the game.

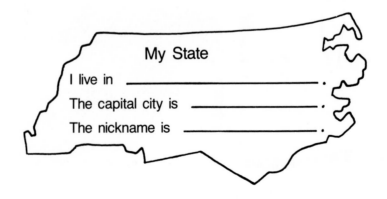

My State

I live in _____ .
The capital city is _____ .
The nickname is _____ .

Variations: (a) My State. The children will fill in pertinent information about their state. They will draw in the state flower, bird, or tree. (b) The children will play the game with neighborhood or city maps.

5. *Where Do You Live?* The students will learn where they live in relationship to earth, continent, country, state, and city with the help of a bulletin board. The bulletin board should have a map of the community, pictures of the earth, continent, country, and state. The students will locate their street on the map and with red yarn draw a line from their street to a name card. They should engage in activities locating their school and places of interest near home and school.

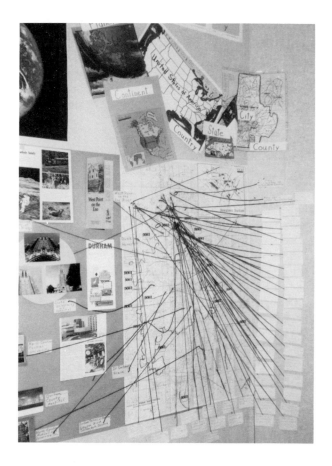

6. *Family Booklet.* The children will write or dictate about their families. They will tell about the kind of house they live in, what each family member looks like, what each member does, and what they do together.

Suggested Activities: The Need for Rules and Laws

1. *Classroom Rules.* The students will formulate a list of no more than six or seven classroom rules with the help of the teacher.
2. *Infractions of Rules.* The students will do a research activity to determine which of the class rules are broken most frequently. They will divide the rules among them and keep a tally sheet of the number of infractions for a specific

amount of time. A large bar graph can be made on which each student can report the number of infractions (Guyton, 1985).

3. *Consequences of No Rules.* The students will realize the importance of rules by setting up a hypothetical situation of a community that has no laws to rule them. The inhabitants are always arguing and are unable to live peacefully and safely. The students will discuss the rules and laws needed for this community and draw a correlation between rules and laws that protect and rules and laws that carry a responsibility.

4. *Future Laws.* The students will engage in a synthesizing activity by projecting into the future and writing some rules and laws for a future community or a community in space.

5. *Conclude That Communities Everywhere Need Rules and Laws.* The students will research another culture and compare their laws with the laws of the United States. This research can be done by interviewing people who have lived in other countries. A recording can be made of the interview and kept in a listening center.

Filmstrips

What Do You Do About Rules?
Citizenship Adventures of the Lollipop Dragon

Suggested Activities: Understanding the Justice System

1. *Fair and Unfair Rules.* The students will engage in a problem-solving activity to determine if the rules most often broken were fair or unfair. If they determine they were unfair, should they be changed or deleted?

2. *Understanding the Difficulty of Fair Judgment.* The students will role-play a modern version of "The Little Red Hen." Some neighborhood children get together to bake cookies. One child has to leave to care for a baby brother while his mother takes his grandmother to the doctor's office. He leaves just before the cookies are ready to go into the oven and returns just after they have baked. The protest is that he should not have any cookies because he did not help with the complete job. His protest is that it was not his fault that he had to leave. What are his rights? What is fair? Should the group allow him to have cookies? (Nelson, 1980)

3. *Understanding Certain Aspects of the Justice System.* The students will recognize laws that protect and laws that constrain by having a lawyer and a police officer visit the class. The students will be better informed of the legal guidelines they must operate within. Both the lawyer and police officer must include drug, alcohol, and sexual abuse in their presentation.

4. *Understanding the Rights of Individuals.* The students will be able to form a mental concept of the reality of their own rights by seeing a framed Bill of Rights. These rights should be read and discussed.

Filmstrips

Careers with a Police Department

Films

Dope Is for Dopes
Good and Bad Touching

Suggested Activities: The Need for Civic Responsibility

1. *Identifying Civic Responsibilities.* The students can participate responsibly in improving their school and community. They will take a tour around the school and make a list of improvements that are needed. They will chart a course of action and set up committees to make the improvements. This idea can be extended into the community. The families, school administrators, and city or county officials can be called upon to help. A newspaper article can be written about the project for the school and local newspaper. (McGowan, 1985)
2. *Rewarding Good Citizenship.* The students will form criteria for a good citizen and vote by secret ballot for the student or students that deserve recognition for taking their civic responsibility seriously.

Filmstrips

Citizenship Adventures of the Lollipop Dragon
The Fight
Values in Action

Films

Rock in the Road

Suggested Activities: Local Government

1. *Elections.* Students will be able to understand the election process by seeing the action at the polls on election day if they are set up in the school. The children can conduct their own election in the room.
2. *Identifying Some Elected Officials.* The students will be able to identify the position and duties of the elected officials if a judge, mayor, commissioner, or other official could visit the classroom.

Filmstrips

Local Government: How It Works

Suggested Activities: Changing Stereotyped Attitudes About Officials and Leaders

1. *Attitude Survey.* The students will discuss what makes a good leader. They will fill out an attitude survey with the knowledge that it will not be graded (Women's Educational Equity Act Program, 1985).

ATTITUDE SURVEY

Name _____

Answer the following questions by writing yes or no.

1. Anyone can be a leader. _____
2. Different kinds of groups need different kinds of leaders. _____
3. Many women have worked to make laws more fair for everyone. _____

4. Leaders need help in making decisions. _____

5. Sometimes 3rd graders are group leaders. _____

Finish this sentence with your own ideas.

I like leaders who are _____

Name two things you think would happen if a woman were President of the United States.

1. _____
   _____

2. _____

---

2. *Become Acquainted with a Leader.* The students will read about the life of Shirley Chisholm. After they have read of her life and leadership, they will take the attitude survey again to see if they have changed their attitudes (Women's Educational Equity Act Program, 1985).

SHIRLEY CHISHOLM
(November 30, 1924–   )

By Dorothy L. Bristol

Have you ever been told to stop fighting? This is the story of a little girl who grew up to be a fighter. She didn't fight by hitting people. She fought by helping them. This little girl was poor. She was black and very small in size. She had trouble speaking. When this little girl grew up, she worked very hard to help people live better. For this reason, she is called a fighter.

The little girl's name is Shirley Chisholm. She was born in 1924 in Brooklyn, New York. Her parents were from Barbados, an island in the Caribbean Sea. Do you know where that is?

Shirley's mother did sewing for people and her father worked in a bakery. The family was very poor. Their apartment had no heat. Sometimes Shirley and her two sisters had to stay in bed just to keep warm in the winter. There was always a lot of love in Shirley's family. Their love for each other kept their hearts warm and feeling good.

Shirley's parents did not have enough money to take care of their children. One day Shirley's mother packed boxes with food and clothing. She took Shirley and her sisters to Barbados by boat. The boat trip took nine days. Shirley was just three years old.

Shirley, her sisters and her mother went to her grandmother's farm in Barbados. Shirley's mother stayed there with the children for six months. Then she went back to New York to work and save money. Shirley and her sisters did not get to see their mother and father again for seven long years.

Shirley loved the farm, and she loved her grandmother. The children had chores to do to help with the farmwork. They carried water. They fed the ducks and chickens. They gathered eggs. They took care of the sheep, goats and cows.

Life on grandmother's farm was not all work. Sometimes the children went swimming in the blue Caribbean Sea. They played in the sand together and enjoyed each other's company. Shirley started school when she was four years old. By the time she was five years old she could read and write.

When Shirley was ten years old, she and her sisters returned to New York. The family

was happy to be living together again. Shirley graduated from high school and went to college in New York. When she finished college she became the director of a nursery school. Later she was in charge of a child care center.

Shirley Chisholm loved children. She also liked to work with adults. She felt many people weren't being treated fairly and she wanted to change this. She decided to try to get elected to the state government. In this way, she could help make laws that would protect people's rights in her state. Shirley told the voters what she wanted to do and they elected her! She served in the state government for four years. Next, she decided to run for a higher government office. Shirley Chisholm became the first Black woman in the entire country to be elected to the House of Representatives. Now she would be able to help decide on laws for the entire country.

While Shirley was working to make new laws, she called herself "fighting Shirley Chisholm." How Shirley did fight! She fought for health care, child care and good housing. She fought for laws to help make people's lives better. She fought for equal rights for women, for Blacks and for other groups of people who are not being treated fairly.

In 1972, Shirley Chisholm tried to be elected President of the United States. She did not win this, but she showed people something. She showed people that you can be a successful fighter if you grew up as a poor, Black girl with a speech impairment.

Shirley Chisholm is now teaching, speaking, and writing. She especially likes to talk to students. She says that America's future depends on our girls and boys. She hopes that the new leaders will be women and men of every color. Shirley Chisholm hopes that these new leaders will be fighters for equal rights for all people, too.

Shirley Chisholm, the first Black woman to have her name placed in nomination for President at a major political party convention. She served in the U.S. House of Representatives and continues to work for better schools and better jobs.

Listening Questions

1. How does Shirley Chisholm "fight"?
2. What kind of work does Shirley do?
3. What does she fight for?

Suggested Activities

Discussion

1. After reading the Chisholm biography, have the students discuss leaders they know who are women. Who are they? What kinds of roles do they fill as leaders? What qualities do these women possess that make them leaders? Don't limit the discussion to elected leaders only. Consider the school principal, the president of the PTA, the head librarian, or school nurse, as well as other women in more political leadership roles.
2. Discuss an election. What does it mean to vote? Have the students hold an election with two candidates running for the same office (they can decide what the office will be). How are candidates chosen? Who gets to vote? Discuss the fact that many people, men and women, black and white, worked hard to get voting rights for Black Americans and women. It was because of their work and the work of other women leaders that Shirley Chisholm was able to run for office. Help the class understand that Shirley Chisholm's candidacy for President was an important step toward the nomination of Geraldine Ferraro for Vice President in 1984.

Activities

1. Help your class learn about their state representatives. Have the class write a letter to their representative. Have them write about issues that they think are important. Have them ask the representative about the issues on which she/he is working.
2. Shirley Chisholm did not see her mother for seven years while she stayed at her grandmother's farm in Barbados. Ask your students if they have ever been apart from someone very special to them for such a long time. Ask them how they felt during that time. Have your students write a letter to someone very special in their lives who they have not seen for a long time.
3. Have your students write a story about Shirley Chisholm. Ask them to write about ways they are like Shirley. Ask them to write about ways they are different from her.

Source: Women's Educational Equity Act Program (1985). *Women as Members of Communities; Third Grade Social Studies.*

Suggested Activities: Understanding Time and Chronology

1. *Telling Time.* The students will learn how to tell time on the hour, before and after, using a clock with movable hands and large numbers. They should engage in an activity that lists the specific times each day that they have certain activities to do and draw clocks showing these times.
2. *Calendar.* The students will learn the months of the year, holidays, birthdays, and other special fun red-letter days, such as the day peanut butter was first made (*Instructor's Big Holiday Book,* 1981). They will mark these red-letter days on a calendar worksheet.

Filmstrips

The Mystery of the Clock
Money and Time Adventure of the Lollipop Dragon

Films

What Time Is It?
Calendar, the Days, Weeks, Months

NOVEMBER

Sunday	Monday	Tuesday	Wednesday	Thursday	Friday	Saturday

NOVEMBER

1. How many days are in November? _____
2. On which day of the week did November begin? _____
3. On which day of the week will November end? _____
4. What is the date today? _____
5. What year is this? _____
6. When is Election Day this year? _____
7. When is Thanksgiving? _____
8. Yesterday was _____
9. Tomorrow is _____
10. What month comes before November? _____
11. What month comes after November? _____
12. What is the date of the first Friday in November? _____
13. On which day of the week does Thanksgiving come? _____
14. Write the names of the boys in your room who have birthdays in November.

_____

15. Write the names of the girls in your room who have birthdays in November.

_____

16. Write the dates of all the Tuesdays in November.

_____

17. Next Friday is _____

18. November is the _____ month of the year.

third   sixth   tenth   eleventh

19. November is a _____ month.

spring   summer   fall   winter

20. How many months are left in this year? _____

Suggested Activities: History

1. *Famous Black Americans Crossword Puzzle.* The children will complete the crossword puzzle, filling in the last name of the famous black American. The children will use pictures as clues, with or without name labels.

Across

1. Famous conductor of the underground railroad
2. Famous professional male tennis player
3. Former slave who discovered many uses for the peanut
4. An important civil rights leader who was assassinated

Down

1. Poet and short story writer
2. Beloved jazz trumpeter

2. *Family Photos.* The children will bring two photos of their families, showing them in the past and present. They will compare and contrast the pictures. They will write or dictate stories about the photos, giving informational data about their families.
3. *Old Book Collection.* The students will bring old textbooks and storybooks from home to compare with the present day textbooks. They will tell what is alike and what is different. They will project into the future and tell what the present ones do not have that future books will have. The students can display the old books near the picture album.
4. *Help Little Red.* The children will play this game according to the rules on the laminated game board. The children will find the cards and answer sheet stored in kraft envelopes and stapled to the back of the game board.

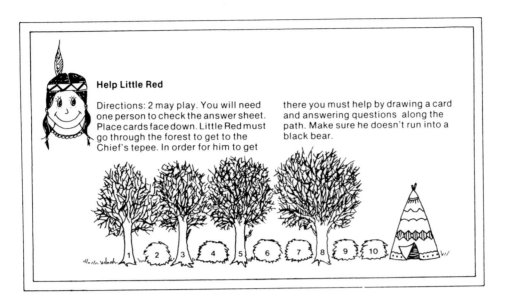

Help Little Red

Directions: 2 may play. You will need one person to check the answer sheet. Place cards face down. Little Red must go through the forest to get to the Chief's tepee. In order for him to get there you must help by drawing a card and answering questions along the path. Make sure he doesn't run into a black bear.

1. What 3 groups of people live in North Carolina?

2. Who were the first people to live in North Carolina?

3. Indians lived in groups called

4. Who was the first child born of English parents?

5. What were the names of the first 2 indians to visit England.

6. From what land did blacks come from?

7. What happened in 1776?

8. What was the first town in North Carolina?

9. Name some dances the colonists enjoyed.

10. What did the Stamp Act require?

Answers: Help Little Red

1. Indians, Europeans, Blacks
2. Indians
3. Tribes
4. Virginia Dare
5. Wanchese, Manteo
6. Africa
7. The United States became free from England.
8. Bath
9. Virginia Reel, Minuet
10. A stamp had to be bought to put on all papers. (Books, newspapers, documents, etc.)

---

5. *Then and Now Museum.* The students will learn how technology has changed life-styles by looking into some old Sears catalogs. They will find clues of kitchen utensils, clothes, toys, home appliances, communication and transportation products, and home and family care products that were used years ago and are no longer needed. The students will look for some of these items in attics, grandparents' homes, and other available places and bring any appropriate ones to school to display (Hatcher, 1985).

6. *New Treasures.* The students will observe the old outmoded objects from the past and determine that they can still have value. The students will make a chart stating the object, its original use, and suggestions for ways it can be used now (Hatcher, 1985).

7. *Presidents.* The children will gather information about the present president and record their findings. They will record the president's full name, state of birth, what he did before he was president, and three interesting facts about him.

   Variation. The children will gather information on one of the 40 presidents and record their findings. They will record the same information as above and include the number of his presidency and the years he lived.

8. *Treasure Hunt.* On the field trip the students will carry along a pencil and pad in order to fill out a treasure hunt list. They will observe the different types of architectural structures, which will increase their sensitivity to the space in which people live today and have lived in the past (Hatcher, 1985).

Treasure Hunt List

1. Identify a structure that has been changed from its original use; for example, a home into a business or a warehouse into a restaurant, etc.
2. Identify a structure that has been modified from its original appearance; for example, a room has been added; remodeling has occurred, or is in process, to the inside or outside.
3. Identify a structure that has been restored.
4. Identify a structure that is over 100 years old.
5. Identify a structure that is an example of a pure architectural style.
6. Identify a building or house of interest to you.
7. Identify a structure that has housed the same family for several generations.

9. *Fashion Show.* The students will model some items of clothing that they brought for the then and now museum. They will do some research and try to find the exact time the fashions were worn and what made the particular fashion popular (Carroll, 1985).

Suggested Activities: Learning to Use Maps and Globes

1. *Map Puzzles.* Students will put together wooden inlay puzzles of continents and oceans. They will feel and see the shapes as well as develop spatial relationships by placing the continents and oceans in the appropriate place.

2. *Map Construction.* The students will learn about space and dimension by using blocks, milk cartons, monopoly hotels, spools, and paper roll tubes as models for buildings and places in the community. A sand table or cabinet top can be used for the streets and roads (Van Cleaf, 1985).

3. *Picture Maps.* The students will construct a picture map by cutting pictures of buildings and places in their community out of magazines or old books. They will place the pictures on a background of poster board. Students can see relationships between the location of home, park, school, church, and shopping centers (Van Cleaf, 1985).

4. *Matching Places with Directions.* Students can learn which direction a place of interest is in the community with a matching activity. Using a map of the community, number the location of a few special places of interest. Number and label strips of paper or pictures of these places. The student matches the numbers and determines in which cardinal direction these places are located.

5. *Draw Maps.* The students will select an area around the school ground or in the classroom to draw, arranging places and items in a logical sequence. This activity is to help develop an understanding of the relationship between objects in the environment and two-dimensional drawings (Van Cleaf, 1985).

6. *East and West.* The students will determine the directions east and west by observing the sunrise and sunset in relation to the direction their home is facing. They are to draw a picture of their house at sunrise and sunset and label *east* and *west* on it.

7. *Using the Globe.* The students are to use a globe to develop the concept that north and south are at opposite ends of the earth, that the globe is a model of the earth, and that north, south, east, and west are cardinal directions.

8. *Computer Crossword Magic.* The students or the teacher can use Crossword Magic and create a puzzle with the seven continents and four oceans to help identify and reinforce the correct spelling of them (Sherman, 1981).

9. *Global Awareness.* The students will construct a diagram with a small circle

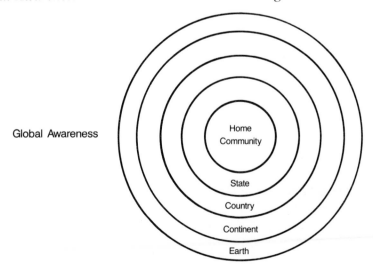

Global Awareness

Home
Community

State

Country

Continent

Earth

in the center with their name and address in it. Out from the center draw larger circles with the global dimensions in the circles (Peters, 1981).

Filmstrips

Maps and Globes
Maps, Globes, and Graphs
Exploring Maps: Map Skills for Today
Globes
Using Maps to Find Locations

Films

Maps are Fun
Maps and Their Uses

Suggested Activities: Environmental Problems

1. *Litter Bags.* The children will make colorful trash bags from large grocery bags to place around the school environment.
2. *Community Menace.* The children will play with a deck of cards with pictures of several familiar community helpers on the cards, including a Community Menace Card (bank robber, litter bug, etc.). They will play the game similar to Old Maid, trying to avoid being "stuck" with the Community Menace card.

Nurse

Fire fighter

Police Officer

Bank Robber

Suggested Activities: Communication

1. *Communication.* The children list ways people communicate today and in the past. They will suggest future methods of communication. The three lists will be compared and contrasted.
2. *Using the Telephone.* The children will practice telephone usage and manners with an unconnected standard telephone.
3. *Telephone Directory.* The children will locate special numbers such as the police, fire department, and businesses in the yellow pages.

Suggested Activities: Transportation

1. *Box Cars and Trucks.* In a study of community, children will make motor vehicles from large cardboard boxes that are used by community helpers. They will draw or paint on details.
2. *Transportation Mobiles.* The children will make transportation mobiles using colorful clothes hangers, string, and pictures of different modes of transportation.
   Variation. The children will paint or draw with chalk a mural showing different modes of transportation.
3. *Land, Water, Air Transportation.* The children will sort laminated pictures of toy cars, planes, boats, trains, and other modes of transportation.
4. *Future Transportation.* The children will construct their own mode of future transportation and tell what it is and how it travels.
5. *Transportation Safety Rules.* In a group, the children will make a list of safety rules for riding the bus, going on a hike, riding in a car, or riding on a boat.

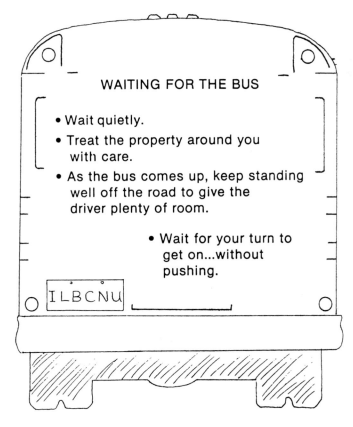

Suggested Activities: Life-Style Comparisons

1. *Community Comparison.* The child will compare life in two different communities, such as city/farm, present year/1900, inner city/middle America, jungle village/home community.

Variation. Two groups of children representing different communities will seek an answer for the same situation.

2. *Story Writing.* The children will write stories about what they think it would be like to live in different kinds of environments, such as inner city, prison, palace. They will illustrate their stories with drawings or magazine pictures.

3. *Indian Chief.* The children will play this game according to directions written beside the Indian head. The answer card and feathers will be stored in a brown kraft envelope and stapled to the back of the game. The teacher will draw an Indian head with a big feather headdress on tagboard and laminate. The teacher will cut out separate feathers and write on each one the word to define.

INDIAN CHIEF

Put the feathers in the Indian's headdress by defining the words on the feathers.

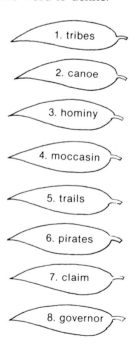

1. tribes
2. canoe
3. hominy
4. moccasin
5. trails
6. pirates
7. claim
8. governor

Answer Card—Indian Chief

1. tribes-groups of Indians
2. canoe-a boat used by Indians
3. hominy-corn hulled and crushed, eaten boiled
4. moccasin-soft shoe of deerskin
5. trails-Indian paths through the forest
6. pirates-ship robbers
7. claim-announced that land is yours
8. governor-ruler of the colony

4. *City Life and Farm Life.* The children will draw background scenes for city and farm life. They will sort laminated figures associated with city and farm life.
5. *Communities.* The children will build different communities, such as igloos, adobe huts, Indian tepees, straw huts, longhouses, and log cabins. They will build miniature communities or a community large enough to have dramatic role-playing.
6. *Dioramas.* The children will make dioramas to depict an Eskimo, Indian, or African village. They will construct their dioramas with shoe boxes, crayons, paints, and cardboard or construction paper cutouts.

Suggested Activities: Appreciating Our American Heritage

1. *Pledge to the Flag.* The students will repeat the "Pledge of Allegiance to the Flag" until they can say it. They must understand the meaning of "allegiance," "indivisible," "liberty," "republic," "pledge," and "justice."
2. *The National Anthem.* The students will become familiar with the National Anthem by listening to a recording. They must understand why citizens stand, and the meaning of the words of the first verse.
3. *American Indian Heritage Week.*
   a. *Pueblo.* The children will arrange different size boxes like an Indian pueblo

on a piece of cardboard or tagboard. They will cover the boxes with thin, brown salt clay, brown paper, or paint. The ladders, windows, and doors will be constructed with a variety of materials such as toothpicks, twigs, heavy paper, or felt-tip pens.

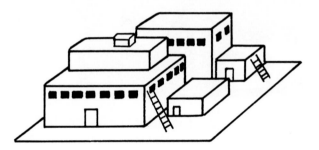

b. *Tree bark tepee.* The children will cut out a large circle from brown paper. They will glue white crepe paper over the circle. They will draw lines on the circle with a brown or black felt-tip pen for bark markings. They will cut a triangle from the edge of the circle making a door. They will roll the circle into a cone and staple or tape it. They will glue three toothpicks or small sticks to the top of the cone.

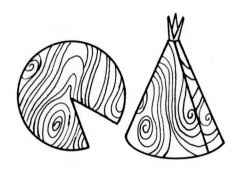

c. *Tepees.* The children will cut out a large circle from paper. They will cut the circle in half and cut a slanted 1″ line on the curved side of the paper for a door. They will color or paint the half-circles with Indian symbols. They will overlap corner A with corner B and staple or tape together.

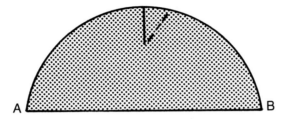

d. *Indian shield.* The children will construct circular shields from various materials such as tagboard, heavy paper, or circular pizza cardboard. They will decorate it with Indian symbols using crayons, paints, felt-tip pens, or paper. They will attach a strip of cardboard on the back for the handle.

e. *Indian bear rug.* The children will cut the shape of a bearskin from a large piece of brown paper. They will draw Indian symbols on it.

f. *Indian tunic.* The children will cut a large brown bag along the dotted lines as shown in the picture. They will cut fringe along the bottom of the tunic and the top of the armholes. They will decorate it with Indian symbols.

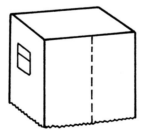 

g. *Indian pictographs.* Indians wrote with pictographs. Display examples and guess what symbols denote. The children will try to guess the meaning of the symbols from a picture.

hunt morning noon evening

teepee campfire rain

deer bird tracks river

look man woman mountain

hear horse tracks talk together

Variation. The children will match one set of cards with symbols to another set of cards with the word giving the meaning of the symbol.

noon

h. *Totem pole.* The children will design a totem pole using a paper tube and a variety of decorating materials such as crayons, felt-tip pens, colored paper, yarn, noodles, scraps of material, and beans.

Films

Our Country's Flag
America's National Anthem
Boyhood of George Washington
Boyhood of Abraham Lincoln

Suggested Activities: Special Holidays

1. *Special Holidays.* The children will compare and contrast how people of different ethnic groups in the same community celebrate a holiday. The students will learn about the celebration of special national holidays as they view films and filmstrips, sing songs, read stories, and look up information appropriate for the special days.
   Variation. The children will make holiday items used by ethnic groups during a holiday, such as a piñata, kite, or Halloween costumes.
2. *Special Foods.* The children will prepare and cook special foods eaten by different ethnic groups or in different countries during a holiday.
3. *Holiday Words Scramble.* The children will unscramble holiday words that have been written on the outline shape of things associated with familiar holidays.

Holiday Word Scramble

kirtc

ppkmniu

shogt

rtee

rteeg

tSnaa

geg

bakest

Variation. The children will make the outlines and write scrambled holiday words on the outline for another child to unscramble.

4. *Halloween:* Tasty Jack-O-Lanterns. The children will spread orange-colored cream cheese onto a rice cake or cracker. They will place raisins on top of the cheese spread to make facial features for a jack-o-lantern.

5. *Thanksgiving Celebration.* The students will engage in a special Thanksgiving celebration. They will learn that it is a true American holiday and that it has many social studies components.

a. *Mural.* The students will illustrate the sequence of events of the first Thanksgiving by drawing a mural with five or six scenes.

b. *Turkey hands.* The children will trace their hands on fall-colored construction paper, cut them out, curl the fingers with a pencil, and glue the hands onto the back of a turkey body for its feathers. The body of the turkey is drawn on tagboard, cut out, and its physical features painted on.

c. *Turkey scraps.* The children will tear a piece of brown construction paper into the shape of a turkey's head and body. The children will tear pieces of other colors of construction paper into the shape of feathers. They will glue all the pieces together.

d. *Thanksgiving feast.* The students will share ideas in a simulated family-style feast at school. While lunch is being enjoyed some children may share facts about the first Thanksgiving. Some children may prepare to show how fruit can be used to make animals that were present at the first feast. Others may sing songs, while still others share family jokes, riddles, or funny family stories.

e. *Log cabins.* The children will make a log cabin from a small empty milk carton or a square box. They will cut a door in the side leaving one side attached. They will cover the sides and top of the box with a variety of materials such as pretzel sticks, popsicle sticks, clothes hanger tubes, or paper (brown or black).

Filmstrips

Indians for Thanksgiving
Squanto and the First Thanksgiving
Thanksgiving Day
The Thanksgiving Story
Lincoln and Washington: Why We Celebrate Their Birthdays

Suggested Activities: Exploration of Other Cultures

1. *Resource People.* The children will learn about other cultures through persons from other countries who live in the community.
2. *Books, Filmstrips, Movies.* The children will experience vicarious visits to other lands through specially selected media.
3. *Letters.* The children will write to children in other countries in the United Nations.
4. *Cook's Tour.* The children will prepare special dishes from different countries with the help and/or suggestions from parents of different nationalities.

5. *Customs from Other Cultures.* The children will research customs in other cultures, such as Christmas in Mexico, Doll's Day in Japan, and the Chinese's New Year.
6. *Crafts from Other Cultures.* The children will make crafts and items from other cultures, such as piñatas, maracas, or tomtoms.
7. *Japanese Paper Folding.* The children will make origami animals from 7-inch squares.

   a. *Origami Dog.*

   1. Fold in half   *2. Fold over corners*   *3. Draw face*

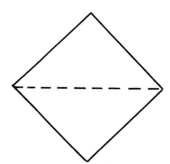   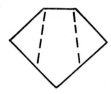   

   b. *Origami Whale*

   1. Fold in half and open again   *2. Fold top and bottom corners to center*

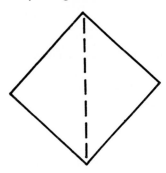   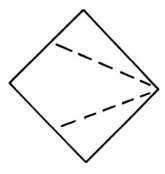

   3. Fold left corner in   *4. Fold bottom to the top*

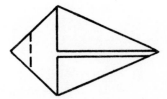   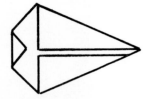

   5. Fold right corner to the left and up

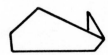

c. *Origami Bird*

1. Fold in half and open again

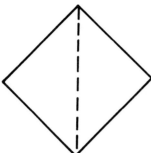

2. Fold left and right corners to center

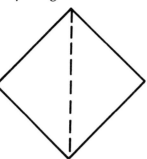

3. Fold top corner

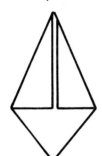

4. Fold left corner over

5. Pull out triangle from center

8. *Japanese Writing.* The children will write some kanji characters, a Japanese writing form of Chinese characters, using black paint or ink and small brushes.

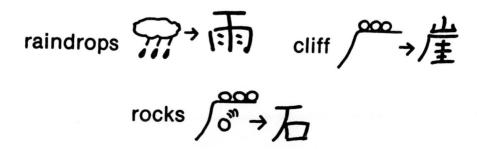

Study this Chinese dictionary.

火 = fire	山 = mountain	天 = sky
口 = mouth	人 = person	木 = tree
大 = big	月 = moon	木木 = forest (2 trees)

Write these Chinese characters in English.

口 _____   火 _____   大 _____

山 _____   木 _____   月 _____

Japanese Writing

The Japanese use three forms of writing. **Hiragana** is like our alphabet. It is made up of fifty-one letters. Each letter stands for a sound. **Katakana** is made up of the same sounds, but this writing is used only for foreign words and telegrams. **Kanji** is a set of Chinese characters. Some of these characters are "pictures" of what they stand for.

Use black paint or ink. Try writing some of these kanji!

① → ▬	一	
	one	
① → ▬ ② → ▬	二	
	two	
① → ② → ③ →	三	
	three	
木	木	
	tree	
森	森	
	forest	

9. *Festival Frolic.* In small groups, the children will research traditional Japanese festivals such as New Year's Day, Festival of the Dolls, Children's Day, and Obon. They will draw or paint a mural showing how these festivals are celebrated.

10. *Haiku.* The children will compose a class haiku poem which has a nature theme and 3 lines, the first of 5 syllables, the second of 7 syllables, and the third of 5 syllables.

    Variation. The children will write their own Haiku and draw a picture about it.

11. *Paper Dolls from Other Lands.* The children will cut outline bodies to color in facial features with crayons, paints, or markers and make native costumes from brightly colored paper or fabric. They will make stands for the dolls from heavy tag- or cardboard.

12. *Tissue Bit Flags.* The children will make flags of their own country and other countries from colored tissue paper bits.

Suggested Activities: Population Education

1. *Language Arts*
    a. The children will listen to stories illustrating various roles of family members, community helpers, and careers.
    b. The children will read about and discuss the alternative roles for adults such as working women, one-parent families, and single adults from supplementary basal readers.
    c. The children will make books or collages about population issues, such as crowding, alternative roles for women, and pollution, from pictures cut from magazines.
    d. The children will write about population issues using story starters in the creative writing center.
    e. The children will go on field trips to a large shopping center, airport, bus terminal, downtown district, or industrial complex to feel the effects of crowding, listen for noise pollution, and observe traffic, construction, and trash. The children will record their results from the field trips on a language experience chart.
    f. The children will observe and list overcrowded conditions in the school, such as trailers, makeshift classrooms in the library, health room, and hallways.
    g. The children will write and put on puppet shows on population concepts such as the advantages and disadvantages of small and large families, conservation, and roles for women.
    h. The children will role-play and pantomine population issues.

2. *Mathematics*
    a. The children will add, subtract, and multiply sets of people.
    b. The children will chart the number of people in their families. They will discuss the average family size. They will compare and contrast aspects of the largest family and the smallest family.
    c. The children will count and record the populations of their families, their neighbor's family, their school, dogs and cats on their street, to discuss census.
    d. The children will solve story problems such as "If a family of two drinks 2 gallons of milk a week, how much would a family of four (six, eight) drink?"

e. Using one-to-one correspondence, the child will divide 12 cookies between two (three, four, six) children.

f. The children will solve money story problems comparing the basic needs of small families with the basic needs of large ones (lunch money, shoes, movies).

3. *Science*

a. The children will observe animals in the classroom and discuss reproduction.

b. The children will plant, grow, and care for plants. They will chart the growth of the plants and identify what plants need in order to grow (sun, water, air).

c. The children will make a bulletin board illustrating land, air, and water pollution.

d. The children will observe the effects of land, water, and air pollution on nature walks.

e. The children will make terrariums and aquariums to observe the balance of nature.

f. The children will collect newspapers, bottles, and alumnium cans to be given to the appropriate organization to be recycled. The children will practice conservation by using both sides of paper, turning off lights when they leave a room, and recycling paper or magazines.

g. The children will gain a better understanding of their dependence on electricity. The teacher will disconnect all electrical equipment (audiovisual aids, lights, etc.) in the morning before the children arrive. The children will have class under these conditions. They will discuss and list all the uses of electricity in the classroom. They will discuss alternatives to electricity.

h. The children will inventory all the electrical appliances in their homes.

4. *Social Studies*

a. The children will role-play different life-styles and roles studying families around the world.

b. The children will explore the classroom for evidence of social and economic interdependence of countries by looking at trademarks on items in the room and discussing vacations they have taken.

c. The children will go on field trips to discover alternative roles for men and women: for example, hospitals employ women doctors and male nurses. The children will ask questions of resource people who visit the classroom.

Suggested Activities: Understanding Economic Resources

1. *Economic Exchange.* To introduce money as an economic exchange, display examples of currency, checks, credit cards, and a flowchart showing the circular flow of money on a bulletin board. On another portion of the board illustrate the concept of bartering.

2. *Goods and Services.* The students will learn which jobs provide goods and which jobs provide services by naming their parents' jobs. The teacher will list them on a chart in the appropriate category: goods, services, or both goods and services.
3. *Community Economic Resources.* The students will develop a chart to identify the resources in the community and be able to recognize the type of resource (Speas, Martelli, Graham, & Cherryholmes, 1983).

(Name of Students' Community) Economic Resources		
People Resources	Natural Resources	Man-Made Resources

4. *Everyone Is a Consumer.* The students will understand how they are consumers. The class should be divided up into groups. They should have access to yellow pages of old telephone books, newspaper ads, and magazine advertisements. They are to make a collage of all the goods that their families consume in a period of a week or a month (Atwood, 1985).
5. *Decision Model.* The students will engage in a problem-solving activity by identifying an economic problem and using a decision model to solve it. The students will learn they can *save* or *spend* money and time, or save some and spend some, but not save and spend at the same time (Speas, Martelli, Graham, & Cherryholmes, 1983).

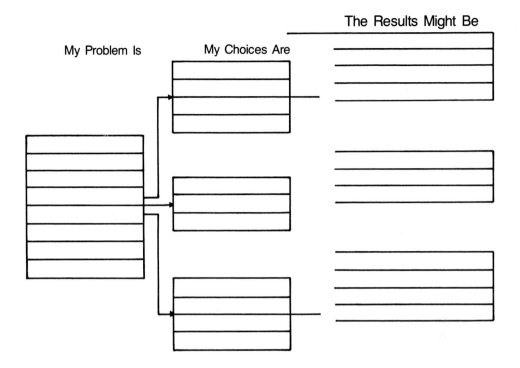

6. ***Economic Resources from Other Communities and Countries.*** The students will learn how many products come from other places by observing labels in clothing and packaging. They should make a list of products and the communities and countries from which they come. They should determine which of these products is not available in their own community or country and how dependent each country is on another.
7. ***Resource Person.*** The students will receive first-hand information about another country's economic resources if a new citizen or visitor from another country or community will visit the classroom.
8. ***Pen Pals.*** The students will be able to compare their own economic way of life with a child in another community or country by having pen pals. They should make a list of questions to ask in their correspondence in order to find out about economic resources as well as other aspects of life in their pen pal's community and country.
9. ***Cupcake Factory.*** The students will learn about the margin of profit, division of labor, and productivity as they become entrepreneurs. They will either simulate or actually carry out an economic project. First they must do market research to find out if the product they decide to produce will sell. Shares of stock will be sold for investment purposes and in order to have capital to buy ingredients and materials needed to make the product. A banker could be invited to talk about loans and interest. Committees will be needed to finance the projects, buy materials, make the product, advertise, sell the product, and handle profits (Yeargan & Hatcher, 1985).
10. ***Taxes.*** The students will define the term *taxes* and make a list of the goods and services that are payed for by tax money. They will engage in a critical thinking activity to determine the best use of tax money. For example, why

is it more efficient for tax money to buy fire trucks than for individuals to provide their own? Students should do a survey and determine the different kinds of taxes their parents pay. The students should try to determine another way to provide goods and services (such as welfare) besides using tax money.

Filmstrips	*Films*
What's Money For?	Why We Use Money
Can You Make Change?	Why We Have Taxes: The Town
Money and Time Adventures of	Who Had No Policeman
the Lollipop Dragon	Story of Our Money System
Basic Concepts in Economics	Making Change for a Dollar
Targo the Job Explorer	

Suggested Activities: Computers in the Social Studies Curriculum

1. *Graphics.* The students will be able to use the computer to draw pictures and symbols and to design charts, tables, and graphs for research reports. The students will use the Basic and Logo programs and, if a printer is available, the graphics can be printed out (Cacha, 1985).
2. *Authoring Systems.* Teachers and students can use authoring systems to create drills, make crossword puzzles, and hidden word puzzles to be used as culminating or supplementary activities in social studies units (Cacha, 1985).
3. *Interactive Programming.* The students will be able to design a simple interactive program about a historical event in which the user must decide between two choices, only one of which is right (Cacha, 1985).

Suggested Activities: General

1. *Music.* The children will learn music activities incorporated into units of study in the social studies program. During the study of transportation, they will learn songs like, "The Glendy Burke" (steamboat), "Little Red Caboose" (train), and "Up, Up and Away" (balloon).
2. *Costumes.* The children will make costumes related to particular units of study. They will use crepe paper and other materials for details.
3. *Museum, Hobby, or Special Exhibit Area.* The children will set up an area in the classroom or hallways to exhibit things.

4. *Special Interest Areas.* The children will use materials on display related to current units of study or as separate units.

5. *Drug Awareness*
   Booklets. Make blank booklets in the shape of a capsule, syringe, marijuana plant, the letters LSD. Have the children use them to write or dictate about drugs.
   Resource person. Have a person from the narcotics squad show various drugs and alert children to the dangers of usage.
   Language master. Use cards for developing vocabulary.
   Filmstrip. Have available with related films.
   Situation. As the unit ends, bring a stranger on the school grounds who will attempt to sell drugs to children. The police might help with this.
6. *Sex Education.* Use male and female small pets (rabbits, chickens, hamsters, guinea pigs, guppies, etc.). Create a chart. Watch and record the changes that occur during pregnancy. Things the children might chart include weight (daily), amount of food eaten (daily), changes in habits, and changes in appearance.
7. *Classroom Newspaper.* The children will write and distribute a class newspaper. The children will examine several newspapers to decide how to set up the editorial staff and what sections to include in the paper, such as classroom, school, community, current national events, comics, sports, and a "Dear Abby" column. They would decide how often to publish it and for how long.
8. *Magazine Articles.* In the social studies center, the children will use magazine articles from children's magazines related to an area of study. They will answer a set of guide questions attached to each research card or set of cards.
9. *Films, Tapes.* The children will see films and hear tapes related to the units of study.
10. *Paper-Stuffed Animals and People.* The children will draw large outlines on evenly folded paper of animals or people, related to a unit of study like the circus, zoo, Thanksgiving. They will cut them out, color, stuff with newspaper, and staple or glue the edges.
11. *Dominoes.* The children will match pictures such as zoo animals, farm animals, means of transportation, community helper, and holiday things.
12. *Build Your Vocabulary.* The children will place a brick on a blank area of the house when they can define or tell something about the vocabulary word written on the brick. They will use special vocabulary related to the unit of study. A large tagboard house may be used or a house drawn on a stencil for duplicating individual worksheets.

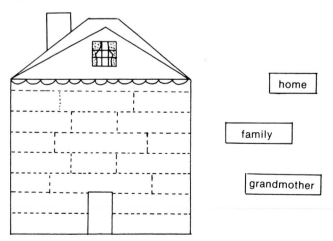

13. *Toss and Answer.* The children will play on this floor-sized game board with pictures of community helpers, famous people, representations of city or rural life, or means of transportation. They will take turns tossing a beanbag onto spaces on the game board. When the beanbag lands, the child names the picture and tells something about it according to the rules of the game. For example, if the pictures are modes of transportation, the child names the picture and tells if it is used on land, water, or air. A spin-and-answer dial could be substituted for a beanbag and game board.

14. *Happy Flower Notecard.* The children will fold pieces of 8½″ × 11″ yellow construction paper and cut it into a large circle leaving about 1″ of a fold as a hinge. They will cut different colors of construction paper into smaller circles. They will overlap and glue the smaller circles around the back of the yellow circle as petals. They will draw a happy face on the front of the yellow circle and a message on the inside.

15. *Gameboard.* The children play games on a versatile game board to reinforce information and skills learned in social studies. The players will move one space on the board for each question answered correctly about a related theme at school, places and things in the community, and famous people.

Suggested Activities: Understanding Life on the Farm

1. *Alphabetical Fruits and Vegetables.* Use a stand-up board with eight hooks positioned in it. (Drapery hooks work well on tagboard.) Have a set of eight cards with a picture on each. Have the child put the cards in alphabetical order.

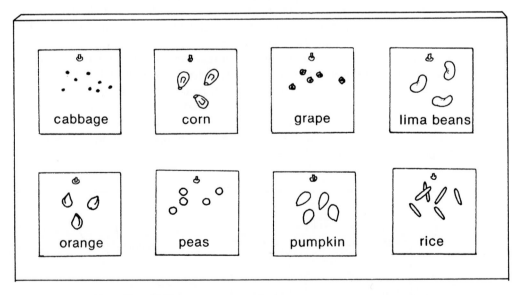

2. *Colorful Pigs.* Cut a pig out of tagboard for each color. Write the color word on the front half of the pig. Put a color square on the back half of the pig. Cut the pig into two puzzle pieces. Be sure to vary the puzzle lines so that each pig is self-correcting.

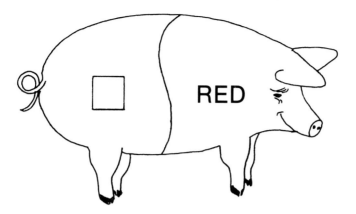

3. ***Planting the Crops.*** A bottle crate is needed for the garden. Make a set of cards with a picture of a fruit or a vegetable on each. The cards are divided evenly among two or three children. The children take turns looking at one card at a time and giving the beginning sound. The correct answer is on the back of the card. If the correct answer is given, the child gets to "plant" his or her crop by placing it in the crate. The child with the most crops planted wins.

4. ***The Farm Game.*** Two or three children can play. Copy the playing board as shown. A set of cards is needed for the well and the egg basket positions in the middle of the board. Plastic farm animals are nice to use for markers. All markers are placed on the star. The game begins by the first child rolling the die and moving that number of blocks. If a player lands on a well or an egg basket, he or she draws a card and counts the number of objects on the card. The player names the number and moves that number of spaces. If the objects are counted incorrectly, the child places the card at the bottom of the stack and does not move forward. The players travel around the board twice. The first player to reach the star on the second trip is the winner.

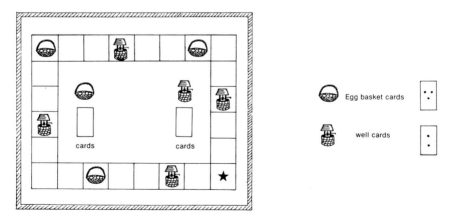

5. ***Language Master Cards.*** Tape a farm vocabulary word on each card. Write the word and an illustration of the word on the card.

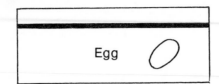

6. ***ABC Duck Puzzles.*** Cut a duck for each letter from yellow tagboard. Put a lower-case letter on the head and a capital letter on the body of the duck. Cut each duck into two puzzle pieces. The child matches each head with its appropriate body. Another version of this can be used with ducks and eggs.

7. ***Animal Puzzles with Names of the Animals.*** Use a piece of tagboard for each animal puzzle. Draw one animal on each card (pig, cow, dog, and cat are good choices). The name of the animal is printed across the top. Cut the puzzle into three sections.

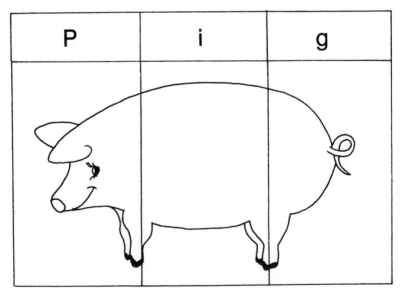

8. ***Word Search Fun Sheets.*** Use some of the new vocabulary words and hide them within the page of letters. The child circles each word as he or she finds it.

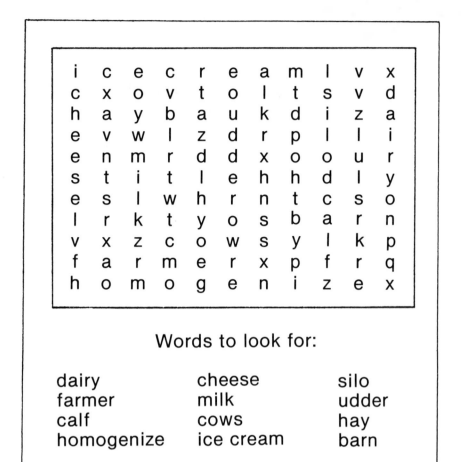

Words to look for:

dairy	cheese	silo
farmer	milk	udder
calf	cows	hay
homogenize	ice cream	barn

9. *Vegetable and Fruit Match.* Make a variety of cards so that when the halves are fitted together the card represents a fruit or a vegetable.

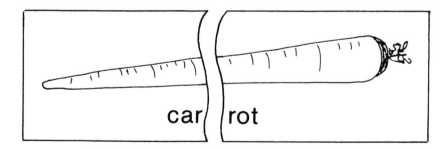

10. *What's Your Name?* Make one card for each animal. On the left side of the card, draw a picture of the animal. On the right side of the card, write the name of the animal. Cut the card into two puzzle pieces. Have the child match the animal to its name.

11. ***Corny Compounds.*** Cut ears of corn from yellow tagboard and husks from green tagboard. Put half of the compound word on the ear of corn and the rest of the word on the husk. The child matches the ear of corn with its appropriate husk. This game can be made self-correcting by placing the answer on the back of the ears of corn or also by providing a list with the answer.

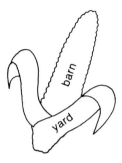

12. ***Barnyard Match Game.*** Draw a game board as shown on a piece of tagboard. A set of cards with math problems is needed. Plastic animals are used as markers. The first child picks up a card and answers the math problem. If the child is correct, he or she moves up one space. If incorrect, the child does not move. Children take turns and the first player to reach his or her barn wins.

| start | start | start | start |

13. ***Animals Made from Shapes.*** Attribute blocks are used. Form simple animal shapes from the attribute blocks. Trace the outer edge of this shape onto tagboard. Label the picture with the name of the animal. The child uses the attribute blocks to completely fill in the outline of the animal. On the back side of the card, the animal is drawn again with the outline of each block drawn in. This side can be used as a simple matching activity or to give the correct answer for the front of the card.

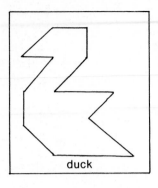

duck

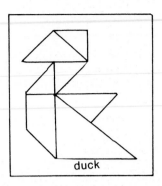

duck

14. *Fence the Animals.* Two or three children play. For each child, draw an animal in the center of a piece of tagboard. Punch eight evenly spaced holes around the animals. At least eight pegs (golf tees may also be used) are needed for each child. Make a set of cards with math problems. The child draws a card and answers the problem. If correct, the child gets to put a peg in his card. The first child to fill in all eight holes with pegs "fences" his or her animal and wins.

15. *Count Your Crops.* Make a stand-up board with hooks. You can use tagboard with drapery hooks inserted. Make four sets of vegetable theme cards to count by 1's, 2's, 5's, and 10's. The child takes a set of cards appropriate for his or her ability and hangs them in order on the board.

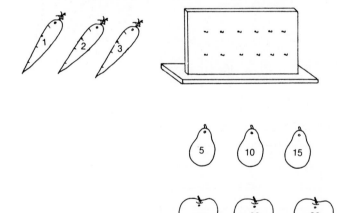

16. *Egg Hatchery.* Numbers are written in the sections of an actual egg carton. Small eggs are cut from tagboard. A math problem is written on each egg. The child solves the math problem on the egg and places the egg in its proper place in the egg carton. Answers to the problems can be written on the back of the eggs so that the child can check his or her own work.

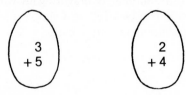

17. *Farmer John Goes Fishing.* An actual fishbowl can be used to hold the fish cut from tagboard. A number is written on each fish and a paper clip is attached to each. Make a fishing pole from a stick with a string and a magnet attached. A game board in the shape of a fishbowl is also made from tagboard. On this board are pictures of fish that have number words on them. The child goes fishing with the magnetic pole. When the child catches a fish, he or she looks at the number on the fish and then matches it to the fish on the game board with the appropriate number word.

18. *Chicken Dominos.* Make domino cards with sets of chicks on them. Two children take turns matching like sets of chicks.

19. *Farm Bingo.* Five to six children play. Each child has a card with five vegetables across the top and five rows of numbers below these vegetables. Beans can be used to cover the numbers as they are called. Let one child be the "caller." Follow Bingo rules. Encourage children to help each other.

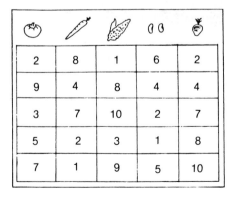

🍅	🥕	🌽	🫛🫛	🥬
2	8	1	6	2
9	4	8	4	4
3	7	10	2	7
5	2	3	1	8
7	1	9	5	10

master card

🍅	🥕	🌽	🫛🫛	🥬
1				
2				
3				
4				
5				
6				
7				
8				
9				
10				

20. *Barn Floor Game.* Three barns are drawn on a large piece of vinyl as shown. Two children play and each child gets a bean bag. The first child tosses a bean bag onto the vinyl. The child checks the number of the barn on which his or her bean bag landed and takes a card that has the same number on it. The child turns the card over and names the shape and color. The children check each other's answers. The game is over when each child has had five turns or when the children tire of the game.

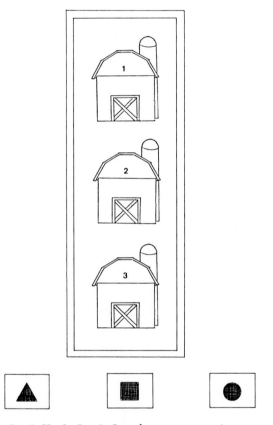

21. *Planting Seeds Task Card.* See the accompanying example.

PLANTING SEED TASK CARD.

> 1. Put soil ⁖ in a cup.
> 2. Plant a seed *o* in the soil
> 3. Put water ʰ⁰ on the seed.
> 4. Look at the cup each day.

22. *Mature Animal—Young Animal Puzzle.* Using tagboard, draw a picture of a mature animal on half of the card. Draw pictures of the young animals on the other half. Label each picture and cut into two puzzle pieces.

duck

ducklings

23. ***Plant Reproduction.*** Let children experiment with various ways of making a new plant.

24. ***Farm Animals and Their Products.*** Divide a piece of tagboard into six sections and paste on pictures of the following: a sheep, a turkey, a cow, a chicken, a pig, and a goose. Small cards are made with pictures of the products we get from each of these animals. The child matches the product to its appropriate animal. Examples are

Sheep: sweater, scarf
Turkey: roast turkey
Cow: milk, butter, steak, cheese, shoes
Chicken: egg, chicken leg
Pig: sausage, bacon, ham
Goose: pillow feathers

25. ***Woodworking Activities:*** Make the following task cards and have the children complete the activities.

Peter Cottontail

1. Sand a triangle.
2. Cut out ears, $0 0$
       eyes, • •
   and a nose. ▽
3. Glue these to triangle.
4. Add pipe cleaner whiskers.
5. Glue on a cotton ball tail. ○

Let's Make a Scarecrow

1. Take 2 popsicle sticks and glue together like this:

   Let dry.

2. Take another popsicle stick and glue to others crossways:
   Let dry.

3. Glue another stick on to form an x. Let dry.

4. Glue a cotton ball on to the top of the scarecrow for the head.

5. Decorate your scarecrow with felt for clothes.

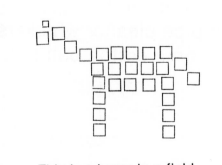

This is a horse in a field.

26. *Farm Mosaics.* The children are given small squares of construction paper and are asked to plan a farm scene on a background sheet of paper. The children are encouraged to plan and "play" with their squares before they glue the squares down.

27. *Cotton Ball Sheep.* Give the children pieces of black construction paper and ask them to cut out the basic shape of a sheep. Then have them glue cotton balls onto the body to symbolize wool.

28. *Playdough Farm Animals.* Each child shapes the farm animal of his or her choice. These can be used to form a farm scene, grouping like animals together and placing them in appropriate areas of the farm.

29. *Vegetable Printing.* After examining and identifying the vegetables, the children are allowed to dip these into paint and print on paper. The children may want to play games with each other, trying to identify the vegetable by the design it made.

30. *Block Center Task Cards.* Draw a picture of a farm scene on the card. Ask the children to tell what they see in the picture. Let the children construct their own farm scenes similar to those on the cards. As a followup to this, the children may wish to dictate experience stories about their constructions.

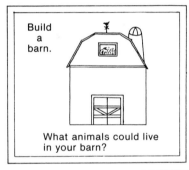

Build a barn.
What animals could live in your barn?

Build a henhouse.
How many blocks did you use?
Show it to a friend.

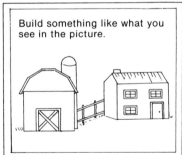

Build something like what you see in the picture.

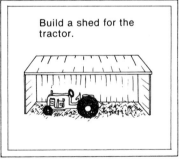

Build a shed for the tractor.

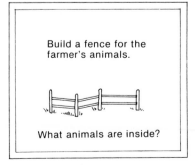

Build a fence for the farmer's animals.
What animals are inside?

31. *Cooking Activities.* The farm lends itself nicely for cooking because of its emphasis on fruits, vegetables, and dairy products. Here are three possibilities:

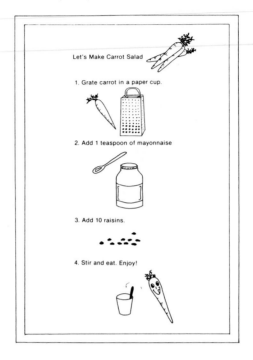

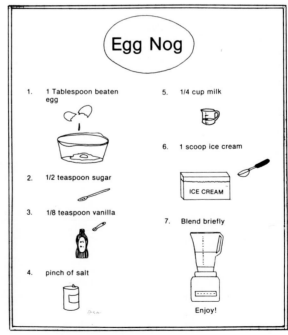

Making Butter

Pour small amounts of whipping cream into small jars (baby food jars are a comfortable size to handle). Children take turns shaking cream until it becomes butter. A bit of salt can be included for added taste. Spread on crackers and enjoy.

32. ***Checklist to Accompany a Field Trip to a Farm.*** A field trip to a farm takes the children beyond the ordinary realm of the classroom and helps to satisfy their natural curiosity. A checklist such as the one that follows is motivating for the child and helps to define the goals of the field trip.

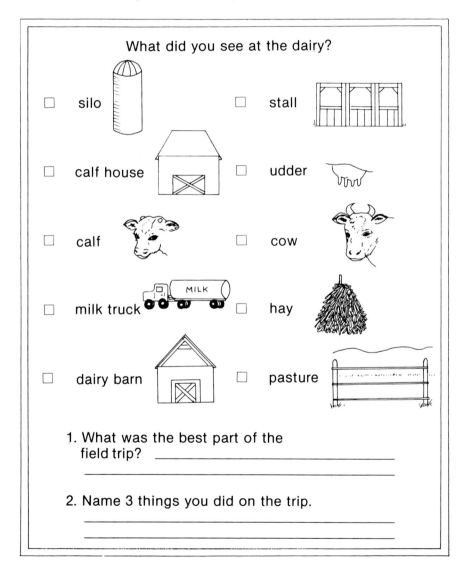

Farmer Brown's Apple Tree

Materials needed:
Lettuce (or Spinach)
Celery Stalks
Cherry tomatoes
Lemons

1.

Arrange 2 pieces of
lettuce to form
a tree top. Put it on a
paper plate.

2.

Add 1 celery stalk
for the tree trunk.

3.

Place 4 cherry
tomatoes on
your tree for apples.

4.

Squeeze lemon juice
on your tree.

5.

Eat and enjoy!

33. *Sing "Old MacDonald Had a Farm."* The children will be able to

Reproduce the words in the song by correctly singing the song with the teacher after having learned the words to the song.

Identify the sounds of a cow, turkey, lamb, hen, pig, and duck by singing the correct sounds for each animal in the song.

Produce the correct animal picture when a certain animal's verse is being sung by holding up the picture of that animal.

Description

a. *Words:*

Old MacDonald had a farm, E-I-E-I-O
And on his farm he had a *cow,*
   E-I-E-I-O.
With a *moo moo* here and a *moo moo* there
Here a *moo,* there a *moo,* everywhere a
   moo-moo.
Old MacDonald had a farm, E-I-E-I-O.

b. *To do:*

Give each child an animal. There are ducks, pigs, turkeys, hens, cows, and lambs. Children are told to keep their animals in their laps when their animals' sound is not being sung. At the end of each round, add another animal sound until six sounds are sung. The children are to hold the animals beside their face when their animal's sound is being sung.

c. *Illustration*

Photocopies of the animals used in "Old MacDonald Had a Farm."

34. *Play Bingo.* The children will be able to

Reproduce the words in the song by correctly singing the song with the teacher after learning the words to the song.

Substitute one letter at a time in the word *Bingo* with a clap as each verse is sung.

Description

a. This song may be sung with a guitar. The song is sung through six times. Each time one more letter is substituted with a clap. By the last verse the children should not be spelling the word at all; they should be clapping out the rhythm.

b. *Words*

There was a farmer had a dog and
   Bingo was his name-o.
B-I-N-G-O, B-I-N-G-O
   B-I-N-G-O and
Bingo was his name-o.

References

Atwood, V. A. (1985). "Bubble-Good Data: Product Testing and Other Sources." *Social Education, 49,* 147–148.

Banks, J., and Clegg, A. (1985). *Teaching Strategies for the Social Studies: Inquiry, Valuing and Decision-making* (3rd ed.). New York: Longman.

Bloom, B. S. (1956) *Taxonomy of Educational Objectives: The Classification of Educational Goals: Handbook I, Cognitive Domain.* New York: David McKay.

Cacha, F. B. (1985). "Microcomputer Capabilities in the Elementary Social Studies Program." *The Social Studies, 75,* 62–64.

Carroll, R. (1985). "Exploring the History of a Neighborhood: A Community Project." *The Social Studies, 77,* 150–154.

Cartledge, G., and Milburn, J. F. (Eds.) (1986). *Teaching Social Skills to Children* (2nd ed). New York: Pergamon Press.

Chilcoat, G. W. (1985). "The Literary Popular Story Paper as Classroom Activity: The Role of Women in Nineteenth Century America." *The Social Studies, 76,* 76–79.

Crossett, B. (1983). "Using Both Halves of the Brain to Teach the Whole Child." *Social Education, 47,* 266–268.

Day, B. (1983). *Early Childhood Education* (2nd ed). New York: Macmillan Publishing Company.

Day, B., and Drake, K. (1983). *Early Childhood Education Curriculum Organization and Classroom Management.* Alexandria, Va.: Association for Supervision and Curriculum Development.

Edwards, B. (1979). *Drawing on the Right Side of the Brain.* Los Angeles: Houghton Mifflin.

Ellis, A. K. (1977). *Teaching and Learning Elementary Social Studies.* Boston: Allyn and Bacon, Inc.

Guyton, E. M. (1985). "The School as a Data Source for Young Learners." *Social Education, 49,* 141–144.

Hatcher, B. (1983). "Putting Young Cartographers 'On the Map.'" *Childhood Education, 59,* 311–315.

Instructor Books. (1981). *Instructor's Big Holiday Book.* New York: Instructor Publications.

Hatcher, B. (1985). "Children's Homes and Neighborhoods: Untapped Treasures from the Past." *The Social Studies, 75,* 155–159.

Jantz, R. K., et al. (1985) Inquiry and Curriculum Change: Perceptions of School and College/University Faculty. *Theory and Research in Social Education, 13* (2), 61–72.

Jarolimek, J. (1986). *Social Studies in Elementary Education* (7th ed.). New York: Macmillan.

Krathwohl, D. R., Bloom, B. S., & Masia, B. B. (1964). *Taxonomy of Educational Objectives: The Classification of Educational Goals: Handbook II, Affective Domain.* New York: David McKay.

Martin, D. S. (1985). "Ethnocentrism Revisited: Another Look at a Persistent Problem." *Social Education, 49,* 604–609.

Martorella, P. (1985). *Elementary Social Studies: Developing Reflective, Competent, and Concerned Citizens.* Boston: Little, Brown & Company.

Maxim, G. (1983). *Social Studies and the Elementary School Child.* Columbus, Ohio: Charles E. Merrill.

McCarthy, B. (1980). *The 4MAT System.* Oakbrook, Ill.: Excel.

McGowan, T. M. et al. (1985). "Teaching About Elections in Indiana Schools." (ERIC Document Reproduction Service No. ED 260 998.)

Michaelis, J. U. (1976). *Social Studies for Children in a Democracy* (6th ed.). Englewood Cliffs, N.J.: Prentice-Hall, Inc.

Miller, J. W. (1985). "Teaching Map Skills: Theory, Research, Practice." *Social Education, 49,* 30–31.

Nelson, M. R. (1980). "Teaching Young Children About Law." *Childhood Education, 56,* 274–277.

North Caroline Department of Public Instruction. (1985). North Carolina Competency Based Curriculum, K-3. Raleigh, N.C.

Peters, R. (1981). "Infusing Global Awareness Components of Environmental Education Programs into the Kindergarten–Grade Twelve Social Studies Curriculum for Purposes of Affecting Student Attitudes and Perspectives." (ERIC Document Reproduction Service No. ED 205 392.)

Schlereth, T. J. (1980). *Artifacts and the American Past*. Nashville, Tenn.: American Association for State and Local History.

Schug, M., Todd, R., and Beery, T. (1984). "Why Kids Don't Like Social Studies." *Social Education, 48,* 382–387.

Scott, K. P. (1985). "Social Interaction Skills: Perspectives on Teaching Cross-Sex Communication." *Social Education, 49,* 610--612.

Seefeldt, C. (1984). *Social Studies for the Preschool—Primary Child* (2nd ed.). Columbus, Ohio: Charles E. Merrill.

Seefeldt, C., and Barbour, N. (1986). *Early Childhood Education: An Introduction*. Columbus, Ohio: Charles E. Merrill.

Self, E. (1977). *Teaching Significant Social Studies in the Elementary School*. Chicago: Rand McNally College Publishing Company.

Sherman, L. (1981). *Crossword Magic*. California: L & S Computerware Company, Sunnyvale, Calif.

Skeel, D. J. (1979). *The Challenge of Teaching Social Studies in the Elementary School* (2nd ed.). Santa Monica, Calif.: Goodyear Publishing Company, Inc.

Speas, J., Martelli, L., Graham, A., and Cherryholmes, L. (1983). *Communities*. New York: Webster Division, McGraw-Hill Book Company.

Stanley, W. B. (1985). "Social Studies Research: Theory into Practice." National Institute of Education, Washington, D.C. (ERIC Document Reproduction Service No ED 268 064.)

Stanley, W., et al. (1985). *Review of Research in Social Studies Education 1976–1983. Bulletin 75* (ISBN–0–89994–303–9). Washington, D.C.: National Council for Social Studies.

Superka, D., Hawke, S., and Morressett, I. (1980). "The Current and Future States of the Social Studies." *Social Education, 44,* 362–369.

U.S. Secretary of Education, Bennett, W. (1986). *First Lessons: A Report on Elementary Education in America*. Washington, D.C.: U.S. Government Printing Office.

Van Cleaf, D. W. (1985). "The Environment as a Data Source: Map Activities for Young Children." *Social Education, 50,* 145–146.

Walsh, H. (1980). *Introducing the Young Child to the Social World*. New York: Macmillan.

Wilkerson, R. (1986). *An Evaluation of the Effects of the 4MAT System of Instruction on Academic Achievement and Retention of Learning*. Unpublished doctoral dissertation, University of North Carolina, Chapel Hill.

Women's Educational Equity Act Program (F D), Washington, D. C. (1985). "Women as Members of Communities: Third Grade Social Studies." (ERIC Document Reproduction Service No. ED 260 998.)

Yeargan, H., and Hatcher, B. (1985). "The Cupcake Factory: Helping Elementary Students Understand Economics." *The Social Studies, 76,* 82–84.

Activities

Beckman, C., Simmons, R., and Thomas, N. (1982). *Channels to Children: Early Childhood Activity Guide for Holidays and Seasons*. Colorado Springs, Colo.: Channels to Children.

Forte, I., Pangle, M., and Tupa, R. (1974). *Pumpkins, Pinwheels and Peppermint Packages*. Nashville, Tenn.: Incentive Publications.

Instructor Books. (1981). *Teacher's Activity Calendar*. New York: The Instructor Publications, Inc.

Kaplan, S., Kaplan, J., Madsen, S., and Gould, B. (1974). *A Young Child Experiences: Activities for Teaching and Learning*. Santa Monica, Calif.: Goodyear.

Schaffer, F. (1985). "Our Fifty States." *Schooldays, 4,* 24–35.

Schaffer, F. (1986). "Let's Explore Japan." *Schooldays, 5,* 3–12.

Schaffer, F. (1986). "Chinese Writing." *Schooldays, 5,* 71.

Stephens, L. (1983). *Developing Thinking Skills Through Real-Life Activities*. Boston: Allyn and Bacon, Inc.

Other References

Finkelstein, J. M., and Nielsen, L. F. (1985). "Celebrating a Centennial: An Approach to Teaching Historical Concepts to Young Children." *The Social Studies, 76,* 100–102.

Monson, D. L. (Ed.) (1985) "Adventuring with Books: A Booklist for Pre-K–Grade 6." (ERIC Document Reproduction Service No. ED 264 588.)

Washington, H., and Davis, R. (1981). "Social Studies in Oregon Schools: A Guide to Developing a Comprehensive Program for Grades Kindergarten Through Twelve." (ERIC Document Reproduction Service No. ED 204 236.)

World Order Values Bibliography. Books and audio-visual materials for children and youth, selected and annotated. (1984). (ERIC Document Reproduction Service No. ED 266 992.)

Films

America's Heroes; George Washington. Coronet
America's National Anthem. Learning Corp. of America
Beginning Responsibility—Taking Care of Things. Coronet
Boyhood of Abraham Lincoln. Coronet
Boyhood of George Washington Carver. Coronet
Calendar: The Days, Weeks, Months. Coronet
Communication: A First Film. Bailey Films
Family of the Island, Her Name Is Wasametha. McGraw-Hill
Home Free. Bailey Films
Making Change for a Dollar. Coronet
Maps Are Fun. Coronet
Maps and Their Uses. ACA
Moving Goods in the Community. Coronet
Our Country's Flag. Coronet
Rock in the Road. A-F-A
Story of Our Money System. Coronet
The Fight. Walt Disney Productions
There's Nobody Else Like You. Film Fair/Film West
Turn Off the Pollution. Encyclopedia Britannica Films
What Is a Friend? McGraw-Hill
What Mary Jo Shared. Bailey Films
What Time Is It? 2nd Ed. Coronet
Why We Have Taxes. Learning Corp. of America
Why We Need Each Other. Learning Corp. of America
Why We Use Money. Learning Corp. of America

Filmstrips

Basic Concepts in Economics. BFA Educational Media
Can You Make Change? Goodman
Careers with a Police Department. Colonial
Citizenship Adventures of the Lollipop Dragon. SVE
Community Services: Many People Serve Our Community. National Geographic
Exploring Maps: Map Skills for Today. Xerox
Getting Along. Scholastic
Globes. January Productions

Indians for Thanksgiving. SVE
Lincoln and Washington: Why We Celebrate Their Birthdays. SVE
Living in Cities. Teaching Resources
Making and Keeping Friends. SVE
Maps and Globes and Graphs. Eye Gate Media
Money and Time Adventure of the Lollipop Dragon. SVE
People Serving Your Community. National Geographic
Personal Success. SVE
Squanto and the First Thanksgiving. SVE
Targo the Job Explorer. SVE
The Tree That Became a Chair. Filmstrip Production Assoc.
Using Globes. CRM/McGraw-Hill
Using Maps to Find Locations. SVE
Values in Action. Holt
What Do You Do About Rules? Guidance Assoc.
What Is a Community? Learning Tree
What Is Responsibility? EBEC
What's Money For? Clearview
Who Am I? Scholastic
Who Do You Think You Are? Guidance Assoc.

Resources

1. The following associations offer publications, educational materials, services and other resources for teachers:

   National Association for the Education of Young Children
   1834 Connecticut Avenue, N.W.
   Washington, DC 20007

   Association for Childhood Education International
   3615 Wisconsin Avenue, N.W.
   Washington, DC 20016

   Child Study Association of America
   9 East 89th Street
   New York, NY 10010

   Administration for Children, Youth, & Families
   Box 1182
   Washington, DC 20013

2. Instructional resources for teaching multiethnic education and ethnic heritage studies.

   The Council on Interracial Books for Children
   1841 Broadway
   New York, NY 10023

   National Council for the Social Studies
   3501 Newark Street, N.W.
   Washington, DC 20016

Anti-Defamation League of B'nai B'rith
345 East 46th Street
New York, NY 10017

Multi-Cultural Understanding
Riverside Unified School District
3954 12th Street
Riverside, CA 92501

EMI
P.O. Box 4272
Madison, WI 53711

3. Law-related education.

Law Day USA
American Bar Association
750 North Lake Shore Drive, 8th Floor
Chicago, IL 60611

4. Resource for publication list and some free materials on teaching about war and peace.

Center for War/Peace Studies
218 East 18th Street
New York, NY 10003

5. Resource provides teachers with newsletter for methods on how to use the newspaper in the classroom.

American Newspaper Publishers Association Foundation
The Newspaper Center
Box 17407
Dallas International Airport
Washington, DC 20041

6. Energy and environment resources.

Humanics Limited
P. O. Box 7447
Atlanta, GA 30304

a. Energy: curriculum for 3 to 5 years olds
b. Aerospace Projects for Young Children: overview of people's mastery of space, beginning with a look at thee sky

National Association for the Advancement of Humane Education
Box 362
East Haddam, CT 06423

a. *People and Animals:* 400 teacher-tested ideas for explaining the interdependency of life resource for environmental education units

Julia A. Fellows, Editor
Energy and Education, NSTA
1742 Coonecticut Avenue, N.W.
Washington, DC 20009

A monthly newsletter published by NSTA on energy education. Free subscription.

Department of Energy Technical Information Center
P. O. Box 62
Oak Ridge, TN 37830

Catalog: *Selected Dept. of Energy Publications Project for the Energy Enriched Curriculum* (PEEC) K-12 interdisciplinary units and a series of Fact Sheets on energy topics

National clearinghouse for energy information with most free information and colorful posters.

7. Resources of free and inexpensive instructional materials.

Educator's Progress Service
Randolph, WI 53956

Dale E. Schaffer
Library Consultant
437 Jennings Avenue
Salem, OH 44460

Sourcebook for Teaching Aides. $4.95
55 page booklet of 1300 items mostly free to librarians and teachers. Posters, charts, maps, study prints, pictures, and colorful pamphlets.

8. Navajo Curriculum Center
Rough Rock Demonstration School
Star Route 1
Rough Rock, AZ 86503

Audio Visual Reference Guide
Journals and Periodicals for Teacher Reference and Classroom Use

11
Sand and Water Play

There is something natural and basic about playing in sand and water—having a tea party in the sun, watching a boat floating, or just engaging in pouring and sorting activities. The motivation is built-in and the fun is there. Younger children might simply enjoy the sensory experiences provided by sand and water, others may learn about letters by drawing in the sand, and still others can learn how cities are built by construction in the sand. As children work with sand and water, there are many possibilities for mathematics in measuring and filling, for language and communication in their play, and for science in experiments with the qualities of sand and water.

Lay-Dopyera and Dopyera (1982) state that materials such as sand and water offer rich learning possibilities for children. These materials take on whatever form and meaning a child imposes upon them and replicate something very specific in the real world. Activity becomes increasingly detailed and elaborate as the child matures and becomes more experienced with the possibilities inherent in the material. When children construct a highway with a sand tunnel or create a rainstorm at the water table, they symbolize these objects and events in their thinking. Their activity may lead them to new discoveries. "For example, as the sand caves in on cars in the highway tunnel, they may begin to wonder what keeps the ground from falling on cars in real tunnels" (La-Dopyera & Dopyera, 1982, p. 219). Lay-Dopyera and Dopyera stress that as the incompleteness of children's knowledge becomes apparent, their curiosity will lead them into more precise observations and further experimentation.

Lay-Dopyera and Dopyera (1982) also note that large muscle activities are predominant in outdoor sand play. Children constantly transporting sand develop strength, balance, and endurance. Children gradually increase their ability to perform these actions with ease and agility. In addition to large muscle development, children also engage in activities that foster small muscle development during sand and water play. Furthermore, a child is able to reduce tension as he or she becomes involved in various sand and water activities.

Lindberg and Swedlow (1980) maintain that children can become engrossed as they play with sand. Children can hold sand in their hands and feel the mass of it get smaller and smaller as it sifts between their fingers. In damp sand they can leave footprints, handprints, or the print of their whole body. Sand can be transferred

520

from containers of many shapes and sizes by pouring, spooning, dumping, or sifting.

Lindberg and Swedlow (1980) stress that children learn many concepts because of the versatility of sand. They learn mathematical concepts as they compare shapes they make with wet sand, discover that wet sand is heavier than dry sand, and use measuring cups to measure amounts of sand. Children engage in scientific processes as they find ways of controlling sand in order to build tunnels, bridges, or roads. In addition, children have experience in communication as they talk with other children about what they are doing.

According to Lindberg and Swedlow (1980), children can also become engrossed in water play. Children can engage in either solitary or group play with water. There is no feeling of failure during water play because water can be used over and over again. If children enjoy what they are doing, they can repeat their actions. If not, they can stop and do something else with the same water.

Children can make many scientific discoveries during water play. For example, some things float on water, while other things sink. When pushed, water generates force. Water takes the shape of its container. It can change from liquid to vapor and become ice or snow. When things are mixed with water, their properties may change. For example, salt forms a solution and dirt forms a mixture.

Playing with water in its various forms commands children's attention. The discovery that some objects float is remarkable to them. At first children test one object after another, yet eventually they observe that some objects always fall to the bottom, while others always remain on top. When detergent is added to water, a child can fill the air with bubbles by blowing through a straw. Ice and snow are particularly exciting to children. Children can catch snowflakes on their tongues, and if there is enough snow, they can build snow figures.

Sand and water play presents various learning possibilities for children. Through this play, they can gain scientific and mathematical knowledge, as well as develop language and communication skills. No matter what the activity, sand and water play results in fun and exciting experiences for children as they learn, develop, and mature.

Environmental Resources

Sand and water table and/or a large galvanized (or plastic) tub
Sheets of plastic, an old shower curtain, or an absorbent rug to place under the tub
Scales (balance)
Plastic aprons for the children
A hose and/or pitchers to fill the tub (the teacher can mark the water line with a magic marker so children can fill the tub to the best level)
Sponges and a pail, a mop for cleanup
Storage space for materials

Materials

Permanent

Plastic containers and lids (all sizes and shapes)
Plastic dishes (cups, bowls, mugs, beakers)
Measuring spoons and measuring containers (cup, pint, quart, gallon, liter)
Weights (ounces, grams)
Bubble pipes, eggbeaters, and other mixers (whisks, spoons)

Meat basters
Corks, sponges
Plastic eyedroppers
Funnels of different sizes
Sieves of all shapes and sizes, sprinkler tops on bottles
Brushes of several sizes
Flexible plastic tubing (of several diameters)
Several lengths of pipe and hose
Rolling pin, shells, stones
Wheelbarrow, trowels, spoons, shovels, buckets, sticks, rakes, ladles, dump trucks, sand combs

Expendable

Straws
Cakes of soap, soap flakes, liquid soap
Food coloring
Tempera paint
Small sponges
Pieces of wood
Styrofoam, cork
Chart paper, markers
Box of objects for sinking and floating (sponge, nail, rubber eraser, pencil, leaf, nickel, paper clip, rock, cork, crayon, twig, acorn, peanut, rubberband, wooden bead, lengths of sticks, spools, odd pieces of wood, scissors)

Teacher-Made Materials

1. Tin cans with varying numbers of holes punched into the middle of the closed ends with a large nail. These can be used for both sand and water play.

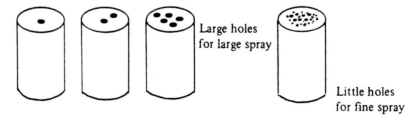

Large holes
for large spray

Little holes
for fine spray

2. Pie tins with holes punched into the bottom can be used for both sand and water play.

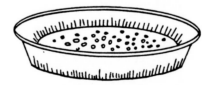

3. Cans with holes punched into the sides can be used for both sand and water play.

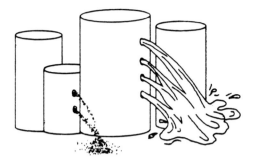

4. Large-sized detergent bottles (plastic) that are cut across the middle can be used for funnels in sand and water play.

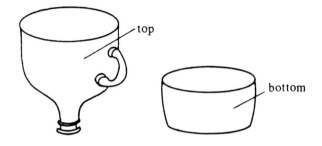

5. Balance for weighing sand and water.

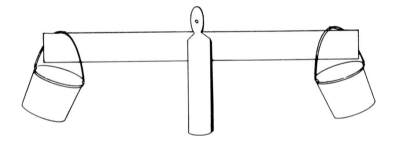

6. A cloth doll that gives children experience in pouring. The doll is made of strong cloth, and sand is poured into her with a large tablespoon or wooden spoon. Drawstrings are are at the top of her head for closing.

7. Shakers made from Awake orange juice cans (because they have rubber tops) are filled to various levels with sand (both fine sand and gravel sand). These could also be used as shakers in music.

8. Shakers made from plastic medicine bottles are filled with sand and a round stick is nailed to the lid of the jar for a handle. Can be used as a rhythm instrument.

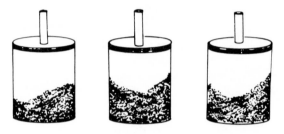

9. Materials for water and sand play.

Indoor play

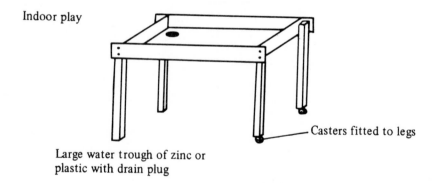

Casters fitted to legs

Large water trough of zinc or plastic with drain plug

Wood sand tray made of a 6″ × 1″ softwood frame and hardboard base strengthened with battens. Stood on chairs for play. Sand may be stored in tin cracker box.

Dishpan and towel on low table or box

Another crude type of sand-box might be cinder blocks just put together to keep sand in an area. Children could sit on the blocks.

Wood-frame sandpit with metal strips across corners. Allow 6" space for foot room from top to level of sand.

Tub of water on two crates

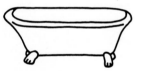

An old bathtub would be ideal for water play.

Objectives

1. To play creatively in the sand or water alone or with others.
2. To use the sand, water, and available materials to seek answers to open-ended questions.
3. To discover equivalences through the use of water and other materials.
4. To use large muscles while digging, hauling, and building with sand.
5. To classify materials that will and will not float; that are absorbent and non-absorbent.
6. To develop writing skills by labeling bottles filled with sand or water and calling them cola, milk, juice, etc.

Suggested Activities

1. *Experiment with Food Color and Water.* Mix colors with water to discover how all colors are made from the primary colors (red, yellow, and blue).

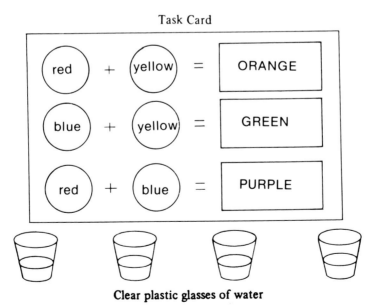

Task Card

Clear plastic glasses of water

2. *Boat Races.* Divide a pan into racing lanes. Children blow boats with straws. Number boats for a math experience; make a chart to record wins and losses.
3. *Creative Water Painting.* Use brushes, sponges, or other materials to make wet imprints on the chalkboard.

4. *Task Cards.* Use teacher-made work cards or directions to suggest methods to help the child to discover the effects of weight on floatation.

Can floating in water

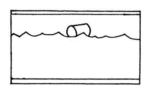

Task Card

1. Put 🌰 in the 🛢

2. What happens?

Task Card

1. Put little ⛵ in 〜〜
2. Put 🌰 on ⛵
3. How many 🌰 make the little ⛵ sink?

Task Card

1. Put big ⛵ in 〜〜.
2. Put 🌰 on ⛵
3. How many 🌰 make the big ⛵ sink?

5. ***Therapy.*** Use sand or water play as a therapeutic technique (playing for the sake of play and for relaxation and release of tensions).

6. ***Water Play Related to Other Centers.*** Other activities that involve water play are cleaning, washing dishes and/or clothes, and imaginary cooking.

7. ***Floating and Sinking Experiment.*** Have a collection of objects that sink and float. (See list under "Materials.") Provide two shoe boxes labeled "Things that sink" and "Things that float." See Table on pages 530–532.

Topic: Sink/Float

Day	Objective	Group Time	Water Center	Other Centers	Research	Writing
1, 2	To observe objects that sink and float.	Discuss the meaning of "sink" and "float" as related to water. Talk about things that sink and float. Introduce activities in centers. Discuss gravity.	Have a tub of clear water in center. Place various objects in the center to experiment with sinking and floating; then classify. Containers for classifying are coded by color and symbol and are in the center. Plastic trash bags are in the center for use as smocks to cover clothing. Background of the center (or bulletin board) demonstrates, pictorially, the concepts of sink and float.	Art—Draw an object floating or sinking and label. Sink and Float float sink	Look up *sink* and *float* in reference to water. Read books about things that float and discuss with the class.	Write a language experience story to go with art center picture, or a story about a mysterious object that sank or floated.
3, 4	Children guess which objects sink and float, test their guesses, and record results.	Discuss what was learned about sinking and floating and the idea of guessing and testing. Introduce the chart to be filled in on an individual small-group basis. (The chart could be written on the contract as part of an individual assignment.)	Same setup as before, including tub of water, but only objects to be tested are placed in the center. A wipe-off chart is hanging nearby. Individual containers for water could be included in lieu of the tub. Chart is as follows: Guess / Test — sink float sink float Sponge / Marble / Ball of foil / Penny Real examples of each object are glued to the chart to aid in matching.	Math—Discuss weight and how it may affect the ability to sink or float. Social Studies—Look at a life preserver and talk about how it works. Guest speaker: A lifeguard; or a scuba diver discusses sinking and floating under water.	Look up and write about what you learn about why some objects float and others sink.	Write a story about a sunken boat or sunken treasure.

5, 6	1) Test *wet* and *dry*. Observe how equilibrium is achieved when a wet object is placed in water. Observe effects of wetness and dryness on floatation. 2) Reinforce previously learned concepts about sinking and floating.	Be sure the children understand the assignment. Discuss how wetness and dryness might affect ability to float. Reiterate previously learned information in relation to sink/float. Discuss outcomes of previous testing. Discuss new centers activities and how to use the chart.	Individual tubs of water and specific objects (both wet and dry examples of each object) are in the center. A wipe-off chart (see the one below) is hanging nearby. Child tests objects in wet and dry states and checks off the chart. Additional activities could involve wetting objects with a substance other than water and testing whether that made a difference. Investigate DRY / WET — Sink, Float, Sink, Float Sponge, Paper towel, Stick of Wood, Piece of towel, Cotton ball, Kleenex	Art—Paint the sidewalk with water. Block—Try floating various sizes of blocks. Sand—Feel wet and dry sand.	Find out about substances, such as oil, that float on water as well as those that sink. Look up gravity, find out how it affects sinking and floating.	Tell a story about floating on a raft down the river. Write about floating in outer space and what it might feel like.
7, 8	1) Observe how salt and sugar change the properties of water in respect to taste and floatation.	Discuss salt and its effect on water. Discuss what happens to salt and sugar when they are placed in water.		Make a clay-salt water animal. Music—Listen to recordings of ocean waves, whale sounds, etc. Movement—Pretend to be swimming in the ocean.	Find out about plants and animals that live in salt water. Look up the Dead Sea and find out how salt affects life under water. Find out where salt and sugar come from.	Make up a story about how the sea became salty. Make a list of what salt does. Write about the difference in the taste of sugar and salt.

Topic: Sink/Float

Day	Objective	Group Time	Water Center	Other Centers	Research	Writing
7, 8	2) Reinforce learning with music, and movement activities.	Introduce activities for centers.	Small containers, paper cups, and a large pan of water are provided along with salt and sugar. Children can add salt, in various amounts, to a container of water. Objects can be placed in the water to see if salt changes their ability to sink or float. Children may do the same for sugar. Children may taste-test samples of salt water and sugar water.	Books—Read about ocean life. Water play—Watch colors mix under water through clear container.	Find out about, and make a list of, things that taste sugary and salty.	
9, 10	Using materials in the center, build a boat that floats.	Discuss materials that sink and float. Discuss boats and their uses and special designs. Introduce activities for centers.	A large container of water is provided, along with plenty of tinfoil, clay, or styrofoam for constructing boats. Children may test materials and determine how to form their boat. After making and testing the boat, the child may put it on display in the center.	Art—Paint a picture of a boat on water. Dress-up—Act out a play you have written about a boating adventure. Books—Read a story about a boat. Math—Measure and record the length, width, and weight of your boat. Social Studies—Look at maps and find out where boats go.	Find out about boat construction and design. Look up different types of boats and write about your favorite. Draw a picture of that boat (sailboat, houseboat, tugboat, steamboat, motorboat, aircraft carrier, submarine, canoe, etc.).	

8. *Vocabulary and Concept Development.* Encourage the children to describe what they are doing and to answer questions about how and why they are doing it.

9. *Water Experiments.* Undertake experiments dealing with (a) how water affects different materials (Kleenex, beans, sugar, clothes) and how and why different materials absorb water and (b) the rate of water flow through various tubes and funnels.

10. *Digging Activities.* Use the sand table or outdoor digging area with spoons, cups, trowels, sticks, and shovels to dig for enjoyment, to experiment with floating and damming, to build canals, and so on.

11. *Map Study.* Use sand (in sand table) for simple map study. Streets, houses, and stores can be constructed and placed on the sand or can be drawn with the child's finger.

12. *"Cooking."* Use sand and water for an imaginary "cooking" experience. A recipe and directions might be placed over the tub to suggest this. This activity is a good follow-up to role playing in the home-living center.

13. *Letters in the Sand.* Use a tactile approach to learning letters, numbers, and shapes by having the children write in the sand or mix sand and water to form letters and numbers.

14. *Exploring Scientific Properties.* Explore the various textures of dirt, temperature of water, and science of waves.

15. *Health.* In conjunction with home living, let the children give the dolls a bath or wash their clothes. This is a good way to teach them about health practices.
16. *Outdoor Digging.* Have an unconstructed digging pile as a part of the outdoor play area.
17. *Comparing Weight.* Children can use a balance scale to discover differences in the weight of wet and dry sand.
18. *Comparing Quantity and Capacity* Discuss how liquids and solids (drinks, medicine, flour, sugar) are measured in everyday situations to introduce measuring experiments. Use transparent measuring containers so children can easily see differences in quantity and capacity.
    a. *Comparing Quantity.* Use two different size containers (e.g., pint and quart) for discovering relative differences in units of measure. Children can chart how many spoonfuls or cups of water or sand each container holds in order to determine which holds more or less.
    b. *Comparing Capacity.* Provide containers that are different shapes but hold the same amount to compare capacity.
19. *Measuring Water for Eating or Drinking.* Children can measure water to make Jello, lemonade, popsicles, and ice cubes.

20. *Dictating or Writing Stories.* Write about experiences playing in the sand (e.g., "How I Made Muffins," "The Sand Village," "If I Were a Sand Castle I Would . . .").

21. *Aquarium.* Make an aquarium with sand on the bottom. Plant water plants in the sand.

22. *Planting and Watering Activities.* Develop planting and watering task cards and perform tasks over a period of a few days.
    1. Put soil in a cup.
    2. Plant a seed in the soil.
    3. Put water on the seed.
    4. Look at the cup every day.
    5. Make pictures of what you see.

    1. Plant two seeds in two paper cups.
    2. Put water in one cup.
    3. Do not put water in the other cup.
    4. Which seeds grow?

    1. Water one plant.
    2. Do not water another plant.
    3. What happened?
    4. Then water both plants.
    5. What happens?

23. *Water Glass Chimes.* Fill glasses of the same size with different amounts of water. Strike rims of glasses lightly with various instruments.

24. *Observation of Water Conduction.* Color a glass of water. Place a stalk of celery in it. Have children observe how the colored water rises up through the celery.

25. *Plastic Toys.* Children can play with plastic ducks, dolphins, and fish in the water.

26. *Listening Experience.* Boil water in a kettle, and let the children listen to the boiling water and the whistle.

27. *Ripples.* Throw stones and rocks in water at a local lake to see the ripple effect. Perhaps some children can make a stone skim the water.

28. *Weather Activities.* Experiments with rain, snow, and ice can be part of a unit on weather. On two rainy days, children can collect rainwater in a pan, pour it in clear measuring cups, and compare how much rain fell each day. After a winter storm, children can melt snow and ice.

29. *Explore Occupations and Services Related to Water.* Discuss what a plumber does. Visit the basement of the school to see the water pipes. Take a field trip to the city water works facility to see how water is processed and how it gets to homes and buildings.

30. *Sand and Water Play—Art-Related Activities*
    Make boats for water play.
       a. Spool boats

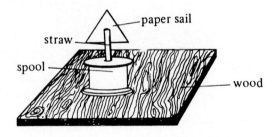

       b. Scrap lumber boats
       c. Newspaper boats
       d. Leaf boats
       e. Jar lid boats

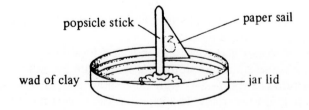

       f. Cork boats

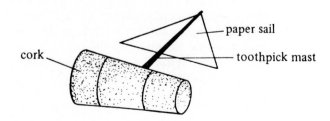

g. Walnut boats

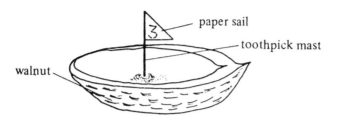

Sand painting. Add 1 part paint powder to 4 parts sand and combine in large shakers. Children shake on paper they have covered with paste.

Elmer's Glue sand painting. Design a picture on a colored piece of construction paper with Elmer's Glue. Scatter sand on top, then brush off. Sand remains where glue was.

Sandpaper projects. Make sandpaper numbers and number charts, letters, and pictures.

Painting with water colors. Children learn that depending on how much water they use, their color will get darker or lighter.

Sand candles. Make a roundish indentation in the sand. Fill with melted (colored) wax and put in a wick. Let dry, then remove from sand and brush off.

Cutouts. Cut out pictures of water in its various forms from magazines.

References

Lay-Dopyera, M., and Dopyera, J. E. (1982). *Becoming a Teacher of Young Children* (2nd ed.). Lexington, Mass.: D.C. Heath and Company.

Lindberg, L., and Swedlow, R. (1980). *Early Childhood Education: A Guide for Observation and Participation* (2nd ed.). Boston: Allyn and Bacon, Inc.

12

Woodworking

The woodworking center has been accepted for the most part in good schools for young children (Rudolph & Cohen, 1984). The National Association for the Education of Young Children adopted 22 goals for children's learning as guidelines for woodworking in early childhood programs (Skeen, Garner, & Cartwright, 1984). Decker and Decker (1984) stated that woodworking centers are popular with children. Rudolph and Cohen (1984), in monitoring children's reaction to the center, found much interest and lasting satisfaction from the time spent there. Most children have watched a grown up use tools at some time or other and long for a chance to use them, too (Adams, 1967).

In addition to children's enthusiasm for woodworking activities, child development theory and research support the developmental appropriateness and value of woodworking. Piaget emphasized that young children learn and develop by interacting with their environment. They touch, pour, taste, or in woodworking activities, hammer, saw, and drill objects in order to learn about them. They obtain important information on the basis of interaction with tangible materials (Leeper, Witherspoon, & Day, 1984).

Evans (1975) stated that motivational theory points to children's need to interact with their environment to cause change, not to maintain the status quo, and that "a variety of stimuli presented across varying sensory modalities will have the effect of maintaining optimal arousal" (Evans, 1975, p. 282). According to Rudolph and Cohen (1984), children "derive sensory pleasure from handling wood and learning the mechanics of fitting, fastening, connecting, and cutting" (Rudolph & Cohen, 1984, p. 161). They enjoy hands-on experience with the physical attributes of the materials employed (roughness, softness, sharpness). As Leeper et al. (1984) have emphasized, in order to ensure children's development, the teacher and the school need to offer many avenues of manipulation that children might not otherwise experience. Woodworking is one such avenue.

Woodworking and carpentry activities incorporate skills from traditional school subjects, such as language arts, math, and science, and provide children with opportunities for cognitive, psychomotor, and affective development. As children compare sizes and shapes, note different textures, and decide which materials and tools to use, they are learning to experiment and solve problems. Measuring, counting, and sorting lead to practical understanding of mathematics. Children learn new vocabulary as they name each tool and woodworking action (Davis, 1980). They develop expressive skills and vocabulary as they describe what they see, hear, do, and feel in woodworking. Manipulating tools promotes the development of large and small muscles. Hammering and sawing provide emotional release. In addition, woodworking fosters creative expression, respect for property, and appreciation for the child's efforts and those of others.

Piaget stated that children may gain as much from their errors as from completed tasks (Evans, 1975). "As children grow they acquire more complex and sophisticated means of interacting with their environment" (Homan, Banet, & Weikart, 1979). "There is a progression from simple one-step activities to more complex ones" (Pitcher et al., 1984). Adams and Taylor (1982) differentiate children's stages of development according to how they grow in woodworking proficiency. "Therefore, by making available activities designed to meet the developmental characteristics found in the specific stages, the needs and interests of each child can be more appropriately met and challenged," (Adams & Taylor, 1982).

In spite of the many developmental benefits of woodworking activities, they are often excluded from the curriculum, or if they are included, they are underutilized by teachers. "Woodworking is one of the first activities to be eliminated from kindergarten programs" (Davis, 1981). Adams and Taylor (1982) cite many instances of carpentry materials put aside or left in a corner.

Why does this part of the curriculum tend to be ignored? Anderson and Hoot (1986) suggest that the noise is objectionable, that the dust and shavings create a mess, and that there are unnecessary safety dangers. Rudolph and Cohen (1984) state that "women kindergarten teachers rarely feel secure and knowledgeable about supervising woodworking." Women comprise 93.7 percent of all children's teachers (Anderson & Hoot, 1986). This may be one reason woodworking centers are excluded. Another factor may be the cost and availability of woodworking materials, tools, and equipment.

Teachers can overcome obstacles to implementing woodworking centers in many ways. To build confidence, they might invite a carpenter or carpentry instructor to visit the classroom and teach them and the children basic woodworking operations and safety techniques. According to Anderson and Hoot (1986), "It is imperative that the teacher feel comfortable using the tools so that the sense of power over the medium is transferred to the students." To obtain resources for a woodworking center, teachers can solicit donations of scraps, tools, and equipment from parents and local businesses. To ensure safety, teachers can carefully supervise and establish clear rules and procedures for woodworking activities.

An important consideration for teachers operating woodworking centers is avoiding sex-role stereotypes and biases (Anderson & Hoot, 1986). Sometimes females play in home living centers while males are encouraged to engage in woodworking activities. Teachers should encourage both to participate in woodworking activities, and should provide the support and assistance needed to make woodworking a successful experience for both sexes.

Pitcher, Feinburg, and Alexander (1984) state that "the teacher sets the stage for inventiveness and safety." Day and Drake (1983) urge teachers to set clear expectations in the early childhood classrooms. The establishment of specific rules sets the "appropriate atmosphere for learning." Adams and Taylor (1982) have established these four rules for the carpentry center:

All equipment and tools have a home. When something is taken out of its home, it needs to be returned to its home.

Each tool has a particular use and is limited to that use only.

No one should hold equipment or a tool for anyone else. Use a tool instead of a person.

If a tool doesn't work or if you need help, ask the teacher or another adult for assistance.

Another set of rules by Adams (1967), in *Creative Woodworking in the Kindergarten,* also establishes guidelines for using woodworking tools:

Hands off cutting edges.

Both hands on the saw handle.

Always have the piece of wood to be cut held firmly against the table with a vise or a clamp, or even two.

The teacher or other resource person should check the tightness of vises or clamps.

Allen and Hart (1984) emphasize that woodworking is a teacher-structured activity which must be supervised at all times. Good monitoring involves listening to and observing children while they are building, in order to gain insights into behavior and growth (Leeper et al., 1984). With appropriate structure, direction, and monitoring, children can learn basic woodworking skills that will be useful throughout their lives.

Environmental Resources

Essential

Center area, free from distractions, away from flow of traffic, in a side room, yet not isolated from supervision and access to other areas for dramatic play (Skeen et al., 1984).

Storage for tools on a wall rack or pegboard.

A workbench or table set out from the wall so that children will not have to reach over the work table to get tools.

Color coding on the floor or carpet to indicate the proper places for equipment and supplies within the woodworking area.

Color coding on the tool rack and/or pegboard to indicate which tools go where. Outlines of tools and clean-up equipment can also be color coded (Skeen et al., 1984; Day & Drake, 1983).

Sturdy workbench or table with
Height proportionate to size of child (approximately waist high).
Top that allows for carrying out basic operations without fear of damage.
Space sufficient to allow movement.

Storage space (a tool cabinet with pegs, shelves, drawers, and containers for other materials).

Important

Sawing bench (may be placed in an outdoor woodworking area).

Nailing block: (30″ × 10″ × 6″) with carpet squares underneath to cut down on noise. This can be moved outdoors (Skeen et al., 1984).

Recommended

Rollers on workbench or table to allow for movement inside and outside.

Rollers with locks on them so table/bench stays still.

Shop vacuum for quick pick ups.

First aid kit for splinters and cuts.

Sink, wash-up area.

Equipment

Essential

Hammer: 7 to 10 oz claw with wooden handle

Screwdrivers: assorted sizes of both slot (standard) and Phillips

"C" clamps; 4″-6″ in length

Nails: variety of penny and heads

Screws: assorted sizes and types

Ruler, measuring tape, and yardstick (that includes metric measurements) (Rudolph & Cohen, 1984)

Keyhole or compass saw that is light and easy for young children to handle (Skeen et al., 1984)

Rasp: a good, safe tool for children to handle (Rudolph & Cohen, 1984)

Hand saws: crosscut and coping

File: cabinet, half-round 8″

Brace and bit
Hand drill and bits or push drill and points

Important

Vise for workbench
Pliers: combination, 6″
Sawhorse
Sure forms: are handled like rasps and files, but cut smoothly and easily (Skeen
    et al., 1984)

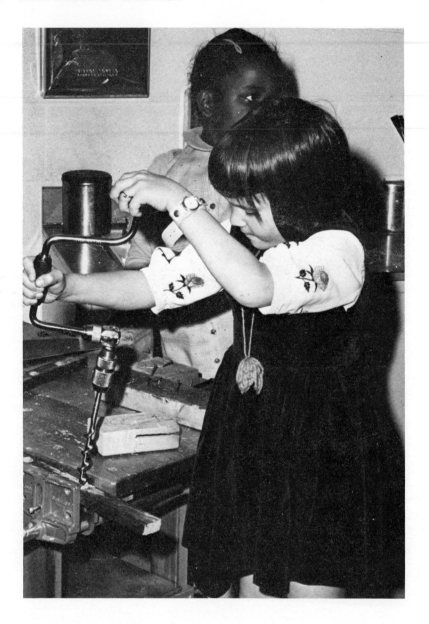

File card for cleaning file
Monkey wrench
Wire cutter
T-square
Awl

Recommended

Planes: block and smoothing
File
Miter box
Paint scraper

Materials

"Large" wood supply—many varied shapes and sizes
  Soft pine or spruce
  White pine rather than yellow pine, grown in U.S. (eastern, western, and sugar
    white pine)
  Spruce (white, black, red, Sitka, and Engelman, grown in U.S.) (Skeen et al.,
    1984)
  Some finished and unfinished wood
  Molding and doweling
  Plywood
"Small" wood supply
  Toothpicks
  Popsicle sticks
  Tongue depressors
  Paint stirrers
  Small branches and sticks

End grain scraps
Box of assorted scrap wood
Cardboard
Tri-wall
Large posterboard boxes

Wood Supply Sources

Local lumber companies
Local hardware stores
Local paint stores
Local cabinet shops
Construction sites
High school industrial arts classes
Parents of students and friends

Supplies

Pencils, scissors, string, wallpaper scraps, tacks, tapes, leather, wire, chicken wire, paper clips, glue
Small wheels, styrofoam, bottle caps, pop-tops from cans
Formica, tile, linoleum
Sandpaper, paint, shellac, brushes
Hinges, knobs, nuts, bolts, hooks
Pulleys, rope
Broom, dustpan, rags
Safety glasses
Work gloves
Magnet
Paint shirts
Band-aids
Mild bath soap

Objectives

1. To use wood as a medium of expression.
2. To discover relationships of equality, inequality, and proportionate comparisons while building and constructing with wood and other materials.
3. To communicate, plan, and work cooperatively with others to solve common problems.
4. To use woodworking as an emotional release and/or as a means of nonverbal expression.
5. To develop fine muscles by working with hammer and nails, and large muscles by working with saw, lifting, and so on.
6. To improve eye-hand coordination by manipulating tools.
7. To experience a legitimate way of making noise.
8. To refine sensory awareness.

Seven Basic Woodworking Operations

1. *Sanding.* The sanding operation underlies almost all woodworking activities. Its purpose is to smooth and shape wood. Mounting sandpaper on wood blocks

makes this operation much easier for children to master and reduces waste of sandpaper supplies.

Steps to Follow

Fold a section of sandpaper to accommodate the approximate area of the wood block.

Bend the sandpaper along the fold several times.

Tear the sandpaper along the straight edge of a table or workbench.

Use a staple gun or glue to secure the sandpaper. Do not allow children to manipulate a staple gun. It is a tool that requires strength and precision to use properly. Its potential danger is great.

Sanding is accomplished with long, even strokes away from the body. Sand with the grain of the wood. If the piece of wood to be sanded is small, students may wish to hold the wood in one hand while using the sanding block with the other. For larger pieces of wood, securing the wood with a "C" clamp or vise will make the sanding operation easier. Allow children to discover the difference varying grades of sandpaper make in the smoothness obtained.

2. *Gluing.* The second woodworking operation is, generally, not difficult for children to master since they have had previous experience with glue. However, make sure that the glue used with wood is suited to that purpose. Popsicle sticks are handy for spreading glue evenly on the two or more areas of wood to be glued together. Putting small amounts of glue in recycled plastic food containers cuts down on waste.

Steps to Follow

Spread glue on surfaces.

Wait for the glue to get tacky. Provide a related activity for children during the waiting time.

Apply a very thin second coat of glue.

Hold or clamp wood together until the product can be put aside to set.

3. *Hammering or Nailing.* This basic woodworking operation is for fastening material together.

Steps to Follow

Use an awl or a nail with a large head to make a pilot hole. The pilot hole anchors the nail and makes it easier for the child to hammer the nail in straight.

Insert the nail in the pilot hole.

Hold the hammer near the end of the handle. While holding the nail with the thumb and forefinger of the other hand, tap the nail lightly with the hammer until it stands by itself.

Remove fingers from the nail and hit harder until the nail is in place.

If the wood splits during the operation, the reason(s) may be that the nail is too near the edge of the wood, the nail shaft is too thick, or there are too many holes in the same grain of wood. The nail is likely to bend if it is too long and thin. Having the work too high may cause the child to hit the nail on an angle. This, in turn, may also cause the nail to bend. A safety precaution for this operation and others is wearing safety glasses. Protective lenses help to prevent getting wood or metal particles into the eyes, and most children find them fun to wear.

4. *Holding.* Vises and "C" clamps hold the wood securely to the work surface during sanding, sawing, drilling, and some fastening operations. For most efficient use of a vise, have it permanently attached to the workbench or table. Placing a piece of heavy cardboard or thin wood between the holding device and the finished product will prevent marring.

5. *Drilling.* The drilling operation has two distinct purposes. The first is to drill holes through wood, and the second is to make pilot holes in which to insert screws. There are many types of drills and bit sizes. One used very frequently with children is a hand drill with a ¼″ chuck that works like an egg-beater. Bits ranging in size from ⅛″ to ¼″ are available to use in this type drill. The push drill is easy for young children to use for making holes ¼″ and smaller. The bits for this type of drill are commonly called "points." A brace and bit is used for holes larger than ¼″. For young children, the appropriate drill point or bit could be chosen and secured by an adult.

Steps to Follow

Secure the wood to the work surface.
Make an initial pilot hole for the drill with the awl.
Use the appropriate drill and bit for the intended purpose.

6. *Fastening with Screws.* The initial step in this operation is choosing the appropriate type screwdriver—slot or Phillips. The size of the screwdriver should be equal to the size of the screwhead. Select the necessary bit or point for the predrilling according to the screw's shank size.

Steps to Follow

Select a screwdriver and bit.

Insert the bit into the drill. Test to make sure that it is secure.

Punch an initial pilot hole with an awl.

Predrill a hole for the screw.

Insert the screw and turn it with the selected screwdriver (clockwise for inserting, counterclockwise to remove).

"Screwdrivers are dangerous. They are best used only by children with advanced skill and coordination. . . . A worn screwdriver tip should be reground or replaced. Applying soap to screw makes driving it easier" (Skeen et al., 1984).

7. *Sawing.* This operation is the most difficult woodworking operation for the majority of children to master. The basic carpenter's saw, a crosscut, 12–16″ long is used for this operation. A good one will have 11 to 16 points per inch. Look for the number of points per inch on the heel of the saw. Before buying a saw, in addition to looking for the appropriate size and number of points per inch, bend the blade over to test the metal. If the blade does not spring back straight, do not buy it. A coping saw is used to cut gradual curves and interior shapes. Buy extra blades since they tend to break frequently.

Steps to Follow

Mark a saw line with a pencil.

Secure the wood with a vise or clamp to saw on the waste-wood side of the line. Use a wood file to make a groove for the saw blade.

With the saw resting in the groove, begin slow, rhythmic back-and-forth motions. Hold the wood with your free hand.

Increase the speed of the motions as the groove deepens.

Slow your motions near completion to help prevent breaking or splintering the wood.

A work glove on the holding hand protects the child from abrasions if the saw happens to slip out of its groove. Lubricate the saw blade with mild bath soap to keep it working smoothly. Also, be sure to have the blade sharpened occasionally.

In addition to the seven basic woodworking operations, children enjoy painting what they construct. Brannen (1978) suggests using a mixture of easel paint and white glue which covers the wood well and does not rub off easily. Brannen also suggests having a rule that some construction must occur before painting; otherwise some children will only paint.

Introduction to Woodworking

1. *Tools and Wood.* Touching the tools and wood helps young children feel secure. By holding and feeling all the materials, children acquire information about weight, balance, strength, and texture. Children will move the wood from one place to another, shake the work table, take out and replace the tools. When children have learned the motions and behaviors appropriate for the center, they will then move to the next level (Davis & Taylor, 1982).

2. *Demonstration.* Always demonstrate the proper use of tools to children. Go through the actual steps children will be using to duplicate a specific woodworking activity. If sequence is important to the process, help the child to understand the rationale for the progression.

3. *Simple Activity Attempts.* Children will begin to enlarge upon their awareness of carpentry by experimenting with some of its uses and the processes involved. Hammering, sanding, gluing, sawing, and placing pieces of wood securely into the vise and removing them are among the basic skills explored (Davis & Taylor, 1982).

4. *Experimentation.* After children have had an opportunity to produce a directed product in woodworking, allow them to experiment with another similar project. The product may be identical to the one produced earlier or may vary in every way from the original. The product is not the goal. What is important here is giving the child an opportunity for expression.

5. *Recipes.* Chart paper or posterboard may be used to make woodworking recipes. Directions for specific woodworking activities are sequentially numbered and written in concise sentences. Illustrations and varying colors for each step in the sequence help children to follow written directions. See the accompanying "recipes."

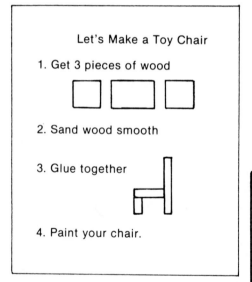

Let's Make a Toy Chair

1. Get 3 pieces of wood

2. Sand wood smooth

3. Glue together

4. Paint your chair.

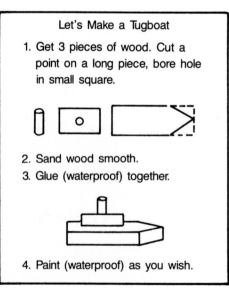

Let's Make a Tugboat

1. Get 3 pieces of wood. Cut a point on a long piece, bore hole in small square.

2. Sand wood smooth.

3. Glue (waterproof) together.

4. Paint (waterproof) as you wish.

Let's Make a Napkin Holder

1. Get 3 pieces of wood

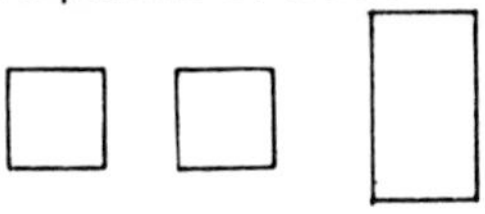

2. Sand wood smooth

3. Glue sides to bottom

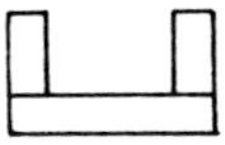

4. Paint, if you wish.

Let's Make An Airplane

1. Get 3 pieces of wood like these:

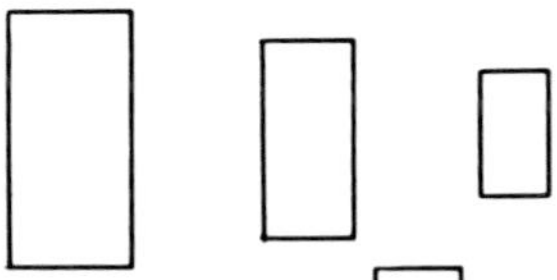

2. Sand wood smooth.

3. Glue front wing on.

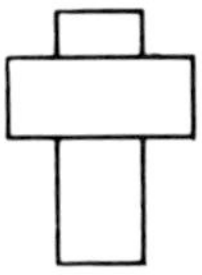

4. Glue back wing on.

5. Paint.

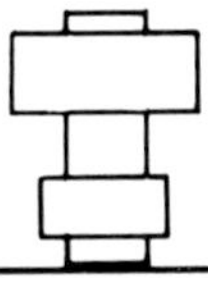

Let's Make a Serving Tray

1. Get 3 pieces of wood.

2. Sand wood smooth.
3. Nail together.

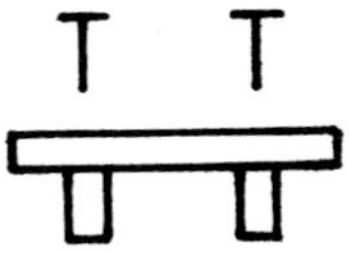

4. Paint as you wish.

6. *Task Cards.* Use posterboard cards with illustrations and written directions for specific woodworking activities. If a precise sequence is necessary, number each card. Otherwise, leave the cards unnumbered and use them to evaluate the child's understanding of the activity. To preserve task cards, laminate or cover with transparent adhesive. Sample tasks cards follow.

Let's
Make A
Key Holder

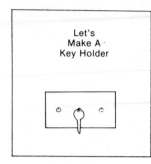

1. Punch wood at
the 3 dots on
the front.

2. Punch wood at
dot on back.

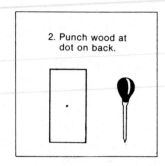

3. Sand the
wood.

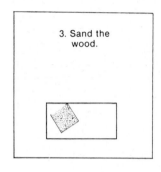

4. Paint wood
with varnish.

5. Let dry
overnight.

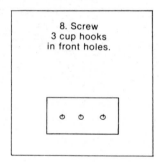

6. Drill the 3
punched holes
on the front.

7. Nail hanger
at back
punched hole.

8. Screw
3 cup hooks
in front holes.

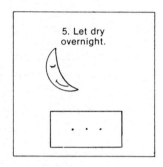

LET'S
MAKE A
BIRDFEEDER

1. Sand a piece of wood like this:

2. Nail 5 bottle caps into each large side of wood.

3. Punch and drill a hole at dot on top of wood.

4. Screw a hook in the top hole.

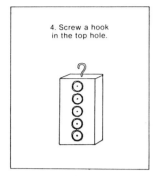

5. Full bottle caps with peanut butter.

6. Press down in birdseed

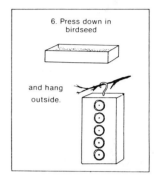

and hang outside.

Let's Make a Stoplight.

1. Bore hole for dowel in bottom piece of wood.

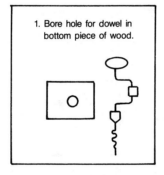

2. Cut dowel to the height you wish.

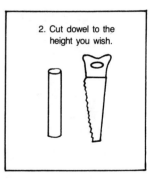

3. Bore hole into bottom of Stoplight piece.

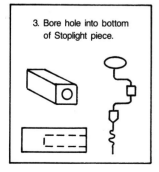

4. Sand all wood.

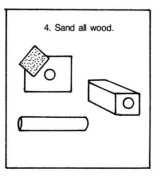

5. Paint wood yellow and/or green.

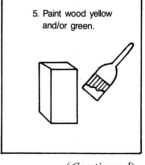

(Continued)

6. Let dry overnight.

7. Tack bottle caps to Stoplight block.

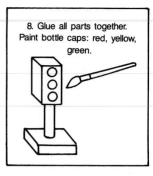

8. Glue all parts together. Paint bottle caps: red, yellow, green.

Suggested Activities

1. *Resource Person.* Invite a local carpenter (preferably a parent or relative of one of your students) to demonstrate proper usage of major tools, the importance of measuring for proper proportions, how to smooth wood with sandpaper, and so on.
2. *Field Trips.* Plan field trips to a construction site, cabinet shop, and/or a lumber yard.
3. *Large Tree Stump.* Add a large tree stump (inside or outside) to this center to use for hammering.
4. *Ideas for Using Cardboard.* Cardboard can be purchased or can be obtained as industrial scrap.

   Stool: Make the base from a large tube, and the top from thin plywood or triwall. Fasten with tape or glue. Small telephone wire spools can also be used to make stools.
   Table: Same as above using several tubes for the base.
   Storage containers: Fasten several tubes together.

5. *Ideas for Using Wood.* Simple objects such as animals and boats can be made by children. Children can build their own creative structures; older children may use simple pictorial directions. The finished product may be painted.

   Trucks and cars. Use assorted sizes of wood blocks for the body of the vehicle. Thumb tacks with red and silver heads serve as lights. Faucet washers, jar lids, or dowels may be used as wheels. All basic woodworking operations are incorporated in this activity.
   Trains. This is similar to the preceding activity with the addition of hooks and catches for connecting train cars.

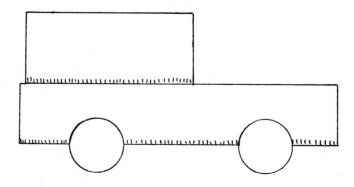

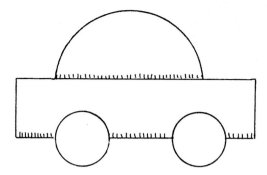

Buildings. With small modifications, the initial structure may be a house, barn, school, or church. Entire minicities may be built.

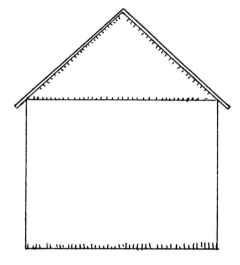

Fences. Wood blocks serve as corner posts and supports with tongue depressors or Popsicle stick rails.

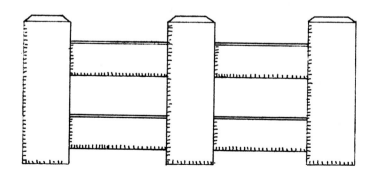

Animal cages. Use tongue depressors and Popsicle sticks. Glue on paper wheels for circus train effect.
Use wood blocks and Popsicle sticks (with or without wheels).

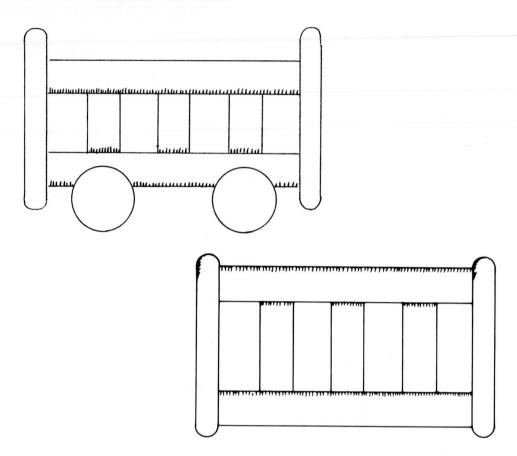

Recipe holders. This may be an all-gluing activity or a combination of any of the fastening operations (gluing, nailing, and/or fastening with screws).

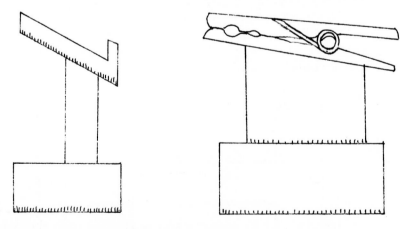

Tomahawks. This is a simple nailing activity.
Puzzles. Use simple shapes with straight edges and/or slight curves.

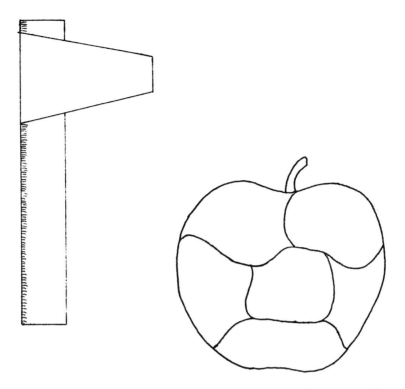

Marvelous monsters. Make these with one or a combination of fastening operations and lots of imagination.

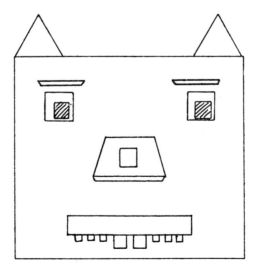

People. Use one or more fastening operations combined with various sizes and shapes of wood. Have newspaper or material scraps available for clothes and other special features.

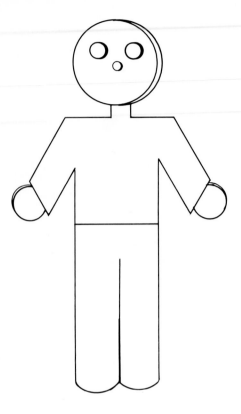

Animals. Imagination makes this an especially creative activity using different sizes and shapes of wood and a combination of fastening operations.

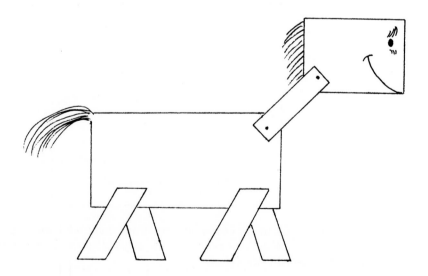

Animal wrap boards. Use yarn or wire to trace outlines of animals on nails.

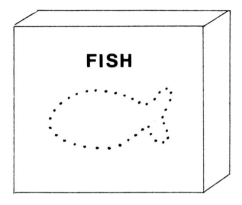

FISH

Rubber band letter boards. Use printed numbers and arrows on boards to help ensure accurate letter formation.

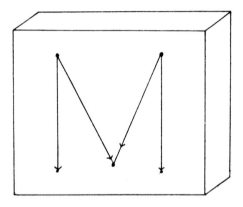

Geoboards. This is a good activity for even very young children who have some hammering experience.

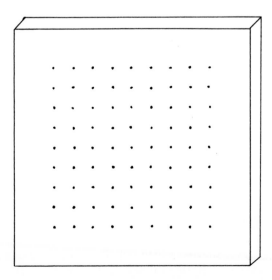

Signs. Let children make traffic signs for use later in the block corner, sand area, or outside.

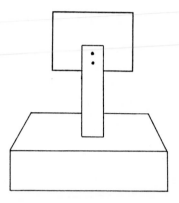

Bird house. This may be a gluing and/or nailing activity. Make sure that glue is waterproof for use outside.

Book holders. Making book holders with fixed ends uses skills in sanding, nailing, and painting. Making bookholders with adjustable ends requires sanding, sawing, drilling, and painting skills.

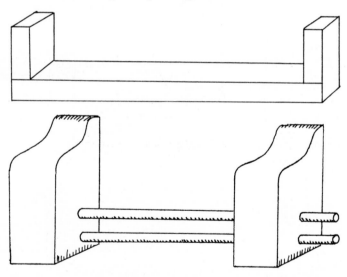

6. *Combined Use of Wood and Cardboard.* Make a mobile with several scraps of decorated wood and cardboard.

Interrelated Center Activities

1. *Language Arts*
    a. Show pictures of construction sites, tool catalogs, tool boxes, and so on to the child. The child is to find and discuss specific woodworking tools in the pictures.
    b. The child draws an object made of wood on a Language Master card. The child tape-records information about the object drawn and listens to his or her own recording and those of other students.

   c. Children match picture cards of tools with word cards of tool names, rhyming words, and scrambled letter cards.

   d. Students look up information about trees, leaves, paper, and so on.

   e. Students write about what they would like to be made into if they were a tree or what they would build from wood if they had their choice of anything in the world.

   f. Read stories such as *The Boy Who Couldn't Get Away from Trees; City Tree, Country Tree; The Playground Tree; The House That Jack Built; The Three Little Pigs; Noah's Ark.*

   g. Children make journals of activities completed. Ask them to share the journals in circle time (Koppelman, 1976).

2. **Games**

   a. Classify pictures and/or objects into correct categories such as tools, toys, clothes, and books.

   b. Cut and paste classification cards of tools, wood products, and people who work with wood from magazines and catalogs.

   c. Make Lotto games with pictures or word cards for children to match.

   d. Design and develop open-ended game boards and information cards in the shape of tools.

   e. Play sorting games for different sizes and/or types of nails or screws.

3. **Blocks.** Build various structures such as houses, schools, trains, and space stations.

4. ***Science and Math***
   a. Children count the annual rings of a tree trunk to determine its approximate age.
   b. Children measure and mark several pieces of wood both in inches and centimeters.
   c. Children add and subtract various marked wood lengths.
   d. Children use scales to weigh different kinds of wood of like size. They chart and compare the different weights.
   e. Students identify ten objects made of wood.
   f. Children make an insect jar by pounding holes in jar lid with hammer and nail (Oklahoma State Dept. of Education, 1983).

5. ***Art***
   a. Make a tree collage. Cut brown and green paper and paste onto a baking sheet.
   b. Paint woodworking projects.
   c. Make seasonal trees. Draw four trees; paint and/or color according to each season.
   d. Make block pictures. Use pictures cut from magazines and decoupage onto wood.
   e. Make leaf prints. Cover leaves with thin paper and color over them with the flat side of a crayon.
   f. Draw and color carpenter's tools.
   g. Make tool boxes with shoe boxes and string handles. Add paper tool cutouts.
   h. Crush old crayon pieces in a paper or cloth bag using hammers. Spread crushed crayon on construction or waxed paper. Fold and melt with a warm iron.
   i. Make a design with glue on paper. Sprinkle sawdust on wet glue. Shake the excess into wastebasket.
   j. Paint on different textures of wood products such as paper, cardboard, paneling, wood blocks.

6. ***Drama***
   a. Students pantomime tools being used.
   b. Provide props for role-playing people who work with wood-forest rangers, lumberjacks, carpenters, and so on.
   c. Stimulate creative dramatics with songs such as "London Bridge" and "If I Had a Hammer."

7. ***Social Studies***
   a. Provide stories such as: *A Day in the Life of a Carpenter; What Can She Be? An Architect,* (Koppelman, 1976,).
   b. Children discuss future use for woodworking in their homes.
   c. Children draw the tools they think a carpenter or an architect uses (Koppelman, 1976).
   d. Children research other jobs that use woodworking and/or carpentry.

References

Adams, P. (1982). *Children's Workshops: Ideal for Carpentry Centers*. Columbus, Ga.: Columbus College, School of Education. (ERIC Document Reproduction Service No. ED 242 387.)

Adams, R. J. (1967). *Creative Woodworking in the Kindergarten*. Minneapolis, Minn.: T. S. Denison.

Allen, K. E., and Hart, B. (1984). *The Early Years, Arrangements for Learning*. Englewood Cliffs, N.J.: Prentice-Hall.

Anderson, S., and Hoot, L. (1986). "Kids, Carpentry and Pre-school Classrooms." *Day Care Early Education, 13,* 12–15.

Brannen, N. (1978). *Woodworking: Arizona HSST/DCA Competency Based Training Module #30*. Coolidge, Ariz.: AZ/NV Child Development Associates. (ERIC Document Reproduction Service No. EDI 180 638.)

Davis, H. G. (1980). "Reading Pressures in the Kindergarten." *Childhood Education, 57* (2), 76–79.

Day, B., and Drake, K. (1983)). *Early Childhood Education: Curriculum Organization and Classroom Management*. Alexandria, Va.: Association for Supervision and Curriculum Development.

Decker, C. A., and Decker, J. R. (1984). *Planning and Administering Early Childhood Programs* (3rd ed.). Columbus, Ohio: Charles E. Merrill.

Evans, E. D. (1975). *Contemporary Influences in Early Childhood Education* (2nd ed.). New York: Holt, Rinehart & Winston.

Hohman, M., Banet, B., and Weikart, D. P. (1979). *Young Children in Action*. Ypsilanti, Mich.: High Scope Educational Research Foundation.

Koppelman, P. (1976). *The House That Jack and Jill Built*. San Francisco, Calif.: Rosenburg Foundation. (ERIC Document Reproduction Service No. EDI 149 013.)

Leeper, S. D., Witherspoon, R. L., and Day, B. (1984). *Good Schools for Young Children* (5th ed.). New York: Macmillan.

Oklahoma State Dept. of Education. (1983). *Growing: Pre-Kindergarten Through 2nd Grade*. Oklahoma City, Okla.: (ERIC Document Reproduction Service No. 239 711.)

Pitcher, E. G., Feinburgh, S. G, and Alexander, D. (1984). *Helping Young Children Learn* (4th ed.). Columbus, Ohio: Charles E. Merrill.

Rudolph, M., and Cohen, D. H. (1984). *Kindergarten and Early Schooling* (2nd ed.). Englewood Cliffs. N.J.: Prentice-Hall.

Skeen, P., Garner, A., and Cartwright, S. (1984). *Woodworking for Young Children*. Washington, D.C.: National Association for the Education of Young Children.

Thompson, D. (1981). *Easy Woodstuff for Kids*. Mount Rainier, Md.: Gryphon House.

13

Evaluating, Assessing, and Recording Creative Learning

Evaluation is an integral part of the educational process. Effective teachers continually monitor and assess students' needs and progress, appraising academic, social, and physical growth, and planning individualized programs to support that growth. Good teachers also regularly evaluate the impact and effectiveness of the general learning environment and the specific activities, materials, and teaching strategies used within it. In order to make the environment more conducive to learning, they investigate new resources, implement changes, and reevaluate (Evertson, Emmer, Clements, Sanford, & Worsham, 1984). In addition, teachers assess their own strengths and weaknesses, and are sensitive to the effectiveness of their interactions with students. Evaluation is an on-going daily process that consciously or unconsciously guides every instructional decision.

According to Bentzen (1985, p. 107), the evaluation process is a "comparison between some event, object, or behavior, and a standard or criterion." The standards that drive evaluation are established at national, state, local, and individual levels. National, state, and local licensing and funding agencies define mandatory minimum program standards. National professional organizations, such as the National Association for the Education of Young Children, define accreditation criteria and standards for optimal program effectiveness. State departments of education and social services, as well as local school boards, parent organizations, and curriculum committees, define goals and standards for local teachers, students, and program content. These standards are then implemented and supplemented by individual teachers as they set the priorities and criteria for their own classrooms (Hildebrand, 1980).

While the specific standards of the many organizations and individuals involved in early childhood education may vary, the central and overriding standard is developmental appropriateness. Two statements, written twenty years apart, indicate the endurance of this standard, and capture the compelling rationale for it:

At the heart of the educational process lies the child. No advances in policy, no acqui-sitions of new equipment have their desired effect unless they are in harmony with the nature of the child, unless they are fundamentally acceptable to him.

Knowledge of the manner in which children develop, therefore, is of prime impor-tance, both in avoiding harmful practices and in introducing effective ones (Plowden et al., 1966)

Given the well-established fact that young children learn differently, the conclusion that educators must draw is a straightforward one: the education of young children must be in keeping with their unique modes of learning. (Elkind, 1986)

As suggested above, knowledge of child development is the cornerstone of high quality early childhood programs (Developmentally Appropriate Practice, 1986). From this foundation, three basic criteria form the framework for evaluating early child-hood programs:

1. Children have unique developmental needs, learning styles, backgrounds, and interests. The individual child's needs, abilities, and interests must determine the curriculum, not a prescribed text, curriculum guide, or time schedule.
2. Young children learn by doing. They learn through play, exploration, concrete sensory experience, and action on the environment. The learning environment must stimulate discovery and learning through children's active participation: playing, experimenting, touching, seeing, discussing, questioning, and prob-lem-solving. In early childhood education, the learning process is as important as the content.
3. The learning environment must be child-centered and focus on children's total development, supporting cognitive, social, affective, and physical growth. A child-centered environment is not only developmentally appropriate, but also pro-vides the respect, affection, and support young children need to develop pos-itive feelings about themselves and about learning.

Within this broad framework, the particular evaluation techniques and criteria used will depend on the purpose and subject of the evaluation. Some commonly used evaluation techniques are:

Achievement Tests	Logbooks
Anecdotal Records	Observation Reports
Aptitude Tests	Performance Charts
Assessment Inventories	Rating Scales
Attitudinal Measures	Role-playing
Basic Skills Inventories	Self-concept Scales
Behavior Inventories	Sociograms
Checklists	Student Contracts
Class Projects	Student Diaries
Creativity Tests	Student Work Samples
Diagnostic Tests	Teacher-Effectiveness Measurements
Discussions	Teacher-made Tests
Interviews	

This chapter explores several of these evaluation techniques as they may be ap-plied in two areas: (1) assessing the impact and effectiveness of the learning environment and (2) assessing individual student needs and progress. Since the learning environment influences the individual and individual needs influence the learning environment, the two areas are inextricably intertwined. Teachers must consider and synthesize the results of evaluations in both areas to develop effective overall and individual learning programs.

Evaluating the Learning Environment

A good starting point for evaluation is to take a broad look at all major aspects of the learning environment: teacher-child relationships, the teaching/learning process, curriculum organization, materials and equipment, the physical environment, and the outdoor environment. The following checklist can serve as a guide for teachers in evaluating and improving their own creative learning environments.

Early Childhood Learning Environment Checklist

Teacher-Child Relationships

Do you serve as a facilitator of learning, a guide, and a resource person, rather than as a dispenser of information?

Do your actions and behavior communicate that enjoying learning, respecting others, and learning how to learn are more important than acquiring specific subject knowledge?

Do you make sure that each child succeeds in something every day?

Do you structure learning so that children are secure in what they know and unafraid of what they don't know? Do you communicate to children that mistakes are learning opportunities to be explored, not problems to be avoided?

Do you offer constructive suggestions and feedback in a positive, sincere manner?

Do you act with respect and trust for children?

Do you believe that children respond to genuine trust and confidence in them with positive, productive, and mature behavior, and that they respond to distrust and lack of confidence with negative, unproductive, and immature behavior?

Do you circulate among the children—encouraging them, asking individual questions, and giving each child individual attention daily?

Do you really listen to questions raised by children, and help them find the answers instead of answering for them? Do you help children understand that some questions have no easy answers and that many questions have several answers?

Do you ask children questions that help them develop logical thinking patterns and independent problem-solving skills?

Do you help children act with independence and confidence by clearly communicating responsibilities and structuring the environment so that children are able to comfortably carry out their responsibilities?

Do you allow and encourage initiative in children by providing choices in selecting learning activities?

Do you support the development of internal discipline and responsibility by establishing clear, consistent rules and expectations and using sound social behavioral discipline techniques?

Teaching/Learning Process

Are many opportunities provided for learning through the senses—feeling, hearing, tasting, smelling, and seeing?

Are children encouraged to interact with (explore, manipulate, and experiment with) their environment?

Do activities stimulate learning through active participation and discovery rather than through passive reception and replication of information?

Is the learning process open-ended and self-correcting so that children can learn independently and explore many answers?

Is the learning process flexible and self-paced, so that children can start at their own levels of competence and progress at their own developmental and learning rates?

Are individual and small-group activities, rather than whole-group instruction emphasized?

Are children learning from each other by observing, imitating, and teaching one another?

Are children encouraged to talk with each other, investigate questions together, and cooperatively seek their own answers?

Is dramatic and creative play a key component of learning experiences in all content areas?

Are exciting hands-on experiences, where children can make their own choices and produce their own results, available?

Are children involved in planning and evaluating their learning activities?

Curriculum Organization

Does the curriculum address all areas of children's development, not just cognitive development?

Is a variety of learning centers available that offers experiences not only in traditional academic areas, but also in music, art, woodworking, creative dramatics, and play with sand, water, and blocks? Does the curriculum also include outdoor play that is an extension of classroom learning and a movement program?

Is the curriculum flexible enough to meet individual needs, learning styles, and interests? Do the children's needs and interests, rather than arbitrary program guides and schedules, drive the curriculum?

Is curriculum content integrated so that children can experience the rich and varied intellectual, creative, and practical applications of what they are learning? Are themes and units of study incorporated in different learning centers and activities so that children can understand the relationships and interdependencies among the skills and knowledge they are acquiring?

Are contracts or other methods used to plan and monitor an appropriate and balanced program for each child?

Does the curriculum allow for spontaneous child or teacher initiated activities?

Materials and Equipment

Is there a wide variety of materials, supplies, and equipment that accommodates different developmental levels and interests?

Are many materials available that provide concrete, sensory learning experiences and can be counted, arranged, rearranged, taken apart, and put together again?

Are informal teacher- and child-made materials utilized in addition to commercial materials?

Are children encouraged to supply their own materials so that their interests are fully appreciated and incorporated in the program?

Are bulletin boards and displays in the classroom organized around children's own handiwork?

Are materials available that promote the growth of both fine and gross motor skills?

Are materials organized through color coding or other methods so that children can independently locate, use, and replace them in the appropriate place.

Are materials and equipment accessible to children? Do they know how to use equipment by themselves and care for it properly?

Are materials and equipment safe, durable, and portable for outdoor as well as indoor use?

Is there an outdoor sandbox with toys, buckets, shovels, water, and measuring containers of various sizes and shapes so that math concepts will be reinforced and dramatic play will be encouraged?

Is there an adequate woodworking table with appropriate tools, materials, and a sawhorse available for outdoor and indoor use?

Is there an outdoor or indoor area available for water play? Is a variety of materials available, such as funnels, rubber hoses, plastic measuring containers, eggbeaters, liquid detergents, boats, sponges, corks, and other objects that sink or float, so that children can experiment with and discover simple math and science concepts?

Are roller tables (or carts) available for transporting art supplies, blocks, or other materials for outdoor use?

Are many large work surfaces available?

Physical Environment

Is the classroom an appealing place with a warm, inviting, homelike atmosphere?

Is there adequate space for active children to explore, create, and move about freely?

Are the rooms well-heated, lighted, and ventilated?

Are there storage areas with adequate individual space for children to store their wraps, completed work, and other possessions?

Does the classroom have open space for movement and large group activities?

Is the classroom decentralized or divided into a variety of learning centers rather than arranged in straight rows of desks or tables and chairs?

Are furniture, equipment, and toilet and water facilities child size, convenient, and accessible to children?

Are quiet and noisy centers and activities separated so that they do not interfere with one another? Are noisy and messy activities done outside when possible?

Is furniture arranged to provide large work surfaces? Is furniture creatively and flexibly arranged and rearranged to construct and divide learning centers?

Are learning centers arranged to best utilize the space available and to promote efficient transitions between centers and activities?

Are there comfortable spots in the room with carpet and pillows for reading, listening, or other quiet individual activities?

Is there provision for easy flow of activities within the classroom, between rooms, and between the indoors and outdoors?

Outdoor Environment

Is the outdoors utilized as a part of the total living-learning environment? Do outdoor activities extend and reinforce classroom learning?

Are children free to move outside as part of an integrated day? Are outdoor experiences enriching rather than restricting?

Is there a nature environment with trees, plants, and flowers so that children can explore, analyze, and learn about natural science?

Are there outdoor animals in pens or cages for children to care for and observe?

Are there vegetable gardens, flower gardens, or potted plants for children to cultivate and observe?

Are children given the opportunity to work and play outside in a variety of ways— alone, in groups, actively, and quietly?

Is there an outside entrance near the classroom so that games, materials, and equipment can be moved in and out easily?

Is the outdoor area visible, preferably through large windows from floor to ceiling, to facilitate supervision and minimize the possibility of accidents?

Is the outdoor area safe—free from glass and sharp metal?

Is there a hard surface area appropriate for playing with blocks, playing with wheeled toys, bouncing balls, and other activities?

Is there a soft grassy area for playing, running, or sitting together and reading, telling, or listening to stories?

Is there a balance of sunny and shady areas?

Is there an outside covered area or roof so that activity can go on even on drizzly days?

Do the equipment and materials provided encourage children to do something based on their own ideas, rather than just watch it operate?

Are open-ended materials (boxes, barrels, rubber tubes, wood strips, kegs with rubber tops for drums) available for children to use in their own creative ways?

Are adequate equipment and space provided for dramatic play, for example, a tree house, fort, teepee, raised platforms, a stripped down car, wooden crates, logs, tree stumps, an outdoor theatre, little houses, or "in and out" places children can crawl through or climb?

Is there a mixture of homemade inexpensive equipment (ropes, tires, telephone spools, sewer pipes, bean bags, newspaper balls, etc.) and commercial equipment (jungle gyms, wheeled toys, slides, rockers, climbing and reaching apparatus, and other stationary equipment)?

Is there a diversity of equipment to provide for a variety of developmental levels among the children?

Are the equipment and space adequate for the development of motor skills and coordination?

Is there climbing equipment and apparatus to help children develop large muscles?

Are there balance beams, logs, posts, or tree stumps to help children develop a sense of balance?

Is there sufficient apparatus to help children develop a sense of motor direction?
Is there a slide or smooth pole children can climb up and slide down?
Are there interesting and challenging swings, such as a knotted rope swing or a tire swing, to help children develop arm and leg muscles?
Is there an outside storage area organized so that children know where to find and replace equipment?

Teachers can use the Early Childhood Learning Environment Checklist to assess the quality of each major component of the learning environment and to target specific areas for improvement. In addition to this overall evaluation, teachers must also assess the effectiveness of the learning environment in terms of its impact on children's behavior and engagement in learning. Developmental classrooms are complex, fluid settings that encompass diverse developmental and learning goals and involve a wide range of individual and group activities. In order to accurately assess the effects of this multifaceted environment, teachers must observe and analyze many variables.

The Wasik-Day Open and Traditional Learning Environment and Children's Classroom Behavior Instrument provides an effective mechanism for correlating student behavior with a number of environmental variables (Day & Drake, 1983). Designed for use in early childhood through sixth-grade classrooms, this instrument provides a specific classroom behavior scale for measuring the effects of six variables: place, group leader, number in group, movement, academic behavior, and communication. The observer using the Wasik-Day Instrument collects data on a specific child for ten consecutive one-minute intervals, checking the appropriate box for each variable at the end of each minute. An example of a completed Wasik-Day Instrument is shown in Figure 1. Definitions of each category on the instrument and instructions for tabulating behaviors are as follows:

Time. Record hour and minute at the beginning of each 10-minute recording session. Note any changes that cause a break in a consecutive 10-minute recording. If a break occurs, go to a new 10-minute set.

Place. Prepare a map of the room and label all areas (see Figure 2).

Home base—circle. Code when the child is in home base for circle activities. Examples of these activities are morning scheduling arrangements, listening to a story, or observing a flannel board activity.

Home base—other. Code when the home base area is used for all other activities (for instance, when the music teacher, parent, or teacher aide uses the home base for other activity). Also code if one or more children are using the home base as a study area.

Study area. Code when specifically designated areas are used for completing individually assigned work.

Center. Code when the child is in a learning center. Denote the center by the following code: A-Art, B-Blocks, G-Sensorimotor, H-Housekeeping, M-Math, U-Music, R-Reading, E-Research, S-Science, O-Social Studies, D-Woodworking, W-Writing, L-Listening, C-Cooking, T-Water, N-Sand, I-Outside, O-Other.

General room space. Includes all space not specifically designated by one of the other categories. These areas should be denoted by shaded areas on the map.

Transition. Code when a child is moving from one area to another, changing activities, gathering materials for work, or cleaning up. Child may be in one of the designated areas.

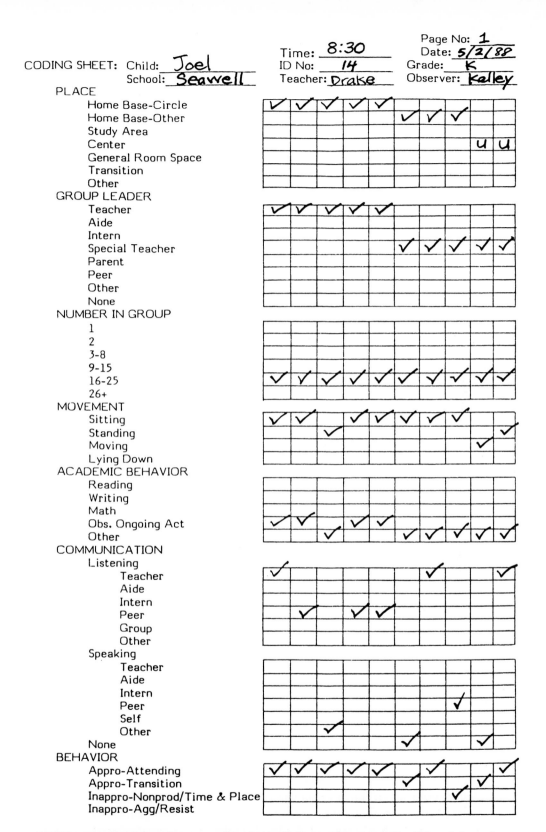

FIGURE 1. Sample of a Completed Wasik-Day Open and Traditional Learning Environments and Children's Classroom Behavior Instrument

571

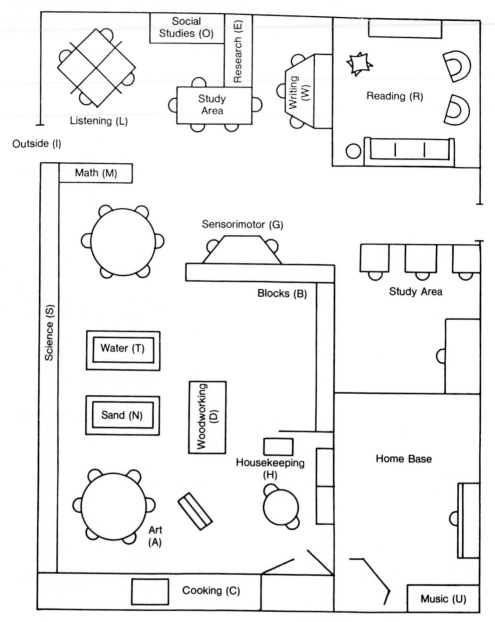

FIGURE 2. *Sample of a Classroom Map for Coding Purposes*

Other. Code if an area is not covered and describe the setting on the back of the code sheet.

Group Leader. Code the individual who is explicitly the leader of the ongoing activity in which the child is involved. The leader does not need to be physically near at all times. If the teacher is in a one-to-one relationship with the child, code the teacher as the leader. If children are together with no designated leader and one child becomes the leader, code group leader as peer. Codes: Teacher, Aide, Intern, Special Teacher, Parent, Peer, Other, and None.

Number in Group. Code the number of children in the group in which the child is involved. For example, count all children sitting on the floor in a common area listening to a story. If the child is sitting at a table with other children, count the total number of children at that table. Do not include adults.

Movement

Sitting. Code sitting behavior regardless of whether the child is sitting on a chair, floor, table, or other structure.

Standing. Code standing regardless of where the child is standing.

Moving. Code when locomotion is involved. Do not code fidgeting as moving.

Lying down. Code when the child is in a prone position, regardless of the classroom activity.

Academic Behavior

Reading. Code when the child has all appearances of reading (looking at pages in books, periodically turning pages). Book must have words.

Writing. Code when the child is using a pencil, crayon, or other writing instrument to print or write letters or words. If the child is reading and writing, code as reading when no writing is being done.

Math. Code if the activity is math and the child is involved with the activity. Code even if the child is reading or writing math problems.

Observing ongoing activity. Code when an activity is being explained or demonstrated or when some topic is being presented and the children are supposed to be listening. Activity must be appropriate for the classroom.

Other. All other academic or appropriate classroom behavior not specified above, including art, music, science, social studies, and clean-up time.

Communication

Listening. Code as listening when the child appears to be attentive to the person who is speaking. Subcategories are teacher, aide, intern, peer, or other.

Speaking. Code the individual to whom the target child is speaking. If the child is talking out loud or singing and has not directed this toward anyone, code as the subcategory self. The subcategories are teacher, aide, intern, peer, self, or other.

None. Code when the child is neither listening nor speaking.

Appropriateness of Behavior

Appropriate-attending. Code the time a child is behaving appropriately and the overt behavior suggests active involvement in learning activities. This includes productive independent activity such as reading, writing, painting, constructing, or working with a teaching device; assertive work such as asking for help or support; contributing information and ideas; cooperative behavior such as talking to or working with peers; and appropriate dependent activity such as answering direct questions and carrying out requests.

Appropriate-transition. Examples of a child's behavior that are classified as appropriate but not as attending include arranging materials for work, waiting for help from a teacher, sitting quietly in a chair but showing no overt productive behavior, and sitting while a teacher presents material but not responding to it.

Inappropriate-nonproductive or inappropriate time or place. Code as non-productive behavior looking around and engaging in repetitive physical movements such as rocking in a chair, swaying back and forth, fidgeting, or aimless wandering. For inappropriate for time and place, code all appropriate behaviors performed outside the time limits or in an inappropriate setting. Examples are continuing with one activity when it is time for another to begin, not being in the appropriate place while carrying out work, speaking out of turn, and interrupting another person.

Inappropriate-aggressive or resistive, attention-getting. For aggressive or resistive behaviors, code direct attack on a child or teacher; grabbing, pushing, hitting, kicking, name calling, destroying property; and physically or verbally resisting instructions or directions. For attention getting, code activities which result in and are being maintained by social attention. Examples would be bothering or annoying others, criticizing, making noise, loud talking, clowning, excessive hand raising, temper tantrums, and excessive requests for assistance.

Before using the Wasik-Day Instrument, observers should be trained in a basic time sampling procedure using the instrument and a stopwatch. For individuals familiar with classroom settings, six to eight hours has been sufficient training time. Observers should first learn the categories on the instrument and the layout of the room from a coded map. They should then practice coding data both from video-tapes and actual observations of children in classroom settings. Observers should familiarize themselves with a new classroom for at least thirty minutes prior to collecting data.

When observing over a long period of time, observers should take breaks after every twenty minutes of recording. In addition to recording observations on the instrument, observers should complete a Daily Schedule Sheet as shown in Figure 3. This sheet provides important information on time, activity, and place that may be necessary to interpret the data on the Wasik-Day Instrument. Observers do not record data during children's rest time, lunch, outside play, and other times when children are outside the classroom.

Before an observer codes data for research or evaluation purposes, overall instrument agreement of 85 percent or higher on ratings of five different children should be obtained with a second observer. Both observers collect ten minutes of data for each comparison. In each comparison, the percentage of total instrument observer agreement can be calculated as follows:

1. Count the total number of actual observer agreements across all categories.
2. Divide the total number of actual agreements by the total number of possible agreements. (70 is the total number of possible agreements in a ten-minute observation: 7 categories × 10 minutes = 70 possible agreements).
3. Multiply the result by 100 to obtain the percentage of total instrument observer agreement.

For example, if two observers had 63 agreements in a ten-minute observation, the total instrument observer agreement would be (63 ÷ 70) × 100 = 90 percent.

In addition to calculating total instrument observer agreement, the percentage of agreement on each of the seven categories should also be calculated. This calculation is the same as above, except that the total number of possible agreements in

A Completed Daily Schedule Sheet

School _Seawell_   Classroom #7
Child _Joel_   Grade _K_
Observer _Kelly_   Date _May 2_

Summary of Daily Schedule

Time	Activity / Place	Comments
8:30	Circle	
8:35-9:10	Special teacher (music)	
9:10-9:30	Circle	
9:30-10:40	Centers	
10:40-11:35	Lunch	
11:35-11:41	Circle	
11:41-12:34	Outside	
12:34-12:37	Transition	
12:37-12:57	TV	
12:57-1:18	Outside skill group (never happened before)	
1:18-2:11	Centers	
1:37-1:58	Helping other child - did his work for him	
1:49-1:50	Bathroom	
2:11-	Recess and home	

FIGURE 3.   *Sample of a Completed Daily Schedule*

each category is 10 (1 category × 10 one-minute intervals). Training should continue until observer agreement on each category is 90 percent or higher.

Figure 1 illustrates one ten-minute observation of a child named Joel. During the first five minutes, Joel was primarily sitting in a large group at home base, observing the on-going activity, and behaving appropriately. During the second five minutes, Joel made a transition to the music center. Another teacher took over as group leader in the home base area, and shortly afterwards Joel moved to the music center, remaining in a large group setting. There was one instance of inappropriate speech with a peer during this time.

Data such as this from the Wasik-Day Instrument can be used for many purposes. Observations of many children can be analyzed over time to determine the overall impact on classroom behavior of different group sizes, learning centers, activities, and leaders (teachers, aides, parents, student teachers, and interns). In addition, many observations of one child can be analyzed to determine the influence of the same variables on individuals and to assess changes in an individual child's behavior over time.

Evaluating Individual Needs and Progress

In addition to evaluating the impact and effectiveness of the learning environment, teachers must also assess individual children's developmental levels, needs, and progress. Individual evaluations serve diagnostic and prescriptive purposes, and provide data for planning, maintaining, and improving appropriate individualized learning programs. Three general types of individual evaluation discussed in this chapter are developmental screening, contracts, and teacher and student records.

Developmental Screening

Early childhood developmental screening provides an overall picture of students' development in key areas, and helps to identify children who may need further in-depth screening or remediation. For example, the screening program developed by the Early Prevention of School Failure Project (EPSF Project) assesses auditory, visual, visual-motor, and motor synthesis maturation levels, as well as children's experiences and adjustments (Werner). The program's objective is to prevent school failure through early detection and remediation of developmental deficiencies in 4- to 6-year-old children. Parent involvement is a key component of the program. Prior to screening, the principal or program coordinator explains the program's purpose, stressing that EPSF gives a reliable evaluation of development and provides teachers with the information they need to select appropriate curricula and materials. Each parent completes a parent evaluation form, and is interviewed as part of the screening process. The screening test battery, administered both in the language the child speaks and in the language in which the child will be instructed, includes the following evaluation instruments:

Peabody Picture Vocabulary Test (PPVT). Provides an estimate of an individual's receptive vocabulary. The test is administered individually to each child. Four different pictures of familiar objects are presented; the examiner names one and the child points to the picture named. Results are recorded as an age equivalent score.

Preschool Language Scale (PLS). Designed to sample five integrated conceptual and experiential areas of language development: Visual-Vocal Integration, Vocabulary, Auditory Response, Integrative Auditory Memory and Discriminative Visual-Auditory Memory. The examiner individually instructs the child in each task. Results are recorded on a point scale. Norms for individual subtests are provided for chronological age.

Developmental Test of Visual-Motor Integration (VMI). Gives the staff an approximation of visual-motor abilities for prognosis of possible writing and reading problems. The child copies scaled drawings. Results are recorded in developmental age.

House-Tree-Person Test (H-T-P). Used to assess visual-motor skills. The H-T-P confirms visual-motor ability but is also more memory loaded. Each child is asked to draw separately a house, tree, and person. The Goodenough scoring of the person provides a development score.

Revised Motor Activity Scale (MAS). Used for evaluating a child's body awareness, manual dexterity and body control. Perceptual-motor skills are one part of a child's nonverbal development and involves both awareness of objects and information through the senses and the ability to perform coordinated movements. The scale is individually given, evaluating such skills as balancing, rhythm, directionality, body image, fine and gross movement, bilateral activities, and dominance. Results are recorded on a point scale.

Speech and Language Evaluation. The speech therapist uses an appropriate screening test such as the Photo Articulation Test to analyze specific speech sounds. Children found to have speech sound errors are tested further at the beginning of the school year. Developmental language problems are noted.

Another example of early childhood development screening is the Early Identification and Intervention Program (EIIP) developed by the Maryland State Department of Education (*A Teacher's Manual: Early Identification and Intervention Program,* 1983). Through specific diagnosis and evaluation, the suspicion of a learning problem is either confirmed or denied, and high-risk children are then placed in programs designed to ameliorate their problems and prevent academic failure. The EIIP consists of screening, review and evaluation, and intervention.

Maryland Observational Screening Checklist for Kindergarten

Item Descriptions

1. *Copies first name or a simple word.* The child should be able to copy a word. A letter reversal is not important, nor is size. This observation must be made more than once.
2. *Repeats a sentence with correct word order.* Given a five to six word simple sentence, the child should be able to repeat the sentence in correct order. The sentence used by the teacher for this observation should be at least five words in length but not more than six (i.e., "My book is on the table." "I have a good friend.").
3. *Asks teacher's help only when needed.* The amount of attention or help the child needs, requires, or demands from the teacher in order to complete assigned tasks is what is observed. The child should be able to work relatively independently for sustained periods of time.
4. *Groups objects by category.* Presented with a variety of objects (such as foods and toys) the child should be able to group the similar items.
5. *Comprehends directional concepts.* The child should have an awareness of directionality on the ability to translate directions into space. He/she should differentiate between up and down, forward and backward, before and after, above and below, in front of and in back of, between, besides, and so forth. Examples could be:
   a. "Put the doll on top of the table."
   b. "Put the dog under the table."
6. *Tells how many objects there are in a group of five.* Given a group of objects that total five, the child should be able to tell the teacher how many there are. The child should be able to say that there are five items.

7. *Follows a verbal direction containing three associated steps.* The child should be able to follow a three step associated (related) direction. The multiple directions should be clear, concise, and meaningful, leading to some conclusion. Examples could be:

   a. "Go to your cubby, get your coat, and put it on."

   b. "Take one of the papers from that table, go to your seat, and draw a picture of an animal."

8. *Retells a story or nursery rhyme in sequential order.* The child should be able to retell a story or rhyme in the same sequence as the original. The recitation of nursery rhymes should be accepted; such as "Jack and Jill" or "Little Miss Muffet."

9. *Recognizes own name in print.* Given the child's name in print and other names, he/she should select his/her name consistently. The teacher should provide the child more than an opportunity to recognize his/her given name consistently.

10. *Speaks in sentences of more than three words.* The child should be able to express himself/herself with language comparable to that of the other children in the class, and should not need to struggle to find the right words or be unable to verbally express a thought clearly. When answering questions presented by the teacher, or in conversation with other children, the child should be able to speak in sentences of more than three words (i.e., "I didn't do it." "Give me that book.").

11. *Names the colors red, yellow, blue, and green.* The child should be able to name each of the colors which the teacher presents.

12. *Usually has good self-control.* The child should demonstrate self-control that is typical for a kindergarten child. Check "no" if the child has a tendency to make spontaneous outbursts (i.e., speaks out of turn and/or speaks without thinking), or is restless (i.e., an inability to sit still), or annoys and bothers others, or does not attend to the lesson, and so forth.

13. *Pays attention to what he/she is doing when other things are going on around him/her.* The child should be able to complete a task despite normal distractions. When the child is able to concentrate in quiet circumstances, but is very susceptible to interruptions from other stimuli such as nearby movement and "people noises," check "no."

14. *Counts by rote 1 to 10.* The child should be able to recite numbers in order from one to ten.

15. *Tells about a picture while looking at it.* The child should be able to verbalize in response to a familiar picture. This need not be an elaborate description or explanation, but merely serve as an indicator that the child can express an idea.

16. *Identifies differences in pictures.* The child should be able to identify one picture that is different from the rest when mixed in with a group of four other pictures or drawings (e.g., a smiling face mixed in with four frowning faces or a lynx cat (nub tail) mixed in with four alley cats).

17. *States full name and age when asked.* The child should be able to state his/her first and last name and numerical age when asked, i.e., nickname or given name plus surname. Age should be stated verbally rather than indicated with fingers.

18. *Recognizes and names upper- and lower-case letters.* The child should be

able to name some upper-case and lower-case letters and to differentiate letters with a fair degree of accuracy.

19. *Copies a circle, cross, and square so that it is recognizable.* The child should be able to accurately copy a circle, cross, and square. The circle must be approximately round and closed (a somewhat elliptical form is acceptable); the lines of the cross must intersect and be relatively straight, although the meeting point does not have to produce a perfect ninety degree angle; the lines of the square must not be broken and the angles must be present.

20. *Interacts well in peer group activities.* The child should be able to work and play cooperatively with one or more peers. The child should be observed for his/her ability to carry out both leadership and membership roles, share materials, and take turns willingly during joint and group classroom activities.

21. *Tells about a recent school activity.* After participating in some school activity, the child should be able to describe the experience in an understandable manner. The verbal description should be fairly typical for kindergarten children at that particular point in the kindergarten year. The teacher should judge the description by the time lapse between the initial activity and the retelling.

22. *Finishes most tasks or projects.* In comparison with other children in the class, the child should consistently complete various tasks and be frequently successful at finishing within the recommended or "normal" time frame. When he or she tends to need more time to complete tasks that are of average difficulty for kindergarten children at this particular point in the kindergarten year, check "no."

23. *Attempts most tasks or projects.* The child should be willing to attempt tasks that the teacher feels are appropriate for the average child in his/her class at that point in the kindergarten year. The item is not scored because the child is successful or unsuccessful in completing the task, but because the child either refuses to try the task or gives up so quickly that it is obvious that the child is not trying.

24. *Speaks so that he/she is usually understood by peers and/or adults.* Given a question or an opportunity to talk freely, the child should usually be able to say words and sentences that are understood by others. The main emphasis should be placed on whether the child's oral language is understandable, not on grammatical accuracy or elaboration.

25. *Arranges three events in correct sequence.* Given three events out of sequence, the child should be able to arrange the events in the correct sequential order. The difficulty level of the task should be what the teacher considers appropriate for kindergarten children at that point in the kindergarten year.

Contracts

Contracts are another form of individual evaluation. They provide a written plan and record of each student's daily activities and progress. They are an excellent and efficient means of monitoring performance, since the children themselves can check off completed activities and evaluate how well they did. Along with self-correcting materials, contracts give children a clear idea of their own progress. Teachers check children's progress as work occurs, and also meet with each child daily to review the day's work. Relevant completed work is stapled to the contract for children to take home so that parents can also monitor progress.

During the daily conferences, teachers can evaluate overall problems and progress and plan the next day's contract accordingly. In this way teachers can assign activities at an appropriate difficulty level, and can also ensure a balanced program. It is important for teachers to be realistic about the amount of work that is included in the contract and to allow flexibiltiy for exploration and new experiences.

Contracts occur along a continuum. First there is the teacher-made, teacher-assigned contract in which the student has little or no input. This type is used most frequently in traditional classrooms, and puts little responsibility for planning in the hands of the students. The second type is the teacher-made, student-assigned contract. With this type, the teacher prepares a bank of contracts, and the student choses one on which to work. The third type is the student-made, student-assigned contract which contains content in an area the student has selected. This might be an area of weakness or an area of particular interest to the student. Teachers can use several different types of contracts and should include some student-assigned activities. The level of contracting depends on the student's reading ability and the student's ability to be self-responsible.

Contracts are the most effective means available to teachers to provide individualized learning programs. They provide for one-on-one evaluation and enable teachers to accommodate individual learning styles and needs. The following sample contracts represent a variety of ability levels as well as varying levels of input on the part of the student. They are intended to be a guide to help teachers implement a contracting system in their own classrooms.

Sample 1

Sample 2

Name	
Date	
Choose at least one activity in each center.	
Games	**Math**
☐ Puzzles	☐ Spool Game
☐ Beads	☐ Measuring
Art	**Writing**
☐ Clay	☐ Write your name in the sand
☐ Cut and Paste	☐ Sesame Street
Choose a center. Where did I go? ____ ____	How did I do? ☐ I learned something new ☐ I worked and had fun ☐ I wasted too much time
Meet with the teacher	My favorite was ____

Name:	
Date:	
Reading	**Math**
☐ I read this book: ☐ Indian Blends	☐ Cuisenaire Rods
Listening Choose one: ☐ Filmstrip ☐ Record	**Science** Choose one: ☐ Draw or write how the baby chick looks ☐ Water Play
Choose a center. Where did I go? ____	Meet with ____
What did you like best about today?	What would you change?

Sample 3

(For a child with no reading ability)

My Contract

Name: Date:

Choose any four

☐ Math	☐ Art
Six 6 1 2 3 4 5	
☐ Reading BINGO A K N E O B	☐ Blocks
☐ Dramatic Play Your Choice	☐ Meet with _____

Sample 4

(For a child with some reading ability)

My Contract

Name: Date:

Choose any four

☐ Outside	☐ Writing
Building	A C R L J Practice Cards
☐ Science Magnet Game	☐ Games Puzzles
☐ Listening Language Master R	Meet with _____

Sample 5

Name:	Week of :
Monday ☐ Reading ☐ Writing ☐ Math ☐ ☐ ☐ with the teacher	**Tuesday** ☐ Reading ☐ Writing ☐ Math ☐ ☐ ☐ with the teacher
Wednesday ☐ Reading ☐ Writing ☐ Math ☐ ☐ ☐ with the teacher	**Thursday** ☐ Reading ☐ Writing ☐ Math ☐ ☐ ☐ with the teacher
Friday ☐ Reading ☐ Writing ☐ Math ☐ ☐ ☐ with the teacher	**How did I do?** ☐ I went to many centers. ☐ I learned something new. ☐ I need to work harder. ☐ I liked _____ best. ☐ ☐

Sample 6

Contract

Name: Date:

Choose any three of the four centers.

☐ Art	Make one of these: a burlap flower, stitchery, a design, weaving
☐ Math	Play one of the games
☐ Reading	Read a book about an animal
☐ Writing	Do one of these: (1) Make up a story using a story starting card (five sentences) (2) Practice your writing using task card: numbers 5 to 8

Meet with _____

What did you like best about today?

What would you change?

Sample 7

Contract	
Name	Date
Choose any four :	

☐ Math
Play the marching
addition game. Keep
your own score.
2^{+2} 4^{+3} 6^{+9}

☐ Art   Choose one:
Junk Collage
Pipe cleaner flowers
Paint a picture
Stitch a picture

☐ Science
(1) Look at the book
   Insects in Our World
(2) Find the centipede
(3) Make a list of things
   you learned about
   centipedes
(4) Make an egg carton
   centipede

☐ Outside Choose one:
Build something that moves
Write or draw something
   on the sidewalk that
   shows how you feel.
   Use colored chalk.

☐ Writing
(1) Choose a picture
(2) Write a story. You may
   use chart paper.
(3) Read   to a friend.
(4) Put it in the center.

☐ Meet with _____

Sample 12

Name	MON	TUES	WED	THUR	FRI
Skill Group					
Language Skill					
Scholastic					
Handwriting					
Science					
Creative Writing					
Spelling					
Language Games					
Math					
Listening					
Reading Enjoyment					
Exploration					
Media Center					
Social Studies					

(CENTERS)

CIRCLE ONE

Art

You and Me _____ game

Reading   Do a book report
Center   Use a   book

Outdoor Group
   Reading group with your teacher
   Worksheets

Language   Red   game
             Yellow   game
Writing   card

Blocks

Library   Visit Pooh   Magazines
Center

Lunch   Story

Math group with your teacher

"Read - in"   Conference

Sample 14   Social Studies Contract for 1 week

Centers	Mon	Tues	Wed	Thurs	Fri
Social Science Look at the filmstrips on Eskimos.					
Creative Writing 1. Choose a card from the "Creative Writing" box. Make up a story. 2. Make up your own story starter. Place it in the "Creative Writing" box.					
Following Directions 1. Play the "Mousetrap" game					
Reading Enjoyment 1. Read __ or more newspaper articles. 2. Read one of the scholastic readers 3. Choose a book to read in our "private" library.					

"My Dinosaur Contract"   Name:

Art — ① Make your favorite dinosaur out of clay. ② Work on the dinosaur mural.

Special — ① Name the dinosaurs in the center ② Number your paper 1-10.

Games — Put together a dinosaur puzzle.

Listening — Watch the dinosaur film.

Blocks — Build a dinosaur. I used __ blocks.

Language Arts — Draw a picture of your favorite dinosaur and write a story to tell why you like it.

Reading — Read a dinosaur book.

Housekeeping — Cook a meal fit for a dinosaur.

Math — Work a dinosaur math sheet.

Seat Work — Do a dinosaur cut and paste.

Project Plan

Name	Date Started

Problem: Area to be researched

Procedure: How I plan to go about it

Some things I want to find out

Resources: Materials I will need

Results: What happened

Teacher Comments:

Current Events

Contract

These activities will help you to learn about things that happen in the world around you. You must do four activities. Decide with the teacher which four you will do and how you will report on each one. You have five days in which to finish this contract.

Objectives

1. To be able to describe three people in the news.
2. To be able to identify three world leaders.
3. To be able to identify four major news media.

Activities

1. Examine photographs of important people in the news. Identify each one by finding his or her picture in a newspaper or a magazine.
2. Draw a cartoon about a person or event in the news that you think is important.
3. Get a friend to help you write an article like one in the newspaper or a magazine.
4. Begin a class newspaper with current news.
5. Make up at least one riddle about a person in the news.
6. Begin a scrapbook of news items that you think are note worthy.
7. Listen to the news on TV or radio for one week. Make a list of important news items.

I agree to the terms of this contract.
_____ (student)
_____ (teacher)

Sample Weekly Contracts

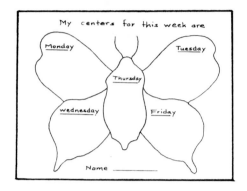

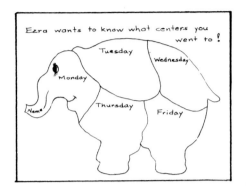

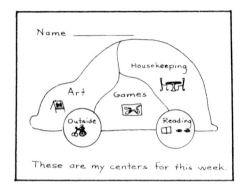

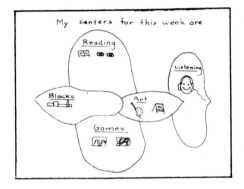

Sample Weekly Language Arts Contract

My Language Arts Contract   Date: May 10 - May 14

Name: _____

	Monday	Tuesday	Wednesday	Thursday	Friday: Children's Museum
Writing	It is national "Be Kind to Animals" week. Make a list of rules to follow for good pet care.	Write a story about a person whom you admire very much.	FREE CHOICE!	SHIPWRECKED 	
Reading	Read with Miss Smith. ☺	Read "Last Stop, City Hall" on P. 43 in Widening Circles.	Library. Read "The People Downstairs" on P. 53.	Read - In ☺	
Skills	① Use these words in a sentence: shovel, bucket, toward, noise, fence, loud, move, breakfast, shout ② Do the Number Words on the board. ③ Skyline! ☺	① Do ▲ Rhyming words on the board ② Do ▲▲ on the board. ③ Copy the poem beside the board (in cursive).	① " " Quotation Marks ② Look these words up in the dictionary and write the first definition: ① seven ② quiet ③ roof ④ thin ⑤ loud	① Do the ● on the board (singular and plural) ② Copy the months. Have a friend call them out to you and see if you can spell them.	

Do the Animal Hunt beside the board.

Work on your Spelling. I would like for you to do two units this week.

* Bonus (to be done any day)	
FREE CHOICE!	
Write a story about how your mouth feels when you eat a pickle.	
Play the Noun Verb game	
Play a game of Consonant Blend Checkers.	
Do the worksheets	
Write a story about what it would be like if animals were the masters and human beings were the pets.	

what Page am I on? _____

Reading Contract for

_____

Do _____:

☐ 1. Read the story _____
_____

☐ 2. Do the question sheet.

☐ 3. Do the sentence sheet.

☐ 4 Do the worksheets. (pages_____
_____

☐ 5. Tell someone about the story you read.

☐ 6. Write down the words you did not know.

"Be a whale of a reader!"

Contract Completed:
yes ☐
no ☐

Self-Evaluation Sheet

Name_____

Date_____

• I finished my work._____

• I had trouble with_____.

• I enjoyed_____most.

• I put my name on all my papers._____

• I did_____work.

Teacher_____

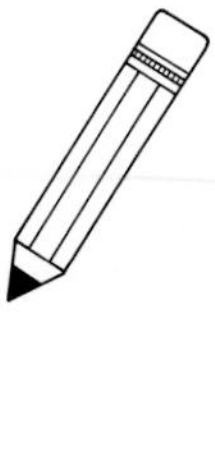

Work Completion Chart
Color a star if you finish your work.
Name_____
"Reach for the Stars"

1. Mon.
2. Tues.
3. Wed.
4. Thurs
5. Fri.
6. Mon.
7. Tues.
8. Wed.
9. Thurs.
10. Fri.

Week 1 -_____
Week 2-_____
Percentage of work
completed_____
Date_____

Teacher and Student Records

Because so many activities occur simultaneously in an early childhood classroom, teachers must be keen observers and careful record-keepers in order to ensure a continuum of purposeful learning. Teacher records might contain the amount of time spent on particular tasks, the different activities in which children participate, the quality of that participation, and recommended next steps. Such records are obtained through direct observation of individual students and through written work that indicates the nature and extent of individual achievement. Student records may be kept in folders or notebooks and on index cards. The information should be concise and descriptive; it should be dated and evaluated monthly, with notations of progress recorded. An example of such a record on one student, Michael B., accompanies this discussion.

Records should indicate general behavior patterns as well as academic achievement. Pleasant or disturbing family occurrences, illnesses, accidents, and highlights at school should all be noted, as these may be important in assessing the child's overall development. These records indicate the social interaction and emotional development to which academic learning is greatly related.

Class records, family grouping records, or team records must also be kept. Through these records an analysis may be made of the activities shared by a larger number of children. The students may help to keep these records, often in the form of charts or lists indicating centers visited; stories read, told, or written; special projects undertaken; commercial and teacher-made games played; and learning task cards completed. Observation of this record should reveal balance in a variety of areas; if lack of variety is indicated steps can be taken to prevent this from happening.

Michael B.

9/21 Art and Experience Story—Drew a picture of a picnic (complete with football playing and eating toasted marshmallows) that took place during the summer vacation; dictated a story, consisting of five sentences, to a parent aide about this experience. Story and pictures reflect creativity as well as good sentence structure.

9/22 Science—Is very much interested in reading and looking at pictures about animals. Together we made up a contract of work for him to complete on beavers and alligators. (Contract to be filed in his folder.)

9/25 Math—Has worked for several days with Cuisenaire rods and learning task cards numbered 15 to 24. Self-correcting cards indicate good progress. Must give him individual achievement test in a few days.

9/13 Blocks—Michael has been the leader in designing the city of Washington, D.C., in the block-building center. This interest stems from a recent family trip there. Additional unit blocks were borrowed from Mrs. Smith's room next door to complete the Washington Monument structure. Labels have been placed on all the structures. Filmstrip, books, and records, and Language Master task cards on Washington have been added to the listening and viewing center. Michael seems more interested in staying in the block center and constructing rather than in reading and viewing. Must be encouraged to visit the listening and viewing center.

10/4 Writing—Had to be encouraged to do his own writing about a recent field trip to the children's museum. Has no trouble remembering his experiences or even adding interesting information to them; needs help in making his writing neater.

10/8 Reading—Is reading very well independently in the book *Adventures at Sea,* 3. Encouraged him to take this book home to read to his parents.

10/13 Social Behavior—Michael is very popular among his classmates in spite of his inability at this time to control his temper if things don't always go his way. We're working on this, paying special attention to rewarding, through praise, his positive actions. Has shown some improvement and is aware that his teachers and parents are concerned about helping him with this. Must work with him on his interfering with Tommy and Susan during math skill group.

Students should also be encouraged to keep records through their own diaries and activities. This diary will help children understand their own progress; it will help the teacher learn what seems to interest the child most or gives the child the greatest satisfaction. Accuracy is not as important in keeping a diary as is the recording of how children feel about the work they are doing as well as about themselves.

Written reports and notes taken from teacher observations, as well as student-kept records, provide the teacher a form of evaluation not only on student performance but on teacher performance as well. Another important means of evaluating teacher and student performance is through the use of tape or video recorders. These recordings allow the teacher to view the learning situation, and what his or her role in it has been, from an objective point of view. By viewing the tape, the teacher becomes an observer rather than a participant and can gain valuable insight into the role of the teacher in the learning process.

Through the use of records (e.g., Michael B.), the teachers' additional records, and the children's diaries and logs, teachers should be able to identify each child's general achievements and the areas where special help is needed. Also, teachers should be able to know the kinds of work that each child has been doing and how the child has progressed in these areas. Overall, record keeping in an early childhood environment is very important, and accurate and detailed reports of the individual child's developmental levels and what he or she is doing must be kept. Record keeping should be an informal, simple process, with records being easy to keep and easy to read. Conferences, observation notes, and comments by both pupil and teacher should be kept. The records may take many forms, among them anecdotal notes, files of children's work, records of formal and informal tests, checklists, and most important, teacher observation—both informal and systematic—often over a long period of time.

In addition to the teachers and the children, however, a third party must also be involved—the parents. Parents play a vital role in the evaluation of each child, from the beginning of the school year and throughout a child's educational program. Home information (i.e., early experiences and language development, position in the family, interests that the child has at home, behavior and attitude among family members) helps teachers to understand the child, since these experiences often affect the child's school experience. Parent-teacher conferences should become a regular part of the school program, as they are helpful not only in keeping parents informed of their child's growth but also in engaging their support in school activities. Parents are entitled to know exactly what the child is learning and what the child might be having difficulty doing. Samples of the child's work should be shown and analyzed during the conference periods. Along with the records the teachers have kept (both individual and total group) and the records and diaries that the individual children have kept, the parent-teacher conferences should provide occasions for shared evaluation.

Conclusion

Evaluation, assessment, and record-keeping are critical components of an effective early education program. Evaluation has many benefits for teachers, students, and their parents. It provides valuable information about academic progress, developmental needs, teacher performance, the learning environment, and overall program effectiveness. Through evaluation, teachers learn about their own effectiveness as well as their students' progress (Lemlech, 1979).

Evaluation and assessment serve not only as measures of success, but also as motivators for improved performance (Rubin, 1980). Students and teachers alike need accurate and constructive feedback in order to meet their goals. Teachers can use evaluation to promote excellence in students and themselves. The purpose of evaluation is to identify strengths as well as weaknesses and to use that information to plan what and how to improve. The teacher's approach to evaluation should be a positive and proactive one in which mistakes are viewed not as failures, but as valuable opportunities for further learning and growth.

Evaluation involves both formal assessment instruments and informal observation and record-keeping. The usefulness of informal observation should not be underestimated. Children's everyday choices and behavior provide important insights into learning needs, interests, and the effectiveness of teaching strategies, activities, and materials. Were the children interested in exploring the new materials in the math center? How long did they remain in the center attempting to solve the problems? Were the children interested enough to want to share their experiences with the teacher, other children, or a classroom observer? What do children decide to do among free-choice activities? Through such observations, discussions with students, and listening to children talk with each other, teachers have a basis for planning classroom and individual program improvements.

Teachers who strive to maintain the most appropriate learning environment constantly evaluate, implement changes, and evaluate again. "Evaluation must be done regularly, continuously, and consistently" (Blake, 1977). Evaluation should be systematic, individualized, and constructive. Effective evaluation enables teachers and children to accomplish their best in an early education program.

References

Bentzen, W. R. (1985). *Seeing Young Children: A Guide to Observing and Recording Behavior* New York: Delmar Publishers, Inc.

Blake, H. E. (1977). *Creating a Learning-Centered Classroom: A Practical Guide for Teachers.* New York: Hart Publishing Company, Inc.

Day, B., and Drake, K. (1983). *Early Childhood Education: Curriculum Organization and Classroom Management.* Association for Supervision and Curriculum Development. Alexandria, Va.

Developmentally Appropriate Practice. (1986). Washington, D.C.: National Association for the Education of Young Children.

Elkind, D. (1986). Formal Education and Early Childhood Education: An Essential Difference. *Phi Delta Kappan, 67,* 631–636.

Evertson, C. M., Emmer, E. T., Clements, B. S., Sanford J. P., and Worsham, M. E. (1984). *Classroom Management for Elementary Schools.* Englewood Cliffs, N.J.: Prentice-Hall, Inc.

Hildebrand, V. (1980). *Guiding Young Children* (2nd ed.). New York: Macmillan Publishing Company.

Lemlech, J. K. (1979). *Classroom Management.* New York: Harper and Row.

Plowden, Lady Bridget, and others. (1966). *Children and Their Primary Schools: A Report of the Central Advisory Council for Education.* London: Her Majesty's Stationery Office.

Rubin, D. (1980). *Teaching Elementary Language Arts* (2nd ed.). New York: Holt, Rinehart and Winston.

A Teacher's Manual: Early Identification and Intervention Program. (1983). Maryland State Department of Education, Division of Instruction, Language and Learning Improvement Branch.

Werner, L. *Early Prevention of School Failure Nationally Validated Program: Diagnosing for School Success.* Peotone: A Nationally Validated Developer-Demonstrator Model Project.

14

Early Childhood Classroom Designs

Early childhood classrooms encourage the flow of movement from center to center and provide for social interaction. There is flexibility in space usage, and the space is seen as being shared rather than as compartmentalized into individual territories. This extension of space expands the pupil's interaction with peers and materials. Communication flows between students and teachers as well as among the students. The following layouts are meant to be used as guides for those interested in opening the space in the classroom. Many require no specific architectural features but can be utilized within any four walls. Learning occurs in good self-contained classrooms just as it does in good open-space environments.

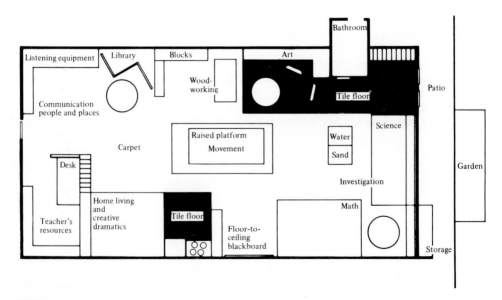

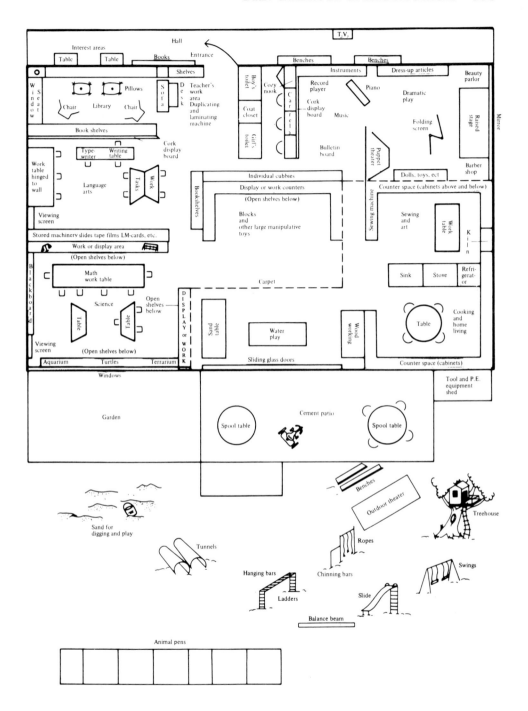

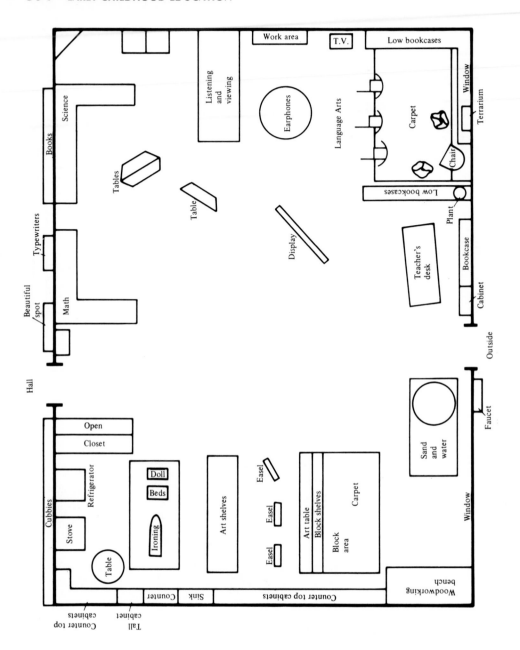

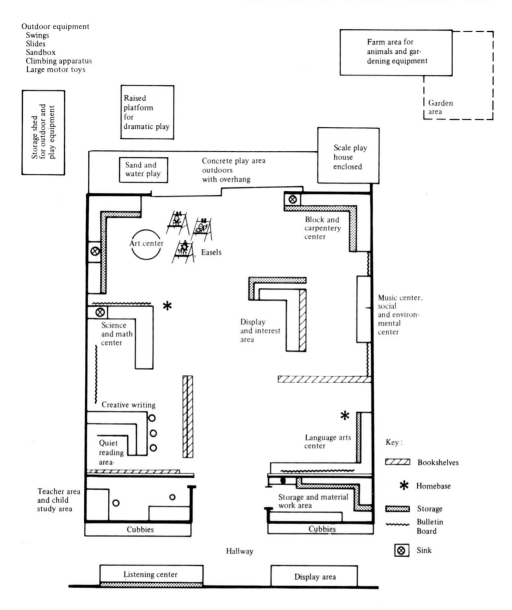

Outdoor equipment
  Swings
  Slides
  Sandbox
  Climbing apparatus
  Large motor toys

Farm area for animals and gardening equipment

Garden area

Storage shed for outdoor and play equipment

Raised platform for dramatic play

Scale play house enclosed

Sand and water play

Concrete play area outdoors with overhang

Art center

Easels

Block and carpentery center

Music center, social and environmental center

Science and math center

Display and interest area

Creative writing

Quiet reading area·

Language arts center

Teacher area and child study area

Storage and material work area

Cubbies

Cubbies

Hallway

Listening center

Display area

Key:

  Bookshelves

  * Homebase

  Storage

  Bulletin Board

  ⊗ Sink

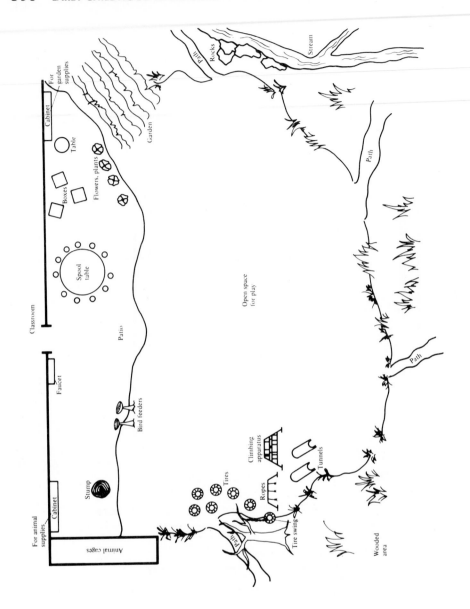

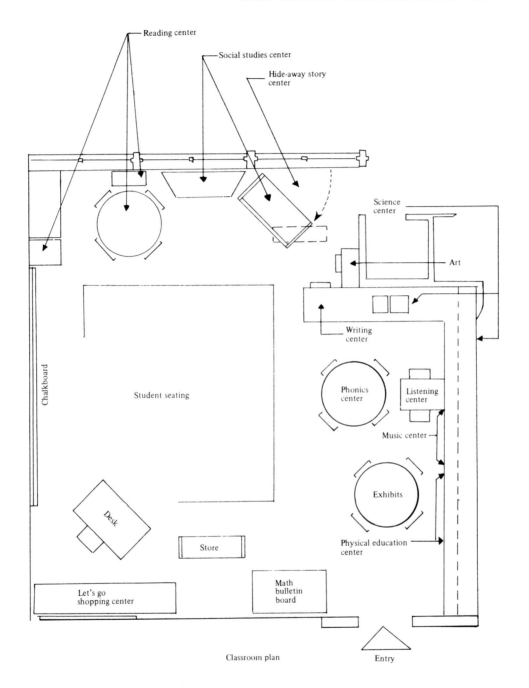

Reading center

Social studies center

Hide-away story center

Science center

Art

Writing center

Chalkboard

Student seating

Phonics center

Listening center

Music center

Exhibits

Desk

Physical education center

Store

Math bulletin board

Let's go shopping center

Classroom plan

Entry

Resource Materials

Appendixes

Appendix A

Resource Books for Teachers

All About Whales, by Roy Chapman. New York: Random House, 1954.

An Introduction to Trees, by John Kieran. New York: Doubleday, 1966.

Animals of the Sea, a Golden Stamp Book, by Millicent Selsam. New York: Scholastic, 1975.

Beginnings, Teacher's Guide, Science Curriculum Improvement Study. Chicago, IL: Rand McNally and Company, 1974.

Bubbles, Rainbows, and Worms: Science Experiments for Pre-School Children, by Sam Brown (Ed.). Mr. Ranier, MD: Gryphon House, 1981.

Collecting Cocoons, by L. J. Hussey and C. Pessino. New York: Thomas Y. Crowell, 1953.

Discovering Plants, by Glenn O. Blough. New York: McGraw-Hill, 1966.

Early Childhood and Science: A Collection of Articles, by Margaret McIntyre. Washington, D.C.: National Science Teachers Association, 1984.

Explore and Create, by Dixie Hibner and Lix Cromwell. Livonia, MI: Partner Press, 1980.

Exploring Earth Science, by Rose Wyler. Racine, WI: Western Publishing, 1973.

Farming in the Classroom—Teachers' Guide. Science Study Aid No. 8, Agricultural Research Service. Washington, DC: U.S. Department of Agriculture, Supt. of Documents, Government Printing Office.

Fish, by Christine Sharr. London: MacDonald & Co., 1971.

Food in History, by Reay Tannahill. New York: Stein and Day Publishers, 1973.

Food Selection for Good Nutrition in Group Feeding. Agricultural Research Service. Washington, DC: Department of Agriculture, U.S. Government Printing Office.

Games That Teach for Children Three Through Six, by Evelyn Kay. Minneapolis, MN: T. S. Denison and Company, 1981.

Gardening in Containers—A Handbook. New York: Brooklyn Botanical Gardens, 1958.

Good Earth Almanac, by Monte Burch. Prairie Village, KS: Andrews-McMeel Publ., 1972.

Houses from the Sea, by Alice E. Goudy. New York: Scribner, 1959.

How Do Your Children Grow? Association for Childhood Education International, 3615 Wisconsin Avenue, N.W., Washington, DC 20016: Assoc. for Childhood Educ. Int'l., 1959.

Hurricanes, Tornadoes and Blizzards, by Kathryn Hitte. New York: Random House, 1960.

I Can Make a Rainbow, by Marjorie Frank. Nashville, TN: Incentive Publications, 1976.

Insect Masquerades, by H. Simon. New York: Viking, 1968.

Insects, A Golden Guide, by Herbert Zim. New York: Golden Press, 1976.

Insects of North America, by A. Kots and E. Kots. New York: Doubleday, 1971.

Leaves, by James Poling. New York: Holt, 1971.

Let's Go Metric (Chapter 7), by Frank Donovan. Weybright and Talley, 1974.

Let's Go to the Seashore, by Harriet Huntington. New York: Doubleday, 1941.

Life Along the Seashore, by Alan Solem. Chicago: Encyclopedia Britannica Press, 1963.

Life in a Bucket of Soil, by Richard Rhine. New York: Lothrop, 1972.

Mammals, A Golden Guide, by Herbert Zim. New York: Golden Press, 1955.

Mathematics Their Way, by Mary Baratta-Lorton. Menlo Park, CA: Addison-Wesley, 1976.

Nature with Children of All Ages, by Edith Sisson. Englewood Cliffs, NJ: Prentice-Hall, 1982.

North Carolina Competency-Based Curriculum, Raleigh, NC, 1985. N.C. Department of Public Instruction.

Number in Preschool and Kindergarten: Educational Implications of Piaget's Theory, by Constance Kamii. Washington, DC: National Association for the Education of Young Children, 1982.

Nutrition and Intellectual Growth in Children, Association for Childhood Education International, 3615 Wisconsin Avenue, N.W., Washington, DC 20016: 1969.

Pets in a Jar, Collecting and Caring for Small Wild Animals, by Seymour Simon. New York: Penguin Books, 1979.

Science Experiences for the Early Childhood Years, by Jean Durgin Harlan. Columbus, OH: Charles E. Merrill, Co., 1976.

Science Experiences You Can Eat, by Vicki Cobb. New York: Lippincott, 1972.

Science from Water Play, Teaching Primary Science, by John Bird. Milwaukee, WI: MacDonald-Raintree, 1979.

Seashells, A Golden Stamp Book, by Carson Ritchie. New York: Western Pub., 1973.

Selection and Care of Fresh Fruits and Vegetables, 1977, United Fresh Fruit and Vegetable Association, 1019 19th Street, N.W., Washington, DC 20036.

Taste and Smell, by Joy Wilt and Terre Watson. Waco, TX: Creative Resources, 1978.

Teaching Children about Science: Ideas and Activities Every Teacher and Parent Can Use, by Elaine Levenson. Englewood Cliffs, NJ: Prentice-Hall, 1985.

Teaching Mathematics to Young Children, by Rosalie Jensen and Debora Spector. Englewood Cliffs, NJ: Prentice-Hall, 1984.

The Amazing Seeds, by Ross E. Hutchins. New York: Dodd & Mead, 1965.

The Crust of the Earth: An Armchair Traveler's Guide to the New Geology, by Chet Raymo. Englewood Cliffs, NJ: Prentice-Hall, 1983.

The Hidden Magic of Seeds, by Dorothy E. Shuttlesworth. Emmaus, PA: Rodale Press, 1976.

The Insects, by P. Farb. New York: Time/Life, 1977.

The Life of Fishes, by Dr. Maunce Burton. London and New York: MacDonald & Co., 1972.

The Organic Living Book, by Bernice Kohn. New York: Viking Press, 1972.

The Story of Ants, by Dorothy Shuttlesworth. New York: Doubleday, 1964.

The Winds of Weather, by A. Harrism Stone and Herbert Spiegel. Englewood Cliffs, NJ: Prentice-Hall, 1969.

Thinking Goes to School: Piaget's Theory in Practice, by Hans G. Furth and Harry Wach. New York: Oxford University Press, 1975.

Trees: A Golden Guide, by Herbert S. Zim and A. C. Martin. Racine, WI: Western, 1956.

Watch the Tides, by David Greenhood. New York: Holiday House, 1961.

Water, by Boris Arnow. New York: Lothrop, Lee and, Shephard, 1980.

Water, Water Everywhere: Science Through Waterplay, by Jean Benish. Winston-Salem, NC: Kaplan Press, 1977.

Weather: A Golden Guide, by Will R. Burnett, Paul E. Lehr, and Herbert Zim. New York: Golden Press, 1975.

Where They Go in Winter, by Margaret Buck. New York: Abingdon Press, 1968.

Young Children Reinvent Arithmetic: Implications of Piaget's Theory, by Kamii, Kazuko, and Goergia DeClark. New York: Teachers College Press, 1985.

Books for Children

A Ball of Clay, by John Hawkinson. Chicago: Albert Whitman & Co., 1974.

A First Look at Animals Without Backbones, by Millicent Selsam. New York: Walker, 1976.

A First Look at Birds, by Millicent Selsam. New York: Scholastic Books, 1981.

A First Look at Leaves, by Millicent E. Selsam and Joyce Hunt. New York: Scholastic Book Services, 1976.

A First Look at the World of Plants, by Millicent E. Selsam and Joyce Hunt. New York: Walker, 1978.

A Gardening Book: Indoors and Outdoors, by Anne B. Walsh. New York: Atheneum, 1976.

A Single Speckled Egg, by Sonia Levitin. New York: Paranassus, 1976.

A Snowy Day, by Ezra Jack Keats. New York: Greenwillow Books, 1963.

A Tree is a Plant, by Clyde Bulla. New York: Thomas Y. Crowell, 1973.

A Tree is Something Wonderful, by Elizabeth Cooper. Chicago: Children's Press, 1972.

A World of Color, by Sylvia Root Tester. Elgin, IL: The Child's World, 1939.

ABC Science Experiments, by Harry Milgrom. New York: Children's Press, 1975.

Air Is All Around You, by Franklin Branley. New York: Thomas Y. Crowell, 1962.

All Butterflies, by Marcia Brown. New York: Charles Scribner's Sons, 1974.

Amazing Air, Science Club, by Henry Smith. New York: Lothrop, Lee and Shepard Books, 1982.

And Everything Nice, by Eliza K. Cooper. New York: Harcourt Brace and World, Inc., 1966.

And Me, Coyote, by Betty Baker. New York: Macmillan Publishers, 1982.

Animals That Give People Milk, by Terrance W. McCabe and Harley W. Mitchell. Chicago, IL: National Diary Council, 1970.

Apple Orchard, by Irmengarde Eberle. New York: Henry Z. Walck, Inc., 1962.

Apricot ABC, by Miska Miles. Boston, MA: Little, Brown, 1969.

Arts of Clay, by Christine Price. New York: Charles Scribner's Sons, 1977.

Bedtime for Frances, by Russell Hoban. New York: Harper and Row, 1960.

Black is Beautiful, by Ann McGovern. New York: Four Winds Press, 1969.

Black is Brown is Tan, by Arnold Adoff. New York: Harper, 1973.

Bodies, by Barbara Brenner. New York: Dutton, 1973.

Black Means . . . , by Barney Grossman and Gladys Broom. New York: Hill and Wang, 1970.

Buckets of Paint, by Edna Becker. Nashville, TN: Abingdon Press, 1949.

Castle, by David McCauley. Boston, MA: Houghton Mifflin, 1977.

Cathedral, by David McCauley. Boston, MA: Houghton Mifflin, 1973.

Cats, F. Henrie. New York: Watts, 1980.

Chickens Aren't the Only Ones, by Ruth Heller. New York: Grosset and Dunlap, 1981.

Circles, Triangles and Squares, by Tana Hoban. New York: Macmillan, 1974.

Discovering Design, by Marion Downer. New York: Lothrop, Lee and Shepard Co., 1947.

Discovering What Earthworms Do, by Seymour Simon. New York: McGraw-Hill, 1969.

Do Bears Have Mothers, Too? by Aileen Lucia Fisher. New York: Crowell, 1973.

Eating and Cooking Around the World, by Erick Barry. New York: John Day Company, 1963.

Eskimo Crafts and Their Cultural Backgrounds, by Jeremy Comins. New York: Lothrop, Lee and Shepard, 1975.

Everyday Trees, by Gertrude Allen. Boston, MA: Houghton Mifflin, 1968.

Find Out by Touching, by Paul Showers. New York: Thomas Y. Crowell, 1961.

Fingerprint Owls and Other Fantasies, by Marjorie Katz. New York: M. Evans and Company, 1972.

First Book of Tree Identification, by Matilda Rodgers. New York: Random House, 1951.

Flash, Crash, Rumble and Roll: Let's Read and Find Out, by Franklyn M. Branley. New York: Thomas Y. Crowell, 1964.

Follow the Wind, by Alvin Tresselt. New York: Lothrop, Lee and Shepard Books, 1950.

Foxfire Books, by Eliot Wigginton. Garden City, NY: Doubleday & Company.

Freight Train, by Donald Crews. New York: Greenwillow, 1978.

Frogs, by Graham Tarrant. Los Angeles: Inter-visual Communications, Inc., 1983.

Fruits We Eat, by Carroll Lane Fenton and Hermine B. Kitchen. New York: John Day Company, 1961.

Good For Me: All About Food in 32 Bites, by Marilyn Burns. New York: Little Brown & Company, 1978.

Grains, by Elizabeth B. Brown. Prentice-Hall, 1977.

Great Big Air Book, by Richard Scarry. New York: Random House, 1971.

Green Says Go, by Ed Emberly. Boston, MA: Little, Brown, 1968.

Growing Up, How We Become Alive, Are Born and Grow, by Karl de Schweinitz. New York: Macmillan Company, 1965.

Hailstones and Halibut Bones, by Mary O'Neil. Garden City, NY: Doubleday, 1961.

Harold and the Purple Crayon, by Crockett Johnson. New York: Harper and Row, 1955.

Hide and Defend, by Kathleen Daly. New York: Golden Press, 1976.

How a Seed Grows, by Jordan. New York: Thomas Y. Crowell, 1960.

How Plants Make Food, by Martin J. Gutnik. Chicago: Children's Press, 1976.

How to Be a Nature Detective, by Millicent Selsam. New York: Harper and Row, 1963.

Hunters Stew and Hangtown Fry, by Lila Perl. Seabury Press, 1977.

I See the Winds, by Lazue Mizumura. New York: Thomas Y. Crowell, 1966.

I Spy: A Picture Book of Objects in a Child's Home Environment, by Lucille Ogle. New York: American Heritage Press, 1970.

If You Were an Ant, by B. Brenner. New York: Harper, 1973.

Indoor Outdoor Gardening Book, by Cynthia and Alvin Koehler. New York: Grosset & Dunlap, Inc. (Wonder Books), 1969.

Inside of Animals, by Gale Cooper. Boston: Little, Brown, 1978.

It Could Always Be Worse, by Margot Zemach, ed. New York: Farrar, 1976.

It's Easy to Have a Caterpillar Visit You, by Allan, Caroline, and Judith O'Hagan. New York: Lothrop, Lee and Shepard, 1980.

It's Easy to Have a Snail Visit You, by Allan, Caroline, and Judith O'Hagan. New York: Lothrop, Lee and Shepard, 1980.

It's Easy to have a Worm Visit You, by Allan, Caroline, and Judith O'Hagan. New York: Lothrop, Lee and Shepard, 1980.

Kids Gardening: First Indoor Outdoor Gardening Book for Children, by Aileen Paul. Doubleday, 1972.

Light and Darkness, by F. M. Branley. New York: Thomas Y. Crowell, 1975.

Liquid Magic, Science Club, by Philip Watson. New York: Lothrop, Lee and Shepard Books, 1982.

Look at Leaves, by Rena K. Kirkpatrick. Milwaukee: Raintree Children's Books, 1978.

Louie, by Ezra Jack Keats. New York: Greenwillow, 1975.

Me and My Bones, by R. A. Gallant. New York: Doubleday, 1971.

Measure with Metric, by Franklyn Branley. T. Crowell, 1975.

Messing Around with Water Pumps and Siphons, by Bernie Zubrowski. Boston: Little, Brown, 1981.

Milk for You, by G. Warren Schloat. Charles Scribner's Sons, New York, 1951.

Millions of Cats, by Wanda Gag. New York: Coward-McCann, Inc., 1928.

My Skyscraper City, by Penny Hammond and Katrina Thomas. Garden City, NY: Doubleday, 1963.

Nothing to Eat But Food, by Frank Jupo. New York: E. P. Dutton and Co., Inc., 1954.

Nuts, by Olive L. Earle and Michael Kantor. New York: Morrow, 1976.

Plants are Like That, by A. Harris Stone and Peter Plascencia. Englewood Cliffs, NJ: Prentice-Hall, 1968.

Plants in the City, by Herman and Nina Schneider. New York: John Day, Co., 1951.

Plants in Winter, by Joanna Cole. New York: Thomas Y. Crowell, 1973.

Plants That Feed the World, by Rose E. Frisch. Princeton, NJ: D. Van Nostrand Company, 1966.

Plants That Feed Us, by Carroll Lane Fenton and Hermine B. Kitchen. New York: John Day & Company, 1971.

Popcorn, by Millicent E. Selsam. New York: Morrow, 1976.

Print Making, by Suellen MacStravic. Minneapolis, MN: Lerner Publishing Company, 1973.

Printmaking, by Harlow Rockwell. Garden City, NY: Doubleday & Co., 1973.

Rain and Hail, Let's Read and Find Out, by Franklyn M. Branley. New York: Thomas Y. Crowell, 1963.

Rice, Food For a Hungry World, by Winnefred Hammond. New York: Coward McCann, Inc., 1961.

Rocks and Gems, by Jay Heavilin. New York: Macmillan, 1964.

Salt, by Augusta Coldin. New York: Thomas Y. Crowell, 1965.

Seasons, by John Burningham. New York: Bobbs-Merrill, 1970.

See What I Caught! by Ann Thomas Piecewicz. Englewood Cliffs, NJ: Prentice-Hall, 1974.

Shadow, by Marcia Brown. New York: Charles Scribner's Sons, 1982.

Shapes, by John J. Reiss. Scarsdale, NY: Bradbury Press, Inc., 1974.

Shapes, by Miriam Schlein. Reading, MA: Addison-Wesley, 1952.

Snow Stumpers, by David Webster. Garden City, NY: The National History Press, 1968.

Spider Silk, by Augusta Goldin. New York: Thomas Y. Crowell, 1965.

Square Is a Shape, by Sharon Lerner. Minneapolis, MN: Lerner Press, 1974.

Sweet and Delicious Fruits of Tree, Bush and Vine, by Elizabeth Cooper. Chicago: Children's Press, 1973.

The Art of the Southwest Indians, by Shirley Glubock. New York: Macmillan Co., 1971.

The Bakery Factory, by Aylette Jenness. New York: T. Crowell, 1978.

The Birth of Sunset's Kittens, by Carla Stevens. New York: William H. Scott, 1969.

The Carrot and Other Root Vegetables, by Millicent E. Selsam. New York: William Morrow & Company, 1970.

The Chemistry of a Lemon, by A. Harris Stone and Peter Plascencia. Englewood Cliffs, NJ: Prentice-Hall, Inc., 1966.

The Cloud Book, by Tomie dePaola. New York: Holiday House, 1975.

The Color Kittens, by Margaret Brown. New York: Golden Press, 1967.

The Colors Book, by Christine Timmons. Chicago: Encyclopedia Britannica, Inc., 1974.

The First American Peanut Growing Book, by Kathy Mandry. New York: Random House, 1976.

The First Book of Food, by Ida Scheib. New York: Franklin Watts Publishers, 1956.

The First Book of Gardening, by Virginia Kirkus. New York: Franklin Watts, Inc., 1956.

The First Book of the Earth, by O. Irene Severy. New York: Franklin Watts, 1958.

The Girl Who Loved Wild Horses, by Paul Goble. Scarsdale, NY: Bradbury, 1978.

The How and Why Wonder Book of Weather, by Paul E. Blackwood. New York: Grosset and Dunlap, 1978.

The Indoor Outdoor Grow It Book, by S. Sinclair Baker. New York: Random House, 1966.

The Little House in the Big Woods, by Laura Ingalls Wilder. New York: Harper & Row, 1953.

The Magic of Color, by Hilda Simon. New York: Lothrop and Lee, 1981.

The Riddle of Seeds, by Winifred G. Hammond. New York: Coward-McCann, 1965.

The Rock Hound Book, by S. Simon. New York: Viking Press, 1973.

The Secret World of the Baby, by Beth Day and Margaret Liley, M.D. New York: Random House, 1968.

The Shape of Me and Other Stuff, by Dr. Seuss. New York: Beginner Books, 1973.

The Stonecutter, by Gerald McDermott. New York: Viking Press, 1975.

The Story of Johnny Appleseed, by Aliki. Englewood Cliffs, NJ: Prentice-Hall, 1963.

The Tomato and Other Fruit Vegetables, by Millicent E. Selsam. New York: William Morrow & Company, 1970.

The Tremendous Tree Book, by Mary Garelick. New York: Scholastic Book Services, 1979.

The True Book of Pebbles and Shells, by Illa Podendorf. Chicago: Children's Press, 1972.

The True Book of Rocks and Minerals, by Illa Podendorf. Chicago: Children's Press, 1972.
The True Book of Science Experiments, by Illa Podendorf. Chicago: Children's Press, 1972.
Twist, Wriggle and Squirm: A Book About Earth Worms, by Lawrence P. Pringle. New York: Thomas Y. Crowell, 1973.
The Wind is Air, by Mary Brewer. New York: Children's Press, 1975.
The Wonderful Egg, by G. Warren Schloat. New York: Charles Scribner's Sons, 1952.
The Wing on a Flea, by Ed Emberly. Boston: Little, Brown, 1961.
The Wonderful World of Food, by John Boyd Orr. New York: Garden City Books, 1958.
The Young Potter, by Denys Val Baker. New York: Frederick Warne Co., 1963.
Tricks Animals Play, by J. N. Clarkson. Washington, DC: National Geographic Society, 1975.
Underground, by David McCauley. Boston, MA: Houghton Mifflin, 1976.
Water All Around, by Tillie Pine and Joseph Levine. New York: Whittlesey House, 1959.
Water for Dinosaurs and You: Let's Read and Find Out, by Roma Gans. New York: Thomas Y. Crowell, 1972.
We Read About Seeds and How They Grow, by Harold E. Tannenbaum and Nathan Sillman. St. Louis, MI: Webster Publishing Company, 1960.
Weather, by Imelda and Robert Updegraff. New York: Penguin Books, 1982.
What Is Your Favorite Thing to Touch? by M. T. Gibson. New York: Grosset & Dunlap, 1965.
What Makes a Shadow? by Clyde R. Bulla. New York: Scholastic Book Services, 1962.
What Makes Day and Night? by F. M. Branley. New York: Thomas Y. Crowell, 1961.
When Cave Men Painted, by Norman Bate. New York: Charles Scribner's Sons, 1963.
When the Wind Stops, by Charlotte Zolotow. New York: Harper and Row, 1962.
When Winter Comes, by Russel Freedman. New York: Dutton, 1981.
Whose Nose is This? by Richard Van Gelden. New York: Walker, 1974.
Wild Foods, by Lawrence Pringle. New York: Charles Scribner's Sons, 1978.
Zoo City, by Stephen Lewis. New York: Greenwillow Books. 1976.

Films

Another Way to Learn. Educational Development Center, 55 Chapel Street, Newton, Mass. 02160.
Battling Brook Primary School (Four Days in September): An Overview Plus Several Vignettes. Education Development Center, 55 Chapel Street, Newton, Mass. 02160.
Blocks. Campus Films, 20 East 46th Street, New York, N.Y. 10017.
Catch a Tiger. Du Art Film Laboratories, 245 West 55th St., New York, N.Y. 10011.
Children Are People. Agathon Press, 150 Fifth Avenue, New York, N.Y. 10011.
Children Dance. Consolidated Film Industries, 959 Sward Street, Hollywood, Calif. 90038.
Discovery and Experience (series includes 10 films): *Learning by Doing, Math Is a Master, Our Own Music, Learning by Design, Finding Out, Movement in Time and Space, The Changeover, City Infants, The Growing Mind, How Children Think.* Produced by British Broadcasting Corporation. Available in the United States from Time-Life Films, 1271 Sixth Avenue, New York, N.Y. 10020.
Dramatic Play. Campus Film Corporation, New York, N.Y. 10017.
Early Expressionists. Contemporary Films, 267 West 25th Street, New York, N.Y. 10001.
First Friends. International Film Bureau, 332 South Michigan Avenue, Chicago, Ill. 60604.
Glasser on Discipline. Media Five, 1011 North Cole Avenue, Hollywood, Calif. 90038.
I Am Here Today. Educational Development Center, 55 Chapel Street, Newton, Mass. 02160.
Infants School. Education Development Center, 55 Chapel Street, Newton, Mass. 02160.
Medbourne Primary School—Four Days in May. Education Development Center, 55 Chapel Street, Newton, Mass. 02160.
My Art Is Me. University of California Extension Media Center, Berkeley, Calif. 94720.
Open Classroom. Sherwin Rubin, 4532 Newton St., Torrance, Calif. 90505.

Piaget's Theory: Classification. Davidson Films, 3701 Buchanan Street, San Francisco, Calif. 94123.

Piaget's Theory: Conservation. Davidson Films, 3701 Buchanan Street, San Francisco, Calif. 94123.

Primary Adventure. Inner London Education Authority, The County Hall, London, SE 1, England.

Primary Education in England: The English Infant School. I/D/E/A, Information Division, P.O. Box 446, Melbourne, Fla. 32901.

Reading: A Language Experience Approach. Promethean Films South, P.O. Box 26363, Birmingham, Ala. 35226.

Room to Learn. Association Films, Madison Avenue, New York, N.Y. 10022.

See My Rainbow. Nassau Film Production, 515 Oxford Street, Westbury, N.Y. 11590.

School Without Failure. Media Five, Film Distributors, 1011 North Cole Avenue, Hollywood, Calif. 90038.

The British Infant School—Southern Style. Promethean Films South, P.O. Box 1489, Auburn, Ala. 36830.

The Informal Classroom. Educational Coordinates, 4325 Pastoria Avenue, Sunnyvale, Calif. 94086.

Westfield Infant School: Two Days in May. Education Development Center, 55 Chapel Street, Newton, Mass. 02160.

What Did You Learn at School Today? Leichestershire Country Library, Clarence Street, Leichestershire LE13RW, England.

Films For Children

America's Heroes: George Washington. Coronet
America's National Anthem. Learning Corporation of America
Beginning Responsibility—Taking Care of Things. Coronet
Boyhood of Abraham Lincoln. Coronet
Boyhood of George Washington Carver. Coronet.
Calendar: The Days, Weeks, Months. Coronet
Communication: A First Film. Bailey Films
Family of the Island, Her Name Is Wasametha. McGraw-Hill
Home Free. Bailey Films
Making Change for a Dollar. Coronet
Maps and Their Uses. ACA
Maps Are Fun. Coronet
Moving Goods in the Community. Coronet
Our Country's Flag. Coronet
Rock in the Road. A–F–A
Story of Our Money System. Coronet
The Fight. Walt Disney Productions
There's Nobody Else Like You. Film Fair/Film West
Turn Off the Pollution. Encyclopedia Britannica Films
What Is a Friend? McGraw-Hill
What Mary Jo Shared. Bailey Films
What Time Is It? 2nd Ed. Coronet
Why We Have Taxes. Learning Corporation of America
Why We Use Money. Learning Corporation of America
Why We Need Each Other. Learning Corporation of America

Film Strips/Cassette Tapes

Early Childhood Education: Curriculum Organization and Classroom Management

This program applies the current research on how children learn to creating an early childhood learning environment. Emphasis is on managing and organizing the classroom in a way that provides for active participation, observation, exploration, and verbalization on the part of the child. Further, the program seeks to meet the needs of the total child—cognitive, affective, and psychomotor—and to match the curriculum to the developmental needs, interests, and learning styles of each child. The materials are designed to help participants implement a complex program step by step. The kit includes four sound filmstrips.

> Filmstrip 1, "The Six Components," introduces the six components of a developmental approach to early childhood education. The three curriculum organization components—learning centers, skills groups, and units of study—and the three classroom management components—color-coding contracts and internal and external discipline techniques—are defined and illustrated in an actual classroom setting.
>
> Filmstrip 2, "A Typical Day," follows an individual child through daily activities in the classroom. Emphasis is on the six components of curriculum organization and classroom management and how they help organize the child's program.
>
> Filmstrip 3, "A Unit of Study," details techniques used to implement an experiential, "hands-on" approach for teaching social studies and science concepts to young children. Units of study are organized and taught through the use of both groups and learning center activities.
>
> Filmstrip 4, "Does It Work?," reviews the rationale for a developmental approach in teaching young children and introduces methods for assessing the effectiveness of early childhood programs. The use of appropriate objective measures of classroom behavior is stressed, including detailed instructions on how to use the Wasik-Day Learning Environments and Children's Classroom Behavior Scale.

The filmstrips are accompanied by materials that allow early childhood practitioners to assess their own philosophies of teaching, plan a learning environment that meets children's developmental needs, design their own contracts, organize plans and develop materials for unit teaching through learning centers, implement small-group instruction in math and reading skills, and apply management techniques such as color coding and internal and external discipline methods to their own classrooms.

The kit is intended for use by early childhood teachers, administrators, curriculum specialists, and university educators. It can be used as the basis for staff development workshops or teacher education classes or as self-instruction by individuals.

The project director is Barbara D. Day, professor of Curriculum and Instruction at the University of North Carolina at Chapel Hill and past president of the Association for Supervision and Curriculum Development. The program may be ordered from the Association for Supervision and Curriculum Development, 225 North Washington Street, Alexandria, Va. 22314.

Filmstrips for Children

Can You Make Change? Goodman
Careers with a Police Department. Colonial
Citizenship Adventures of the Lollipop Dragon. SVE
Community Services: Many People Serve Our Community. National Geographic
Exploring Maps: Maps Skills for Today. Xerox
Getting Along. Scholastic
Globes. January Productions
Indians for Thanksgiving. SVE
Lincoln and Washington: Why We Celebrate Their Birthdays. SVE
Living in Cities. Teaching Resources
Making and Keeping Friends. SVE
Maps and Globes and Graphs. Eye Gate Media
Money and Time Adventures of the Lollipop Dragon. SVE
People Serving Your Community. National Geographic
Personal Success. SVE
Squanto and the First Thanksgiving. SVE
Targo the Job Explorer. SVE
The Tree That Became a Chair. Filmstrip Production Association
Using Globes. CRM/McGraw-Hill
Using Maps to Find Locations. SVE
Values in Action. Holt
What Do You Do About Rules? Guidance Association
What Is a Community? Learning Tree
What Is Responsibility? EBEC
What's Money For? Clearview
Who Am I? Scholastic
Who Do You Think You Are? Guidance Association

Appendix B

Materials for Learning Centers

Language Arts Center

1. Reading games, commercial and teacher-made
2. Reading skills kits
3. Flannel boards and cutouts
4. Large alphabet blocks
5. Puzzles
6. Sequence cards
7. Chalkboards
8. Magnetic board
9. Pictures and objects for classifying
10. Magazines and catalogs
11. Writing paper of different sizes and shapes

12. Pencils, colored marking pens, crayons
13. Poems and story starters
14. Blank booklets
15. Dictionaries
16. Book jackets
17. Word boxes
18. Typewriter
19. Feel box
20. Magic slates
21. Word cards
22. Filmstrips, tapes, records related to reading
23. Manipulative devices for visual discrimination and motor coordination
24. Tape recorder, earphones
25. Paper: lined and unlined, white and colored
26. Sentence strips
27. Paints and brushes
28. Various scrap materials that can be used for book covers
29. Manipulative letters: wood, sandpaper, pipe cleaners, plastic, cardboard
30. Cans labeled with a letter each: small cans with small letters, large cans with capital letters in another color
31. Pictures: wild and farm animals, vegetables, fruits, birds, flowers, various other pictures of different groups of things and places
32. Wide variety of books of interest to children
33. Series of pictures (for putting in correct sequence)
34. Dramatic play equipment (dress-up clothes, props, furniture)
35. Cards for children to write their own words on
36. Groups of cards with rhyming words (self-correcting)
37. Groups of cards with rhyming pictures (self-correcting)
38. ABC Bingo game
39. Groups of pictures with one different for visual discrimination
40. Tiles with letters on each
41. Play and real telephones
42. Mirror (full child body length)

Reading Center

1. Large area rug or carpet
2. Pillows or floor cushions
3. Rocking chairs
4. Easy chairs and couch
5. Assortment of books (library books, basal readers)
6. Magazines and catalogs
7. Encyclopedias
8. Child-made books
9. Shelves (low)
10. Flannel board, story characters, and objects
11. Puppets
12. Viewmasters and slides of stories
13. Filmstrips of stories

14. Tape recorder for children to tape themselves reading
15. Record player and records with corresponding book
16. Tape recorder and tapes with corresponding books
17. Books with coordinating filmstrips
18. Newspapers: class, local, and city (current)
19. Stories: child-written and commercial
20. Talk-starter picture cards
21. Magnetic board and letters
22. Lotto games
23. Matching picture and letter games
24. Parquetry blocks, designs
25. Puzzles (variety of types and number of pieces)
26. Spelling and reading games
27. Crossword puzzles
28. Tapes: blank, teacher-made
29. 1 to 2 tables and 2 to 4 chairs each
30. Small table with typewriter
31. Low shelves used also as a divider
32. Book rack
33. Open storage for records and tapes
34. Carrels for individual usage
35. Electrical outlets

Block Center

1. Set of solid wooden blocks: unit blocks, double unit blocks, quadruple unit blocks, ramps, curves (elliptical and circular), Y shapes, triangles, cylinders
2. Set of hollow-ply blocks (varying in size)
3. Riding wheel toys (tractor and trailer, derrick truck, open van truck)
4. Small vehicles (airplane, helicopter, dump truck, steamroller, train, firetruck)
5. Block bin
6. Block cart
7. Rubber zoo and farm animals
8. Rubber people (farmer, police officer, fire fighter)
9. Traffic signs
10. Tiles, carpet squares, wallpaper (can be used as floors)
11. Miniature furniture
12. Magic markers, pencils, small cards, sentence strips (for labeling; store in small boxes or cans covered with contact paper)
13. Puppets
14. Tool kits (for dramatic play)
15. Thin pieces of rubber tubing (for gasoline pumps)
16. Pulleys
17. Dry cell batteries with lights (to illuminate building interiors)
18. Planks
19. Packing crates, boxes, ropes
20. Books related to building and construction
21. Objects used to "decorate" buildings: dominoes, shells (scallop, clam), variety of small plastic containers and lids, popsicle sticks, large dried beans,

small colored cubes (1" or 2 cm), spools (thread and textile mill), parquetry blocks, assorted colored wooden table blocks, lumber scraps (sanded), pebbles, stones

22. Other building materials: Lego blocks (large and small), Tinker Toys, Lincoln Logs, large hollow blocks (plastic or wooden)
23. Easter grass (excellent for animal life)
24. Scraps of fabric
25. Styrofoam pebbles
26. Small flags
27. Art box (paper, crayons, string, clay, scissors, scotch tape, masking tape, etc.)

Math Center

1. Counters (blocks, beads, sticks, straws, buttons, clothespins, bottle caps)
2. Scales and objects to weigh
3. Rulers, yardstick, tape measure
4. Thermometers
5. Clocks
6. Measuring devices (spoons, cups, containers, various sizes)
7. Math books
8. Commercial and teacher-made games (see directions for making)
9. Bead or counting frame
10. Cuisenaire rods
11. Number lines
12. Balances
13. Play money
14. Geoboards and rubber bands
15. Flannel board and cutouts
16. Pegs and pegboard
17. Dominoes
18. Problem or activity cards
19. Acetate folders for worksheets
20. Place value charts
21. Magnetic letters and numbers, magnetic board
22. Fractional parts and fractional board
23. Playing cards, checkers and board, chess set and board
24. Rope (for encompassing areas), puzzles, logs
25. Blocks of all shapes and sizes, number blocks, parquetry, attribute blocks
26. Flash cards
27. Sum stick, adding machine, calculator
28. Trundle wheel, compass, measuring rods and containers
29. Abacus
30. Collections of all types (buttons, coins, stones, sticks, stirrers, macaroni, beans, yarn, marbles, bottle caps)
31. Egg cartons for making sets
32. Books (interest and reference)
33. Catalogs, newspaper ads
34. Geometric wire forms and patterns
35. Metric step-on scales, metric platform scale, metric plastic measure set (spoons and cups, 1 ml to 250 ml), balance scale with metric weights (1 g to 50 g)

36. Coin stamps
37. Unifix cubes
38. Rice and sand (for measuring)

Woodworking Center

1. Workbench
2. Sawhorse
3. Storage shelves
4. Hand drill with several bits
5. 4″–6″ "C" clamps
6. File, cabinet, half round 8″
7. File card for cleaning file
8. Hammers 7 to 10 oz. (claw) with wooden handles
9. Pliers, combination, 6 in.
10. Saw, hand crosscut, 16 and 11 pt.
11. Saw, coping (for cutting curves)
12. Screwdrivers, slotted and Phillip's head type
13. Vice for workbench
14. Backsaw
15. T-square
16. Miter box
17. Paint scraper
18. Brush
19. Hole punch, center
20. Plane
21. Rasp (for smoothing edges)
22. Broom, dustpan
23. Nails (variety)
24. Hooks and screws
25. Paint
26. Trash can with lid
27. Paint stain
28. Paintbrushes
29. Wood scraps
30. Rulers, yardstick
31. Rags
32. Glue (Elmer's)
33. Nailing block
34. Shop vacuum
35. First aid kit
36. Sink
37. Keyhole or compass saw
38. Brace and bit
39. Sure forms
40. Monkey wrench
41. Wire cutter
42. Awl
43. "Large" wood supply (soft pine or spruce, finished or unfinished wood, molding and doweling, plywood)

44. "Small" wood supply (toothpicks, popsicle sticks, tongue depressors, paint stirrers, small branches and sticks, "end grain" scrips, box of assorted scrap wood)
45. Cardboard (tri-wall, large posterboard boxes)
46. Pencils, scissors, string, wallpaper scraps, tacks, tapes, leather, wire, chicken wire, paper clips, glue
47. Small wheels, styrofoam, bottle caps, pop-tops from cans
48. Formica, tile, linoleum
49. Sandpaper, paint, shellac, brushes
50. Hinges, knobs, nuts, bolts, hooks
51. Pulleys, rope
52. Broom, dustpan, rags
53. Safety glasses
54. Work gloves
55. Magnets
56. Paint shirts
57. Band-aids
58. Mild bath soap

Science Center

1. Large aquarium
2. Bird-feeding station
3. Magnifying glass (hand, tripod), microscope, telescope
4. Cage for insects, bug house
5. Cages for live animals, animal food
6. Different kinds of soil
7. Magnets (bar, U, horseshoe)
8. Science kits
9. Prisms
10. Seeds to plant and classify
11. Watering cans, trowel, flower pots, incubators
12. Objects that float and sink
13. Terrarium
14. Objects to smell, taste, hear, touch, see
15. Thermometers (outdoor and indoor, Celsius and Fahrenheit), barometer
16. Things to take apart and put together
17. Pulleys, levers, inclined planes, screws, wheels and axles, bolts, gears
18. Simple machines
19. Electrical equipment, electrical bell, bulbs, switches, hot plate, flashlight
20. Compass
21. Shapes
22. Things to classify
23. Flower boxes
24. Rock and shell collections
25. Rugs
26. Tables
27. Low shelving for puzzles, games, displays
28. Windows (preferably low enough for the children to see out)
29. Clear plastic containers with labels for "raw materials"

30. Plastic tubs for storing materials and supplies
31. A sink, preferably with hot and cold water
32. Tuning forks
33. Wood, wire, glass
34. Bottles
35. Candles
36. Batteries
37. Magazines (especially farm and science magazines)
38. Resource material, pleasurable nature reading (e.g. Ranger Rick)
39. Pendulums, pendulum frame, pendulum bobs
40. Scales (balance, kitchen, spring), weights, assorted materials for balancing
41. Mirrors and lenses
42. Kaleidoscope, color paddles
43. Calendars, clocks, hour glass, egg timer, sundial
44. Tape measures, yardstick, meter stick, rulers, dry and liquid measure containers
45. Rope, drinking straws, food coloring, stopwatch, stethoscope, sponges, keys
46. Kite, locks, iron filings, mechanical junk, slinky, strings
47. An assortment of chemicals from home: vinegar, baking soda, table salt, baking powder, sugar, cream of tartar, rubbing alcohol, epsom salts, iodine, ammonia, hydrogen peroxide
48. Fibers: nylon, silk, rayon, linen
49. Heat, water
50. Paper and pen for labeling
51. Chart and graph paper

Social Studies Center

1. Maps (city, neighborhood, state, U.S., world)
2. Globe (primary)
3. Pictures and study prints
4. Magazines and catalogs
5. Question and problem cards
6. Teacher-made activity cards
7. Social studies books
8. Encyclopedias
9. Filmstrips relating to social studies
10. Class books about social studies topics
11. Charts of information
12. Models of workers, stores, indians, vehicles, radios
13. Equipment such as telephone to take apart
14. Scrapbooks
15. Materials to make a diorama, peep box, models
16. Activity kits (e.g., Community Helpers)
17. Graphs
18. Cartoons
19. Real objects (flags, coins, costumes)
20. Typewriter
21. Cassette player, cassettes, and headsets
22. Record player, headset, and records

23. Dukane (filmstrips, tapes or records)
24. Film loop projector and film loop
25. Overhead projector and transparencies
26. Slide projector and color transparency slides
27. Radio, television
28. Microcomputer and software
29. Works of art (paintings, drawings, sculptures, basketing, pottery, architecture)
30. Paper for writing, construction, chart
31. Art materials (paints, easels, chalk, crayons, clay, paste)
32. Cartons and boxes
33. Blocks and transportation toys
34. Telephone
35. Envelopes and stamps
36. Cooking equipment and utensils
37. Clothing for dramatic/role play

Home Living and Creative Dramatics

1. Puppets/puppet theater
2. Materials for making puppets (scissors, glue, pens, markers, cloth scraps, paper bags, boxes, costumes, yarn, buttons, trinkets, styrofoam balls, styrofoam cups, handkerchiefs, tongue depressors, string, socks, paper plates, spools, cardboard rolls, pint-sized milk cartons, clay or playdough)
3. Brooms, mop, dustpan
4. Brushes
5. Clothes rack
6. Dish pan
7. Child-sized wooden sink, stove, refrigerator, cupboard
8. Small table, chairs, bed
9. Small rug
10. Shelves
11. Chest for dress-up clothes, shoes, hats
12. Dolls
13. Doll clothes
14. Doll bed and other furniture
15. Cooking supplies (measuring spoons and cups, minute timer, mixing bowls, hot plate, toaster oven, saucepans, wooden spoons, eggbeater, paring knife, cookie cutter, pot holder, aprons or smocks, dishpans, rolling pin, muffin tin, cookie sheets, paper towels, plates, napkins, recipe task cards or chart, spatula, grater, sifter, whisk, blender, aluminum foil, cutting board, electric fry pan, colander, vegetable brush)
16. Sponges, cloths, potholders, aprons
17. Doll carriage
18. Dishes, silverware
19. Mirror
20. Rocking chair
21. Curtains for window
22. Artificial fruits, vegetables
23. Telephone, classroom telephone book, datebook
24. Ironing board, iron

25. Pails, sponges
26. Jewelry, shoes, handbags, hats (including various occupational hats such as fireman, policeman, hardhat, nurse, helmet, cap, etc.), coats, scarves, dresses for play, props for playing doctor, beauty parlor
27. Flower vase with flowers
28. Books, magazines, newspapers
29. Added objects as needed for special emphasis
30. Sufficient space to allow free movement

Fine Arts Center

Music

1. Rhythm instruments
2. Small boxes
3. Dowel sticks
4. Record player
5. Records
6. Earphones
7. Autoharp (and cards made out with markings for familiar songs)
8. Music books and charts of songs to play
9. Glasses of water and spoons
10. Manuscript paper for children to write songs
11. Scarves for dancing
12. Materials for children to make their own instruments (boxes, paper plates, bottle caps, pebbles, stones, beans, cans)
13. Kalimba (with cards)
14. Zither (and cards)
15. Piano
16. Tape records and tapes
17. Models of staff and notes, separate notes (to match and read), clef signs (traditional and invented)
18. Zim—Gar bells (20 notes)
19. Rhythm instruments, bought and/or homemade (sticks, bells, cymbals, drums, triangles, tambourines, claves, etc.)
20. Other musical instruments (guitar, ukelele, recorder, etc.)
21. Songs written on chart
22. Double-headed tom-tom
23. Carpet or rug
24. Shelves
25. Space

Art

1. Materials for weaving, stitchery
2. Box of materials for collages
3. Bags
4. Socks
5. Art prints and art objects
6. Books of crafts, artists, pictures of paintings
7. Box of paper scraps and material scraps
8. Magazines and catalogs, greeting cards, newspapers

9. Wallpaper samples
10. Aprons, old shirts, or smocks
11. Cans: coffee, juice, spice
12. Corn starch, laundry starch
13. Flour, salt (for play-dough)
14. Drying rack
15. Florists' wire
16. Electrical wire
17. Telephone wire
18. Colored toothpicks
19. Plastic garbage can with lid for clay (pottery)
20. Cake tins for modeling clay
21. Containers with lids for mixed paints
22. Clay boards ($9'' \times 12''$ hot mats), cafeteria trays
23. Paper clips, brads, staples, pins
24. Food coloring
25. Buttons, different shapes of macaroni, nuts, bottle caps
26. Wood scraps
27. Scissors
28. Paint (tempera)
29. Paste
30. Glue (Elmer's)
31. Glue sticks
32. Tape
33. Rubber cement
34. Stapler
35. Magic markers
36. Pencils (lead, colored)
37. Finger paint
38. Rulers
39. Plaster of paris
40. Colored chalk and pastels
41. Pipe cleaners
42. Looms
43. Yarn
44. Water colors
45. Charcoal
46. Modeling clay
47. Pottery clay
48. Paintbrushes
49. Crayons
50. Construction paper
51. Fingerpainting paper
52. Art tissue
53. Crepe paper
54. Fadeless paper
55. Corrugated cardboard
56. Instant papier-mache
57. Straws, needles
58. Hair spray

59. Talcum powder
60. Coat hangers
61. Iron
62. Sponges
63. Aluminum foil, waxed paper
64. Boxes of many shapes and sizes
65. Styrofoam trays
66. Play dough
67. Inner tubes
68. Lace, ribbon, felt
69. Shells, seeds, dried flowers
70. Jewelry
71. Blankets and sheets
72. Cord, yarn, string, and thread
73. Architect's drawing paper
74. Newsprint
75. Butcher block paper
76. White drawing paper
77. Posterboard
78. Manila paper
79. Sticky tack
80. Compasses
81. Paper punch
82. India ink and stamp pad
83. Working space: tables, easels, countertops, floor and outdoor space
84. Cleanup equipment: buckets, sponges, and mops (should be accessible to the children)

Quiet Area

1. Rugs
2. Pillows
3. Rocking chair
4. Screen or drape of material to eliminate noise of other classroom activities

This should be a quiet place where a child may go to be alone to think or do what he or she wishes. It should be a comfortable relaxing area but include no specific materials. Children may bring their own materials to this center.

Outdoor Centers

1. Sand and water play table with top
2. Aluminum sand utensils
3. Sailboat
4. Jungle gym
5. Sandbox
6. Swings (tire or leather seats)
7. Platforms for climbing and swinging
8. Large sewer pipes (set in cement)
9. Tree trunks
10. Low turning bars

11. Low horizontal ladders
12. Safety climbing tree
13. Low climbing ropes
14. Wading pool
15. Walking boards (cleated and of various lengths, 4' to 6' and 8" to 12" wide)
16. Sawhorses (various heights)
17. Ladders (cleats at each end, 3" to 5')
18. Wooden steps, wooden ladder
19. Heavy wooden benches
20. Low balance beams
21. Bales of straw
22. Tires: tractor, automobile, bicycle
23. Balls (various sizes, 8" to 24")
24. Bean bags
25. Jump ropes (long and individual)
26. Riding toys (wagons, tricycles, wheelbarrows)
27. Sand toys
28. Tools for gardening (shovels, rakes, hoes)
29. Building blocks
30. Tools for woodwork
31. Water hose
32. Large packing boxes
33. Equipment for crawling and tunneling
34. Scrap lumber for large construction
35. Wooden boxes, packing crates, rope handles, cardboard cartons
36. Planks
37. Steering wheel and column attached to a heavy box
38. Parent-made equipment and materials (storage unit to build, wooden climbing structure, telephone spools, wooden bridges and structures, cans and barrels, tire constructions, rolling slide, trees encircled with brick, nets for climbing)

Sand and Water Center

1. Sand and water table and/or a large galvanized (or plastic) tub
2. Sheets of plastic, and old shower curtain, or an absorbent rug to place under the tub
3. Scales (balance)
4. Plastic aprons for the children
5. A hose and/or pitchers to fill the tub (the teacher can mark the water line with a magic marker so children can fill the tub to the best level)
6. Sponges and a pail, mop for cleanup
7. Storage space for materials
8. Plastic containers and lids
9. Plastic dishes (cups, bowls, mugs, beakers)
10. Measuring spoons and containers
11. Weights (ounces, grams)
12. Bubble pipes, egg beaters, and other mixers (whisks, spoons)
13. Meat basters
14. Corks, sponges

15. Plastic eyedroppers
16. Funnels of different sizes
17. Sieves of all shapes and sizes, sprinkler tops on bottles
18. Brushes of several sizes
19. Flexible plastic tubing (of several diameters)
20. Several lengths of pipe and hose
21. Rolling pin, shells, stones
22. Wheelbarrow, trowels, spoons, shovels, buckets, sticks, rakes, ladles, dump trucks, sand combs
23. Straws
24. Cakes of soap, soap flakes, liquid soap
25. Food coloring
26. Tempera paint
27. Small sponges
28. Pieces of wood
29. Styrofoam cork
30. Chart paper, markers
31. Box of objects for sinking and floating (sponge, nail, rubber eraser, pencil, leaf, nickel, paper clip, rock, cork, crayon, twig, acorn, peanut, rubberband, wooden bead, lengths of sticks, spools, odd pieces of wood, scissors)

Appendix C

Suggested References on Production of Teacher-Made Materials

Allen, Roach Van, and Claryce Allen. *Language Experience Activities.* Boston: Houghton Mifflin, 1976.

Baratta-Lorton, Mary. *Mathematics Their Way.* Reading, Mass.: Addison-Wesley, 1976.

——. *Workjobs: Activity-Centered Learning for Early Childhood Education.* Reading, Mass.: Addison-Wesley, 1972.

——. *Workjobs II: Number Activities for Early Childhood.* Reading, Mass.: Addison-Wesley, 1979.

Blake, Jim, and Barbara Ernst. *The Great Perpetual Learning Machine: Being a Stupendous Collection of Ideas, Games, Experiments, Activities, and Recommendations for Further Exploration.* Boston: Little, Brown, 1976.

Croft, Doreen J., and Robert D. Hess, *An Activities Handbook for Teachers of Young Children.* Boston: Houghton Mifflin, 1976.

Espich, James E., and Bill Williams. *Developing Programmed Instructional Materials.* Belmont, Calif.: Lear Siegler, 1967.

Flemming, Bonnie Mack, Darlene Softley Hamilton, and JoAnne Deal Hicks. *Resources for Creative Teaching in Early Childhood Education.* New York: Harcourt Brace Jovanovich, 1977.

Forgan, Harry W. *The Reading Corner: Ideas, Games, and Activities for Individualizing Reading.* Pacific Palisades, Calif.: Goodyear, 1977.

Forte, Imogene, and Mary Ann Pangle. *Mini-Center Stuff.* Nashville, Tenn.: Incentive Publications, 1976.

Glazier, Raye. *How to Design Educational Games.* Cambridge, Mass.: ABT Associates, 1971.

Hayett, William. *Display and Exhibit Handbook.* New York: Reinhold, 1967.

Kaplan, Sandra Nina, Jo Ann Butom Kaplan, Sheila Kunishima Madsen, and Bette K. Taylor. *Change for Children: Ideas and Activities for Individualizing Learning.* Pacific Palisades, Calif.: Goodyear, 1973.

————. Jo Ann Butom Kaplan, Sheila Kunishima Madsen, and Bette Taylor Gould. *A Young Child Experiences: Activities for Teaching and Learning.* Pacific Palisades, Calif.: Goodyear, 1975.

Kohl, Herbert R. *Math, Writing, and Games.* New York: New York Review/Vintage Books, 1974.

Liu, Sarah, and Mary Lou Vittitow. *Games Without Losers: Learning Games and Independent Activities for Elementary Classrooms.* Nashville, Tenn.: Incentive Publications, 1975.

Matterson, E. M. *Play and Playthings for the Pre-School Child.* Baltimore: Penguin Books, 1970.

Michener, Dorothy, and Beverly Muschlitz. *Teacher's Gold Mine.* Nashville, Tenn.: Incentive Publications, 1979.

Petty Walter R., and Mary E. Bowen. *Slithery Snakes and Other Aids to Children's Writing.* New York: Appleton-Century-Crofts, 1967.

Smith, Hayden R., and Thomas S. Nagel. *Instructional Media in the Learning Process.* Columbus, Ohio: Merrill, 1972.

Smith, James A. Boston: Allyn & Bacon, Series in Creative Teaching.

————. *Creative Teaching of the Language Arts,* 1973

————. *Creative Teaching of Reading and Literature,* 1975

————. *Creative Teaching of the Creative Arts,* 1967.

————. *Creative Teaching of the Social Studies,* 1983.

————. *Creative Teaching of Mathematics,* 1978.

————. *Creative Teaching of Science in the Elementary School,* 1974.

Stone Mountain Education Projects. *Preschool Equipment.* Conway, Mass.: SMEP, 1972.

Turner, Ethel M. *Teaching Aids for Elementary Mathematics.* New York: Holt, Rinehart and Winston, 1966.

Voight, Ralph Claude. *Invitation to Learning—The Learning Center Handbook.* Washington, D.C.: Acropolis Books, 1971.

Appendix D

Early Childhood Commercial Suppliers

ABC School Supply, Inc.
6500 Peachtree Industrial Blvd.
P.O. Box 4750
Norcross, Georgia 30071

American Guidance Service
Publisher's Building
Circle Pines, Minnesota 55014

American Science and Engineering, Inc.
Education Division
955 Massachusetts Avenue
Cambridge, Massachusetts 02139

Carolina School Supply
2619 West Boulevard
P.O. Box RRR
Charlotte, North Carolina 28203

Childcraft Educational Corporation
20 Kilmer Road
Edison, New Jersey 08818

Community Playthings
Rifton, New York 12471

Constructive Playthings
1040 East 85th Street
Kansas City, Missouri 64131

Creative Publications
3977 East Bayshore Road
P.O. Box 10328
Palo Alto, California 94303

McGraw-Hill Book Company
Webster Division
1221 Avenue of the Americas
New York, New York 10020

Nienhuis Montessori U.S.A., Inc.
320 Pioneer Way, Department 4
Mountain View, California 94041

Scholastic Book Services
904 Sylvan Avenue
Englewood Cliffs, New Jersey 07632

Cuisenaire Company of America, Inc.
12 Church Street, Box D
New Rochelle, New York 10805

Cypress Publishing Corporation
1763 Gardena Avenue, Suite 100
Glendale, California 91204

Delta Education, Inc.
P.O. Box M
Nashua, New Hampshire 03061

Developmental Learning Materials
P.O. Box 4000, One DLM Park
Allen, Texas 75002

Didax Educational Resources
6 Doulton Place
Peabody, Massachusetts 01960

Educational Teaching Aids
159 West Kinzie Street
Chicago, Illinois 60610

Leicestershire Learning Systems
Chestnut Street
Lewiston, Maine 04240

Listening Library, Inc.
P.O. Box L
Old Greenwich, Connecticut 06870

Stones Southern School Supply
3800 Holly Springs Road
Raleigh, North Carolina 27606

Teaching Resources Corporation
50 Pond Park Road
Hingham, Massachusetts 02043

Weston Woods
Weston, Connecticut 06883

Bibliography

Accreditation Criteria and Procedures. (1986). Washington, D.C.: National Association for the Education of Young Children.

Adams, P. (1982). *Children's Workshops: Ideal for Carpentry Centers.* Columbus, Ga.: Columbus College, School of Education. (ERIC Document Reproduction Service No. ED 242 387.)

Adams, R. J. (1967). *Creative Woodworking in the Kindergarten.* Minneapolis, Minn.: T. S. Denison.

Adkins, J. (1973). *Toolchest.* New York: Walker.

Alexander, J. (Ed.). (1983). *Teaching Reading* (2nd ed.). Boston: Little, Brown and Company.

Allen, K. E., and Hart, B. (1984). *The Early Years: Arrangements for Learning.* Englewood Cliffs, N.J.: Prentice-Hall.

Almy, M., and Genishi, C. (1979). *Ways of Studying Children.* New York: Teacher's College Press.

Altman, I., and Wohlwill, J. F. (1978). *Children and the Environment.* New York: Plenum.

Anderson, S., and Hoot, L. (1986). "Kids, Carpentry and Pre-School Classrooms." *Day Care Early Education, 13,* 12–15.

Andrews, M. F. (1980). "The Consonance Between Right Brain and Affection, Subconscious, and Multi-Sensory Functions." *The Journal of Creative Behavior, 14,* 77–87.

Arieti, S. (1976). *Creativity: The Magic Synthesis.* New York: Basic Books, Inc.

Athey, I. J., and Rubadeau, D. O. (Eds.). (1970). *Implications of Piaget's Theory.* Waltham, Mass.: Ginn-Blaisdell.

Atwood, V. A. (1985). "Bubble-Good Data: Product Testing and Other Sources." *Social Education, 49,* 147–148.

Baer, G. (1979). *Paste, Pencils, Scissors, and Crayons.* West Nyack, N.Y.: Parker Publishing Company.

———. (1982). *Imaginative Art Lessons for Kids and Their Teachers.* West Nyack, N.Y.: Parker Publishing Company.

Baker, K. R. (1966). *Let's Play Outdoors* (Rev. ed.). Washington, D.C.: National Association for the Education of Young Children.

Baker, L. (1979). *The Art Teacher's Resource Book.* Reston, Va.: Reston Publishing Company.

Banks, J., and Clegg, A. (1985). *Teaching Strategies for the Social Studies: Inquiry, Valuing and Decision-making* (3rd ed.). New York: Longman.

Baratta-Lorton, M. (1976). *Mathematics Their Way.* Menlo Park, Calif.: Addison-Wesley.

Barnett, R. R. (1981). *Let Out the Sunshine: A Montessori Approach to Creative Activities.* Dubuque, Iowa: William C. Brown.

Beaney, J. (1970). *Adventures with Collage.* New York: Frederick Warne & Company.

Beaty, J. V. (1986). *Observing Development of the Young Child.* Columbus, Ohio: Charles E. Merrill Publishing Company.

Beckman, C., Simmons, R., and Thomas, N. (1982). *Channels to Children: Early Childhood Activity Guide for Holidays and Seasons.* Colorado Springs, Colo.: Channels to Children.

Bentzen, W. R. (1985). *Seeing Young Children: A Guide to Observing and Recording Behavior.* New York: Delmar Publishers, Inc.

Berliner, D. C. (1979). "Tempus Educare." In P. L. Peterson & H. J. Wahlberg (Eds.), *Research on Teaching* (pp. 120–135). Berkeley, Calif.: McCrutchen.

Beswick, B. A. (1983). *Every Child an Artist.* West Nyack, N.Y.: Parker.

Bicanich, D. D., and Manke, C. W. (1978). *Sensori-motor Activity Guide for Preschoolers from Birth to Age Five.* West St. Paul, Minn.: Bicanich & Manke.

Bilus, P., and Sachs, K. (1981). *Integrating Arts with the Curriculum Areas.* Washington, D.C.: Department of Education.

Blake, H. E. (1977). *Creating a Learning-Centered Classroom: A Practical Guide for Teachers.* New York: Hart Publishing Company.

Blake, J., and Ernst, B. (1976). *The Great Perpetual Learning Machine.* Boston: Little, Brown.

Blau, R. (1977). *Activities for School-Age Child Care.* Washington, D.C.: National Association for the Education of Young Children.

Bloom, B. S. (1981). *All Our Children Learning.* New York: McGraw-Hill.

———. (1982). *Human Characteristics & School Learning* (2nd ed.). New York: McGraw-Hill.

Boardman, E., and Andress, B. (1981). *The Music Book.* New York: Holt, Rinehart and Winston.

Bostley, E. J. (1985). "How to Teach Music as a Daily Discipline." *The School Administrator, Vol. 42,* No. 10, p. 26. Arlington, Va. American Association of School Administrators.

———. (1986). "Children's Musical Cognition as Revealed in Their Created Music Notations," *The Proceedings of the 1986 Southeastern Music Education Symposium.* Athens, Ga.: The University of Georgia Center for Continuing Education.

Boy Scouts of America. (1970). *Woodwork.* North Brunswick, N.J.: Author.

Brannen, N. (1978). *Woodworking: Arizona HSST/CDA Competency Based Training Module #30.* Coolidge, Ariz.: AZ/NV Child Development Associates. (ERIC Document Reproduction Service No. ED 180 638.)

Brittain, W. L. (1979). *Creativity, Art, and the Young Child.* New York: Macmillan Publishing Co.

Brock, R. (1974). *Now You Need a Toolbox.* New York: Dell.

Brophy, J. E. (1979). "Teacher Behavior and Its Effects." *Journal of Educational Psychology, 71,* 733–750.

Broshnahan, J. A. P., and Milne, B. W. (1978). *A Calendar of Home/School Activities.* Santa Monica, Calif.: Goodyear.

Brown, S. (Ed.). (1981). *Bubbles, Rainbows and Worms.* Mount Ranier, N.Y.: Gryphon House.

Bruner, J. S. (1966). *Toward a Theory of Instruction.* Cambridge, Mass.: Harvard University Press.

———. (1969). *The Process of Education.* Cambridge, Mass.: Harvard University Press.

Bryant, J. C. (1983). *Why Art, How Art.* Seattle, Wash.: Special Child Publications.

Burke, E. M. (1986). *Early Childhood Literature: For Love of Child and Book.* Boston: Allyn and Bacon, Inc.

Burns, P. C., and Broman, B. L. (1983). *The Language Arts in Childhood Education* (5th ed.). Boston: Houghton Mifflin Co.

Busse, T. V., and Mansfield, R. S. (1980). "Theories of the Creative Process: A Review and a Perspective." *The Journal of Creative Behavior, 14,* 91–103.

Cacha, F. B. (1985). "Microcomputer Capabilities in the Elementary Social Studies Program." *The Social Studies, 75,* 62–64.

Carroll, J. B. (1963). "A Model of School Learning." *Teachers College Record, 64,* 722–723.

Carroll, R. (1985). "Exploring the History of a Neighborhood: A Community Project." *The Social Studies, 77,* 150–154.

Cartledge, G., and Milburn, J. F. (Eds.). (1986). *Teaching Social Skills to Children* (2nd ed.). New York: Pergamon.

Cartwright, C. A., and Cartwright, G. P. (1974). *Developing Observation Skills.* New York: McGraw-Hill Book Company.

Cheek, M. C., and Cheek, E. H. (1980). *Diagnostic-Prescriptive Reading Instruction.* Dubuque, Iowa: Wm. C. Brown Company Publishers.

Chilcoat, G. W. (1985). "The Literary Popular Story Paper as Classroom Activity: The Role of Women in Nineteenth Century America." *The Social Studies, 76,* 76–79.

Chosky, L. (1986). *Teaching Music in the Twentieth Century.* Englewood Cliffs, N.J.: Prentice-Hall, Inc.

Cliatt, M. J. P., Shaw, J. M., and Sherwood, J. M. (1980). "Effects of Training on the Divergent-Thinking Abilities of Kindergarten Children." *Child Development, 51,* 1061–1064.

Cohen, M. D. (Ed.). (1976). *Selecting Educational Equipment and Materials for School and Home.* Washington, D.C.: Association for Childhood Education International.

Cohen, S., and Oden, S. (1974). "An Examination of Creativity and Locus of Control in Children." *The Journal of Genetic Psychology, 124,* 179–185.

Cole, A., Haas, C., Heller, E., and Weinberg, B. (1976). *A Pumpkin in a Pear Tree.* Boston: Little, Brown and Company.

Cole, N. R. (1940). *The Arts in the Classroom.* New York: John Day Co.

Coleman, M. (1984–85). "Play, Games and Sport: Their Use and Misuse." *Childhood Education, 61,* 192–197.

Collier, M. J., Forte, I., and MacKenzie, J. (1981). *Kids' Stuff.* Nashville, Tenn.: Incentive Publications.

Colvin, M. P. (1979). *Big Holiday Book.* Dansville, N.Y.: Instructor Publications.

Comins, J. (1975). *Eskimo Craft and Their Cultural Backgrounds.* New York: Lothrop, Lee and Shepherd.

Cooley, W., and Leinhardt, G. (1980). "The Instructional Dimensions Study." *Educational Evaluation and Policy Analysis, 2,* 7–24.

Cornbleth, C., and Korth, W. (1980). "Context Factors and Individual Differences in Pupil Involvement in Learning Activities." *Journal of Educational Research, Vol. 73, No. 6,* pp. 318–323.

Crane, D. (Ed.). (1982). "Arts and Crafts for Everyone." *Instructor, 92,* 70–79.

Crary, E. (1979). *Without Spanking or Spoiling: A Practical Approach to Toddler and Preschool Guidance.* Seattle, Wash.: Parenting Press.

Criteria for Selecting Play Equipment. (1981). Rifton, N.Y.: Community Playthings.

Crook, E., Reimer, B., and Walker, D. S. (1981). *Music.* Morristown, N.J.: Silver Burdett.

Crossett, B. (1983). "Using Both Halves of the Brain to Teach the Whole Child." *Social Education, 47,* 266–268.

Curwin, R. L., and Mendler, A. N. (1980). *The Discipline Book: A Complete Guide to School and Classroom Management.* Reston, Va.: Reston Publishing Company, Inc.

D'Amato, J., and D'Amato, A. (1969). *African Crafts for You to Make.* New York: Messner.

Davidson, L., McKernon, P., and Gardner, H. (1981). "The Acquisition of Song." *Documentary Report of the Application of Psychology to the Teaching of Music.* Reston, Va.: MENC.

Davidson, T. (1976). *The Learning Center Book: An Integrated Approach.* Santa Monica, Calif.: Goodyear.

Davis, H. G. (1980). "Reading Pressures in the Kindergarten." *Childhood Education, 57* (2), 76–79.

Day, B. D. (1983). *Early Childhood Education: Creative Learning Activities* (2nd ed.). New York: Macmillan Publishing Company.

Day, B. D., and Drake, K. N. (1983). *Early Childhood Education: Curriculum Organization and Classroom Management.* Alexandria, Va.: Association for Supervision and Curriculum Development.

———. (1986). "Developmental and Experimental Programs: The Key to Quality Education and Care of Young Children." *Educational Leadership, 44* (3), 24–27.

Decker, C. A., and Decker, J. R. (1984). *Planning and Administering Early Childhood Programs* (3rd ed.). Columbus, Ohio: Charles E. Merrill.

Developmentally Appropriate Practice. (1986). Washington, D.C.: National Association for the Education of Young Children.

Dice, M. L. (1976). "In Search of Creativity: Some Current Literature." *The Gifted Child Quarterly, 20,* 196–203.

Dickson, W., and Raymond, M. W. (1984). *Language Arts Computer Book.* Reston, Va.: Reston Publishing Company, Inc.

DiStefano, P., Dole, J., and Marzano, R. (1984). *Elementary Language Arts.* New York: John Wiley & Sons.

Dotts, M. F., and Dotts, M. A. J. (1974). *Clues to Creativity, Vol. I.* New York: Friendship Press.

———. (1975). *Clues to Creativity, Vol. II.* New York: Friendship Press.

Doyle, W. (1977). "Learning the Classroom Environment: An Ecological Analysis." *Journal of Teacher Education, 28,* 51–55.

Dudek, S. Z. (1974). "Creativity in Young Children: Attitude or Ability?" *The Journal of Creative Behavior, 8,* 282–292.

Easton, J. Q., Muirhead, R. S., Frederick, W. C., and Vanderwicken, S. (1979). *Relationships Among Student Time on Task Orientation of Teachers, and Instructional Grouping in Elementary Reading Classes.* Paper presented at the meeting of the American Educational Research Association, San Francisco. (ERIC Document Reproduction Service No. ED 169 503.)

Edwards, B. (1979). *Drawing on the Right Side of the Brain.* Los Angeles: Houghton Mifflin.

Eheart, B. K., and Leavitt, R. L. (1985). "Supporting Toddler Play." *Young Children, 3,* 18–22.

Eisner, E. W. (1982). *Cognition and Curriculum.* New York: Longman.

Elkind, D. (1986). "Formal Education and Early Childhood Education: An Essential Difference." *Phi Delta Kappan, 67,* 631–636.

Ellis, A. K. (1977). *Teaching and Learning Elementary Social Studies.* Boston: Allyn and Bacon, Inc.

Ellis, A. (1959). *Music with Children.* New York: McGraw-Hill.

Engstrom, G. (Ed.). (1971). *The Significance of the Young Child's Motor Development.* Washington, D.C.: National Association for the Education of Young Children.

Epstein, C. (1979). *Classroom Management and Teaching: Persistent Problems and Rational Solutions.* Reston, Va.: Reston Publishing Company, Inc.

Evans, E. D. (1975). *Contemporary Influences in Early Childhood Education* (2nd ed.). New York: Holt, Rinehart and Winston, Inc.

Evertson, C. M., Emmer, E. T., Clements, B. S., Sanford, J. P., and Worsham, M. E. (1984). *Classroom Management for Elementary Schools.* Englewood Cliffs, N.J.: Prentice-Hall, Inc.

Eyring, J. (1968). "Scientific Creativity." In H. A. Anderson (Ed.), *Creativity and Its Cultivation.* New York: Harper and Brothers.

Faber, A., and Mazlish, E. (1980). *How to Talk So Kids Will Listen and Listen So Kids Will Talk.* New York: Avon Books.

Fein, G. G. (1982). "Pretend Play: New Perspectives." In J. F. Brown (Ed.), *Curriculum Planning for Young Children* (p. 23). Washington, D.C.: National Association for the Education of Young Children.

Filby, N. (1978). "How Teachers Produce 'Academic Learning Time': Instructional Variables Related to Student Engagement." In C. W. Fisher (Ed.), *Selected Findings from Phase III-B of the Beginning Teacher Evaluation Study.* San Francisco: Far West Laboratory for Educational Research. (ERIC Document Reproduction Service No. ED 160 639.)

Finkelstein, J. M., and Nielsen, L. F. (1985). "Celebrating a Centennial: An Approach to Teaching Historical Concepts to Young Children." *The Social Studies, 76,* 100–102.

Fisker, L. E. (1966). *The Cabinetmakers.* New York: Franklin Watts.

Fleming, B. M., and Hamilton, D. (1977). *Resources for Creative Teaching in Early Childhood Education.* New York: Harcourt Brace Jovanovich.

Forte, I., and MacKenzie, J. (1975). *Kids' Stuff: Reading and Language Experiences.* Nashville, Tenn.: Incentive Publications.

Forte, I., and Pangle, M. A. (1976). *More Center Stuff for Nooks, Crannies and Corners.* Nashville, Tenn.: Incentive Publications.

Forte, I., Pangle, M., and Tupa, R. (1974). *Pumpkins, Pinwheels, and Peppermint Patties.* Nashville, Tenn.: Incentive Publications.

Foust, S. J., Vurnakes, C. D., Simpson, R. J., Bemer, L., and Wolf, K. (1984). *Centers Galore (Book 5).* Greensboro, N.C.: The Education Center.

Fox, S. E., and Allen, V. G. *The Language Arts: An Integrated Approach.* New York: Holt, Rinehart and Winston.

Frost, J. L., and Klein, B. L. (1983). *Children's Play and Playgrounds.* Austin, Tex.: Playscapes International.

Gagné, R. (1977). *Conditions of Learning* (3rd ed.). New York: Holt, Rinehart and Winston.

Gaitskell, C. D. (1970). *Children and Their Art.* New York: Harcourt Brace and World, Inc.

Gardner, H. (1970). *Juilliard Repertory Library.* Cincinnati, Ohio: Canyon Press Inc.

———. (1983). *Frames of Mind: The Theory of Multiple Intelligences.* New York: Basic Books, Inc.

Gerard, R. W. (1946). "The Biological Basis of the Imagination." In B. Ghiselin. (1952). *The Creative Process* (pp. 226–251). New York: New American Library.

Getzels, J. W. (1985). "Creativity and Human Development." In T. Husen and T. N. Postlehwaite (Eds.), *The International Encyclopedia of Education.* Oxford: Pergamon Press.

———. "Problem-Finding and the Inventiveness of Solutions." *The Journal of Creative Behavior, 9,* 12–18.

Geyer, G. A. (1987, July 30). "Creativity Has Powered America's Success." *The News and Observer,* p. 19A.

Ghiselin, B. (1952). *The Creative Process.* New York: New American Library.

Glasser, W. (1978, February). "Lecture Notes." Lecture presented at the University of North Carolina, Greensboro, N.C.

Goetz, E. M. (1984). *The Training of Creativity as an Operant in Young Children.* Paper presented as part of the symposium, *Current Issues in the Study of Creativity as Operant Behavior,* American Psychological Association, Toronto, Canada. (ERIC Document Reproduction Service No. ED 257 263.)

Gordon, T. (1974). *Teacher Effectiveness Training.* New York: Peter H. Wyden.

Gowan, J. C. (1977). "Some New Thoughts on the Development of Creativity." *The Journal of Creative Behavior, 11,* 77–90.

Gowan, J. C., and Olson, M. (1979). "The Society Which Maximizes Creativity." *The Journal of Creative Behavior, 13,* 194–210.

Green, C. (1959). *I Want to Be a Carpenter.* Chicago: Children's Press.

Greenberg, M. (1979). *Your Child Needs Music.* Englewood Cliffs, N.J.: Prentice-Hall.

Guilford, J. P. (1968). *Intelligence, Creativity, and Their Educational Implications.* San Diego: Robert R. Knapp.

Gump, P. V. (1967). *The Classroom Behavior Setting: Its Nature and Relation to Student Behavior.* (U.S. Office of Education Final Report, Project No. 2453. Bureau Report No. 5-0334.) Lawrence, Kans.: University of Kansas Press.

Guyton, E. M. (1985). "The School as a Data Source for Young Learners." *Social Education, 49,* 141–144.

Harlow, H., and Rockwell, A. (1971). *The Toolbox.* New York: Collier Books.

Hatcher, B. (1985). "Children's Homes and Neighborhoods: Untapped Treasures from the Past." *The Social Studies, 75,* 155–159.

Hatcher, B. (1983). "Putting Young Cartographers 'on the Map.'" *Childhood Education, 59,* 311–315.

Hawkinson, J. (1970). *Paint a Rainbow.* Chicago, Ill.: Albert Whitman.

Heinig, R. B., and Stillwell, L. (1974). *Creative Dramatics for the Classroom Teacher.* Englewood Cliffs, N.J.: Prentice-Hall.

Hendrick, J. (1984). "Enhancing Creativity." In J. Hendrick, *The Whole Child: Early Education for the Eighties* (pp. 279–359). St. Louis: Times Mirror/Mosby College Publishing.

Hess, R. D., and Takanishi, R. (1974). *The Relationship of Teacher Behavior and School Characteristics to Students Engagement.* (Technical Report No. 42.) Standard, Calif.: Stanford Center for Research and Development in Teaching.

Higgenbotham, B. (1980). "Small Cage Habit." *The Journal of Creative Behavior, 14,* i–iv.

Hildebrand, V. (1980). *Guiding Young Children* (2nd ed.). New York: Macmillan Publishing Company.

Hilgard, E. (1959). "Creativity and Problem Solving." In H. A. Anderson (Ed.), *Creativity and Its Implications.* New York: Harper and Brothers.

Hill, B. (1980). "Art Workshop of Classroom Teachers, Part 2." *Instructor, 89,* 77–80.

Hohman, M., Banet, B., and Weikart, D. P. (1979). *Young Children in Action.* Ypsilanti, Mich.: High Scope Educational Research Foundation.

Homan, D. (1981). *In Christina's Toolbox.* Chapel Hill, N.C.: Lollipop Power.

Horwitz, E. L. (1975). *Contemporary American Folk Artists.* Philadelphia: J. P. Lippincott.

Hutt, C., and Bhavnani, R. (1976). "Predictions from Play." In J. S. Bruner (Ed.), *Play: Its Role in Development and Evolution* (pp. 216–219). New York: Basic.

Instructor Books. (1981). *Teacher's Activity Calendar.* New York: The Instructor Publications, Inc.

Jackson, P. W. (1968). *Life in Classrooms.* New York: Holt, Rinehart & Winston.

Jalongo, M. R. (1985). "When Young Children Move." *Young Children, 6,* 51–57.

Jarolimek, J. (1986). *Social Studies in Elementary Education* (7th ed.). New York: Macmillan.

Jenkins, K. S. (1982). *Kinder-Krunchies.* Pleasant Hill, Calif.: Discovery Toys.

Jensen, R., and Spector, D. (1984). *Teaching Mathematics to Young Children.* Englewood Cliffs, N.J.: Prentice-Hall.

Jewell, M. G., and Zintz, M. V. (1986). *Learning to Read Naturally.* Dubuque, Iowa: Kendall/Hunt Publishing Company.

Johnson, H. (1962). *The Act of Block Building.* New York: Bank Street College Publications.

Jones, E. (1973). *Dimensions of Teaching-Learning Environments: Handbook for Teachers.* Pasadena, Calif.: Pacific Oaks College Bookstore.

Joyce, M. (1973). *First Steps in Teaching Creative Dance: A Handbook for Teachers of Children, Kindergarten Through Sixth Grade.* Palo Alto, Calif.: Mayfield Publishing Co.

Kamii, C. (1982). *Number in Preschool and Kindergarten: Educational Implications of Piaget's Theory.* Washington, D.C.: National Association for the Education of Young Children.

Kamii, C. (1973). "Pedagogical Principles Derived from Piaget's Theory: Relevance for Educational Practice." In M. Schwebel and J. Raph (Eds.), *Piaget in the Classroom.* New York: Basic.

Kamii, C., and DeVries, R. (1977). "Piaget for Early Education." In M. C. Day and R. Parker (Eds.), *The Preschool in Action.* Boston: Allyn and Bacon.

———. (1980). *Group Games in Early Education: Implications of Piaget's Theory.* Washington, D.C.: National Association for the Education of Young Children.

Kamii, K., and DeClark, G. (1985). *Young Children Reinvent Arithmetic: Implications of Piaget's Theory.* New York: Teachers College Press.

Kaplan, S. N., Kaplan, J., Madsen, S., and Gould, B. (1975). *A Young Child Experiences: Activities for Teaching and Learning.* Santa Monica, Calif.: Goodyear.

Kay, E. (1981). *Games That Teach for Children Three Through Six.* Minneapolis, Minn.: T. S. Denison and Company.

Khatena, J. (1971). "Teaching Disadvantaged Preschool Children to Think Creatively with Pictures." *Journal of Psychology, 62* (5), 384–386.

King, R. G. (1982). "A General System Model of the Creative Process." *Gifted International: World Council for Gifted and Talented Children, 1,* 17–41.

Kogan, S. (1982). *Step by Step: A Complete Movement Education Curriculum from Preschool to 6th Grade.* Byron, Calif.: Front Row Experience.

Kohl, M. A. F. (1985). *Scribble Cookies.* Bellingham, Wash.: Bright Ring Publishing Company.

Koppelman, P. (1976). *The House that Jack and Jill Built.* San Francisco, Calif.: Rosenburg Foundation. (ERIC Document Reproduction Service No. ED 149 013.)

Kostelnik, M. J., Whiren, A. P., and Stein, L. C. (1986). "Living with He-Man." *Young Children, 4,* 3–9.

Kounin, J. S. (1970). *Discipline and Group Management in Classrooms.* New York: Holt, Rinehart & Winston.

Kounin, J. S., Freisen, W., and Norton, A. E. (1966). "Managing Emotionally Disturbed Children in Regular Classrooms." *Journal of Educational Psychology, 57,* 1–13.

Kounin, J. S., and Sherman, L. W. (1979). "School Environments as Behavior Settings." *Theory into Practice, 13,* 145–151.

Kranz, S., and Deley, J. (1970). *The Fourth "R": Art for the Urban School.* New York: Van Nostrand Reinhold.

Kritchevsky, S., Prescott, E., and Walling, L. (1977). *Planning Environments for Young Children: Physical Space* (2nd ed.). Washington, D.C.: National Association for the Education of Young Children.

Kubie, L. S. (1961). *Neurotic Distortion of the Creative Process.* University of Kansas Press: The Noonday Press.

———. (1967). "Blocks to Creativity." In R. L. Mooney and T. A. Razik (Eds.), *Explorations in Creativity* (pp. 33–42). New York: Harper & Row.

Kuslan, D. M. (1980). "The Art of Reading." *Instructor, 89,* 102–104.

LaPenta, M. (1983). *Macmillan Early Skills Program: Listening Skills.* New York: Macmillan Educational Company.

Lansing, K., and Richards, A. E. (1981). *The Elementary Teacher's Art Handbook.* New York: Holt, Rinehart and Winston.

LaRocque, G. E. (1973). "Educating for Creativity." *English Education, 5,* 5–20.

Lasky, L., and Mukerji, R. (1980). *Art: Basic for Young Children.* Washington, D.C.: National Association for the Education of Young People.

Lasson, R. (1974). *If I Had a Hammer.* New York: E. P. Dutton.

———. (1975). *Carpentry for Children.* New York: Sterling.

Lay-Dopyera, M., and Dopyera, J. E. (1982). *Becoming a Teacher of Young Children* (2nd ed.). Lexington, Mass.: D. C. Heath and Company.

Leavitt, J. E. (1975). *The True Book of Tools for Building.* Chicago: Children's Press.

Leeper, S. H. (1974). *Good Schools for Young Children: A Guide for Working with Three-, Four-, and Five-year-old Children.* New York: Macmillan.

Leeper, S. H., Witherspoon, R. L., and Day, B. D. (1984). *Good Schools for Young Children* (5th ed.). New York: Macmillan Publishing Company.

Lemlech, J. K. (1979). *Classroom Management.* New York: Harper and Row, Publishers.

Lindberg, L., and Swedlow, R. (1980). *Early Childhood Education: A Guide for Observation and Participation* (2nd ed.). Boston: Allyn and Bacon, Inc.

Lindstrom, M. (1957). *A Study of Normal Development in Children's Modes of Visualization.* Berkeley, Calif.: University of California Press.

Linn, M. C. (1980). "Free-Choice Experiences: How Do They Help Children Learn?" *Science Education, 64,* 237–248.

Long, N., and Newman, R. (1980). "Managing Surface Behavior of Children in School." *Conflict in the Classroom.* Belmont, Calif.: Wadsworth.

Lord, T. R. (1984). "A Plea for Right Brain Usage." *JCST, Vol. 14, No. 2,* pp. 100–102.

Lorton, J. W., and Walley, B. L. (1979). *Introduction to Early Childhood Education.* New York: D. Van Nostrand Company.

Lowenfeld, V., and Brittain, W. L. (1982). *Creative and Mental Growth* (7th ed.). New York: Macmillan.

Lowenfeld, V. (1957). *Your Child and His Art.* New York: Macmillan.

Lynch-Fraser, D. (1982). *Dance Play: Creative Movement for Very Young Children.* New York: Walker and Company.

MMCP Final Report. (1970). Washington, D.C.: U.S. Office of Education. (ERIC Document Reproduction Service No. ED 045 865.)

Mark, M. L. (1986). *Contemporary Music Education.* New York: Schirmer Books.

Marotz, L., Rush, J., and Cross, M. (1985). *Health, Safety, and Nutrition for the Young Child.* Albany, N.Y.: Delmar Publications.

Martin, D. S. (1985). "Ethnocentrism Revisited: Another Look at a Persistent Problem." *Social Education, 49,* 604–609.

Martin, J. H. (1985). *A Day in the Life of a Carpenter.* Mahway, N.J.: Troll Associates.

Martorella, P. (1985). *Elementary Social Studies Developing Reflective, Competent, and Concerned Citizens.* Boston: Little, Brown & Company.

Mason, B. (1946). *The Book of Indian Crafts and Costumes.* New York: A. S. Barnes.

Mason, J. M., and Au, K. H. (1986). *Reading Instruction for Today.* Glenview, Ill.: Scott, Foresman and Company.

Matthews, P. W. (1953). *You Can Teach Music.* New York: E. P. Dutton & Co., Inc.

Maxim, G. (1983). *Social Studies and the Elementary School Child.* Columbus, Ohio: Charles E. Merrill.

Maxim, G. W. (1985). "Creativity: Encouraging the Spirit of Wonder and Magic." In G. W. Maxim (Ed.), *The Very Young* (pp. 359–402). Belmont, Calif.: Wadsworth Publishing Company.

Mayesky, M. (1986). *Creative Activities for Children in the Early Primary Grades.* Albany, N.Y.: Delmar Publishers, Inc.

Mayesky, M., Neuman, D., and Wlodkowski, R. J. (1985). *Creative Activities for Young Children* (3rd ed.). New York: Delmar Publishers.

McCallum, H. S., and Glynn, S. M. (1979). "Hemispheric Specialization and Creative Behavior." *The Journal of Creative Behavior, 13,* 263–273.

McCarthy, B. (1980). *The 4MAT System.* Oakbrook, Ill.: Excel.

McDonald, F. J., and Elias, P. J. (1976). "The Effects of Teaching Performance on Pupil Learning." *Beginning Teacher Evaluation Study, Phase II, Vol. 1.* Princeton, N.J.: ETS.

McFee, J. K. (1961). *Preparation for Art.* San Francisco: Wadsworth.

McGowan, T. M. (1985). *Teaching About Elections in Indiana Schools.* (ERIC Document Reproduction Service No. ED 260 998.)

McNairy, M. (1985). "Sciencing: Science Education for Early Childhood." *School Science and Math, 85* (5), 383–393.

Mead, M. (1962). "A Creative Life for Young Children." Washington, D.C.: *Children's Bureau Welfare Administration U.S. DEW.* (ERIC Document Reproduction Service No. ED 001 838.)

Medley, D. M. (1979). "The Effectiveness of Teachers." In P. L. Petersen and H. J. Walberg (Eds.), *Research on Teaching* (pp. 11–27). Berkeley, Calif.: McCutchan.

Melzi, K. (1967). *Art in the Primary Schools.* Oxford, England: Alden and Mowbray.

Michealis, J. U. (1976). *Social Studies for Children in a Democracy* (6th ed.). Englewood Cliffs, N.J.: Prentice-Hall, Inc.

Milgram, R. M., Milgram, N. A., Rosenbloom, G. S., and Rabkin, L. (1978). "Quantity and Quality of Creative Thinking in Children and Adolescents." *Child Development, 49,* 385–388.

Miller, J. W. (1985). "Teaching Map Skills: Theory, Research, Practice." *Social Education, 49,* 30–31.

Monson, D. L. (Ed.). (1985). *Adventuring with Books: A Booklist for Pre-K–Grade 6* (new ed.). (ERIC Document Reproduction Service No. ED 264 588.)

Moore, J. G. (1968). *The Many Ways of Seeing.* Cleveland, Ohio: The World Publishing Co.

Moran, J. D., Milgram, R. M., Sawyers, J. K., and Fu, V. R. (1983). "Original Thinking in Preschool Children." *Child Development, 54,* 921–926.

Moran, J. D., Sayers, J., and Fu, V. R. (1983, May). *Measuring Creativity in Preschool Children.* (ERIC Document Reproduction Service No. ED 224 584.)

Morrow, L. M., and Weinstein, C. S. (1982). "Increasing Children's Use of Literature Through Program and Physical Design Changes." *The Elementary School Journal, 83,* 131–137.

Murdock, C. V. (1984). *Macmillan Early Skills Program: Writing Skills.* New York: Macmillan Educational Company.

Myers, L. K. (1950). *Teaching Music in the Elementary School.* Englewood Cliffs, N.J.: Prentice-Hall.

Nelson, M. R. (1980). "Teaching Young Children About Law." *Childhood Education, 56,* 274–277.

Newman, G. (1984). *Teaching Children Music* (2nd ed.). Dubuque, Iowa: William C. Brown.

North Carolina Department of Public Instruction. (1985). *North Carolina Competency Based Curriculum, K–3.* Raleigh, N.C.: Author.

Norton, D. E. (1985). *The Effective Teaching of Language Arts* (2nd ed.). Columbus, Ohio: Charles E. Merrill Publishing Co.

Oklahoma State Department of Education. (1983). *Growing: Pre-Kindergarten Through 2nd Grade.* Oklahoma City: Author. (ERIC Document Reproduction Service No. 239 711.)

Oliver, S. D., and Musgrave, K. O. (1984). *Nutrition: A Teacher Sourcebook of Integrated Activities.* Newton, Mass.: Allyn and Bacon.

Olmstead, P. (1979). *Parent Roles in Parent Involvement, Parent Education Follow-Through Program.* Lecture presented at the University of North Carolina, Chapel Hill, N.C.

Ott, R. W., and Hurtwitz, A. (Ed.). (1984). *Art in Education: An International Perspective.* University Park, Penn.: Pennsylvania State University Press.

Ozgener, E. S. (1970). *Teachers Need to Ask Creative Type Questions.* (ERIC Document Reproduction Service No. 160-207.)

Pagano, A. L. (1979). "Learning and Creativity." *The Journal of Creative Behavior, 13,* 127–139. (ERIC Document Reproduction Service No. ED 224 584.)

Paine, I. L. (1949). *Art Aids* (5th ed.). Minneapolis, Minn.: Burgess.

Paliska, C. V. (1964). *Music in Our Schools: A Search for Improvement.* Report of the Yale Seminar on Music Education. (Report No. OE-33033, bulletin 1964, number 28.) Washington, D.C.: U.S. Department of Health, Education, and Welfare, Office of Education.

Papousek, M. (1982). *Musical Elements in Mother-Infant Dialogues.* Paper presented at the International Conference on Infant Studies, Austin, Tex.

Pattemore, A. W. (1974). *Art and Environment.* New York: Van Nostrand Reinhold.

Peck, S. (1978). *The Road Less Traveled.* New York: Simon & Schuster.

Peters, G. D., and Miller, R. F. (1982). *Music Teaching and Learning.* New York: Longman.

Peters, R. (1981). *Infusing Global Awareness Components of Environmental Education Programs into the Kindergarten–Grade Twelve Social Studies Curriculum for Purposes of Affecting Student Attitudes and Perspectives.* (ERIC Document Reproduction Service No. ED 205 392.)

Petersen, P. L. (1979). "Direct Instruction Reconsidered." In P. L. Petersen and H. J. Walberg (Eds.). *Research on Teaching* (pp. 57–69). Berkeley, Calif.: McCutchen.

Petersen, P. L., Marx, R., and Clark, C. (1978). "Teacher Planning, Teacher Behavior, and Student Achievement." *American Educational Research Journal, 15,* 417–432.

Petzold, R. G. (1966). *Auditory Perception of Musical Sounds by Children in the First Six Grades.* (Cooperative Research Project No. 1051.) Washington, D.C.: Office of Education.

Pflug, B. (1971). *Boxed-in Doll Houses.* Philadelphia: J. B. Lippincott.

Phyfe-Perkins, E. (1979). *Children's Behavior in Preschool Settings: A Review of Research Concerning the Influence of the Physical Environment.* (ERIC Document Reproduction Service No. ED 168 722.)

Phyfe-Perkins, E. (1981). "An Ecological Assessment of Two Preschool Environments." Cited in E. Phyfe-Perkins, *Effects of Teacher Behavior on Preschool Children: A Review of Research.* (ERIC Document Reproduction Service No. ED 211 176.)

Piaget, J. (1952). *The Origins of Intelligence in Children.* New York: International Universities Press.

Piaget, J. (1966). *Psychology of Intelligence.* (M. Piercy & D. E. Berlyne, Trans.). Totowa, N.J.: Littlefield, Adams.

Piaget, J., and Inhelder, B. (1985). *The Growth of Logical Thinking from Childhood to Adolescence*. New York: Basic Books.

Pitcher, E. G., Feinburg, S. G., and Alexander, D. (1984). *Helping Young Children Learn* (4th ed.). Columbus, Ohio: Charles E. Merrill.

Platts, M. E. (1972). *Launch*. Stevensville, Mich.: Educational Service Incorporated.

Plowden, B. et al. (1966). *Children and Their Primary Schools: A Report of the Central Advisory Council for Education*. London: Her Majesty's Stationery Office.

Price, C. (1977). *Arts of Clay*. New York: Charles Scribner's Sons.

Probst, D. (1980). *A Study of Time on Task in Three Teachers' Classrooms Using Different Instructional Modes*. (Technical Report No. 562.) Madison, Wis.: University of Wisconsin, Research and Development Center for Individualized Schooling.

Raebeck, L., and Wheeler, L. (1964). *New Approaches to Music in the Elementary School*. Dubuque, Iowa: William C. Brown.

Ragan, W.B. (1966). *Modern Elementary Curriculum*. New York: Holt, Rinehart and Winston.

Read, H. (1945). *Education Through Art*. New York: Pantheon Books.

Renfro, N. (1983). "It's in the Bag." *Instructor, 93,* 18–20.

Rinne, C. H. (1984). *Attention: The Fundamentals of Classroom Control*. Columbus, Ohio: Charles E. Merrill Publishing Company.

Rose, K. (1982). *Teaching Language Arts to Children*. New York: Harcourt Brace Jovanovich, Inc.

Rosenshine, B. V. (1979). "Content Time and Direct Instruction." In P. L. Petersen and H. J. Walberg (Eds.). *Research on Teaching* (pp. 28–56). Berkeley, Calif.: McCutchan.

Rosenthal, B. A. (1974). "An Ecological Study of Free Play in the Nursery School (doctoral dissertation, Wayne State University, 1973). *Dissertation Abstracts International, 34,* 4004A–4005A.

Roucher, N. "Enter a Personal Moment," *Instructor, 96,* 88: 1986.

———. "Step Up to a Stage." *Instructor, 96,* 42: 1986.

———. "Walk a Surreal Dog." *Instructor, 96,* 58: 1986.

Rubin, D. (1980). *Teaching Elementary Language Arts* (2nd ed.). New York: Holt, Rinehart and Winston.

Rudolph, M., and Cohen, D. H. (1984). *Kindergarten and Early Schooling* (2nd ed.). Englewood Cliffs, N.J.: Prentice-Hall.

Ruff, F. (1978). *Instructional Variables and Student Achievement in Reading and Mathematics: A Synthesis of Recent Process-Product Research*. Unpublished manuscript, Philadelphia, Research for Better School.

Salomon, J. H. (1928). *The Book of Indian Crafts and Indian Lore*. New York: Harper and Bros.

Schaffer, F. (1985). "Our Fifty States." *Schooldays, 4,* 24–35.

———. (1986). "Chinese Writing." *Schooldays, 5,* 71.

———. (1986). "Let's Explore Japan." *Schooldays, 5,* 3–12.

Schafer, R. M. (1976). *Creative Music Education*. New York: Schirmer Books.

Schickedanz, J. A., York, M. E., Stewart, I. S., and White, D. (1977). *Strategies for Teaching Young Children*. Englewood Cliffs, N.J.: Prentice-Hall, Inc.

Schlereth, R. J. (1980). *Artifacts and the American Past*. Nashville, Tenn.: American Association for State and Local History.

Schug, M., Todd, R., and Beery, R. (1984). "Why Kids Don't Like Social Studies." *Social Education, 48,* 382–387.

Schwebel, M., and Ralph, J. (1973). *Piaget in the Classroom*. New York: Basic Books.

Schweinhart, L. J. (1986). Research Findings Support Child Development Programs. *Educational Leadership, 44* (3), 16.

Schweinhart, L. J. Weikart, D. P., and Larner, M. B. (1986). Consequences of Three Curriculum Models Through Age 15. *Early Childhood Research Quarterly, 1,* 15–35.

Scott, K. P. (1985). "Social Interaction Skills: Perspectives on Teaching Cross-Sex Communication." *Social Education, 49,* 610–612.

Seefeldt, C. (1984). *Social Studies for the Preschool-Primary Child* (2nd ed.). Columbus, Ohio: Charles E. Merrill.

Seefeldt, C., and Barbour, N. (1986). *Early Childhood Education: An Introduction.* Columbus, Ohio: Charles E. Merrill.

Sefkow, P. D., and Berger, H. L. (1981). *All Children Create.* Homes Beach, Fla.: Learning Publications.

Self, E. (1977). *Teaching Significant Social Studies in the Elementary School.* Chicago: Rand McNally College Publishing Company.

Selph, A., and Street, B. G. (1975). *Alphabet Soup* (1st ed.). Durham, N.C.: American Printers Limited.

Severeide, R., and Sugawara, A. I. (1985). *The Effectiveness of Creative Experiences in Enhancing Creative Development.* (ERIC Document Reproduction Service No. ED 258 375.)

Shaklee, B. D., and Amos, N. G. (1985). *The Effectiveness of Teaching Creative Problem Solving Techniques to Enhance the Problem Solving Ability of Kindergarten Students.* (ERIC Document Reproduction Service No. 264 292.)

Sharan, S. (1980). "Cooperative Learning in Small Groups: Recent Methods and Effects on Achievement, Attitudes, and Ethnic Relations." *Review of Educational Research, 50,* 241–271.

Shaw, J. M. (1977). "Teacher-Pupil Communications in Selected Nursery Schools." *Dissertations Abstracts International, Vol. 38,* pp. 161–162.

Sherman, L. (1981). *Crossword Magic.* Sunnyvale, Calif.: L & S Computerware Company.

Sime, M. (1973). *A Child's Eye View.* New York: Harper and Row.

Skeel, D. J. (1979). *The Challenge of Teaching Social Studies in the Elementary School* (2nd ed.). Santa Monica, Calif.: Goodyear Publishing Company, Inc.

Skeen, P., Garner, A., & Cartwright, S. (1984). *Woodworking for Young Children.* Washington, D.C.: National Association for the Education of Young Children.

Slavin, R. E. (1980). "Effects of Student Teams and Peer Tutoring on Academic Achievement and Time on Task." *Journal of Experimental Education, 48,* 253–257.

Smith, J. A. (1966). *Setting Conditions for Creative Teaching in the Elementary School.* Boston: Allyn and Bacon, Inc.

Smith, P. K., and Dutton, S. (1979). "Play and Training in Direct and Innovative Problem-Solving." *Child Development, 50,* 830–836.

Smith, R. F. (1981). "Early Childhood Science Education, a Piagetian Perspective." *Young Children, 36,* 7–9.

Sobol, H. (1978). *Pete's House.* New York: Macmillan.

Spache, G. D., and Spache, E. B. (1986). *Reading in the Elementary School* (5th ed.). Boston: Allyn and Bacon, Inc.

Speas, J., Martelli, L., Graham, A., and Cherryholmes, L. (1983). *Communities.* New York: Webster Division, McGraw-Hill Book Company.

Stallings, J. A. (1980). "Allocated Academic Learning Time Revisited or Beyond Time on Task." *Educational Researcher, 19* (11), 11–16.

Stanley, W. et al. (1985). *Review of Research in Social Studies Education 1976–1983. Bulletin 75.* (ISBN–0–89994–303–9). Washington, D.C.: National Council for Social Studies.

Stanley, W. B. (1985). *Social Studies Research: Theory into Practice.* Washington, D.C.: National Institute of Education. (ERIC Document Reproductive Service No. ED 268 064.)

Stanton, J., Weisberg, A., and the faculty of the Bank Street School for Children. (1967). *Play Equipment for the Nursery School.* New York: Bank Street College of Education.

Stecher, M. B., McElheny, H., and Greenwood, M. (1972). *Joy and Learning Through Music and Movement Improvisations.* New York: Macmillan.

Serafine, M. L. (1979). "Aesthetic Creativity: Thoughts on Children's Activities." *The Journal of Creative Behavior, 17,* 1–8.

Stephens, L. S. (1983). *Developing Thinking Skills Through Real-Life Activities.* Boston: Allyn and Bacon, Inc.

Steven, H. (1963). *Ways with Art.* New York: Reinhold.

Stewig, J. W. (1982). *Teaching Language Arts in Early Childhood.* New York: Holt, Rinehart and Winston.

Stewig, J. W. (1983). *Exploring Language Arts in the Elementary Classroom.* New York: Holt, Rinehart and Winston.

Sukus, J. (1977). *My Toolbox Book.* Racine, Wis.: Golden Press.

Sullivan, M. (1982). *Feeling Strong, Feeling Free: Movement Exploration for Young Children.* Washington, D.C.: Association for the Education of Young Children.

Superka, D., Hawke, S., and Morressett, I. (1980). "The Current and Future Status of the Social Studies." *Social Education, 44,* 362–369.

Sutherland, Z. (1980). *The Best in Children's Books.* Chicago: University of Chicago Press.

Suzuki, S. (1969). *Nurtured by Love.* New York: Exposition Press.

A Teacher's Manual: Early Identification and Intervention Program. (1983). Maryland State Department of Education, Baltimore, MD.

Thompson, D. (1981). *Easy Woodstuff for Kids.* Mount Ranier, Md.: Gryphon House.

Torrance, E. P. (1962). *Guiding Creative Talent.* Englewood Cliffs, N.J.: Prentice-Hall, Inc.

Torrance, E. P. (1969). *A 3-year Study of the Influence of a Creative-Aesthetic Approach to School Readiness and Beginning Reading and Arithmetic on Creative Development.* (ERIC Document Reproduction Service No. 41 419.)

Torrance E. P., and Torrance P. (1973). "Is Creativity Teachable?" *Phi Delta Kappan.* Bloomington, Indiana: Phi Delta Kappa Educational Foundation.

Torre, F. D. (1978). *Woodworking for Kids.* Garden City, N.Y.: Doubleday.

Trostle, S. L., and Yawkey, T. D. (1981). *Creative Thinking and the Education of Young Children: The Fourth Basic Skill.* (ERIC Document Reproduction Service No. 204 015.)

Tryon, C., and Lilienthl, J. W. (1950). *Developmental Tasks: The Concept and Its Importance, Fostering Mental Health in Our Schools.* Alexandria, Va.: ASCD.

U.S. Secretary of Education, Bennett, W. (1986). *First Lessons: A Report on Elementary Education in America.* Washington, D.C.: U.S. Government Printing Office.

Val Baker, D. (1963). *The Young Potter.* New York: Frederick Warne & Company.

Van Cleaf, D. W. (1985). "The Environment as a Data Source: Map Activities for Young Children." *Social Education, 50,* 145–146.

Viguers, R. H. et al. (1946–1956). *Illustrators of Children's Books.* Boston: The Horn Book.

Wachowiak, F. (1985). *Emphasis Art* (4th ed.). New York: Harper & Row.

Wadsworth, B. (1978). *Piaget for the Classroom Teacher.* New York: Longman.

Wallach, M. A. (1970). "Creativity." In P. H. Mussen (Ed.), *Carmichael's Manual of Child Psychology* (3rd ed.) (pp. 1211–1272). New York: John Wiley and Sons.

Wallas, G. (1926). *The Art of Thought.* New York: Harcourt Brace and Company.

Walsh, H. (1980). *Introducing the Young Child to the Social World.* New York: Macmillan.

Warren, J. (1983). *Crafts.* Palo Alto, Calif.: Monday Morning Books.

Warren, J. (1983). *Super Snacks.* Alderwood Manor, Wash.: Warren Publishing House.

Warren, J. (1985). *1.2.3. Art.* Everett, Wash.: Warren Publishing House.

Washington, H., and Davis, R. (1981). "Social Studies in Oregon Schools: A Guide to Developing a Comprehensive Program for Grades Kindergarten Through Twelve." (ERIC Document Reproduction Service No. ED 204 236.)

Way, B. (1967). *Development Through Drama.* Atlantic Highlands, N.J.: Humanities Press.

Webb, N. M. (1982). "Student Interaction on Learning in Small Groups." *Review of Educational Research, 50,* 421–455.

Weikart, D. P., Epstein, A. S., Schweinhart, L. J., & Bond, J. T. (1978). The Ypsilanti Preschool Curriculum Demonstration Project: Preschool Years and Longitudinal Results. *Monographs of the High/Scope Educational Research Foundation, 4.* Ypsilanti, MI: High/Scope Press.

Weininger, O. (1977). "Some Thoughts on Creativity in the Classroom." *The Journal of Creative Behavior, 11,* 109–118.

Weinstein, C. S. (1979). "The Physical Environment of the School: A Review of the Research." *Review of Educational Research, 49,* 594–600.

Welsh, G. S. (1973), "Perspectives in the Study of Creativity." *The Journal of Creative Behavior, 7,* 231–246.

Werner, L. *Early Prevention of School Failure: Nationally Validated Program-Diagnosing for School Success.* Peotone: A Nationally Validated Developer-Demonstrator Model Project.

White, J. D. (1968). *Understanding and Enjoying Music.* New York: Dodd Mead and Company.

Wilkerson, R. (1986). *An Evaluation of the Effects of the 4MAT System of Instruction on Academic Achievement and Retention of Learning.* Unpublished doctoral dissertation, University of North Carolina, Chapel Hill.

Wilson, B. L. (1983, April). *Effect of Task and Authority Structures on Student Task Engagement.* Paper presented at the meeting of the American Educational Research Association, Montreal, Quebec, Canada. (ERIC Document Reproduction Service No. ED 230 416.)

Winner, E. (1982). *Invented Worlds: The Psychology of the Arts.* Cambridge, Mass.: Harvard University Press.

Wolf, A. D. (1984). *Mommy, It's a Renoir.* Altoona, Penn.: Parent Child Press.

Wolfgang, C. H., Mackender, B., and Wolfgang, M. E. (1981). *Growing and Learning Through Play.* New York: McGraw-Hill.

Women as Members of Communities: Third Grade Social Studies. (1985). Washington, D.C.: Women's Educational Equity Act Program (F D). (ERIC Document Reproduction Service No. ED 260 998.)

World Order Values Bibliography. (1984). *Books and Audio-Visual Materials for Children and Youth, Selected and Annotated.* (ERIC Document Reproduction Service No. ED 266 992.)

Yawkey, T. D., Askov, E. N., Cartwright, C. A., Dupuis, M. M., Fairchild, S. H., and Yawkey, M. L. (1981). *Language Arts and the Young Child.* Itasca, Ill.: F. E. Peacock Publishers, Inc.

Yeargan, H., and Hatcher, B. (1985). "The Cupcake Factory: Helping Elementary Students Understand Economics." *The Social Studies, 76,* 82–84.

Zimmerman, M. P. (1971). *Musical Characteristics of Children.* Reston, Va.: MENC.

Zion, L. et al. (1986). *The Physical Side of Thinking.* Springfield, Ill.: Charles C. Thomas.

Index